lonely planet

Los Angeles

Andrea Schulte-Peevers

LONELY PLANET PUBLICATIONS
Melbourne • Oakland • London • Paris

Los Angeles
3rd edition – November 2001
First published – April 1996

Published by
Lonely Planet Publications Pty Ltd ABN 36 005 607 983
90 Maribyrnong St, Footscray, Victoria 3011, Australia

Lonely Planet Offices
Australia Locked Bag 1, Footscray, Victoria 3011
USA 150 Linden St, Oakland, CA 94607
UK 10a Spring Place, London NW5 3BH
France 1 rue du Dahomey, 75011 Paris

Photographs
Many of the images in this guide are available for licensing from
Lonely Planet Images.
W www.lonelyplanetimages.com

Front cover photograph
Chevrolet in car dance competition (STONE/Robert Yager)

Map section photograph
Library Tower & Biltmore Hotel (Jonathan Selig)

ISBN 1 74059 021 X

Contents

INTRODUCTION 9

FACTS ABOUT LOS ANGELES 11

History 11
Geography & Geology . . 18
Climate 18
Ecology & Environment . . 19
Government & Politics . . . 20
Economy 21
Population & People 21
Education 22
Arts 22
Religion 31
Language 32

LOS ANGELES ARCHITECTURE 33

FACTS FOR THE VISITOR 49

When To Go 49
Orientation 49
Maps 50
Responsible Tourism 50
Tourist Offices 50
Travel Agencies 51
Documents 51
Embassies & Consulates . . 53
Customs 54
Money 55
Post & Communications . 57
Digital Resources 60
Books 61
Newspapers & Magazines 63
Radio & TV 63
Photography & Video . . . 64
Time 65
Electricity 65
Weights & Measures 66
Laundry 66
Toilets 66
Luggage Storage 66
Health 66
Women Travelers 68
Gay & Lesbian Travelers . 68
Disabled Travelers 69
Senior Travelers 70
Los Angeles for Children . 70
Useful Organizations 70
Libraries 71
Universities 71
Cultural Centers 72
Dangers & Annoyances . . 72
Emergencies 73
Legal Matters 74
Business Hours 74
Public Holidays & Special
Events 74
Doing Business 77
Work 77

GETTING THERE & AWAY 78

Air 78
Bus 82
Train 84
Car & Motorcycle 84
Hitchhiking 85
Organized Tours 85

GETTING AROUND 86

To/From the Airports 86
Bus 87
Train 89
Car & Motorcycle 91
Taxi 95
Bicycle 96
Walking 96
Organized Tours 96

THINGS TO SEE & DO 98

Downtown Los Angeles . . 98
Financial District Walking
Tour 98
Historic Core Walking
Tour 101
Civic Center 105
El Pueblo de los Angeles 106
Chinatown 108
Little Tokyo 108
South Park & Around . . . 110
Arts District 112
Echo Park 113
Elysian Park 113
Exposition Park Area . . . 114
Griffith Park & Around . . 118

2   Contents

Griffith Park 118
Los Feliz & Silver Lake . . 121
Hollywood 122
Central Hollywood 122
Hollywood Hills 130
Melrose Avenue 131
Fairfax District 131
West Hollywood 133
Mid-City 134
MacArthur Park 135
Koreatown 135
Miracle Mile District 136
Westside 139
Beverly Hills 139
Bel Air & Brentwood . . . 144
Westwood 146
Century City 148
Culver City 149
Coastal Communities . . 151
Malibu & Topanga 151
Pacific Palisades 154
Santa Monica 155
Venice 158

Marina del Rey 159
South Bay 160
Palos Verdes Peninsula . . 162
San Pedro 163
Wilmington 164
Long Beach 165
Naples 167
South Central 167
West Adams 168
Central Avenue 169
Leimert Park 169
City of Vernon 170
Watts 170
East LA 172
Breed Street Shul 172
Mariachi Plaza 172
Self-Help Graphics
Gallery 173
El Mercado 173
Plaza de la Raza 173
North Central 174
Southwest Museum . . . 174
El Alisal 174

Heritage Square
Museum 174
San Gabriel Valley 175
Pasadena 176
San Gabriel 181
San Fernando Valley . . . 183
Glendale 183
Burbank 186
North Hollywood 187
Universal City 187
Elsewhere in the Valley . . 189
Mountains 189
San Gabriel Mountains . . 189
Santa Monica Mountains 190
Activities 191
Bicycling & In-line
Skating 191
Hiking 191
Golfing 193
Health Clubs 194
Horseback Riding 194
Running 195
Tennis 195

PLACES TO STAY   196

Camping 197
Hostels 197
B&Bs 200
Hotels 201
Long-term Rentals 216

PLACES TO EAT   218

Downtown 219
Chinatown 222
Koreatown 222
Los Feliz & Silver Lake . . 223
Central Hollywood 224
Melrose/La Brea 226
West Hollywood 227
Beverly Center District . . 228
Fairfax District 230

Beverly Hills 231
Westwood 233
Culver City 233
Malibu 233
Santa Monica 234
Venice & Marina del Rey 236
South Bay 238
San Pedro & Long Beach 240
East LA 241

Monterey Park 241
Leimert Park 242
Pasadena 242
Glendale 243
Burbank 243
North Hollywood &
Universal City 244
Ventura Blvd 244
Markets 246

ENTERTAINMENT   247

Cinemas 247
Theater 248
Comedy Clubs 253
Classical Music & Opera 253
Dance 254

Clubs 255
Jazz & Blues 258
Swing 260
Latin Music 260
Country & Western 261

Bars 261
Pubs & Microbreweries . . 264
Coffeehouses 265
Gay & Lesbian Venues . . 267
Spectator Sports 269

SHOPPING

271

Where To Shop 271   What To Buy 277

EXCURSIONS

285

Anaheim 285   Big Bear Lake 298   Santa Barbara 303
Santa Catalina Island . . . 291   Six Flags Magic   Las Vegas 309
Laguna Beach 294   Mountain 303
Glen Ivy Hot Springs . . . 298   Hurricane Harbor 303

THANKS

313

INDEX

315

LOS ANGELES MAP SECTION

329

MAP LEGEND

360

The Author

Andrea Schulte-Peevers

Andrea is a Los Angeles–based writer, editor and translator who caught the travel bug early in life, hitting all continents but Antarctica by the time she turned 18. After finishing high school in Germany, Andrea decided the world was too big to stay in one place and moved first to London, then to Los Angeles. Armed with a degree from UCLA, she managed to turn her wanderlust into a career as a travel writer and may still chase penguins around the South Pole one of these days. Since joining the LP team in 1995, Andrea has authored and/or updated the guides to *Berlin*, *Germany*, *Baja California*, *San Diego & Tijuana*, *California & Nevada* and *Spain*.

FROM THE AUTHOR

Many thanks to everyone who's contributed tips and insights into the complex tapestry that is Los Angeles. My greatest debt goes to my husband David who worked with me on the previous edition of this book and who once again sustained me with support, love and advice throughout this project. As always, I also owe Carol Martinez and Stacy Litz of the LACVB who once again assisted me ably and helped me make all the right connections.

At the LP Oakland office, a heartfelt thanks to Mariah Bear for letting me update my favorite Lonely Planet book, to Michele Posner for a fun lunch and brainstorming session, to China Williams for competently shepherding my prose from computer to paper and to the lead cartographer, John Culp, and the designer, Henia Miedzinski, for making the book look good.

This Book

The first edition of *Los Angeles* was written by John Gottberg. Andrea Schulte-Peevers and David Peevers collaborated on the second edition. Some sassy sidebars were contributed by David Peevers and Paige R Penland.

FROM THE PUBLISHER

Like sand through an hourglass, these are the days at Lonely Planet. China Williams, after recovering from amnesia, edited the third edition of *Los Angeles* with immense help from Susan Shook Malloy. Sage guidance was provided by Michele Posner and Kate Hoffman, who in tandem saved Happy Oaktown. China, Susan and Gabi Knight proofed and Ken DellaPenta indexed the book. Kerri Thomsen reviewed the Disneyland section.

John Culp, with help from Eric Thomsen, fended off his evil twin brother for control of the mapping empire. Alex Guilbert, Monica Lepe and Tracey Croom oversaw the mapping efforts from their wood-paneled board room. Bart Wright, Ivy Feibelman and Tim Lohnes kept the map-controlling devices in good working order.

While working undercover as dockhands, Hugh D'Andrade, Hayden Foell, Beca Lafore, Justin Marler, Henia Miedzinski, Hannah Reineck, Lora Santiago, Lisa Summers and Wendy Yanagihara drew the illustrations. Henia Miedzinski renounced her family fortune to design the book and the colorwraps, and Susan Rimerman risked banishment from Happy Oaktown's country club to supervise design matters. No one's secret love child was discovered during the production of this book.

ACKNOWLEDGMENTS

Several images in this book have been reproduced with permission from the Los Angeles Public Library: the 1907 image of Vine St looking north from Hollywood Blvd, from the library's photo collection; the 1953 image of the freeway express bus, from the *Herald Examiner* Collection; and the 1940 image of an officer marking a parked car, also from the *Herald Examiner* Collection.

The 1942 photograph of the Japanese-American child being evacuated with his parents to Owens Valley was reproduced from the Library of Congress' Office of War Information Photograph Collection.

Foreword

ABOUT LONELY PLANET GUIDEBOOKS

The story begins with a classic travel adventure: Tony and Maureen Wheeler's 1972 journey across Europe and Asia to Australia. Useful information about the overland trail did not exist at that time, so Tony and Maureen published the first Lonely Planet guidebook to meet a growing need.

From a kitchen table, then from a tiny office in Melbourne (Australia), Lonely Planet has become the largest independent travel publisher in the world, an international company with offices in Melbourne, Oakland (USA), London (UK) and Paris (France).

Today Lonely Planet guidebooks cover the globe. There is an ever-growing list of books, and there's information in a variety of forms and media. Some things haven't changed. The main aim is still to help make it possible for adventurous travelers to get out there – to explore and better understand the world.

At Lonely Planet we believe travelers can make a positive contribution to the countries they visit – if they respect their host communities and spend their money wisely. Since 1986 a percentage of the income from each book has been donated to aid projects and human-rights campaigns.

Updates Lonely Planet thoroughly updates each guidebook as often as possible. This usually means there are around two years between editions, although for more unusual or more stable destinations the gap can be longer. Check the imprint page (following the title page at the beginning of the book) for publication dates.

Between editions, up-to-date information is available in two free newsletters – the paper *Planet Talk* and email *Comet* (to subscribe, contact any Lonely Planet office) – and on our Web site at www.lonelyplanet.com. The *Upgrades* section of the Web site covers a number of important and volatile destinations and is regularly updated by Lonely Planet authors. *Scoop* covers news and current affairs relevant to travelers. And, lastly, the *Thorn Tree* bulletin board and *Postcards* section of the site carry unverified, but fascinating, reports from travelers.

Correspondence The process of creating new editions begins with the letters, postcards and emails received from travelers. This correspondence often includes suggestions, criticisms and comments about the current editions. Interesting excerpts are immediately passed on via newsletters and the Web site, and everything goes to our authors to be verified when they're researching on the road. We're keen to get more feedback from organizations or individuals who represent communities visited by travelers.

Lonely Planet gathers information for everyone who's curious about the planet – and especially for those who explore it firsthand. Through guidebooks, phrasebooks, activity guides, maps, literature, newsletters, image library, TV series and Web site, we act as an information exchange for a worldwide community of travelers.

Research Authors aim to gather sufficient practical information to enable travelers to make informed choices and to make the mechanics of a journey run smoothly. They also research historical and cultural background to help enrich the travel experience and allow travelers to understand and respond appropriately to cultural and environmental issues.

Authors don't stay in every hotel because that would mean spending a couple of months in each medium-size city and, no, they don't eat at every restaurant because that would mean stretching belts beyond capacity. They do visit hotels and restaurants to check standards and prices, but feedback based on readers' direct experiences can be very helpful.

Many of our authors work undercover; others aren't so secretive. None of them accept freebies in exchange for positive writeups. And none of our guidebooks contain any advertising.

Production Authors submit their raw manuscripts and maps to offices in Australia, the USA, the UK or France. Editors and cartographers – all experienced travelers themselves – then begin the process of assembling the pieces. When the book finally hits the shops, some things are already out of date, we start getting feedback from readers and the process begins again....

WARNING & REQUEST

Things change – prices go up, schedules change, good places go bad and bad places go bankrupt – nothing stays the same. So, if you find things better or worse, recently opened or long since closed, please tell us and help make the next edition even more accurate and useful. We genuinely value all the feedback we receive. A well-traveled team reads and acknowledges every letter, postcard and email and ensures that every morsel of information finds its way to the appropriate authors, editors and cartographers for verification.

Everyone who writes to us will find their name listed in the next edition of the appropriate guidebook. They will also receive the latest issue of *Planet Talk*, our quarterly printed newsletter, or *Comet*, our monthly email newsletter. Subscriptions to both newsletters are free. The very best contributions will be rewarded with a free guidebook.

We may edit, reproduce and incorporate your comments in all Lonely Planet products, such as guidebooks, Web sites and digital products, so let us know if you don't want your comments reproduced or your name acknowledged.

Send all correspondence to the Lonely Planet office closest to you:

Australia: Locked Bag 1, Footscray, Victoria 3011
USA: 150 Linden St, Oakland, CA 94607
UK: 10a Spring Place, London NW5 3BH
France: 1 rue du Dahomey, 75011 Paris

Or email us at: talk2us@lonelyplanet.com.au

For news, views and updates, see our Web site: www.lonelyplanet.com

HOW TO USE A LONELY PLANET GUIDEBOOK

The best way to use a Lonely Planet guidebook is any way you choose. At Lonely Planet, we believe the most memorable travel experiences are often those that are unexpected, and the finest discoveries are those you make yourself. Guidebooks are not intended to be used as if they provided a detailed set of infallible instructions!

Contents All Lonely Planet guidebooks follow the same format. The Facts about the Country chapters or sections give background information ranging from history to weather. Facts for the Visitor gives practical information on issues like visas and health. Getting There & Away gives a brief starting point for researching travel to and from the destination. Getting Around gives an overview of the transport options available when you arrive.

The peculiar demands of each destination determine how subsequent chapters are broken up, but some things remain constant. We always start with background, then proceed to sights, places to stay, places to eat, entertainment, getting there and away, and getting around information – in that order.

Heading Hierarchy Lonely Planet headings are used in a strict hierarchical structure that can be visualized as a set of Russian dolls. Each heading (and its following text) is encompassed by any preceding heading that is higher on the hierarchical ladder.

Entry Points We do not assume guidebooks will be read from beginning to end, but that people will dip into them. The traditional entry points are the list of contents and the index. In addition, however, some books have a complete list of maps and an index map illustrating map coverage.

There may also be a color map that shows highlights. These highlights are dealt with in greater detail later in the book, along with planning questions. Each chapter covering a geographical region usually begins with a locator map and another list of highlights. Once you find something of interest in a list of highlights, turn to the index.

Maps Maps play a crucial role in Lonely Planet guidebooks and include a huge amount of information. A legend is printed on the back page. We seek to have complete consistency between maps and text, and to have every important place in the text captured on a map. Map key numbers usually start in the top left corner.

Although inclusion in a guidebook usually implies a recommendation, we cannot list every good place. Exclusion does not necessarily imply criticism. In fact, there are a number of reasons why we might exclude a place – sometimes it is simply inappropriate to encourage an influx of travelers.

Introduction

Overwhelming. Intimidating. Frightening. Or even, where *is* it? No other city on earth is so talked about, yet so misunderstood. Los Angeles is feared for its natural disasters, dreaded for its crime and violence, disparaged for its jammed freeways and poor air quality and scorned for what some call a plastic personality. Many visitors who land at LAX don't even bother spending time in the city, instead quickly heading off to more human-scale destinations like San Francisco, Santa Barbara and the natural wonders of the Southwest. But because you bought this book, you're obviously not one of them. Congratulations! You're about to discover one of the world's most fascinating cities.

Here's the deal: LA is not an easy place to grasp. It doesn't feel like any city you've ever known. It's vast and amorphous, with no clearly defined center. But the key to understanding – and appreciating – the place is to throw out the notion that it's a city at all. In fact, it's a conglomeration of 88 independent cities, some of them with quite distinct identities (Santa Monica, Pasadena and Long Beach among them), many others merely nondescript sprawls, blending anonymously into the urban maelstrom.

LA is sometimes called the 'Big Orange' (a moniker intended to counter New York's 'Big Apple'). But you might think of it as the 'Big Onion,' a city where you continually peel away the layers – one by one – until you arrive at your own feeling of what it's all about. There are things about LA that will make you weep. Other layers will make you feel excited about the prospects for humankind.

Best known, perhaps, is Creative LA, the epicenter of the world's movie and media industries. Then there's Global LA, a cutting-edge experiment in how the nations of the world might one day live in relative harmony. Consider Historical LA, where monuments and buildings allow us to trace the city's evolution from Native American tribal ground and Spanish mission settlement to Wild West outpost and 20th-century megalopolis. Natural LA, a place where you can surf in the morning, hike in midday and ski at night: It's no dream.

But the most important facet is perhaps Innovative LA. This is where the latest technology – from animation to satellites to medical equipment – is dreamed up. Trends are born here, ideas that swim out of LA's stream of consciousness and make their way around the world. Surfing, shopping malls, drive-thru culture, step aerobics and hip-hop music all conquered the globe from here.

What makes LA so fascinating is its wealth of human experience, its endless menu of intriguing flavors and textures. Any time the mood strikes, you can explore a different culture, food, music – or even a historical period – simply by driving a few miles across town. Savor authentic chow mein in Chinatown, top-notch sushi in Little Tokyo, matzo soup in the Fairfax District, California cuisine in Beverly Hills or burritos in East LA. Dancing? You could don zoot suits and do the jitterbug or go for salsa and merengue, or perhaps just good old-fashioned rock 'n' roll. Watch Pacific Islanders perform their traditional dances one weekend, jam with jazz greats on Central Ave on another, or wave at celebrities participating in the Hollywood Christmas Parade. Impressionist paintings at the Getty Center, indigenous pottery at the Southwest Museum, black sculptures at the California African American Museum, Latino murals in East LA...the choices are endless. 'Boredom' does not make an appearance in the Los Angeles lexicon.

Getting to know LA as a visitor means exploring it bit by bit, layer by layer, neighborhood by neighborhood. Don't expect to pack in a visit to the Getty Center, a beachside lunch in Santa Monica, shopping in Beverly Hills and strolling the Hollywood Walk of Fame all in one day. Sure, it can be done, but you will be exhausted. Instead, restrict your visit to certain neighborhoods that interest you. Use this book for some pre-trip research, and then budget at least one full day in each area. Changing your accommodations every other day is a good idea, as it will minimize long drives.

As you peel away layer after layer, the City of Angels will reveal itself to you in all its mesmerizing and seductive complexity, offering you a rewarding and memorable experience.

Facts about Los Angeles

HISTORY

The earliest residents of the Los Angeles area were the Gabrieleño (the Spanish name for the Shoshone) and the Chumash Indians, who arrived in this desert region between 5000 and 6000 BC. The Gabrieleño were inland hunters and gatherers whose staple food was the acorn, which was finely ground and made into bread or porridge. They were also fine weavers and used root fibers to make watertight baskets. The Chumash, who lived on the coast, built 25-foot long boats that carried them to offshore islands.

Rain was too scarce and inconsistent for permanent agriculture. The Gabrieleño swapped their seeds and skins to the Chumash for fish and soapstone pots. In religious matters both tribes were animistic, placing special importance in the powers of the eagle and crow, as well as the porpoise, which was considered a sort of guardian spirit. Earthquakes were blamed on the restlessness of seven giants who held the entire world on their shoulders. Warfare was rare and horses were unknown before the Spanish arrived.

The first European known to have laid eyes upon the Los Angeles basin was Portuguese sailor Juan Rodríguez Cabrillo, who sailed the coast in 1542. From present-day Santa Monica Bay, he observed a brown haze over the landscape – no doubt from campfires at the Gabrieleño village of Yangna, located near modern Downtown LA. Cabrillo named the bay Bahia de los Fumos, or 'Bay of Smokes.'

Mission Era

The Spanish had been in Mexico for more than two centuries before they finally undertook exploring the northern wilderness of Alta (Upper) California. In 1769, California governor Don Gaspar de Portolá and Franciscan Father Junípero Serra led an expedition from San Diego north to Monterey, looking all the while for likely sites on which to build missions so they could Christianize the native peoples.

Follow-up expeditions established 21 California missions along El Camino Real, 'The King's Highway,' under the direction of Father Serra. There were two in greater Los Angeles: the Mission San Gabriel Archangel, built in 1771, and the Mission San Fernando Rey de España, founded in 1797. (Restorations can still be visited.) The Gabrieleño who gathered at these missions and built their communities around them had no previous concept of heaven or hell, but they began trading hard labor for supposed salvation. In the process, the Gabrieleño were exposed to a variety of diseases, from measles to syphilis, that decimated the tribes.

In 1781, the missions embarked on a plan to create separate agricultural communities to produce food and support their expansion. Forty-four *pobladores*, or settlers, were assigned from San Gabriel to establish a new town near the village of Yangna, on the banks of a cottonwood-lined stream about 9 miles southwest of the mission. The town they established, El Pueblo de Nuestro Señora la Reina de los Angeles del Río Porciúncula (The Town of Our Lady the Queen of the Angels of the Porciúncula River), was named after a saint whose feast day had recently been celebrated.

The pobladores – most were mestizos (mixed Spanish and Indian blood) – had a daunting task. Half of them were children, and their town site lacked both a harbor and a navigable river. What's more, the Anza Trail – an overland supply route to Mexico blazed in 1774 by Juan Bautista de Anza – had been severed at the Colorado River (a few days' ride east of the pueblo) by hostile Yuma Indians. There would be no supplementary goods coming by land and only rare shipments by sea.

But Los Angeles, as the pueblo became known, grew into a thriving farming community. Taking full advantage of long sunny days and sufficient water, the settlers developed orange and olive groves, vineyards, wheat fields, and herds of cattle, sheep and horses. It was fortunate the community had achieved such self-sufficiency: during the Mexican War of Independence (1810–21) – during which Mexico won independence from Spain – Alta California was virtually cut off, and Los Angeles and other pueblos were entirely on their own.

Ranchos

By the early 19th century California was already well known to foreign sea merchants. Until Mexican independence, foreign trade was officially banned by the Spanish, but the lure of imported luxuries in so remote a location was irresistible. *Contrabandistas* traded where and when they pleased, anchoring in secluded coves, paying bribes when necessary and thumbing their noses at the weak territorial administration.

Initially sea otters were the primary draw; a single adult pelt earned $300 worth of tea, silks, spices and ceramics in China. New England whalers also worked this coast, harvesting the great mammals as they migrated north from Baja California. But cattle provided the primary products. Tallow (for soap and candles) and hides (for shoes) were exported to the US East Coast in exchange for such manufactured goods as cloth, footwear, tools and cutlery.

Upon Mexican independence in 1821, many of that new nation's citizens looked to California to satisfy their thirst for private land. By the mid-1830s, the missions had been secularized, with a series of governors doling out hundreds of free land grants. This process gave birth to the rancho system. *Rancheros*, as the new landowners were called, prospered and quickly became the social, cultural and political fulcrums of California. The average rancho was 16,000 acres in size

As a River, It's a Washout

All rivers have a history and find their destiny in the sea. But few have had to suffer the ignominious fate of the 58-mile-long Los Angeles River. The lush appearance of this limpid, tree-lined stream in 1829 caused the great fur trader Kit Carson to pronounce the Los Angeles area 'truly a paradise on earth.' For more than 3000 years – until the Spanish set up a pueblo near what is now Downtown LA – the wetlands formed by the river were the exclusive domain of the Shoshone Indians (also known as the Gabrieleño).

What the Indians could have told the Spanish – if they'd been asked – was that this river had an unpredictable and even freakish nature. Throughout the city's infancy, the river made itself repeatedly felt and feared. Whenever the rains came to the local mountains, the river jumped its banks, flooding fields and homes. And in the fierce winter of 1824-25, it actually changed course altogether, heading south and emptying into the sea at San Pedro instead of Santa Monica Bay.

In 1914 rains swelled the river to the point where its flow equaled that of the mighty Colorado River. Heavy flooding and more course changes continued until 1934, when the entire LA County area was deluged by four days of torrential rains, resulting in millions of dollars of damage and the loss of 113 lives. LA declared war on the river and called in the US Army Corps of Engineers.

In 1938 the Corps canalized the river; 10,000 workers applied 3 million barrels of concrete by hand, resulting in what you see today. The vegetation of the river survives only along short stretches of remaining natural riverbed, which accounts for only 17% of its entire length. The rest of the riverbed is a concrete sluiceway – the brunt of many cruel jokes and the sight of epic Schwarzenegger truck crashes – that leads the river to its current outlet in Long Beach.

Still, in winter months when the rains come, Angelenos eye their only real river nervously, and perhaps wistfully ponder how yet another LA landmark came to an inglorious concrete ending.

and largely given over to livestock to supply the hide-and-tallow trade.

Enterprising *Californios* often sold 75,000 or more hides a year, for an average price of $2 apiece. Although some made fortunes – they paid no taxes and footed no public-works projects – California rancheros were largely illiterate and lived in nonpermanent dwellings. They had no schools and their homes generally lacked wooden floors, windows or running water.

Immigrants from the USA became the merchant class. Joseph Chapman, a Boston millwright-cum-pirate, became the first Yankee, or *Yanqui*, Angeleno in 1818; he was known as El Inglés or 'The Englishman.' Others followed slowly; by the mid-1830s there were still only 29 US citizens residing in Los Angeles. But these few bought entire shiploads of imported goods from seafarers, and in exchange delivered full cargoes of 40,000 hides. In setting up a system of credit for rancheros, they established California's first banking system.

An overland route to other parts of the US was established by the colorful and well-traveled fur trapper Jedediah Smith, who arrived at the San Gabriel mission via the Sierra Nevada in 1826. Kit Carson, a legend of the American West, helped forge the Santa Fe Trail to Los Angeles in 1832. But most Easterners didn't know much about California until 1840, when the publication of Richard Henry Dana's *Two Years Before the Mast* gave an account of his mid-1830s experience in the coastal hide-and-tallow trade. 'In the hands of an enterprising people, what a country this might be,' Dana wrote of Los Angeles, which then had a population of just over 1200.

Bear Flag Republic & Statehood

Impressed by California's potential wealth and imbued with Manifest Destiny (the imperialist doctrine to extend the US border from coast to coast), the US President Andrew Jackson sent an emissary to offer the financially strapped Mexican government $500,000 for California. Though American settlers were by then showing up by the hundreds, especially in Northern California, Jackson's emissary was tersely rejected. A political stew was brewing.

In 1836, Texas seceded from Mexico and declared itself an independent republic. When the US in turn annexed Texas in 1845, Mexico broke off diplomatic relations and ordered all foreigners without proper papers deported from California. Outraged Northern California settlers revolted, captured the nearest Mexican official and, supported by a company of US soldiers, led by Captain John C Frémont, declared California's independence in June 1846 by raising their 'Bear Flag' over the town of Sonoma.

The Bear Flag Republic existed for all of one month. (The banner lives on, however, as the California state flag.) War had broken out in Texas in May after Mexican and US patrols clashed over disputed territory. That gave the US all the justification it needed to invade Mexico. By July, US naval units occupied every port on the California coast, including the capital, Monterey. On August 13, troops led by Frémont and Commodore Robert F Stockton overtook Los Angeles without a shot being fired. Final opposition was squelched the following January after a skirmish at Paso de Bartolo on the San Gabriel River.

US troops captured Mexico City in September 1847, putting an end to the war. As a part of the 1848 Treaty of Guadalupe Hidalgo, the US paid $15 million for all Mexican territories west of the Rio Grande and north of the Gila River (in Arizona), including California.

Only two years later, California was admitted as the 31st of the United States. The primary reason behind this accelerated recognition was gold, which suddenly appeared in quantity enough to provide full monetary support for US coinage. Los Angeles was also incorporated in 1850 (on April 4) and made the seat of Los Angeles County. It was an unruly city of dirt streets, adobe homes, saloons, brothels and gambling houses that thrived on the fast buck. But by 1854, Northern California's gold rush had peaked and the state was thrust into a depression. While unemployed miners swarmed to LA and other cities, banks and businesses that had harnessed their futures to miners' fortunes closed their doors.

Making matters worse for the rancheros was the land commission sent west by Congress in 1851. Everyone who had received a land grant two decades earlier was now forced to prove its legitimacy with documents and witnesses. By 1857 some 800 cases had been reviewed by tribunal, 500 in favor of the original, pre-rancho landowners. Many ranchos now passed into the hands of the US government. Landowners that endured the tribunal were again tested by declining cattle prices and a brutal three-year drought (1862–65). Many Californios were bankrupted, their ranchos mortgaged, subdivided, fenced and planted by the new Angelenos.

Hatred of Anglo domination spread quickly through the Californio community, provoked in part by an 1855 state edict, known as the 'Greaser Law,' which levied a $20-per-month tax on foreign nationals. Many of the newly poor Mexicans resorted to highway robbery, both of Wells, Fargo & Co stagecoaches (holdups averaged twice a month for 14 years) and – beginning in the 1870s – railroads.

From Small Town to Big City

When the first transcontinental railroad, the Central Pacific (later renamed the Southern

Water for a Thirsty Giant

The growth of semi-arid Los Angeles into a megalopolis is inextricably linked to water. When the city's population surged to 200,000 people in the early 20th century, ground-water levels were insufficient to meet the city's needs, let alone sustain further growth. It was apparent that water had to be imported. Fred Eaton, a former LA mayor, and William Mulholland, the city water bureau superintendent, knew just how and where to get it: by aqueduct from the Owens River Valley, at the foot of the Eastern Sierras, some 250 miles northeast.

The fact that Owens Valley itself was settled by farmers who needed the water for irrigation purposes didn't bother either the men or the federal government, which actively supported the city in acquiring land and securing water rights in the valley area.

Voters gave Mulholland the $24.5 million he needed to build an aqueduct that would carry melted snow from the mountains to the city. Work on the aqueduct began in 1908. An amazing feat of engineering – crossing barren desert floor as well as rugged mountain terrain for 233 miles – it opened to great fanfare on November 5, 1913. An extension to the Mono Basin in 1940 lengthened the aqueduct by 105 miles. The Owens Valley, though, would never be the same. With most of Owens Lake drained, the once-fertile valley became barren, causing farms to close and businesses to go bust. A bitter feud between valley residents and the city ensued; some foes even used dynamite to sabotage the aqueduct. Formal arbitration in 1929 ended with LA making a few concessions. It's against the backdrop of these 'water wars' that Roman Polanski's Academy Award–winning *Chinatown* is set.

To this day, LA's Department of Water and Power owns 307,000 acres in the Inyo and Mono Counties and the system supplies more than 75% of the city's water. But residents at the water's source still resent the thirsty giant to the south.

Pacific), was completed in 1869, San Francisco was far and away California's metropolitan center. Los Angeles' parched climate, its distance from both fresh water and mining resources, and its vulnerability to major earthquakes made it unattractive to the San Francisco power brokers who owned the Central Pacific. But a bit of wheeling and dealing brought a spur line to LA in 1876, via the San Joaquin Valley. In 1885, the Atchison, Topeka & Santa Fe Railroad directly linked Los Angeles across the Arizona desert to the East Coast.

Coinciding with the arrival of the railroad was the establishment of an orange-growing industry in Southern California. Around 1874, three Brazilian navel (seedless) orange trees were shipped from the US Department of Agriculture to Eliza and Luther Tibbetts, botanists in Riverside, a town east of Los Angeles. So successful were these trees, which produce their fruit in winter, that a second crop of summer-producing Valencia oranges was established in what is now Orange County. By 1889 more than 13,000 acres in six counties were planted with orange trees, dramatically improving the previously woebegone local economy.

Unlike many fruits, oranges easily survive long-distance rail shipping. As California oranges found their way onto New York grocery shelves, coupled with a hard-sell advertising campaign, Easterners heeded the advice of crusading magazine and newspaper editor Horace Greeley to 'Go West, young man.' Los Angeles' population jumped from 2300 in 1860 to 11,000 in 1880, and to more than 50,000 in 1890. It reached 100,000 in 1900.

Never mind that there was no natural harbor, or that the supply of fresh water was inadequate to support even a small town. Sharp minds and willing spirits would overcome these obstacles. The first of these needs was addressed by the construction of a harbor at San Pedro, 23 miles south of City Hall. Work began in 1899 and the first wharf opened in 1914, the year the Panama Canal was completed. Suddenly 8000 miles closer to the Atlantic seaboard by virtue of this new passageway, San Pedro became the busiest harbor on the West Coast.

The sporadic flow of the Los Angeles River (as the Río Porciúncula was now known) may have been adequate for the original pueblo, but even when supplemented by scattered artesian wells, the local water supply wasn't nearly sufficient. Bringing drinkable water to the growing city required a much more complex solution. See the boxed text 'Water for a Thirsty Giant.'

Growing Strong: Oil, Military & Movies

LA's population had soared to 1 million by 1920, 2 million by 1930. This time it was the discovery of oil that brought exponential growth. Though the presence of black gold had much earlier called attention to an abundance of crude oil, it wasn't until 1892, when Edward Doheny drilled a well near Downtown LA, that a sophisticated and highly profitable regional oil industry took off. Local refineries were constructed and storage methods were developed. Meanwhile, the introduction of the automobile generated a growing need for fuel; enormous profits awaited those who could pump their oil fast enough. New strikes were still being made at Santa Fe Springs and Signal Hill in the early 1920s. The demand for exporting much of that oil also caused a boom in shipping and related harbor industries.

During WWI, the Lockheed brothers and Donald Douglas – making note of Los Angeles' ideal test-flight weather and its capacity to house large work forces – established aircraft manufacturing plants in the area. Two decades later, with another world war brewing, the aviation industry employed enough people to help lift LA out of the Great Depression. By the end of WWII, billions of federal dollars had been poured into Southern California military contracts, and thousands of families had moved to the region to work at the plants. Through the Cold War years, increased dependence on federal spending led some critics to call Los Angeles a 'Federal City.'

Capitalizing on the influx of aviation employees brought about whole new suburbs south of Los Angeles. Lakewood, just north of Long Beach, is the classic example: the entire city was developed almost overnight to house employees of McDonnell-Douglas. It is said that in a single hour of one day in 1946, 107 new tract houses were sold there.

During the war and the years immediately following, the railroads drew thousands of African American maintenance workers from Texas and Louisiana to Los Angeles. Still more arrived when it became apparent that a vibrant black community

The WWII Battle of LA

Los Angeles old-timers can tell you that less than three months after the Japanese attack on Pearl Harbor, a mysterious battle took place in the skies over Los Angeles.

On February 23, 1942, a Japanese submarine surfaced near Santa Barbara and shot several rounds into a beachside oil field. The entire West Coast tensed in anticipation of further attacks. They didn't have to wait long.

Just two nights later, at 7pm, warning came of a possible attack. By midnight, radar screens picked up an unidentified flying object approaching Los Angeles. Three hours later, an object resembling a balloon of some sort was sighted just over Santa Monica. Anti-aircraft guns opened fire. Tracers lit up the sky. Reportedly some 1400 rounds were fired skyward, but no bombs fell in retaliation. Whoever – whatever – it was that 'attacked' Los Angeles that night disappeared into thin air. At the war's end, Japanese military spokespeople denied having had anything to do with it.

Oddly, the submarine attack that precipitated this paranoia may have been a personal vendetta rather than a military assignment. Legend has it that the submarine's commander, Kozo Nishino, had sworn revenge on the oil field 10 years earlier when his oil tanker visited Southern California. Apparently he accidentally sat on a prickly pear cactus and some locals rudely laughed at him.

was developing in South Central LA. What had been just a small colony before the war became a thriving cultural center by 1950.

But it is the film industry that has symbolized 20th-century Los Angeles. In modern LA, it's known simply as 'The Industry.' Independent producers were attracted here beginning in 1908 for numerous reasons. Southern California's sunny climate allowed indoor scenes to be shot outdoors – essential given the unsophisticated photo technology of the day. Any location, from ocean to desert to alpine forest, could be realized nearby. What's more, the proximity of the Mexican border enabled filmmakers to rush their equipment to safety when challenged by the collection agents of patent holders such as Thomas Edison.

Studios were constructed in Culver City and Universal City, but the capital of filmdom was the LA suburb of Hollywood. Soon moviegoers were succumbing to the romance of Southern California and fashion fads flowed from popular movies shaped styles around the world.

Zoom to the Present

Ever since studios first found their home in Los Angeles, the city has raced to live up to the hype created by the film industry. That vision helped attract two new breeds of immigrants: the eccentric artisan – from writers and musicians to painters and architects – and the fashionable hedonist drawn by the broad sandy beaches and the temptations of Hollywood.

But all the while, trouble was brewing in the city. Policy-makers had turned a blind eye to growing ethnic friction for decades, including a week-long spell of urban warfare between Anglo sailors and Latino teenagers in 1943, known as the Zoot Suit Riots. In the 1960s, South Central LA was faced with increasing tension as the quality of life there continued to decline. The unrest came to a boil in August 1965 in one of the nation's worst race riots: The primarily black neighborhood of Watts exploded with six days of burning and looting. Thirty-four people died in the riots, and more than a thousand were wounded.

The Los Angeles Riots: 1992 & 1965

April 29, 1992: 'Not Guilty.' The words cut through the stifling air of a hushed Simi Valley court-room like a dagger through silk, their gravity still a notion unfathomed. More than a year earlier, a cuadrilla of LAPD officers had stopped Rodney King, an African American, for driving erratically and appearing to be under the influence. After King initially resisted arrest, they tried to subdue him both verbally and physically. A neighbor, George Halliday, witnessed the incident and recorded the infamous videotape, which showed the cops brutally kicking, beating and shouting at King as he crouched on the asphalt. The images were beamed across the globe immediately.

'Not Guilty.' The verdict that acquitted three of the four officers of all charges unleashed a torrent of fury that would consume LA for three days. Thousands of enraged residents, mostly in South Central, gathered on the streets to protest; rioting and looting soon followed. Stores in their own community were set ablaze and innocent bystanders were assaulted. Like wildfire, the rioting quickly enveloped other neighborhoods. Businesses and schools closed and a dusk curfew was imposed, leaving frightened Angelenos huddled in their homes watching events unfold on television. A tear-ful Rodney King sobbed, 'Can't we all just get along?' – an appeal that was as naive as it was futile. National Guardsmen, positioned on rooftops, patrolling the streets with machine guns and sta-tioned with armored vehicles at places like Venice Beach, were called in to restore order. The shock-ing toll: 54 dead, 2000 injured, 12,000 arrested and $1 billion in property damage.

The riots of 1992 were eerily reminiscent of the Watts Riots a generation earlier. Back in August 1965, it was a traffic stop of a black youth that triggered an explosion of rage in the most down-trodden areas, which were determined to pay LA back for decades of oppression, injustice and dis-crimination. As the city began to lick its wounds six days later, then-Governor Pat Brown appointed a commission to study the causes of the riots. It found high unemployment in south LA (double that in the rest of the city), overcrowded and underfunded classrooms, and discriminatory housing laws that kept African Americans ghettoized and in sub-standard homes. Little has changed since.

In 1991, Rodney King became an instant symbol of American racism and police brutality. Because of the incident many had to recognize that discrimination still exists, that treatment of whites and non-whites by the police and courts is different and that South Central's schools and in-frastructure are inferior to those in wealthy Westside communities. But some Angelenos were split about the motives of the '92 riots. There's also a lingering suspicion in some circles that the riots were not politically motivated but rather an expression of simple material greed as evidenced by TV images of laughing hordes hauling everything from sneakers to VCRs from ravaged stores and triumphantly posing with their loot for the cameras.

Meanwhile, the LAPD continues to stay in the headlines with accusations of racial profiling, ex-cessive force and corruption. The Rampart scandal of the late 1990s, which, among other things, revealed that anti-gang officers had planted evidence, was just the latest installment. Clearly, the road to recovery for LA is still a long one.

South Central, populated mainly by blacks and Latinos, saw subsequent riots in 1979 and 1992. The latter – a direct result of the acquittal of LAPD members charged with beating Rodney King – cost 54 lives and $1 billion in property damage. (For more on the riots, see the boxed text 'The Los Angeles Riots: 1992 & 1965.')

In LA history, the 1990s was the decade 'from hell,' and not just because of the riots. Heavy rain in 1992 and 1994–95 caused major flooding, mudslides and property damage, especially in coastal towns like Malibu. Brush fires, fanned by the Santa Ana desert winds, made many more people homeless in 1993. And then, of course, there was the Northridge earthquake of 1994, which registered 6.9 magnitude and brought down freeways, apartment and nervous systems.

Police brutality continued to stay in the news headlines and, at the end of the decade, became coupled with police corruption in the so-called 'Rampart scandal.' LAPD officers assigned to the Rampart area near Downtown LA, one of the most gang-infested and crime-ridden districts, had employed illegal tactics of violence and planted evidence in order to curtail gang activity. Crime did drop, but the price was the LAPD's integrity.

GEOGRAPHY & GEOLOGY

Los Angeles County encompasses geographical extremes from a subtropical desert and 76 miles of coast to an offshore island and at least one peak above 10,000 feet. The county covers 4081 sq miles, spread over a broad coastal plain, bordered on its west and south by the Pacific Ocean, on its north by the San Gabriel Mountains, and on its east by smaller ranges that run to the Mojave Desert. The Santa Monica Mountains separate Hollywood and Beverly Hills from the San Fernando Valley to the north.

But the most notable aspect of LA's geography is that it straddles one of the world's major earthquake fault zones. The great San Andreas Fault runs northwest to southeast within 33 miles of Downtown LA at its nearest point. More than three dozen lesser faults also crisscross the metropolitan area like tremulous cracks on an eggshell.

Angelenos live in fearful knowledge that 'The Big One' may strike any moment. Earthquakes rated above 6.0 have wreaked death and destruction in LA five times this century – with epicenters near Long Beach in 1933, in the San Fernando Valley in 1971 (Sylmar) and 1994 (Northridge), and two in 1992 in the Big Bear region.

CLIMATE

One of LA's greatest assets is its temperate Mediterranean climate, a prime reason why so many people are drawn here. Most of the

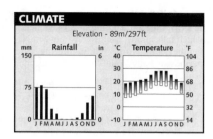

county is protected from extremes of temperature and humidity by the mountain ranges to its north and east. August and September are the hottest months; January and February the coolest and wettest.

Temperatures

Those who keep track of such things say downtown Los Angeles gets 186 days of sunshine a year; the beaches get 137. The highest temperature ever recorded was 110°F (42.9°C) in 1955 and the lowest was 27.9°F (-2.2°C) in 1949. The city's average temperature, though, is around 70°F (21°C), with summer highs usually in the mid 80s to low 90s and winter lows typically in the mid 50s to low 60s. How high the mercury climbs depends very much on location, with temperatures rising the farther you get away from the ocean. Offshore breezes keep beach communities 10°F to 15°F cooler than areas farther inland or in the San Fernando Valley, which is the hottest area during summer. Coastal fog also contributes to the cooling effect, though it usually burns off by noon. Evenings tend to be cool throughout the city, even at the peak of summer. In fall and winter, daily temperature variations can be extreme – from daytime highs of 100°F (37°C) to nighttime lows of 50°F (9°C) are not that uncommon.

Elevation is another climate-determiner. During most winters, the temperature falls far enough below freezing to support ski resorts in the San Gabriel Mountains, often without using artificial snow. Driving into the mountains in those months may mean leaving the valley floor in a T-shirt and putting on snow chains an hour later.

Rainfall & Winds

LA's average annual rainfall is 14.68 inches, which falls almost exclusively between November and April. While not the rule, periods of heavy rain sometimes occur in January and February.

From August to November, the Santa Ana winds occasionally rush into Los Angeles from the high desert to the east, racing down canyons (where they are heated by compression) as fast as 70mph. The Santa Anas are usually accompanied by clear skies and warm weather – and perhaps something more intangible in the air. Raymond Chandler wrote that during Santa Anas 'meek little wives feel the edge of the carving knife and study their husbands' necks.'

Because of LA's hot, dry summers, winds are feared primarily for the fire danger they create. The chaparral-covered slopes of the Santa Monica and San Gabriel Mountains and the Laguna Hills are susceptible to wildfires at these times. In 1993, more than a thousand homes in Malibu, Laguna Beach and Altadena (near Pasadena) were destroyed and 240 sq miles of private and national forest land burned by brush fires. Complicating matters are the winter rains, which guarantee severe mudslides on slopes that have been denuded by summer fires.

ECOLOGY & ENVIRONMENT
Smog

There's no denying that for decades, one of LA's biggest environmental problems has been smog, a composite term of 'smoke' and 'fog.' In recent years, though, tougher environmental regulations have contributed to a significant decline in pollution levels. In general, air pollution is less of a problem in the coastal areas, where offshore breezes provide some relief; the worst air can be found in the inland valleys (San Fernando and San Gabriel). Pollution concentration also varies by season, changing as weather conditions shift. While carbon monoxide and particulate matter levels are highest in fall and winter, ozone levels reach their peak during sun-intensive summer days. Summer also brings the greatest number of inversion days, when a warm air layer traps the noxious fumes.

Cars and factories were first identified as the main sources of air pollution in the late 1940s when the first air quality regulatory body formed. Since the mid-1970s, the South Coast Air Quality Management District (SCAQMD) regulate emissions and enforce federal, state and local air pollution laws. The SCAQMD has a toll-free, taped information service with hourly updates of air pollution levels in the Los Angeles area (☎ 800-288-7664).

Water

The aqueduct built by William Mulholland and Fred Eaton in 1908 – together with a newer one completed in 1970 – still delivers 75% of LA's water supply today (also see the boxed text 'Water for a Thirsty Giant'). Its flow has been increased from 26 million gallons daily when it opened to 525 million gallons. A further 10% is being coaxed from the Colorado River and brought here via a third 300-mile aqueduct. Only the remaining 15% comes from natural local aquifers. The largest such catchment is the San Fernando Valley Groundwater Basin, which holds the equivalent of a two-year water supply for a million people.

Most of the used water eventually ends up in Santa Monica Bay, usually after treatment in sewage plants. About 100 million gallons a day are reclaimed at two major plants and used for landscaping, maintaining local golf courses and cooling power plants.

From 1987 to 1993, California experienced one of its worst droughts in history, with precipitation ranging between 61% and 90% below normal. As a result, the state has made revolutionary progress in cutting back on water use. Water suppliers signed a conservation agreement with environmental groups, requiring water utilities to adopt such conservation practices as offering consumer rebates on low-flush toilets and providing free water audits to those who implement the practices with the most force. Furthermore, the Department of Water Resources set up a water bank that bought surplus water and sold it to those with shortages.

For information about LA's water quality, see Health in the Facts for the Visitor chapter.

GOVERNMENT & POLITICS

The city of Los Angeles is governed by a mayor (the executive branch) and a 15-member council (the legislative branch), each of whom is elected by the people for a four-year term. Other elective offices are those of the controller and of the city attorney. In 1993, Richard Riordan – a lawyer, entrepreneur and self-made millionaire – succeeded five-term mayor Tom Bradley. Riordan was elected again in 1997. The 2001 mayoral bid resulted in a well-publicized run-off election between two liberal candidates: James K Hahn, the city attorney, and Antonio Villaraigosa, former speaker of the California State Assembly. Hahn, the more conservative of the two, won. The LA mayor has considerable powers that include creating an annual budget, approving or vetoing ordinances, appointing city officials and commissioners and playing host to foreign and domestic dignitaries.

The city council keeps itself busy enacting ordinances, levying taxes, authorizing public improvements, ordering elections and adopting traffic regulations, among other responsibilities. Currently, the council reflects the rainbow of diversity that is characteristic of LA and includes black, Latino, Asian, white and gay members. Day-to-day

Tom Bradley – An LA Icon

Tom Bradley (1917–1998) was Los Angeles' first African American mayor and, by many accounts, also its most successful. He served five successive terms from 1973 to 1993, during which the city emerged as the most powerful on the West Coast. His unabashed boosterism, quiet and dignified style and level-headed pragmatism won him countless supporters from the political and racial spectrum: Westside liberals to inner-city blacks, business leaders to Latino farm workers and unionists. While in office, Bradley opened up city government to minorities and women, expanded social services to the poor and disadvantaged, helped reform the LAPD and brought in major investment from domestic and international corporations. During his tenure, LA's Downtown skyline grew

from that of a mid-size, Midwestern town to today's majestic forest of steel and glass.

The son of Texas sharecroppers, Bradley came to LA with his family in 1924 at age seven. An accomplished athlete, he attended UCLA, then joined the police department in 1940 from which he retired as lieutenant in 1961. That same year, he became the first African American to be elected to the city council; he served until 1969. Bradley's first mayoral run – against long-time incumbent Sam Yorty – failed but he came back four years later and the rest is history. The 1984 Olympic Games, which went off without a hitch and were the first ever to become financially profitable, are considered his crowning achievement. The Rodney King Riots in 1992, though, marked the low point of his career. He retired shortly thereafter and died of a heart attack in 1998 at age 80.

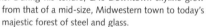

administrative duties are distributed among 36 departments and bureaus, including the Department of Water and Power and the Housing Authority, which are controlled by boards appointed by the mayor.

LA County, comprising 88 independent cities including Los Angeles, is governed by the Board of Supervisors. Also elected to four-year terms, its five members have vast executive and legislative powers. This process results in a jurisdictional nightmare of some 700 separate government units, including various police and fire departments, which all compete for tax revenues.

ECONOMY

After weathering a series of problems in the early 1990s (high unemployment, an eroding tax base and federal spending cuts among them), LA rebounded and began the new millennium triumphantly. The county now ranks in 19th position (21st in 1995) in terms of gross product when compared with the countries of the world, just ahead of Switzerland, Belgium and Sweden.

While LA certainly benefited from the strong national economy in the late 1990s, major economic restructuring – and a move away from the traditional three-tiered economy of aerospace, entertainment and tourism – is primarily responsible for improved balance sheets. This is borne out of a dramatic drop in the unemployment rate, from 9.8% in 1993 to 5.5% in September 2000.

According to the Los Angeles Economic Development Corporation (LAEDC), Los Angeles is the second-largest manufacturing center in the US, with the apparel industry alone employing some 164,000 people. Another 212,000 work in software development and for such technology companies as Boeing, DirecTV and NASA's Jet Propulsion Lab. Los Angeles is also a center of design, be it of cars, furniture, household products or toys.

The motion picture industry continues to flourish, largely because of an insatiable appetite for filmic fare in the US and abroad as well as new and enhanced technologies. Between 1990 and 1998, employment in

'The Industry' skyrocketed from 143,300 to 250,000, and it generated more than $31 billion in revenue.

Tourism is another dependable source of income. In 1998, 23.5 million overnight visitors infused about $11.9 billion into the local economy and provided employment for 287,000 people. Of all arrivals, 5.5 million come from abroad, mostly from Mexico, followed by Japan, the UK, Canada and Germany.

As in most industrialized nations, the service industry, though, represents by far the biggest sector, providing about 29% of all jobs (most of them in the business and professional management fields). In second position is trade and retail, which tallies in at 22%. Manufacturing takes third place with 20% or 834,000 workers, and the remainder is split among smaller sectors such as transportation, communication, public utilities, finance, insurance and real estate.

LA has the nation's highest number of women-owned businesses: around 233,000. There are also almost 250,000 minority-owned firms, including 109,000 Latino, 32,500 African American and 90,000 Asian companies.

POPULATION & PEOPLE

There's much confusion about how many people live in LA, largely because there's confusion about what constitutes LA in the first place. The largest unit, and the one most frequently cited by economists, is the so-called LA Five County area. Counting 15.8 million inhabitants, it comprises the counties of Los Angeles, Orange, San Bernardino, Riverside and Ventura, which themselves are divided into 178 separate cities.

The most useful figure, though, is that of LA County, which consists of 88 incorporated cities with a population of 9.9 million; it is the largest county in the US. The smallest city in LA County is Vernon with just 85 inhabitants, while the largest is the city of Los Angeles proper, home to 3.82 million people. Other well-known incorporated cities are Santa Monica, Beverly Hills, Long Beach and West Hollywood. About 29% of all Californians live in the county, which is predicted to swell to 11.6 million people by 2020.

For all intents and purposes, we use LA County figures in this book, unless mentioned otherwise.

The ethnic makeup of LA County is considerably diverse, with Hispanics accounting for 45.6% (37.8% in 1990), whites for 32.2% (41%), Asians and Pacific Islanders for 12.6% (10.3%), African American for 9.4% (10.5%) and Native American for 0.2% (0.4%). As the 1990 figures show, LA's ethnic composition is changing rapidly, with Latinos (+20.6%) and Asians (+22.3%) being the fastest-growing groups.

In fact, nearly half of the Spanish-speaking population of California lives in LA County, especially in East LA and surrounding communities. African Americans predominate in Inglewood, Watts and Compton, mainly south of the I-10 (Santa Monica) Fwy between the I-405 and I-110 Fwys to Long Beach. Traditional Asian communities – Chinatown and Little Tokyo – can be found just a few blocks north and east of City Hall, respectively. Farther east of Downtown, Monterey Park has become a largely Chinese American enclave. The recent influx of Koreans is most visible around Vermont Ave and Olympic Blvd. Long Beach is the home of approximately 40,000 Cambodians, the largest Cambodian community in the USA.

EDUCATION

There are 215 institutes of higher education in the Greater LA area, more than there are in all of Texas. Some of them, such as the University of California Los Angeles, the University of Southern California, the California Institute of Technology and the Art Center College of Design, are world-class. But below the college level, the news isn't all that good, in fact it is disastrous.

According to an article published in the *San Francisco Examiner*, LA's public school district (with 722,000 students the nation's second largest) is 'dysfunctional' – classrooms are overcrowded, school buildings are crumbling, textbooks and other supplies are in short supply. In statewide standardized tests, LA's schools performed sub-par in all grades and in all disciplines, including math, language and reading. About 30% of students never graduate high school.

A bloated bureaucracy has been given part of the blame, but it's also the extremely heterogeneous student body that challenges an inflexible institution. The ethnic breakdown shows that about 70% are of Hispanic origin, 13.2% are African American, 10% are white and 4.2% are Asian. Many children come from poor households, don't speak English fluently and have parents with little education. A lack of qualified teachers is another problem. With classroom conditions so difficult and pay so poor (starting salary is $37,000), the district finds it difficult to attract and retain qualified teachers. One in four teaches on emergency credentials and almost 40% have fewer than two years experience.

In June 2000, former Colorado governor Roy Romer was hired as district superintendent, the sixth in 10 years. He has promised to cut the bureaucracy, improve teacher training and bring down class size.

ARTS

No city in America can claim the artistic versatility that Los Angeles has. And since the beginning of the 20th century, no other city can claim the cultural influence – both high and low – that LA exerts worldwide.

Film

Los Angeles culture is unique in that the city's primary art form – film – is also a major export. It's a medium with a powerful presence in the lives of not only Americans, but of people around the world. Consequently, images of Los Angeles are distributed far beyond the city's limits, ultimately reflecting back on the city itself. Few people can come to Los Angeles without some cinematic reference to the place, and many who have settled here make every effort to live up to the image.

The movie industry is hardly unaware of the relationship between cinema and Los Angeles. With ever-increasing regularity, films feature the city not only as a setting but as a topic – and in some cases, almost as a character.

Drama Perhaps the greatest film about Los Angeles is *Chinatown* (1974). Directed by Roman Polanski and starring Jack Nicholson and Faye Dunaway, this is the story of LA's early-20th-century water wars. Robert Towne's brilliant screenplay deftly deals with the shrewd deceptions that helped make Los Angeles what it is today.

Blade Runner (1982) is a sci-fi thriller directed by Ridley Scott and starring Harrison Ford, Rutger Hauer and Sean Young. The film projects modern Los Angeles far into the 21st century, with newer buildings reaching farther into the sky – icy fortresses contrasting starkly with chaotic, neglected streets. A multilingual pidgin (including Spanish and Japanese) is quite convincingly the street language, and LA's water problems are ironically solved by a moist, greenhouse-effect climate.

John Singleton's *Boyz 'N the Hood* (1991), starring Cuba Gooding Jr, offers a major reality check on coming of age as a black teen in today's inner city. Meanwhile, Lawrence Kasdan's *Grand Canyon* (1991), starring Danny Glover and Kevin Kline, presents a glimmer of hope as black and white families cope with the sobering realities of racial tensions in modern LA. *Falling Down* (1992) offers a much more cynical treatment of racial issues in Los Angeles. It stars Michael Douglas as a frustrated white man who goes on an angry rampage through the city's ethnic neighborhoods.

Robert Altman's *Short Cuts* (1993) poignantly weaves together several stories by Raymond Carver to show a sadly depraved Los Angeles. Populated by characters of all walks of life, played by the likes of Lily Tomlin, Andie MacDowell, Tim Robbins and Robert Downey Jr, this film leaves no aspect of LA culture unexamined.

Hollywood on Hollywood The film industry itself is a popular subject in the movies. Stories about regular people who come to Hollywood and struggle to make it big are especially popular. *A Star is Born*, first made in 1937 by director David O Selznick, stars Janet Gaynor as a woman who rises to stardom at the same time her movie-star husband (Fredric March) declines in popularity. Obviously, this story has a timeless appeal: it was remade in '54 with Judy Garland, and again in 1976 with Barbra Streisand.

The '50s produced a pair of major critiques of The Industry. Billy Wilder's *Sunset Boulevard* (1950), starring Gloria Swanson and William Holden, is a fascinating study of the way in which Hollywood discards its aging stars. The Paramount lot and Schwab's Drugstore (no longer there) are two of its many local settings. Vincent Minelli's *The Bad and the Beautiful* (1952) takes a good, hard look at the filmmaking business, with Lana Turner recalling the exploits of an aggressive, egotistic film producer, played by Kirk Douglas.

A more contemporary comment on Hollywood is Robert Altman's *The Player*, released in 1992. Starring Tim Robbins and Fred Ward, this is a classic satire on the movie-making machinery, featuring dozens of cameos by the very actors and actresses being spoofed.

Crime With so many hardboiled detective novels coming out of Los Angeles, it's only natural that a distinct style of film adaptations followed. Movie trailers simply called them thrillers – but the French, taking note of the original new style, called it *noir* and the name stuck. You can discover the dark side of 'Los Angeleez' from the '40s to the present through many noir classics available on videocassette.

See if you can keep up with the rapid-fire, racy patter of Fred MacMurray and Barbara Stanwyck in Billy Wilder's *Double Indemnity* (1944). Based on James M Cain's short novel, this film ironically features Edward G Robinson as the honest good guy. And if you really enjoy tense, snappy dialogue, check out Humphrey Bogart and Lauren Bacall in *The Big Sleep*. Both of these films make free use of Los Angeles as a dark, foreboding backdrop.

A star-studded mural on Hollywood Blvd at Wilcox Ave

The original *Dragnet* movie – released in 1954, directed by and starring Jack Webb – is basically a big screen pilot for the long-running television show. But in following the daily doings of Sergeant Joe Friday of the LAPD, you will get some sense of the criminal aspect of 1950s Los Angeles and a tour of various locations throughout LA as a bonus. You might miss the cynicism and irony of more hardboiled noir classics, though.

Recent crime films set in Los Angeles include *The Grifters* (1991), starring John Cusack as a slick con-man living in the Bryson Hotel on Wilshire Blvd, and *Devil in a Blue Dress* (1995), starring Denzel Washington as reluctant South Central detective Easy Rawlins.

The films of Quentin Tarantino are self-consciously influenced by noir classics, westerns, and even Hong Kong thrillers, and prominently feature modern-day Los Angeles. *True Romance* (1993), written by Tarantino, stars Christian Slater as a naive and unbelievably lucky fugitive who de-flects his trouble toward greedy film tycoons. *Pulp Fiction* (1994), written and directed by Tarantino, is a humorous and ironic view of LA from the bottom up. In very Chandleresque fashion, Tarantino creates a surreal Los Angeles through convincing original dialogue. For all of its action, the film is quite realistically stuck much of the time in cars cruising LA's streets.

In 1997, the visceral and brilliant *LA Confidential* (1997), starring Kevin Spacey, Kim Basinger and the wonderfully slimy Danny DeVito proved another brilliant entry in the noir department. 'Hard-hitting' doesn't begin to describe the violent world of deals, sexual betrayal and double-crossing that drive both good and bad cops to hubristic destinies – and deaths – in the LA of the crime-ridden '50s.

Comedy The flip-side of noir must be comedy, which allows for equally suitable presentations of Los Angeles. Who would deny that the LA lifestyle can be downright silly?

Perhaps the most outrageously sardonic comment on LA is Tony Richardson's *The Loved One* (1965). With a screen adaptation by Terry Southern and Christopher Isherwood and loosely based on the Evelyn Waugh novel, this film is certain to delight and disgust you. It features such stars as Sir John Gielgud and Liberace (appearing as a huckstering mortician).

A pair of Paul Mazursky films capture different aspects of Los Angeles in ironic fashion: *Down and Out in Beverly Hills* (1985) is an eccentric comedy featuring Nick Nolte as a homeless man who cons his way to become a permanent family member of a wealthy Beverly Hills couple (played by Richard Dreyfuss and Bette Midler). And *Scenes from a Mall* is just that – the movie is shot almost entirely in a shopping mall. Woody Allen and Bette Midler go through much of the modern-day LA experience while trying to shop.

In *LA Story* (1991), comedian Steve Martin parodies the city that he calls home. Just about every aspect of LA life – from enemas to earthquakes to cappuccino – gets the irreverent Martin treatment.

Music

Throughout the 20th century, Los Angeles has been a mecca for musical talent, whether native or imported.

European Composers Several important early-20th-century composers joined LA's community of exiled European artists in the '30s and '40s. Their ranks included Otto Klemperer, who later became music director of the LA Philharmonic, Kurt Weill and Arnold Schoenberg, who arrived in 1936, took a professorship at UCLA and composed his *Fourth Quartet*. Igor Stravinsky settled in Hollywood in 1940 and as an Angeleno wrote his *Symphony in C* and the opera *Rake's Progress*.

Jazz Jazz began to flourish in LA in the 1920s when horn player Kid Ory became conductor of a recording orchestra made up entirely of black musicians. Throughout the 1920s, jazz was played throughout town and eventually merged with swing and, under the leadership of Benny Goodman, became part of Big Band music.

In the 1940s jazz arrived in a big way, especially on Central Avenue, the main commercial strip of the African American community. Other major venues were the Swanee Inn on Westwood Blvd and the Hi-De-Ho just west of Downtown. It was while holding a nightly gig in Hollywood that Charlie Parker was offered a seven-month engagement in Camarillo State Hospital's drug rehab ward. Looking back on that experience, Parker later recorded 'Relaxing at Camarillo' for LA's Dial label. Many great jazzmen were born in Los Angeles, Dexter Gordon, Charles Mingus and Art Pepper among them.

In the '50s, West Coast Jazz was born with artists such as Pepper, Buddy Collette, Gerry Mulligan, Chet Baker and Shelly Manne performing under LA's relaxing influence. At clubs such as Shelly's Manne-Hole in Hollywood and the Lighthouse at Hermosa Beach (still there), they created a soothing, harmonically sophisticated style of jazz that took the edge off the East Coast-oriented bop scene. Jazz fell into a slump in the '60s, as other styles like rhythm & blues and soul became more popular and musicians sought more fertile ground in Europe, leaving only underground avant-garde artists to hold the torch in LA. The scene picked up again in the 1980s and today jazz is as popular as ever, evidenced by the proliferation of public jazz concert series and jazz music played in restaurants and nightclubs. Several venues in Leimert Park Village function as incubators of a new generation of LA jazz artists.

Rhythm & Blues From the '40s through the '60s, South Central was home to a number of outstanding nightclubs presenting blues, R&B, jazz and soul. Watts churned out vocal groups in the doo-wop tradition, including the Penguins, who first recorded 'Earth Angel' for Doo-Tone records. A juke joint crawl in the mid-'50s would likely have included sets played by T-Bone Walker, Amos Milburn or Charles Brown.

At the hub of a thriving Watts musical scene, Johnny Otis brought many forms of music to the public's attention with his popular Johnny Otis Orchestra – featuring Little Esther Phillips – and his record label, DIG. Starting in the early '60s, Sam Cooke performed hit after hit and ran his SAR record label, attracting soul and gospel talent from around the country to Los Angeles.

Rock 'n' Roll Though rock 'n' roll was from its beginning recorded in LA, the first homegrown talent to make it big in the '50s was Richie Valens, whose 'La Bamba' was a rockified traditional Mexican folk song. In the early '60s, LA's beaches and suburbs were treated to a highly popular style of rock 'n' roll called surf music. Dick Dale and his Del-Tones, the Beach Boys, and Jan and Dean were all local talent. In the mid-'60s, a group of UCLA students – among them the 'lizard king,' Jim Morrison – formed the Doors, who grooved on the Sunset Strip for half a decade.

LA has produced two of rock's most original writers and performers. With his band, the Mothers of Invention, Frank Zappa began his indescribable career with the album *Freak Out* in the mid-'60s. With a voice rusted by bottom-shelf bourbon and filterless cigarettes, Tom Waits has brought the world music built on sounds dragged out from a tin pan alley junkyard, influenced by the varied likes of Louis Armstrong, Kurt Weill and Charles Bukowski.

Perhaps the definitive LA rock band is X. Though not strictly punk, X's combination – the vocals of Exene Cervenka and John Doe over the rockabilly guitar licks of Billy Zoom – created an original, decidedly Angeleno sound that simply blew the doors off the local punk scene. For a more pronounced punk sound, Black Flag led the way with the rants of singer Henry Rollins.

In the mid-'80s, Los Lobos emerged from East LA with a Mexican-influenced rock sound that crossed racial boundaries around the country. Out of Downey came Dave and Phil Alvin and the Blasters, which led the rockabilly revival. Also bred locally, the Red Hot Chili Peppers exploded on the national scene in the late '80s with a highly charged, funk-punk sound.

Rap & Hip-Hop The area stretching from South Central LA down to Long Beach is the local rap hotbed. Seminal rappers Eazy E, Ice Cube and Dr Dre all got their start in the group NWA, the band that put Compton and West Coast rap on the map. Dr Dre went on to found Death Row Records with Suge Knight, launching such popular artists as Tupac Shakur and Snoop Doggy Dog. Eazy-E, NWA's driving force, went on to found Ruthless Records, which launched acts including Kid Frost (one of the first well-known Latino rappers) and Grammy Award–winning Bone Thugs-n-Harmony. Cypress Hill, a uniquely successful crossover hip-hop outfit, emerged from the LA scene, as have popular rappers such as Coolio and Eminem.

Today known as hip-hop, Southern California's vibrant youth subculture has come a long way since local radio station KDAY became America's first commercial rap station. What began a decade ago as a grassroots art form has become one of the city's most popular cultural exports, from baggy jeans to billion-dollar movie deals.

Traditional Mexican Music LA's large Mexican immigrant population – which hails primarily from rural parts of its southern neighbor – has introduced several styles of traditional regional music, most notably *banda*, *norteña* and *ranchera*.

Norteña has roots in *corridos*, folk ballads dealing with Latino-Anglo strife in the borderlands in the 19th century, and themes from the Mexican Revolution. Today's songs focus more on the trials and tribulations of small-time smugglers or drug-runners trying to survive amid big-time corruption and crime. The accordion is the most characteristic instrument, although backing for the singer is also guitar-based, with bass and drums. Los Tucanes de

Tijuana and Los Tigres del Norte from Mexicali are the most popular bands.

Banda is a fairly recent derivative of norteña, substituting large brass sections for guitars and accordion and playing a combination of Latin and more traditional Mexican rhythms. Banda Machos, Banda Cuisillos and Banda Aguacaliente are big names.

Ranchera is Mexico's urban 'country' music. Developed in the expanding towns and cities of the 20th century, it's mostly melodramatic stuff with a nostalgia for rural roots: vocalist-and-combo music, maybe with a mariachi backing. Eugenia León, Juan Gabriel and Alejandro Fernández are among the leading ranchera artists.

mariachi band

Literature

Los Angeles has been a temporary home to many illustrious 20th-century writers, among them William Faulkner, F Scott Fitzgerald and Aldous Huxley. During WWII, German writers Bertolt Brecht and Thomas Mann resided in LA, exiled from their war-torn homeland. While much of the local writing talent seems to be harnessed to the film industry – even Faulkner and Fitzgerald were in LA primarily to make a living writing screenplays – Los Angeles provides an immense wealth of irresistible material to writers. Bookworms will find that novels about the city make for fascinating reading.

Novels LA has been a favorite subject of novelists since the 1920s. Many have regarded LA in political terms, often viewing it unfavorably as the ultimate capitalist city. Classics in this vein include Upton Sinclair's *Oil!* (1927), a work of muckraking historical fiction with socialist overtones.

Nathanael West's *The Day of the Locust* (1939) is one of the best – and most cynical – novels about Hollywood ever written. Every paragraph seems to place one little observation upon another, which strangely (for this city that so steadfastly insists on revising itself) still hold true a half century later.

John Fante's *Ask the Dust* (1939) is a tour of Depression-era Los Angeles. The fame and fortune fantasies of struggling writer Arturo Bandini jar violently against the grim reality of LA's dusty Downtown streets, where 'the smell of gasoline makes the sight of palm trees seem sad.' Aldous Huxley's novel *After Many a Summer Dies the Swan* (1939) is a fine and ironic work based on the life of publisher William Randolph Hearst (as was Orson Welles' film *Citizen Kane*).

More recent examples of LA fiction include several books published in 1970: Terry Southern's *Blue Movie* concerns the decadent side of Hollywood; Joan Didion's *Play It as It Lays* looks at Angelenos with a dry, not-too-kind wit; *Post Office*, by poet-novelist Charles Bukowski, captures the down-and-out side of Downtown (Bukowski himself worked at Downtown's Terminal Annex); and *Chicano*, by Richard Vasquez, takes a dramatic look at the Latino barrio of East LA.

The mid-'80s brought the startling revelations of Bret Easton Ellis' *Less Than Zero*, about the twisted lives of wealthy Beverly Hills teenagers. Covering quite a different terrain, Richard Rayner's *Los Angeles Without a Map* (1988) is about a British man who gets lost in his Hollywood fantasies.

Literary Potshots

Many literary giants of the early 20th century came to Hollywood at one time or another, offering up their talents to the studio gods. Unfortunately, few left feeling they'd raised Hollywood's standards for screenwriting, and even fewer enjoyed the experience. F Scott Fitzgerald never left, but not necessarily by choice: a notorious drunk, he died in Hollywood of a heart attack at the age of 44. Nathanael West was killed in a car crash at 36. Whether in parting or not, they all managed to fire off a salvo or two about the screen trade.

Nelson Algren (on working with director Otto Preminger) 'If I took him seriously, I couldn't take myself seriously.'

Raymond Chandler 'If my books had been any worse, I would not have been invited to Hollywood. If they had been any better, I would not have come.'

Graham Greene 'If there was any truth in the original, it had been carefully altered. If anything had been left unchanged, it was because it was untrue.'

Ernest Hemingway 'Take your manuscript and pitch it across. No, on second thought…first let them toss the money over. Then you throw it over, pick up the money, and get the hell out of there.'

Evelyn Waugh 'Each book purchased for motion pictures has some individual quality, good or bad, that has made it remarkable. It is the work of a great array of highly paid and incompatible writers to distinguish this quality, separate it, and obliterate it.'

Nathanael West 'There's no fooling here. All the writers sit in cells in a row, and the minute a typewriter stops, someone pokes his head in the door to see if you are thinking.'

The novels of Carolyn See, who teaches at UCLA, are well-crafted and inspiring, the most recent being *The Handyman* (1999). It's the story of an aspiring artist who returns to LA from Paris, earns his living as a handyman, hooks up with an eccentric cast of characters and ends up rescuing several by transferring his own humanity onto them.

The novels of Japanese American writer Cynthia Kadohata are emotional yet written in a straight-forward uncluttered way. *In the Heart of the Valley of Love* (1997) is the story of survival of a young girl in a near-apocalyptic LA in 2052 and explores human relationships and struggles in the face of adversity.

Crime For all the literary attention placed on the city, it is crime fiction – traditionally called 'pulp fiction' for the cheap, pulpy paper formerly used by paperback publishers – that really captures Los Angeles. The city has such a short, dense history, with fortunes shifting so dramatically and the inflated hype of the American dream contrasting so sharply with the ever-present specter of desperate, downtrodden hangers-on, that pulp fiction has struck a natural and resounding chord with the American public – as has its big-screen manifestation, film noir.

The undisputed king of LA pulp is Raymond Chandler, who wrote several books from the '30s to the '50s featuring the struggling private investigator Philip Marlowe. Chandler's works are filled with troubled characters riding the tide of evil forces that seem to govern the metropolis – before they sink to the bottom. If you start with Chandler's best-known work, *The Big Sleep* (1939), chances are you'll want to read all of the others, too – among them *The Lady in the Lake* and *The Long Goodbye*.

Another LA pulp writer is James M Cain, who continues to enjoy a popularity that rivals Chandler's. Cain's books – including *The Postman Always Rings Twice* (1934), *Mildred Pierce* (1941) and *Double Indemnity* (1943) – are tense concoctions mixing sex and crime, always with a pervading sense of the enormous opportunities waiting to be seized in Los Angeles.

In Steve Fisher's *I Wake Up Screaming* (1941), inside Hollywood dope scene serves as backdrop to the tale of a blonde beauty, on the brink of stardom, who suddenly turns up dead. When this one was made into a movie, sensitive filmmakers took out the Hollywood dirt and set the story in New York. But crime and the movies turned out to be a popular combination. *The Woman Chaser* (1960), by Charles Willeford, is about a sleazy and successful used car salesman who gives up his business and dives headlong into writing, producing and directing a motion picture – sticking at all costs to his own artistic vision.

The Grifters (1963) is by novelist Jim Thompson, who has been described as a sort of bastard child of Chandler and Hammett. Strange as *that* sounds, Thompson is even weirder. *The Grifters* is about a slick young con-man who preys on the suckers of LA, and his unusually possessive mother who won't leave him alone. Since the '50s, Ross MacDonald has continued to mine the Chandler vein, with Los Angeles figuring prominently in novels such as *The Moving Target* and *The Barbarous Coast*.

In recent years, crime fiction set in LA has enjoyed an enormous resurgence. In 1990 Elmore Leonard came out with *Get Shorty*, about a Florida loan shark who comes to Southern California to collect a large sum of money from a Hollywood producer. Instead – or perhaps inevitably – he gets mixed up in the film business.

Walter Mosley's Easy Rawlins novels, set in Watts, have been hugely popular. *Devil in a Blue Dress, A Red Death, White Butterfly, Black Betty* and *A Little Yellow Dog* place hero Rawlins in a series of situations – always with historically accurate contexts – that test his desire to remain an honest citizen.

James Ellroy's acclaimed quartet of LA police novels, *The Black Dahlia, The Big Nowhere, LA Confidential* and *White Jazz*, are a dizzying time trip through decades of LA's corruption-filled history. After you've read those, check out *Hollywood Nocturnes*, in which Ellroy vividly captures Hollywood at its raciest in the hyper-delusional, over-sexed story of hip-talking accordion player Dick Contino.

Women too have jumped into the mystery fray. Mercedes Lambert's two recent novels *(Dogtown*, 1991, and *Southtown*, 1996) revolve around the adventures of LA lawyer Whitney Logan as she delves into the bowels of Koreatown along with her cohort – and former prostitute – Lupe Ramos.

Michael Nava is another writer who's broken through the boundaries of the mystery genre. The star of his LA-based crime series (including *How Town* and *The Burning Plain*, 1998) is Henry Rios, a gay Mexican American lawyer who is thrown into the dark side of the city of lights.

Theater

After New York, LA is the country's second most influential and important city for live theater. It's a lively scene, fueled by the fact that LA is home to one quarter of the nation's professional actors. The Music Center in Downtown houses two of LA's most important stages, the Ahmanson Theater, which does Broadway productions, and the Mark Taper Forum, which often presents experimental works. Century City's Shubert Theater also hosts major musicals. Other famous theaters include the Pantages in Hollywood and the Pasadena Playhouse.

In recent decades, small independent theaters, the equivalent of off-Broadway and off-off Broadway stages, have flourished in West Hollywood, Hollywood and North Hollywood. Many of them are housed in converted structures, warehouses, retail stores and even a natural forest. Under the Equity Waiver Program, theaters of 99 seats or fewer are allowed to pay non-equity (nonunion) rates to their actors, often resulting in professional actors working alongside amateurs.

Architecture

Despite the city's relative youth, Los Angeles' building styles have gone through a seemingly continual evolution.

The Mission style was popular in the late 19th century. In the early 20th, it was the California bungalow, the paradigm of which is the Gamble House in Pasadena. Frank Lloyd Wright was commissioned to build several homes in Los Angeles between 1917 and 1923; the Hollyhock House in Eastern Hollywood and the Ennis-Brown House near Griffith Park offer some of his finest work. The designs of Irving Gill and of Austrians Rudolph Schindler and Richard Neutra, who introduced the International (or Modernist) style to Los Angeles, are also highly acclaimed.

Downtown Los Angeles still features some of the city's finest buildings. Among them are the 1893 Bradbury Building, a Victorian treasure, and the 1939 Union Passenger Terminal, a fine example of Mission Revival. Parts of Hollywood in particular seem to stand as monuments to the fantastic Art Deco style so popular in the 1920s and '30s. For details on some of the finest in LA architecture, see the Los Angeles Architecture special section.

Painting & Sculpture

The city's first art schools date to the 1880s and include the LA School of Art and Design, founded by Louisa Garden MacLeod, and the College of Fine Arts at the University of Southern California. A decade or so later, the young city saw an influx of painters migrating to sunnier climes from the East Coast and San Francisco. Many settled around the Arroyo Seco in Pasadena as well as in Topanga Canyon, Laguna Beach (Orange County) and Avalon on Catalina Island. Known as the 'Eucalyptus

A Helping Hand for Public Art

Nothing bridges social gaps like the visual arts. Surrounded by speakers of some 90 languages – many living in poverty and unable to afford the 'high' arts – LA-area artists are taking steps to ensure their messages are heard by those residents who need it most.

The Social & Public Art Resource Center (SPARC; ☎ 310-822-9560, www.sparcmurals.org; Map 13), 685 Venice Blvd, Venice, is one such group dedicating itself to the production, exhibition and preservation of multiethnic art projects, notably the city's more than 1000 murals.

Founded in 1976 by three women artists, SPARC has provided countless opportunities for established artists and youth apprentices to embellish their neighborhoods. Some spectacular projects include the **Great Wall of Los Angeles**, a half-mile mural along the Tujunga Wash in the San Fernando Valley, showing the history of California from prehistoric times to the 1950s. It was painted over six summers from 1974–79 by about 400 children and teenagers under the leadership of SPARC cofounder and artistic director, Judith Baca.

In 1988 the Great Walls Unlimited: Neighborhood Pride program was conceived, which, cosponsored by LA's Cultural Affairs Department, has resulted in some 70 murals, mostly in East LA and South Central but also in Koreatown, Long Beach and parts of the San Fernando Valley. SPARC headquarters, in a former jail, also contains a Mural Resource and Education Center and an art gallery.

School,' these painters specialized in pleasant Impressionist-style landscapes with natural and pastel color palettes.

The seeds of Modernism were laid in 1916. Stanton Macdonald-Wright and Rex Slinkard founded the Modern Art Society, whose memebers were largely artists returning to LA from the East Coast or Europe, where they had picked up Cubism, Expressionism and Fauvism. The Otis Art Institute, another important college that survives, also dates to this time. Major Modernists from the '20s to the '40s included Jackson Pollock, Charles White, Man Ray, Eugene Berman, Albert King and Oskar Fischinger. While many were thematically inspired by the California landscape and lighting, by the '40s and '50s, attention turned to the materialism, consumerism and technological progress that characterized the era.

The trend continued through the '60s when LA experienced a major art boom, with a slew of new galleries and museums opening and painters migrating to the city from all over the world. Among them flourished a gaggle of avant-garde artists including Edward Kienholz, Robert Irwin and John Mason, whose works were pioneered by the Ferus Gallery. Other major artists were David Hockney, who had come here from England, Richard Diebenkorn and Ed Ruscha. The '70s saw an emergence of art by ethnic artists, notably the Latino group Los Four (Frank Romero, Beto de la Rocha, Gilbert Lujan and Carlos Almaraz), which focused on public art and gave the city many colorful murals and extravagant sculptures. Women artists were always underrepresented, although muralist Judith Baca has certainly left her mark all over the city.

LA still has a lively art scene, with many museums and private galleries concentrated in Beverly Hills, West Hollywood and Santa Monica. For an easy overview of the latest in local art, visit the several dozen galleries at the Bergamot Station in Santa Monica. Galleries also cluster on the Avenues of Arts & Design in West Hollywood and on La Brea Ave near Melrose Ave. Many established artists live in Venice, including Laddie John Dill; the annual Venice Art Walk lets art lovers sneak a peek into the studios of many of them. The place to be for up-and-coming artists is the rather industrial Arts District in Downtown LA near Little Tokyo and at The Brewery, a nearby artists' colony in an abandoned brewery. The main publication keeping tabs on all current exhibits is *Artscene*, a free monthly that lists dozens of galleries.

RELIGION

Los Angeles may have a reputation as a secular Babylon, a soulless Sodom and Gomorra, but the fact is that religion in all its diversity has always thrived here, especially in the first half of the 20th century. LA gave birth to a number of churches – some might be more suitably called cults – including the Church of the Nazarene in 1908, Aimee Semple McPherson's International Church of the Foursquare Gospel in 1923, the Church of Scientology in 1958 and the Metropolitan Community Churches (catering to gays and lesbians). Evangelist Billy Graham launched his national career here during the Los Angeles crusade of 1949. Disillusionment with traditional faiths and an interest in spirituality in recent decades also generated the New Age movement, which has spread from LA across the country and beyond.

Though Protestant evangelism, brought here by early migrants from the Midwest, dominated in LA until the middle of the 20th century, increased immigration from all over the world has led to immense religious diversification. These days more than 600 religious groupings can be identified in the LA area, making it more diverse than London and New York. Christianity dominates, with more than 3 million Catholics alone. Large Protestant faiths include Methodist, Presbyterian, Episcopalian, Lutheran and Baptist. Evangelical and Pentecostal Christians and Mormons are among the fast-growing congregations. Forty percent of all Buddhists living in the US reside in the LA area, and there are more Jews here (about half a million) than in Tel Aviv.

LANGUAGE

English is Los Angeles' primary and 'official' language, though Spanish is almost as widely spoken. There are entire neighborhoods where foreign languages dominate. Koreatown, for instance, has many store signs in Korean letters only; signs also appear in local languages in Chinatown and of course sections of East LA where Mexican Americans dominate. Spanish is the first language of some 80% of those whose native tongue is not English. Other large linguistic niches are Vietnamese, Hmong and Cantonese.

LOS ANGELES ARCHITECTURE

A rchitecture in LA is as multifaceted as the city's image. In a place where anything goes, the buildings too have pushed creative boundaries, reflecting the different lifestyles, incomes and tastes of its heterogeneous population.

After 1850, the simple adobe and mud constructions of the early Spanish and Mexican settlers had gradually been replaced by structures made from wood and brick. Styles such as Greek Revival, Italianate, Queen Anne and Colonial Revival began to proliferate, making the city look very much like a sunbelt Minnesota. A major turning point in LA history – and its architecture – came in the early 20th century as LA experienced exponential growth and bringing with it young architects eager to build with new styles and materials. Space was abundant and land was cheap. One of the dominant forms developed early on was the bungalow, an outgrowth of the Arts and Crafts movement (also known as Craftsman) and inspired by buildings from the Far East.

DAVID PEEVERS

Craftsman, in many ways, laid the foundation for the Modernist style that was to follow. One of its basic tenets was to adapt the form of the building to its natural environment. Frank Lloyd Wright gave the impetus with his Hollyhock House and drew to LA a slew of other architects, including Rudolph Schindler and Richard Neutra. In true LA fashion, other forms such as Art Deco, Streamline Moderne and Mission Revival flourished simultaneously. The Modernist style prevailed.

After WWII, an ambitious building program covered the suburbs with miles of tract housing – cheap digs for the growing city. But LA's Downtown changed noticeably only in the 1960s and '70s when the city

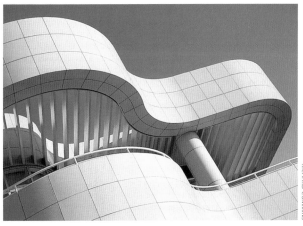

RICHARD CUMMINS

Above: Detail from the Oviatt Building

Right: Getty Center

RICK GERHARTER

repealed the 150-foot height limit (enforced because of the earthquake danger). New technology made it possible to build tall structures capable of withstanding major tremors. Looking at Downtown today, it's hard to imagine that clusters of high-rises didn't take shape until the early '80s.

New architects have since begun experimenting with fragmentation and unconventional building materials. Though influential, not all these architects have proven successful. But as the $1 billion Getty Center (designed by Richard Meier) illustrates, a nearly bottomless budget often begets the grandest designs.

Architects

Frank Lloyd Wright (1867–1959) Frank Lloyd Wright is considered one of the most prolific and influential architects in the USA. Wright came to LA in 1917 to work on the Hollyhock House (see Hollywood in the Things to See & Do chapter). Built in a style he called California Romanza, it incorporated pre-Columbian motifs. Inspired by a set of building blocks he played with as a child, Wright also created 'textile block' houses, made from blocks of prefab concrete. He worked feverishly until his death at the age of 92, dedicated to architecture – which he poetically defined as 'music frozen in time.'

Lloyd Wright (1890–1978) Frank's eldest son, Lloyd, began his career as a landscape architect for the Boston-based firm of Olmsted & Olmsted in 1911, eventually coming to California and joining the firm of Irving Gill. After stints as a set and airplane designer, Lloyd began collaborating with his father on the Hollyhock

Above: Frank Lloyd Wright's Hollyhock House, with Observatory in the far background

Left: Mayan-inspired detail from the Hollyhock House
(RICK GERHARTER)

House. Although he was a prolific architect in his own right, his work has largely been overshadowed by his father's.

Greene & Greene The brothers Charles (1868–1957) and Henry (1870–1954) Greene were educated at the Massachusetts Institute of Technology and arrived in LA in 1893, when the Arts and Crafts movement (also known as Craftsman) was beginning to take hold. They earned their place in architectural history for their invention of the Craftsman bungalow, hugely popular in the early 20th century. Many of their homes survive, especially in Pasadena (see Tour II).

Rudolph Schindler (1887–1953) A great admirer of Frank Lloyd Wright, the Austrian-born Schindler took a job with an architectural firm in Chicago, where Wright's firm was located, hoping that one day he would meet his idol and perhaps work for him. Schindler's dream came true when he became a Wright associate and moved to LA in 1920 to work on the Hollyhock House. Though inspired by Wright, Schindler also created his own more radically Modernist designs, evident in his own home at 833 Kings Rd in West Hollywood (see the Things to See & Do chapter). Some of its elements went on to become staples of Southern California architecture, such as sliding doors, concrete-slab flooring and rooms opening onto a central courtyard.

Richard Neutra (1892–1970) In his mid-20s, Richard Neutra confessed to his diary that he was anxious to leave his native Vienna, Austria, to find a place 'where one does not have to fear the winter, where one does not have to slave, but finds time to think and more importantly, to be a free spirit.' In 1924 Neutra found such a place in LA. He is considered one of the most influential Modernists, obsessed with the concept he called 'bio-realism': achieving organic harmony between the spatial needs of humans and the natural environment. Neutra made ample use of windows and terraces, glass, lightweight steel and other materials suited to the Southern California climate (see Tour III).

Frank Gehry (born 1929) LA-based Frank Gehry is widely regarded as the world's most outstanding contemporary architect. He often uses unconventional materials such as plastic sheering and wire-mesh screens in his designs, which still seem to integrate into their respective environments. Gehry has received several honorary doctorate degrees and countless awards, including the prestigious Pritzker Prize for Architecture (1989). His public designs in LA include the Santa Monica Place shopping mall (1981), the Cabrillo Maritime Museum (1981), the Geffen Contemporary (1983) and **Right:** The Frank Gehry House Loyola Law School (1984). Downtown's Walt Disney Hall, due to be

DAVID PEEVERS

DAVID PEEVERS

completed in 2003, is another Gehry design. (See the Things to See & Do chapter, for more coverage of select Gehry designs.)

Richard Meier (born 1934) Meier is another architect who, like Gehry, has managed to perfect and transcend the Modernist visions of early-20th-century architects such as Schindler and Neutra. Until now, his pinnacle of achievement has been the Getty Center, a commission he received after an illustrious career. For the Getty, he departed from his signature gleaming, white-paneled facades, to using travertine marble instead. Meier also designed the Museum of Television and Radio in Beverly Hills (see the Things to See & Do chapter).

Styles

Victorian Better known as Queen Anne/Eastlake style in California, Victorian architecture was popular in the late 19th and early 20th century. Mostly residential, it consists of multistory homes accented by gables, turrets, mansard roofs, wrap-around porches, heavy detailing and ornamentation, and painted facades in a variety of textures. Few examples survive in LA, but Angelino Heights in Echo Park has a whole cluster (see Downtown in the Things to See & Do chapter).

Mission Revival With its simpler classical lines, Spanish Colonial architecture – as the Mission style is also called – was a reaction to the more elaborate Queen Anne style and a nostalgic hearkening back to the early days of California missions. Hallmarks are arched doors and windows, solid walls and red-tile roofs (used mostly for public buildings but also for residences). The style's heyday lasted from 1890 to 1915. Noteworthy examples in Los Angeles are Union Station in Downtown and the Southwest Museum in Mt Washington (see Things to See & Do).

Craftsman The Craftsman style, which emerged between 1900 and 1920, was a reaction to the Industrial Age and the frilliness of Victorian architecture. Simplicity and harmony were key design principles as practitioners blended Asian, European and American influences into single-family homes that were well-crafted and both functional and comfortable.

Left: The Craftsman-style Gamble House, Pasadena

Houses are distinguished by a boxy shape topped by a low-pitched gabled roof, often with exposed rafters. Wood is the primary material but boulders sometimes constitute the foundations, lower wall sections and chimneys. Overhanging eaves, terraces and sleeping porches function as transitions between, and extensions of, the house and its natural setting (see Tour II).

Revivals In the 1920s, it was very popular to copy earlier styles, often blending them and thus creating an architectural hodgepodge that was surprisingly aesthetic. No style was safe, including Neoclassical, baroque, Tudor, pueblo and French Norman; exotic elements were even borrowed from Mayan, Aztec and Egyptian architecture. Examples abound in Los Angeles, including the houses of worship on the Wilshire Corridor (see Tour IV) and several buildings Downtown (see Tour I).

Art Deco Art Deco was a favorite style in the 1920s and '30s, especially for public and office buildings. The style is characterized by vertical lines and symmetry that create a soaring effect, often mitigated by a stepped pattern toward the top. Ornamentation is heavy, especially above doors and windows, and may consist of floral motifs, sunbursts or zigzags. Excellent examples are the Eastern Columbia Building in Downtown and the Wiltern Theater and former Bullocks Wilshire department store, both in Koreatown (see the Things to See & Do chapter).

Streamline Moderne Related to Art Deco, Streamline Moderne sought to incorporate the machine aesthetic, in particular the aerodynamic aspects of airplanes and ocean liners. Horizontal bands of smallish, circular windows – like ship portholes – and smooth curved facades were

Top right: The Art Deco Eastern Columbia Building, Downtown

Right: The Streamline Moderne Coca-Cola Bottling Plant

typical elements, as were simulated railings and the use of aluminum and stainless steel. Look for this style in the Coca-Cola Bottling Plant in Downtown and in the Crossroads of the World building on Sunset Blvd in Hollywood (see the Things to See & Do chapter).

Modernist Also called the International Style Modern, this style was initiated in Europe (mostly Germany) by Bauhaus architect Walter Gropius, Mies van der Rohe and Le Corbusier. In LA, Rudolph Schindler and Richard Neutra were its early practitioners. Both in its residential and public forms, Modernist characteristics include a boxlike shape, open floor plans, flat roofs, plain and unadorned facades and interior walls, and the abundant use of glass. Examples concentrate in Silver Lake (see Tour III).

Tour I – The Glamour Years: Downtown

Other Downtown architectural gems are covered in the Historic Core Walking Tour in the Things to See & Do chapter.

Central Library, 630 W 5th St The Downtown Central Library was designed in 1922 by Bertram Goodhue who, inspired by the discovery of King Tut's tomb the same year, incorporated numerous Egyptian motifs. Note the sphinxes on either side of the 5th St entrance and the gilded pyramidal tower. Another noteworthy feature is the 2nd-floor cathedral-like Lodwrick M Cook Rotunda. It is almost entirely swathed in a colorful 1933 mural showing snapshots of LA history, such as the founding of the missions and the advent of the railroads. The adjacent Children's Room has a stunning Spanish-Colonial painted wood-beamed ceiling and another historical mural.

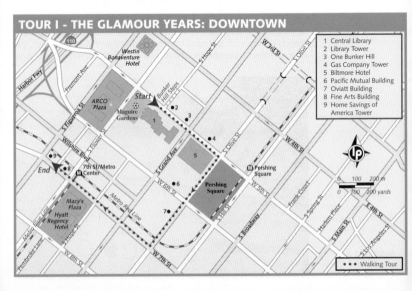

TOUR I - THE GLAMOUR YEARS: DOWNTOWN

1 Central Library
2 Library Tower
3 One Bunker Hill
4 Gas Company Tower
5 Biltmore Hotel
6 Pacific Mutual Building
7 Oviatt Building
8 Fine Arts Building
9 Home Savings of America Tower

The Tom Bradley Wing is an eight-story glass atrium (four stories above ground, four below) added in 1993 and named for a former mayor. Its whimsical chandeliers represent the three types of information available in the library: the natural world, the human-made world and the spiritual world.

DAVID PEEVERS

Library Tower, 633 W 5th St The tallest building in LA has 73 floors and juts 1017 feet into the air. Designed by Henry Cobb, an architect from the New York firm of IM Pei, the Library Tower was attacked by an alien spaceship in the 1996 movie *Independence Day*. Take a peek into the lobby; the walls are adorned with several angel murals.

One Bunker Hill, 601 W 5th St This 12-story Art Deco Moderne office tower with classical elements dates to 1931 (Allison & Allison) and is a composition of limestone and terra-cotta. The reliefs above the entrance recall the building's former occupant, the Southern California Edison company, and depict energy, light and power. The monumental 40-foot-high lobby features 17 types of marble, gold-leaf ceilings and a mural by Hugo Ballin, a set designer for Cecil B DeMille.

Gas Company Tower, 555 W 5th St If you've seen the movie *Speed*, you might recognize this modern office tower squatting on the northeast corner of Pershing Square (1991; Richard Keating). Its monotonous blue-glass facade is broken up on the top floors by an oval wedge (supposedly in the shape of a gas flame). The lobby is reached via two flights of escalators. Through a glass wall you can glimpse the 35,000-sq-foot mural 'Dusk' by Frank Stella on the adjacent building. Integrated into the lobby floor are rows of inverted fountains, which continue outside beyond the glass wall to spurt forth from the ground.

Biltmore Hotel, 515 S Olive St Dominating the Olive St side of Pershing Square is one of LA's grandest and oldest hotels. Designed by the team that also created New York's Waldorf Astoria, it has hosted presidents, the 1960 Democratic National Convention and eight Academy Awards ceremonies. The hotel's sumptuous interior boasts carved and gilded ceilings, marble floors, grand staircases and palatial ballrooms in styles ranging from Renaissance to Baroque to Neoclassical. The Pershing Square entrance leads to a chapel-like side lobby with a carved and painted wooden ceiling. The double staircase with an ornamental railing leads to the Rendezvous Court, modeled after the court of Spain's Queen Isabella.

Right: One Bunker Hill lobby

Pacific Mutual Building, 523 W 6th St An impressive Beaux Arts structure from 1922 (Dodd & Richards), the Pacific Mutual Building boasts a facade that faintly resembles a Greek temple. There's a suggestion of fluted Corinthian columns that visually support the three-story arched entrance topped by terra-cotta sculptures. The lobby's vaulted ceiling and its marble floors, walls and staircase are worth a look, too.

Oviatt Building, 617 S Olive St The 1928 Oviatt is an Art Deco gem conceived by the mildly eccentric James Oviatt, owner of the men's clothing store previously on the premises (now the Cicada restaurant). Oviatt fell in love with Art Deco on a visit to Paris and subsequently had

Los Angeles Conservancy Tours

RICK GERHARTER

The Los Angeles Conservancy (☎ 213-623-2489) is a nonprofit organization with a mission to preserve and raise awareness of the historical buildings in LA. Trained docents conduct a series of entertaining and informative walking tours through the Downtown area. Tours are thematic and, except where noted, meet at 10am, last about 2½ hours and cost $8. Reservations are required.

Angelino Heights (1st & 3rd Sat of the month; $10) – tour LA's first suburb, with its late-19th-century Victorian homes, including interior visits of two.

Art Deco (every Sat) – spotlight the various landmarks built in this jazzy, geometric style en vogue in the 1920s and '30s.

Biltmore Hotel (2nd Sat of the month at 11am; 90 mins) – go behind-the-scenes, including the health club, kitchen and presidential suite.

Broadway Theaters (every Sat) – tour the historic theater district including the insides of accessible theaters.

Little Tokyo (1st Sat of the month) – learn about the history of this Japanese enclave and visit the interiors of a church and temple.

Marble Masterpieces (2nd Sat of the month) – explore the use of marble in lobbies of modern and historic office buildings and hotels.

Mecca for Merchants (4th Sat of the month) – travel 7th St, the birthplace of many of the city's department stores.

Pershing Square (every Sat) – visit the square's architectural and historic landmarks.

Spring Street (2nd & 4th Sat of the month) – stroll along LA's 'Wall Street of the West,' once the heart of the old financial district and now the focus of revitalization.

Union Station (3rd & 4th Sat of the month) – tour the last great railway station built in the US (1939) and the 1993 Transit Gateway addition.

Left: Union Station, Downtown

carpets, draperies and fixtures shipped over from France, including the purportedly largest shipment of etched decorative glass by René Lalique ever to cross the Atlantic. Note the bronze doors and carved wooden interiors of the elevators. Oviatt himself lived in the building's huge, two-story penthouse, complete with pool, roof garden and tennis court.

Fine Arts Building, 811 W 7th St This 12-story 1927 Walker & Eisen structure is a visual feast inside and out. The facade is awash in floral and animal ornamentation; sculptures peer down from arcaded upstairs windows. The cathedral-like lobby, though, is especially striking. Built in Spanish Renaissance style, it has a galleried mezzanine from which large sculptures representing the arts gaze down. It's all topped by a flat-beamed and painted wooden ceiling and anchored by a delightful fountain. Flanking rows of glass alcoves are used for changing art exhibits.

Home Savings of America Tower, 660 S Figueroa St Rising above the Metro Rail station at 7th and Figueroa Sts is this remarkable structure, designed by Tim Vreeland. Travertine and green marble cover the base of the tower, while two floral glass murals rise to a height of 40 feet. Take the elevator to the 7th-floor Sky Lobby, decked out in polished marble in natural and burgundy tones and crowned by a mural of a romanticized portrayal of LA by Richard Haas.

Tour II – Craftsman & Beyond in Pasadena

This tour covers a small area in western Pasadena, near the Norton Simon Museum, that teems with exemplary Craftsman bungalows by Charles and Henry Greene. Homes by other architects of the style cluster in the Bungalow Heaven neighborhood in northern Pasadena

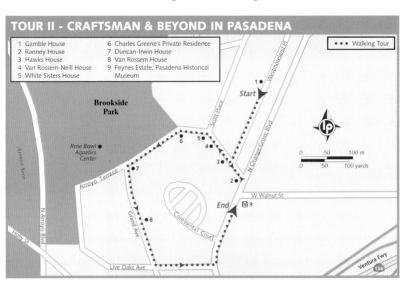

TOUR II - CRAFTSMAN & BEYOND IN PASADENA

1 Gamble House
2 Ranney House
3 Hawks House
4 Van Rossem-Neill House
5 White Sisters House
6 Charles Greene's Private Residence
7 Duncan-Irwin House
8 Van Rossem House
9 Feynes Estate; Pasadena Historical Museum

••• Walking Tour

Brookside Park

Start

Rose Bowl ● Aquatics Center

End 🏛 9

W Walnut St

0   50   100 m
0   50   100 yards

Arroyo Seco

Arroyo Terrace

Grand Ave

Continental Court

Live Oaks Ave

N Arroyo Blvd

Holly St

Westmoreland Pl

Scott Place

N Orange Grove Blvd

Ventura Fwy

134

ANDREA SCHULTE-PEEVERS

between Mountain St and Washington Blvd and Wilson Ave and Holliston Ave. Stop by the Pasadena Visitors & Convention Bureau (see the Facts for the Visitor chapter) for a pamphlet outlining a self-guided tour of this latter area.

Gamble House, 4 Westmoreland Place
The Gamble House is a 1908 Greene & Greene design considered the world's best example of Craftsman architecture. It features terraces, bedroom porches for outdoor sleeping and overhanging eaves to keep out the sun. A designated National Historic Landmark, it is now a study center for the USC School of Architecture. Original furnishings, also designed by the brothers, share attention with the rare and dark woods – teak, maple, oak, redwood – and the leaded art glass, especially in the front door. The Gamble House starred as the home of mad scientist Doc Brown (Christopher Lloyd) in the three *Back to the Future* movies. Guided one-hour tours (☎ 626-793-3334) depart roughly every 20 minutes noon to 3 pm Thursday to Sunday except major holidays. Tours are $5/4/3/free for adults/seniors/students/children.

Other Greene & Greene Homes Tranquil Arroyo Terrace has the highest concentration of homes by the brothers, including **Charles' private residence** at 368 Arroyo Terrace, begun in 1902 but altered and enlarged numerous times. Other examples include **Hawks House** (1906), 408 Arroyo Terrace; **Ranney House** (1907), 440 Arroyo Terrace; **Van Rossem-Neill House** (1903–6), 400 Arroyo Terrace; **White Sisters House** (1903 for Charles' sister-in-law), 370 Arroyo Terrace.

More structures are on Grand Ave, around the corner from Arroyo Terrace, including the large **Duncan-Irwin House** (1900–06) with a beautiful facade at 240 Grand Ave, and the **Van Rossem House** (1904) at 210 Grand Ave.

Feynes Estate, 470 W Walnut St This beautiful 18-room mansion is home of the Pasadena Historical Society (☎ 626-577-1660). Built in 1907 by Robert Farquhar in Beaux Arts style, it was once owned by the Finnish consul, which explains the small display of Finnish folk art in the former garden sauna. The main house has a local history museum with antique furnishings, paintings and Oriental rugs adorning the main floor and archival photos in the basement. Guided tours are offered at 1pm, 2pm and 3pm Thursday to Sunday (closed holidays) and cost $4, $3 for seniors & students, free for children.

Top Left: Duncan-Irwin House, Pasadena

Left: Feynes Estate, Pasadena
(ANDREA SCHULTE-PEEVERS)

Tour III – Modernist Visions in Silver Lake

Silver Lake – especially the streets framing the Silver Lake reservoir – has a great concentration of milestone residential architecture, allowing for a quick survey of LA's best-known Modernists, Richard Neutra and Rudolph Schindler. Except for the Neutra homes, which date primarily to the 1950s and '60s, most were built during the 1920s and '30. All are private homes, so please do not disturb the residents. Note that this is not a walking tour, as the homes are spread across many miles.

Richard Neutra Private Residence, 2300 E Silver Lake Blvd Having spent his early LA years living in Schindler's house on N Kings Rd, Neutra was able to create his own residential vision in 1933 thanks to a $3000 grant by Dutch patron CH Van der Leeuw. The Silver Lake reservoir is visible from the upper floor, where he placed the private quarters, including living room, sleeping porches and roof deck. His studio and guest quarters are on the lower floor. The house burned down in 1963 and was re-created by Neutra's son Dion. It is now owned by Cal Poly Pomona's School of Environmental Design and may be viewed by appointment only (☎ 909-869-2667). Neutra's ashes are buried beneath a eucalyptus tree in the garden.

Neutra Colony The full extent of Neutra's architectural vision shines through in a convenient cluster of private homes built just south of his

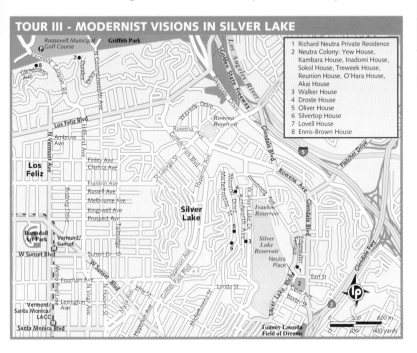

TOUR III - MODERNIST VISIONS IN SILVER LAKE

1 Richard Neutra Private Residence
2 Neutra Colony: Yew House,
   Kambara House, Inadomi House,
   Sokol House, Treweek House,
   Reunion House, O'Hara House,
   Akai House
3 Walker House
4 Droste House
5 Oliver House
6 Silvertop House
7 Lovell House
8 Ennis-Brown House

DAVID PEEVERS

own in the area where Silver Lake Blvd intersects with Earl St and Cove Ave. They include the following:

Yew House (1957), 2226 Silver Lake Blvd; **Kambara House** (1960), 2232 Silver Lake Blvd; **Inadomi House** (1960), 2238 Silver Lake Blvd; **Sokol House** (1948), 2242 Silver Lake Blvd; **Treweek House** (1948), 2250 Silver Lake Blvd; **Reunion House** (1949), 2240 Earl St; **O'Hara House** (1961), 2210 Neutra Place; **Akai House** (1961), 2200 Neutra Place.

Kenilworth Ave & Micheltorena St Rudolph Schindler designed several houses on this quiet street. The mint-colored Walker House (1936), whose dramatic garden side is unfortunately not visible from the street, is at 2100 Kenilworth Ave. What is visible are the sliding front doors and two-door garage. Atop a slope at 2025 Kenilworth Ave is the slightly crumbling Droste House (1940), painted in the same color.

Schindler's Oliver House (1933), 2236 Micheltorena St, has a modest street-side exterior that belies the gabled roofline facing the garden and the wooden rooftop sundeck. One of the most remarkable buildings is expressionist John Lautner's Silvertop House (1957), 2128 Micheltorena St, which features angular and round forms, a cantilevered driveway and a pool.

Lovell House, 4616 Dundee Dr The Lovell House was the structure that catapulted Richard Neutra to architectural stardom. Built in 1929, it is quintessential International Style, featuring modern-age materials such as a lightweight steel frame that took only 40 hours to erect. Its open, free-flowing floor plan and suspended balconies are typical of Neutra's vision. This house was prominently featured in the movie *LA Confidential*.

Ennis-Brown House, 2607 Glendower Ave Not far from the Lovell House is this 1924 Frank Lloyd Wright structure on a hillside overlooking the city and is the last of his four 'textile block' houses. Inspired by Mayan architecture, it has a highly ornamented and organized facade. Some two dozen forms of prefab concrete blocks, held together with steel spikes, were used in the construction. The main living area is on the upper floor, reached via a marble staircase. Besides offering great views, the living room also has a fireplace topped by a glass mosaic. *Blade*

Left: Part of the Neutra Colony, Silver Lake

Right: Wilshire Boulevard Temple

Runner, Twin Peaks and a Ricky Martin video are among the filmings that have taken place here. Tours are offered on the second Saturday of every odd month by reservation only (☎ 323-660-0607); the cost is $10 for adults, $5 for students & seniors. If you're not in town at that time, you can call and arrange for a private tour on another date – the price is the same but there's a three-person (or $30) minimum.

Tour IV – Religious Buildings on Wilshire

Wilshire Blvd between Western Ave and Hoover St has the greatest concentration of religious structures in LA. Most date back to the 1920s, when Wilshire was being developed as a fashionable thoroughfare, and the buildings' size and elaborate features reflect pre-Depression prosperity. These days, most are supported and maintained by Korean and Latino immigrant congregations. Stylistically, these churches are a theatrical hodgepodge of various styles borrowed from different time periods and places around the world. It's not unusual to find soaring Gothic arches paired with a Byzantine dome and a Romanesque rose window.

While purists might scorn this seemingly incongruous blending, in most cases architects managed to come up with aesthetically pleasing and functional creations.

Christ Church, 635 S Manhattan Place Originally a synagogue, this Renaissance Revival was built by Russell & Alpaugh in 1924 and is now a nondenominational congregation. It sports a triple-arched entryway topped by a row of arched bays separated by carved medallions.

Wilshire Boulevard Temple, 3663 Wilshire Blvd This dignified synagogue houses the largest and oldest Jewish Reform synagogue in LA, with a congregation of more than 2400 families. A short staircase leads to a Romanesque three-arched

Judson Studios: A Legacy of Stained Glass

Those with an interest in LA churches are likely to come across superb stained-glass windows of near supernatural luster and transparency. These windows may well be the product of the Judson Studios (☎ 323-255-0131), a small workshop hidden away in a rambling villa at 200 S Ave 66 in the Highland Park neighborhood, northeast of Downtown.

In business for five generations, Judson Studios has created pieces primarily for churches, though they've also created a football-field-size vaulted ceiling for the Tropicana Hotel in Las Vegas from their diminutive digs. Here in LA, examples of their work include the rotunda of the Natural History Museum in Exposition Park and the windows of St James Episcopal Church on Wilshire Blvd. The latter features the work of three generations of Judsons, each employing a different style. Look for the Craftsman window (1926) in the north elevation, the Neo-Gothic one (1952) in the south elevation and the contemporary Gothic (1995) in the clerestory. Tours of the studios ($5) are offered by appointment on Wednesday for groups only, but individual visitors are welcome to join in. Call ahead to see if a tour is scheduled. There's also a gallery, open from 10am to 4pm Monday to Friday (free admission).

portal, topped by a rose window and lorded over by an enormous dome. Inspired by a synagogue in Florence, Italy, it was designed by a team of architects that included Abram M Edelman, the son of the temple's first rabbi, and was built in 1929. The sanctuary is a breathtaking symphony of black marble, gilded altar fixtures, stained-glass windows, hardwood doors, wainscoting and bronze chandeliers – and above it all a soaring cupola. Of particular note is the frieze mural that wraps around the entire interior. Donated by the movie-mogul Warner brothers and painted by Hugo Ballin, it depicts 3000 years of Jewish history, culminating with an eerie foreshadowing of the Holocaust. The history of LA Jews is shown in

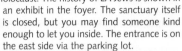

DAVID PEEVERS

an exhibit in the foyer. The sanctuary itself is closed, but you may find someone kind enough to let you inside. The entrance is on the east side via the parking lot.

St Basil's Roman Catholic Church, 3535 W 6th St Designed in 1974, St Basil's is one of the rare modern churches on Wilshire Blvd. A fairly typical example of 1970s aesthetics, its exterior is reminiscent of Pablo Picasso at the height of his Cubist period. Unadorned concrete columns seem to support each other at odd angles and are intersected by floor-to-ceiling abstract stained-glass windows. Sculptures inside the church depict the Stations of the Cross.

Wilshire Christian Church, 634 S Normandie Ave The work of Robert Orr (1923), this is an extravagant pile of reinforced concrete

Left: St Basil's Roman Catholic Church

inspired by the hugely popular Northern Italian Romanesque style. This church features an octagonal campanile with a red-tile roof and a French rose window.

Immanuel Presbyterian Church, 3300 Wilshire Blvd This church dates from 1927, and with its very prominent tower of 200 feet, stylistically emulates the 15th-century French Gothic cathedrals. The vaulted nave is decorated with colored stencil drawings. The church's floors are done in tile, and there are plenty of carved-wood fixtures, including the pulpit.

First Congregational Church, 540 S Commonwealth Ave One block north of Wilshire Blvd, this Gothic-style church was built by LA architect David Allison in 1932 and is topped by a tower inspired by that of Magdalen College at Oxford University in England. The cruciform sanctuary exudes a dignified air, with muted light slicing through kaleidoscopic stained glass windows designed by the Judson Studios (see boxed text). The entrance is through an arched portal with cast-bronze doors depicting scenes from the life of Christ. The church's Great Organ boasts over 20,000 pipes and ranks among the world's largest; recitals take place regularly. Ask the receptionist at the adjacent school for permission to enter if the doors are closed.

Tour V – The Cutting Edge

Frank Gehry and Richard Meier are the two major architects that have made their mark in LA in the '80s and '90s. Both have taken on large and small-scale commercial and residential commissions that have stretched the frontier of LA architecture. You'll need a car to see all of these places in a single day.

Right: Richard Meier's cutting-edge landmark, the Getty Center

RICHARD CUMMINS

The Getty Center, 1200 Getty Center Dr (Map 2) The most remarkable work of architecture in recent LA history is the hilltop Getty Center (1998). Its fortresslike appearance from vantage points below vanishes the moment you find yourself face to face with the complex. Architect Richard Meier has made perfect use of the hill's natural shape, placing buildings along the outline of a ridge. Openness is the connecting element between each of the structures, as they all lead to courtyards and terraces and are angled and spaced to provide different views of the city and the mountains at every turn. There's no building taller than two stories, but Meier built additional subterranean floors connected by corridors.

The museum consists of five sequential pavilions entered from a central courtyard accented by an elongated fountain. Also accessible from here are the circular garden, a cafe and other facilities. Sensuously curved buildings are juxtaposed with geometric ones. Add the California sunshine to the mix and you get a most remarkable alchemy of light and shadow. It's an effect further enhanced by the stone used in the Getty's construction: cream-colored, cleft-cut, textured and fossilized travertine marble. Reflecting the sunlight in the early morning, the marble literally seems to absorb the rays in the afternoon before radiating a golden warmth.

Free architecture tours of the Getty are offered continuously throughout the day. Check at the information desk for the next available tour.

Chiat/Day Building, 340 Main St, Venice (Map 13) The West Coast headquarters of this international advertising agency is a world-famous Frank Gehry landmark. The building's visual focus is a giant pair of binoculars, designed by Claes Oldenburg and Coosje van Bruggen, leading to the parking garage. It is flanked by two wings: one white, curved and streamlined to resemble an oceanliner, the other a surreally angled group of copper-plated pillars that are an abstract rendition of a forest.

Gehry House, 1002 22nd St, Santa Monica (Map 13) For his 1978 private residence, Frank Gehry converted a rather mundane two-story clapboard home into a deconstructivist postmodern collage. He stripped and gutted the structure, then wrapped it into an oddly angular shell made from such materials as corrugated aluminum siding, plywood, glass and chain-link fencing. Although aesthetically pleasing as a whole, the Gehry House juxtaposes visually incongruous elements, creating the effect of an abstract sculpture.

RICK GERHARTER

Left: Chiat/Day Building, a Frank Gehry design, Venice

Facts for the Visitor

WHEN TO GO

Los Angeles, blessed by sunshine and moderate temperatures, is a year-round destination. The best months are usually April to June and September and October. The beaches are liveliest in summer, but hotel prices rise accordingly. During shoulder seasons, tourist crowds are smaller, prices are lower, and most attractions are still operating. The winter months, while cooler and with a greater chance of rain, can still be a good time to travel to LA. In fact, this is when the city often looks positively stunning: clear skies, summer temperatures, dreamy sunsets and the Downtown skyline set against the backdrop of 10,000-foot mountains doused in snow. Hotel prices are at their all-time-low. On the downside, many points of interest have shorter hours.

ORIENTATION

Most first-time visitors to Los Angeles are instantly confused, even intimidated, by its size and sprawl. Unlike other metropolises, like New York or Paris, LA is a decentralized hodgepodge with no clearly defined center. In order to understand this phenomenon, it helps to know that what is commonly referred to as 'LA' is really 'LA County,' a conglomeration of 88 cities of which Los Angeles is just one. Others are such well-known locales as Santa Monica, Pasadena, Beverly Hills and Long Beach, each one of them a city in its own right, with its own government, business district, residential areas, parks and attractions.

The heart of the city of Los Angeles is Downtown, about 12 miles east of the ocean and hemmed in by the I-10, I-5 and US 101. Northeast of here is the city of Pasadena, the main city in the San Gabriel Valley and home to the Rose Bowl and prominent universities and research centers. East of Downtown is East LA, where immigrants from Mexico and other Latin American countries have recreated a community resembling those they left behind. Latinos have also increasingly moved into such historically African American neighborhoods as Watts, Compton and Inglewood, located south and southwest of Downtown LA.

Most areas of interest to visitors are west of Downtown LA. Hollywood is a vast area that encompasses such neighborhoods as bohemian-turned-trendy Silver Lake and fashionable Melrose Avenue. On its western edge is the city of West Hollywood, the epicenter of gay and lesbian culture. Farther west are the 'three Bs': Bel Air, Brentwood and the city of Beverly Hills, which collectively epitomize the 'lifestyles of the rich and famous.' Hugging the northern county coast are three more posh areas: the beachside city of Malibu, Pacific Palisades and the city of Santa Monica. Farther south along the coast, Venice, Marina del Rey and the South Bay cities of Manhattan Beach, Hermosa Beach and Redondo Beach are all relaxed, middle-class enclaves with a strong beach culture of surfing, tanning, volleyball, etc. The South Bay spills into the craggy Palos Verdes peninsula, home to three master-planned, wealthy communities shared by people, horses and, yes, peacocks. San Pedro and Long Beach, the southern beach towns, are both characterized by their

The Shoestring Corridor

The most interesting aspect of the shape of Los Angeles is the long narrow strip known as the Shoestring Corridor, which was annexed by the city in 1906. Sixteen miles long, but just half a mile wide, this strip connects central LA to the city's harbor in San Pedro, slicing through the cities of Gardena, Carson, Torrance and Lomita. On any clearly demarcated map, it appears that the City of Angels has the tail of a devil.

ports. Offshore, thinly populated Santa Catalina Island has a Mediterranean flavor and makes for a nice day trip.

The Hollywood Hills, a continuation of the Santa Monica Mountains, are a physical and, some might say, ideological separation between Los Angeles 'proper' and the San Fernando Valley, which forms the northern boundary of LA County. The quintessential suburbia, it is characterized by unsightly strip malls but also by major TV and movie studios and related facilities.

MAPS

In most cases, the maps in this book are comprehensive enough for you to navigate within particular neighborhoods without getting lost. Handout maps from hotels, car-rental agencies and tourist offices may be insufficient if you plan on spending any length of time exploring the nooks and crannies of LA County. To cover the entire area, you most likely need several maps. The driver's bible is the annually updated, fully indexed *Thomas Guide* ($19.95) with detailed maps of the entire county. Call ☎ 800-899-6277 to order, or visit any local bookstore.

Other good maps are those by the American Automobile Association, available at the organization's offices (see Useful Organizations, later in this chapter, for details) and free to members. Lonely Planet produces a Los Angeles map, available in bookstores or through the company's Web site (www.lonelyplanet.com).

RESPONSIBLE TOURISM

Water is a precious resource and too much of it gets wasted every single day. You can help LA maintain its water reservoir by taking short showers and by being conservative in your use of towels; don't use three when one will suffice. To help conserve energy, turn off lights and the air-conditioning when leaving your hotel room. Littering is loathed and incurs hefty fines. While hiking in the woods, stay on the trails and don't pick wildflowers. Take out everything you bring in – this includes *any* kind of garbage you create.

TOURIST OFFICES
Local Tourist Offices

Maps, brochures, lodging information and tickets to theme parks and other attractions are available through the Los Angeles Convention and Visitors Bureau (LACVB). The Downtown office (☎ 213-689-8822, fax 213-624-1992; Map 5), 685 S Figueroa St, Los Angeles, CA 90017, is open 8am-5pm Monday to Friday, and 8:30am Saturday. The Hollywood Visitor Information Center (☎ 213-689-8822; Map 9), in Janes House at 6541 Hollywood Blvd, is open 9am-5pm, Monday to Saturday. The LACVB also maintains a 24-hour multilingual events hotline at ☎ 213-689-8822; its Web site is at www.lacvb.com.

The California Welcome Center (☎ 310-854-7616), 8500 Beverly Blvd, on the ground floor of the Beverly Center, is open 10am-6pm daily and has plenty of free brochures about sights and hotels throughout the entire state. The staff also sells tickets to local attractions, museums and events and can help with hotel reservations.

Many of the independent cities within LA County either provide information through their tourist offices or chambers of commerce. Contact any of these agencies for specific information about lodgings or attractions in that particular city only.

Beverly Hills Visitors Bureau (☎ 310-248-1015, 800-345-2210, www.bhvb.org; Map 11) 239 S Beverly Dr, Beverly Hills, CA 90212

Hermosa Beach Chamber of Commerce (☎ 310-376-0951, www.hbchamber.net/home; Map 14) 1007 Hermosa Ave, Hermosa Beach, CA 90254

Hollywood Chamber of Commerce (☎ 323-469-8311, http://chamber.hollywood.com; Map 9) 7018 Hollywood Blvd, Hollywood, CA 90028

Long Beach Area Convention & Visitors Bureau (☎ 562-436-3645, 800-452-7829, www.golongbeach.org; Map 16) 1 World Trade Center, Suite 300, Long Beach, CA 90831

Malibu Chamber of Commerce (☎ 310-456-9025, fax 310-456-0195, www.malibu.org) 23805 Stuart Ranch Rd, Malibu, CA 90265

Manhattan Beach Chamber of Commerce (☎ 310-545-5313, http://manhattanbeachchamber.net; Map 14) 425 15th St, Manhattan Beach, CA 90266

Marina del Rey Visitors Center (☎ 310-305-9546; Map 13) 4701 Admiralty Way, Marina del Rey, CA 90292

Pasadena Convention & Visitors Bureau (☎ 626-795-9311, http://pasadenacal.com; Map 17) 171 S Los Robles Ave, Pasadena, CA 91101

Redondo Beach Chamber of Commerce & Visitors Bureau (☎ 310-374-2171, 800-282-0333, http://redondochamber.org; Map 14) 200 N Pacific Coast Hwy, Redondo Beach, CA 90277

San Pedro Chamber of Commerce (☎ 310-832-7272, sanpedrochamber.com; Map 15) 390 W 7th St, San Pedro, CA 90731

Santa Monica Convention & Visitors Bureau (☎ 310-393-7593, www.santamonica.com; Map 13) 1400 Ocean Blvd, Santa Monica, CA 90401

West Hollywood Convention & Visitors Bureau (☎ 310-289-2525, 800-368-6020, fax 310-289-2529; www.visitwesthollywood.com; Map 10) 8687 Melrose Ave, M-38, Pacific Design Center, West Hollywood, CA 90069

Tourist Offices Abroad

The LACVB has trained a network of travel agents in Australia, Germany, Mexico, Britain and Japan who can help with travel plans to Los Angeles. See the LACVB Web site (link to LA Travel Experts) for contact information if you live in one of those countries.

The California Division of Tourism in Sacramento publishes an annual California Official State Visitor's Guide, available for free via the Internet (www.gocalif.ca.gov) or by calling ☎ 800-862-2543. Much of the information is also contained on the Web site itself.

TRAVEL AGENCIES

Budget and student travel specialists include Council Travel with offices in Westwood at 931 Westwood Blvd (☎ 310-208-3551; Map 11); in Santa Monica at 531 Santa Monica Blvd (☎ 310-656-9991; Map 13); in Pasadena inside Distant Lands bookstore at 56 S Raymond Ave (☎ 626-793-5598; Map 17); and in Long Beach at 4706 E 2nd St (☎ 562-621-6603; Map 4). The Santa Monica branch is a so-called 'gateway office,' meaning it sells books tours and tickets to local and regional attractions; it also offers Internet access.

STA Travel has offices in Westwood at 920 Westwood Blvd (☎ 310-824-1574; Map 11); in Santa Monica at 411 Santa Monica Blvd (☎ 310-394-5126; Map 13) and in Hollywood at 7202 Melrose Ave (☎ 323-934-8722; Map 10).

DOCUMENTS

With the exception of Canadians, who need only proper proof of Canadian citizenship, all foreign visitors to the US must have a passport and most are required to have a US visa. Your passport should be valid for at least six months longer than your intended stay in the USA.

Although most US visitors ultimately have no problem entering the country, immigration and customs officials at Los Angeles International Airport are not famous for their people skills. They may try to intimidate you by firing off a barrage of questions concerning the length of your stay, the amount of money you're carrying, whether you have relatives in the US, where you will be staying or traveling to, and so on. Be prepared to show your return flight ticket; try to remain as calm as possible and answer all questions politely. Be aware that until you have passed through the last formality, you have few rights.

If you feel you have been harassed by an immigration officer (sexist comments have been among the unpleasantries experienced by the author), request to speak with a supervisor immediately. You can state your complaint to them directly or fill out a complaint form. Normally this is all you need to do, but as a further step you can call the US Immigration Service at ☎ 310-215-2101. If you feel that you've been treated inappropriately by a US Customs agent, again request to speak with a supervisor or contact the US Customs offices at ☎ 310-215-2414 (or 2415).

Visas

A reciprocal visa-waiver program applies to citizens of certain countries who may enter the USA for stays of 90 days or less without a visa. Currently these countries are Andorra, Argentina, Australia, Austria,

HIV & Entering the USA

Anyone entering the USA who isn't a US citizen is subject to the authority of the Immigration and Naturalization Service (INS), which has the final say about whether you enter or not. Being HIV-positive is not grounds for deportation, but it is grounds for exclusion. What this means is that once in the US, you cannot be deported for being HIV-positive, but you can be prevented from entering the US.

Though the INS does not test people for HIV when they try to enter the US, however, exclusion may result from answering 'yes' to the question 'Have you ever been afflicted with a communicable disease of public health significance?' on the nonimmigrant visa application form.

If you are HIV-positive but are the spouse, parent or child of a US citizen or legal resident (green-card holder), you are exempt from the exclusionary rule.

For legal information and referrals to immigration advocates, contact the National Immigration Project of the National Lawyers Guild (☎ 617-227-9727), 14 Beacon St, Suite 506, Boston, MA 02108; or the Immigrant HIV Assistance Project, Bar Association of San Francisco (☎ 415-267-0795), 685 Market St, Suite 700, San Francisco, CA 94105.

Belgium, Brunei, Denmark, Finland, France, Germany, Iceland, Ireland, Italy, Japan, Liechtenstein, Luxembourg, Monaco, The Netherlands, New Zealand, Norway, San Marino, Slovenia, Spain, Sweden, Switzerland and the UK. Under this program you must have a round-trip ticket on an airline that participates in the program, proof of financial solvency and a signed form waiving the right to a deportation hearing; you will also not be allowed to extend your stay beyond the 90 days. Consult with your travel agent or contact airlines for more information.

All other travelers will need to obtain a visa from a US consulate or embassy, a process that can usually be done by mail in most countries. Visa applicants may be required to 'demonstrate binding obligations' that will ensure their return back home. Because of this requirement, those planning to travel through other countries before arriving in the USA are generally better off applying for their US visa before they leave their home country, rather than doing so on the road.

The most common visa is a Non-Immigrant Visitor's Visa, B1 for business purposes, B2 for tourism or visiting friends and relatives. A visitor's visa is good for one or five years with multiple entries, and it specifically prohibits taking paid employment in the USA.

If you're coming to the USA to work, you will need a different type of visa, your company or institution should make the arrangements. Allow six months in advance of your planned arrival for processing the application.

Visa Extensions If you want to extend your stay in the USA beyond the date stamped on your passport, apply for an extension *before* the stamped date. Since immigration officers usually assume that you intend to work illegally, you should come prepared with concrete evidence that you've been traveling extensively and will continue to be a model tourist rather than joining the 9-to-5 brigade. A wad of traveler's checks looks much better than a solid bank account. It's also a good idea to bring a US citizen with you to vouch for your character.

Extensions are handled in person by the US Government's Justice Department's Immigration & Naturalization Service (INS; ☎ 213-526-7647), 300 N Los Angeles St, open 6am-3pm most weekdays except to 1pm Thursday. Information over the telephone is dispensed from 7am to 5:30pm weekdays.

Travel Insurance

No matter how you're traveling, make sure you take out travel insurance. Ideally, coverage should not only include medical expenses and luggage theft or loss, but also cover you in case of cancellations or delays in your travel arrangements. The best policies are those that also extend to the worst possible scenario, such as an accident that requires hospitalization and return flight home. Check your medical policy at home, since some may already provide worldwide coverage, in which case you only need to protect yourself against other problems.

Ask both your insurer and your ticket-issuing agency to explain the finer points, especially what supporting documentation is required in case you need to file a claim. STA Travel and Council Travel offer travel insurance options at reasonable prices. Buy travel insurance as early as possible. If you buy it the week before you leave, you may find that, for instance, you're not covered for delays to your flight caused by strikes or other industrial action that may have been in force before you took out the insurance.

Other Documents

Bring your driver's license if you intend to drive a car. If you're a foreign visitor, an International Driving Permit (IDP) is a useful, though not mandatory, accessory. They're usually available for a small fee from your national automobile association and valid for one year. Also bring your valid national license, since it will need to be presented with the IDP. Driver's licenses are also a useful form of identification when seeking access to bars, shows or other age-restricted facilities.

A couple of hostels in Los Angeles are part of Hostelling International/American Youth Hostel (HI/AYH; www.iyhf.org), which is affiliated with the International Youth Hostel Federation (IYHF). You don't need an HI/AYH card in order to stay at these hostels, but having one saves you $3 a night. You can also buy one at the hostel when checking in.

If you're a student, bring along an International Student Identification Card (ISIC),

a plastic ID card with your photograph. These are available at your university or at student-oriented travel agencies and often entitle you to discounts on transportation (including airlines and local public transport) and on admission to museums and sights and meals at university cafeterias. If you're a US student, carry your school or university's ID card.

People over the age of 65 (sometimes 60 or 62) usually qualify for the same discounts as students; a driver's license with your birth date should suffice.

Copies

Before you leave home, you should photocopy all important documents (passport data and visa page, credit cards, travel insurance policy, air/bus/train tickets, driver's license, etc). Leave one copy with someone at home and keep another with you, separate from the originals.

It's also a good idea to store details of your vital travel documents in Lonely Planet's free online Travel Vault in case you lose the photocopies or can't be bothered with them. Your password-protected Travel Vault is accessible online anywhere in the world – to create an account go to www .ekno.lonelyplanet.com.

EMBASSIES & CONSULATES
US Embassies & Consulates

US diplomatic offices abroad include the following:

Australia (☎ 2-6270-5000) 21 Moonah Place, Yarralumla ACT 2600
(☎ 2-9373-9200) Level 59 MLC Center 19-29 Martin Place, Sydney NSW 2000
(☎ 3-9526-5900) 553 St Kilda Rd, Melbourne, Victoria

Canada (☎ 613-238-5335) 100 Wellington St, Ottawa, Ontario K1P 5T1
(☎ 604-685-1930) 1095 W Pender St, Vancouver, BC V6E 2M6
(☎ 514-398-9695) 1155 rue St-Alexandre, Montreal, Quebec

France (☎ 01 42 96 12 02) 2 rue Saint Florentin, 75001 Paris

Germany Embassy: (☎ 030-238 51 74) Neustädtische Kirchstrasse 4-5, Berlin

Consulate: (☎ 030-832 92 33) Clayallee 170, Berlin

Ireland (☎ 1-687-122) 42 Elgin Rd, Ballsbridge, Dublin

Japan (☎ 3-224-5000) 1-10-5 Akasaka Chome, Minato-ku, Tokyo

Mexico (☎ 5-211-0042) Paseo de la Reforma 305, 06500 Mexico City

The Netherlands (☎ 70-310-9209) Lange Voorhout 102, 2514 EJ The Hague (☎ 20-310-9209) Museumplein 19, 1071 DJ Amsterdam

New Zealand (☎ 4-722-068) 29 Fitzherbert Terrace, Thorndon, Wellington

UK (☎ 0171-499-9000) 5 Upper Grosvenor St, London W1 (☎ 31-556-8315) 3 Regent Terrace, Edinburgh EH7 5BW (☎ 232-328-239) Queens House, Belfast BT1 6EQ

Consulates in Los Angeles
Most foreign embassies in the US are located in Washington, DC, but a lot of countries, including the following, have consular offices in Los Angeles. For addresses and telephone numbers of other consulates, please consult the Yellow Pages under Consulates & Other Foreign Government Representatives.

Australia (☎ 310-229-4800, fax 310-277-2258) 2049 Century Park E, 19th floor, 90067

Canada (☎ 213-346-2700, fax 213-346-2767 550 S Hope St, 9th floor, 90071

France (☎ 310-235-3200, fax 310-479-4813) 10990 Wilshire Blvd, Suite 300, 90024

Germany (☎ 323-930-2703, fax 323-930-2805) 6222 Wilshire Blvd, Suite 500, 90048

Japan (☎ 213-617-6700, fax 213-617-6727) 350 S Grand Ave, Suite 1700, 90071

Mexico (☎ 213-351-6800, fax 213-389-9249) 2401 W 6th St, 90057

New Zealand (☎ 310-207-1605, fax 310-207-3605) 12400 Wilshire Blvd, Suite 1150, 90025

UK (☎ 310-477-3322, fax 310-575-1450) 11766 Wilshire Blvd, Suite 400, 90025

Your Own Embassy
As a tourist, it's important to realize what the embassy or consulate of which you are a citizen can and can't do while you're in the US. Generally speaking, it won't be much help in emergencies if the trouble you're in is remotely your own fault. Remember at all times that you are bound by local law and not your own country's. Your embassy may not be sympathetic if you end up in jail after committing a crime locally, even if such actions are legal in your own country.

In genuine emergencies, you might get some assistance, but only if other channels have been exhausted. If all your money and documents are stolen, for instance, it will help you get a new passport. Having a photocopy of the important pages of your passport will make replacement that much easier. But forget about a free ticket if you need to get home urgently – after all, that's what travel insurance is for.

Some embassies used to keep letters for travelers or have a small reading room with home country newspapers, but these days, the mail-holding service has usually been stopped, and even newspapers tend to be out-of-date.

CUSTOMS
US Customs allows each person over the age of 21 to bring 1 liter of liquor and 200 cigarettes duty-free into the USA. US citizens are allowed to import, duty-free, $400 worth of gifts from abroad, and non-US citizens are allowed to bring in $100 worth.

Amounts over $10,000 in US or foreign cash, traveler's checks, money orders or the like need to be declared. There is no legal restriction on the amount that may be imported, but undeclared sums in excess of $10,000 may be subject to confiscation. Under no circumstances should you attempt to import non-prescription narcotic drugs, including marijuana, unless you have a hankering to try out American prisons.

If you arrive directly at LAX from overseas, you will undergo customs and immigration formalities there. If your flight makes an intermediate stop at another US port, even if you did not change flights, you will go through customs and immigration at that first point of entry into the USA.

Even if you have nothing to declare, you may be directed to follow the red line to an inspector, who will x-ray and perhaps hand-search your entire luggage. Occasionally, the 'dog detectives' employed by the Drug Enforcement Agency may sniff you and your luggage for narcotics or illegal foodstuff. Luckier travelers are sent along the green line and spared this procedure.

California is an important agricultural state, so most food products – especially fresh, dried and canned meat, fruit, vegetables and plants – may not be brought into LA to prevent the spread of pests, fungi and other diseases. It's safest not to bring any such food items. If you suddenly remember that pineapple in your backpack, leave it on the plane or chuck it in the trash before you reach customs. Bakery items or cured cheeses are admissible. There's the threat of potential fines and jail time if you break this law, though in reality the items in question are more likely to be simply confiscated.

If you drive into California across the border from Mexico or the neighboring states of Oregon, Nevada or Arizona, you may have to stop for a quick inspection and questioning by officials of the state Department of Food and Agriculture.

If you want to bring your dog, be sure to carry certificates stating that it is free of diseases communicable to humans and has been vaccinated against rabies.

MONEY
Currency
The US dollar is divided into 100 cents (¢). Coins come in denominations of 1¢ (penny), 5¢ (nickel), 10¢ (dime), 25¢ (quarter), and the seldom seen 50¢ (half dollar). Quarters are the most commonly used coins in vending machines and parking meters, so it's handy to have a stash of them. They're available in $10 rolls at all banks. Notes, commonly called bills, come in $1, $2, $5, $10, $20, $50, and $100 denominations – $2 bills are rare, but perfectly legal. There is also a rarely seen $1 coin that you may get as change from ticket and stamp machines. Be aware that they look similar to quarters.

Exchange Rates
At press time, exchange rates were:

country	unit		US dollars
Australia	A$1	=	$0.53
Canada	C$1	=	$0.66
European Union	€1	=	$0.86
Hong Kong	HK$10	=	$0.13
Japan	¥100	=	$0.01
New Zealand	NZ$1	=	$0.41
UK	£1	=	$1.40

Exchanging Money
Most major currencies and leading brands of traveler's checks are easily exchanged in Los Angeles. Banks usually offer the best rates and are typically open 10am to 5pm Monday to Thursday, to 6pm Friday and to 1pm Saturday. LAX has currency-exchange offices in all terminals, but exchange rates are not great; you may want to change your money into dollars or traveler's checks in your home country.

There are literally hundreds of banks around Los Angeles, the most prevalent being Bank of America, Washington Mutual and Wells Fargo. Among the foreign-exchange brokers, one of the most dependable is Thomas Cook (☎ 800-287-7362), with locations in Beverly Hills at 452 N Bedford St (Map 11), in Santa Monica at 401 Wilshire Blvd, and in West Hollywood at 8901 Santa Monica Blvd (Map 10). American Express also exchanges cash and travelers' checks and has locations in the Beverly Center District at 8493 W 3rd St (☎ 310-659-1682; Map 10), in Downtown in the 7+Fig mall at 735 S Figueroa St (☎ 213-627-4800; Map 5) and in Santa Monica at 1250 4th St (☎ 310-395-9588; Map 13).

Cash & Traveler's Checks Though carrying cash is more risky, it's still a good idea to travel with some ($50 or so) for the convenience. Cash is useful for tipping and for small purchases. However, any cash you lose is gone forever and very few travel insurers will come to your rescue. Those that will usually limit the amount to about $300.

Traveler's checks offer greater protection from theft or loss and can be used as cash in many places. American Express and Thomas Cook are widely accepted and have efficient replacement policies. Keeping a record of the check numbers and the checks you have used is vital when it comes to replacing lost checks. Keep this record separate from the checks themselves. For refunds for lost or stolen traveler's checks call American Express (☎ 800-221-7220) or Thomas Cook (☎ 800-223-7373).

Be sure to buy traveler's checks in US dollars. Restaurants, hotels and most stores accept US-dollar traveler's checks as if they were cash, so you'll rarely have to use a bank or pay an exchange fee. Take most of the checks in large denominations. It's only toward the end of a stay that you may want to change a smaller check to make sure you aren't left with too much local currency.

ATMs Automatic teller machines are perhaps the best, safest and most convenient way of obtaining cash. For a nominal service charge (usually $1 or $2), you can withdraw cash from an ATM using a bank card linked to your personal checking account. Credit card withdrawals usually have a 2% fee with a $2 minimum. Practically all banks now have these 24-hour machines. The Plus, Cirrus and Star systems are the most prevalent networks in LA.

Foreign visitors should note that the exchange rate with an ATM is usually the best available, though high service fees may cancel out that advantage. Check the fees and availability of services with your home bank before you leave. When using an ATM, it's best to pick one in a crowded area, as the risk of being robbed is as real here as anywhere else in the world. Avoid using ATMs at night.

Many ATM cards now double as debit cards and are increasingly accepted at gas stations, supermarkets, movie theaters and other businesses. To make a purchase or withdraw cash, you just slide your card through and key in your PIN (personal identification number). Always keep handy the number of where to report lost or stolen cards.

Credit Cards Major credit cards are accepted at most hotels, restaurants, supermarkets, gas stations, shops, car-rental agencies, movie theaters and other places. In fact, you'll find certain transactions – like purchases or bookings (tickets, rooms, cars, etc) over the telephone or Internet – impossible to perform without that little piece of plastic. Even if you don't make a habit out of using credit cards, it's a good idea to have one for emergencies. Visa or MasterCard are more widely accepted than American Express or Discover.

Carry copies of your credit card numbers separately from the cards. If you lose your credit cards or they get stolen, contact the company immediately.

American Express	☎ 800-528-4800
Discover	☎ 800-347-2683
MasterCard	☎ 800-826-2181
Visa	☎ 800-336-8472

Security
Be cautious – but not paranoid – about carrying money. Use the safe at your hotel or hostel for your valuables and excess cash. Don't display large amounts of cash in public. A money belt worn under your clothes is a good place to carry excess currency when you're on the move or otherwise unable to stash it in a safe. Avoid carrying your wallet in a back pocket of your pants. This is a prime target for pickpockets, as are handbags and the outside pockets of day packs.

Costs
Naturally, spending lots of money in LA is not hard, but it's a bit harder to spend little. The secret to staying within budget is to cut costs where you can, such as with accommodations and food. If you're very economical, you can expect to survive in LA on $40 a day per person. If you can afford to spend twice that, you'll start living quite comfortably.

If money is a concern, don't travel during the summer peak months (July and August), when hotel rates sometimes go up by 20% to 50%. Hostels charge the same year-round, about $15 to $20 for bunk bed.

Dining out is a wonderful treat but does not have to put a major strain on your pocketbook. The Places to Eat chapter lists lots of good restaurants where meals cost less than $10. If you're interested in experiencing the latest chichi restaurant, expect to pay $40 and up per person for dinner. Overall, you can cut costs by having the day's main meal at lunch and by having few or no alcoholic drinks. Those on a shoestring could keep themselves going by stocking up at supermarkets.

Public transportation is fairly inexpensive but, given the sprawl that is Los Angeles, getting around can be time consuming. Car rentals are fairly reasonable, and gasoline costs considerably less than in Europe or other countries. Parking fees, however, can add up. For more information on operating a car, see the Getting Around chapter.

Tipping

Gratuities are not really optional in the US, as most people in service industries are paid minimum wages (currently at $5.75/hour but a $1 hike was being considered at the time of writing) and rely upon making a reasonable living through tips. However, if service is truly appalling, don't tip (in which case a complaint to the manager is probably warranted). Here's a guide to customary tipping amounts:

Bellhops, skycaps in airports – $1 to $1.50 per bag

Concierges – nothing for simple information (directions or restaurant recommendations) to $5 to $20 for special services like securing hard-to-get concert tickets

Housekeeping staff – $1 to $2 per guest, left on the pillow each day

Parking valets – $1 to $2 unless posted signs call for more when you retrieve your car

Restaurant servers, bartenders – 15-20% of the pretax bill

Taxi drivers – 10% to 15%

Taxes

Unlike many countries of the world, the USA has no federal value-added tax. Each state, instead, sets its own tax; California has both sales tax and state income tax.

In some cases, the tax is included in the advertised price (eg, gasoline, drinks in a bar and admission tickets for museums or theaters). Restaurant meals and drinks, accommodations and most other purchases are taxed, and this is added to the advertised cost. Unless otherwise stated, prices given in this book don't include sales tax.

In LA County, the state sales tax of 8% applies to all restaurant bills as well as most shopping. Most food items are tax-exempt, although alcohol is not. Services such as manicures, haircuts and taxi rides, are not taxed. A 'transient occupancy tax' is added to room rates at hotels and motels; it is usually included in hostel rates. As this tax is levied by the individual cities, it can range from 11.85% in Pasadena to 12% in Santa Monica and Long Beach, 13% in West Hollywood and 14% in Los Angeles and Beverly Hills.

POST & COMMUNICATIONS
Postal Rates

Postage rates increase every few years. At the time of writing, rates for 1st-class mail within the USA are 34¢ for letters up to 1oz (22¢ for each additional ounce) and 20¢ for postcards.

International airmail rates (except to Canada and Mexico) are 60¢ for a half-ounce letter, $1 for a 1oz letter and 40¢ for each additional half ounce. International postcards and aerogrammes cost 50¢. Letters to Canada are 46¢ for a half-ounce letter, 52¢ for a 1oz letter and 40¢ for a postcard. Letters to Mexico are 40¢ for a half-ounce letter, 46¢ for a 1oz letter and 35¢ for a postcard.

The cost for parcels airmailed anywhere within the USA is $3.20 for 2 pounds or less, increasing by $1 per pound up to $6 for 5 pounds. For heavier items, the rates differ according to the distance mailed. Books, periodicals and computer disks can be sent by a cheaper 4th-class rate.

Sending Mail

Generally, stamps are available at post offices only, though some supermarkets sell booklets of 20 stamps as well. Stamp-dispensing machines, commonly found in convenience stores and hotel lobbies, can be a rip-off, charging you more than face value and sometimes not giving change.

If you have the correct postage, drop your mail into any blue mailbox. If you don't know the postage amount or are sending a package weighing 16oz or more, you must bring it to a post office. There are dozens, if not hundreds, of post office branches in LA County. Most have restricted opening hours, usually 9am to 5pm Monday to Friday and to noon Saturday. The main post office (☎ 213-617-4543; Map 5) is the Terminal Annex next to Downtown's Union Station at 900 N Alameda St. For a post office nearest to you, check the phone book or call ☎ 800-275-8777.

Letters sent within Los Angeles usually take one day for delivery; delivery time for intrastate and interstate mail depends on the distance and remoteness of the addressee and the type of service you have selected. First-class mail is much faster than second-class mail, but not as fast as express mail. Mail sent overseas usually takes about four to seven days, though this varies from country to country. For guaranteed fast delivery, most people rely on more costly private carrier services such as FedEx and UPS.

Receiving Mail

You can have mail sent to you care of 'General Delivery' at any post office that has its own five-digit zip (postal) code. Select a convenient post office, ask them for the correct address and pick-up times. Mail is usually held for 10 days before it's returned to the sender. Ask your correspondents to write 'hold for arrival' on their letters. Mail should be addressed like this:

Lucy Chang
c/o General Delivery
Los Angeles, CA 90025

If you have an American Express Card or traveler's checks, you may have mail sent to an American Express office (see Money, earlier in this chapter). To avoid the $2 service charge, present your card or checks upon pick-up. The sender should make sure that the words 'Client's Mail' appear somewhere on the envelope. American Express will hold mail for 30 days but won't accept registered post or parcels.

Telephone

All phone numbers within the US consist of a three-digit area code followed by a seven-digit local number. If you call locally, just dial the seven-digit number. If you are calling outside your area code, dial 1 + the three-digit area code + the seven-digit number. If you're calling from abroad, the country code for the USA is 1. For directory assistance anywhere in the US, dial ☎ 411.

In LA County there are five area codes; the telephone numbers in this book are accompanied with the appropriate area code. Calls within Los Angeles cost a minimum of 35¢, and rates go up with distance. Long-distance rates depend on the destination and telephone company – call the operator (☎ 0) for rate information. Be sure to decline the operator's offer to put your call through, though, because operator-assisted calls are considerably more expensive than direct-dial calls.

If you're staying at an expensive hotel, it's best to resist making calls from your room. Most add a service charge of 50¢ to $1.50 per call even for local, calling card, credit card or toll-free calls and have especially hefty surcharges for direct long-distance calls. Paradoxically, the cheaper hotel, the lower the surcharge; sometimes local calls are free.

The 800 and 888 area codes are designated for toll-free numbers within the US and sometimes Canada as well. For directory assistance on a toll-free number, dial ☎ 800-555-1212 (no charge). Numbers beginning with 900 – phone sex, horoscopes, jokes, etc – charge premium rates.

Many businesses use letters instead of numbers for their telephone numbers in an

The telephone is this girl's best friend.

attempt to make it snappy and memorable (1 – none; 2 – ABC; 3 – DEF; 4 – GHI; 5 – JKL; 6 – MNO; 7 – PRS; 8 – TUV; 9 – WXY).

International Calls For a direct international call, dial 011 + the country code + the area code and phone number. (To find the country code, check a local phone book or call the international operator at ☎ 00.) International rates depend on the destination and the telephone company you use.

Making international calls with cash from pay phones can be expensive and frustrating, because phones are only equipped to take quarters. From many phones you'll be required to deposit sufficient coins to pay for the first three minutes. Some pay phones allow the use of credit cards, but be sure to read the small print about rates before punching in your number. You can save if the person you're calling is willing to call you back; but determine if the pay phone is equipped to handle incoming calls (some are blocked from doing so).

The lowest international rates available are for calls made from phones in private homes. So if you're staying with someone, find out what they pay, then reimburse them.

Prepaid Calling Cards Prepaid calling cards allow purchasers to pay in advance, then make calls from any phone by dialing a toll-free 800 number, followed by the card code (both listed on the card itself); at the prompt, you then enter the number you're trying to reach. The company's computer keeps track of how much value you have left. These cards are often a good deal and more convenient than coins when using pay phones.

Lonely Planet's eKno global communication service provides low-cost international calls, free messaging services, email and other travel services. You can join online at www.ekno.lonelyplanet.com, where you will find the local-access numbers for the 24-hour customer-service center. Once you have joined, always check the eKno Web site for the latest access numbers for each country and updates on new features.

For local calls, though, you may be better off with a local card, usually available in amounts of $10 and $20. These are sold at some supermarkets, convenience stores and gas stations. Note that some cards don't just charge per-minute rates but also a per-call 'connection fee.' There have also been recent reports of fraud where the cards promised more minutes of calls than they actually offered. Also be cautious of people watching you dial in the card code – thieves memorize numbers and use them to make costly calls.

Fax

Shops that specialize in office services are the best and most reasonably-priced locations from which to send and receive facsimiles. Check the Yellow Pages for the nearest Mail Boxes Etc and the 24-hour Kinko's Copies franchises in Los Angeles. Hotel business service centers may charge as much as $1.50 per page within the US and up to $10 per page overseas. However, some hotels don't charge for receiving faxes.

Email & Internet Access

A multimedia megalopolis, Los Angeles won't hinder anyone wishing to use that fine new friend to travelers, the Internet. If you're traveling with your own laptop and modem, one of the easiest ways to log on is from your hotel room, which, in many cases, might have an in-room data port. Check with your Internet service provider (ISP) for local access numbers within LA for dial-up connection.

Most hostels now have Internet kiosks that usually charge $1 per 10 minutes. The same prices apply at the Santa Monica branch office of Council Travel (see Travel Agencies, earlier in this chapter), which has several high-speed terminals. Access at public libraries is usually free but computers and telephone connections may not be state-of-the-art. Sometimes you may only be able to surf but not to access email. Library cards are usually not needed, though you may be asked to show picture ID.

Other locations for getting on-line are cybercafes, which charge from $6 to $9 per hour and usually offer fast connections. See the boxed text 'Where to Log On' for details.

If you set up an email account with a free Internet service, such as Hotmail (www.hotmail.com) or Yahoo (www.yahoo.com), you can access your email from any computer with a Web connection. For computer and Internet problems you might encounter, and how to solve them, check out www.teleadapt.com.

DIGITAL RESOURCES

The World Wide Web is a rich resource for travelers. You can research your trip, hunt down bargain air fares, book hotels, check on weather conditions or chat with locals and other travelers about the best places to visit (or avoid!).

Where to Log On

Sip your latte while catching up on the news and staying in touch with friends at any of these cybercafes.

In Santa Monica, **EtherTable: LA Bridge Internet** (☎ 310-450-5686; Map 13), 2507 Main St, inside Mäni's Bakery, has a handful of state-of-the-art computers with all three operating systems (MacOS, Windows 98, Linux) and Internet and graphics applications. Computer usage fee is 10¢ to 15¢ per minute, plus a $2 log-on fee. They also have wireless network connections for notebook carriers.

Near Third Street Promenade, the **Interactive Cafe** (☎ 310-395-5009; Map 13), 215 Broadway, has several terminals as well as an international newsstand. It's open 6am to 1am Sunday to Thursday and to 2:30am Friday and Saturday and charges $1 for 10 minutes.

Hollywood has **Cyber Java** (☎ 323-466-5600; Map 9), 7080 Hollywood Blvd at La Brea Blvd. This popular place has enough gadgets to give you an office away from the office. Besides Macs and PCs with fast Internet connections and word processing programs, there's a scanner, a fax and copy machine and printers. Internet access is $2.50 for 15 minutes and $9 for an hour. It's open until midnight.

On hip Melrose Ave, at No 7200, is **@Coffee** (☎ 323-930-1122; Map 10), which charges $7 per hour with a 10-minute minimum. Hours vary, but it's usually open till 8pm.

In West Hollywood, the **WeHo Lounge** (☎ 310-659-6180; Map 10), a friendly coffeehouse at 8861 Santa Monica Blvd, has two terminals at $6 per hour and is open till 2am.

Silver Lake has the **i2i World Café** (☎ 323-660-2999; Map 9), 3823 Sunset Blvd, which has DSL connections and a couple of computers loaded with software; usage is $8 per hour.

The best prices are in Pasadena (Map 17), where both **Equator Coffeehouse** (☎ 626-564-8656), 22 Mills Place, and **Opus** (☎ 626-685-2800), 38 E Colorado Blvd, charge just $3.50 per hour.

There's no better place to start your Web explorations than the Lonely Planet Web site (www.lonelyplanet.com). Here you'll find succinct summaries on traveling to most places on earth, postcards from other travelers and the Thorn Tree bulletin board, where you can ask questions before you go or dispense advice when you get back. You can also find travel news and updates to many of Lonely Planet's most popular guidebooks, and the subWWWay section links you to the most useful travel resources elsewhere on the Web.

CitySync *Los Angeles* is Lonely Planet's digital city guide for Palm OS handheld devices. With CitySync you can quickly search, sort and bookmark hundreds of LA's restaurants, hotels, attractions, clubs and more – all pinpointed on scrollable street maps. Sections on activities, transport and local events means you get the big picture plus all the little details. You can purchase or demo CitySync *Los Angeles* at www.citysync.com.

Web resources abound for Los Angeles. Many of the following are useful in planning and researching your trip; others are just for fun.

General Interest

@LA www.at-la.com – This has got to be the Godzilla of Web sites: it is well-organized and searchable and has links to more than 70,000 sites covering everything from arts to tourism.

Official City of Los Angeles www.ci.la.ca.us – This comprehensive site covers everything from city news and the city council agenda to city-sponsored events. There are links to the LA Police Department, libraries, museums, events and more.

Digital City Los Angeles www.digitalcity.com/losangeles – This extensive site is constantly updated and has a newsy format, visitor guide, white and yellow pages, reviews of restaurants and clubs by locals and lots more.

Online Publications

Los Angeles Times www.latimes.com – This online version of the daily newspaper has international and local news as well as the latest headlines.

www.calendarlive.com – For up-to-date news on what's on in LA, this exhaustive listing is hard to beat. There are links to hotels, museums, festivals, books, activities and more; many of them are reviewed by an *LA Times* staffer.

LA Weekly www.laweekly.com – LA's main entertainment weekly has a fairly good online version with access to a back-issue archive.

Downtown News www.downtownnews.com – This is an excellent weekly newspaper focused exclusively on developments and events in Downtown LA. The site also has tours, descriptions of landmarks, shopping tips, a restaurant guide and lots more.

Transportation

Metropolitan Transit Authority www.mta.net – This huge Web site has information on all MTA public transport options, including the Blue Line, Green Line and Red Line rail lines and all buses.

Big Blue Bus www.bigbluebus.com – This is the Web site of the Santa Monica–based Big Blue Bus company with information on routes, schedules, fares, points of interest as well as maps.

BOOKS

Most books are published in different editions by different publishers in different countries. As a result, a book might be a hardcover rarity in one country while it's readily available in paperback in another. Fortunately, bookshops and libraries can search by title or author, so your local bookstore or library are the best places to find out if the following recommendations are available.

Lonely Planet

Lonely Planet publishes several other titles that visitors to LA might find useful. For detailed information on destinations beyond the scope of this book, check out the comprehensive *California & Nevada* guide. LP also publishes Pisces diving & snorkeling guides, including *Southern California*. All are available at bookstores or may be ordered from the Lonely Planet Web site at www.lonelyplanet.com.

Guidebooks

There's a slew of specialized Los Angeles guides worth considering. One of the best and most intelligently researched and written is *Discover Los Angeles* by Letitia Burns O'Connor and published by the J Paul Getty Trust. The author provides thorough descriptions of major sights and destinations throughout LA County and supplements them with essays about cultural topics such as music, literature and theater. She also adds insightful passages about the various neighborhoods.

Museum Companion to Los Angeles by Borislav Stanic tells you all about the city's museums – large and small – with their hours, parking information and other details. *Off the Beaten Path in Southern California* by Kathy Strong is full of ideas for short getaways and explorations of lesser-known areas in Southern California.

For a different look at LA, consider the excellent *LA Bizarro* by scenesters Anthony R Lovett and Matt Maranian, who unearthed some truly weird nooks and crannies in LA and introduce them in amusingly written essays. A good source for gay and lesbian travelers is Andrew Collins' *Gay Guide to Los Angeles and Southern California*, with lots of snappily written detailed information on hotels, bars, restaurants and more.

Other guides to consider are *LA Times* columnist John McKinney's series of hiking guides, including the *Day Hiker's Guide to Southern California* and *Walking Los Angeles: Adventures on the Urban Edge*. Also good a read is *Fun Places to Go with Children in Southern California* by Stephanie Kegan.

History & Politics

One of the best and most comprehensive sources for just about anything you ever wanted to know about LA is *Los Angeles A to Z* (1997), a heavy encyclopedia meticulously researched and written by Leonard and Dale Pitt and published by the University of California. The 600-page tome covers it all, from AAA to Zuma County Beach, followed by several appendices.

For LA history, check out *Southern California Country: An Island Upon the Land* (1946) by Carey McWilliams, *City-Makers*

(1948) by Remi Nadeau, *Los Angeles: The Enormous Village, 1781–1981* (1981) by John D Weave, *Ethnic LA* (1990) by Zena Pearlstone, and a pair of books by state librarian of California Kevin Starr, *Inventing the Dream* (1985) and *Material Dreams* (1990). Also worth considering is *A Short History of Los Angeles* by Gordon DeMarco.

Biographies

Bookstores are usually overflowing with biographies and autobiographies of Hollywood legends past and present. The following provide background to Hollywood and The Industry: *My Autobiography* (1964) by Charles Chaplin, *Norma Jean: The Life of Marilyn Monroe* (1969) by Fred Lawrence Guiles, *Hollywood's Master Showman: The Legendary Sid Grauman* (1983) by Charles Beardsley, *Hollywood Days, Hollywood Nights* (1988) by Ben Stein, and *Goldwyn* (1989) by A Scott Berg.

General

A good introduction to LA's architecture is *Architecture in Los Angeles* (1985) by David Gebhard and Robert Winter. For a more social view of the city's architecture, check out *City of Quartz: Excavating the Future in Los Angeles* (1990) by Mike Davis, and *Los Angeles: The Architecture of Four Ecologies* (1971) by Rainer Banham.

For books relating to the film industry, look for any of the following: *Hollywood: The Pioneers* (1979) by Kevin Brownlow and John Kobal, *Adventures in the Screen Trade* (1985) by William Goldman, *City of Nets: A Portrait of Hollywood in the 1940s* (1986) by Otto Friedrich, *Behind the Scenes* (1989) by Rudy Behlmer or *The Devil's Candy* (1991) by Julie Salamon.

If you're on a mission to tour the steamy side of Tinseltown, take a look at Kenneth Anger's *Hollywood Babylon* (1975) or read Richard Alleman's *The Moviegoer's Guide to Hollywood* (1985).

For the morbidly interested, *Death in Paradise: An Illustrated History of the LA County Department of Coroner* (1998), by

Tony Blanche and Brad Schreiber, documents the behind-the-scenes crime-solving heroics performed by coroners in some of the most celebrated cases, including the 1871 Chinese Massacre and the 1994 Simpson/Goldman murders.

NEWSPAPERS & MAGAZINES
Los Angeles Times
The *Los Angeles Times* (35¢ daily, $2 Sunday) is the one of the largest daily newspapers in the US joining the ranks of the *Wall Street Journal* and the *New York Times*. Its daily circulation is 1.15 million; the Sunday edition is 1.4 million. The newspaper was founded in 1881 and later purchased by Harrison Gray Otis, then a conservative voice in the burgeoning city. More than 23 Pulitzer Prizes have been awarded to individual writers and for team coverage, including reports on the 1992 Rodney King riots and the 1994 Northridge earthquake. After being privately owned since its inception, the *Times* was sold to media giant the Tribune Company in 2000. Los Angeles is waiting to see the effects of corporate ownership on the *Times'* independence. The Sunday edition includes an expanded calendar section, an excellent source for finding out about cultural events.

Other Newspapers
Over the last decade, the *LA Times* has managed to squash almost all local competition, leaving only the San Fernando Valley–based *Daily News* (circulation 200,000, Sunday 212,000) to provide an alternative voice. The third-largest paper is the Spanish-language *La Opinión* with a circulation of 117,558 weekdays and 72,013 Sunday.

Some of the cities within LA County have their own local papers, including the *Long Beach Press-Telegram*, *Pasadena Star News* and *Daily Breeze*, which serve the Santa Monica Bay communities.

An excellent free source is the *LA Weekly*, issued on Thursday and available at bookstores, video stores, restaurants and convenience stores. It is required reading

for the latest scenes, trends and events. Other freebie event rags include the *New Times* and *The Argonaut*.

International newspapers and those from major US cities are widely available in large bookstores, such as Borders and Barnes & Noble. Major newsstands – particularly prevalent in Santa Monica, West Hollywood and Hollywood – are another good source to try.

Magazines
The monthly *Los Angeles Magazine* is a high-brow glossy that tries hard to capture LA's constantly evolving zeitgeist. Features can be anything from gushy to cynical and cover the spectrum from fluff to investigative, celebrities to the homeless, esoteric to the practical. Its extensive restaurant listings and reviews are digested with gusto by locals.

An alternative is the gossipy *Glue Magazine*, a bimonthly about fashion and the arts in an off-beat and often irreverent way. The writing is pretty sophomoric but columns such as those by cult phenomenon 'Dr' Vaginal Davis, a transsexual scene queen, certainly keep things lively. There's also a pretty useful guide to clubs and restaurants in back.

For insider showbiz news, consult 'the trades': *Variety* and the *Hollywood Reporter*.

RADIO & TV
Greater Los Angeles has 14 television stations and 34 radio stations, a substantial number of them serving the thriving non-English-speaking populations.

The major network affiliates are KCBS, Channel 2; KNBC, Channel 4; KABC, Channel 7; and KTTV (Fox), Channel 11. Independent stations are KTLA, Channel 5; and KCOP, Channel 13. KCET, Channel 28, is affiliated with the Public Broadcasting System. The Spanish-language KMEX, Channel 34, is a Univision affiliate.

For radio, check into KNX 1070 AM or KFWB 980 AM for all-day news and traffic. (See the next page for a list of LA's music stations.)

frequency	station	type of music
88.1	KLON	jazz & blues
89.9	KCRW	public radio/eclectic
91.5	KUSC	classical
93.1	KCBS	classic rock
93.9	KZLA	country
94.7	KTWV	contemporary jazz
95.5	KLOS	rock
98.7	KYSR	modern rock/Top 40
101.1	KRTH	'50s & '60s rock
101.9	KSCA	Mexican regional
102.7	KIIS	top 40
103.1	KACD	Spanish pop/rock
104.3	KBIG	adult contemporary
105.1	KKGO	classical
105.9	KPWR	hip-hop/R&B
106.7	KROQ	modern rock

PHOTOGRAPHY & VIDEO

Print film is widely available at supermarkets and discount drugstores. For general-purpose shooting – for either prints or slides – 100 ASA film is just about the most useful and versatile; it gives you good color and enough speed to capture most situations on film. If you plan to shoot in dark areas or in brightly lit night scenes without a tripod, switch to 400 ASA.

The best and most widely available films are made by Fuji and Kodak. Fuji Velvia and Kodak Elite are easy to process and provide good slide images. Try to avoid Kodachrome: it's difficult to process quickly and generates lots of headaches if not handled properly. For print film, you can't beat Kodak Gold, though Fuji is comparable and Agfa is coming along. Film can be damaged by excessive heat, so avoid leaving your camera and film in the car or placing them on the dashboard while driving.

It's worth carrying a spare battery for your camera to avoid disappointment when your camera dies in the middle of nowhere. If you're buying a new camera for your trip, do so several weeks before you leave and practice using it.

Drugstores are a good place to get your film processed cheaply. If you drop the film off by noon, you can usually pick it up the next day. A roll of 100 ASA 35 mm color film with 24 exposures will cost about $6 to be processed. Many venues offer double sets of prints for much less than double the cost. However, one-hour processing services charge up to $11 per 24-exposure roll. For professional processing and electronic imaging, A&I and its imaging component, A&I Digital, are highly recommended. A&I is in Hollywood at 933 N Highland Ave (☎ 323-856-5255; Map 9) and in Santa Monica at 1550 17th St (☎ 310-264-2622; Map 13).

One of the finest camera and film house on the West Coast is the legendary Samy's Camera (☎ 323-938-2420; Map 10) in the Fairfax District at 431 S Fairfax Ave and now in Venice (☎ 310-450-4551; Map 13) at 585 Venice Blvd. In Westwood the biggest and best is Bel-Air Camera (☎ 310-208-5150; Map 11) at 10925 Kinross Ave. For good, neighborly service in Santa Monica, go to Boulevard Camera (☎ 310-451-0707; Map 13) at 1201 Wilshire Blvd.

If your Nikons or Hasselblads take a nosedive just when you're heading out to shoot Pamela Anderson, go directly to Camera Service Center (☎ 310-397-0072; Map 12), 4355 S Sepulveda Blvd in Culver City. And right next door, at 4353 Sepulveda, you'll find Cary Photo Lab (☎ 310-398-2484; Map 12) for excellent black-and-white work.

Overseas visitors videotaping highlights of their trip should remember that the US uses the National Television System Committee (NTSC) color TV standard, which, unless converted, is not compatible with other standards (PAL or SECAM) used in Africa, Europe, Asia and Australia. Be sure to bring blank tapes that are compatible with your camcorder.

Technical Tips

Los Angeles usually offers plenty of light for photography. When sunlight is strong, and the sun is high in the sky, photographs tend to have harsh shadows. It's best to shoot during early morning and late afternoon, when the sun is low in the sky and the light is softer. A polarizing filter is a useful piece of gear as it deepens the blue of the

Arches, azure and aspirations – public art, Downtown

Welcome to the City of Angels.

'Why did the Sphinx cross the road?' Traffic on Hollywood Blvd

Angels Flight, Downtown LA

This theater premiered Chaplin's *City Lights*.

Tailfins to die for

Best Shots in LA

LA offers a plethora of terrific images. The following list suggests places where you are likely to bag some real 'grabbers.'

Gardens & architecture Huntington Gardens in Pasadena, Getty Museum in Brentwood, Virginia Robinson Gardens in Beverly Hills, and Downtown LA, central Hollywood and Koreatown (Wilshire Blvd)

'The LA scene' (trends, tattoos, etc) Melrose Ave, Los Feliz Village, Silver Lake, Sunset Strip at night, Third Street Promenade in Santa Monica, Venice Boardwalk

Viewpoints of the city, ocean and mountains Griffith Park Observatory, Yamashiro restaurant, Runyon Canyon Park, Palisades Park in Santa Monica, Palos Verdes Peninsula

Definitive shots of the Hollywood sign Top of Beachwood Drive off Franklin in Hollywood, Griffith Park Observatory (Note: The sign is trademarked and copyrighted by the Hollywood Chamber of Commerce, which loves to sue for commercial use of its 'real estate.')

People pictures Santa Monica, Hermosa Beach, Zuma Beach, Manhattan Beach, Malibu (for beach babes, dudes and surfers); along Broadway in Downtown (for bustling Latino life); Chinatown and Little Tokyo (Note: Politely ask for permission to take photos of people.)

---

sky and water, can eliminate many reflections and make clouds appear quite dramatic. The effect of a polarizer is strongest when you point your camera 90 degrees away from the sun. By spinning the filter around you'll see a pretty fair approximation of what the effect will be on film.

In places where light levels are low, using fast film or your camera's fill-flash function may be helpful. Just remember: normal camera flash is only effective from 10-15 feet (3-5m), so don't waste it trying to light up an entire stadium. A monopod or lightweight tripod is an invaluable piece of gear for 'steadying up' your camera for slow exposures or when using a telephoto lens. These will also allow you to take those great night shots of neon, theater marquees and those 'streaking taillights' shots of cars rushing by. Lacking the above gear, jam your camera against anything at hand – a church pew, a tree, a street sign – to steady up. And remember: 'Blurry is a worry. Steady is ready.'

One more tip: All flight passengers have to pass their luggage through x-ray machines, which are capable of destroying unprocessed film. To be on the safe side, it's best to carry film and loaded cameras in your hand-luggage and ask airport security people to inspect them manually. Pack all your film into a clear plastic bag that you can quickly whip out of your luggage. This not only saves time at the inspection points but also helps minimize confrontations with security staff.

TIME

California is in the Pacific Time Zone, which is Greenwich Mean Time minus eight hours. Therefore, when the time is noon in Los Angeles, it is 8pm in London, 9am in Honolulu, 3pm in New York, 4am (the next day) in Singapore and 6am (the next day) in Sydney or Auckland.

Daylight saving time is in effect from the last Sunday in April to the last Sunday in October. Clocks are set ahead one hour in the spring ('spring forward'), and set back one hour in the fall ('fall back'), meaning that sunset is an hour later during the long days of summer.

ELECTRICITY

Electric current in the US is 110V and outlets are suited for flat two-prong or three-prong (two flat, one round) plugs. If your appliance is made for another electrical system, you will need a transformer or adapter; if you didn't bring one, check drugstores, hardware or consumer-electronics stores such as Radio Shack (check the Yellow Pages for the closest location).

WEIGHTS & MEASURES

When it comes to measurement, LA is no different from the rest of the US, which clings stubbornly to the Imperial system. Distances are in inches, feet, yards and miles. Three feet equal 1 yard; 1760 yards or 5280 feet equal 1 mile. For additional details, see the Metric Conversion chart on the inside back cover of this book.

LAUNDRY

Most hostel-style accommodations and many mid-priced motels offer laundry facilities at coin-op rates. Larger hotels, however, charge exorbitant prices for one-day service. (How does $2 for a pair of underpants sound?) In such cases, you may want to do your own wash in your bathroom, or deliver your load to a laundry that will charge you as much per pound as the hotel charged for washing those skivvies. No matter where you're staying, you're never far from a coin-operated laundry. If you haven't already spotted one while driving around, ask your hotel for directions to the nearest Laundromat.

TOILETS

Foreign visitors should know that the puritanical prudishness, so prevalent in the US, even extends to this most basic human need. Toilets are never called 'toilets' but a slew of euphemisms, including restroom, bathroom, powder room, washroom, men's and ladies' rooms, and little boys' and little girls' rooms.

Public toilets are basically nonexistent, so you have to be assertive and creative in finding facilities. Shopping malls and department stores, hotel lobbies, museums and other public places are your best bets. Ducking into a bar is an OK alternative, though keep in mind that you have to be over 21 to even enter and should probably buy a drink. Casual restaurants such as diners and cafes are usually an option, though fancy ones (where you have to pass the host or hostess) may refuse you. Many of the beaches, such as Zuma, Santa Monica, Venice and Manhattan Beach, have decent public facilities.

LUGGAGE STORAGE

At Los Angeles International Airport, lockers ($1.25-7.50) are in the boarding areas of all terminals and may be used for a maximum of 48 hours (24 hours in the Tom Bradley International Terminal). If your luggage is too big for the lockers or needs to be stored longer, you can leave it with the International Baggage Service on the upper floor of the international terminal, which also has a luggage repair station.

HEALTH

Los Angeles is a typical first-world destination when it comes to health. The only foreign visitors who may be required to have immunizations are those coming from areas with a history of cholera and yellow fever.

Precautions

While LA water is safe to drink, it does not taste great and most people prefer bottled water. The ocean water quality of Santa Monica Bay has seen dramatic improvement, making swimming and surfing at most beaches much safer today than a mere decade ago. Thanks to efforts led in part by the Santa Monica–based advocacy group Heal the Bay, tougher laws and regulations are now in force. For example, the extension of the discharge pipe of the Chevron plant in El Segundo, the diversion of dry-weather runoff from storm drains, and a reduction of sludge discharge all have contributed to healthier conditions. But only water spilling into ocean via storm drains is not treated at all, which makes swimming in the bay after major rains a health hazard. In general, avoid swimming in the ocean for three days after a storm.

Heal the Bay issues a monthly Beach Report Card, which evaluates ocean water quality based on a grading system from A+ to F. The report is available by calling Heal the Bay at ☎ 310-453-0395 or ☎ 800-432-5229 (within CA only) or by visiting its Web site at www.healthebay.org.

It's the sun, though, that presents far greater health risks. Unless you fancy having the complexion of a lobster or are foolish enough to ignore skin cancer warnings, cover every exposed body part with high protection sunscreen whenever outdoors – and not just when lying by the pool or going to the beach. Days often start out cool and overcast only to turn gloriously sunny by lunchtime, so carry a small tube with you.

Coastal communities aside, summers can get unbearably hot, making heat exhaustion a common problem. It's easily avoided by drinking lots of liquids, preferably plain water.

Health Insurance

Health care in Los Angeles is outstanding but it's also very expensive, and without insurance even minor health concerns can easily bust your entire travel budget. Unless your health plan at home provides worldwide coverage, definitely take out travel health insurance. Without evidence of insurance, hospitals may refuse care in all but life-threatening emergencies and refer you instead to the county hospital where you may have to endure agonizingly long waits.

Some policies specifically exclude 'dangerous activities' like scuba diving, motorcycling and even trekking. If these activities are on your agenda, search for policies that include them. While you may find a policy that pays doctors or hospitals directly, be aware that many private doctors and clinics will demand payment at the time of service. Unless you need acute treatment, it's best to call around and choose one willing to accept your insurance. No matter what the circumstances, be sure to keep all receipts and documentation. Some policies ask you to call back (reverse charges) to a center in your home country for an immediate assessment of your problem. Also check whether the policy covers ambulance fees or an

emergency flight home. See Travel Insurance, earlier in this chapter, for additional information.

Medical Services

If you've had an accident resulting in injuries that require immediate treatment or have an acute illness, call the emergency number ☎ 911. This is a free call from any phone, and no coins are needed if you're using a pay phone. It will connect you to an emergency operator, who will dispatch an ambulance to transport you to the emergency room of the nearest hospital. For outpatient treatment of non-life threatening ailments – such as a sprained ankle, a bladder infection or a serious flu – ask at your hotel or someone you know to recommend a doctor or check under Clinics in the Yellow Pages.

Major hospitals include Hollywood Presbyterian Hospital (☎ 323-660-5350; Map 9), 1300 N Vermont Ave near Barnsdall Park; the Cedars-Sinai Medical Center (☎ 310-855-5000; Map 10), 8700 Beverly Blvd in West Hollywood; or the UCLA Medical Center (☎ 310-825-9111; Map 11), 10833 LeConte Ave in Westwood. If you are uninsured, the government-funded LA County/USC Medical Center (☎ 323-226-2622; Map 3), 1200 N State S in East LA, may be a more affordable but not necessarily convenient option.

If you don't have insurance or have a plan with a high deductible, you can keep costs down by going to a state-subsidized clinic catering to low-income people. These are usually well equipped and staffed with nurse practitioners (highly qualified nurses), volunteer doctors or doctors in residency. Often you can get an appointment on the same day. Fees are sliding-scale, assessed on your ability to pay. Venice Family Clinic (☎ 310-392-8630; Map 13), 604 Rose Ave in Venice, is among the best for general health concerns. The Women's Clinic (☎ 310-203-8899; Map 11), 9911 Pico Blvd, Suite 500 in Century City, provides gynecological care, and is a good place to go – for both women and men – when suspecting venereal disease. Progressive Health Services

(☎ 323-650-1508; Map 10), 8240 Santa Monica Blvd in West Hollywood, offers holistic health for men and women for family planning, HIV testing and lesbigay healthcare. The Los Angeles Free Clinic has two branches, one (☎ 323-462-4158; Map 9), 6043 Hollywood Blvd in Hollywood, and another (☎ 323-653-1990; Map 10), 8405 Beverly Blvd near the Beverly Center mall.

For AIDS- and HIV-related questions, contact the AIDS Hotline of Southern California (☎ 800-922-2437), the National AIDS/HIV Hotline (☎ 800-342-2437) or the AIDS Healthcare Foundation (☎ 800-243-2101). AIDS Project Los Angeles (APLA; ☎ 323-993-1600) has offices at 1313 N Vine St in Hollywood.

Nonprescription medications, as well as condoms, are available in major drugstores. Condoms are also often sold from vending machines in public restrooms at universities, bars and night clubs and in some restaurants and hotels. Prescription drugs are filled at every pharmacy, which are conveniently located in 24-hour drugstores chains, such as Sav-On or Rite Aid.

WOMEN TRAVELERS

Women don't need to exercise special caution while visiting Los Angeles. The usual common sense rules – don't walk alone at night, be aware of your surroundings, avoid 'bad' neighborhoods – apply here as much as anywhere else.

Given strict US anti-sexual harassment laws, getting hassled by men is a much rarer occurrence here than in other countries. Some men may interpret a woman drinking alone in a bar as a bid for male company, but most will respect a firm but polite 'no thank you.' If someone continues to harass you, protesting loudly will often will make the offender slink away with embarrassment – or will at least draw attention to your predicament. If you are assaulted, call the police (☎ 911) or the 24-hour Rape and Battering Hotline (☎ 310-392-8381) operated by the Los Angeles Commission on Assaults Against Women. The Santa Monica–UCLA Medical Center at 1250 16th St in Santa Monica has a dedicated 24-hour Rape Treatment Center (☎ 310-319-4000; Map 13). To ward off potential offenders, some women protect themselves with a whistle, mace, pepper spray or self-defense training.

To find out about local happenings, drop by the Sisterhood Bookstore (☎ 310-477-7300; Map 11), 1351 Westwood Blvd. The store's travel section offers many books geared towards women travelers as well as *The Women's Yellow Pages*, which is an excellent resource.

The YWCA has several locations in Los Angeles, including one in Leimert Park at 2501 W Vernon Ave (☎ 323-295-4288; Map 2) and in Santa Monica at 2019 14th St (☎ 310-452-3881; Map 13).

Planned Parenthood (☎ 800-230-7526) has 10 clinics in the Los Angeles area, providing gynecological care, birth control, and testing for pregnancy and sexually transmitted diseases. The branch (☎ 323-223-4462) at 1920 Marengo St, right by the USC County Medical Center, is open 24 hours. Other clinics sensitive to women's healthcare issues are the Progressive Health Services and the Women's Clinic (see Health, earlier in this chapter).

The Women Helping Women Services has a talk line (☎ 213-655-3807), which provides counseling.

GAY & LESBIAN TRAVELERS

As the cosmopolitan capital of California, it's no surprise that LA boasts a high concentration of the state's gay population. Outdone in sheer number only by San Francisco's Castro district, West Hollywood is by far the gayest community in LA with countless restaurants, bars, clubs, cinemas and shops owned by, and largely catering to, a homosexual audience. The beach cities of Santa Monica and Venice also have established gay and lesbian communities, as do Silver Lake, North Hollywood and Studio City. Long Beach also has a large gay and especially lesbian contingent.

Tolerance of homosexuality is generally high in LA, and the sight of couples holding hands or kissing is not uncommon, especially – of course – in gay communities.

Gay and lesbian magazines are excellent sources for catching up on the latest trends, dance clubs, health & fitness centers and restaurants. You'll find stacks of these free periodicals by the entrances to gay-friendly establishments. See the Shopping chapter for bookstores serving the gay community.

The best gay travel guide is the annually updated *Damron's Women's Traveller* with listings for lesbians and *Damron's Men's Travel Guide* for men, both published by Damron Company (www.damron.com). Also available is Fodor's *Gay Guide to Los Angeles & Southern California* by Andrew Collins.

The LA Gay & Lesbian Center (☎ 323-993-7400, www.gay-lesbian-center.org: Map 9), 1625 N Schrader Blvd in West Hollywood, is a one-stop service and health agency. Besides operating several clinics, it also offers legal services, a packed schedule of activities and a youth center. Most services are free or low cost. Other clinics sensitive to lesbigay healthcare issues include the Progressive Health Services and the Women's Clinic (see Medical Services, earlier in this chapter, for contact information for these organizations).

If you've been harassed, threatened or assaulted, you can report the incident to the Gay & Lesbian Alliance Against Defamation (Gladd; ☎ 800-429-6334), the Anti-Violence Project (☎ 323-993-7673) or the City of West Hollywood – Gay Bashing Complaints (☎ 323-848-6470). The ACLU – Gay & Lesbian Rights Chapter (☎ 323-977-9500) is an advocate group with offices at 1616 Beverly Blvd.

DISABLED TRAVELERS

Public buildings are required by law to be wheelchair accessible and to have special restroom facilities. Public transportation services (buses, trains and taxis) must be accessible to all, including those in wheelchairs.

Getting around Los Angeles on public transport while confined to a wheelchair is possible but requires some planning. The Metropolitan Transportation Authority and the Big Blue Bus company of Santa Monica operate a fleet of wheelchair-accessible buses. For schedule information, call ☎ 213-626-4455 (or TDD ☎ 800-252-9040). The Paratransit Referral Service Info Line (☎ 800-431-7882) refers mobility-impaired people to door-to-door transportation services in LA County. For information about traveling to and from Los Angeles International Airport, contact Travelers Aid (☎ 310-646-2270), or visit one of their many booths at the airport (the largest is in the Tom Bradley Terminal). Car rental companies can supply hand-controlled vehicles at a day or two's notice, and taxi services can provide vans to accommodate wheelchairs.

Larger private and chain hotels (see the Places to Stay chapter for listings) have suites for disabled guests. Telephone companies are required to provide relay operators for the hearing impaired; call ☎ 800-735-2922 (voice) or ☎ 800-735-2929 (TDD/TTY). Many banks now provide ATM instructions in Braille, and you will find audible crossing signals (such as the famed 'cuckoo-crossings' in Santa Monica) as well as dropped curbs at busier roadway intersections.

All major airlines, Greyhound buses and Amtrak trains allow service animals to accompany passengers, and frequently sell two-for-one packages when attendants of seriously disabled passengers are required. Airlines will also provide assistance for connecting, boarding and deplaning the flight – just ask when making your reservation. (Note: Airlines must accept wheelchairs as checked baggage and have an onboard chair available, though some advance notice may be required on smaller aircraft.)

A central clearinghouse for information, referrals and tips about accessibility and service availability is the LA County Commission on Disabilities (☎ 213-974-1053 or TDD ☎ 213-974-1707). Other useful numbers include the Center for the Partially Sighted (☎ 310-458-3501), which provides counseling, equipment and health information programs; the 24-hour Crisis Line for the Handicapped (☎ 800-426-4263), which offers volunteer counseling, support, information and referrals; and the

Greater LA Council on Deafness (GLAD; ☎ 213-478-8000 voice and TDD) for counseling, interpretation, information and referrals. The Society for the Advancement of Travel for the Handicapped (SATH; ☎ 212-447-7284), 347 Fifth Ave, No 610, New York, NY 10016, can provide travel information through its quarterly magazine.

SENIOR TRAVELERS

Although the age at which one qualifies for benefits varies with the attraction, people 50 years and up can expect to receive discounts and benefits at many Los Angeles attractions and accommodations.

It's certainly worth contacting the American Association of Retired Persons (AARP; ☎ 202-434-2277, 800-424-3410, www.aarp.org), 601 E St NW, Washington, DC 20049 – a flash of its membership card (available at just $9 a year to US residents over the age of 50) is often enough to get discounts on hotels, car rentals, etc. It also arranges travel for members through AARP Travel Experience.

Elderhostel (☎ 877-426-8056, ☎ 877-426-2167 TTY, www.elderhostel.org), 75 Federal St, Boston, MA 02110, organizes educational programs in most US cities, including Los Angeles. Grand Circle Travel (☎ 617-350-7500, 800-597-3644, www.gct.com), 347 Congress St, Boston, MA 02210, offers senior travelers escorted tours and travel information. It also provides a free booklet entitled *Going Abroad: 101 Tips for Mature Travelers* that will prove useful in planning for domestic travel as well.

LOS ANGELES FOR CHILDREN

Traveling successfully with young children requires planning and effort. Don't try to overdo things; even for adults, packing too much into the time available can cause problems. And make sure the activities include the kids as well – balance a day at the Getty Center with a visit to the zoo or the beach. Include the kids in the trip planning; if they've helped to work out where you are going, they will be much more interested when they get there. LP's *Travel with Children* by Maureen Wheeler is a good

source of information for this kind of thing. For area-specific information, also consider *Fun Places to Go with Children in Southern California* (1997) by Stephanie Kegan.

Most car-rental firms have children's safety seats for hire at a nominal cost, but be sure to book them in advance. The same goes for highchairs and cots (cribs); they're common in many restaurants and hotels, but in limited numbers. The choice of baby food, infant formulas, soy and cow's milk, disposable nappies (diapers) and the like is great in LA supermarkets. Diaper changing stations can be found in many public restrooms in malls, department stores and in family-oriented restaurants.

It's perfectly fine to bring your kids, even toddlers, along to casual restaurants, cafes and daytime events; though upscale restaurants might not be as welcoming. Some of the larger hotels offer a baby-sitting service, and others may be able to help you arrange one. Alternatively, there are a number of agencies you can contact. Be sure to ask whether your sitter is licensed and bonded, what the person charges per hour, whether there's a minimum fee and whether the sitter charges extra for meals and transportation. Established agencies you might try include the Baby Sitters Guild (☎ 323-658-8792), Best Babysitters Service (☎ 323-857-0023) and also Buckingham Nannies (☎ 310-247-1877, 800-200-7161).

See the boxed text 'Especially for Kids' in the Things to See & Do chapter, for recommendations for activities with children.

USEFUL ORGANIZATIONS

Headquarters of the Automobile Association of Southern California (☎ 213-741-3111; Map 5), a subdivision of the American Automobile Association (AAA), is in a Spanish colonial mansion at 2601 S Figueroa St, but there are numerous other offices throughout LA. AAA provides its members and those of affiliated foreign clubs with motoring information, maps, tour books, car insurance and travel planning in general. Most importantly, perhaps, it offers free emergency road services and towing (☎ 800-400-4222).

LIBRARIES

The Downtown Central Library (☎ 213-228-7000; Map 5), 630 W 5th St, in a historic building designed by Bertram Goodhue, is the repository of more than 2 million books and a prized archive of historical photographs. The collection is supplemented with several galleries and an active calendar of events. Library hours are 10am to 8pm Monday to Thursday, 10am to 6pm Friday and Saturday and 1pm to 5pm Sunday. For more on this historic building, see Downtown in the Things to See & Do chapter and the Los Angeles Architecture special section.

Other excellent public libraries are the Beverly Hills Library (☎ 310-288-2220; Map 11), 444 N Rexford Dr, which has strong collections of local history and fine arts; the Santa Monica Library (☎ 310-458-8600; Map 13), 1343 6th St, which has selections in art, business, fiction and history; and the Glendale Central Library (☎ 818-548-2020), 222 E Harvard St, which focuses on business and California and local history.

The University of California at Los Angeles (UCLA; ☎ 310-825-4321; Map 11), on Westwood Blvd in Westwood, has a vast library containing 6.6 million volumes spread over 10 departments in separate buildings. Of greatest general interest is the Research Library (☎ 310-825-4732, reference 310-825-1323). UCLA also operates the historic William Andrews Clark Memorial Library in the West Adams district (see Things to See & Do for details).

The University of Southern California (USC; ☎ 213-740-6050; Map 6), just north of Exposition Park, has a network of 17 libraries with a total of 2.8 million books, 3 million photographs, and electronic databases. USC's collections in architecture, cinema, international and public affairs, American literature, regional history, marine science, philosophy, Latin American studies and Korean studies are particularly noteworthy. The main repository is the Doheny Memorial Library (☎ 213-740-4039).

Other university libraries in LA County can be found at Art Center College of Design (☎ 626-396-2233), 1700 Lida St in Pasadena; Caltech (☎ 626-395-6405; Map 17) at 1201 E California Blvd in Pasadena; Cal State Northridge (☎ 818-677-2285), 18111 Nordhoff St; and the Cal State Los Angeles (☎ 213-343-4927), 5151 State University Dr.

UNIVERSITIES

Los Angeles has dozens of public and private institutions of higher learning. The most prestigious is UCLA (☎ 310-825-4321; Map 11), 405 Hilgard Ave, established in 1919 and the largest of the 10 UC campuses. It has some 36,500 students, enrolled in more than 100 programs, including medicine, law, film and TV, and performing arts and has produced five Nobel Prize laureates. Research milestones include being the birthplace of the Internet in 1969. Alumni include Francis Ford Coppola, track and field athlete Jackie Joyner-Kersee and former LA mayor Tom Bradley. Admission to UCLA is highly selective.

Close behind – and a fierce crosstown rival in college football and basketball – is the private USC (☎ 213-740-2311; Map 6), University Park Campus, with one Nobel Prize among its accomplishment. In 1999, it enrolled 28,766 students, including the second-largest foreign student contingent in the nation. Because of its exorbitant tuition fees (about $30,000/year), it has been nicknamed 'University of Spoiled Children.'

LA is also home to four campuses of the California State University system, located in Long Beach, Northridge, Downtown LA and Dominguez Hills. Their combined enrollment was just over 90,000 in 1999. Occidental College is a distinguished private liberal arts college. Specialized schools of international renown include Art Center College of Design and California Institute for the Arts and the California Institute of Technology (Caltech).

About 300,000 students are also enrolled in Los Angeles area's two-year community colleges, of which Santa Monica College (SMC) enjoys the best reputation. It transfers more students to UCLA or UC Berkeley than any other community college in California; this accomplishment has earned it the nickname 'Stanford-on-Pico,' likening the community college to the preeminent school of Stanford. Alumni include Arnold Schwarzenegger, Dustin Hoffman and astronaut Buzz Aldrin. The Santa Monica Track Club, which has produced 27 Olympic-medal winners and launched the careers of Carl Lewis and other athletes, is based at the college.

For more information about LA's major schools, see the Things to See & Do chapter.

CULTURAL CENTERS

The French Alliance Française de LA (☎ 310-652-0306) is at 215 S La Cienega Blvd in Beverly Hills. The German Goethe Institute (Map 10; ☎ 323-525-3388) is at 5750 Wilshire Blvd, Suite 100, in the Miracle Mile district.

DANGERS & ANNOYANCES

Much has been written about crime in Los Angeles, though overall crime figures have gone down in recent years. If you take ordinary precautions, chances are you won't be victimized.

Walking around in the daytime is generally no problem anywhere, although extra caution should be exercised in East LA, South Central, some sections of Hollywood and the MacArthur Park neighborhood west of Downtown, which are plagued by interracial gang activity, drugs, prostitution, or a combination thereof. It's best to stay away from these districts after dark; if you do venture there, use a private vehicle (car or taxi) and don't walk around much.

The streets of Hollywood yield dangers from drug addicts and crazed people, and should be avoided after nightfall; ditto for Venice. Exercise a bit of extra caution in Silver Lake and West Hollywood. Westside communities like Westwood and Beverly Hills, as well as the beach towns (except Venice), are generally among the safer areas (the 1999 killing of a German tourist in Santa Monica notwithstanding), as is Pasadena.

Although media coverage of gangs suggest otherwise, greater Los Angeles is no war zone. A truce between the Bloods and the Crips has been in effect since 1992 – an encouraging precedent. And the only gang activity seen by the majority of Angelenos is the work of graffiti-happy 'homeboys.' But areas to avoid are the poorest sections of South Central, East LA, Long Beach and Unglued.

In general, be aware of your surroundings and who may be watching you. Avoid walking on dimly lit streets at night, particularly when alone. Walk purposefully. Avoid unnecessary displays of money or jewelry. Divide money and credit cards to avoid losing everything. Always aim to use ATM machines in well-trafficked areas and keep your eyes open.

Car thefts are more common here than in other areas of the country, although the number of carjackings has actually come down. Always lock your car and put your

Northridge earthquake damage, Santa Monica

valuables out of sight, even if leaving the car for just a moment. Never leave anything of value – cameras, video cameras, purses, etc – in the back seat. Rent a car with a lockable trunk, but try not to leave valuables behind when you park. Keep your windows closed and your doors locked if anyone approaches your vehicle. If your car is bumped from behind in a remote area, don't stop until reaching a well-lit, busy area, police station or gas station. Gangs who orchestrate freeway 'accidents' and then sue are not uncommon. However, freeway shootings, a plague in the early '90s, are now extremely rare.

Thefts are rare in major hotels with good security, but they are not uncommon in cheap motels. Keep your room locked when you're gone, and take advantage of the office safe for jewelry or documents you may not be carrying with you. Never leave money or cameras in view in restaurants or bars. Beware of pickpockets and petty thieves in large crowds. Keep tight hold of your purse or bag, or you can wear your money and passport in a secure place on your person. If you are unlucky enough to have something stolen, report it immediately to your hotel's front desk or to the nearest police station (see Emergency for contact information).

Street people and panhandlers abound in areas such as Downtown and Santa Monica. Nearly all are harmless. It's your judgment call whether it's appropriate to offer them money or anything else.

EMERGENCIES

In case of emergency, dial ☎ 911 and request assistance from the police, fire department,

---

Shake, Rattle & Roll: Earthquakes in LA

Earthquakes occur in greater number than most people realize – in fact, LA experiences dozens a week. Most are of a magnitude that makes them detectable only by sensitive seismological instruments. Occasionally, a tremor of 4.5 or 5.0 magnitude may give you a start and rattle a few glasses; it will pass in a moment, leaving only heart palpitations.

Many Angelenos are prepared with an emergency kit for major earthquakes. Ideally, it includes a first-aid kit, portable radio, flashlights and extra batteries, blankets, essential medications, three days' worth of food and three gallons of water per person.

In the extremely unlikely event that you're in Los Angeles during a major earthquake the LA Fire Department recommends you do the following:

- If you are indoors, stay indoors. Immediately take cover under a desk or table, or under a doorway. Stay clear of windows, mirrors, or anything in danger of falling, such as bookshelves or file cabinets. Don't use the elevators. If you're in a shopping mall or large public building, expect the alarm or sprinkler systems to come on.

- If you are outdoors, get into an open area away from buildings, trees and power lines. If you are driving, pull over to the side of the road away from bridges, overpasses and power lines. Stay inside the car until the shaking stops.

- If you are on a sidewalk near buildings, duck into a doorway to protect yourself from falling bricks, glass and debris.

- Prepare for aftershocks.

- Afterward, check first for personal injuries, then for fire hazards (such as gas leaks or electrical-line damage) and spilled chemicals or medicines. As the city water supply may become polluted, you should boil any tap water before drinking it until notified otherwise. Use the telephone only if absolutely necessary. Turn on the radio and listen for bulletins.

ambulance or paramedics. Some other contacts include:

AIDS Hot Line	☎ 800-342-2437
Alcohol & Drug Referral Hotline	☎ 800-252-6465
Crisis Response Unit	☎ 800-833-3376
Poison Information Center	☎ 800-777-6476
Rape & Battering Hotline	☎ 310-392-8381
Suicide Prevention Hotline	☎ 800-333-4444

Local telephone directories have a First Aid & Survival Guide, which includes advice on surviving an earthquake and a list of steps in performing CPR.

If you have something stolen, report it to the police – in many cases, you'll need a police report to make a claim if you have a travel insurance policy. If your credit cards, cash cards, or traveler's checks have been stolen, notify your bank or the relevant company as soon as possible. (See Money, earlier in this chapter, for contact information for major credit card companies.)

Foreign visitors who lose their passport should contact their consulates (see Foreign Embassies & Consulates, earlier in this chapter).

LEGAL MATTERS

If you are stopped by the police for a traffic offense, you'll usually be given a ticket stating the amount of the fine, which you have 30 days to pay. There is usually no point in getting into a discussion, which may only make your predicament worse. (Also see Car & Motorcycle in the Getting Around chapter for automobile-related concerns.)

Nude sunbathing, or going topless in the case of women, is against the law on LA beaches and you may be fined – and will certainly draw a huge crowd!

It's generally forbidden to have an open container of an alcoholic beverage in public, regardless of whether you're in a car, on the beach, in a park or on the sidewalk. The drinking age is 21 and is strictly enforced. If you look even close to 21, you will likely be asked to show a picture ID to prove your age. You could incur stiff fines, jail time and penalties if caught driving under the influ-

ence of alcohol. Drug use also generates zero tolerance among police officers and can get you into serious trouble with the law.

Many cities, especially Santa Monica, have recently begun to crack down on jaywalking. Fines can be as high as $40.

If you are arrested, you are allowed to remain silent. There is no legal obligation to speak to a police officer if you don't wish, but never walk away from one until given permission. Anyone who is arrested is legally allowed (and given) the right to make one phone call. If you don't have a lawyer or family member to help you, call your consulate. The police will give you the number upon request.

BUSINESS HOURS

Regular business hours are 9am to 5pm, but there are certainly no hard and fast rules. Smaller retail shops generally stay open 9am to 6pm Monday to Saturday, but malls usually don't close until 8pm or 9pm weekdays and 6pm or 7pm weekends. Finding 24-hour supermarkets, convenience stores and gas stations should be no problem anywhere in Los Angeles. Post offices are open 9am to 5pm Monday to Friday; some also open on Saturday. Bank hours are typically 9am or 10am to 5pm or 6pm Monday to Friday; a few are also open to 1pm or 2pm on Saturday.

PUBLIC HOLIDAYS & SPECIAL EVENTS

California observes most US national holidays. On these days, all government offices (including post offices) and banks will be closed. Some individual businesses, museums and restaurants may close as well, particularly on Thanksgiving, Christmas and New Year's Day. Many holidays are observed on the nearest Monday.

New Year's Day January 1
Martin Luther King Jr Day 3rd Monday in January
Presidents' Day 3rd Monday in February
Memorial Day Last Monday in May
Independence Day (4th of July) July 4
Labor Day 1st Monday in September
Columbus Day 2nd Monday in October

Veterans' Day November 11
Thanksgiving Day 4th Thursday in November
Christmas Day December 25

Los Angeles has a packed calendar of special events, with many festivities celebrating the traditions and culture of a particular ethnic group. Dates for most events shift slightly from year to year, so for specifics call the number listed with each entry below or the Los Angeles Convention & Visitors Bureau events hotline at ☎ 213-689-8822. Details are also published in the *Los Angeles Times* and *LA Weekly*. An admission fee applies to all events listed in this section that are not designated as free.

January

Tournament of Roses Parade & Rose Bowl – January 1. Marching bands, grinning celebrities and enormous flower-coated floats, proceeding along Pasadena's Colorado Blvd before the Rose Bowl, a famous college football game between champions of the Midwest and West Coast divisions (☎ 626-449-4100); post-parade viewing of floats at Victory Park, Pasadena (☎ 626-449-7673)

Dr Martin Luther King Birthday Unity Parade – mid January. Free street parade, starting at 1950 Lemon Ave in Long Beach, celebrating the civil rights activist (☎ 562-570-6816)

February

Chinese New Year – late January/early February. Free festivities, fireworks, paper dragons, carnival rides and other traditional revels in the heart of Chinatown (☎ 213-617-0396)

Pan African Film & Art Festival – throughout the month. The largest such festival in the US showcasing different types of films from Africa, the Caribbean, Latin America, Europe and North America portraying the complexity of black cinema (☎ 213-896-8221)

Los Angeles Bach Festival – dates vary. An annual concert series since 1934 (the oldest such classical music festival in the US) at the magnificent First Congregational Church, 540 S Commonwealth Ave (☎ 213-385-1345)

Nissan Open Golf Tournament – last week of February. Prestigious golf tournament at the Riviera Country Club in Pacific Palisade (☎ 800-752-6736)

March

LA Marathon & Bike Tour – first Sunday in March. A 26-mile race from Figueroa and 6th Sts in Downtown through Chinatown, Hollywood and Echo Park (☎ 310-444-5544)

Cowboy Poetry & Music Festival – late March. Western poets and country music in Santa Clarita (☎ 800-305-0755)

April

Toyota Grand Prix of Long Beach – early to mid-April. A week-long auto-racing spectacle drawing world-class drivers (☎ 888-827-7333)

Blessing of the Animals – Saturday before Easter. A draw for pets and people from all parts of Southern California to Downtown LA's Olvera St (☎ 213-625-5045)

Easter – Religious holiday in April or March

***Los Angeles Times* Festival of Books** – third weekend in April. Free fair with author readings and discussions, storytelling, children's activities on UCLA campus in Westwood (☎ 800-528-4637, ext 72665)

Fiesta Broadway – last Sunday in April. Free Cinco de Mayo street fair celebration with entertainment from renowned Latino singers along historic Broadway in Downtown (☎ 310-914-0015)

May

Cinco de Mayo Celebration – early May. Celebration of the Mexican victory over the French at the Battle of Puebla (1862); free festivities abound in the Pueblo area around Olvera St in Downtown (☎ 213-625-5045)

Venice Art Walk – mid-May. Private studio tour of Venice-based artists along with tastings of gourmet dishes from local restaurants (☎ 310-392-9255)

Topanga Banjo Fiddle Contest – mid-May. Bluegrass music festival with more than 100 contestants at Paramount Ranch in the Santa Monica Mountains (☎ 818-382-4819)

Los Angeles Cuban Cultural Festival – 3rd Sunday in May. Echo Park celebration of the cultural heritage and contributions of the Cuban community (☎ 310-914-0015)

June

Grand Performances Moonlight & Matinee Series – June to September. LA's top-caliber series of free music, dance and theater in the fabulous setting of the California Plaza Watercourt in Downtown LA, featuring local, national and

international artists (☎ 213-687-2190, www
.grandperformances.org)

Old School Jam – mid-June. Concert, festival and
food and craft fair celebrating reggae and Caribbean culture and history (☎ 310-515-3322)

Jazz & Blues Festival – mid- or late June. Performances by jazz and blues masters and their pro-
tégés, Leimert Park Village at 43rd Place and
Crenshaw Blvd (☎ 213-473-4296, 213-485-0709)

Mariachi USA Festival – third weekend in June.
Big fiesta celebrating the finest mariachi music
and ballet folklórico, Hollywood Bowl, 2301 N
Highland Ave, Hollywood (☎ 213-848-7717)

Los Angeles Gay & Lesbian Pride Celebration -
late June. The largest such celebration west of
the Mississippi with live entertainment, 250
vendors and food stalls throughout West Hollywood (☎ 323-860-0701)

July

Lotus Festival – first weekend after July 4th. Asian
Pacific festival at Echo Park Lake, the largest
lotus bed outside China (☎ 213-485-5448)

Outfest – LA Gay & Lesbian Film Festival – mid-
to late July. Huge film festival by and for gay,
lesbian, bisexual and transgender people (☎ 323-
960-9200, www.outfest.org)

LA Latino Film Festival – late July. More than 70
films, documentaries and shorts from the US and
the rest of the Americas at the Egyptian Theater,
6712 Hollywood Blvd (☎ 323-469-9066, www
.latinofilm.org)

Malibu Art Festival – last weekend in July. Paintings, sculptures, jewelry, photography, textiles
and crafts, along with free live entertainment
and the Malibu Food Fair at the Malibu Civic
Center (☎ 310-456-9025)

Mercedes Benz Cup Tennis Tournament – late
July. International tennis tournament at the
UCLA campus in Westwood (☎ 310-824-1010)

Gourmet LA – late July. Tasty dishes from 20 to 30
of LA's top restaurants, nonstop live music, chef
demonstrations, lectures and food-related seminars at Santa Monica Civic Auditorium, 1855
Main St (www.efestival.com)

August

Nisei Week Japanese Festival – early to mid-
August. A free Japanese festival in Little Tokyo,
with a parade, karaoke, kimono-clad dancers
and crafts demonstrations (☎ 213-687-7193)

African Marketplace and Cultural Faire – mid- to
late August. A free celebration of African
culture, with more than 350 crafts booths and

lots of entertainment and music, Rancho
Cienega Park, 5001 Rodeo Blvd, Downtown
(☎ 323-734-1164)

Sunset Junction Street Faire – mid August. On
Sunset Blvd in the 3600 to 4600 blocks, a free
street fair celebrating the ethnic diversity and
cultural wackiness of Silver Lake, Echo Park and
Los Feliz neighborhoods (☎ 323-661-7771)

September

Los Angeles County Fair – second Thursday after
Labor Day. Huge fair that runs for 18 days with
carnival rides, prizes, livestock exhibits and live
country entertainment at the LA County Fair-
grounds in Pomona (☎ 909-623-3111)

Oktoberfest – early September to late October.
The largest Southern California Oktoberfest, with
beer, sausages, oompah bands and chicken
dancing at Alpine Village, 833 W Torrance Blvd,
Torrance (☎ 310-327-4384, www.alpinevillage.net)

Mexican Independence Festival – weekend closest
to September 16. On Olvera St in Downtown, a
free celebration of Mexico's independence from
Spain with live performers, food, historic displays and celebrities from Mexico (☎ 213-624-
3660)

Simon Rodia Watts Towers Jazz Festival – late
September. Free jazz, gospel and blues festival
surrounding the Watts Towers at 1727 E 107th St
(☎ 213-847-4646)

**Simon Rodia Watts Towers Day of the Drum Fes-
tival** – late September. Free festival that attracts
drummers from around the world (☎ 213-847-
4646)

Festival of Philippine Arts & Culture – mid-September. Free festivities include dance and music
performances, film, theater and food at Cabrillo
Beach in San Pedro (☎ 213-389-3050)

October

South Bay Greek Festival – early October. Free
festival with music, dancing, Greek crafts and
food at St Katherine Greek Orthodox Church,
722 Knob Hill, Redondo Beach (☎ 310-540-
2434)

Halloween Party – October 31. Free rambunctious
street fair with eccentric, and occasionally X-
rated, costumes all along Santa Monica Blvd in
West Hollywood

November

Día de los Muertos – November 2. Day of the
Dead (a Mexican festival of the return of the
dead to earth for one day each year) with a large

candlelight procession, decorated altars and skull-shaped candy on Olvera St in Downtown (☎ 213-485-9777)

Mariachi Fesival – mid-November. Free Mariachi music and ballet folklórico at Mariachi Plaza in Boyle Heights (☎ 213-485-2437)

Doo Dah Parade – Saturday after Thanksgiving. Free wacky parody of the traditional Rose Parade, on Colorado Blvd in Pasadena, with such staple marchers as a precision briefcase drill team, a roving volleyball game and the West Hollywood Cheerleaders; beware of artificial seagulls 'anointing' unsuspecting onlookers (☎ 626-440-7379)

Hollywood Christmas Parade – late November or early December. Free parade featuring celebrities from film and TV ringing in the season by waving at bystanders from flashy floats along Hollywood Blvd in Hollywood (☎ 323-469-2337)

December

Holiday Festival of Lights – throughout December. Largest lighting display in Southern California in Griffith Park (☎ 323-913-4688)

Christmas Boat Parade – mid-December. Many beautifully decorated and twinkling yachts illuminate the harbor in Marina del Rey; best viewed from Burton Chase Park (☎ 310-821-7614; free)

Las Posadas – daily on the eight days before Christmas. Free candlelight processions that relive Mary and Joseph's journey to Bethlehem, followed by piñata-breaking for kids on Olvera St and surrounding streets (☎ 213-625-5045)

DOING BUSINESS

Los Angeles is the largest business, financial and industrial center on the West Coast and is currently experiencing a boom, which attracts talented workers from the country's more moribund areas. The city has become ever more progressive in beating the business drum and now has a host of advocacy and outreach programs designed to make doing business here well-oiled and successful. The following is only a brief outline of partnerships and resource centers to help you understand local practices, provide referrals to important agencies, and obtain business-related publications.

Los Angeles Economic Development Corporation (☎ 888-452-3321, nfo@laedc.org, www.laedc .org;

Map 5) 515 S Flower St, 32nd floor in Downtown LA.

US Small Business Association (☎ 818-552-3210, www.sba.gov/ca/la) 330 N Brand, Suite 1200, Glendale

Los Angeles Chamber of Commerce (☎ 213-580-7500, www.lachamber.net) 350 S Bixel St

Los Angeles Business Council (☎ 310-475-4574) 10880 Wilshire Blvd, Suite 1003 in Westwood

To find out what's happening at street level, pick up a copy of the *Los Angeles Business Journal*, sold at bookstores, newsstands and some convenience markets. Another useful resource is Pacific Bell's *Business to Business Yellow Pages* (available at libraries), which lists businesses and agencies by category.

For translation or interpreting services, try Berlitz (☎ 310-260-7100, 800-367-4336), 525 Broadway, Suite 300, Santa Monica.

WORK

If you're not a US citizen or legal resident (with a 'green card'), there's a lot of red tape involved in getting work in the US, and rather severe penalties (a heavy fine for your employer, deportation for yourself) if you're caught working illegally. If you have particular skills, as well as a sponsoring employer or close relative living in the US, you have a reasonable chance of getting a special working visa from an American embassy before you leave your own country.

The type of visa varies depending on how long you're staying and the kind of work you plan to do. Generally, you need either a J-1 visa, which you can obtain by joining a visitor-exchange program, or a H-2B visa, which you get when being sponsored by a US employer. The latter is not easy to obtain (since the employer has to prove that no US citizen or permanent resident is available to do the job); the former is issued mostly to students for work in summer camps. If you lack connections, it's unlikely you'll be granted a working visa.

Information on legal student employment opportunities is best obtained from a university, either in your own country or in the US.

Getting There & Away

AIR

If you're flying into Los Angeles, you'll most likely land at Los Angeles International Airport, 17 miles southwest of Downtown LA. Smaller regional airports, handling mostly short-distance domestic travel, are Burbank-Glendale-Pasadena Airport (☎ 818-840-8840), 14 miles northwest of Downtown, and Long Beach Airport (☎ 310-421-8293), 22 miles south.

Outside of LA County are John Wayne-Orange County Airport in Newport Beach (☎ 714-252-5006), 40 miles southeast, and Ontario International Airport in San Bernardino County (☎ 909-983-8282), 40 miles east. The Getting Around chapter has details on how to travel to and from LA County airports.

Airports

Los Angeles International Airport (LAX; ☎ 310-646-5252, www.lawa.org; Map 2) handles all overseas and most domestic

flights in and out of the city and is the fourth-busiest airport in the world (behind Chicago O'Hare, Atlanta Hartsfield and Dallas-Fort Worth). Some 64 million passengers, a quarter of them traveling from other countries, pass through LAX's nine terminals each year. Ticketing and check-in are on the upper (departure) level of each terminal, while baggage claim areas are on the lower (arrival) level.

Some 80 passenger carriers and 20 cargo carriers serve LAX. The hub for most international airlines is the Tom Bradley International Terminal (TBIT), named after LA's first African American mayor.

The Burbank-Glendale-Pasadena Airport (☎ 818-840-8840, 800-835-9287, www.bur .com; Maps 2 & 18), 2627 Hollywood Way, is small and easily accessed. It is an excellent alternative to LAX for certain domestic flights ranging from Albuquerque, New Mexico, to Wichita, Kansas.

Departure Tax

Airport departure taxes are normally included in the cost of tickets bought in the USA, though they may not be included with tickets purchased abroad. There's a $6 airport departure tax charged to all passengers bound for any foreign destination. However, this fee – in addition to a $6.50 North American Free Trade Agreement (NAFTA) tax charged to passengers entering the USA from a foreign country – are hidden taxes added to the purchase price of your ticket.

Buying Tickets

If you're flying to Los Angeles from overseas, the airfare is likely to be the biggest expense in your budget. Fortunately, stiff competition has resulted in widespread discounting. Get your ticket as early as possible, because some of the cheapest fares must be bought weeks or months in advance, and popular flights sell out early. Lower fares are generally available by traveling

Warning

The information in this chapter is particularly vulnerable to change. Prices for international travel are volatile, routes are introduced and canceled, schedules change, special deals come and go, and rules and visa requirements are amended. Airlines and governments seem to take a perverse pleasure in making price structures and regulations as complicated as possible. In addition, the travel industry is highly competitive and there are many hidden costs and benefits.

The upshot of this is that you should get quotes and advice from as many airlines and travel agents as possible, and make sure you understand how a fare (and any ticket you may buy) works before you part with your hard-earned cash. The details given in this chapter should be regarded as pointers and are not a substitute for your own careful, up-to-date research.

midweek, staying over a Saturday night and taking advantage of short-lived promotional offers. To ensure that you get the best deal, set aside a few hours to research the market. The Internet is a useful resource and most travel agencies and airlines have their own Web sites.

The days when some travel agents routinely fleeced travelers by running off with their money are, happily, almost over. Paying by credit card generally offers protection, as most card issuers provide refunds if you can prove you didn't get what you paid for. You may decide to pay slightly more than the rock-bottom fare by opting for the safety of an established travel agent. Firms such as STA Travel and Council Travel with offices worldwide, Travel CUTS in Canada, Usit Campus (formerly Campus Travel) in the UK and Flight Centre in Australia are not going to disappear overnight, and they do offer good prices to most destinations. These companies also sell discounted tickets for students and people under 26.

Air Passes Most US airlines offer air passes to overseas visitors. These are essentially books of coupons each good for one flight within the US that non-US citizens buy in their home countries in conjunction with an international airline ticket. Savings over single tickets purchased within the US are usually substantial. The minimum number of coupons is usually three or four and the maximum is eight or 10. One catch is that if a connection is not a direct flight (ie, it involves a change of flight number), it counts as two coupons.

Some airlines require you to plan your itinerary in advance and to complete all flights within 60 days of arrival, but rules vary among individual airlines. Some may allow you to use coupons on standby, in which case call the airline a day or two before the flight and make a 'standby reservation.' Such a reservation gives you priority over all other travelers who just appear hoping to get on the flight the same day.

Major airlines offering air pass programs that serve Los Angeles include American, Alaska, Continental, Southwest, North-western, United, America West, Air Canada and US Airways.

Other Parts of the USA

Discount travel agents in the US are known as consolidators (although you won't see a sign on the door saying 'Consolidator'). San Francisco is the country's consolidator capital, although good deals can be found in most big cities. Consolidators are listed in the Yellow Pages (under Travel Agents) and also advertise in the weekly travel section of the major daily newspapers, such as the *New York Times*, the *Chicago Tribune* and the *San Francisco Chronicle*.

Council Travel, the USA's largest student travel organization, has around 60 offices in the country; its head office (☎ 800-226-8624) is at 205 E 42nd St, New York, NY 10017. Call for the office nearest you or visit its Web site at www.ciee.org. STA Travel (☎ 800-777-0112) also has offices around the country. Call the toll-free number for locations or visit its Web site at www.statravel.com.

Canada

Canadian discount air ticket sellers are also known as consolidators. The *Globe & Mail*, the *Toronto Star*, the *Montreal Gazette* and the *Vancouver Sun* carry travel agents' ads and are good places to look for cheap fares. Travel CUTS (☎ 800-667-2887) is Canada's national student travel agency with offices in all major cities. Its Web address is www.travelcuts.com.

Australia & New Zealand

The main carriers across the Pacific are Qantas, Air New Zealand and United. Prices are higher if you wish to stop over in Hawaii or plan to stay abroad for more than two months.

The weekend travel sections of big newspapers, such as the Melbourne *Age*, the *Sydney Morning Herald* and the *New Zealand Herald* are good sources for discounted airfares. For the best fares, try STA Travel and Flight Centre. STA Travel (☎ 03-9349 2411) is headquartered at 224 Faraday St, Carlton, VIC 3053 and has branches in other major cities and on some university

Air Travel Glossary

Alliances Many of the world's leading airlines are now intimately involved with each other, sharing everything from reservations systems and check-in to aircraft and frequent-flyer schemes. Opponents say that alliances restrict competition. Whatever the arguments, there is no doubt that big alliances are the way of the future.

Courier Fares Businesses often need to send urgent documents or freight securely and quickly. Courier companies hire people to accompany the package through customs and, in return, offer a discount ticket that is sometimes a bargain. However, you may have to surrender all your baggage allowance and take only carry-on luggage.

Fares Airlines traditionally offer 1st-class (coded F), business-class (coded J) and economy-class (coded Y) tickets. These days, there are so many promotional and discounted fares available that few passengers pay full fare.

Lost Tickets If you lose your airline ticket, an airline will usually treat it as a travelers check and, after inquiries, issue another one to you. Legally, however, an airline is entitled to treat it as cash, so if you lose it, then it could be gone forever. Take very good care of your tickets.

Onward Tickets An entry requirement for many countries is that you have a ticket out of the country. If you're unsure of your next move, the easiest solution is to buy the cheapest onward ticket to a neighboring country or a ticket (from a reliable airline) that can later be refunded if you do not use it.

Open-Jaw Tickets These are return tickets used to fly out to one place but return from another. If available, this can save you from having to backtrack to your arrival point.

Overbooking Since every flight has some passengers who fail to show up, airlines often book more passengers than they have seats. Usually excess passengers make up for the no-shows, but occasionally somebody gets 'bumped' onto the next available flight. Who is it most likely to be? The passengers who check in late. If you do get 'bumped,' you are normally offered some form of compensation.

Reconfirmation Some airlines require you to reconfirm your flight at least 72 hours prior to departure. Check your travel documents to see if this is the case.

Restrictions Discounted tickets often have various restrictions on them – such as mandatory advance payment and penalties for alterations or cancellations. Others have restrictions on the minimum and maximum period you must be away.

Round-the-World Tickets RTW tickets give you a limited period (usually a year) in which to circumnavigate the globe. You can go anywhere the carrying airlines go, as long as you don't backtrack. The number of stopovers or the total number of separate flights is decided before you set off, and these tickets usually cost a bit more than a basic return flight.

Ticketless Travel Airlines are gradually waking up to the realization that paper tickets are unnecessary encumbrances. On simple one-way or return trips, reservations details can be held on computer, and the passengers merely show identification to claim their seats.

Transferred Tickets Airline tickets cannot be transferred from one person to another. Travelers sometimes try to sell the return half of their tickets, but at check-in you will be asked for identification that matches the name on the ticket.

campuses. Call (☎ 131 776 Australiawide) for your nearest branch, or visit its Web site at www.statravel.com.au. Flight Centre (☎ 131 600 Australiawide) has a central office at 82 Elizabeth St in Sydney and dozens more throughout Australia. Its Web address is www.flightcentre.com.au.

In New Zealand, Flight Centre (☎ 09-309 6171) has a big office in Auckland at National Bank Towers (corner of Queen and Darby Sts) and many branches throughout the country. STA Travel (☎ 09-309 0458) has its main office at 10 High St, Auckland, plus other branches in Auckland, as well as in Hamilton, Palmerston North, Wellington, Christchurch and Dunedin.

The UK

Many airlines, including British Airways, United Airlines and Virgin Atlantic, have nonstop services between London and Los Angeles. In the UK, airline ticket discounters are known as bucket shops. Travel agent ads appear in the travel pages of the Saturday edition of the *Independent* and the Sunday *Times*. Also look for free magazines, such as *TNT*, widely available in London outside the main railway and underground stations.

STA Travel (☎ 020-7361 6161) is at 86 Old Brompton Rd, London SW7 3LQ and has other offices in London and Manchester (www.statravel.co.uk). Usit Campus (☎ 020-7730 3402), 52 Grosvenor Gardens, London SW1 W0AG has branches throughout the UK (www.usitcampus.com). Both agencies sell tickets to all travelers but cater especially to young people and students.

Other recommended travel agencies include Bridge the World (☎ 020-7734 7447), 4 Regent Place, London W1R 5FB; Flightbookers (☎ 020-7757 2000), 177-178 Tottenham Court Rd, London W1P 9LF; and Trailfinders (☎ 020-7938 3939), 194 Kensington High St, London W8 7RG.

Continental Europe

Though London is the travel discount capital of Europe, a range of good deals is also available from other major cities. From continental Europe, KLM flies from Amsterdam, Air France from Paris, Swissair from Zurich, Lufthansa from Frankfurt and Iberia from Madrid.

France has a network of travel agencies that sells discount tickets to travelers of all ages. OTU Voyages (☎ 01 44 41 38 50) has a central Paris office at 39 Ave Georges Bernanos (5e) and 42 offices around the country. The Web address is www.otu.fr. Acceuil des Jeunes en France (☎ 01 42 77 87 80), 119 Rue Saint Martin (4e), is another popular discount travel agency. Other bargain-oriented Paris agencies are Nouvelles Frontières (☎ 08 03 33 33 33), 5 Ave de l'Opéra (1er), www.nouvelles-frontieres .com; and Voyageurs du Monde (☎ 01 42 86 16 00), 55 Rue Sainte Anne (2e).

In Belgium, Acotra Student Travel Agency (☎ 02-512 86 07), at 51 Rue de la Madeline, Brussels, and WATS Reizen (☎ 03-226 16 26), at de Keyserlei 44, Antwerp, are both well-known agencies. In Switzerland, SSR Voyages (☎ 01-297 11 11), which specializes in student, youth and budget fares, has branches in major Swiss cities, including Zurich at Leonhardstrasse 10. The Web address is www.ssr.ch. In the Netherlands, NBBS Reizen is the official student travel agency with offices around the country; the one in Amsterdam (☎ 020-624 09 89) is at Rokin 66.

Asia

Although most Asian countries now offer fairly competitive airfare deals, Bangkok, Singapore and Hong Kong are still the best places to shop around for discount tickets.

Khao San Rd in Bangkok is the budget travelers' headquarters. Bangkok has a number of good travel agents, but there are also some suspect ones; ask the advice of other travelers before handing over your cash. STA Travel (☎ 02-236 0262), 33 Surawong Rd, is a good and reliable place to start.

In Singapore, STA Travel (☎ 737 7188), in the Orchard Parade Hotel, 1 Tanglin Rd, offers competitive discount fares for Asian destinations and beyond. Singapore, like Bangkok, has hundreds of travel agents. The Chinatown Point shopping center on New Bridge Rd has a good selection of travel agents.

Major Airlines Serving LA

The following airlines serve LAX and offer toll-free telephone numbers.

US-based Airlines

Alaska Airlines	☎ 800-426-0333	www.alaskaair.com
Aloha Airlines	☎ 800-367-5250	www.alohaair.com
American Airlines	☎ 800-433-7300	www.aa.com
America West	☎ 800-235-9292	www.americawest.com
Continental Airlines	☎ 800-231-0856	www.continental.com
Delta Airlines	☎ 800-221-1212	www.delta-air.com
Hawaiian Airlines	☎ 800-367-5320	www.hawaiianair.com
Northwestern	☎ 800-225-2525	www.nwa.com
Reno Air	☎ 800-736-6247	www.renoair.com
Southwest	☎ 800-435-9792	www.iflyswa.com
TWA	☎ 800-221-2000	www.twa.com
United	☎ 800-241-6522	www.ual.com
US Airways	☎ 800-428-4322	www.usairways.com

International Airlines

Aer Lingus	☎ 800-223-6537	www.aerlingus.ie
Aeroméxico	☎ 800-237-6639	www.aeromexico.com
Air Canada	☎ 800-776-3000	www.aircanada.ca
Air France	☎ 800-237-2747	www.airfrance.com
Air New Zealand	☎ 800-262-1234	www.airnz.co.nz
British Airways	☎ 800-247-9297	www.british-airways.com
Cathay Pacific	☎ 800-233-2742	www.cathaypacific.com
Japan Airlines	☎ 800-525-3663	www.japanair.com
KLM – Royal Dutch Airlines	☎ 800-374-7747	www.klm.com
LTU International Airways	☎ 800-888-0200	www.ltu.de
Lufthansa Airlines	☎ 800-645-3880	www.Lufthansa.com
Mexicana Airlines	☎ 800-531-7921	www.mexicana.com
Qantas	☎ 800-227-4500	www.Qantas.com.au
Singapore Airlines	☎ 800-742-3333	www.singaporeair.com
Varig Brazilian Airlines	☎ 800-468-2744	www.varig.com
Virgin Atlantic	☎ 800-862-8621	www.fly.virgin.com

Hong Kong has a number of excellent, reliable travel agencies and some not-so-reliable ones. A good way to check the reputation of a travel agent is to look it up in the phone book: Fly-by-night operators don't usually stay around long enough to get listed. Many travelers use the Hong Kong Student Travel Bureau (☎ 2730 3269), 8th floor, Star House, Tsimshatsui. You could also try Phoenix Services (☎ 2722 7378), 7th floor, Milton Mansion, 96 Nathan Rd, Tsimshatsui.

BUS

Several independent companies operate shuttle service between LA and other West Coast cities, including Las Vegas.

Greyhound

Greyhound (☎ 800-231-2222), the only nationwide bus company, serves Los Angeles from cities all over North America. Buses are clean and comfortable and equipped with air-conditioning, toilets and reclining seats. Smoking is not permitted. Ticket prices are reasonable, though bargain air-fares can occasionally match or undercut its fares (for example to San Francisco). On shorter routes, it may be cheaper and more convenient to rent a car than to ride the bus, especially if there's more than one of you traveling.

The 24-hour main LA terminal (☎ 213-629-8421; Map 5) is at 1716 E 7th St at Alameda St in Downtown. The area is a bit rough, but the station itself is safe enough inside. Other LA-area Greyhound stations are at 1715 N Cahuenga Blvd, Hollywood (☎ 323-466-6381; Map 9); 645 E Walnut Ave, Pasadena (☎ 626-792-5116; Map 17) and 464 W 3rd St in Long Beach (☎ 562-432-1842; Map 16).

The standard one-way/roundtrip to/from San Diego costs $13/22; buses depart from Downtown LA almost every half hour and the journey takes from 2¼ to 3¾ hours, de-pending on the number of stops en route. Service to Santa Barbara is $14/24, with about a dozen buses a day making the trip in two to three hours. San Francisco is served almost hourly, with trips costing $42/78 and taking anything from 7½ to 11 hours. Buses to Las Vegas depart about hourly and take between five and 7½ hours ($33/60). Anaheim is served at least once hourly in 1/2 to 1½ hours ($8/16). For other destinations, call Greyhound or check its Web site at www.greyhound.com.

All fares listed above are for midweek travel. Fares for weekend travel are slightly higher; children, students and seniors qualify for discounted fares. Tickets are also cheaper if purchased seven or 14 days in advance. If there's two of you, you may qualify for the 'companion fare' which allows two people to travel for the price of one. Tickets may be bought in person at the terminal, through a ticket agent, over the phone or on the Internet with a major credit card. They can be mailed to a US address or be picked up at the terminal with proper identification.

Greyhound's unlimited travel pass, called the Ameripass, is available for seven, 10, 15, 21, 30, 45 or 60 days online or in person at the terminal (but not by phone). In 2001, rates were $185/235/285/335/385/419/509, respectively. Overseas travelers qualify for the discounted International Ameripass ($155/209/235/285/335/355/449), but tickets must be purchased at least three weeks before departure and are only sold online or by a few select ticket agents.

Other Bus Companies

Hop On Hop Off Bus (☎ 415-336-9800, hoponbus@aol.com) is a backpacker-oriented bus service between LA and San Francisco for a veritable steal of $33 (let's hope they stay in business). Comfortable 12-passenger buses depart LA around 7:30am on odd days and San Francisco at the same time on even days. The bus will pick you up at your hostel and drop you off at another hostel in your destination city. Buses stop in Santa Barbara, San Luis Obispo, Monterey and Santa Cruz. You can get off at any stop and hop back on for free within a seven-day period. Each additional pick-up is $3.

Green Tortoise Adventure Travel (☎ 415-956-7500, 800-867-8647 from outside of the Bay Area, tortoise@greentortoise.com) operates its 'North/South Alternative Com-muter' bus between Seattle and Los An-geles weekly with stops in San Francisco and Portland. You can get off in whatever city you wish. Sample one-way fares from LA are $35 to San Francisco, $69 to Eugene, $79 to Portland, and $89 to Seattle. Travel-ing with the Green Tortoise is a throwback to Ken Kesey's Merry Pranksters of the late '60s and the nearest thing in America to the 'Magic Bus.' Buses are like a mobile com-mune. You travel in converted sleeper coaches outfitted with mattresses on raised platforms and bunk beds; there are couches, tables, kitchen appliances and stereos but no restrooms (the bus will make stops 'as necessary'). Smoking and alcohol are not allowed on the bus.

Another company, the Missing Link Tours (☎ 702-453-7193, 800-209-8586, info@ themissinglinktours.com), operates a $39 shuttle to Las Vegas on Monday and Friday. They too pick up from some area hostels. Return trips from Las Vegas run on Thurs-day and Sunday.

TRAIN

America's national rail system, Amtrak (☎ 800-872-7245, www.amtrak.com), operates up and down the California coast and all over the USA. In LA, trains arrive and depart from Union Station (☎ 213-624-0171; Map 5) at 800 N Alameda St in Downtown LA. Reservations can be made online, by phone or in person at the station.

Since summer 2000, the sleek double-deck cars of the *Pacific Surfliner* have been chugging along the California coast between San Diego and San Luis Obispo with a stop in LA. Seating is available in coach and business class. All seats have laptop computer outlets, and there's a cafe car as well. The *Surfliner* makes nine roundtrips between LA and San Diego daily; four trains head north to Santa Barbara and one of these continues on to San Luis Obispo. The trip itself, which hugs the coastline for much of the route, is a treat because of the beautiful scenery

Interstate trains stopping in LA are the *Coast Starlight*, going daily between LA and Seattle with stops including San Luis Obispo, Oakland, Sacramento, Klamath Falls and Portland; the *Southwest Chief*, with daily departures to Chicago via Flagstaff, Albuquerque and Kansas City; and the *Sunset Limited*, with service thrice weekly to Orlando via Tucson, El Paso, Houston, New Orleans and Jacksonville.

Fares & Passes

Standard coach fares between Los Angeles and San Diego are $25 each way and the trip takes 2¾ hours. The trip to/from San Francisco aboard the *Coast Starlight* to Oakland, then shuttle bus from there, is $46 each way and takes roughly 12 hours. Trips to/from Santa Barbara are $16 each way and take 1½ hours. Children, students and seniors qualify for discounted fares. Advance bookings are suggested during summer and around major holidays.

If you're planning on doing a lot of traveling, look into a rail pass. Different passes become available all the time and all offer substantial savings over individual tickets. At the time of writing, offers included the California Pass, which allows for seven days of travel within a 21-day period throughout the entire state for $159. The Southern California Pass is good for five days of travel within a seven-day period in Southern California only and costs $99. You may not use long-distance trains (the *Coast Starlight*, *Southwest Chief* and *Sunset Limited*).

CAR & MOTORCYCLE

If you're driving a car or riding a motorcycle into LA, there are several routes by which you might enter the metropolitan area.

From San Francisco and Northern California, the fastest route to LA (about six hours) is via I-5, a heavily traveled freeway through the San Joaquin Valley, which is miserably hot in the summer and always boring. I-5 enters LA County at the 4183-foot Tejon Pass ('The Grapevine'); it is known as the Golden State Fwy through Burbank to Downtown, the Santa Ana Fwy through Anaheim to Irvine, and then the San Diego Fwy as it hits the coast at Capistrano Beach and continues to the Mexican border.

The alternative to I-5 from San Francisco, taking about eight hours, is the US 101, a curvy and picturesque freeway that follows the inland edge of the coastal ranges south from San Jose to San Luis Obispo. US 101 enters LA as the Ventura Fwy, turns into the Hollywood Fwy in Studio City and finally merges with the I-5 in Downtown.

By far the most scenic – and slowest – route is via the Pacific Coast Hwy (also known as PCH, or simply Hwy 1), which takes at least 10 hours. This road clings to the cliffs of the Big Sur coast between the Monterey Peninsula and San Luis Obispo, where it joins the US 101. While the views are spectacular, the curve-riddled PCH is subject to fog, landslides and other hazards.

From San Diego and other points south, I-5 is the obvious route. At Irvine, the I-405 (San Diego Fwy) branches off I-5 and takes a westerly route to Long Beach and Santa Monica, bypassing Downtown LA and rejoining I-5 near San Fernando. This route can be a time-saver if you're headed to the Westside.

If you're coming into LA from Las Vegas or the Grand Canyon, you'll want to take I-15 to the I-10, near Ontario. The I-10 is the main east-west artery through LA and leads on through Downtown before ending in Santa Monica. For more information about Los Angeles' labyrinthine highways, see the boxed text 'Major Freeways' in the Getting Around chapter.

The normal freeway speed limit is 65mph (104km/h) but may occasionally be raised to 70mph (112km/h) on open road. Most drivers push their speed 5 to 10mph higher than the posted limits. Any faster than that and you risk being pulled over by the California Highway Patrol.

HITCHHIKING

Hitching is never entirely safe anywhere in the world and is not recommended. Travelers undeterred by the potential risk should be aware that on the whole, hitchhiking is uncommon in modern-day America and hitchers are generally viewed with suspicion. Few motorists are willing to stop for a thumb. Use extreme caution, both when hitchhiking and picking up hitchhikers.

At the risk of sounding sexist, women should never hitchhike alone or even with another woman. Drivers are often reluctant to pick up lone men, so a man and a woman together have the best chance of getting a ride and of being safe. You can hitchhike on roads and highways; on freeways you must stand at the on-ramp. The best method for hitching a ride might be to ask someone pulling into a gas station; this also allows you to check out the person (and vice versa). Be prepared for more refusals than offers.

ORGANIZED TOURS

Group travel can be a good and often economical way to go, especially for single travelers who are sociable. Try to pick a tour that will suit you in terms of age, gender and interests. Tours usually include a mix of nationalities but few Americans. This can be a drawback, since you'll only be stopping briefly at most destinations, making an immersion in local culture less likely. The best source for organized travel is a travel agent

back in your home country. The companies mentioned below have all been around for decades and enjoy a good reputation.

Trek America (☎ 973-983-1144, 800-221-0596, in the UK ☎ 01296-256 777, www.trekamerica.com) offers activity-oriented bus tours, traveling in 12- or 14-seat vans rather than full-size buses. Most nights are spent camping in tents, and everyone helps with the camping chores. Stops are often for two or three nights to permit hiking and more individual sightseeing. The standard Trek America trips are for the 18- to 38-year-old age group, but the 'Footloose' trips are designed for older travelers. Los Angeles is included in several of their seven-day and two-week trips. 'Western Wonder,' for instance, starts in San Francisco and takes in Yosemite National Park, Las Vegas and the Grand Canyon before ending up in LA. The 10-day 'Southwest Trail' runs from Denver to LA via the Rockies, Monument Valley, the Grand Canyon and Las Vegas.

AmeriCan & Roadrunner (☎ 310-324-3562, 800-873-5872, amadlax@aol.com, www.americanadventures.com) is based in LA and offers similar small-size group tours around the West for the budget-conscious. Eight of their tours start in the city, including the 12-day 'Pacific Coast' trip (from $599) to Seattle with scheduled stops in Yosemite, San Francisco, Mt Rainier National Park and other wonderful places. The 13-day 'Western Safari' (from $809) takes in many of the national parks, including Bryce Canyon, Zion and Grand Canyon, as well as Las Vegas and San Francisco. Group size is limited to 13; nights are spent camping or in hostels or budget hotels. Tours are open to anyone over 18. Bookings and inquiries from outside the US or Canada should be directed to the UK office (☎ 892-51-27-00, fax 892-51-18-96, amadsales@twins.co.uk), 64 Mt Pleasant Ave, Tunbridge Wells, Kent TN1 1QY.

The Missing Link Tours (☎ 702-453-7193, 800-209-8586, info@themissinglinktours.com) runs tours to Las Vegas, the Grand Canyon and Bryce and Zion Canyon that are geared toward backpackers. Tours run three to seven days and start at $200.

Getting Around

Contrary to popular belief, LA does have a very comprehensive and even fairly efficient public transportation system. Nearly all communities are served by buses, and a fast light- and heavy-rail system hits many of the major area attractions, such as Hollywood and Universal Studios. Still, the automobile remains by far the area's most popular mode of transportation. Before rushing headlong into the bumper-to-bumper melee, though, consider all of your transportation options.

TO/FROM THE AIRPORTS
Los Angeles International Airport (Map 2)
Practically all hostels and airport-area hotels offer free pickups from LAX. Check the accommodation boards or information kiosks at the airport or the Places to Stay chapter in this book for details. QuickAid touchscreen computer monitors, located in all terminals, provide free information about ground transportation, costs and other subjects. Travelers Aid (☎ 310-646-2270) information booths are on the arrival level of each terminal and are staffed 7am to 10pm weekdays and 9am to 9pm weekends. Near these booths, there are TDD telephones for the hearing-impaired; the TDD telephone number for information is ☎ 310-417-0439 and California Relay Service for the Deaf is ☎ 800-735-2929. Free courtesy phones provide similar information and can be found in all terminals.

Getting Around LAX To travel between terminals, board the free Shuttle A beneath the LAX Shuttle sign on islands outside each terminal on the lower level. Hotel courtesy shuttles stop here as well. A free minibus equipped with a wheelchair lift for the disabled can be ordered by calling ☎ 310-646-6402.

Door-to-Door Van Service Several companies operate door-to-door shuttles from all terminals; vans stop on the lower level of each terminal beneath the signs marked 'Shuttle.' If you are travelling solo, shuttles are usually cheaper than a taxi and faster than public transportation. The three dominant companies are Prime Time (☎ 800-473-3743), Super Shuttle (☎ 310-782-6600) and Xpress Shuttle (☎ 800-427-7483). Of these the last usually has the best prices. Expect to pay $12 to Downtown, $19 to Hollywood and $14 to Santa Monica. The fare depends on distance.

Most shuttles operate 24 hours a day and drop you off right at your destination, but you may have to wait your turn along the route, as other passengers are accommodated as well.

Public Transportation The budget-conscious approach is to take the free 24-hour Shuttle C bus, which stops outside each terminal every 10 to 20 minutes, to the LAX Transit Center at 96th St and Vicksburg Ave (Map 2). Here you can connect to public buses that will take you anywhere in the greater Los Angeles area. For more information, see Bus, later in this chapter, and the boxed text 'Important Bus Routes.' If you're headed for Pasadena, you can also board the AirportBus (☎ 800-938-8933), which runs every two hours from 9:15am to 7:15pm and costs $12 each way.

LAX is not directly served by trains, but the closest station, a 10-minute bus trip away, is Aviation, on the Metro Rail Green Line. Take the free Shuttle G bus that stops on the lower (arrival) airport level beneath the LAX Shuttle signs. The Metro Rail Green Line runs south to Redondo Beach and then east to Norwalk. On an eastbound train, you can transfer at the Rosa Parks (Imperial/Wilmington) station to the Metro Rail Blue Line, which will take you north to Downtown LA or south to Long Beach. The fare is just $1.35. See Train, later in this chapter, for more about the Metro Rail system.

Car & Taxi It is advisable to reserve a rental car prior to your arrival; but if you do not already have a reservation, you can make a booking from courtesy phones in the arrival areas. Rental offices are outside the airport, with each company operating a free shuttle. For details on renting a car, see Car Rental, later in this chapter.

If driving to or from the airport, the closest freeway passing by LAX is the I-105 (Century Fwy), although the more useful is the I-405 (San Diego Fwy). Heading north on the I-405 will take you to the intersection with the I-10 (Santa Monica Fwy), which travels west to Santa Monica and east to Downtown (with turn-offs to Beverly Hills, West Hollywood and Hollywood). Traveling south on the I-405 takes you to the South Bay cities of Hermosa Beach and Manhattan Beach, as well as Long Beach. The fastest route to Venice is along Lincoln Blvd.

Outside each terminal are curbside taxi dispatchers who will summon a cab for you. Average fares are $20 to $25 to Santa Monica, $25 to $30 to Downtown or Hollywood and up to $80 to Anaheim (Disneyland). A $2.50 airport surcharge will be tacked onto your fare, and there may be additional fees for excess luggage. Taxis are the fastest and most convenient way to go to and from the airport; with two or three people to share the expense, they can also be relatively inexpensive.

Burbank-Glendale-Pasadena Airport (Maps 2 & 18)

You'll find basically the same transportation options at this airport as at LAX. Public buses leave from the intersection of Hollywood Way and Burbank Airport Exit. Bus No 163 South goes straight to Hollywood in about half an hour ($1.35); bus No 394 South travels to Downtown LA in about one hour ($1.35) and bus No 094 South goes to Pasadena with a change to bus No 180 East at San Fernando & Los Feliz ($1.60, request a transfer). An Amtrak/Metrolink station (for the Ventura County Line) is also near the airport and is connected to it by a free shuttle bus.

BUS

Only 10% of the LA County population relies upon public transportation to get them around the city each day. A network of 208 separate bus routes spans the sprawling metropolis.

Metropolitan Transportation Authority

For maps, timetables and passes, the MTA (☎ 800-266-6883 within LA County, www .mta.net) has several customer centers in LA. In Downtown, the MTA center (Map 5) is in Level C of ARCO Plaza, 515 S Flower St and is open 7:30am to 3:30pm; in the Miracle Mile district in Mid-City, the center (Map 10) is at 5301 Wilshire Blvd and is open 9am to 5pm; in the San Fernando Valley, the office is at 14435 Sherman Way, No 107, in Van Nuys, and is open 10am to 6pm. The MTA Downtown headquarters is at Union Station in the Transit Center-East Portal and is open 6am to 6:30pm. All MTA offices are closed on weekends.

The regular base fare is $1.35 for unlimited local travel on a single bus or rail line in one direction (exact change is required). Transfers are 25¢ each use. Freeway express buses cost $1.85 to $3.85, depending on the route and distance. Weekly passes are $11 for unlimited local travel throughout the network and are issued from Sunday to Saturday. Monthly passes, good for travel during any calendar month, are $42. Semimonthly passes – valid either for the first or second half of the month – are $21. Another way to save is by buying tokens, which cost $9 for 10 tokens (90¢ versus $1.35 per trip). Passes and tokens are sold at MTA customer centers and 750 other locations, such as supermarkets, bookstores or check cashing places (see the Web site for a full list).

Metro Rapid Metro Rapid is a fast and frequent priority bus service that operates on two routes. Bus No 720 travels along Wilshire Blvd and Whittier Blvd from Santa Monica to Montebello via Westwood, Beverly Hills, Fairfax, Mid-Wilshire, Downtown and East LA in about 90 minutes. Traveling the entire distance is a cheap

Important Bus Routes

For those short on cash but rich in time, public transport is the preferred method of transport. For more route or schedule information, visit the MTA Web site at www.mta.net (which has a customized route planner), the Santa Monica's Big Blue Bus Web site at www.bigbluebus.com, or LADOT's Web site at www.ladottransit.com (select DASH route service).

From LAX To Anywhere

From LAX, take the free Shuttle C bus to the LAX Transit Center, where you can catch public buses in all directions.

Hollywood – MTA No 42 West to Overhill and La Brea Aves, transfer to MTA No 212 on the southeast corner of Overhill and La Brea Aves, arrive at Hollywood Blvd and Highland Ave; duration: 1¼ hours *or* MTA No 111 East to La Brea and Florence Aves, transfer to MTA No 212 on the southeast corner of La Brea and Florence Aves, arrive at Hollywood Blvd and Highland Ave; duration: 1½ hours

Downtown – MTA No 42 West to Downtown; duration: 1 hour

Santa Monica – Big Blue Bus No 3 West to downtown Santa Monica; duration: 1½ hours

South Bay – MTA No 232 West to Sepulveda and Imperial Aves, transfer to MTA No 439 West on the northwest corner of Sepulveda and Imperial Aves, arrive in downtown Manhattan or Hermosa Beaches; duration: 30 minutes *or* MTA No 232 West to Pacific Coast Hwy and Torrance Blvd (near the Redondo Beach Pier); duration: 30 minutes; *or* No 439 South to Manhattan, Hermosa and Redondo Beach (express); duration: 30-60 minutes

From Downtown to Anywhere

Most services run from 5am to 2am at intervals of every 15 minutes or so.

Beverly Hills – MTA No 720 (Metro Rapid)

Burbank Studios – MTA No 96

Disneyland – MTA No 460 (express)

Huntington Library, Art Collection and Botanical Gardens (Pasadena) – MTA No 79

Long Beach – MTA No 60 or MTA No 456 (express)

Melrose Ave – MTA No 10

San Pedro – MTA No 446 (express)

Santa Monica Blvd – MTA No 4 (runs 24 hours)

Santa Monica via Wilshire Blvd – MTA No 22

Sunset Blvd – MTA No 2

Wilshire Blvd – MTA No 20 (runs 24 hours)

Venice Beach – MTA No 33 or MTA No 436 (express)

Beauty and the bus (1953)

introduction to some of the LA's most interesting neighborhoods and an opportunity to get a sense of the city's vast dimensions. The other route, bus No 750, connects Universal City in the eastern San Fernando Valley with Woodland Hills near the Valley's western end, traveling along Ventura Blvd. Standard fares apply.

Big Blue Bus

Santa Monica's Big Blue Bus (BBB; ☎ 310-451-5444, www.bigbluebus.com) operates a clean and efficient fleet throughout much of the Westside, including Westwood (UCLA), Pacific Palisades, LAX and, of course, Santa Monica and Venice. Bus No 14 goes to the Getty Center. The fare is only 50¢ and transfers to another Blue Bus are free (those to an MTA or Culver City bus are 25¢). The fastest and most comfortable way to get to Downtown LA from Santa Monica is via express bus No 10 ($1.25). Bus No 3 serves LAX.

The BBB also operates the electric Tide Shuttle, which connects the shopping districts of downtown Santa Monica and Main St at 15-minute intervals for 25¢.

Culver City Bus

The Culver City Bus (☎ 310-253-6500) provides service throughout Culver City and the Westside, including LAX. Buses operate between 5:30am to 11pm weekdays and 6am to 11pm weekends. The fare is 60¢ and transfers to the Big Blue Bus or MTA buses are 25¢.

LADOT/DASH

Los Angeles Department of Transportation (LADOT; www.ladottransit.com) operates a fleet of clean-fuel local shuttle buses called DASH. Smaller and more comfortable than city buses, they operate in 19 communities, including Hollywood, the Fairfax District, Koreatown, Watts and Mid-City. Since these buses are geared to local residents, they usually connect residential areas with business districts and area attractions, making them useful for visitors staying in the area as well. Buses run at frequent intervals throughout the day until about 7pm;

most lines operate Monday to Saturday and the fare is just 25¢ each trip.

Of special note is the DASH line that operates daily in Downtown LA; it is a great way to see that part of the city and spare yourself the hassle and expense of parking. Six separate routes hit all the area hot spots from Chinatown in the north to Exposition Park in the south, and from the Financial District and Central Library in the west to Little Tokyo and the Arts District in the east. For more information, call the area code you are currently in, plus ☎ 808-2273. Maps are available from this number, the Web site, at tourist offices or on DASH buses.

TRAIN
Metro Rail

The MTA also operates Metro Rail, a network of two light-rail lines and one heavy-rail line that connects Downtown LA and Hollywood, North Hollywood, Long Beach, Redondo Beach and Norwalk. These trains offer a clean and inexpensive way to travel and can be faster than the freeways. One-way tickets are $1.35 and are dispensed by coin-operated machines. For Metro Rail information, call ☎ 800-266-6883 within LA County or check www.mta.net.

Red Line From a visitor's standpoint, this is the most useful of the Metro Rail lines because it connects three attraction-packed neighborhoods: Downtown, Hollywood and Universal City. If you're staying near a station in any of these areas, you'll find getting around without private transportation a snap. The Red Line runs underground from Union Station through Downtown to central Hollywood and on to Universal Studios and North Hollywood. Red Line trains run every five to 10 minutes between 5am and 11:15pm daily.

Blue Line This line connects Downtown LA with downtown Long Beach and is an excellent way to travel between the two cities. It operates between Downtown LA's Metro Center station at 7th and Flower Sts and downtown Long Beach from 5am to

Big Red Cars

Youngsters are often amazed that a complete light-rail network existed in LA: It seems so anti-thetical to today's Auto-topia. But in the late 19th century, long before LA's freeways were built – even before William Mulholland brought water to the Los Angeles Basin – all corners of this fast-growing city were served by a network of electric railways. By 1901 these 'Big Red Cars' were consolidated under Henry E Huntington's Pacific Electric Railway. Huntington also owned a streetcar system called the Yellow Cars, which operated in Downtown LA. When he got bored with his trains in 1910, Huntington sold his empire to the Southern Pacific Railroad.

At their peak, the Red Cars covered over 1100 miles of track stretching as far east as San Bernardino, west to the Pacific Ocean, north to San Fernando and south to Huntington Beach. Trains traveled at speeds of up to 50mph on private rights-of-way.

The growth of the city's suburbs was directly tied to the rail network. As dozens of housing sub-divisions along the Pacific Electric tracks were developed, Midwesterners and Easterners, lured by the sun and inexpensive and plentiful land, moved to Southern California by the millions.

Ultimately, automobiles spelled the doom of fixed-rail transit in Los Angeles. Not only did cars intrude on the trains' rights-of-way, but public funds shifted toward the building of more roads. From the late 1930s onward, the Red Car lines declined steadily until the last train ended its final run (from Downtown to Long Beach) in April of 1961.

The total shift from rails to cars has in recent years prompted theories of a conspiracy on the part of the auto and oil industries. In the 1930s, a group of large corporations, including Firestone Tire and General Motors, set up a surrogate company called National City Lines to buy up and destroy public rail systems throughout the USA. A federal court found them guilty of anti-trust vi-olations in 1949 and imposed a moderate fine.

12:20pm (northbound) and 11:25pm (south-bound) daily. Trains travel at intervals of six to 20 minutes. The Red and Blue Lines meet at the Metro Center station in Downtown LA. The Blue Line connects with the Green Line at the Rosa Parks (Imperial/Wilming-ton) stop.

Green Line The 20-mile Green Line runs west from Norwalk parallel to the I-105 (Century Fwy). It connects with the Blue Line at the Rosa Parks (Imperial/Wilming-ton) stop, then curves south, bypassing LAX and terminating at Marine Ave on the northern border of Redondo Beach. Unfor-tunately, it does not stop anywhere near the coast, making it more of interest to com-muters than to visitors. There's a free shuttle bus between LAX and the Aviation station (a 10-minute ride). Trains operate 4:30am to 11:30pm daily at intervals of six to 20 minutes.

Metrolink

Metrolink (☎ 800-371-5465) is a 416-mile system of six commuter train lines operated by the Southern California Regional Rail Authority. It connects Downtown LA's Union Station with the four counties sur-rounding Los Angeles – Orange, Riverside, San Bernardino and Ventura – as well as northern San Diego County. Lines in opera-tion are the Ventura County Line (which stops at Burbank Airport), the Antelope Valley Line, the San Bernardino Line, the Riverside Line and the Orange County Line (which ends in Anaheim). A sixth line, the Inland Empire Line, connects San Bernardino and Riverside with Orange County. Most trains run during peak commute hours; some lines offer restricted Saturday service and the San Bernardino Line also operates on Sunday.

You can purchase tickets from vending machines on station platforms or from the ticket window at Union Station. Amtrak tickets are not valid on Metrolink, and vice versa. Fares are zone-based (for example, the one-way fare from Union Station to Burbank Airport is two zones=$5, to Anaheim is three zones=$6). There's a 25% discount for off-peak travel (8:30am to 3:30pm Monday to Friday, all day weekends).

CAR & MOTORCYCLE

In Los Angeles, there is one car for every 1.8 residents, a statistic that includes children and other nondrivers. The city sprawls across such a huge geographical area that you'll likely spend some time behind the wheel. Don't let horror stories about LA freeways (all 1000 miles' worth) scare you off. The pretzel-shaped interchanges and access ramps seem daunting at first and traffic can jam up for miles, but outside the peak commuter hours the city's celebrated freeways are by far the fastest and easiest way to get around – surely, 9.9 million people can't be wrong.

In terms of volume, Los Angeles has the densest traffic in the USA, and it is best to avoid travel during the heaviest commuter hours (7am to 10am and 3pm to 7pm weekdays). Weekend travel is generally a lot smoother, except between 5pm and 8pm. Unfortunately, there's no guarantee that you'll avoid tie-ups, which are usually the result of an accident and can easily double your travel time.

Except for short distances, surface streets are usually poor alternatives to freeways. The city – stoplights and all – is just too large to traverse quickly. Reasonably fast surface roads traveling north-south are La Brea Ave and La Cienega Blvd; narrow Fairfax Ave is often clogged. Olympic Blvd is the best east-west route, though Santa Monica Blvd can be OK; Wilshire Blvd is comparatively slow. The most scenic cross-town road is Sunset Blvd, though with its dangerous curves and high speeds, it's not always the safest to negotiate. The areas of Beverly Hills and West Hollywood are not served by freeways.

It will help to memorize LA's major freeways by name as well as by number (see the

Accidents Do Happen

Accidents are an unfortunate but common occurrence in auto-dependent LA. As a visitor, it's good to know the appropriate protocol when involved in a 'fender-bender.'

• Don't drive away! Remain at the scene of the accident unless you care to check out the interior of the local jail.

• Call the police at ☎ 911 (and an ambulance, if needed) immediately and give the operator as much specific information as possible (your location, if there are any injuries involved etc).

• Get the other driver's name, address, driver's license number, license plate number and insurance information. Be prepared to provide similar documentation, such as your passport, international driver's license and insurance documents.

• Tell your story to the police carefully. Refrain from answering any questions until you feel comfortable doing so (with a lawyer present, if need be). That's your right under the law. The only insurance information you need to reveal is the name of your insurance carrier and your policy number.

• Always comply with an alcohol Breathalyzer test. If you opt not to take the test, you'll almost certainly find yourself with an automatic suspension of your driving privileges.

• If you're driving a rental car, call the rental company promptly.

boxed text 'Major Freeways'). If you get lost, don't fret: There are emergency call boxes every mile or so, and frequent on-ramps and off-ramps where you can exit the freeway and pull into the nearest gas station to ask directions.

Driving Conduct & Special Rules

Many Angelenos banish manners from their cars and turn into maniacs who cherish cutting you off, riding your bumper or not letting you change lanes. In these situations, it's best to stay as calm as possible and not be provoked, especially if you don't know your way around.

Speed limits, unless posted otherwise, are 35mph (56 km/h) on city streets and 65mph (104km/h) on freeways. Most drivers exceed these limits by a few miles per hour, however. Keep in mind that tickets can be given for driving too slowly as well as driving dangerously fast. Watch for school zones, which are strictly enforced at 15mph during school hours. *Never* pass a school bus when its rear red lights are flashing: Children are getting off the bus at these times. If you encounter an ambulance with its siren wailing, you should safely steer over to the right curb and halt, allowing it to pass.

Seatbelts – and motorcycle helmets – must be worn at all times. It's illegal for anybody in the car (not just the driver) to consume alcohol while driving. Any open containers of booze must be stashed in the trunk. Keep your driver's license, registration papers and insurance information with you, in case you get stopped by the police.

LA drivers live and die by their *Thomas Guides*, voluminous, spiral-bound books of street maps with detailed indexes that pinpoint every address in LA County. Equally important to the average Angeleno are 'eye-in-the-sky' traffic reports, carried on the AM stations KNX 1070 and KFWB 980 every six minutes. Airborne pilots report freeway jam-ups as they occur and suggest alternate routes.

A few hints for first-time US drivers: Unless a sign indicates otherwise, you can turn right after stopping at a red light as long as you don't impede intersecting traffic – which has the right of way. At intersections with four-way stop signs, cars proceed in the order in which they arrived. If two cars arrive simultaneously, the one on the right has the right of way. This can be an iffy situation as opinions may differ over who arrived first: Better to be safe than sorry.

On freeways, you may pass slower cars on either the left or the right side; if two cars are trying to get into the same central lane, the one farther right has priority. The far-left lane is often separated by two double yellow lines, meaning it's a 'diamond lane' and reserved for car pools of two, three or more passengers. Posted signs give the minimum number of passengers required for using the diamond lanes, and fines for disobeying the minimum number are prohibitively stiff (up to $271).

Parking

Parking is one of the biggest bugaboos for LA drivers. Metered parking often costs 25¢ per 15 minutes and may be limited to as little as 30 minutes. Be aware of colored curbs (red=no parking, yellow=loading zone, white=loading zone, green=20-minute limit, blue=disabled parking), since parking patrols issue tickets relentlessly. You may pay as much as $30 for simply being 30 seconds late in returning to your vehicle. Always study signposts for restrictions. Parking on residential streets – especially those near nightlife areas – is often reserved for residents. You can't park on certain streets during street cleaning hours – usually early on a weekday morning – which are posted as well. And of course, don't block driveways or park too closely to fire hydrants or bus stops.

Naturally, it's safest to put your car in a parking garage, though this may cost you a bundle. To cut costs, look for city-run public garages, more prevalent in smaller cities like Santa Monica, Beverly Hills and West Hollywood. These usually offer two hours of free parking and low rates thereafter. Parking in business districts such as Century City or Downtown can cost as much as an insane $3.50 for each 20-minute period. In

HERALD EXAMINER COLLECTION/LOS ANGELES PUBLIC LIBRARY

An LAPD officer chalks the tires of a parked car (1940).

Downtown, this can easily be avoided by choosing a lot on the area's perimeter, which may charge just $3 all day.

Parking at motels and cheaper hotels is usually free, while fancier ones charge anywhere from $5 to $20 a day in addition to the room rate. Valet parking at nicer restaurants and hotels is ubiquitous and can be both a convenience and a scam. In areas where there is basically no public parking (Melrose Ave, for example), the valets are a welcome sight. But in places such as the Yamashiro restaurant in Hollywood, where you watch the attendant drive your car a few feet to the restaurant's parking lot and then charge you $3.50 for the 'convenience,' it can be infuriating.

Car Rental

Although car-rental agencies are located throughout the LA area, you may find that your bargaining power goes farthest at LAX, where the competition is greatest. Costs are highest in summer and during major holiday periods and lowest on weekends, when business travel is down. Rental rates for mid-size cars range from $25 to $45 per day, $120 to $200 per week, more in peak season; larger or luxury cars are considerably more expensive. It's definitely worth shopping around since prices vary widely, even from day to day within the same company.

In order to rent a car, you will need a credit card and a drivers' license. Most rental agencies require that drivers be at least 21 years old; drivers under 25 must normally pay a surcharge of $5 to $15 per day. Rates do not include the 8% sales tax…or insurance.

Many North American travelers have credit cards that provide collision insurance if the card is used to pay for the car rental. If you are an overseas visitor, check with your credit card company to see if this option is available to you (your home auto insurance will not cover you in the US). Otherwise, you'll have to pay about $9 to $11 a day for a loss-damage waiver (covering any damage to the rental agency's car) and again for a liability insurance supplement (covering personal injury as well as damage to the other car). Paying this additional $20 or so on top of the rental cost is usually optional, but considering your liability if you *do* have an accident, insurance is highly advisable.

Gasoline in the US is quite inexpensive by foreign standards but prices fluctuate, sometimes drastically. At the time of writing, the average price per US gallon (3.8 liters) was $2, double the price 12 months earlier, and expected to increase within the coming months. Be sure to return your rental car with the same amount of gas you drove away with, or you'll be charged exorbitant refueling rates.

Only some agencies permit their rental cars to be taken into Mexico and only if you buy supplemental Mexican car insurance, which adds $18 to $25 per day.

Major car-rental agencies with offices at LAX and elsewhere include the following:

Alamo	☎ 800-462-5266	www.goalamo.com
Avis	☎ 800-331-1084	www.avis.com
Budget	☎ 800-472-3325	www.drivebudget.com
Dollar	☎ 800-800-4000	www.dollar.com
Enterprise	☎ 800-325-8007	www.enterprise.com
Hertz	☎ 800-654-3131	www.hertz.com
National	☎ 800-227-7368	www.nationalcar.com
Thrifty	☎ 800-847-4389	www.thrifty.com

Some independent agencies that may have lower rates include Avon (☎ 310-277-4455), 1100 S Beverly Dr, Beverly Hills; Midway (☎ 800-366-0643), 1901 Ocean Ave, Santa Monica; Rapid (☎ 323-467-7368), 6848 W Sunset Blvd, Hollywood; and Rent-A-Wreck (☎ 310-478-0676), 12333 W Pico Blvd, West LA.

If money is no object, you can rent everything from a Rolls Royce to a Porsche at Beverly Hills Rent-A-Car (☎ 800-479-5996), Exotic Car Rental (☎ 800-385-8888), Rent A Classic Convertible (☎ 310-828-3014) or Sunbelt Sports Car Rental (☎ 310-410-2025).

Major Freeways

Angelenos live and die by their freeways. Most freeways are known both by their number and their name, which can get confusing. In general, those going east-west have even numbers and those running north-south have odd numbers.

I-5 – Golden State Fwy	From Downtown northwest to Bakersfield
I-5 – Santa Ana Fwy	From Downtown southeast to Irvine
I-10 – San Bernardino Fwy	From Downtown east to San Bernardino
I-10 – Santa Monica Fwy	From Downtown west to Santa Monica
I-105 – Century Fwy	From El Segundo east to Norwalk
I-110 – Harbor Fwy	From US101 Downtown south to San Pedro
I-110 – Pasadena Fwy	From US 101 Downtown north to Pasadena
I-210 – Foothill Fwy	From I-5 in Sylmar east to I-10 in Pomona
I-405 – San Diego Fwy	From I-5 in San Fernando southeast to I-5 at Irvine
I-605 – San Gabriel River Fwy	From I-210 in Duarte south to I-405 in Long Beach
I-710 – Long Beach Fwy	From I-10 in Alhambra south to Long Beach
Hwy 60 – Pomona Fwy	From I-5 Downtown east to I-10 at Beaumont
Hwy 118 – Ronald Reagan Fwy	From Simi Valley east to San Fernando
Hwy 134 – Ventura Fwy	From Studio City east to Pasadena
US 101 – Hollywood Fwy	From I-5 and I-10 Downtown northwest to Hwy 170 in North Hollywood
US 101 – Ventura Fwy	From Hwy 134 in North Hollywood west to Ventura

If you're a budding movie star, want to make a grand entrance at a party or just enjoy tooling around town behind tinted windows, you might consider renting a chauffeur-driven limo. Rates start at $60 per hour for a six-passenger stretch limo (from $75 for a 10-seater). There's usually a three-hour minimum, and tax and tip are not included. Check the Yellow Pages or try Diva Limousine (☎ 310-278-3482), Fox Limousine (☎ 818-780-8898), Limos for Less (☎ 800-689-8005) or Pacific Limousine (☎ 310-649-5466).

The Southern California climate is biker-friendly, though LA traffic is not. Still, for that *Easy Rider* feeling, hop on a Harley and drive along Route 66 or the Pacific Coast Hwy. Among the companies worth trying are Eagle Rider Motorcycle Rental (☎ 800-501-8687), 11860 S La Cienega Blvd, 2 miles south of LAX, and Route 66 Harley Davidson Rentals (☎ 888-434-4473), 4161 Lincoln Blvd in Marina del Rey. Both have multilingual staff and provide helmets, leather jackets and basic liability insurance. Models to choose from include the Bad Boy and the Heritage Softtail Classic. Most rentals go for $75 to $165 a day. Bartels' Harley-Davidson (☎ 310-823-1112), 4141 Lincoln Blvd, has officially licensed T-shirts, motor clothes and accessories. Make sure you get a helmet for yourself and any passenger: Helmets are required by law in California, and the law is strictly enforced.

Car Purchase

If you're spending several months in LA, a used vehicle is worth considering, though purchasing one can be quite a hassle. If you don't have experience working on cars, it is best to spend $50 to have a mechanic check the car for defects before you buy (stay away from vendors who refuse to let you do this). You can find out the official value of a used car by looking it up in the *Blue Book*, which is available in libraries and bookstores and lists cars by make, model and year issued and the average resale price.

Although used-car dealers can simplify the process, purchasing a car from a private individual is usually cheaper. Check the classified ads in the *LA Times* as well as the various free weeklies and the *Recycler*, a weekly newspaper with classified ads for secondhand items. If you purchase a car from an individual, you must have the car's emissions smog-tested at a garage and get a certificate that verifies the vehicle meets state standards (cars sold by dealers have already been tested).

You must also purchase an auto insurance policy, which can be rather expensive. Insurance rates depend on a variety of factors such as your age and driving record, the make and year of the car, whether it has airbags or security devices, and where you live. The annual premium for a 1991 Honda Civic with a purchase price of $1500, for example, would be about $500 for liability insurance only (the required minimum) and about $700 for full coverage (including theft and collision insurance).

To register your car, take the smog certificate and proof of insurance, along with the ownership title and bill of sale, to the Department of Motor Vehicles (DMV; www.dmv.ca.gov). You can make an appointment or show up at a DMV office and plan on spending several hours waiting in line. If you buy from a dealer, you can usually skip the DMV: The paperwork is done for you and the registration bill follows in the mail.

As your departure from the US approaches, you must set aside time to sell the car. Rather than sell it to a used-car dealer for a pittance, take out an ad in a local newspaper or in the *Recycler* (☎ 323-660-8900), which does not charge for noncommercial ads.

TAXI

Unlike New York, Chicago and other big cities, you can't just thrust your arm out and expect to hail a taxi in LA. Except for those lined up outside airports, train stations, bus stations and major hotels, cabbies respond to phone calls rather than hand waves. Fares are metered; you pay $2 at flag fall, $1.80 per mile. Occasionally there are additional charges for luggage (50¢ per piece) and passengers in excess of three (75¢ per person).

Checker	☎ 800-300-5007
Independent	☎ 800-521-8294
United Independent	☎ 800-822-8294
Yellow Cab	☎ 800-200-1085

BICYCLE

Cyclists are entitled to their share of any city street in Los Angeles. Freeways, on the other hand, are reserved for automobiles and motorcycles. Be aware that the number of cyclists on LA streets is relatively small, and riding aggressively is likely to antagonize already jangled motorists. Wear a helmet; it's the law and just makes sense. For details on recreational biking, see Activities in the Things to See & Do chapter.

Many MTA buses are now equipped with bike racks and bikes ride for free, although you must securely load and unload your bike yourself. In order to take your bike on Metro Rail, you need a free permit obtained from MTA customer centers (see MTA section earlier in the chapter) or by calling ☎ 800-266-6883. Bikes are not allowed during rush hours (6am to 9am and 3pm to 7pm). Metrolink trains allow bikes aboard at no charge any time, without permits.

WALKING

Tell an Angeleno, 'I'll just walk,' and they're bound to try talking you out of it. In Los Angeles, dispersion is the rule of city planning and all but a few strips were developed with motorists, rather than pedestrians, in mind. If you hate to see all those sidewalks going to waste, sections of Downtown, Santa Monica, Beverly Hills and central Hollywood are areas where 'hoofing it' will prove worthwhile – but you'll probably have to drive or take a bus there first. Several walking tours are outlined in the Things to See & Do chapter and Los Angeles Architecture special section.

ORGANIZED TOURS

Most Los Angeles tour companies operate year-round, with stepped-up schedules during the peak visitor periods of summer and the Christmas holiday. You can book directly with the tour operators, through your hotel front desk or with any tourist office. Discounted tours are available at hostels; for tours with no fee, see the boxed text 'Free Tours.'

Walking & Biking Tours

Angel City Tours (☎ 310-470-4463, info@ angelcitytours.com) offers an introduction to the historical and architectural highlights of Downtown in a friendly, informal and personable manner. The two-hour tours ($12.50, plus $3 transit fares; offered by appointment) start at Union Station and also cover the Grand Central Market, the Bradbury Building and El Pueblo de Los Angeles.

Beyond the Glitz Tours (☎ 323-658-7920, 877-999-9925, www.beyondtheglitz.com) is tailored to the 'cultured explorer in you.' The schedule changes quarterly and may include the Hollywoodland & Hollywood Sign Walk ($15) or the Santa Monica Canyon Walk ($15). The company also offers themed bus/walking tours, such as the Homes by Frank Lloyd Wright ($39) and the Final Resting Places of Hollywood Royalty tours.

For tours operated by the Los Angeles Conservancy, see the related boxed text in the Los Angeles Architecture special section.

A fun chance to combine sightseeing and a workout is by joining the enthusiastic staff of LA Bike Tours (☎ 323-466-5890, 888-775-2453, www.labiketours.com) on one of their five trips around the city. Tours focus on particular neighborhoods and last three to four hours. Snacks, bottled water, bike and helmet are part of the package, which goes for $39.50.

The Los Angeles chapter of the Sierra Club (☎ 213-387-4287, www.angeleschapter .org/ics) and the National Park Service (☎ 805-370-2300, www.nps.gov/samo) lead hundreds of guided hikes throughout the year, covering all corners of the Santa Monica Mountains. Tours range from family strolls to strenuous workouts. They take place morning, noon and night, last a few hours to several days and attract a mixed bag of hiking enthusiasts from Westside families to Silver Lake grungies to Leimert

Park yuppies. All hikes are open to the public and are usually free. Copies of both organizations' quarterly events calendars are available by calling the numbers listed previously.

For educational guided tours in small groups, offered in several languages, there's Hiking in LA (☎ 818-501-1005), founded and operated by Jost Rhodius. Tours are easy to tough, last three to five hours and explore various trails in the Santa Monica Mountains. En route you'll be introduced to the region's flora and fauna, geology and history, with special emphasis on Native Americans. Fees include water, snacks and a tour summary and cost from $25 to $40. There's a two-person minimum; otherwise you pay a surcharge. Rhodius also offers an excellent five-hour walking tour of Downtown LA ($40).

Bus & Boat Tours

Several companies offer essentially the same kind of tours at roughly the same prices. City tours provide an overview, covering everything from Downtown LA to Hollywood, Beverly Hills and some stars' homes. Basic one-day tours cost around $40, with night tours ranging from $45 to $60. Theme park tours going to Universal Studios, Disneyland, Knott's Berry Farm and Six Flags Magic Mountain are priced between $60 and $75, admission included. Children's discounts are available.

Some of the larger tour companies are Starline Tours of Hollywood (☎ 800-959-3131), LA Tours (☎ 323-937-3361), LA City Tours (☎ 888-800-7878), VIP Tours (☎ 310-641-8114, 800-438-1814), GuideLine Tours (☎ 323-465-3004, 800-604-8433) and EuroPacific Tours (☎ 800-303-3005). Trolleywood Tours (☎ 323-469-8184) offers fun and

fact-filled one-hour tours of Hollywood aboard a cute trolley ($16), and two-hour tours of about 60 Beverly Hills celebrities' homes in a van ($31).

Easily the favorite ocean trip for LA visitors and residents alike is a roundtrip day cruise to Santa Catalina Island. Boats depart daily for the town of Avalon from several mainland harbors, including Long Beach and San Pedro (see Santa Catalina Island in the Excursions chapter).

Other tours include whale watching, harbor sightseeing or dinner cruising; for more information, contact Hornblower Cruises (☎ 310-301-6000), 13755 Fiji Way, Marina del Rey; Shoreline Village Cruises (☎ 562-495-5884), 429 Shoreline Village Dr, Long Beach; and Spirit Cruises (☎ 310-548-8080), Berth 77, Ports O'Call, San Pedro.

Things to See & Do

Los Angeles is a vast place with enough to keep you busy for a few years. Places of interest, museums, sights and other diversions are described in this chapter by neighborhood. Recreational activities are at the end.

Downtown Los Angeles

Perennial doubters and incorrigible cynics will never believe it, but LA does have a center. Yes, there is a *there* there. The place where tens of thousands of commuters work, where powerful international banks and corporations are headquartered and where skyscrapers rise against the backdrop of the San Gabriel Mountains: Few areas of LA have as much to offer per square mile as Downtown. It is rich in history (this is, after all, the birthplace of the city), wonderful architecture, exciting restaurants, superior cultural institutions and countless smaller surprises. In fact, it is possible to 'travel around the world' in just a day as you make your way from enclaves like Chinatown and Little Tokyo to the Mexican marketplaces of Olvera St and Broadway to the bazaarlike Fashion District and back to the 21st-century America of the Financial District.

Orient yourself at the Civic Center, America's second-largest complex of government buildings (after Washington, DC). Northeast of here, across the US-101 (Hollywood Fwy), are El Pueblo de Los Angeles and Chinatown. Southeast is Little Tokyo; southwest is the main business district. Farther south are the Fashion District, the Staples Center and Convention Center, and, past the I-10 (Santa Monica Fwy), Exposition Park. North of Downtown proper are some of LA's earliest suburban communities and Dodger Stadium.

Getting around Downtown is easy; most places of interest are quickly reached by walking. For the foot-weary, there's a great

public transport system: DASH mini-buses, which operate at five to 10-minute intervals and cost just 25¢ per ride. See the boxed text 'Important Bus Routes' in the Getting Around chapter for route highlights. If you arrive by car, park in a cheap lot on the periphery rather than in the extortionary lots in the center.

FINANCIAL DISTRICT WALKING TOUR

LA's modern business and financial district extends seven blocks south from the Civic Center to 8th St, and from the I-110 (Harbor Fwy) six blocks east to Hill St. Much of the area sprawls across Bunker Hill, which, a century ago, was Los Angeles' most trendy neighborhood. Flecked with stately mansions built in the Queen Anne/Eastlake styles, this chic enclave deteriorated into a slum following an influx of transients in the 1920s. After WWII, it took the city almost 20 years to decide whether to restore or raze the neighborhood. In the end, the demand for progress resulted in the forest of glass and concrete high-rises that now crowns the hill. Grand Ave bisects the two main complexes: the Wells Fargo Center to the west and California Plaza to the east. Also here are large condominium complexes and the futuristic Westin Bonaventure Hotel, which has a quintet of cylindrical glass towers instantly recognizable to moviegoers from *Terminator* and *In the Line of Fire*.

Central Library

This tour begins at the historic 1922 Downtown Central Library (☎ 213-228-7000, 630 W 5th St; free guided tours at 12:30pm Mon-Fri, 11am & 2pm Sat, 2pm Sun). This enormous repository contains about 2.5 million books and historical photographs; the building itself also brims with art and architectural detail. Of note are the two galleries – the Getty Gallery on the 2nd floor and the Photography Gallery on the ground floor – both of which host imaginatively curated changing exhibits (free).

In 1986, a pair of devastating fires roared through the library, destroying or damaging more than a million books. When the complex reopened – 7 years and $214 million later – an eight-story glass-roofed atrium and the stylish **Maguire Gardens** had been added. The tranquil 1½-acre garden features cypress, olive and other trees flanking sinuous walkways, where benches offer a respite. The three reflecting pools and adjoining steps that bisect the park are actually an artwork called *Spine* (1993) by Jud Fine. The animal figures in the pools depict the evolution of life, while the symbols carved into the risers of the steps trace the development of communication.

For more on the library, see the Los Angeles Architecture special section; for hours, see Libraries in the Facts for the Visitor chapter.

Bunker Hill Steps

Walk to the 5th St exit of the library. Rising up for five stories from the foot of the Library Tower, LA's tallest building, are the attractive Bunker Hill steps. They culminate at a fountain featuring a female nude by Robert Graham called *Source Figure*. Just beyond, on your left, is the **Ketchum YMCA**, where Downtown suits work off stress. Terraces with outdoor cafes invite a quick bite or drink. From here, continue straight (north) on Hope St.

Public Art on Hope Street

The freeform sculpture on your right, outside the Mellon Bank Center, is Alexander Liberman's *Ulysses* (1988). Farther on, the red sculpture outside the ARCO world headquarters (not to be confused with ARCO Plaza, a few blocks west) is Alexander Calder's *Four Arches* (1974). Just next to the sculpture is the Plaza Orchard, a small park, where three waterfalls plunge into a lower-level pool. Cross the street and enter the Wells Fargo Center; note Jean Dubuffet's cartoonish sculpture *Le Dandy* (1982) in the window by the entrance. The escalator whisks you to a glassy atrium with a

Highlights

- Explore the wacky neighborhoods of Los Feliz (especially Vermont Ave), Silver Lake (Sunset Junction), Melrose Ave, Broadway or the Fashion District (in Downtown).

- Feast your eyes on Old Masters and new visions at the Huntington, LACMA and Getty Center art museums.

- Test the boundaries of reality and perception at the Museum of Jurassic Technology.

- Catch up on cutting-edge art at Bergamot Station in Santa Monica, The Brewery in Downtown or Self-Help Graphics in East LA.

- Work out with the stars at Crunch Gym in Hollywood or Gold's Gym in Venice.

- Discover LA's 'wild side' during a hike in the Santa Monica Mountains.

- Track down dead legends at Hollywood Forever, Westwood Memorial Park or other star-studded cemeteries.

- Feast on gourmet cuisine with a birds-eye view of city lights (restaurants on or above Sunset Blvd are good choices).

- Slurp hot soup and stock up on produce at Downtown's Grand Central Market.

- Rent a convertible and careen (carefully, of course) into the sunset along Sunset Blvd from Downtown to the Pacific Ocean.

- Get close up – if not personal – with your favorite sitcom stars during a live taping.

- Sun, swim and surf at Zuma, Santa Monica or Manhattan Beach.

- Come to Venice Boardwalk for the SoCal beach scene and even a henna tattoo, transcendental massage or tarot card reading.

- Enjoy sandwiches, wine & Mozart at the Hollywood Bowl.

For comparison, here are the top ten attractions sought out by overnight visitors (based on surveys conducted for the Los Angeles Convention & Visitors Bureau): Universal Studios Hollywood, Disneyland, Hollywood Walk of Fame, Rodeo Dr, Venice Beach, Mann's Chinese Theater, Sunset Blvd, Santa Monica Beach & Pier, Knott's Berry Farm and Marina del Rey.

FINANCIAL DISTRICT WALKING TOUR

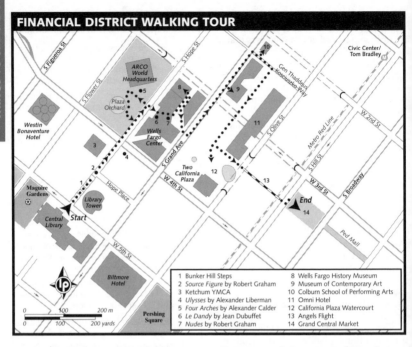

1 Bunker Hill Steps	8 Wells Fargo History Museum
2 *Source Figure* by Robert Graham	9 Museum of Contemporary Art
3 Ketchum YMCA	10 Colburn School of Performing Arts
4 *Ulysses* by Alexander Liberman	11 Omni Hotel
5 *Four Arches* by Alexander Calder	12 California Plaza Watercourt
6 *Le Dandy* by Jean Dubuffet	13 Angels Flight
7 *Nudes* by Robert Graham	14 Grand Central Market

tropical fountain garden accented by more Robert Graham nudes.

Turn left and exit through the door to get to the Wells Fargo History Museum.

Wells Fargo History Museum

Well worth a visit is this interesting little museum (☎ 213-253-7166, 333 S Grand Ave; admission free; open 9am-5pm Mon-Fri). Established in the wake of the great California gold rush of the late 1840s, the Wells Fargo Company grew to be synonymous with the maturation of the American West through its banking and stagecoach operations. This museum relives that era with maps, guns, traveling paraphernalia, an original stagecoach and a 2lb gold nugget. The friendly docent is only too happy to answer questions or start the 15-minute video.

Exit the museum, turn right, walk to Grand Ave, turn left and head toward the pyramid rooftop of the Museum of Contemporary Art.

Museum of Contemporary Art

On the east side of Grand Ave, MOCA is Downtown's most touted museum (☎ 213-626-6222, 250 S Grand Ave; admission adults $6, students & seniors $4, children under 12 free; open 11am-5pm Tues-Sun, to 8pm Thur). The building itself is a work of art. Japanese architect Arata Isozaki combined cubes, pyramids and barrel-vaulted shapes with glass, aluminum and red sandstone to create a unique structure that suits its purpose perfectly. Inside is a maze of galleries filled with paintings, sculptures and photographs from the 1940s to the present.

Exhibits drawn from MOCA's permanent collection, considered one of the world's most important of the period, are supplemented with international traveling exhibits. Styles represented include Abstract Expressionism, Pop Art, Minimalism and conceptual art by such artists as Robert Rauschenberg, Mark Rothko, Jackson Pollock, Willem de Kooning, Andy Warhol and Alberto Giacometti. Free 30-minute tours take place at noon, 1pm and 2pm Tues-Sun. The shop stocks a good range of unusual souvenir and gift items.

Tickets are also good for same-day admission to MOCA's satellite museums, the MOCA Geffen Contemporary (see the Little Tokyo section, later in this chapter) and the MOCA Gallery at the Pacific Design Center (see the West Hollywood section).

Exit MOCA at the northeast side and cross General Thaddeus Kosciuszko Way to the Colburn School of Performing Arts.

Colburn School of Performing Arts

Just north of MOCA, the idiosyncratic structure with the oversized zinc-clad roof is the Colburn School of Performing Arts (☎ 213-621-2200, 200 S Grand Ave), a pre-college, non-degree granting music school with around 1300 students. It started in 1950 as an outgrowth of the School of Music of the University of Southern California but has been independent since 1980. Students and faculty regularly perform in the two recital halls, as do other groups like the LA Mozart Players. Alumni include San Francisco Symphony director Michael Tilson Thomas, jazz pianists Patrice Rushen, Eric Reed and Donald Vega and violinist Anne Akiko Myers.

Walk southwest past MOCA (it's now on your right) and the Omni Hotel (previously the Hotel Inter-Continental), where jurors of the OJ Simpson trial were sequestered for months. This will get you to the California Plaza Watercourt, the site of summer lunchtime and evening concerts. On the plaza's southeastern side is Angels Flight.

Angels Flight

Billed as 'the shortest railway in the world,' Angels Flights was conceived in 1901 as a way for the gentlefolk residing in manses atop Bunker Hill to descend the steep incline between California Plaza and Hill St to the shopping district below. In 1960 it was mothballed to make room for Bunker Hill's high-rises. Nineties nostalgia finally breathed new life into the little trains, which

provided a literal and metaphorical link between the corporate world of the Financial District and the Latino shopping district around Broadway.

The antique funicular had only been back in business for five years when a deadly accident brought operation to a sudden halt. On February 2, 2001, one of the two rail cars broke lose, rocketing downhill and slamming into its twin, which was stopped at the bottom. The accident killed an 83-year-old passenger and seriously injured seven others. Operation was suspended while the accident was being investigated and the fate of Angels Flight remained uncertain at the time of writing.

Unless operation has resumed, walk downhill along the steps paralleling the track. At the bottom, cross Hill St and conclude the tour with a snack or refreshment at the **Grand Central Market** (for details, see the Places to Eat chapter).

HISTORIC CORE WALKING TOUR

Pershing Square and the area southeast of it form LA's historic Downtown core, once an elegant business district. Allowed to decay into a shabby neighborhood for decades, it's been on the rebound for several years now and is a vibrant part of town, filled with striking architecture, landmark buildings and a weird and wonderful collection of bargain-basement stores catering mostly to Latino shoppers. Homelessness and poverty are prevalent but this shouldn't stop you from daytime exploration of this fascinating place. This tour can be combined with Tour I of the Los Angeles Architecture special section.

Pershing Square

This tour starts at LA's oldest public park (1886), framed by 5th, 6th, Olive and Hill Sts. Pershing Square got a $14 million facelift in 1994, intended to create a revitalized nexus for the Downtown community. The park remains sadly underutilized, even though it's no longer the 'grime and crime' scene it was as recently as the mid-1980s. A 120-foot purple tower and plenty of public art – such as a stylized earthquake fault line and historical ceramic postcards embedded in concrete benches – are attractive features.

Jewelry District

From Pershing Square head south on Hill St, which cuts right through LA's Jewelry District. Silver and gold jewelry, watches, gemstones and other trinkets are sold here at discount prices. Don't be too dazzled to gaze up at the facade of the **Pantages/ Warner Brothers Theater** *(401–421 W 7th St)*. Built in 1919 by Alexander Pantages, it features a rounded-corner tower and a white terra-cotta mantle with floral decorations and fluted columns. In the 1940s, it became a Warner Brothers movie theater, but in 1988 the building was gutted to become yet another jewelry mart. Inside you can still see parts of the auditorium, including the baroque ceiling, the balcony seats and the proscenium. Continue south on Hill St, then turn left (east) on 9th St for the one-block walk to Broadway.

Broadway Theater & Commercial District

Broadway – especially between 3rd and 9th Sts – could very well be the busiest commercial street west of Chicago. Cacophonous, pungent and garish: this Latino retail hub pulses with activity. Mariachi music blares, shop windows display billowy wedding gowns, and huge signs advertise everything 'cut-rate.' But Broadway's main attraction is its great density of historic buildings – especially the 11 movie palaces built between 1913 and 1931 that – earned it a listing on the National Register of Historic Places. In the pre-Depression days of filmmaking, Mary Pickford, Douglas Fairbanks, Charlie Chaplin and other Hollywood glitterati leapt from limousines to attend lavish premieres at Broadway's theaters.

Architecturally, the theaters are a marvelous hodgepodge of styles, from Spanish Gothic to French Baroque. Their dramatic facades and flamboyant interiors were inspired by European churches, palaces and castles. Sadly, many have been allowed to crumble or been converted into retail space.

Several, though, still show movies and at least a couple have been reincarnated as churches. Most of the buildings can only be seen from the outside – unless you're on an LA Conservancy tour (see the related boxed text in the Los Angeles Architecture special section). For superb photographs of the lavish interiors, check out the coffee-table book called *The Last Remaining Seats* by Robert Berger and Anne Conser.

The first building you encounter, though, is not a theater at all but the **Eastern Columbia Building** *(1927; 849 Broadway)*, the former home of two clothing stores called Columbia and Eastern Outfitting. Magnificent in its turquoise terra-cotta mantle, it is a premier example of the Art Deco Zigzag Moderne style. Look for the plant motifs, gilded sunburst pattern above the entrance and the clock faces on the soaring tower.

Half a block south of here is the Spanish Gothic **United Artists Theater** *(1927, 933 Broadway)*, which is now a church and only open during Sunday services. It was designed by Walker & Eisen, the same architecture team that gave the world the Fine Arts Building and the Oviatt Building (see the Los Angeles Architecture special section for more information). It was the only theater on Broadway affiliated with a major studio and was bankrolled by the ubiquitous trio of Chaplin, Pickford and Fairbanks.

Turn around and head north on Broadway. Across the street you'll see the French Renaissance **Orpheum Theater** *(1926; 842 Broadway)*, which reopened in 1999 as a first-run movie theater. It's a spectacular building with a 90-foot-high auditorium capped by a gold-leaf coffered ceiling and wrought-iron chandeliers; it even has a still functional Wurlitzer pipe organ. Just north of here are the sad remains of the **Rialto Theater** *(1917, 812 Broadway)* whose splendor has been reduced to a couple of pathetic stores.

A little farther on is the **Tower Theater** *(1927; 802 Broadway)*, the first built expressly for showing 'talkies.' *The Jazz Singer*, the first all-talkie, actually premiered here in 1927. This was the project on which

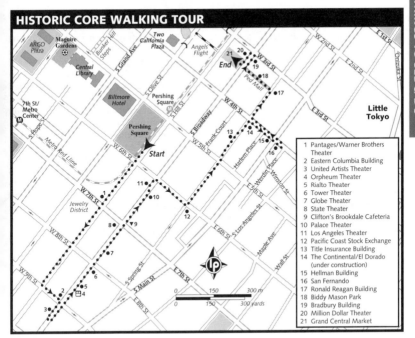

HISTORIC CORE WALKING TOUR

1 Pantages/Warner Brothers Theater
2 Eastern Columbia Building
3 United Artists Theater
4 Orpheum Theater
5 Rialto Theater
6 Tower Theater
7 Globe Theater
8 State Theater
9 Clifton's Brookdale Cafeteria
10 Palace Theater
11 Los Angeles Theater
12 Pacific Coast Stock Exchange
13 Title Insurance Building
14 The Continental/El Dorado (under construction)
15 Hellman Building
16 San Fernando
17 Ronald Reagan Building
18 Biddy Mason Park
19 Bradbury Building
20 Million Dollar Theater
21 Grand Central Market

Charles Lee cut his teeth before becoming Los Angeles' premier theater designer during the '30s and '40s. Largely Baroque, it incorporates elements from such European landmarks as the Paris Opera House. The tower's top was lowered after a 1971 earthquake. The splendid interior is often used as a movie location.

On the next block stands the **Globe Theater** *(1913; 744 Broadway)*, the first Broadway theater to show feature-length films. Little is left of its Beaux Arts design after it was gutted and turned over to the storeowners. Across the street, the **State Theater** *(1921; 703 Broadway)* was taken over by a Spanish-language evangelical church in 2000. Its style is Spanish Renaissance and the magnificent interior can be admired during church services or whenever doors are open.

Next up is the **Los Angeles Theater** *(1931; 615 Broadway)*, the last movie palace built by Charles Lee in a style so lavish that the Phantom of the Opera would approve. Seating more than 2000 in its French Baroque setting, the theater features opulent details such as a vaulted, coffered ceiling, a central staircase leading to a crystal fountain and Corinthian columns. It opened with the premiere of Chaplin's *City Lights*, but has been dark since 1994. En route you'll pass by the venerable **Clifton's Brookdale Cafeteria** *(☎ 213-627-1673, 648 Broadway)*, an eccentric Downtown eatery (see the Places to Eat chapter).

Spring Street

Turn right on 6th St to get to Spring St. In the 1920s, this street was a major center of finance and wore with pride the title 'Wall Street of the West.' Decline began as the new financial district mushroomed on Bunker Hill in the 1960s, and today Spring St is one of Downtown's less savory thoroughfares, its former splendor concealed by a coat of grime and neglect. Because of its many stately buildings, it was declared a Historic District in the 1990s and efforts to bring the street back to life are underway.

Architecture fans may want to take a closer look at the gray, monumental **Pacific Coast Stock Exchange** *(1930; 618 Spring St)*, with its fluted pilasters. As you continue north, another place worth ducking into is the lovely lobby of the Art Deco **Title Insurance Building** *(1928; 433 Spring St)*. The corner of Spring and 4th Sts marks the western end of the so-called 'Old Bank District,' which extends one block east to Main St. Here, developer and Downtown booster Tom Gilmore is trying to breathe life into a trio of dilapidated beauties: the **Continental/El Dorado Building** *(corner of Spring & 4th Sts)*, a future boutique hotel; the **Hellman Building** *(corner of Main & 4th Sts)*; and, across the street, the **San Fernando**, which has already been converted into postmodern loft apartments.

Backtrack to Spring St and turn right where you'll encounter the massive **Ronald Reagan Building** *(300 Spring St)*, whose lobby features a large-scale, feverishly colorful mural by Carlos Almaraz and Elsa Flores called *California Dreamscape*. (Legend has it that the building was originally to be called the Reagan State Office Building before someone realized that its abbreviation would read, 'Reagan SOB.')

Duck through the little passageway of 333 S Spring St (across from the Reagan Building) to get to the tiny **Biddy Mason Park** *(open 8am-8pm Mon-Fri, 9am-8pm Sat-Sun)*. A series of plaques by artists Betye Saar and Sheila Levrant de Bretville chronicle the life of the amazing Biddy Mason, a former slave turned property owner and midwife. She went on to found the city's First African Methodist Episcopal Church, still the most influential African American church in LA. Her house, where she lived from 1866–1891, stood near the spot now occupied by the little park that is a popular hangout of (usually peaceful) homeless people. It is accented by a fountain consisting of a phalanx of pipes and shaded by jacaranda trees.

Other Historic Buildings

Biddy Mason Park leads you back onto bustling Broadway. Turn right to arrive at one of LA's architectural highlights, the elegant **Bradbury Building** *(1893; ☎ 213-626-1893, 304 Broadway; lobby open 9am-6pm Mon-Fri, 9am-5pm Sat-Sun)*. Now an office building, the Bradbury is often used as a movie set, making an especially memorable appearance in *Blade Runner*. Its modest exterior only accentuates the interior splendor: Behind heavy oak doors, a five-story galleried atrium is flooded by daylight streaming through a tent-shaped glass roof. The black filigree of the cast-iron banisters is offset by walls of tawny glazed bricks and red marble staircases. A pair of manually operated open-cage elevators takes employees, unhurriedly, to their offices.

The Bradbury was the final project of mining millionaire turned real estate developer Lewis Bradbury. According to legend, the architect George Wyman – a mere draftsman – accepted the commission after communicating with his dead brother via a Ouija board. For inspiration, Wyman drew upon an 1887 novel by Edward Bellamy, *Looking Backward*, about a utopian civilization in the year 2000. The building was Wyman's only success, and Bradbury died a few months before its completion. You're free to step into the lobby, though security guards may prevent you from walking up the stairs or taking the elevator.

Across the street is another historic theater, the 1918 **Million Dollar Theater** *(307 Broadway)*. Note the squiggly, heavily ornamented facade in Spanish Churrigueresque style; if you're lucky, you may be able to pop inside for a look at the neat coffered ceiling.

The tour concludes at the **Grand Central Market** a few steps south. This vibrant food bazaar has been in business since 1917 and is crammed with stalls selling herbs, spices, cheeses and candy, plus nearly every vegetable, fruit and animal that grows – all at rock-bottom prices. Numerous food stalls provide delicious sustenance and character galore. (Also see the Places to Eat chapter.)

CIVIC CENTER (MAP 5)

Extending 8 blocks east to west from San Pedro to Figueroa Sts, the Civic Center contains most of LA's city, county, state and federal office buildings. In addition to the buildings discussed in detail below, the (in)famous Criminal Courts Building (*210 W Temple St*), where the OJ Simpson murder trial took place in 1995, and Parker Center (*150 N Los Angeles St*), the LAPD headquarters, are also part of the mix.

City Hall

Anyone who grew up watching television in the '50s and '60s can tell you about Los Angeles City Hall (*200 N Spring St*), which cameoed in the *Superman* series as the Daily Planet building from which the show's hero would leap into the sky. City Hall was also featured as Los Angeles' main police station in *Dragnet*.

Built in 1928 in a jumble of styles including Art Deco, Byzantine and Romanesque, the 28-story building (Downtown's tallest until 1966) has recently – like many of LA's aging stars – undergone a face-lift. About $235 million-worth of snips and tucks have restored its most distinctive feature, the sleek tower capped with a stepped pyramid. Inside, impressive marble columns and a colorful ceramic-tile dome add stateliness to the City Hall rotunda. Eclectic artworks – including a Shinto shrine from Japan and a giant holographic portrait of former mayor Tom Bradley – serve notice that LA is no ordinary city. Tours were suspended during restoration work but may have resumed; contact the tourist office (☎ *213-689-8822*) or the City Hall Volunteer Center (☎ *213-485-6984*) for more information.

Los Angeles Times

Catercorner from City Hall in a subdued Art Deco 10-story building is western North America's largest daily newspaper (☎ *213-237-5757, 202 W 1st St; tours at 1:30pm Tues & Thur by reservation; 10 years & older only*). Free 45-minute tours introduce visitors to the inner workings of this print-media giant. There's free parking in the

Purple People Greeters

The Downtown Center District of Los Angeles is an affiliation of property owners and merchants who realized that to many people 'going Downtown' meant a highly unsavory if not outright dangerous experience. To battle this image they hired a small army of mostly young people to patrol the streets on foot, by bike or in cars. The Purple People Greeters answer questions, provide directions, make referrals or even call the LAPD when things get rough.

It's easy to spot these welcoming folks: Traveling in pairs like Mormon missionaries, they all wear purple T-shirts with 'District Safety' or 'Downtown Guide' emblazoned on the back. You can also visit them at their Service Center (☎ 213-624-2425) at 801 S Hill St.

garage at 213 S Spring St. Reservations must be made at least one week in advance. Tours of the *Times'* Olympic Plant printing facility, 2000 E 8th St, which has a pressroom twice the length of a football field, are also offered on occasion (call for details).

Music Center of LA County

The complex of three theaters known collectively as the Music Center (☎ *213-972-7211, 135 N Grand Ave*) dominates the northwestern end of the Civic Center mall between 1st and Temple Sts. The sculpture surrounding a lusty fountain is by Jacques Lipschitz. Also note the whimsical bronze door designed by Robert Graham.

With 3200 seats, the **Dorothy Chandler Pavilion** is the largest of the three theaters and is also the oldest, dating to 1964. Besides being the main venue of the Los Angeles Philharmonic, the Los Angeles Opera and the Los Angeles Master Chorale, it has also hosted several Academy Awards ceremonies. Visiting Broadway musicals can be seen at the 2084-seat **Ahmanson Theater**, while the 742-seat **Mark Taper**

Forum presents a wide variety of theater productions, from avant-garde drama to literary satire.

The center offers one-hour guided **tours** (*☎ 213-972-7483; admission free; tours 10am, 10:30am, 11:30am, noon, 1pm, 1:30pm Tues, Thur-Sat May-Oct; reservations not required but call for schedule confirmation and winter hours).* Tours depart from the main entrance of the Dorothy Chandler Pavilion.

Walt Disney Hall

On Grand Avenue, just south of the Music Center, the future home of the LA Philharmonic is taking shape, poised to become another LA landmark: The Walt Disney Hall, designed by Frank Gehry, will be a concert hall like no other. Its exterior is a choreography of dynamically curving and folding walls that could be seen as an abstract interpretation of a ship caught in a rough sea. The facade is to be clad in a skin of brushed stainless steel sheets. The vaguely nautical theme continues in the main hall itself, which has been likened to a 'ceremonial barge' and is made primarily of blonde hardwood. It has a fragmented sail-like ceiling that curves and billows upwards, and the tiered and sectioned audience seating completely wraps around the orchestra pit. A vast organ, with pipes arranged in a haphazard fashion like a bag of French fries, juts forth from amongst the seats.

Also part of the 3.6-acre site will be the Roy and Edna Disney CalArts Theater (REDCAT) and an art gallery featuring the work of CalArts students and other artists.

Construction has been repeatedly delayed because of financial problems but it was going forward full steam at the time of writing. If all goes according to plan, Disney Hall will set sail in 2003.

Cathedral of Our Lady of the Angels

In the same general vicinity, but this time east of the Music Center, another future landmark was emerging at the time of writing: LA's new Catholic cathedral – the seat of Cardinal Roger Mahoney. This new cathedral is scheduled to open in 2002 and will replace the old Cathedral of St Vibiana (1876) on Main St, which was condemned after the 1994 earthquake.

Sitting on 5½ acres on Temple St between Grand Ave and Hill St, the new cathedral was designed by Spanish star architect José Rafael Moneo and is unapologetically modern – almost an exercise in geometry – and completely without right angles. Employing the latest in earthquake technology, the structure is supposed to withstand a potential 8.3 'Big One.' Instead of stained glass, the windows are made of milky alabaster said to bathe the vast interior, which seats up to 3000, in a rosy glow. A monumental illuminated cross tops the edifice. Another important design feature is the Great Bronze Doors (30 feet x 30 feet) conceived by Venice (California) sculptor Robert Graham, whose iconography celebrates the cathedral's namesake, Our Lady of the Angels.

A generous plaza leads up to the cathedral entrance. Also part of the complex are the cardinal's residence, a conference center and office space as well as a 156-foot campanile (a freestanding bell tower).

EL PUEBLO DE LOS ANGELES (MAP 5)

This 44-acre historic park northeast of the Civic Center commemorates the site where the city was founded in 1781 and preserves many of its earliest buildings. The site – originally named El Pueblo de los Angeles – was declared a state historic park in 1953. Inside the historic Sepulveda House (enter from Olvera St) is the visitors center (*☎ 213-680-2381 tour information, ☎ 213-625-3800 general information, 622 N Main St; office opens 10am-3pm Mon-Sat; exhibits open 11am-2pm Mon-Sat).* The center also shows a free film of LA history. Volunteers lead guided walking tours describing 27 historic buildings; tours leave hourly between 10am and 1pm, Tuesday through Saturday. Reservations are required. Alternatively, pick up a free pamphlet outlining a self-guided tour of the area. Fiestas and celebrations, such as Mardi Gras, the Blessing of the Animals, Cinco de Mayo and Las Posadas, take place in the pueblo throughout the year.

Olvera Street

The park's main visitor attraction is Olvera St, a narrow, block-long passageway. Known as Wine St through most of the 18th century, it was renamed in 1877 to honor the first LA County judge. By the early 20th century, Olvera St had devolved into a slum, with many of its buildings empty and crumbling. A visit from civic champion Christine Sterling in 1926 turned things around. Putting her power behind rescuing this historic lane, she solicited help and money from her famous friends, such as *LA Times* publisher Harry Chandler; prison laborers were hauled in to grade and pave the street.

Olvera St reopened in 1930 as an open-air Mexican marketplace and has been a tourist attraction ever since. Shops, restaurants and the stalls of vendors selling hand-woven clothing, leather belts and bags, handmade candles and piñatas line the brick alley. Shops are open daily 10am-6pm, later in summer.

Olvera St boasts LA's oldest existing house, the **Avila Adobe** *(1818; admission free; open 9am-5pm daily, shorter hours in winter)*. Built by Don Francisco Avila, a wealthy ranchero and one-time LA mayor, it was later a military headquarters, boarding house and restaurant. The rooms, which are restored and furnished in period style, are open for self-guided tours. Christine Sterling herself, affectionately nicknamed the 'Mother of Olvera St,' lived here until her death in 1963.

The 1887 **Sepulveda House** *(622 N Main St)* contains the visitors center. A two-story Eastlake Victorian built during the boom of the 1880s, it's an architectural hybrid of Mexican and American traditions. Its 2nd floor was originally a boarding house, then contained a puppet theater before becoming a USO canteen during WWII. The house was restored in the 1980s. Also on Olvera St is the **Pelanconi House** (1855), LA's first brick building, once occupied by a winery.

Old Plaza & Around

Olvera St spills into the Old Plaza, the central square of the original pueblo. Statues of Felipe de Neve, who led the first group of settlers, and Spanish king Carlos III, who ruled at that time, are here along with an ornate bandstand and Australian Moreton Bay fig trees.

West of the plaza is the **Church of Our Lady the Queen of the Angels** *(1822; ☎ 213-629-3101, 535 N Main St)*, built by Franciscan friars and indigenous laborers. The current structure replicates the original two-story adobe church with a tile roof and bell tower and still serves Los Angeles' huge Latino population.

The area south of the plaza boasts various other early structures, including the 1858 **Masonic Hall** *(☎ 213-626-4933, 416 N Main St; admission free; open 10am-3pm Tues-Fri)*. This two-story Italian Renaissance building houses a collection of Masonic memorabilia. The 1870 **Pico House** *(430 N Main St)* was once an elegant hotel built by Pio Pico, the last Mexican governor of California. The adjacent Italianate **Merced Theater** *(422 N Main St)* dates from the same time. In 1884 the city built its first fire station, the **Old Plaza Firehouse** *(☎ 213-625-3741, 134 Paseo de la Plaza; admission free; open 10am-3pm Tues-Sun)*. After incarnations as a saloon, boarding house and stores, it is now a museum of 19th-century fire-fighting equipment and photographs.

Union Station

Southeast of El Pueblo is Union Station *(1939; 800 N Alameda St)*, the last of the great railroad stations in the US. It harmoniously blends Spanish Mission style with Streamline Moderne elements and features a 135-foot clock tower, a marble-floored waiting room and massive original chandeliers dangling above clunky leather armchairs. The station is often used as a movie location; you may have seen it in *Bugsy*, *The Way We Were* or *Union Station*.

The beautiful, double-domed building north of the station is the **Terminal Annex**, LA's central post office. This is where

Charles Bukowski worked for years, inspiring the novel *Post Office* in 1971.

CHINATOWN (MAP 5)

Chinatown covers the 16-sq-block area north of El Pueblo along Broadway and Hill St between Sunset Blvd and Bernard St. Chinese people have been a presence in Los Angeles since the 1850 census recorded two male house servants – Ah Fou and Ah Luce. The population quickly grew in the late 19th century as more Chinese immigrated to the Los Angeles area for the numerous railroad-building jobs. Others toiled as cooks, servants, ranch hands or farm help. Discrimination was rampant and often turned violent, as evidenced by the Chinese Massacre of 1871, which left 19 Chinese men and boys dead. To add insult to injury, the original Chinatown was demolished in the 1930s to make room for Union Station, forcing its residents to relocate a few blocks north to present-day Chinatown. Fewer than 5% of LA's 200,000 Chinese Americans make their home here today; the majority live in suburban Monterey Park east of Downtown.

Chinatown, however, is still a social and cultural center. In February Chinatown's streets become a feast for the senses as giant dragons, decorated floats and lion dancers take part in the spectacular Chinese New Year parade. On any day of the year you can enjoy fresh Cantonese or Sichuan delicacies at dozens of restaurants, or browse in shops for cheap kitsch to exquisite silk clothing and art. Other shops display a profusion of bizarre produce and culinary oddities such as dried sea cucumber, elk antlers and pickled ginseng. Huge assortments of boxed exotic teas are sold along with medicinal potions mixed by herbalists following ancient recipes. Peer into the meat and fish shops for a glimpse of how fresh the food can be in the local restaurants: many of the animals – including frogs – are sold alive. **Superior Poultry** (☎ 213-628-7645, 750 N Broadway) has been in business for more than half a century and is the last place in the entire city to sell live poultry. Customers make their selections from dozens of cluck-ing chickens crammed in metal cages in the front room; the chosen ones are then dispatched, plucked, drawn and cut up by a league of uniformed executioners in the back room.

The more touristy section of Chinatown is a plaza of gift shops and restaurants called **Gin Ling Way** on the northern end of Broadway. Near the elaborately decorated entrance gate is a statue of Sun Yat-sen, an early 20th-century revolutionary regarded as the 'George Washington of the Republic of China.' Farther on is a whimsical wishing well and a five-tiered pagoda housing the legendary Hop Louie restaurant. Also note the curvilinear rooflines, many featuring animal figures that protect the building from evil.

South of here is the **Kong Chow Temple** *(2nd floor, 931 N Broadway)* above the East West Federal Bank. To enter, ring the bell and someone will let you in. Near the altar of this Buddhist temple, there will be a wooden cup containing 100 bamboo sticks engraved with Chinese numbers. Hold the cup in both hands and shake it at an angle until one stick pops out. The number on the stick will correspond with a fortune, which the caretaker can look up in a booklet. One fortune included the enchanting message: 'Keep your ideas about things and people to yourself.'

At the time of writing, the opening of a new **Chinese American Museum** dedicated to the Chinese American experience and history in Southern California was scheduled for fall 2001. It will be housed in the historic **Garnier Building** *(1891, 423 N Los Angeles St)*, one of the oldest and most important surviving buildings of LA's original Chinatown. The Garnier Building once housed stores, a fraternal organization and even served as Chinatown's 'city hall.' For more information about the museum call ☎ 213-626-5240.

LITTLE TOKYO (MAP 5)

Immediately south of the Civic Center is Little Tokyo, roughly bounded by 1st and 4th Sts on the north and south, Alameda St on the east, and Los Angeles St on the west.

RUSSELL LEE/LIBRARY OF CONGRESS

Japanese-American child being removed from LA to an Owens Valley internment camp (1942)

This bustling neighborhood was first settled by early Japanese immigrants in the 1880s. During WWII, it was effectively decimated by the removal of US-born Japanese to internment camps. The attack on Pearl Harbor coupled with military moves by Japan created the fear of a Japanese invasion of the West Coast and suspicion of US-born Japanese. As a result, President Roosevelt's Executive Order 9066, issued on February 19, 1942, authorized the building of so-called relocation centers (essentially barbed-wire camps) where people of Japanese descent would be 'contained' during the conflict. There were a total of 10 camps, including two in California (in Manzanar and Tule Lake). The Japanese community left behind their homes, businesses and reputations – all of which were not easily reclaimed upon their return. After the war, it took the community decades to recover.

Today Little Tokyo – or 'J-Town' – is again the social, economic and cultural center for nearly a quarter million Japanese Americans. For maps and information, drop in at the **Little Tokyo Visitor Center** (☎ 213-613-1911, 307 E 1st St, open 10am-6pm Mon-Sat). See the boxed text 'LA Conservancy Tours' in the Los Angeles Architecture special section for information about formal tours of Little Tokyo.

Japanese American National Museum

Start your exploration of Little Tokyo at the Japanese American National Museum (☎ 213-625-0414, 369 E 1st St; admission adults $6, seniors $5, students $3, children under 5 free; open 10am-5pm Tues-Sun, to 7:30pm Thur). The museum originally opened in 1992 in the historic Nishi Hongwanji Buddhist temple (1925). In 1998, a second building adjacent to the original opened, increasing exhibit space fivefold.

The museum is the country's first dedicated to the Japanese American experience. Objects of work and worship, photographs and art from the past 130 years show emigration to the US, foundation of an American life and the painful chapter of the WWII camps. The interactive Legacy Center contains a database of concentration camp records, allowing visitors to scan lists for relatives and friends. Another section explains and encourages experimentation with origami. Other exhibits highlight the history of particular Japanese communities, and there's a pleasant Japanese garden as well.

MOCA Geffen Contemporary

Frank Gehry cleverly converted a former warehouse into this vast exhibition space (☎ 213-626-6222, 152 N Central Ave; admission adults $6, seniors & students $4, children under 12 free; open 11am-5pm Tues-Sun, to 8pm Thur). Located right behind the Japanese American National Museum, it was originally called the Temporary Contemporary because it housed MOCA's collection while that museum's permanent facility was being constructed in California Plaza. Renamed for entertainment mogul David Geffen, a major patron, it is now used primarily for large-scale installations. Tickets are also good for same-day admission to MOCA at California Plaza and the MOCA Gallery at the Pacific Design Center.

Elsewhere in Little Tokyo

Across 1st St from the Japanese American National Museum is the **Japanese Village Plaza** (☎ 213-620-8861, 335 E 2nd St), a winding block-long pedestrian mall designed to resemble a rural hamlet in Japan. It's lined with about 40 traditional shops and restaurants (see Frying Fish Sushi or Shabu Shabu House in the Places to Eat chapter). A *yagura*, or medieval lookout tower, marks the village's 1st St entrance. Also note the haiku and tanka poems on wooden boards above a bench usually occupied by community elders. The plaza is often the site of celebrations, such as Buddha's birthday, the Cherry Blossom Festival and Tanabata, the Festival of Lovers. A few steps west of the 1st St entrance is the small **Koyasan Buddhist Temple** at the end of a plain driveway.

The mall's southern border is 2nd St. Farther south, you'll find the modern **Japanese American Cultural & Community Center** (☎ 213-628-2725, 244 S San Pedro St), which contains a gallery, bookstore and library. Just south of the building is the beautifully landscaped **James Irvine Garden**, also called Seiryu-en, or 'the Garden of the Clear Stream.' The fan-shaped building east of the center houses the **Japan American Theater** (☎ 213-680-3700), where you might witness Kabuki or Noh, stylized dance-dramas, or Bunraku, traditional puppet shows. Two blocks east of here is the huge **Mitsuwa Marketplace** (on Alameda & 3rd Sts), which incorporates a department store, a food hall and several restaurants.

Also worth a quick look are the traditional **Japanese garden** (4th floor of the New Otani Hotel at 120 S Los Angeles St), and the **Astronaut Ellison S Onizuka St**, a pedestrian mall dedicated to the Japanese American space explorer who died in the space shuttle *Challenger* tragedy of 1986.

SOUTH PARK & AROUND (MAP 5)

The South Park district is roughly bordered by the I-110 (Harbor Fwy) and Hill St to the west and east, respectively, and 9th St and the I-10 (Santa Monica Fwy) north and south. It is home to the Convention Center and the slick Staples Center, as well as several hotels. Farther east shoppers will have to visit the Fashion District and the flower market.

Grand Hope Park

Peaceful Grand Hope Park, south of 9th St between Grand and Hope Sts, was completed in 1993 as one of the first South Park beautification developments. Designed by Lawrence Halprin, the park features a clock tower, flower-festooned pergolas, a decorative fountain, a playground and coyote statues. Flanking its Grand Ave side is the **Fashion Institute of Design and Merchandising** (☎ 213-624-1200, 919 S Grand Ave), attended by some 3000 students from 45 countries.

Museum of Neon Art

On the park's southwest corner, a rocking Elvis and serene Mona Lisa are just two of the vibrant neon signs on view at the Museum of Neon Art (MONA; ☎ 213-489-9918, 501 W Olympic Blvd; admission adults $5, seniors & students $3.50, children under

12 free; open 11am-5pm Wed-Sat, noon-5pm Sun). The only permanent facility of its kind, the unusual museum showcases changing exhibits of artists working in neon, electric and kinetic art. Works from the museum collection also grace some facades at Universal City Walk. Neon devotees may want to join MONA's nighttime bus tours of signs, movie marquees and public art offered monthly for $45 (reservations are required).

La Plata Cigar Factory & Shop

At LA's only cigar factory *(☎ 213-747-8561, 1026 Grand Ave)*, you can watch these decidedly phallic smokes being rolled by hand in the diminutive back room. In business for over 50 years, the place is owned by Victor Migenes Jr who holds to the same traditions and standards as his father did before him. One of the company's Cuban-born rollers has been in the trade – developing the 'touch' – for half a century. The tobaccos are primarily Dominican and Ecuadorian, and up to nine kinds of leaf may find their way into each smoke. If you want to get a real education in cigar-ese, try to get yourself locked into La Plata's humidor for 10 minutes or so with Migenes or one of his salespeople. There, drenched in aroma that immediately makes you want to go off and fight in the hills, you will hear true connoisseurs speak about cigars in a way that only deep love can kindle.

Staples Center

One of LA's newest landmarks, the Staples Center *(☎ 877-305-1111, box office ☎ 213-742-7340, 1111 S Figueroa St)* opened in late 1999. It is a $175-million sports and entertainment arena with a futuristic design and outfitted with the latest technology, including a Bose sound system and $2 million worth of lighting. This is the home of LA's basketball teams, the Lakers and Clippers, as well as its hockey team, the Kings; the center also hosted the 2000 Democratic National Convention. It seats up to 20,000 spectators and has 160 luxury suites, 2500 premier-level seats, five concourse levels, two restaurants, shops and business centers.

Fashion District

Formerly known as the Garment District, this 56-block area toward the southern end of Downtown (framed by Broadway and Wall Sts, and 7th St and Pico Blvd) is the heart of LA's clothing manufacturing and wholesale trade. For bargain shoppers, it's fashion nirvana.

Strolling around here is more Middle Eastern souk than American mall. Overstuffed racks of Technicolor swimsuits, flowery summer dresses and Tommy Hilfiger knockoff track suits spill from tiny storefronts onto the sidewalks. Piles of scarves, cotton socks and cheap T-shirts compete for space with men's blazers and leather belts slung over rails like dead snakes. The most cacophonous artery is Santee Alley where peddlers wink, clap, shout and do whatever they must to get your attention. Things are quieter at more traditional shops, although they're more expensive and not nearly as much fun. See the Shopping chapter for details on how and where to shop in the Fashion District.

Southern California Flower Market

If you walked along the 700 blocks of Wall St and Maple Ave in the afternoon, you'd never know that only a few hours earlier a mad hubbub had enlivened the quiet streets. During the wee hours the warehouses swarm with buyers, grasping bunches of blossoms and flitting from stall to stall like feeding bees. An intense mélange of scents – from tangy Hawaiian ginger to sweet roses – wafts through the air. Buckets of snapdragons in profuse color and other posies are heaped onto waiting trucks for delivery to flower shops throughout Southern California.

Employing nearly 2000 people, this is the country's largest cut-flower market *(☎ 213-627-2482; admission $2 Mon-Fri, $1 Sat; open to public 8am-noon Mon, Wed, Fri, 6am-noon Tues, Thur, Sat)*. Flower cultivation in the city began in 1892 when Japanese American farmers planted fields south of Downtown and in Santa Monica. The flower market itself dates to 1913 and moved to its current location in 1923. To soak up some

The Story Behind the Garment Glitz

Clothing manufacturing has been an important industry in LA since the 1920s and it is now the largest in the country, having overtaken New York City. In 1998, the rag trade pumped $17.2 billion into the economy and put money into the pockets of about 164,000 Angelenos. Unfortunately, there's a sad flip side to this impressive economic success.

A study by the US Department of Labor found that working conditions in nearly all apparel factories in LA range from substandard to scandalous. Nearly two-thirds are in violation of minimum wage and overtime laws and practically all ignore health and safety standards. Sewing-machine operators usually toil under inhuman conditions, crammed like cattle into crumbling warehouses with no air-conditioning and poor sanitary facilities. Workers get paid on a piecework basis, often earning less than the legal minimum hourly wage, and are hired and dismissed at will. The classic sweatshop, in other words, is alive and well.

Most garment workers are recent immigrants (often undocumented) with little or no English skills and low educational attainment. About 70% are women and the vast majority is Latino, primarily Mexican; about 10% are Asian. Employers exploit their vulnerability and lack of legal recourse. Although conditions may be barely tolerable, few ever dare to speak up; those who do are usually fired instantly.

After the discovery of a virtual slave house in 1995, where 72 Thai women had been forced to work 17-hour days at $2 an hour, some clothing companies hired private monitoring services to assess working conditions. Little has changed, though, as many choose to ignore the results in favor of the bottom line. The cry for more stringent regulations has fizzled faster than last season's fashions.

of the atmosphere and scarf down a hearty breakfast, drop in at the Flower Market Coffee Shop on Wall St.

Coca-Cola Bottling Plant

This 1937 plant (*1334 S Central Ave*) is a perfect example of the Streamline Moderne style inspired by the sleek forms of ocean liners and airplanes. Located in an otherwise unattractive industrial section of Downtown, the plant has a facade featuring design elements like a ship's bridge, porthole windows, ship doors and metal balconies. Its corners sport two oversized Coke bottles.

ARTS DISTRICT

In the dilapidated industrial section on the eastern edge of Downtown, a lively loft arts district has sprung up. There are plenty of artists' studios and galleries, mostly filled with highly unusual and experimental art. **Brewery Art Complex** (*2100 N Main St; Map 3*) is a self-contained artist colony on the

site of what used to be the Pabst Brewing Company plant. Artists work in many media, including sculpture, architecture, painting, photography and design. Studios are closed to the public except during the twice-annual free Brewery Art Walks (usually in spring and fall, call ☎ 213-694-2911 for dates), though you can wander around to examine the large installations – usually works in progress – scattered throughout.

See the Shopping chapter for coverage of the Brewery's noteworthy galleries.

San Antonio Winery (Map 5)

The last remaining winery in the city is the San Antonio Winery (*☎ 323-223-1401, 737 Lamar St; admission & tastings free; open 10am-6pm Sun-Tues, 10am-7pm Wed-Sat*). It takes a vivid imagination to realize that the barren industrial wasteland just north of the US-101 (Hollywood Fwy) and west of I-5 (Golden State Fwy) was once the germ cell of California's fecund wine industry. In the early 1830s, Frenchman Jean Louis Vignes was among the pioneers to bring the cherished grape to Los Angeles, then hardly more than a far-flung outpost on the country's edge. But as the California gold rush and railroad construction brought an influx of new immigrants – including many from Mediterranean Europe – the demand for wine skyrocketed and new vineyards popped up all across the state.

In 1917, the year when Italian immigrant Santo Cambianica founded San Antonio Winery, LA already had nearly 100 wineries. The fledgling business managed to tough out the Prohibition years by producing sacramental wine and by selling grapes to home wine makers. By the '50s, it was one of California's largest wineries, producing mostly inexpensive table varieties. In the late '70s, San Antonio started making quality vintage wines, specializing in oaky chardonnay and full-bodied cabernet sauvignon. You will not find any of its vineyards beneath smoggy LA skies; they are all in Monterey, Napa and Sonoma counties near San Francisco.

All wines may be sampled in the tasting room, where affable patriarch Steve Riboli, a descendant of Santo Cambianica, is usually on hand to answer questions. Self-guided tours behind the scenes are free as well, and there's a restaurant to help sop up the wine.

ECHO PARK (MAP 5)

This community is named after the 26-acre park, at Glendale Blvd and Park Ave, which surrounds a nicely landscaped lake with paddleboats available for hire. The lake is blanketed by the largest lotus bed outside China and is the setting of the Lotus Festival, a celebration of Asian Pacific culture that takes place every July.

A few blocks east of the lake is **Angelino Heights**, LA's original commuter suburb, which grew on a hillside in the 1880s and was linked to Downtown by a trolley line. Its greatest appeal is its cluster of beautifully restored and lovingly maintained Victorian homes, especially in the 1300 block of Carroll Ave. (There are a few more

on Kellam Ave, one block north.) All are private residences and can only be admired from the outside, though the interior of some may be viewed during the walking tours given monthly by the LA Conservancy (see the related boxed text in the Los Angeles Architecture special section).

Angelus Temple

Opposite the north end of Echo Park is the mammoth circular and domed Angelus Temple, the headquarters of the International Church of the Foursquare Gospel, founded by the eccentric and charismatic Aimee Semple McPherson (1890–1944) in 1923. The angelic-looking McPherson distinguished herself by recognizing the power of a new technology – the radio – to spread her faith and philosophy. Through her showbiz-style *Sunshine Hour* broadcast on the church-owned radio station, she essentially pioneered the televangelism industry of today. (KFSG is still in operation today at 96.3 FM.)

Though hugely popular, Sister Aimee was not without controversy. In 1926, she disappeared into the ocean in Santa Monica, only to 'resurface' four weeks later, claiming that she had been kidnapped. Rumor has it that she had really been holed up with a lover at a remote site. She was charged with conspiracy, though the district attorney eventually dropped the case. Mentally unstable for years, Sister Aimee went the way of so many flamboyant Hollywood stars: She overdosed on drugs. Her church, however, still has about 17 million members worldwide. The Angelus Temple seats up to 5000 people and is impressive with stained-glass windows and a stage-like altar.

ELYSIAN PARK (MAP 5)

Just east of Echo Park is this neighborhood, whose focal point is Dodger Stadium and the park from which it derives its name. Created in 1886 as a recreational refuge, Elysian Park has changed much over the years. Reshaped by a landslide in 1937, a large section was handed over to the LA Police Department, which still maintains its training academy here. In 1940 the I-110

(Pasadena Fwy) took another big chunk out, as did Dodger Stadium in 1959.

Dodger Stadium

Squatting on a chaparral-cloaked hilltop overlooking Downtown is LA's historic baseball stadium (☎ 323-224-1500, 1000 Elysian Park Ave; tour price adults $8, children $4; tours 10am, 11:30am & 1:30pm Wed-Sat). The stadium, which recently underwent a $50 million renovation, is home to the Los Angeles Dodgers. One of Major League baseball's most popular teams, the Dodgers moved to LA from Brooklyn in 1958. (The name 'Dodgers,' by the way, is an abbreviation of 'Trolley Dodgers' and refers to the trolley tracks crisscrossing the area surrounding their Brooklyn ball field in the team's early days during the 1890s.) The move to LA came about because Walter O'Malley, president and chief stockholder of the team since 1950, felt his team needed to play on a new and improved field. When Brooklyn balked at spending the money, O'Malley shocked the world of sports by moving his team to LA, essentially inventing the mobile professional sports franchise.

LA welcomed the team with open arms and the promise to build the state-of-the-art Dodger Stadium. The stadium seats 56,000 and is widely regarded as one of the most magnificent ballparks in the US.

The team responded by producing a string of legends that included Duke Snider, Jackie Robinson, Roy Campanella, Pee Wee Reese, Gil Hodges, Don Drysdale, Sandy Koufax, Tommy Davis, Frank Howard, Fernando Valenzuela and Orel Hershiser. Walter Alston, manager since 1954, guided the team through 23 seasons, 2042 wins, four world championships and seven National League pennants. The O'Malley family maintained ownership until selling out to publishing tycoon Rupert Murdoch in 1998.

The one-hour tour takes you to the press box, dugout, luxury suites, stadium field and the warning track as well as the Dugout Club where trophies, photographs and memorabilia trace the Dodgers' history. (For game information, see Spectator Sports in the Entertainment chapter).

EXPOSITION PARK AREA (MAP 6)

This section covers the area southwest of downtown and includes Exposition Park and the University of Southern California.

Exposition Park

Exposition Park, which began as an agricultural fairground in 1872, covers the equivalent of 25 sq city blocks south of Exposition Blvd and west of Figueroa St. When this became a public park in the early 20th century, its master plan called for a cluster of museums that are still its main attraction. The main outdoor attraction is the 1927 **Rose Garden** (admission free; open 8:30am-sunset Apr-Dec). This groomed sprawl of 15,000 bushes represents some 150 varieties of the noble blossom and is a popular wedding spot.

North of the park is the sprawling campus of the University of Southern California (USC). The surrounding area, once one of LA's grandest residential districts, is marked by many Victorian, Queen Anne and Art Deco structures.

Natural History Museum of LA County

On the park's northwestern edge sits an imposing 1913 Spanish Renaissance structure, home to the Natural History Museum of LA County (☎ 213-763-3466, www.nhm.org, 900 Exposition Blvd; admission adults $8, students & seniors $5.50, children 5-12 $2; open 9:30am-5pm Mon-Fri, 10am-5pm Sat-Sun). The museum's vast collections chronicle the earth's 4.5-billion-year evolution and showcase the astonishing diversity of natural life. On the ground level, two huge habitat halls present **African and North American mammals**, but it's the dinosaurs that are the most reliable crowd-pleasers: a Tyrannosaurus rex and a Triceratops are pitched in battle in the foyer.

For more in-depth study, visit the **Dinosaur Hall** to view a complete Tyrannosaurus skull and skeletons and models of other dinosaurs. Also on this floor, the **Gem & Mineral Hall** dazzles with some 2000 specimens, including 300 pounds of gold. Many of the treasures are imaginatively displayed in a walk-through vault.

Several smaller galleries on the ground floor are dedicated to American history from the pre-Columbian era to 1914. A particular highlight is the **Times Mirror Hall of Native American Cultures** with its collections of Navajo textiles, baskets from California and the Great Basin, beadwork from the Plains and a re-created pueblo cliff dwelling. For a thorough survey of 400 years of **California history**, head to the lower level.

The mezzanine level is home to the **Insect Zoo** of local and exotic creepy crawlies, including tarantulas, Madagascan hissing cockroaches, butterflies, scarab beetles and even a giant ant farm. Farther upstairs, you'll find the **Schreiber Hall of Birds** with 27 interactive learning stations and three imaginatively presented walk-through habitats. In the **Marine Life Hall** on the same floor, dioramas showcase California sea life from the intertidal to the deep-sea zones. Also here is one of the museum's most prized species: a preserved 14½-foot-long megamouth, one of the world's rarest sharks.

If you're traveling with young children, you might want to check out the **Discovery Gallery** on the ground floor, where assistants help select 'discovery boxes,' filled with stuffed animals, building blocks, a puzzle or an animal bone.

California Science Center

If your memory of school science makes you groan, then a visit to the California Science Center should convince you that, gee, science *can* be fun. One of LA's favorite family destinations, the center is a hands-on, interactive, state-of-the-art facility (☎ 213-744-7400, 700 State Dr; admission free; parking $5 at Figueroa & 39th Sts, street parking free; open 10am-5pm daily).

The exhibits begin in the **Science Plaza**, a cylindrical pavilion embellished with 1578 golden spheres (called *The Aerial*) suspended above a central double helix-like sculpture called *DNA Bench*; both pieces of art are by Larry Kirkland. Off to the side is the **California Gate**, which juxtaposes two granite plates connected by negative space in the outline of the state of California.

The museum doors lead to the **Science Court**, a three-story glass atrium where you'll find fast-food eateries as well as a museum store (there's also a more 'grown-up' cafe on the 3rd floor). Suspended from the ceiling is a kinetic sculpture called a hyperbolic paraboloid, or Hypar, which slowly expands and contracts to form bizarre shapes. Also in the atrium is the High Wire Bicycle, a physics lesson disguised as a circus act. Junior daredevils – strapped into a harness – pedal along a thick cable, counterbalanced by a weight. Rides are $2.

The two main exhibition areas are on the 2nd floor. Off to the left is **World of Life**, which is based on the concept that all forms of life – from amoebae to cacti to Homo sapiens – share the same basic processes, from reproduction to the intake and processing of energy to the disposal of waste. You can compare the human heart to that of a mouse or an elephant, or hop on a red blood cell for a computer fly-through of the circulatory system. Learn about digestion from Gertie's Guts or look at the developmental stages of an embryo as it turns into a fetus and eventually into a fully-grown baby. Drop in at the Surgery Theater to watch a video of an open-chest surgery, then recover by observing newly hatched chicks in the nearby incubator.

The museum highlight is the **Bodyworks theater**. It stars a techno-doll named Tess who's billed as '50 feet of brains, beauty and biology.' Cutaways show Tess' organs, bones, muscles and veins. Interacting with her cartoon sidekick, Walt, via a video screen, Tess 'comes to life' in a 15-minute multimedia show. Small children may still have trouble understanding the science, but they *will* remember Tess.

Virtual reality games, high-tech simulators, laser animation and other such gadgetry await in the **Creative World** exhibit. The focus here is on human innovations in communication, transportation and structures. In the Communication area, you can send and receive video messages, participate in digital jam sessions or play virtual soccer or volleyball. The Structures Gallery explains static principles of bridges and

Especially for Kids

It's easy to keep kids entertained in LA, given the myriad choices for outdoor explorations along the beaches, in the mountains and even in the urban core. Amusement parks such as Disneyland, Knott's Berry Farm and Universal Studios Hollywood are of course hugely popular, but they're also very expensive and exhausting for everyone in the family.

Here is a short list of alternatives to the typical amusement park activities (see the relevant sections in this chapter for detailed coverage).

Aquarium of the Pacific (Long Beach)
Autry Museum of Western Heritage (Griffith Park)
California Science Center (Exposition Park)
Griffith Observatory & Planetarium (Griffith Park)
Kidspace (Pasadena)
La Brea Tar Pits and Page Museum at La Brea Discoveries (Miracle Mile District)
Los Angeles Zoo (Griffith Park)
Museum of Flying (Santa Monica)
Natural History Museum of LA County (Exposition Park)
UCLA Ocean Discovery Center (Santa Monica)

LA also has a few galleries dedicated to children, usually with an active schedule of storytelling, reading and workshops. Try Every Picture Tells a Story (☎ 323-932-6070, 7525 Beverly Blvd; Map 10); Storyopolis (☎ 310-358-2500, 116 N Robertson Blvd; Map 10) or Children's Book World (☎ 310-559-2665, 10580½ W Pico Blvd, West LA).

Generations of Angelenos have grown up with Bob Baker Marionette Theater (☎ 213-250-9995, 1345 W 1st St, Echo Park; admission $10; show times 10:30am Tues-Fri, 2:30pm Sat & Sun; Map 5). Since 1963, it has enthralled kids ages two to 12 with its adorable singing and dancing marionettes and stuffed animals that interact with their young audiences seated on a carpet. It's pure magic. (There's free parking next to the theater.)

In Santa Monica, the Puppet and Magic Center (☎ 310-656-0483, 1255 2nd St; admission $6.50) is a 40-seat theater with regularly scheduled performances as well as puppet workshops and a puppet museum.

Other theaters that occasionally stage shows for children include the Santa Monica Playhouse, the Coronet Theatre and the Will Geer Theatricum Botanicum (for details on these, check out the Entertainment chapter). Also check the Calendar section of the LA Times.

buildings. A highlight here is the earthquake simulator. Finally, there's the Transportation Gallery, where you get a close-up look at a solar-powered car and learn what makes planes fly and boats sail.

IMAX Theater

Next to the California Science Center is the Frank Gehry–designed IMAX Theater (☎ 213-744-7400; admission adults $6.50, students $5, children $3.75, $1 surcharge for 3D films; call for show times). The theater's 7-story high and 91-feet wide screen and six-channel digital surround-sound system presents awe-inspiring nature films. A 3D projector uses two 15,000-watt xenon bulbs, bright enough to be seen with the naked eye if they were on the moon.

California African American Museum

In the park's most northeasterly corner is the state-owned California African American Museum (☎ 213-744-7432, 600 State Dr;

admission free; open 10am-5pm Tues-Sun). This museum does an excellent job at presenting the complex range of African and African American art and artifacts in an educational and pleasing environment. Items from the permanent collection of fine art include works by painters of the 1920s Harlem Renaissance, when black American artists established a cultural identity in the various media. Examples are shown on a rotating basis, along with crafts such as fertility figures, ceremonial implements, funeral statues, masks and headdresses. Temporary exhibits often focus on historical themes or on distinguished African Americans in politics, sports and science. Lectures, theater, music and other cultural programming complement the exhibits.

Memorial Coliseum & Sports Arena

The Los Angeles Memorial Coliseum *(☎ 213-748-6131, 3911 S Figueroa St)*, south of the California Science Center, has played host not only to the 1932 and 1984 Summer Olympic Games, but also to the baseball World Series in 1959 and to Super Bowl I and VII. In 1960, Democratic presidential nominee John F Kennedy and his running mate, Lyndon B Johnson, gave their acceptance speeches here. Built in 1923 and enlarged in 1932, the monumental stadium seats 106,000 people. The headless bronze bodies of both a female and a male nude – designed by LA artist Robert Graham for the 1984 Olympics – greet visitors approaching the characteristic Art Deco eastern entrance. Major damage during the 1994 earthquake resulted in thorough retrofitting.

The adjacent Los Angeles Memorial Sports Arena *(☎ 213-748-6136, 3939 S Figueroa St)* dates from 1959 and hosts rock concerts, ice shows, a circus and even the occasional rodeo.

University of Southern California

Founded in 1880, University of Southern California *(USC; ☎ 213-740-5371, www.usc .edu)* is one of the oldest private research universities in the American West. Its 155-acre campus, just north of Exposition Park,

consists of the College of Letters, Arts and Sciences as well as 17 professional schools. In 2001 student enrollment was 28,100, including 4200 foreign students, mostly from Asian countries. USC is particularly noted for its School of Cinema-Television, the oldest (since 1929) and the highest ranked in the country. Distinguished alumni include directors George Lucas, Ron Howard and Robert Zemeckis. Other alumni include John Wayne, architect Frank Gehry, astronauts Neil Armstrong and Charles Bolden, Gulf War general Norman Schwarzkopf and OJ Simpson. Free 50-minute walking tours of the campus are offered 10am-3pm Monday to Friday; just show up at the admissions center or call ☎ 213-740-6605 for reservations.

Fisher Gallery In 1939 Elizabeth Holmes Fisher founded the Fisher Gallery *(☎ 213-740-4561, 823 Exposition Blvd; admission free; open noon-5pm Tues-Sat, closed May-Aug)*. Its permanent collection includes Thomas Doughty's *Along the Mohawk* (1828) and other 19th-century American landscapes. Works by Thomas Gainsborough, Sir Joshua Reynolds, Benjamin West and other British artists are as much a part of the collection as paintings from the 19th-century French Barbizon School, including Théodore Rousseau's *The Lake in the Forest* and Camille Corot's *Le Lac*. Several rooms are reserved for changing exhibitions showcasing the work of student artists, emerging local and national artists and contemporary international artists.

Shrine Auditorium

At the northeast corner of campus is the double-domed Shrine Auditorium *(☎ 213-749-5123, 665 W Jefferson Blvd)*. When completed in Moorish style in 1926, it was the largest theater in the US, seating almost 6500. Its pipe organ is still the biggest of any theater in the world. Besides being the occasional home of the Grammy Awards, the American Music Awards and the Academy Awards, it is also the gathering place and headquarters of the Al-Malaikah Temple, a subdivision of the Arabic Order of Nobles of the Mystic Shrine, who are also known as Shriners.

Architectural Landmarks (Map 5)

Three corners of the intersection of Adams Blvd and Figueroa St are occupied by historical buildings, two of them churches. Despite its mission-like appearance, the structure in the southwest corner is actually just the headquarters of the Automobile Club of Southern California (☎ 213-741-3111, 2601 S Figueroa St). It was built in 1923 and features octagonal towers, topped with a domed cupola, as well as an impressive lobby.

Standing tall at a 45° angle to the northwest corner is **St Vincent De Paul Catholic Church** (1925; ☎ 213-749-8950, 621 W Adams Blvd; admission free; open 7am-4:30pm). Its exterior is a fine example of Spanish Colonial Revival with a heavily ornamented Churrigueresque main facade. It features a bell tower ringed by statues of the four Evangelists and a dome covered in kaleidoscopic tiles. Inside, notice the Italian Renaissance stained-glass windows, the carved choir stalls and the gold-leafed main altar. The ceiling mural is the work of Vatican painter Giovanni Smeraldi. St Vincent's has an active congregation, with several masses held daily in either English or Spanish.

Somewhat removed from the southeast corner, you will find **St John's Episcopal Church** (1925; ☎ 213-747-6285, 514 W Adams Blvd; hours vary). Enter by ringing the bell of the office to the left of the church. The design of St John's was inspired by a Romanesque church in a village near Rome. Italian artisans crafted the elaborate exterior, including the depiction of the Evangelists around the rose window. Inside, St John's is a three-nave structure with narrow side aisles separated from the central nave by slender Corinthian columns. The wood-beamed, hand-painted ceiling is an exact replica from an 11th-century Tuscan church. Most eye-catching, though, are the patterned marble walls and mosaics of the chancel area, and the gold-drenched Lady Chapel to the right of the altar. If you look carefully, you may also find the tiny footprints in the tiled floor next to the last seat on the right of the 10th pew; these were supposedly left by a child of one of the masons working on the church.

Griffith Park & Around

This section covers the area northeast of downtown and includes Griffith Park and the neighborhoods of Silver Lake and Los Feliz.

GRIFFITH PARK (MAP 8)

Spreading across a rugged mountainous area, Griffith Park (open 6am-10pm) is five times the size of New York City's Central Park and is the nation's largest municipal park. California oak, wild sage and manzanita blanket much of its 4107 acres, with elevations ranging from 384 feet to 1625 feet (Mt Hollywood). The famous Hollywood sign is atop Mt Lee, on the western edge.

Griffith Park got its name from Colonel Griffith J Griffith, an immigrant from South Wales who'd made his millions in gold mining speculation. He donated more than 3000 acres to the city in 1896 on the condition that it 'must be made a place of recreation and rest for the masses.' Upon his death in 1919, Griffith bequeathed additional money for the construction of an amphitheater and an observatory. (Note that Griffith wasn't all Mr Nice Guy: He spent two years in San Quentin prison for attempted murder of his wife.)

It's fair to assume that Griffith would be pleased with the results. Griffith Park remains a respite from urbanity. Within its boundaries are not just the theater and observatory he envisioned, but also a zoo, a major museum, golf courses, tennis courts, playgrounds, bridle paths and hiking trails.

Griffith Park is bounded by Hwy 134 (Ventura Fwy) to the north, the I-5 (Golden State Fwy) to the east, Los Feliz Blvd to the south and the US-101 (Hollywood Fwy) to the west. Approaching from the south, the most direct route into the park is via Vermont Ave. You can also enter via Western or Canyon Aves. Get directly onto either Griffith Park Dr or Zoo Dr by taking the respective exit from I-5.

Roads and bridle and hiking trails close at sunset (except the one leading to the observatory). Outdoor activities are detailed in the appropriately named Activities section, later in this chapter.

Griffith Observatory & Planetarium

Narrow winding roads – or, for the physically adept, trails – lead up to the Griffith Observatory & Planetarium (☎ 323-664-1191, www.griffithobs.org, 2800 E Observatory Rd). Located on the southern slopes of Mt Hollywood, facing the city, the snowy white facade and shiny copper domes have been a landmark since 1935. The view from here alone – especially on a clear day or at night – is worth making the trip. The entire Los Angeles basin, from the mountains to the east via the high-rises of Downtown to the gleaming Pacific in the distance, sprawls below you. James Dean fans will probably recognize the observatory grounds as the setting of the switchblade fight in *Rebel Without a Cause*; look for a small bust of the actor near the entrance to the building.

A thorough renovation of the observatory is scheduled to begin in January 2002 and will keep the complex closed until at least late 2004.

Greek Theater

Just within the park's southern boundary is the Greek Theater (☎ 323-665-1927, 2700 N Vermont Ave), which showcases popular musical talent as well as ballet and other dance performances from May to October in an open-air amphitheater. Also built with funds left by Griffith, the Greek Theater opened in 1930 and offers seating to audiences of around 6000. A Wall of Fame features handprints and signatures of the stars – including Johnny Mathis, Harry Belafonte and Santana – who have sold more than 100,000 tickets at the Greek.

Los Angeles Zoo

In the northeast corner of the park is the LA Zoo (☎ 323-644-6400, 5333 Zoo Dr; admission adults $8.25, seniors $5.25, children 2-12 $3.25; open 10am-5pm daily, to 6pm or 7pm in summer). It is the triumphant successor to two earlier animal parks. Selig Zoo, the first, was in Downtown and dates back to 1885, while the second, Griffith Park Zoo, opened in 1912 stocked primarily with circus animals no longer capable of holding a job. The modern Los Angeles Zoo opened its doors in 1966 and is home to some 1200 animals representing 350 species. Some of them have lived at the zoo since its beginning, including the elephant Gita, the alligator Methuselah and the Indian rhino Herman.

The undisputed highlight is the exhibit of 13 chimpanzees living in a re-created habitat of the Tanzanian Mahale Mountains. It's an exhibit – complete with waterfall and 'abandoned' buildings – that will make even the most impassioned animal lover feel that zoos might sometimes do a valuable service. It's part of a $15 million Great Ape Forest expansion project that might see completion in 2002.

The zoo has around a dozen habitats laid out over 80 acres according to the animals' continental origins: North and South America, Africa, Australia and Eurasia. On view are mammals, birds, amphibians and reptiles. A crowd favorite is the Ahmanson Koala House, which simulates dawn and dusk to allow visitors to witness these cuddly creatures at their most active. There is also an aquatic section, a reptile house and a big aviary. Adventure Island is an interactive area geared towards small children and focused on animals in the Southwest. The LA Zoo has also been instrumental in helping the world's population of California condors inch its way back from near extinction. Many other rare animals – skinks to mountain tapirs – have also been successfully bred here.

THINGS TO SEE & DO

Autry Museum of Western Heritage

Anyone interested in the history of the American West will hit the mother lode at this delightful museum (☎ 323-667-2000, www.autry-museum.org, 4700 Western Heritage Way; admission adults $7.50, seniors & students $5, children 2-12 $3; open 10am-5pm Tues-Sun, to 8pm Thurs). On the eastern edge of Griffith Park, the museum opened in 1988 and was financed with a $54-million donation from the Gene Autry Foundation; it features 10 galleries that skillfully combine scholarship and showmanship.

Gene Autry (1907–1998) became a millionaire several times over as an actor and singer, earning him the title of 'The Singing Cowboy.' In the 1940s, Autry opened the rodeo scene to a larger audience by bringing in entertainers during shows. Autry also recorded nine gold records – including 'Rudolph, the Red-Nosed Reindeer' and 'Back in the Saddle Again.' He parlayed his earnings into three music publishing companies, four radio stations, a Palm Springs resort and a Major League baseball team, the Anaheim Angels.

Start your tour of the permanent galleries on the main level in the Spirit of Discovery gallery, which shows how the West was 'discovered' again and again by various peoples, from prehistoric tribes to Native Americans to missionaries. Then head to the basement for a look at the panoramic mural by Guy Deel. The first gallery on your right documents the harsh realities of overland transportation and life on the Western trails. Included in this coverage is the tragic Trail of Tears when 4000 Native Americans lost their lives after being forced from their lands in the East.

Ensuing galleries deal with the clashes between conquerors and Native Americans, including General Custer's (in)famous Last Stand at Little Bighorn, and the roles played by Europeans, Chinese, Mexicans, Mormons and Canadians lured to California during the gold rush. A huge carved mahogany saloon bar from 1880, gaming tables and cheating devices illustrate aspects of that era's freewheeling social life. The flip side of that coin – a prevailing climate of violence and lawlessness – is given poignant emphasis in the Colt Collection. From here swagger over to the Spirit of the Cowboy Gallery, which sheds light on the lives of real cowboys of yore and today. Back upstairs, other rooms show how the West has been glorified and romanticized in fine art, movies, radio, TV and advertising.

The museum also offers concerts, gallery talks, symposia, panel discussions, film screenings and storytelling sessions for children.

Travel Town Museum

Railroad buffs will not want to miss this nostalgic museum (☎ 323-662-5874, 5200 W Zoo Dr; admission free; open 10am-5pm Mon-Fri, 10am-6pm Sat & Sun Apr-Sept; to 5pm the rest of the year). On the northern edge of Griffith Park, Travel Town is an outdoor transportation museum that specializes in pre-WWII railroad antiques. Highlights include 14 vintage steam locomotives (the oldest from 1864, the 'youngest' from 1925), as well as two still-functioning diesel locomotives. Also part of the collection are freight and passenger cars (including several sleepers) and several cabooses, two of which are used in demonstrations. Kids of any age may climb onto some of the locomotives and imagine themselves as engineers. There's also a warehouse-size hall displaying historical fire engines and firefighting equipment as well as a huge model-train network, which a dedicated local hobby club operates, usually on weekends from 10am-4pm.

The best day to visit Travel Town is the first full weekend of every month, when volunteers run free rides (donations are appreciated) on a caboose pulled by a diesel engine. Rides operate continuously from 10:10am to 5:30pm (in winter to 4:30pm). There are also trips on a miniature train (admission adults $2, seniors $1.25, children $1.50).

Other Things to See & Do

Located just east of the Travel Town Museum, the **Los Angeles Live Steamers** is a club devoted to live steam, gas-mechanical and electronic railroad technology (☎ 323-669-9729, 5202 Zoo Dr; free rides; open 11am-3pm Sun). Come early, as lines can get quite long for the rides on the one-eighth-size model trains.

Kids' attractions, centered in the park's southeast corner, include the **Griffith Park Southern Railroad** (☎ 323-664-6788; rides adults $1.75, seniors $1.25, children $1.50; 10am-4:30pm Mon-Fri, 10am-5pm Sat & Sun). This miniature train ride has operated since 1948 and makes a 1-mile loop past pony rides, through an old Western town and a Native American village. Nearby, generations of Angelenos and visitors have also delighted in riding the richly festooned 1926 **merry-go-round** (☎ 323-665-3051; rides $1; 11am-5pm daily in summer, weekends only in winter). To get to this area, follow Crystal Springs Dr along the park's eastern flank.

Forest Lawn Memorial Park – Hollywood Hills

Just west of Griffith Park is this 340-acre cemetery (☎ 323-254-7251, 6300 Forest Lawn Dr; admission free – unless you're planning to stay forever; open 8am-6pm daily), which boasts sculptures and artwork, plus a fine catalog of dead celebrities, including Lucille Ball, Liberace, Bette Davis and Stan Laurel. (For background on Forest Lawn cemeteries, see the even more grandiose Glendale branch, later in the chapter.)

The Court of Liberty is quite a patriotic homage to America's founding fathers. From the center of the terraced court of Albert Speer–like proportions soars a statue of George Washington. Note the grave of Stan Laurel on your right as you walk toward a gigantic mosaic mural. Here,

millions of minuscule tiles form a sentimental but nonetheless impressive depiction of the country's founding.

Behind follows the Hall of Liberty (open 10am-4:45pm), which contains a replica of the Liberty Bell as well as a Mexican history museum. Just west of here is the Lincoln Terrace with a memorial statue of the president and a smaller mosaic with scenes from his life.

LOS FELIZ & SILVER LAKE (MAP 9)

These side-by-side neighborhoods east of Hollywood have a reputation as hip and wacky hangouts of artists, musicians, lesbigays and bohemians of all stripes. But, as with other LA areas of this ilk, such as Venice, they too are under threat of yuppification. Moneyed folk from the Industry and other trades, wanting to partake in the thrift-shop chic, are actually undermining exactly what attracted them to the 'hood in the first place. Rents and home prices have shot up and the 'days of cool' could be numbered. In the meantime, though, come here to browse bizarre stores, have an eclectic dining experience or sip a martini at a retro bar. Vermont Ave in Los Feliz and the area where Sunset Blvd meets Hollywood Blvd (Sunset Junction) in Silver Lake are good places to start your explorations.

Both neighborhoods are also dappled with great Modernist architecture by Richard Neutra, Rudolph Schindler and others (see Tour III in the Los Angeles Architecture special section). The closest Metro Rail stop is the Vermont/Sunset station on the Red Line.

Barnsdall Art Park

Occupying an olive-shrouded hill on Vermont Ave between Hollywood and Sunset Blvds (enter from Hollywood Blvd), Barnsdall Art Park is a city-owned cultural and arts center offering low-cost art classes to children and adults. The center's art galleries showcase contemporary works by students, faculty and community artists from throughout Southern California. The park was closed for restoration at the time of writing but should be reopened by 2002. The park's main attraction, though, the 1921 **Hollyhock House**, is getting a thorough $10-million face-lift and will be closed until least 2003.

This was Frank Lloyd Wright's first LA project, commissioned by oil heiress Aline Barnsdall (1882–1946), a progressive and philanthropic single mother dedicated to arts and theater as well as the controversial topics of birth control and socialism. It was Wright's first attempt at integrating architecture with the Southern California environment, a style he later labeled California Romanza. His dramatic interpretation extends the interior living space by juxtaposing each room with an equivalent outdoor space. He used skylit walkways, glass doors, porches and colonnades to establish relationships between the two. Other elements are a central courtyard with a small amphitheater and rooftop terraces with great views of the Hollywood Hills and the city. Varying ceiling and floor levels serve as transitional elements between rooms. Stylized renditions of the hollyhock, Aline's favorite flower, are incorporated throughout.

KCET Studios

LA's public TV studio, KCET *(☎ 323-953-5289, 4401 Sunset Blvd)* is well-known nationally for its – sometimes award-winning – shows including *Life & Times Tonight* and *California Gold*. It is headquartered in the longest continuously producing movie lot in Hollywood; the first film was shot in 1912. The brick complex was originally the home of Monogram Pictures, a small studio that made mostly low-budget B movies, including *Queen of Outer Space* starring Zsa Zsa Gabor.

As a public service, KCET offers free tours of the studio, usually on Friday. The one-hour tour takes in the historic sound stages, a modern TV control room, current sets and a director's booth. There's nothing glamorous about this tour and things can get a bit technical at times, but it is a great way to gain genuine insight into movie and TV production. Cameras are allowed. Call ahead for reservations.

Hollywood

CENTRAL HOLLYWOOD (MAP 9)

Hollywood is back – at least if the dreams of developers and city boosters come true. For many decades, glamour was banished from this fabled part of Los Angeles. Most of the studios had moved on to greener and bigger pastures in places like Culver City, Burbank and Studio City. Hollywood's streets were left to decay into grit and grime, peopled by teenage runaways, junkies and other unsavory characters. A major tourist attraction despite such drawbacks, the district has seen numerous half-hearted attempts at revitalization. Finally, though, a number of factors might have coalesced to write a new chapter in the history of the former dream factory.

Some of the historic movie palaces – the El Capitan and the Egyptian – have already been restored and are enjoying great popularity. Nearby, the Pantages Theater is undergoing a renaissance with the staging of *The Lion King* musical. And the opening of the Metro Rail Red Line station has made getting here from Downtown or Universal City a matter of minutes. But the revival's pièce de résistance is Hollywood & Highland, the vast glitzy entertainment center taking shape next to Mann's Chinese Theater. The complex's Kodak Theater will host the Academy Awards. While it will most certainly bring in visitors by the droves, the complex is also meant to lure locals to its restaurants, stores and nightclubs, a major gamble given the sanitized playground being created. Whether the 'new Hollywood' will be just a giant tourist trap or a dynamic urban haven remains to be seen. But if all goes according to plan, Hollywood's tawdry recent past will come to an end worthy of a Gable and DeHavilland kiss.

Hollywood is connected to Downtown LA and the San Fernando Valley via the Metro Rail Red Line. The stop at Hollywood Blvd and Highland Ave puts you into the thick of things. Local DASH-Hollywood buses make a loop from Vermont Ave via Franklin Ave to Hollywood Blvd and Highland Ave, then back east via Fountain Ave.

Historic Hollywood Walking Tour
This tour takes in major sights – new and old – along historic Hollywood Blvd. It starts at the shiny silver sculpture at the intersection with La Brea Ave and ends at fabled Hollywood & Vine, about 1½ miles farther east. Also look out for the historic sign markers posted along Hollywood Blvd for information supplementing this tour.

Hollywood Walk of Fame Big Bird, Bob Hope, Marilyn Monroe and Sting are just a few of the celebrities being sought out, admired, photographed – and stepped on – day after day. Conceived by businessman Harry Sugarman as a tribute to the artists and entertainers that put Hollywood on the map, the Walk of Fame has for decades faithfully fulfilled its other purpose – luring tourists to Tinseltown. Joanne Woodward was the first to be honored in 1960. Now there are some 2000 marble-and-bronze stars on Hollywood Blvd between La Brea Ave and Gower St and along Vine St between Yucca St and Sunset Blvd. Each star bears the celebrity's name and an emblem identifying his or her artistic field – movies, TV, radio, recording or live theater.

If you can't find your favorite star along the walk consider buying one as a gift. The stars are fee-based rather than merit-based and can be bought through the Hollywood Chamber of Commerce. Studios sometimes spring for stars, but, in many cases, it's the fan clubs that get the ball rolling. They're also usually the ones who keep the star clean and shiny. The local fan club of crooner Julio Iglesias meets on a fixed date every month toting Ajax, bronze cleaner, sponges and whatnot; as they clean and polish, they exchange the latest gossip about their man.

Induction ceremonies are held once or twice a month. Call the Hollywood Chamber of Commerce at ☎ 323-489-8311 for the schedule.

Hollywood Entertainment Museum Just a few stars west of Mann's Chinese Theater, state-of-the-art technology unravels the history and mystery of moviemaking at the Hollywood Entertainment Museum (☎ 323-465-7900, 7021 Hollywood Blvd; admission adults $7.50, seniors & students $4.50, children 5-12 $4; open 11am-6pm daily Memorial Day to Labor Day; closed Wed the rest of year).

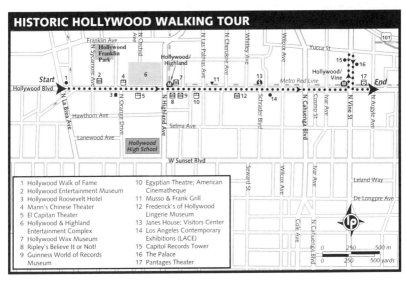

Visits start in the central rotunda lorded over by the Goddess of Entertainment, looking suspiciously like Oscar's cousin. This is the only section that may be explored without a guide, so take your time to admire the gigantic model of '30s Hollywood incorporated into the elevated stage. Also here are costumes and selections from the Max Factor Collection, including an ominous metal device called a 'beauty calibrator,' used by make-up artists to determine imperfections in an actress' face. While here, you'll also experience a multi-screen video presentation chronicling the history of Hollywood.

A guide then takes you on the Studio Tour, which introduces various phases of the filmmaking process, including a prop room, a Foley room (where sound effects are created), the wardrobe department and an art director's office. You'll see original items from movies including *Forrest Gump, The Addams Family* and *Star Trek*, but the real tour highlight (and not just for Trekkies) is when you'll be beamed up to the USS *Enterprise* via the Transporter Room. Sit in the captain's chair or zero in on *Star Trek* trivia on interactive screens. More down-to-earth is the place where everybody knows your name – the original set of *Cheers* – next door. Also popular is the interactive Kodak Spotlight Theatre where you learn about the creation of special effects.

Hollywood Roosevelt Hotel Elegant interior architecture and rich history rendezvous in the distinguished Hollywood Roosevelt Hotel (☎ 323-466-7000, 7000 Hollywood Blvd). Even more interesting is the excellent historical exhibit about Hollywood's bygone heyday on the hotel's mezzanine level. The exhibit is free and always open.

Several of the old photographs on display reveal moments in the history of the hotel itself, which began attracting luminaries shortly after its 1927 opening. In 1929, Douglas Fairbanks hosted the first Academy Awards ceremony here, doling out what was then called the Merit Awards

to Janet Gaynor (best actress) and Emil Jannings (best actor).

In the '30s, the hotel's Cineclub jazz lounge saw Errol Flynn, F Scott Fitzgerald and Salvador Dalí – the latter in town to make movie sets – quenching their thirst. (The Cineclub is now called Cinegrill, which is covered in more detail in the Entertainment chapter.)

For those who believe in such things, the hotel cleverly hones a reputation of being haunted. There are tall tales of calls made from a room without a phone, reflections of Marilyn Monroe in a mirror and Montgomery Clift's ghost slamming doors. More earthly are the Roosevelt's impressive lobby with its hand-painted ceiling and wrought-iron grill work, and the pool with its faded mural by David Hockney. (For more information, see the Places to Stay chapter.)

Mann's Chinese Theater In 1927 movie mogul Sid Grauman conceived what would become the most famous of Hollywood movie palaces, Mann's Chinese Theater (☎ 323-464-8111, 6925 Hollywood Blvd). To see the exotic interior you have to buy a ticket for the first-run films still being shown here. However, access to the famous forecourt, where more than 150 screen legends have left their mark, is free. Leaving one's foot or handprints in wet cement has been a special honor since Douglas Fairbanks, Mary Pickford (who co-owned the theater) and Norma Talmadge started the tradition, though some celebrities have chosen to immortalize other body parts such as their nose (Jimmy Durante) and legs (Betty Grable). Today the forecourt is graced with the imprints of some 180 stars. Some recent ones are Tom Hanks (1998), Denzel Washington (1998), Richard Gere (1999) and Sean Connery (1999).

Hollywood & Highland Developers and politicians are betting the bank that this new mega-entertainment complex will be the cornerstone of the 'Hollywood Renaissance.' The $567-million project, named for its location, is planned as an ambitious

Ghost Expeditions: If the Spirit Moves You...

There was a chill in the air and a fearful sense of foreboding as the ancient gate creaked open and…all right, we're exaggerating. It was a usual balmy night in Hollywood – but it was midnight and the gate at the entrance to the Vogue Theater did creak a little as we met with kindred and curious souls and our guides to the beyond. We were in search of the paranormal, a term that has enormous irony when applied to LA. The dead – like nearly everyone else in LA – are apparently uneasy.

We were entering the Vogue as guests of the International Society for Paranormal Research (ISPR) to hunt up the spooks in this 'very active' site. ISPR's director, Dr Larry Montz, and his psychic sidekick, Daena Smoller, would lead us into realms where the rational never go. We were there to plumb the psychic depths and find if we were adepts ourselves or just hopeless realists.

Through musty tunnels beneath the theater's stage, in the claustrophobic room where a projectionist had died – and periodically reappears – we held onto dowsing rods and nosed around for psychic currents in the rooms, hoping for the ultimate reward: a sighting. Our rods were emphatically still, but those of others whirled like the blades of a helicopter. One woman swooned, saying, 'She's blowing on the back of my neck' – an allusion to one of the children who died in a schoolhouse fire on this very spot at the turn of the 20th century. We were clearly missing something. Not a screech, not an unexplained stench, not so much as a raised hair on the back of the neck. But weird, anyway.

About 3am, having this book to write and feeling cross-eyed with fatigue, we left our wide-eyed cohorts sniffing for the eternal. We headed home with apologies to these very nice people who had at least made our initial ghost hunt fun. And then…on the freeway our car went berserk: strange rattlings, the loss of gears, and we were suddenly filled with inexplicable feelings of dread. The next day we got word that our repairs would only amount to a cheap 28¢ part. What was it that Daena had told us? Ah, yes, 'The children's spirits in this theater like to play little tricks. And they do like to travel around, just like us.' Nah, it couldn't be.

ISPR Ghost Expeditions take place regularly at several LA haunts. Call them at ☎ 323-644-8866 or check their Web site at www.hauntings.com. The cost is $45 per person.

---

playground of stores, restaurants, nightclubs, a small TV studio, a luxury hotel and a 40,000-sq-ft Grand Ballroom catered by Wolfgang Puck. The structure that is getting the most attention, though, is the 180,000-sq-foot auditorium that will host the Academy Awards for 20 years starting in 2002. The opening of the grand facility will quite literally be a 'Kodak moment,' for that company has bought naming rights to the theater and allegedly paid $75 million for the privilege. It will also host other mega-entertainment events and shows year-round. Visually the most unusual element will be the Babylon Court, which, if the renderings are to be believed, will resemble an epic Cecil B DeMille movie set; anchoring the circular plaza will be a huge, freestanding triumphal arch decorated with neo-Babylonian motifs and lorded over by a pompous pachyderm perched on a lofty pedestal. Construction was moving speedily ahead at the time of writing and may well be finished by the time you're reading this.

El Capitan Theater Across the street, El Capitan (☎ *323-467-7674, 6838 Hollywood Blvd*) has an impressively ornate Spanish Colonial facade and a flamboyant East Indian–inspired interior. Built for live performances in 1926, it was converted to a movie house in the 1940s when it premiered *Citizen Kane*. Now owned by Disney, the newly restored theater has state-of-the-art sound and an awesome glitter curtain. It now shows first-run films, including Disney musicals, which are sometimes preceded by short live shows.

Ripley's Believe It or Not! The rooftop replica of a T-rex beckons passers-by to examine the 300 exhibits of the weird and wild at Ripley's Believe It or Not! (*☎ 323-466-6335, 6780 Hollywood Blvd; admission adults $9.95, seniors & students $8.95, children 5-12 $6.95; open 10am-11pm daily).* An adventurer, reporter and collector, Robert Ripley traveled the world in search of curiosities, introducing them through his syndicated newspaper cartoons after 1918. Inside this amusing, if sensationalist, 'odditorium' are images of the giraffe-necked African woman, a two-headed goat, a six-legged cow and a man with a 4-foot crowbar stuck through his head. Also on display is a shrunken human head and a sculpture of Marilyn Monroe made from 264,000 discarded $1 bills.

Guinness World of Records Museum Practically next door is the gaudy entrance to the Guinness World of Records Museum (*☎ 323-462-8860, 6764 Hollywood Blvd; admission adults $10.95, seniors $8.50, children 6-12 $6.95; open 10am-midnight Sun-Thur, 10am-2am Fri & Sat).* This homage to the extreme is housed in a former movie theater. While some of the exhibits reflect general knowledge (the tallest mountain, biggest planet), others illustrate bizarre records, such as the woman with the most tattoos and the most time spent asleep on a tight rope (185 days). Combination tickets with the Hollywood Wax Museum are $15.95/ 12.95/8.95 for adults/seniors/children.

Hollywood Wax Museum No celebrities around to snare your stare? Don't fret: fantasy can be reality at the Hollywood Wax Museum (*☎ 323-462-5991, 6767 Hollywood Blvd; admission adults $10.95, seniors $8.50, children 6-12 $6.95; open 10am-midnight Sun-Thur, 10am-1am Fri & Sat).* The wax figures of 220 celebrities are frozen like deer

in the headlights for your amusement. You'll see passable waxen images of showbiz greats such as Liz Taylor, Tom Cruise and (ooh… look!) Leonardo DiCaprio. American presidents, prominent athletes and even religious figures are also here. The icky chamber of horrors is good fun, as is the marvelously ironic monster gallery inhabited by Hannibal Lecter, King Kong and…Mike Tyson! If you feel you must visit both this and the Guinness Museum, you can save with a combination ticket costing $15.95/12.95/8.95.

Egyptian Theatre Site of the first Hollywood premiere *(Robin Hood* in 1922), the 1100-seat Egyptian Theatre (*☎ 323-466-3456, 6712 Hollywood Blvd)* is Hollywood's oldest cinema. It was built in 1922 in an exotic design inspired by the discovery of King Tut's tomb that same year and features a splendid sunburst ceiling, hieroglyphs and sphinx heads. In its heyday, it had live caged monkeys and usherettes clad in Cleopatra-style garb.

After a comprehensive restoration in the late 1990s, the Egyptian became the permanent home of the American Cinematheque, a nonprofit film organization dedicated to introducing the public to non-mainstream, specialty films. It also shows *Forever Hollywood,* a one-hour visitor-oriented documentary about the history of Hollywood narrated by Sharon Stone. (For movie information, see the Entertainment chapter.)

Musso & Frank Grill On the next block is the Musso & Frank Grill (*☎ 323-467-7788, 6667 Hollywood Blvd),* a survivor and legend. The oldest restaurant in Hollywood (since 1919), it counted Hollywood darlings Mary Pickford and Douglas Fairbanks among its first guests. Literary lions such as William Faulkner and F Scott Fitzgerald followed in the '40s as members of the Algonquin Round Table West, and the restaurant is still a favorite Industry hangout today. Decor and menu have changed little since those days of yore (see the Places to Eat chapter).

Frederick's of Hollywood Lingerie Museum You'll have to navigate through a denser maze of bras, negligees, panties and garter belts than you'd find at a '60s Hollywood pool party to get to Frederick's Lingerie Museum and Celebrity Lingerie Hall of Fame (☎ 323-466-8506, 6608 Hollywood Blvd; admission free; open 10am-6pm Mon-Sat, noon-5pm Sun). In a small back room, you can admire such 'flimsies' as a tasseled bustier worn by Madonna, Joan Crawford's billowy underskirt and boxers once sported by Robert Redford. You will also get a not-so-serious look at the evolving shape of bra fashions.

Janes House The Janes House (6541 Hollywood Blvd), set back off the street at the end of a courtyard, is a rare remnant of the mansions that once lined Hollywood Blvd – then known as Prospect Ave – in the early part of the 20th century. Built in 1903 in turreted Queen Anne style, it was a longtime family-run school for Industry children and now houses the Hollywood Visitor Information Center.

LA Contemporary Exhibitions This artist-run shopfront gallery has absolutely nothing to do with Frederick's Lingerie, although its acronym (LACE) might suggest otherwise (☎ 323-957-1777, 6522 Hollywood Blvd; $3 suggested donation; open 10am-6pm Tues-Thur, noon-6pm Sat & Sun). The gallery provides artists on the cutting edge of painting, sculpture, video, photography, music and performance art a place to showcase their multifaceted work. Primarily local and regional artists present largely conceptual and often site-specific works. Performance art and film screenings supplement the exhibit schedule, which changes approximately every two months.

Museum of Death Check your stomach at the door, or at least get ready for it making some serious flips, while perusing the displays at this den of the deceased (☎ 323-466-8011, 6340 Hollywood Blvd, enter from Ivar Ave; admission $7; open noon-10pm Sun-Thur, till midnight Fri & Sat). This museum is the brainchild of a woman who – speaking of brain – scooped up (from the sidewalk) the brain of a man who had leapt to his death from a balcony; her husband is a one-time collector of animal skeletons. The couple moved from San Diego – where they operated a precursor to the current museum in a former mortuary – in 1999 and opened the Hollywood version a year later. Their macabre compilation includes the whole gamut of death-related artifacts, memorabilia, photographs and even art. You'll be treated to the bloody T-shirt of a man executed in Florida's electric chair, and photos of a murdered Sharon Tate and John F Kennedy. Antique morticians' equipment and stuffed celebrity pets, including Liberace's cat Candy also await. Original art work by the mass murderer Charles Manson and serial killer John Wayne Gacy decorate one of the rooms. It's sick, it's twisted, it's *sooooo* LA.

Hollywood & Vine The days when this fabled intersection bustled with actors and studio execs are long gone but the mystique certainly lives on. Walk a few steps north on Vine St to the famous **Capitol Records Tower** (1750 N Vine St), designed to look like a stack of records. At its foot is an interesting mural of jazz legends painted by the ingeniously named Richard Mural.

Across the street is the 1924 Art Deco **The Palace** (1735 N Vine St), whose current incarnation as a nightclub follows stints as a stage theater, radio studio, variety theater and TV production studio (also see the Entertainment chapter).

A few yards east of the intersection is the **Pantages Theater** (☎ 323-468-1770, 6233 Hollywood Blvd), considered one of America's finest examples of Art Deco architecture. Its vaulted lobby holds statues of a movie director and an aviatrix, presumably in their only Hollywood coupling. Opened in 1930, the Pantages was bought by Howard Hughes in 1949 and hosted the Academy Awards throughout the 1950s and the Emmys in the '70s. A movie palace

PHOTO COLLECTION/LOS ANGELES PUBLIC LIBRARY

LOOKING NORTH FROM HOLLYWOOD MEMORIAL CHAPEL.   SHOWING RESIDENCE OF A. G. BARTLETT.

Before the days of glitterati, Hollywood and Vine hosted orchards and farmland (1907).

until 1977, it was converted into a theater and now often hosts elaborate Broadway musicals and concerts (also see the Entertainment chapter). The walking tour concludes here.

Cinerama Dome

Looking like half of a giant golf ball, the Cinerama Dome (☎ 323-466-3401, 6360 Sunset Blvd) opened in 1963, and its design as a geodesic dome was a complete novelty and technological masterpiece. It was created to screen 'Cinerama' movies, an early wide-screen format that required three 35mm projectors. The building itself may be round, but the auditorium is not, although the screen itself is gently curved.

In 2000, the theater closed to be renovated and outfitted with state-of-the-art technology. It will be the centerpiece of a three-story mall that will also feature an additional 15-screen movieplex, restaurants, stores, a health club and offices. The complex is set to open in 2002.

Hollywood Athletic Club

Built in 1923 in Spanish-Mediterranean style, this beautiful building (6525 Sunset Blvd) once boasted a pool, gym, fitness room and star-studded (no pun intended) male-only membership. Johnny Weissmuller and Buster Crabbe, both famous for playing Tarzan, as well as Rudolph Valentino, John Wayne and other hunks, were among those who swam laps and pumped iron here. The first Emmy broadcast came from here in 1949 (with TV in its infancy, there weren't that many awards).

Crossroads of the World

This cluster of buildings (6671 Sunset Blvd) was designed as one of Los Angeles' earliest shopping malls in 1936 by Robert Derrah, a noted Streamline Moderne architect who also designed the Coca-Cola Bottling Plant on Central Ave in Downtown. Derrah once again applied a nautical theme here, building the central structure in ship shape, its bow topped by a tower, which is crowned by a rotating globe. European-style cottages, many in mock-Tudor, flank this structure and now contain offices.

Hollywood High School

Hollywood High School (1521 N Highland Ave) has an impressive roster of alumni, but because of changing demographics it's no longer a celluloid breeding farm. This Art Deco high-school building still looks impressive, especially the science building with its bas-relief by Bartolo Mako above the entrance.

Famous Alumni

Want to find out where your favorite celeb studied algebra and French? Visit any of the following schools; all are public, except Immaculate Heart and Harvard-Westlake:

Beverly Hills High
241 S Moreno Dr (Map 11)
Corbin Bernsen, Albert Brooks, Nicolas Cage, Richard Chamberlain, Jamie Lee Curtis, Richard Dreyfuss, Carrie Fisher, Lenny Kravitz, Swoosie Kurtz, Rob Reiner, Pauly Shore

Fairfax High
7850 Melrose Ave at Fairfax Ave (Map 10)
Slash of Guns N Roses

Glendale High
1440 E Broadway
John Wayne

Hollywood High
1521 N Highland Ave at Sunset Blvd (Map 9)
Carol Burnett, Linda Evans, Judy Garland, James Garner, Barbara Hershey, John Ritter, Jason Robards, Mickey Rooney, Charlene Tilton

Immaculate Heart High
5515 Franklin Ave (Map 9)
Tyra Banks, Natalie Cole, Mary Tyler Moore

Le Lycée Français
10361 W Pico Blvd (West LA)
Jodie Foster

Los Angeles High
4650 W Olympic Blvd (Mid-City)
Dustin Hoffman

Marshall High
3939 Tracy St (Silver Lake)
Leonardo DiCaprio

Narbonne High
24300 Western Ave
(Harbor City)
Quentin Tarantino

Polytechnic High
1600 Atlantic Ave
(Long Beach)
Snoop Doggy Dog

Redondo Union High
631 Vincent Park
(Redondo Beach)
Demi Moore

Santa Monica High
601 Pico Blvd
Glenn Ford, Rob Lowe, Chris Penn, Sean Penn, Charlie Sheen

University High
11800 Texas Ave (Map 13)
Jeff Bridges, Randy Newman, Nancy Sinatra, Elizabeth Taylor, Tone Loc

Van Nuys High
5535 Cedros Ave
Marilyn Monroe, Robert Redford

Venice High
13000 Venice Blvd
Myrna Loy

Westlake School for Girls
(now Harvard-Westlake)
700 N Faring Rd, Bel Air
Candice Bergen, Debby Boone, Bridget Fonda, Tracy Nelson, Sally Ride, Tori Spelling, Shirley Temple

Hollywood Sign

Visible from just about anywhere, this is Hollywood's, and indeed LA's, most recognizable landmark. Located on Mt Lee in Griffith Park, it was built in 1923 at a cost of $21,000 as an advertising gimmick for a real estate development called Hollywoodland. In 1932 a young actress named Peggy, who was despondent over her nonexistent career, jumped to her death from the letter H. Until 1939 a caretaker, living behind an L, maintained the sign. In 1945, the land was deeded to the city, which – recognizing the sign's promotional value – merely chopped off the last four letters. Each letter is 50 feet tall and made of sheet metal. The sign has always been a favorite with pranksters: The sign read 'Ollywood' during the Iran-Contra hearings and dope-heads once turned it into 'Hollyweed.' To prevent people from following Peggy's or the pranksters' examples, the city has made it illegal to hike to the sign. For good views of it, head to the Griffith Park Observatory or to the top of Beachwood Canyon Dr.

Paramount Studios

The only movie studio still in Hollywood proper is Paramount Studios (☎ 323-956-1777, 5555 Melrose Ave; tour price $15; tours hourly, 9am-2pm daily). Its frilly wrought-iron gate has made movie history itself, notably in *Sunset Boulevard* (1950) when an aging diva (Gloria Swanson) drove onto the lot believing her career was about to be revived. The gate is at the corner of Bronson Ave and Marathon St and is not to be confused with the main gate on Melrose Ave. Founded in 1914, Paramount is the home of the original *Star Trek* TV series and the current *Star Trek: Voyager*. Its roster of blockbuster movies ranges from the 1921 *The Sheik* with Rudolph Valentino to the *Indiana Jones* trilogy and *Forrest Gump*.

Guided two-hour walking tours give you some insight into the inner workings of a major studio; if you're lucky, you may get to see a working set, though this is not guaranteed. To buy tickets, go to the gate at 860 N Gower St and ask for the visitor center. Reservations are not necessary; cameras are not allowed and neither are children under 10.

Hollywood Forever Cemetery

Just north of Paramount, the famous 'immortals' crowd into this equally famous cemetery (☎ 323-469-1181, 6000 Santa Monica Blvd; grounds usually open 7am-6pm, mausoleum open 8am-5:30pm). More than 300 Hollywood legends have been interred here since 1899, including Rudolph Valentino, Peter Lorre and Peter Finch (all in the Cathedral Mausoleum). Around the pond, you'll find the graves of Tyrone Power, who died during a dueling scene on a set in Madrid, and Jayne Mansfield, who

lost her head – literally – in a car accident. Cecil B DeMille resides here in a white sarcophagus alongside his wife. John Huston, whose last film was an adaptation of James Joyce's *The Dead*, now rests here after a life of lust and genius. West of the Cathedral Mausoleum is a reflecting pool with the tomb of Douglas Fairbanks. Farther east is the Jewish cemetery – Beth Olam – where notorious gangster Bugsy Siegel is buried in the southwest corner.

The cemetery almost closed in the late 1990s after years of neglect, but in 1998, Forever Enterprises purchased and cleaned it up. The company has written a new chapter in the marketing of death by selling 'video biographies' of the deceased; these videos can be viewed in the Forever Theater and at three kiosks.

A detailed map ($5) to the stars' graves is available in the flower shop on the right past the entrance. Shop hours vary but are shorter than grounds' hours.

Rock Walk of Fame

If you want to see the hands of such legends as BB King, ZZ Top, Steeley Dan, the Doobie Brothers and dozens more immortalized in concrete, pay a visit to the Guitar Center (☎ 323-874-1060, 7425 Sunset Blvd). While here, check out the amazing store, a veritable musician's mecca: it has a wall-to-wall, floor-to-ceiling selection of any guitar imaginable – acoustic, electric, bass, plastic. The vintage collection in the basement, where prized treasures like Martin guitars cost up to $10,000, is worth a look. Upstairs are the drum and percussion departments. The staff is super-friendly, even if all you want to do is browse.

HOLLYWOOD HILLS (MAP 9)

Two to three generations ago, stars such as Ethel Barrymore and Gloria Swanson made their homes along the rugged ridges above Hollywood and in canyons such as Laurel, Nichols, Runyon and Beachwood. More recently, Lou Diamond Phillips and Rebecca de Mornay have made their homes here. More stars live in Whitley Heights, a series of Italian villa-style houses built into the hillside above Franklin and Highland Aves by architect Hobart J Whitley.

Better known is the **Freeman House** (☎ 323-851-0671 or ☎ 213-740-2723, 1962 Glencoe Way at Hillcrest Rd), designed by Frank Lloyd Wright in 1924. It's another of Wright's experimental homes using textile-block construction technology that required laying 12,000 handmade concrete tiles. There's a distinct Mayan influence as well as such modernist design elements as corner-to-corner glass windows. The building, which is owned by USC, experienced considerable structural damage in the 1994 Northridge earthquake and is currently under restoration.

Each summer, these homes echo with some of the world's finest live music wafting upwards from the **Hollywood Bowl** (☎ 323-850-2000, 2301 Highland Ave), an outdoor amphitheater that looks like a giant beehive in aerial photographs. It's the summer home of the LA Philharmonic Orchestra (see the Entertainment chapter). The Bowl opened in 1916 with a performance of *Julius Caesar* and a who's who cast including Douglas Fairbanks and Tyrone Power. The first concerts were held in 1922, with the orchestra seated on an old barn door. Lloyd Wright, Frank's son, built the first concert shell two years later, but it has always been riddled with problems and was modified several times, the last time by Frank Gehry in 1982. In 2000, it was decided to demolish the historic shell and replace it with a larger one with superior acoustics. Preservationists have opposed this idea and filed a lawsuit.

History and special exhibits can be found on the grounds of the Hollywood Bowl in the **Hollywood Bowl Museum** (☎ 323-850-2058, 2301 N Highland Ave; admission free; open 10am-8:30pm Tues-Sat, call for Sun hours July 1-Sep 16; 10am-4:30pm Tues-Sat rest of year).

Nearby stands one of the Industry's most important structures: **the site of Hollywood's first feature**, the original horse barn used by pioneering movie director Cecil B DeMille's to shoot *The Squaw Man*. It was originally located at Selma and Vine St, moved to the Paramount Studios lot in 1927

and arrived at its present spot in 1985. After suffering through a fire in 1996, it has been fully restored and presently houses the **Hollywood Studio Museum** (☎ 323-874-2276, 2100 N Highland Ave; admission $2; open 11am-3:45pm Sat & Sun). Inside are exhibits on early filmmaking, including costumes, projectors and cameras as well as a replica of DeMille's office.

Nearby is the **John Anson Ford Theater** (☎ 323-466-1767, 2580 Cahuenga Blvd). Built in the 1930s, the Ford has a hillside backdrop of palms and cypress that gives it a particularly intimate feeling (also see the boxed text 'Outdoor Venues' in the Entertainment chapter).

MELROSE AVENUE (MAP 10)

Melrose Ave is LA's former and once-again center of cool. Countless boutiques, many of the wacky and unique variety, flank both sides of this thoroughfare. Restaurants, bars and theaters are also part of the eclectic mix, making Melrose one of the funnest places in town to stroll around. The action concentrates in the section between Fairfax and La Brea Aves, but in recent years the area around the Pacific Design Center has also gained in popularity.

Don't even bother showing up before noon on any day, and if you can, come on Saturday for people-watching at its finest. This is when you'll see magenta-and-lime-haired grunge rockers, skinhead motorcyclists, pierced-nosed headbangers and Armani-clad record execs dazzling wide-eyed tourists. Wild shop windows and freakishly colorful facades reflect the diversity of humankind. And it should be noted: for a stark contrast to the trendy frenzy that is Melrose, most residents on the surrounding side streets are Orthodox Jews.

FAIRFAX DISTRICT (MAP 10)

The spine of LA's principal Jewish neighborhood is Fairfax Ave – sometimes affectionately called 'Kosher Canyon' – between Santa Monica and Wilshire Blvds. Though many liberal Jews have scattered to the four winds within the metropolis, Orthodox and Hassidic Jews (who moved here from East

Body Modifications

They say beauty is only skin deep, and many Angelenos can tell you from personal experience that, indeed, this is true. From full-body tattoos to collagen-injected lips, Los Angeles is America's body shop, ready and willing to provide whatever modifications you need to fit into the mold of your choice.

For a relatively subtle form of rebellion, try a piercing at one of LA's many studios. While a nose ring may be enough to shock your grandmother, there are plenty of other piercing options available, including eyebrows, nipples and, of course, genitalia. Piercing studios abound, but sensitive types may want to try Funny Farm (☎ 323-913-7043, 4651 Melbourne Ave in Los Feliz Village; Map 9).

If you feel you can't hit the beach without a little color, ink-wielding artists abound throughout the city – check out some of these tattoo studios for the best in tinted flesh. Celebrity entries include The Purple Panther (☎ 323-882-8165, 7560 W Sunset Blvd), where Dave Navarro of the Red Hot Chili Peppers was inked. Others to look into include Body Electric Tattoo (☎ 323-954-0408, 7274½ Melrose Ave) and Art & Soul Tattoo (☎ 310-202-7203, 2604 S Robertson Blvd). Bert Grimms Tattooing (☎ 562-432-9304, 22 S Chestnut Place, Long Beach), was LA County's first tattoo parlor (purportedly Bonnie Parker was once a client). Of course, if you spot some local color you really like, just ask the proud owner about the artist. Be sure to observe several artists' work, as well as the shop's overall cleanliness and professionalism, before committing to a tattoo. Even if you are on a budget, this is one area where you probably won't want to skimp.

If you get a tattoo and decide you don't like it, there's no reason to worry. Check the Yellow Pages or www.plastic-surgery.net for a referral to the laser surgeon nearest you. They'll clean that ink up in no time – for a price (and a little more pain).

Have you suspected that all those bronzed bods baking in the California sunshine are a little too good to be true? You're right. LA may be the only place on earth where women routinely write off breast enhancements on their taxes as a 'business expense.' You didn't think all those model/actresses were born that way, did you? Body sculpting isn't just for the famous in this town, although being rich certainly helps. Cosmetic surgeons performing liposuction, facial sculpting, buttock lifts and, yes, 'vaginal rejuvenation' are waiting to transform you into the next Miss America – or, more likely, the next Ms May.

Men are not immune to the desire for perfection. LA's plastic surgeons offer a gamut of services to keep you looking like a decathlon athlete even if you never leave the tanning salon. Hair implants are only the beginning; tummy tucks, biceps enhancement and pectoral implants will surely attract the mate of your dreams. And, for the gift that keeps on giving, finish it all off with penile augmentation surgery, to 'gain length and thickness.' It's just the thing to go with your Prince Albert piercing.

It's no use wondering whether public health in Los Angeles would improve if more of the city's doctors were dedicated to healing the sick rather than beautifying the healthy, just as there's little point in musing that LA's art scene would rise to greater heights if more local geniuses painted on canvas instead of skin. Such weighty concerns inspire little pause for thought in the City of Angels. This is a place where the body is not a temple – it's an investment. Enjoy the scenery!

– Paige R Penland

LA's Boyle Heights as new Latino immigrants flooded into that area) maintain a strong presence. There are lots of yeshivas (gender-segregated Orthodox day schools) as well as scores of delis, Kosher butcher shops, antique furniture stores and other small businesses.

For visitors, the main point of interest is the **Farmers' Market** (☎ *323-933-9211, 6333 W 3rd St*). The 150-plus well-established vendors offer an international array of hot and cold foods as well as fresh produce and unique gift items. It's also a great place to grab a freshly baked pastry and a cup of coffee or fruit juice, and spend time people-watching. Just north of the market looms **CBS Television City** (☎ *323-852-2624, 7800 Beverly Blvd*). Offices of network executives dominate the structure, but a handful of game shows are produced here. Just south, toward Olympic Blvd, Fairfax Ave becomes dominated by Ethiopian immigrants, numbering about 35,000. There are several excellent Ethiopian restaurants here (see Places to Eat for restaurant recommendations in this area).

Local buses on the DASH-Fairfax route travel past the Farmer's Market, Fairfax High School, then west along Melrose to the Beverly Center District along La Cienega and Robertson Blvds.

WEST HOLLYWOOD (MAP 10)

West Hollywood is one of LA's hippest areas, teeming with nightclubs, restaurants and elegant hotels, many of them legendary. The Pacific Design Center and galleries add an artsy touch, and trendy shops cater to fashion fanatics from around the world. West Hollywood is also the heart of LA's gay and – to a lesser extent, lesbian – community, which accounts for one third of the area's 36,000 residents. During June's Gay Pride Parade and the outrageous Halloween Carnival, Santa Monica Blvd explodes in a partying frenzy with hundreds of thousands of visitors (of all stripes) joining locals.

West Hollywood was incorporated as a city in 1984 as a result of an unlikely alliance between (mostly Jewish) senior citizens and the gay and lesbian population. Statistically, about one third of the residents are over the age of 55; recent Russian Jewish immigrants account for another 12%.

Pacific Design Center & Around

Designed by Cesar Pelli in 1975, this architectural landmark was nicknamed the 'Blue Whale' for its behemoth dimensions and shiny blue glass facade (☎ *310-657-0800, 8687 Melrose Ave; tours 10am weekdays, call ahead*). In 1985, two more structures, one sheathed in green, the other in maroon glass, were added. The Pacific Design Center (PDC) houses 150 designer showrooms for home and office furniture for the trade only. This means you can walk around and look but you can't buy except during floor sample sales once or twice a year. On the mezzanine level is the West Hollywood Convention & Visitors Bureau (see the Facts for the Visitor chapter for contact information and hours).

Surrounding streets – mainly Melrose Ave and Robertson and Beverly Blvds – are called the **Avenues of Art & Design** because they contain some 300 additional design shops and showrooms. There are another three dozen art galleries in the vicinity, including the **Margo Leavin Gallery** (☎ *310-273-0603, 812 N Robertson Blvd*), unmistakable for Claes Oldenburg's *Knife Slicing Through Wall* sculpture, which makes a statement in its facade.

MOCA Gallery at PDC

The newest addition to the renowned Museum of Contemporary Art is the free-standing MOCA Gallery (☎ *310-657-0800, 8687 Melrose Ave, courtyard of the PDC; admission $3; open 11am-5pm Tues-Sun, to 8pm Thur*). The 3000-sq-foot gallery opened in January 2001 and presents a lively schedule of work by new and established artists from around the world, with a particular emphasis on architecture and design themes. (See Downtown, earlier in this chapter, for coverage of the main branch of the Museum of Contemporary Art.)

Sunset Strip

On Sunset Blvd, wrote Henry Miller in 1945, a visitor will discover:

...eurythmic dancing, ballroom dancing, tap dancing, artistic photography, ordinary photography, lousy photography, electro-fever treatment, internal douche treatment, ultraviolet-ray treatment, elocution lessons, psychic readings, institutes of religion, astrological demonstrations, hands read, feet manicured, elbows massaged, faces lifted... flatulence dissipated, business improved, limousines rented, the future made clear, the war made comprehensible, octane made higher and butane lower...Chinese herbs are very good for you, and without a Coca-Cola life is unthinkable.

More than half a century has passed, and everything – and nothing – has changed on the fabled Strip – Sunset Blvd between Laurel Canyon Blvd and Doheny Dr. The cast of characters is different now, but the street scene is as eclectic as ever, swarming with dancers, photographers, and medical and spiritual charlatans. Sunset is also the billboard capital of the world. These enormous and imaginative vanity boards are one-of-a-kind placards for new movies, album releases, wannabe stars and, recently, anti-smoking campaigns.

Along here, you'll find a 'where's where' of LA rock history: the Whisky A Go Go, The Roxy, Rainbow Bar & Grill, and the former Gazzarri's (now Key Club) are among the legendary haunts where many a career was launched. The Doors, Jimi Hendrix, Bob Marley, Bruce Springsteen and Van Halen are among the many who have performed at these clubs. And if you're into Hollywood history, it was at the Rainbow (then the Villa Nova) where actress Marilyn Monroe and baseball star Joe DiMaggio met on a blind date in 1953.

Porno Walk of Fame

LA's XXX-rated walk of fame is right outside the Tomkat gay movie theater *(7734 Santa Monica Blvd)*, in the heart of West Hollywood's 'Borscht Belt,' where recent Russian immigrants have set up their own slice of home. Even those who wouldn't touch a porn movie with a 10-inch pole probably know the names of such legendary hard-core divas and studs as Linda Lovelace and Harry Reems of *Deep Throat* fame, or Marilyn Chambers from *Behind the Green Door*. Alas, voyeuristic types expecting cement prints of performers' signature body parts may be disappointed: it's PG-rated hands and feet only.

Schindler House

Once the home of Viennese architect Rudolph Schindler (1887–1953), this is a must-see for Modernist-architecture fans *(☎ 323-651-1510, 835 N Kings Rd; admission $5; open 11am-6pm Wed-Sun; docent tours weekends only)*. Schindler was a Frank Lloyd Wright disciple and built the house and studio in 1921. In the '20s and '30s, it was a gathering place for intellectuals, including novelist Theodore Dreiser and composer John Cage. Schindler's house has Craftsman elements, such as large rooms and canopied outdoor sleeping areas, but the architect also provided prototypes for design elements that have since become staples of California architecture. The flat-roofed building is divided into stark studio-like rooms with concrete walls and flooring; one side of each room has a glass front opening onto a courtyard with sliding doors. In 1925, Schindler shared the house with his associate Richard Neutra, also an Austrian architect; Schindler lived there until he died in 1953.

Heavily altered after Schindler's death, the house was meticulously restored to its original state by the Friends of the Schindler House (FOSH). Since 1994 it has been jointly maintained by FOSH and the Austrian Museum of Applied Arts and functions as a think tank for current issues in art and architecture through public lectures, performances, workshops, symposia and exhibitions.

Mid-City

This section describes the area wedged between the Westside (discussed in the next section) and Downtown, north of the I-10 (Santa Monica Fwy) but south of Hollywood. Its principal artery is Wilshire Blvd, which cuts east to west over a total length of 16 miles. Once a path followed by the Yangna Indians between their village in the Elysian Hills and the La Brea Tar Pits, it was extended from the city to the sea in the late 19th century and named for local entrepreneur H Gaylord Wilshire. En route, it passes through a variety of neighborhoods: Koreatown, Hancock Park, Miracle Mile, the Fairfax District, Beverly Hills, Westwood and Santa Monica, terminating at the Pacific Ocean. Metro Rapid bus No 720 runs along its entire length.

MACARTHUR PARK (MAP 5)

Located just over a mile west of Downtown, MacArthur Park (named after General Douglas MacArthur) is a likely location to begin a westbound exploration of the Mid-City district via Wilshire Blvd. The park itself has been a household name since Richard Harris released the ridiculously epic pop song of the same name some 25 years ago. This former swampland is now at the heart of a largely Latino and Asian community. Come in the daytime to see 80 species of trees and shrubs, a dozen city-commissioned avant-garde sculptures and a lake with paddleboats. This could be a nice spot to hang out or have a picnic, but unfortunately the park is a preferred gathering place for the homeless, drug dealers, low-level prostitutes and other people you probably don't want to share your sandwich with. Definitely stay away after dark.

KOREATOWN (MAP 7)

Koreatown is an amorphous area west of Downtown and south of MacArthur Park. Although culturally dominated by Koreans, it is shared by large numbers of immigrants from Mexico and Central and South America. It's a steadily growing neighborhood, both in population and physical borders, with expansion especially creeping north toward Hollywood. Koreatown was especially hard hit during the 1992 riots but has since recovered beautifully and sports spiffed-up sidewalks and fashionable new malls and grocery stores. Architecturally, however, it remains undistinguished, aside

from a few 1920s buildings and churches, some of which are described in detail in Tour IV of the Los Angeles Architecture special section.

Wiltern Theater

This lovely Art Deco theater, inside a fabulous Zigzag Moderne high-rise called the Pellissier Building (1931), gets its name from its location – at the southeast corner of *Wil*shire and Wes*tern* Blvds. It has the same turquoise facade as the Bullocks Wilshire, about a mile east. In 1982, its date with the demolition crew already set, the Wiltern received a last-minute reprieve thanks to efforts by the LA Conservancy, then got a new lease on life from a preservation-minded developer who bought and restored it to original specifications.

Ambassador Hotel

One of LA's earliest and grandest hotels, the Ambassador Hotel *(1922; 3400 Wilshire Blvd)* now sits abandoned in a lot after closing its doors in 1990 (it is now owned by Donald Trump). In its heyday, it could accommodate 3000 guests, many of LA's leading families, movie greats and presidents among them. The most fashionable boogied to big band music at the Coconut Grove nightclub. In 1968, the hotel gained notoriety when Sirhan Sirhan assassinated Robert Kennedy there. (RFK had just won the California Democratic primary election.) No buyer has been found and it looks as if another landmark will be allowed to crumble. Meanwhile, film crews use it for location shots; it can be spotted in the movies *Pretty Woman*, *Forrest Gump* and *Man on the Moon*.

Bullocks Wilshire

When the Bullocks Wilshire department store *(3050 Wilshire Blvd)* opened in 1929, it was an overnight sensation. On opening day, hundreds of thousands of people crammed through the doors of what is often regarded as the first suburban department store in the USA. A prime example of 1920s Art Deco, it features terra-cotta walls clad with copper and a central tower jutting skyward from the five-floor base structure, which gives it the stature and appearance of a public building.

Boasting a large parking lot, Bullocks Wilshire was the first store to cater to customers arriving by car. It became *the* place to shop and cap successful sprees with afternoon tea in the 5th-floor tearoom, a tradition that survived until the store closed in 1992. No longer located in a fashionable location, it was looted in that year's riots, causing its owners to abandon it shortly thereafter. Fortunately, this lovely landmark was rescued by Southwestern University School of Law in 1997. The building now functions as its law library and administrative offices; interior decorations remain intact. Public tours are conducted on occasion. Call ☎ 323-738-6731 for information.

St Sophia Cathedral

Experience the sensation of walking into a giant's treasure chest, spilling over with gold, crystal and jewels as you enter the opulent St Sophia Cathedral *(☎ 323-737-2424, 1324 S Normandie Ave; admission free; open 10am-2pm Tues-Sat)*. The central place of worship for Southern California's Greek Orthodox population, this 850-seat church perfectly illustrates symbiosis of modern technology and ancient architecture. Completed in 1952, its Byzantine-style interior is devoid of supporting pillars, allowing an unobstructed view of the ornately carved, gold-leafed altar screen. Every square inch of the sumptuous interior is swathed with murals depicting Biblical scenes and illuminated by muted light streaming through radiant stained-glass windows depicting the apostles. Crystal chandeliers from the former Czechoslovakia provide additional light sources.

St Sophia was the brainchild of Greek immigrant and movie theater mogul Charles P Skouros. Skouros almost single-handedly raised the money, then hired the best artisans from the theater industry to build his vision. His goal was for the church 'to be so grand and so beautifully

appointed that when our people come to pray, they will be uplifted and feel closer to God.' See for yourself if he succeeded.

MIRACLE MILE DISTRICT (MAP 10)

The stretch of Wilshire Blvd between La Brea and Fairfax Aves earned the epithet 'Miracle Mile' after an entrepreneur, AW Ross, bought land beside the Rancho La Brea Tar Pits in 1920 and turned it into the city's first commercial district outside of Downtown. Many famous retailers opened branches here, but by the '60s other areas, most notably the suburban shopping malls, put an end to the miracle. Today, the strip is also known as 'Museum Row.'

La Brea Tar Pits

Here's clarification on a common misconception: The La Brea Tar Pits are not filled with tar but with asphalt. While tar is a by-product of the destructive distilling of coal or peat, asphalt is the lowest grade of crude oil. This oil formed from marine plankton deposited in an ocean basin between 5 and 25 million years ago and gathered in a subterranean oil field. Over the past 40,000 years, this asphalt seeped to the surface creating the gooey slick filling the pits today. It wasn't until 1906 that scientists realized that the bubbling ooze had acted like flypaper, entrapping animal and plant life during the Pleistocene Ice Age, 40,000 to 10,000 years ago. The large lake pit outside the Page Museum at La Brea Discoveries graphically

Mommy!

illustrates this process with fiberglass models of a mammoth family. Pit excavations have yielded more than 1 million fossilized skeleton parts, including those of long-extinct mammals such as saber-toothed cats, ground sloths, mammoths and mastodons, along with 200 different bird, reptile, insect and plant species.

Excavations still take place – usually from July to mid-September – when visitors may observe the process from the Pit 91 Visitors Observation Station (☎ 323-934-7243; admission free; open 10am-4pm Wed-Sun).

Page Museum at La Brea Discoveries

Tar pit discoveries are exhibited in the adjacent museum (☎ 323-934-7243, www.tarpits .org, 5801 Wilshire Blvd; admission adults $6, seniors & students $3.50, children 5-12 $2; open 9:30am-5pm Mon-Fri, 10am-5pm Sat & Sun, call for summer hours). The museum opened in 1977 and was named after its founder, a local millionaire and philanthropist. At the museum, you can study the fossilized skeletons of long-extinct mammals that once roamed the LA Basin. The fierce saber-toothed cat (incidentally the state fossil of California) was capable of killing much larger animals, including young mammoths, with its giant jaw and dagger-like fangs. Also here are a mastodon and a 15-foot imperial mammoth with tusks of royal proportions. Both are ancestors of today's elephants. The most prevalent animal, the dire wolf, is given its own Wall of Fame – 404 mounted skulls. The least represented species is Homo sapiens; the only human remains found are those of a young woman believed to have been murdered about 9000 years ago.

Nearby is the glass-encased Paleontology Laboratory where scientists in white robes fuss over an astounding assortment of bones. New discoveries are carefully cleaned, identified, cataloged and stored. But the biggest crowds gather for the film starring everyone's favorite reptile: the dinosaurs. This is especially ironic because dinosaurs had long become extinct by the time the La Brea Tar Pits had formed; in any case, dinosaurs avoided LA altogether. But catering to the current dino-craze, the museum continually shows this film explaining the daily life of these giant lizards with surprisingly realistically re-created animals and natural environments.

Los Angeles County Museum of Art

Just west of the tar pits in Hancock Park is the LA County Museum of Art (LACMA; ☎ 323-857-6000, 5905 Wilshire Blvd; admission adults $7, seniors & students $5, children 6-17 $1; open noon-8pm Mon, Tues & Thur, to 9pm Fri, Japanese Pavilion to 5pm; 11am-8pm Sat & Sun). This museum is considered one of the leading art museums in the US (and, indeed, the world) for its size and variety, not to mention the importance of its works. Several buildings surround a central courtyard. Largest is the four-level Ahmanson Building with a staggering permanent collection encompassing art, sculptures and decorative arts from Europe, Asia and America. Highlights of the latter include works by George Bellows, John Singer Sargent, Mary Cassatt, Winslow Homer and Diego Rivera. But the collection is especially strong in European painting and sculpture and is recognized for its collection of Italian Baroque paintings and works from such masters as Rembrandt, Degas and Gauguin.

Also on display are ancient and Islamic art spanning eight millennia, with pieces from Egypt, Greece, Rome, Turkey and Iran. The museum's assemblage of Southeast Asian art encompasses stone and bronze sculpture, painting and decorative arts. Its Far Eastern section has works from as early as the Neolithic period (400 to 1800 BC) as well as items from the Imperial and Song dynasties and a replica of a Ming-period scholar's studio. A highlight of the Pavilion for Japanese Art is the collection of rare Shin'enkan temple paintings.

With more than 150,000 works, LACMA's collection is so huge that only 5% of its treasures can be exhibited at any one time. In addition, the museum mounts several special exhibits annually, drawn from its own collection, and also hosts high-caliber visiting shows (eg, exhibits of Pablo Picasso, Vincent Van Gogh, Diego Rivera). The 500-seat Bing Center auditorium hosts a film series, concerts and the museum store.

If your understanding of art is limited but you're keen to learn, consider renting the audio tour, which explains some 250 works (adult $3, children 5-17 $1).

LA at a Discount

Everybody likes to save a buck, and this may just help you do it.

Hollywood City Pass This is a ticket booklet with coupons good for one-time admission to the following attractions within a 30-day period: Universal Studios Hollywood, American Cinematheque at the Egyptian Theatre, Autry Museum of Western Heritage, Museum of Television & Radio, Hollywood Entertainment Museum and Petersen Automotive Museum. A city tour with Starline Tours of Hollywood is also part of the package. The booklet costs $59 for adults ($39 children 3-11) and is available at any of the participating places and at the Los Angeles Visitors & Convention Bureau offices in Downtown and Hollywood. Participants in the program are subject to change; check www.citypass.net/Hollywood for updated information.

ArtsCard LA This is another way to save, but it requires some advance planning. This pass is issued free by LA's Cultural Affairs Department and provides discounts of 10% to 50% on museum admissions; theater, dance and concert tickets; and even meals. Participating venues include Miceli's restaurant, House of Blues, the Mark Taper Forum and the El Cid Flamenco Show. To sign up for the card, either call ☎ 213-485-2787 or go to www.ci.la.ca.us/cad/artscardla. After a few weeks, you'll receive your card in the mail, along with a complete list of participating venues (also available on the Web site).

In late 1998, LACMA took over the space of a former May Company department store a few blocks west of the original museum at the corner of Fairfax Ave and Wilshire Blvd. Called LACMA West, the annex is used for traveling exhibits (the touring Van Gogh was its inaugural show).

Craft & Folk Art Museum

Since 1973, traditional folk arts and handcrafted objects have been the focus of this museum (☎ 323-937-4230, 5814 Wilshire Blvd; admission adults $3.50, seniors & students $2.50, children under 12 free; open 11am-5pm Wed-Sun). Exhibits reflect the polyglot melting pot that is Southern California and showcase primarily the work of local and regional artists. For nearly three decades, the museum has organized the biennial International Festival of Masks, usually held in October, with a parade, performances and workshops.

Petersen Automotive Museum

LA's love affair with the automobile is celebrated at the Petersen Automotive Museum (☎ 323-930-2277, www.petersen.org, 6060 Wilshire Blvd; admission adults $7, seniors & students $5, children 5-12 $3; open 10am-6pm Tues-Sun). Named after the publisher who provided the seed money for the $40-million facility, it is housed in a former department store that has been imaginatively converted into three floors of exhibition space.

Even non-car buffs will enjoy the ground-floor exhibit, which leads you through a mock streetscape of LA in the '20s and '30s to the megacity of today and exemplifies the tandem evolution of the automobile and the city. Several inventions, such as gas stations, billboards, mini-malls, drive-in restaurants and movie theaters, were spawned as cars became commonplace. Expansive galleries on the 2nd floor are devoted to rotating exhibits, which may feature hot rods, race cars, classic cars, muscle cars, a fleet of Duesenbergs, vehicles used in movies or cars driven by celebrities. The 3rd floor houses a discovery center, which teaches kids science by way of the automobile.

Westside

Ask five people what they consider to be Los Angeles' Westside and you'll get five different answers. Some will say it encompasses everything west of La Cienega Blvd; for others, the border is the I-405 (San Diego Fwy); some even include anything west of Downtown. In this book, however, Westside is defined as the stretch of communities that separate the coastal communities (Santa Monica, Venice, Marina del Rey) from Hollywood. From north to south, Westside consists of Bel Air, Brentwood, Westwood, Beverly Hills, Century City and Culver City.

BEVERLY HILLS (MAP 11)

Everywhere in the world, the mere mention of Beverly Hills conjures an image of fame and wealth. TV and film have done their part in reinforcing this image. In TV's *Beverly Hillbillies*, Buddy Ebsen and Irene Ryan discovered the pleasures and pitfalls of mansion life. Julia Roberts learned the joys of a Rodeo Dr shopping spree and a suite at the Regent Beverly Wilshire in the movie *Pretty Woman*. And Robin Leach's *Lifestyles of the Rich and Famous* probably spent more time in Beverly Hills than in any other location.

The reality of Beverly Hills is not so different from the myth. Stylish and sophisticated, this city-within-a-city is indeed a place where the rich and famous frolic. Rodeo Dr is lined with a veritable Who's Who of haute couture fashion designers. Opulent manors face manicured grounds on palm-shaded avenues winding gently uphill on the north side of Santa Monica Blvd, while south of Wilshire Blvd are the simpler, but no less elegant, bungalows of the merely upper class.

Golden Triangle

An exploration of Beverly Hills should start in the Golden Triangle district, bordered on the south by Wilshire Blvd, on the northwest by Santa Monica Blvd and on the northeast by Cañon Dr. Rodeo Dr cuts through the heart of the Triangle, beginning at the front doors of the Regent Beverly Wilshire Hotel at 9500 Wilshire Blvd. Other streets to walk are Wilshire Blvd, Beverly Dr and Camden Dr.

Rodeo Drive

Connecting Santa Monica and Wilshire Blvds, Rodeo Drive is a 3-block artery of style that to many visitors represents the holy grail of fashion. But unless you were born with a trust fund or feel like flagrantly maxing out your credit cards, you'll find little to do here other than sauntering down one side of the street and up the other. Lined in a glimmering row are the Pradas, Guccis and Armanis of this world, precious bastions of good taste supplied by the fickle minds of designers halfway around the world.

Julia Roberts' humiliating experience in *Pretty Woman* may come to mind when dealing with waifish salesgirls with an attitude that belies their rather humble station in life. Venturing inside one of these emporia will put you close to noble woods and polished marble arranged in Zen-like minimalism. Price tags will be hard to find, the unspoken maxim being 'if you have to ask, you can't afford it.' And instead of seeing a celebrity – who usually arrive after shop hours – you're more likely to be sidling up to T-shirted tourists from Dubuque or Tokyo.

With a few exceptions, the architecture along Rodeo Dr is rather plain. Look out for **Anderton Court** *(1953; 322 Rodeo Dr)*, a zany Zigzag construction by Frank Lloyd Wright (but it's not considered among his best work). The **Rodeo Collection** *(1981; 421 N Rodeo Dr)*, a recessed multilevel shopping mall with a sunken courtyard, is quite nice as well.

Most people gravitate to **Two Rodeo** *(1990; northeast corner of Rodeo Dr and Wilshire Blvd)*, a raised and curved lane lined by even more shops. Whether it truly resembles a Tuscan hillside village, as its creators intended, could be debated, but its design and ambience are rather attractive. Among the many restaurants here is McCormick's & Schmick, which has one of the city's best happy hours (see the boxed text

'LA's Best Happy Hours' in the Entertainment chapter).

Curious Homes

If you venture farther north on Rodeo Dr, beyond Santa Monica Blvd, you'll quickly come across the **O'Neill House** *(1986; 507 Rodeo Dr)*. A freeform Art Nouveau structure in the tradition of Catalan architect Antonio Gaudí, it has art glass windows, mosaic tilework, skylights and stucco finish. For another perspective, go to the alley behind the building.

A few blocks west of Rodeo Dr is the **Spadena House** *(1921; 516 N Walden Dr)*, which is appropriately called the 'Witch's House.' Originally built as a silent-film set and office in Culver City, it was moved here in the 1930s. With its pitched, thatched roof and wildly romantic garden, it does look like something conjured up by the Brothers Grimm.

Beverly Hills Public Buildings

Public buildings are usually grayish behemoths built with little money and even less imagination. Not so in Beverly Hills whose **City Hall** looks as splendid and dignified as a royal palace. A 1932 Spanish Renaissance confection at 455 N Rexford Dr, it consists of a classical base topped by an eight-story tower with a tiled cupola and gilded pinnacle. It is harmoniously integrated into the contemporary **Civic Center** complex, which is also home to the excellent **Beverly Hills Library** *(☎ 310-288-2200, 444 N Rexford Dr)*.

Center for Motion Picture Study

The Academy of Motion Picture Arts and Sciences maintains a remarkable repository of film history, the Center for Motion Picture Study *(☎ 310-247-3020/35, 333 S La Cienega Blvd; admission free; open 10am-6pm every weekday except Wed)*. It's housed in the former Beverly Hills Waterworks, another project instigated by Douglas Fairbanks in the 1920s. The academy salvaged the crumbling Spanish Romanesque facility in the late 1980s, then spent three years and $6 million breathing new life into this beautiful structure. The building now houses a staggering archive of 6 million still photographs, 20,000 books, 60,000 scripts, 1400 periodicals, 17,000 posters, production files on nearly 100,000 movies, and biographic files on more than 80,000 filmmakers. Add to that the private collections of John Huston, Alfred Hitchcock and Mary Pickford.

The heart of this research facility is the noncirculating Margaret Herrick Library, which is open to the public, but with very tight security. Besides signing in and out, you must lock up your belongings and leave a photo ID. The special collections may only be viewed by prior appointment.

The Academy of Motion Picture Arts and Sciences is the professional organization, composed of Industry heavies, that brings you the annual Academy Awards. Born in 1927, the academy, headed by Douglas Fairbanks, originally handed out Merit Awards. According to Hollywood lore, the prized trophy – the Oscar – got its rather mundane name from academy librarian and later executive director, Margaret Herrick, who innocently mentioned its faint resemblance to her uncle Oscar. Current academy board members include Ed Begley Jr and Gregory Peck.

Virginia Robinson Gardens

These spectacular gardens are one of the best kept secrets in Beverly Hills and rewarding any time of year. They are named for Virginia Robinson, wife of department store magnate Harry Robinson; the estate is one of the city's oldest *(1911; ☎ 310-276-5367, 1008 Elden Way; tour price adults/discounts $8/4; guided 90-minute tours Tues-Thur 10am and 1pm, Fri 10 am, by appointment only)*. The lavish Beaux Art mansion is juxtaposed with a pavilion; the two structures are connected by a swimming pool and expansive lawn. The surrounding 6 acres of gardens are a symphony of terraced hillsides, flower-festooned patios, statuettes and fountains, brick stairs and shaded footpaths. Some 1000 plant varieties are harmoniously tossed together in a profusion of color and fragrance. Besides magnolias, roses and kaffir lilies, there are 50 types of camellias, including one named in honor of Virginia. The huge palm garden boasts the largest grove of king palms outside of Australia. The 6000-sq-foot mansion, where the Robinsons once threw lavish parties for the Hollywood elite, has been left in the state of opulence enjoyed by the couple.

Museum of Television & Radio

An enormous archive of original works of two of the 20th century's breakthrough media can be found at the Museum of Television and Radio (☎ 310-786-1000, www.mtr .org, 465 N Beverly Dr; admission adults $6, seniors & students $4, children under 13 $3; open noon-5pm Wed, Fri-Sun, to 9pm Thur). It is housed in a striking building by Getty Center architect Richard Meier, who designed a starkly white environment with soaring open spaces and natural light surging in through glass fronts.

The heart of the museum beats in the Stanley Hubbard Library, a repository of some 100,000 broadcasts spanning 75 years. Come here to view the 1958 pilot of the Zorro TV series, a 1962 Frank Sinatra concert, interviews with James Dean or other rare and historic footage. Start by searching the computerized database, which is sorted by name, show title and subject category, at easy-to-use touchscreen terminals. After you've made your selection, reserve it at the desk before proceeding to a private viewing console, where you gain access by punching in a three-digit number. You can view portions or an entire program, fast-forward to a particular frame, or watch the same scene over and over. Except when people are waiting, there's no limit on your time at the console.

Aside from the library, the museum offers a daily changing schedule of screenings, three galleries, a radio listening room with pre-recorded programs, seminars and the occasional live broadcast. Pick up a schedule at the information desk in the lobby.

Beverly Hills Hotel

Featured on the cover of the Eagles' Hotel California album, the Beverly Hills Hotel (☎ 310-887-2887, 9641 Sunset Blvd) is as revered in LA as the countless Hollywood legends who have cavorted here (and still do). Affectionately known as the 'Pink Palace,' this swank hotel – with its inimitable Polo Lounge and discreet bungalows – has served as unofficial hobnobbing headquarters of the power elite since 1912. In the '20s, it was Chaplin, Swanson and Valentino holding court in this Disney-esque version of the Alamo. By the '40s, the Polo Lounge became the notorious post-chukker hangout of the lords of the polo crowd, including Darryl F Zanuck, Spencer Tracy and Will Rogers. Marlene Dietrich had her very own 7-by-8-foot bed installed in Bungalow 11, and Howard Hughes, the billionaire recluse, went progressively off his nut during 30 years of delusional semi-residence here.

By the time the '50s rolled around, genuine royalty began rubbing shoulders with such Hollywood aristocracy as Frank Sinatra's Rat Pack, who boozed and brawled away long nights. Elizabeth Taylor bedded six of her eight husbands here in various bungalows. While filming Let's Make Love, Yves Montand and Marilyn Monroe were probably doing just that; Marilyn is also reported to have 'bungalowed' both JFK and RFK here as well.

By the '70s, the Pink Palace had lost its luster and the stars went elsewhere to frolic. For years, the hotel was tossed back and forth among financial titans, only to become – on its 75th birthday – another vessel in the fleet of its current owner, the Sultan of Brunei. Having spent an alleged $176 million to acquire it, the Sultan sank another $100 million into its restoration. When she reopened in 1995, the grand dame had regained her blush, lurid wink and ability to seduce the power players. Scripts are once again read, and deals cut, by the pool where young starlets stretch languidly in the hopes of 'discovery.' (Also see the Places to Stay chapter.)

Finally an infamous postscript: The public bathroom in Will Rogers Memorial Park on Sunset across from the hotel was where ex-Wham-mie George Michael was booked for playing with his 'Mr Pudgey' in front of an undercover police officer.

Tour of the Stars' Homes

It's on the winding, tree-lined streets that climb the Santa Monica Mountain foothills where you'll find the lavish estates of Beverly Hills' famous denizens, from Douglas Fairbanks to Warren Beatty. Many of the sprawling Spanish haciendas, stately Tudor mansions and French Provençal farmhouses were and are home to celebrities that have shaped Hollywood history. This is where they live, frolic – and die. The area is most comfortably explored on a bus tour. (See Organized Tours in the Getting Around chapter for more information.)

Charlie Chaplin and his Breakaway House

If you have a car, you can save some money by doing your own touring. Maps to the stars' homes are hawked for a few dollars in souvenir shops and by street vendors positioned along Sunset and Santa Monica Blvds. Addresses of living stars change with some frequency, though, and these maps may not always be up to date.

The following is a tour of the glamorous, the notorious, the frivolous and the ostentatious. A caveat: Seeing an actual star is highly unlikely. In fact, you may not even see the actual homes thanks to huge privacy walls, dense canopies of trees and security patrols. Often, wealth and fame are measured in security features, which can include robotic cameras, armed guards and fierce dogs. In general, stars don't like tourists pulling up to their mansions, but legally there's little they can do as long as you remain on public grounds. Finally, it goes without saying (but here it is anyway) that under no circumstances should you disturb the residents. This tour takes about two to 2½ hours.

Start at the intersection of Sunset Blvd and Benedict Canyon, both of them rich turf for the starstruck. Head north on the canyon road, turn right onto Summit Dr and proceed to the top. It was **Mary Pickford** and **Douglas Fairbanks** who first brought glamour to Beverly Hills when they expanded Fairbanks' hunting lodge into a hilltop home, known as Pickfair, 1143 Summit Dr. The house itself is gone, demolished by later owner Pia Zadora, but the

generous grounds are still visible through the wrought-iron gates, which sport the name 'Pickfair.' Just below, at 1085 Summit Dr (corner of Cove), is the Spanish-style former home of **Charlie Chaplin**, which earned the nickname 'Breakaway House' because things were always falling apart. Rumor has it that a chintzy Chaplin hired studio carpenters to build it in their spare time. Only the driveway is visible.

Head back downhill, continue north on Benedict Canyon, then turn left on Green Acres Dr, which culminates outside the extraordinary 48,000-sq-foot estate built by comedian **Harold Lloyd** at 1740 Green Acres Dr. Lloyd lived here for 40 years until his death in 1971, but almost nothing of the lavish mansion with its 44 rooms and 26 bathrooms is visible from the street (nor can you see the grounds' waterfall, Olympic-size pool and nine-hole golf course).

Backtrack to Benedict Canyon, continue north to Cielo Dr and turn left, which takes you into a narrow side canyon. The dark and spooky driveway at 10048 Cielo Dr leads to the house where followers of Charles Manson butchered actress **Sharon Tate** (highly pregnant with a child from husband Roman Polanski) and four other victims on August 9, 1969. The complex was demolished in 1994 and replaced by another mansion.

Just off Cielo Dr is Bella Dr, a steep unkempt road leading up to Falcon Lair, the fortress-like former residence of **Rudolph Valentino**. Its current owners managed to have the access road declared private, making it off-limits to the public. For glimpses of the estate look up as you drive west on Cielo Dr. Head back down, then turn left to get to 1579 Benedict Canyon (at Philbert Dr), the modest cottage where 1950s 'Superman' **George Reeves** died on June 16, 1959. The death was officially ruled a suicide, but the fact that the smoking gun didn't have any fingerprints and the walls were riddled with other bullet holes made this case one of Hollywood's great unsolved mysteries.

Return south on Benedict Canyon, turn right on Lexington Rd, then right on Whittier Dr and left on Monovale Dr. The house at 144 Monovale Dr was the LA residence of **Elvis Presley** from 1967 to 1975; you can glimpse the house, tennis court and gardens. Farther on, Monovale Dr merges with Carolwood Dr where, at 245 Carolwood Dr, stands the rather plain former home once occupied by **Burt Reynolds** and **Loni Anderson**, and before that by Beatle **George Harrison**. While here check out the partly visible modern sculpture that adorns the front lawns of the adjacent homes at 265 and 275 Carolwood Dr. Turn around, then follow Carolwood Dr south to Sunset Blvd.

As you turn right, the pink confection immediately in front you, at 10100 Sunset, is the former home of bombshell **Jayne Mansfield**. It was nicknamed the 'Pink Palace' (not to be confused with the Beverly Hills Hotel) because she had everything, down to the sinks, fireplace and swimming pool, painted pink and in the shape of a heart. Rumor has it that the crack in the heart carved into the driveway cement happened at the exact moment she was decapitated in a car accident at age 34 in 1967. The villa's current owner is Engelbert Humperdinck. The impressive mansion behind the Pink Palace is called **Owlwood** and was at one time or other occupied by Marilyn Monroe, Sonny and Cher, and Tony Curtis.

Heading west on Sunset, turn left into Charing Cross Rd, and watch out for bunnies as you make your way past Hugh Hefner's **Playboy Mansion**, 10236 Charing Cross Rd. The driveway is guarded by a Madonna sculpture. The mansion is big, but not as big as the chateau of TV producer **Aaron Spelling**, 594 N Mapleton Dr at Club View, next to Holmby Park (follow Charing Cross, then go left on Mapleton). Spelling's otherworldly digs are commensurate with his extraordinary success with TV's *Charlie's Angels*, *The Love Boat*, *Dynasty*, *Beverly Hills 90210* and *Melrose Place*. The cream-colored mansion allegedly has 123 rooms and at one time was inhabited (not counting domestics) only by Spelling and his wife, Candy, and their children, Randy and Tori. While here, also note the house at 595 Mapleton Dr, an off-white near windowless cube, which takes minimalism to its extreme.

Work your way back to Sunset Blvd, turn left, then head north (right) on Bel Air Rd through the gates of swank Bel Air. Turn right on St Pierre Rd and follow it up and back down the hill. On your right at 486 St Pierre Rd is the abandoned hillside estate of actor **Johnny Weissmuller** of *Tarzan* fame. Easily spied through the trees are the jungle-like terraced gardens where the actor had a swimming pool in the shape of a moat installed to keep those muscles in shape. Turn around, then head right on St Cloud Rd.

The house at 345 St Pierre Rd, at the intersection, was where, in 1942, **Errol Flynn**, known for his appetite for under-age girls, bedded a 17-year-old during a wild party. He was subsequently charged with – and acquitted of – statutory rape, an incident that didn't damage his reputation; it was revealed that the act had been consensual and Flynn wore nothing but his shoes and socks. His film *They Died with Their Boots On* was released shortly thereafter. Marlene Dietrich and Greta Garbo were among those who also lived here later on.

St Cloud veers off to the right and skirts the vast compound of former president and first lady **Ronald and Nancy Reagan**, their home since vacating the White House. The entrance to the house is at 668 Bel Air Rd, where St Cloud joins Bel Air Rd. The original address was 666 Bel Air Rd, but Nancy got it changed because that number is associated with the Sign of the Beast in the New Testament. Turn left and follow Bel Air Rd south back onto Sunset Blvd, where you turn left.

Follow Sunset Blvd east, then turn right on Whittier Dr and left on Linden Dr. You're now in the Beverly 'Flats,' where mansions are more visible. The house immediately on your left at 810 Linden Dr was where gangster **Bugsy Siegel** was gunned down on June 20, 1947 as he was reading a newspaper in his living room. Siegel is often given credit as the founder of modern Las Vegas because he saw its potential as a gambling resort; in 1991 his story was retold in the movie *Bugsy*.

Back on Sunset Blvd, continue east, then turn right onto Bedford Dr. The building at 730 Bedford was where in 1958 Cheryl Crane, the 15-year-old daughter of actress **Lana Turner**, stabbed to death her mother's abusive lover, gangster Johnny Stompanato, with a kitchen knife. She was acquitted on the grounds that it was justifiable homicide. Two blocks south, the small and humble house at 512 Bedford Dr is the former residence of 1920s actress **Clara Bow** of 'It Girl' fame. The apparent nymphomaniac allegedly bedded the entire USC football team, including then linebacker Marion Morrison (the later John Wayne), during one wild night in 1927.

This concludes the tour. Santa Monica Blvd and the commercial heart of Beverly Hills are just south of here.

Greystone Park & Mansion (Map 10)

Wedding parties and film producers are no strangers to the sweeping city views of this 22-acre hilltop park (☎ 310-550-4654, 905 Loma Vista Dr; admission free; grounds open 10am-6pm daily May-Oct; 10am-5pm daily rest of the year). The 55-room mansion (1928) – named for the drab blend of Indiana limestone used in its construction – was a wedding present from oil tycoon Edward L Doheny to his only son Ned. The couple didn't remain happy for long, for on the night of February 6, 1929, Ned was shot in a murder-suicide by his male secretary. The building itself, which sits rather forlornly in the middle of the park, is off-limits to the public but is often used for filming. Scenes from such blockbusters as *The Bodyguard*, *The Witches of Eastwick*, *All of Me*, *Ghostbusters* and *Indecent Proposal* were shot here. An air of neglect hangs over the rambling gardens whose fountains are waterless and lawns ungroomed.

BEL AIR & BRENTWOOD (MAP 2)

The three most prestigious, expensive and star-studded communities in Los Angeles all start with the letter B. Next to Beverly Hills, Brentwood and Bel Air sprawl on the western and eastern sides of the I-405 (San Diego Fwy), respectively. Bel Air, founded in the 1920s by Alphonzo E Bell, is a purely residential neighborhood with a pretzel-shaped network of streets. It is a favorite hideaway of stars whose sybaritic homes are generally out of sight behind security gates and dense foliage. Heavy wrought-iron gates off Sunset Blvd announce that you have arrived. Despite appearances, this is not a gated community, meaning you are free to drive and walk around, as long as you don't trespass onto private property.

Brentwood is comparatively low-key, accessible and less exclusive. Popular with young professionals, it also has its fair share of celebrities. Marilyn Monroe died in her house at 12305 5th Helena Dr on August 4, 1962, reportedly of a drug overdose. But it was the death of Nicole Simpson and Ron Goldman on June 12, 1994 – and the subsequent trials of Nicole's former husband, football great OJ Simpson – that made Brentwood a household name. For months after the trials, Nicole's condominium at 875 Bundy Dr (now 871), where the murders took place, and the Simpson estate at 360 Rockingham Ave, were besieged by tourists.

Interest has since waned, and to further purge the area of such horrible associations, OJ's mansion was recently demolished by its new owner.

Among Brentwood's most attractive streets is the stretch of San Vicente Blvd between Wilshire Blvd and the beach. Its wide, grassy median strip, lined by mature trees, is popular with joggers, while the area surrounding the intersection with Barrington Ave is its commercial and culinary heart.

Getty Center

Fourteen years of planning and construction and $1 billion went into the December 1998 unveiling of the Getty Center (☎ 310-440-7300, 1200 Getty Center Dr; admission free; open 10am-7pm Tues & Wed, 10am-9pm Thur & Fri, 10am-6pm Sat & Sun). The 110-acre campus unites the art collections assembled by the oil magnate J Paul Getty with several Getty-sponsored institutes focused on conservation, art research and education. It hunkers atop a hillside like an impregnable medieval fortress but, oddly, is a rather welcoming place – once you arrive within its vast courtyards.

Four two-story pavilions house the permanent collection, while a fifth presents changing exhibitions. The upper floors of each building focus on paintings; the lower floors, to sculptures, illuminated manuscripts, drawings and furniture. Also here is Getty's collection of 18th-century French decorative arts, which ranks as one of the most prominent in the US, as does his antiquities collection. Paintings never interested Getty much, but since his death in 1976, the Getty Trust has managed to acquire some impressive works, with a focus on pre-20th-century Europeans. This collection now includes masterpieces of the Italian Renaissance, 15th- to 17th-century Dutch works and French 18th- and 19th-century paintings. The string of heavy hitters represented extends from Fra Bartolommeo, Mantegna, Pontormo, Rubens, Van Dyck and Goya to the perennially crowd-pleasing French impressionists Monet, Renoir, Degas and Cézanne as well as Van Gogh.

What distinguishes the Getty from other museums is that its curators haven't assumed that visitors are art experts; they strive instead to educate and make art accessible to all. Next to each gallery entrance are portable gallery cards with backgrounds on an artist, a period, an art form or a method. Each of the pavilions has an Art Access room with easy-to-use computer terminals for more in-depth study. Maps and guides are available in many languages, including Spanish, German and Japanese, and audioguides ($3) allow you to customize your own tour. The Family Room in the Museum Courtyard near the East Pavilion offers displays, hands-on activities and games that make learning about art fun for children. Gallery talks, architecture and garden tours are offered several times daily, and there's also a daily program of lectures, films, concerts and other events.

To many, even more impressive than the art itself is the Getty Center's architecture and design (for more details, see Tour V of the Los Angeles Architecture special section). Open spaces and low buildings placed around a central courtyard collaborate with fountains, exotic landscaping and the sun to create intricate interplay between light and shadow. On clear days, the 360° views extend from a silvery sliver of ocean across the city sprawl to the often snow-capped San Gabriel Mountains and back to the Santa Monica Mountains, bringing into focus the juxtaposition of urbanity and nature that is LA.

Even getting to the Getty is an experience. With parking structures banished to the bottom of the hill, you'll be whisked to the campus aboard driverless trams. Parking reservations (☎ 310-440-7300; $5) are mandatory – except weekdays after 4 pm and all day weekends; college students are exempt from needing parking reservations, as is anyone arriving by MTA bus No 561 or the Big Blue Bus No 14.

Skirball Cultural Center

A cluster of galleries, performance spaces and exhibits takes visitors on a journey through the history of the Jewish people at the Skirball Cultural Center *(☎ 310-440-4500, 2701 N Sepulveda Blvd; admission adults $8, seniors & students $6, children under 12 free; open noon-5pm Tues-Sat, 11am-5pm Sun)*. Exhibits showcase their contributions to the world and to America, often with refreshing irreverence. Unlike most Jewish museums, the Skirball goes far beyond the events of the Holocaust; the simple yet powerful memorial to that time consists of half a dozen photographs of Jewish victims and a single burning lamp. With this dignified display, the museum seems to be saying, 'enough said.'

The $65 million center, which opened in 1996, was designed by noted architect Moshe Safdie and named after Jack Skirball, an ordained rabbi, producer of Hitchcock films and real estate tycoon. The Stephen S Wise Temple (the largest Reform congregation with 4000 families), the University of Judaism and the Milken Jewish High School are nearby.

Judaica displayed at the Skirball is an outgrowth of the collection begun at Hebrew Union College in Cincinnati, Ohio, in 1875. Through photographs and paintings, archeological finds, ceremonial pieces and objects as old as 6000 years, exhibits trace the evolution of Jews – their subjugation under the Egyptians, Romans and Nazis, the epoch of the Diaspora and the founding of Israel. Other galleries examine the history of Jewish holidays and rituals, the importance of synagogue life and the significance of the Torah and menorah. An eye-opening exhibit about Harry Truman expresses admiration for this US president who – against fierce opposition – fought for the establishment of Israel. The most charming exhibits deal with the arrival of European Jews in successive waves of immigration to America. The center owns the original 1935 Nuremberg Laws, which took away citizenship and civil rights from Jews and other non-Aryans; it's signed by Hitler himself.

Interactive touchscreens and video displays add just the right touch of 'tech,' and children should delight in the Discovery Center, where they become hobby archeologists, digging into the past – literally – by

unearthing ancient artifacts. There is a free summer outdoor concert series on Thursday evenings as well as a packed schedule of lectures, concerts and performances (prices vary).

WESTWOOD (MAP 11)

Westwood is best known as the home of the University of California, Los Angeles (UCLA). South of campus, Westwood Village is an attractive pedestrian shopping and restaurant district with a Mediterranean flavor. It fell out of favor after a gang-related shooting in the mid-1980s and recovery came at molasses speed. In 2000, the arrival of a pair of fashionable restaurants and hotels finally rejuvenated the area. Westwood Village is dappled with historic movie theaters, including Fox's 1931 **Westwood Village Theatre**, 961 Broxton Ave, and the 1937 Art Deco **Bruin Theatre**, 948 Broxton Ave.

University of California, Los Angeles

Established in 1919, UCLA has about 36,500 students and is one of the premier institutions of higher learning in the US *(☎ 310-825-4321, www.ucla.edu, 405 Hilgard Ave; free student-guided tours 10:30am and 1:30pm weekdays; reservations required, ☎ 310-825-8764)*.

The 419-acre campus is beautifully landscaped and contains several buildings of architectural interest, as well as museums and exhibit spaces. A self-guided tour might start on **Westwood Plaza**, just north of the terminus of Westwood Blvd, at the bronze Bruin Bear statue, the university mascot. Concerts and public gatherings also take place here. On the right, Ackermann Union has restaurants, shops and the main bookstore. To the left is Pauley Pavilion, the 13,000-seat arena for basketball and volleyball games. Farther west is the LA Tennis Center, the site of the annual Los Angeles Open.

From Westwood Plaza, head east along Bruin Walk to **Royce Quad**, flanked by UCLA's original buildings, which are modeled after famous Romanesque landmarks

What's Free

Fame may not be free in Los Angeles but many of the city's museums and attractions don't charge admission or offer free admission on certain days and times.

Museums (always free)

Cabrillo Marine Aquarium (San Pedro)
California African American Museum (Exposition Park)
California Science Center (Exposition Park)
The Center – Civil Rights Museum (Watts)
Fisher Gallery (University of Southern California)
Fort MacArthur Military Museum (San Pedro)
Franklin D Murphy Sculpture Garden, UCLA (Westwood)
Frederick's of Hollywood Lingerie Museum (Central Hollywood)
Getty Center (Bel Air & Brentwood)
Hollywood Bowl Museum (Hollywood Hills)
Malibu Lagoon Museum (Malibu)
Roundhouse Marine Studies Lab & Aquarium (South Bay)
Museum in Black (Leimert Park)
Museum of African American Art (Leimert Park)
Travel Town Museum (Griffith Park)
Watts Towers Art Center (Watts)
Wells Fargo History Museum (Financial District)

Historic Sights (always free)

Avila Adobe and Olvera St (El Pueblo de Los Angeles)
Camera Obscura (Santa Monica)
Center for Motion Picture Study (Beverly Hills)
William Andrews Clark Memorial Library (West Adams)
El Alisal/Lummis House (Mt Washington)
El Molino Viejo (Pasadena)
Greystone Park & Mansion (Beverly Hills)
Paramount Ranch (San Fernando Valley)
St Sophia Cathedral (Koreatown)
Self-Realization Fellowship Lake Shrine (Pacific Palisades)
Will Rogers State Historical Park (Pacific Palisades)
Wrigley Mansion & Gardens (Pasadena)

Museums (free on the following days)

Autry Museum of Western Heritage (Griffith Park) – 2nd Tuesday of the month
Heritage Square Museum (North Central) – every Friday
Huntington Library, Art Collection & Botanical Gardens (Pasadena) – 1st Thursday of the month
Japanese American National Museum (Little Tokyo) – 3rd Thursday of the month and after 5pm every Thursday
Long Beach Museum of Art (Long Beach) – 1st Friday of the month
Museum of Contemporary Art (Financial District) – Thursday 5pm-8pm
MOCA Geffen Contemporary (Little Tokyo) – Thursday 5pm-8pm
Museum of Neon Art (South Park) – 2nd Thursday of the month after 5pm
Page Museum at La Brea Discoveries (Miracle Mile District) – 1st Tuesday of the month
South Coast Botanical Garden (Palos Verdes Peninsula) – 3rd Tuesday of the month
UCLA Hammer Museum (Westwood) – every Thursday

in Italy: Royce Hall, on the northern side, recalls the Cathedral of Milan, while Powell Library, on the opposite side, is topped by an octagonal tower resembling that of a church in Bologna.

Head down Janss Steps, located at the western end of Royce Quad, to get to the **Fowler Museum of Cultural History** (☎ 310-825-4361; admission adults/discounts $5/3; open noon-5pm Wed & Fri-Sun, noon-8pm Thur). This gallery has a world-class collection of art and artifacts from non-Western cultures. Also on view is the family silver of the Fowlers, the museum's major donors.

Towards the northeastern corner of the campus is the quiet and picturesque **Franklin D Murphy Sculpture Garden** with 70 works by Rodin, Moore, Calder and other American and European artists. On the opposite end of campus (the southeastern corner) is another delightful green oasis: the **Mildred E Mathias Botanical Garden** (enter on Tiverton Ave). It has more than 4000 native and exotic plants and flowers as well as 'The Nest,' a public outdoor classroom. Free docent-led tours take place at 1pm and 2pm on the first Sunday of the month.

UCLA Hammer Museum

In less than a decade, what started as a mere vanity project for its main benefactor, the late industrialist Armand Hammer, has graduated to a respected contemporary and period art museum (☎ 310-443-7000, 10899 Wilshire Blvd; admission adults $4.50, seniors $3, students and children under 17 free; open 11am-7pm Tues-Wed & Fri-Sat, to 9pm Thur, to 5pm Sun). Concurrent, changing exhibits draw from several sources: Hammer's collection of Impressionist and post-Impressionist art (including Pissarro, Cassatt and Van Gogh); Hammer's Honoré Daumier & Contemporaries collection of lithographs, paintings and sculpture satirizing French 19th-century culture and society; and the UCLA Grunwald Center for the Graphic Arts, which owns some 35,000 works on paper from the Renaissance to today. In addition, museum curators mount

courageous and often fascinating exhibits of emerging and established contemporary artists, often from California. An ambitious cultural program of scholarly lectures, readings, discussions, book signings and the Filmforum, an avant-garde film and video series, rounds out the offerings.

Westwood Memorial Park

This small, star-studded cemetery (☎ 310-474-1570, 1218 Glendon Ave) is a bit hard to find, hidden as it is behind Westwood's office stalagmites. (From Wilshire Blvd, turn south onto Glendon Ave and look for the driveway immediately to your left.) Here you'll find the crypt of Marilyn Monroe; Joe DiMaggio sent roses every week until 1982, and Hugh Hefner has allegedly reserved the adjacent box to be close to the ultimate Hollywood babe. Other famous deceased include Natalie Wood, Burt Lancaster, Mel Torme, Roy Orbison and Frank Zappa (in an unmarked grave). Also here are two child actresses from *Poltergeist* – Heather O'Rourke (Carol Anne) and Dominique Dunne (Dana) – both died violently and young.

The writer Truman Capote lies in a space formerly occupied by Peter Lawford. Rumor has it that Capote's ashes were stolen from the home of Joanne Carson (former wife of Johnny Carson) but ultimately returned. Meanwhile, Lawford's crypt had been vacated for defaulting on payments, so Carson bought it and had Capote interred there.

It's a small cemetery, so you should be able to find most graves without too much looking. Otherwise, ask the friendly staff at the office for help.

CENTURY CITY (MAP 11)

Adjoining Beverly Hills to the southwest is Century City, once the backlot of 20th Century Fox Studios. As the Tom Petty song goes, 'Don't want to live in Century City,' and indeed not many people do. High-rise office buildings shoot skyward along Ave of the Stars, which is the main artery of this important business and entertainment center.

Museum of Tolerance

Confront your own closely held beliefs while learning about racism and bigotry at the Museum of Tolerance (☎ 310-553-8403, www.wiesenthal.com, 9786 W Pico Blvd; admission adults $8, seniors $6, students $5, children $3; open Mon-Fri & Sun, call for hours; advance ticket purchase suggested). It's an enlightening, scary and painful experience. The 28,000-sq-foot exhibition with the latest interactive technologies contains two main thematic sections: the **Tolerancenter**, focusing on racism and prejudice in America, and the **Holocaust section**, chronicling the history of the Holocaust as it pertains to Jews. The only way to experience this museum is by taking a 2½- to three-hour tour; tours depart continuously throughout the day.

The tone is set up front, when you must choose from two doors leading to the Tolerancenter. One says 'Prejudiced,' the other 'Not Prejudiced.' Those choosing the latter will find it closed. The highlight of this section is the Point of View Diner, a re-created '50s American diner, where you'll be served with the message of personal responsibility. Sitting at individual video terminals, each person inputs their opinions about a staged newscast involving drunk driving or a hate speech. The results are tabulated instantly.

The Holocaust section first examines the roots of the rise of Nazi power in 1920s Germany. Then – as soft carpeting gives way to rough concrete – you enter a concentration camp, including a 'gas chamber' where you're showered with film footage from actual camps. At the beginning, each visitor is given a photo passport of a child, which is fed into various terminals along the way to reveal his or her fate.

In the **Multimedia Learning Center**, on the 2nd floor, you can research a variety of Holocaust-related topics. Also here are such artifacts as letters by Anne Frank, a bunk bed from the Majdanek camp and Göring's dress uniform cap.

This museum, conceived and implemented by the adjacent Simon Wiesenthal Center, clearly and effectively communicates important messages. One might wish that it were a bit more inclusive in its historical portrayal, however, especially in the Holocaust section. Little mention is made of the fate of non-Jewish groups or the existence of German resistance groups. No attempt is made to put the 12 years of Nazi rule into the context of Germany's history, leaving at least some of the visitors filled with predictable loathing for that country.

Other Things to See & Do

Near the Century City Shopping Center is the **Shubert Theater** (☎ 800-447-7400, 10250 Santa Monica Blvd), one of Los Angeles' leading venues for Broadway productions. The theater is part of the ABC Entertainment Center and Century Plaza Towers, a huge business and theater complex built in 1975 and designed by Minoru Yamasaki, the architect of New York City's World Trade Center. Yamasaki also designed the Century Plaza Hotel, across the street at 2025 Ave of the Stars (see the Places to Stay chapter).

At the foot of Century City, still clinging tenaciously to its original piece of real estate, you'll find the **20th Century Fox Studios** (10201 W Pico Blvd). Tours are no longer offered by this studio, but if you peer through its front gate, you can get a glimpse of a turn-of-the-19th-century New York street set. This studio was home to Marilyn Monroe, Shirley Temple, and many, many other stars.

CULVER CITY (MAP 12)

Few people realize that, in the '30s and '40s, about half of the nation's movies were made in this rather modest-looking city, about 6 miles southwest of Hollywood. Thanks to the initiative of real estate developer and Culver City founder, Harry Culver, movie studios began settling here as early as 1915. The largest studio was Metro-Goldwyn-Mayer (MGM), though there were also a number of others, attracting such moguls as Cecil B DeMille, Samuel Goldwyn, Orson Welles and David O Selznick.

Sony Pictures Studios

In 1990, the vast studio lot that was home (from 1924 until 1986) of the most powerful studio in Hollywood – MGM – was acquired by Sony Pictures Entertainment (☎ 310-520-8687, 10202 W Washington Blvd; tour price $20; tours 9am-3pm weekdays; reservations required; children under 12 not permitted). It was MGM that gave the world such classics as The Wizard of Oz, Ben Hur and The Thin Man mysteries starring William Powell and Myrna Loy. MGM had so many stars under contract (Spencer Tracy, Katharine Hepburn, Elizabeth Taylor, Jimmy Stewart, to drop just a few names) that its motto became, 'More stars than there are in heaven.' MGM was bought out in the 1970s and stopped making movies shortly thereafter, although the roaring lion logo still graced the studio lot until 1986.

These days, Columbia Pictures and Tristar Pictures, both divisions of Sony, are once again making movies and television programs here. The game show Jeopardy is the studio's bread and butter, while recent feature successes have included the remake of Charlie's Angels, As Good as It Gets and Men in Black.

Despite the historical connection to MGM, the two-hour walking tour focuses mostly on Sony productions. Highlights include a visit to the Jeopardy set and sound stage 27 where you can still see the 'Yellow Brick Road.' Tickets also give access to the commissary (restaurant) and the studio store. Tours start in the atrium of the Sony Pictures Plaza building at the corner of Washington Blvd and Overland Ave, where there's also a small exhibit about current and past Sony productions.

Culver Studios

These historic studios (☎ 310-836-5537, 9336 W Washington Blvd) are distinguished by a main building that copies George Washington's white mansion at Mt Vernon. Now owned by Sony as well, it's much smaller than the former MGM lot, but has generated some of the most memorable movies ever, including Citizen Kane (1941) and Gone with the Wind (1939). Blockbuster TV series like Batman and Lassie were also filmed on its backlot. More recently, The Nanny and Mad About You were taped here. At one time, the studio was owned by Lucille Ball's Desilu Studios.

Since no tours are offered, the only way to get onto the lot is by obtaining a ticket to a TV show taping (for details, see the boxed text 'Getting Into a Studio' in the Entertainment chapter).

Museum of Jurassic Technology

You may begin to laugh helplessly at some point when perusing the dark labyrinths of the Museum of Jurassic Technology (MJT; ☎ 310-836-6131, 9341 Venice Blvd; admission adults $4, seniors & students $2.50, children under 12 free; open 2pm-8pm Thur, noon-6pm Fri-Sun). Madness may begin to nibble at your mind. If this feeling persists, exit immediately – or risk becoming an exhibit yourself. The MJT is an assemblage of improbably weird, obscure and arcane displays, seemingly compiled from combing the garage sales of a parallel – but niftily twisted – universe. As you wander from room to room, the lines between reality, imagination and perception become a hazy blur.

Right by the entrance is a small booth where the MJT's history and its spiritual and metaphysical goals are announced in the voice of God Almighty, while a crude video of some object like the Tower of Babel is encircled in smoke. Then you will encounter a 'mouse sandwich,' once known as a cure for the croup, a sculpture of Pope John Paul II (in the eye of a needle) created by a failed violin teacher, a NASA-like plotting map of bright pins on a darkened outline of the USA showing the location of 1937 trailer parks and a sculpture of a duck breathing into a child's mouth – a bit of medical 'quackery.'

By now you are gasping, 'WHAT?!?' The MJT may or may not be an actual museum (some actually consider it artwork). It may be a set designed by Borges or a complete exercise in ironic near-hysteria by MJT curator David Wilson. The state-of-the-art display in a tiny space, sound systems that gently massage and direct you as you helplessly meander – it's maddening, irksome, weird to a fault and howlingly funny even when you feel like Anthony Perkins is watching you through some knothole. There is nothing Jurassic about any of it, and you can find more technology in a bicycle shop. But one thing about the MJT is true above all else: It will stay in your mind for a long, long time.

Coastal Communities

The Pacific Ocean is LA's greatest natural asset, and the communities along the coast are among the most sought-after and expensive places to live. This chapter covers them all, from Malibu in the north to Long Beach near the Orange County line.

MALIBU & TOPANGA (MAP 2)

The history of Malibu and its development into a celebrity enclave is directly tied to the Rindge family from Massachusetts; they were the last owners of the Spanish land grant called Malibu and its 27 miles of coastline. When Frederick H Rindge acquired the land in 1892, it was remote and largely undeveloped. After his death in 1905, his widow, May, fought to prevent first the Southern Pacific Railroad from laying tracks across her land and then the state of California from building a highway.

The railroad was never built, but May's loss to the state in 1923 gave the world the Pacific Coast Highway (PCH). Around the same time, in order to replenish her empty coffers, May also leased some land west of the Malibu Lagoon to movie stars. Clara Bow and Barbara Stanwyck were among the first to move here and the Malibu Colony grew from there. Today, it is home to such major headliners as Mel Gibson, Sting, Tom Hanks and Barbra Streisand. Stars still prize their privacy in this gated and well-policed community. While it's impossible to get past the gate, it is legal to walk along the

beach – as long as you stay below the high-tide mark.

Another flock of entertainment industry bigwigs – stars, producers, directors – lives on Carbon Beach. It is accessible by walking west from the storm-damaged Malibu Pier, which is still awaiting restoration. On the beach is a boulder that's been appropriately nicknamed 'Dealmaker's Rock' because so many movie deals have been struck right here.

A handful of state parks and state beaches offer the best access. Traveling over a stretch of about 25 miles, they include Malibu Surfrider, Point Dume, Zuma and Leo Carrillo (see the boxed text 'Life's a Beach').

The rugged mountains that rise abruptly behind Malibu are encompassed by the Santa Monica Mountains National Recreation Area (see the related section, later in this chapter). More than 150,000 acres of erratically forested hills with many miles of trails are under National Park Service control.

Adamson House & Malibu Lagoon Museum

Built on a prime spot of coast along Malibu Creek is the **Adamson House** (☎ 310-456-8432, 23200 Pacific Coast Hwy; free tours 11am, noon, 1pm & 2pm Wed-Sat). It's a beautiful Spanish Colonial villa laced with Moorish elements in enchanting surroundings and was built for May's daughter, Rhoda Rindge Adamson, in 1928. The house itself, as well as fountains, the pool and bathhouse, is famous for being lavishly decorated with patterned glazed ceramic tiles, manufactured at the Malibu Potteries Tile Company, which was owned by the Rindges between 1926 and 1932.

Adjacent to the Adamson House is the **Malibu Lagoon Museum** (☎ 310-456-8432; admission free; open 11am-3pm Wed-Sat). This local history museum has exhibits on the history of Malibu, from its days as a Chumash Indian habitat to its period as Rancho Malibu, and the evolution of the Malibu Colony. The history of surfing is covered and there's also a display of Malibu Potteries tile.

Life's a Beach

Beaches beckon all along the LA County coastline. Plenty of sunshine and lots of activities draw people to the shorefront year-round. Surfing, sailing, swimming, sunbathing, volleyball, beach-combing – or simply strolling through the sand – are all enjoyed by locals and visitors alike.

Water temperatures become tolerable by late spring and are highest (about 70°F) in August and September. In winter the Pacific becomes chilly, which doesn't stop surfers from hitting the swells in wetsuits. Many beaches have showers and restrooms, lifeguards, snack stands and regular clean-up. With miles and miles of wide sandy shores to enjoy, the beaches rarely get packed with people. The most popular and populated ones are in Santa Monica, Venice and Manhattan Beach.

Hazards are few but shouldn't be ignored. Swimming is usually prohibited for three days after major storms be-

Life's a beach...with a babe or two.

cause of dangerously high pollution levels from untreated runoff sweeping into the ocean through storm drains. The local nonprofit organization Heal the Bay issues a monthly Beach Report Card, which evaluates ocean water quality based on a grading system from A+ to F. Call ☎ 310-453-0395 or ☎ 800-432-5229 (within CA only) or visit its website at www.healthebay.org.

Another element of danger is strong currents, called riptides, which occur when different currents collide, dragging swimmers away from the shore. Look for white, frothy water and flat waves. People getting caught in riptides account for 80% of lifeguard rescues. To check on weather or tide conditions, call the following numbers:

North Beaches (Zuma area)	☎ 310-457-9701
Central Beaches (Santa Monica area)	☎ 310-578-0478
South Beaches (Hermosa area)	☎ 310-379-8471

The following beaches (north to south), though by no means a complete list, are some of our favorites:

Leo Carrillo State Beach (☎ 805-488-5223) is the northernmost in LA County, about 30 miles north of Santa Monica. It's popular with sunbathers who hang out in the section west of the Sequit Point dividing line, while surfers dominate the territory east of the point. There's also a nature trail, tide pools and caves carved into the cliffs.

El Pescador, El Matador & La Piedra Beaches, a few miles south of Leo Carrillo, are secluded hideaways popular with trendy Angelenos willing to make the drive up the coast. They're small and can get crowded, though limited parking provides built-in crowd control. To get to the sand, you must descend steep paths leading down from Pacific Coast Hwy. El Matador is the most scenic, with its eroded rock formations and natural arches, and nude sunbathing is popular here. Watch out for dangerous riptides.

THINGS TO SEE & DO

Life's a Beach

Zuma Beach County Park is one of LA's most beautiful beaches, a wide white sandy strip more than 2 miles long. It's great for ogling strapping lifeguards and scantily clad teens, but most people come for the excellent swimming and body surfing; the water is clean and the waves are large. There's a parking lot (for a fee) and free street parking, though look out for restrictions.

Westward Beach (☎ 310-457-9891) is immediately to the south of Zuma and a better choice for families.

Point Dume Beach is even farther south and is best reached by taking the trail from Westward Beach to the top of the bluff and descending the stairway on the other side; this takes you to a small cove that is LA's unofficial nude beach.

Malibu Lagoon State Beach (☎ 310-456-9497), also known as Surfrider Beach, has some of the best surfing, with superb swells and extended rides. Even those not handy with the board enjoy the spectacle of watching dedicated dudes and dudettes riding the waves to shore. Unfortunately, the water quality here leaves much to be desired; after heavy rains the Heal the Bay score is regularly an F, the result of spillage from the algae-rich lagoon.

Will Rogers State Beach (☎ 310-394-3266), 3 miles long and narrow, is quite a favorite with families. There are several playgrounds and the surf is not very strong, which is why it's also good for surfing novices. At the foot of Chautauqua Blvd you can watch the athletically inclined bump, set and spike on the volleyball courts. Avoid the section at the mouth of Santa Monica Canyon (near San Vicente Blvd) where a storm drain discharges right into the sea.

Santa Monica State & Venice City Beaches are among LA's most popular beaches, offering something for everyone. There's a paved shoreline walk with separate lanes for bicyclers and skaters, children's playgrounds abound and sanitary facilities are spaced only a few hundred yards apart. Snack bars and rental stations for boogie boards, skates and bikes are everywhere. The Santa Monica Pier is an attraction in itself (see the Santa Monica section). The beaches are reasonably clean, though relatively crowded. The nicest stretch is about half a mile south of the Santa Monica Pier. Parking in beach lots is pricey (about $6-10). You can typically park inexpensively in Santa Monica's municipal lots, on 2nd and 4th Sts, and walk to the shore, or you can hunt for street parking a few blocks inland, though spaces are scarce and the meters are monitored constantly.

South Bay Beaches – including Manhattan Beach, Hermosa Beach and Redondo Beach – typify the laid-back SoCal beach scene. Homes here literally fringe the sand. Surfers like the area near the pier in Manhattan, but the large waves make this stretch less suited for small children. Both Hermosa and Manhattan are beach-volleyball capitals. Hermosa is very much a party and pick-up beach with beer-swilling college kids spilling out of pubs that line the Strand and Pier Ave. Redondo Beach is narrower and more family-friendly. A popular summer adventure is a visit to the Seaside Lagoon (see South Bay).

Long Beach, with its more than 10 miles of shorefront, is certainly no misnomer. Thanks to a breakwater 2 miles offshore, however, the water here is eerily flat with few waves, which is good for swimming and windsurfing, though obviously not for boogie boarding or surfing. Long Beach trains its own lifeguards, a tradition in force since 1919. The beach along Appian Way, on the north side of Naples Island, is a good place to come with small children. Horny Beach, next to the Gondola Getaway pier at 5437 E Ocean Blvd, is the area's gathering spot for hormone-crazed teens.

Topanga Canyon

Perhaps the most intriguing drive from Malibu into the mountains is via Topanga Canyon. An alternative-lifestyle community even before it was discovered by hippies in the '60s, Topanga still embraces a collection of homes that range from ramshackle to modern rustic. The emphasis today is on New Age philosophy, as exemplified by the music and cuisine at the Inn of the Seventh Ray (see the Places to Eat chapter).

Will Geer Theatricum Botanicum (☎ 310-455-3723, 1419 N Topanga Canyon Rd) serves the artistic community with a summer series of Shakespeare and other plays in an outdoor amphitheater (also see the Entertainment chapter). It was founded in 1953 as an artistic outlet by the actor Will Geer (best known as Grandpa Walton in the TV series), who, along with others, was blacklisted during the McCarthy era.

The eastern section of **Topanga State Park** (20825 Entrada Rd) climbs the mountain ridge and a network of trails extends through its 9000 acres all the way to Will Rogers State Historic Park (see Pacific Palisades, later in this chapter).

Other Things to See

Long before the Getty Center opened, there was the original **J Paul Getty Museum** at 17985 Pacific Coast Hwy, housed in the replica Roman Villa dei Papiri. It's scheduled to be renovated but a reopening date had not been set at press time.

Rising above a grassy slope with views of the Pacific and the mountains, **Pepperdine University** (☎ 310-456-4000, 24255 Pacific Coast Hwy) surely has one of the most beautiful campuses in the world. Affiliated with the Church of Christ, it was founded in 1937 by George Pepperdine, who had made a fortune selling car supplies.

PACIFIC PALISADES (MAP 2)

Pacific Palisades is an upscale community north of Santa Monica, rife with celebrities (including Arnold Schwarzenegger, Tom Cruise and Tracy Ullman) and common millionaires. They live ensconced in gorgeous Mediterranean-style villas nestled into five major canyons cutting through the Santa Monica Mountains all the way to the ocean.

This region was already a popular seaside resort for wealthy Angelenos in the late 19th century. The actual colony of Pacific Palisades was founded in 1922 by a group of Methodists (led by Charles C Scott) to serve as a place of cultural, educational and religious edification. Founders purchased lots at $1000 each and settled on the mesa above Potrero Canyon. When the Depression hit, the group was forced to sell off land to private investors. Neighborhoods sprang up all around, many of them luring a sizable community of artists and writers in the 1920s to 1940s. Today, Pacific Palisades' pleasures are still largely natural with easy access to rambling hiking trails with sweeping vistas over the Santa Monica Bay.

Will Rogers State Historic Park

Cowboy personality Will Rogers (1875–1935) once made his home in this Santa Monica Mountain park (☎ 310-454-8212; admission free, $5 parking; park open 8am-sunset daily, ranch house open 10am-5pm daily). Rogers made a name for himself as a humorist and actor and through his acerbic commentary on the radio and in newspaper columns. In the late 1920s, Rogers traded Beverly Hills for this ranch estate, where he lived until he died in a plane crash in Alaska in 1935. His wife, who survived him by eight years, deeded the ranch to the state in 1944.

Today, visitors can explore the chaparral-covered hills once wandered by Rogers and check out his private polo field where he was often joined by buddies Spencer Tracy and Walt Disney. (A polo club now hosts matches here on weekends April to September.) Rogers' home is open to the public and still contains his personal furnishings. A short film about Rogers' life and career is shown at the visitors center. The park entrance is west off Sunset Blvd and is marked by signs.

Self-Realization Fellowship Lake Shrine

Whatever negative feelings or stress you may have are likely to evaporate on a visit to the Self-Realization Fellowship Lake Shrine (☎ 310-454-4114, 17190 Sunset Blvd; admission free; open 9am-4:30pm Tues-Sat, 12:30pm-4:30pm Sun). The 10-acre site is a natural amphitheater of paradisiacal beauty and serenity. Stroll along the narrow paths, around a spring-fed lake, through the sunken gardens, ponds, waterfalls and lush vegetation.

Founded in 1920 by Paramahansa Yogananda, a widely admired spiritual leader born and educated in India, the fellowship is dedicated to helping people of all races, creeds and cultures on their spiritual search. Sri Yogananda spent 30 years of his life in the US, and opened the Lake Shrine to the public in 1950.

Highlights of the grounds are the Court of Religions, where each of the five principal religions is acknowledged with its symbol; the Windmill Chapel, a reproduction of a 16th-century Dutch windmill; the Golden Lotus Archway, topped by gilded copper lotus flowers; and the Gandhi World Peace Memorial where a portion of Mahatma Gandhi's ashes is interred in a stone sarcophagus. Towering atop the hillside is the New Temple, an octagonal edifice adorned with stained glass, tile and wood and again crowned by a gilded lotus.

SANTA MONICA (MAP 13)

In recent years, Santa Moncia has undergone an amazing metamorphosis that is the envy of urban planners around the country. It has gone from a quaint, slightly wacky seaside resort to glitzy beach town with a cosmopolitan flair. Once called the 'People's Republic of Santa Monica' for its liberal politics, cheap rent-controlled apartments and tolerance for the homeless, it's now definitely more Cannes than Beijing. Third Street Promenade, at one time a tacky mall you could shoot a cannonball through without hitting anyone, is a commercial runaway success. The air quality, shopping, dining and entertainment are better than almost anywhere in LA.

Santa Monica's hipness factor has also drawn such giants of the entertainment world as Sony, MGM and MTV, which now have corporate offices here. Executives soon fell in love with the city's livability and snapped up fairly humble Spanish villas, replacing them with giant estates built right to the property line. This phenomenon, which has been dubbed the 'mansionification' of Santa Monica, is especially evident in the area north of Montana Ave. Abolition of rent control soon followed, thus driving lower-income people out of the city. Santa Monica's demographics are definitely changing.

For travelers, Santa Monica is a great destination. The freak killing of a German tourist in 1997 notwithstanding, it is a safe place to stay and even to walk around in (but do avoid the beach at night). Most attractions are easily explored on foot. Highlights are the pleasure pier, Third Street Promenade and Santa Monica Place mall, the shopping areas of Main St and Montana Ave, and a cliffside park overlooking the ocean. (See the Shopping chapter for more information on the Santa Monica Place mall and Montana Ave.)

To travel between downtown Santa Monica, the shops on Main St and the southern Santa Monica beaches, hop on the electric Tide Shuttle (25¢ per ride), which runs every 15 minutes between noon and 10pm (to midnight on weekends). The shuttle does a loop starting roughly on the Broadway side of Santa Monica Place, runs west on Broadway, then south on Ocean Ave (which turns into Barnard Way), then east on Marine and back north on Main St; then it jags east on Bicknell and continues north on 4th St before turning west on Broadway, thus completing the loop

Finally, a word of caution: Do not jaywalk – Santa Monica Police will not look the other way and citations can get costly.

Santa Monica Pier & Around
Most likely you know the Santa Monica Pier, even if you have never been there in real life. Just about every movie or TV program set in LA features at least one establishing shot of the pier's historic lighted arch. Behind it, a steep incline spans Pacific Coast Hwy and leads to the most lively and

beloved pier in the entire county. It offers great views of the beach and the Santa Monica skyline and is studded with restaurants, nightclubs and family entertainments. The pier was plagued with gang activity for many years, but the presence of a police station right in the middle of it keeps most trouble away, or at least at bay.

The historic Santa Monica Pier originally consisted of two adjacent quays: a municipal pier, built in 1909 for fishing and strolling, and a pleasure pier with amusements and food venues dating from 1916. The two are joined together today. A remnant from that era is the Hippodrome, home of a quaint **Loof Carousel** that starred with Paul Newman and Robert Redford in the film classic *The Sting*. It's a lovely old-fashioned affair, and its cheerfully hand-painted horses endear it to children large and small.

The pier's main draw is the **Pacific Park** *(☎ 310-260-8744; rides $1.50-4.50, unlimited rides $8.95/15.95 under/over 42 inches tall; open 10am-10pm Sun-Thur, to midnight Fri-Sat; call for shorter winter hours)*. Highlights of this small-scale amusement park are the West Coaster, a comparatively tame but still fun roller coaster, and the full-size Pacific Wheel, the world's first solar-powered Ferris wheel, which is worth riding for the views alone. There are also a host of kiddy rides and arcade games.

Right beneath the Hippodrome is the **UCLA Ocean Discovery Center** *(☎ 310-393-6149, admission adults $3, free for children under 2; 3pm-6pm Tues-Fri, 11am-6pm Sat, 11am-5pm Sun July 1 to Labor Day; 11am-5pm Sat & Sun rest of the year)*. This children-oriented facility demystifies the denizens of Santa Monica Bay. Operated by UCLA's marine science department, the center's 4000 sq feet contain several aquariums inhabited by such local marine life as jellyfish and sharks. Touch tanks allow visitors to interact with urchins, bat rays and sea cucumbers. Friendly young volunteers stand by to answer questions.

On Thursday nights in summer, the pier comes to life with the **Twilight Dance Series**, free outdoor concerts featuring major local and national talent. Past performers have included Bo Diddley, Queen Ida and LA's own Ozomatli. Concerts start at 7:30pm.

Just south of the pier is the newly refurbished **International Chess Park**, where people from all walks of life – sharing an enthusiasm for the game and a leisurely lifestyle – gather. Nearby is the site of the **Original Muscle Beach**, where the Southern California exercise craze began in the mid-20th century. Brand-new equipment once again draws new generations of gymnasts, bodybuilders and other athletes to the historic venue.

Palisades Park

Palisades Park hugs the sandstone bluff that parallels the ocean, separating the city from PCH and the wide, sandy beach. Lorded over by gracefully swaying Washington palm trees, a vast sweep of Santa Monica Bay opens before you. It's a great place to sit quietly on a bench or watch the flocks of joggers, parents and baby strollers, sunset meditators, lovers, tai chi practitioners and Russian immigrants holding their klatsches.

The park begins just north of the pier. This is also where you'll find one of Santa Monica's oldest attractions, the **Camera Obscura** *(Senior Recreation Center, 1450 Ocean Ave; admission free; open 9am-4pm Mon-Fri, 11am-4pm Sat & Sun)*. An early version of the single-lens reflex camera, the Camera Obscura was quite a sensation when it opened in 1899. Ask for the key, then head up the stairway to discover a completely dark room where a 5-foot circular image of Ocean Ave is projected onto a table.

As you stroll north from here, you will notice several gun emplacements built to hold off possible Japanese attacks during WWII. Farther north, where Santa Monica Blvd meets the park, is a commemorative plaque marking the western terminus of the Will Rogers Hwy, also known as Route 66, the 'Main Street of America.' A couple of blocks north, right at Wilshire Blvd, is a statue of the city's namesake, St Monica, an absurdly phallic minimalist rendition.

Third Street Promenade

Before its ambitious revamping in 1989, this walking mall between Broadway and Wilshire Blvds was home to dusty shops, dilapidated facades and homeless people. Then the city spent a few million dollars, and one of the nicest pedestrian-only zones in all of LA County was born. Peruvian flutes mingle with bluegrass guitar and classical cellos in a parade of free street entertainment. Stores, restaurants and cafes with outdoor seating, and no fewer than 17 movie screens draw the crowds to one of the most happening places in the county.

But then, over the course of the last few years, Third Street entered yet another phase. As popularity translated into higher rents, many of the funky, one-of-a-kind boutiques were pushed out. In their stead came the same chain retail stores that can be found everywhere in the world. Flagship stores like the Gap, Pottery Barn, Restoration Hardware, Urban Outfitters, Banana Republic and scores more now dominate this increasingly overcommercialized strip.

Bergamot Station

The nearly 40 galleries berthed within the sprawling industrial grounds of Bergamot Station (☎ 310-453-7535, 2525 Michigan Ave) have been a nexus of the LA art scene since the complex's opening in 1994. Bergamot Station was originally a stop on the Red Line dating to 1875 (see the boxed text 'Big Red Cars' in the Getting Around chapter). Later, the area became an industrial site before being abandoned. It took the vision of an art dealer to look beyond the ramshackle corrugated tin buildings to create one of the most esteemed exhibit spaces in LA.

In addition to housing the Santa Monica Museum of Art, Bergamot Station boasts established galleries like those of Sherry Frumkin and Shoshana Wayne. But it's also home to lesser-known galleries specializing in handmade paper, traditional Japanese ukiyo-e art, contemporary photography and jewelry. Bergamot Station prints a guide to the galleries (available at the sites) or see the Shopping chapter for recommendations of specific galleries.

Santa Monica Museum of Art Copious skylights in a corrugated tin roof shed light on the exhibits at the Santa Monica Museum of Art (☎ 310-586-6488, Bergamot Station; admission adults $3, students & seniors & artists $2; open 11am-6pm Tues-Sat, noon-5pm Sun). This museum is a saucy and irreverent home for changing contemporary art exhibits. Both local and national artists – fledgling to big-name – are showcased; most artists work in new and experimental media. Curators also host an intrepid schedule of public community events. The popular Friday-night salon series is right at the edge of the local scene: You might encounter performance artists or get involved in discussions about surrealist cooking or the symbolic power of trees.

John Drescher Planetarium

Located at Santa Monica College, big crowds flock to the state-of-the-art planetarium (☎ 310-452-9223, 1900 Pico Blvd; show only $4, show and lecture $7). The popular Night Sky Shows explain mysteries from quarks to quasars in three dimensions by a Digistar projection system (the only one on the West Coast). The shows are followed by lectures given by scientists from the Jet Propulsion Lab, Caltech and other eminent research facilities.

Main Street

Main St is flanked by one-of-a-kind boutiques and galleries and is a joy to shop in, albeit a rather pricey one. In between the stores, you'll find the **Edgemar Complex** (1988; 2427–29 Main St), a bold, angular design by local boy Frank Gehry built on the site of a former dairy. It looks more like a giant abstract sculpture than a building: two passageways culminate in a freeform courtyard; facades are made from different materials, including sheet metal and stucco. Nearby is the **California Heritage Museum** (☎ 310-392-8537, 2612 Main St), which has rooms filled with Craftsman-era furniture and historic photographs and a 2nd-floor gallery with changing exhibits about a historical or cultural theme.

Museum of Flying

You don't have to be an airplane aficionado to enjoy the excellent Museum of Flying (☎ 310-392-8822, 2772 Donald Douglas Loop N; admission adults $7, seniors $5, children 3-17 $3; open 10am-5pm Wed-Sun), right at the Santa Monica Municipal Airport, which is entered from Ocean Park Blvd. Housed in an enormous hangar on the grounds of what used to be the Douglas Aircraft Corporation, are three floors of exhibits with such legends of flight as the Mitsubishi Zero, the P-51 Mustang, WWI Fokkers and a replica of the Voyager, the first aircraft to make a nonstop flight around the world.

Take a self-guided tour to exhibits on flight's beginnings, milestones and pioneers. You'll pass several aircraft dangling midair in eerie quiet and aeronautic elegance. There are also interactive 'build a plane' displays, a flight simulator for kids and models of futuristic spacecraft that will have the young ones speculating about their future on Mars.

VENICE (MAP 13)

The quintessential bohemian playground, Venice is famous for its oceanfront boardwalk and Muscle Beach, its canals and unique blend of hippies, New Agers, artists, Industry types and students. In recent years, though, gentrification and rising real estate prices have begun whittling away at the community's character, and it is becoming increasingly yuppified. The boardwalk has been given a face-lift, and young, affluent professionals – especially from the creative and computer fields – are snapping up aging bungalows and replacing them with modern mini-mansions. Chic restaurants, galleries and boutiques now bring life to previously stale streets like Abbot Kinney Blvd, named for the man who founded Venice.

Abbot Kinney (1850–1920) was a visionary, a dreamer and a developer – three hats

that helped him turn what had been nothing but dreary swampland into a thriving beachfront community he dubbed 'Venice of America.' He had the marshes drained and dug a 16-mile network of canals, which began to attract scores of new residents and merchants. He built a promenade, pier and theater for dance and theater performances. Gondoliers imported from Italy poled people through his artificial paradise, which opened – spectacularly, by all accounts – on July 4, 1905.

Kinney's original plan of making his Venice as much a high-brow cultural mecca as the original in Italy faded once the businessman in him realized that people were more interested in entertainment than edification. He brought in a Ferris wheel, a hydrogen-filled balloon, the Rapids water ride (which predated Disneyland's Thunder Mountain by decades) and other such amusements. The park's decline set in during Prohibition soon after Kinney's death in 1920. Speakeasies and gambling moved in, and in 1925 residents asked to be annexed by the city of LA, which paved over most of the canals.

Kinney may have been a little kooky, but he unwittingly set the trend for the Venice of the 20th century, which attracted any and all currents in the counterculture, be it Lawrence Lipton and Stuart Perkoff of the '50s Beat generation, Jim Morrison and his band, The Doors, and other hippies of the '60s, the New Agers of the '70s and '80s, or the roller-blading, image-obsessed babes and dudes of the '90s. Despite the recent changes, Venice still represents the image of a freewheeling, laid-back, slightly crazed but creative and cutting-edge city.

Venice Boardwalk

Bikini-clad bicyclists, chainsaw-juggling entertainers, wanna-be Schwarzeneggers flexing their biceps in an outdoor gym, a roller-skating Sikh minstrel, 'meat is murder' activists, henna tattoo artists – the Venice Boardwalk (officially known as Ocean Front Walk) is a scene that must be seen to be believed. Strolling, bicycling or

Muscle Beach

co-op; a mid-century furniture store; and a building shared by three Euro-style restaurants, a nursery, a yoga studio and an exclusive shoemaker. There are stores specializing in hand-painted tiles, remaindered dishes or essential oils and artwork galore. Once a year, usually in September, the Abbot Kinney St Festival draws thousands of revelers to a party of music, food and entertainment.

Arts Community

Many artists call Venice home, a presence reflected in the numerous galleries and abundant public art. Prime examples of the latter are Jonathan Borofsky's 34-foot **Ballerina Clown**, which balances on the facade of the Venice Renaissance Building, at Rose Ave and Main St. Nearby, four-story binoculars designed by Claes Oldenburg and Coosje van Bruggen decorate the front of the Chiat/Day Building at 340 Main St (see Tour V – The Cutting Edge in the Los Angeles Architecture special section).

Venice also enjoys a strong mural tradition and is home to the nonprofit Social & Public Art Resource Center (SPARC; see the boxed text 'A Helping Hand for Public Art' in the Facts about Los Angeles chapter). The Venice Boardwalk, in fact, is rife with famous murals, including *Chagall Returns to Venice* (1991) by Christina Schlesinger at the synagogue at 201 Ocean Front Walk and Ozone, and Rip Cronk's *Venice Reconstituted* (1989) at 25 Windward Ave.

During the Venice Art Walk, a fundraiser for the Venice Family Clinic and usually held over a May weekend, many artists open up their studios to the public for self-guided or docent-led tours. For more on Venice's numerous galleries, see the Shopping chapter.

skating along this 1½-mile stretch between Marine St in the north to the Venice Pier near the border with Marina del Rey ranks among the top things to do for LA visitors. It's the circus-like atmosphere that draws most, but other good reasons include the wide ribbon of sandy beach and some pretty good restaurants. For maximum sensory impact, come on a warm weekend afternoon.

Venice Canalwalk

Three miles of Venice's canals were restored and cleaned up in 1993 and are now lined by picturesque million-dollar-plus homes. The Canalwalk threads through this idyllic neighborhood, paralleling the tranquil waters inhabited by geese and ducks and spanned by Venetian-style bridges. It's accessed from either Venice or Washington Blvds near Dell Ave.

Abbot Kinney Boulevard

Abbot Kinney would probably be delighted to find that one of Venice's most individualistic streets bears his name. It's been a slow but steady resurgence for this cottage- and bungalow-lined boulevard, which some have called a 'seaside Melrose Ave' but with an unmistakably 'Venetian' flair. As you stroll the 1-mile stretch between Main St and Venice Blvd, you'll pass such one-of-a-kind establishments as an all-women artists'

MARINA DEL REY (MAP 13)

Just south of Venice Beach, some 6000 private sailboats and motor yachts are moored in what locals call simply 'the Marina,' the largest artificial small-craft harbor in the US. Many of the Marina's single professionals live on boats; many more inhabit apartment complexes that surround the slips on streets named after idyllic Pacific isles: Bora Bora, Tahiti, Marquesas, Panay, Palawan, Bali, Mindanao and Fiji. Don't be fooled by the names; the architecture itself is more 1960s sterile than tropical.

The Marina's leading tourist site is **Fishermen's Village** (☎ *310-823-5411, 13755 Fiji Way*), a hokey strip supposed to resemble a Cape Cod village. You *can* go fishing from here – book a trip with Marina del Rey Sportfishing (☎ 310-822-3625) – but most visitors settle for taking a harbor sightseeing cruise or browsing the diverse novelty and souvenir shops.

Just south of the Marina, in an area called Playa Vista, are the **Ballona Wetlands**, the last remaining wetlands in LA County. Fed by both salt and fresh water, they are home to hundreds of bird species, including the great blue heron, as well as fish and plant life. Once owned by Howard Hughes, the land has been in the hands of developers Maguire Thomas Partners since 1989. This company is responsible for constructing a new community atop the marshy lands, a project fought by environmentalists for two decades. Under a court-ordered compromise, the company has been allowed to go ahead with the development, with the provision that it also keeps a large chunk of the area as a bird preserve.

SOUTH BAY (MAP 14)

Manhattan Beach, Hermosa Beach and Redondo Beach form the trio of all-American beach towns ringing the southernmost part of Santa Monica Bay between LAX and the Palos Verdes Peninsula. They are beautiful, peaceful and largely Caucasian enclaves that seem a world removed from the grit and velocity that characterizes most other LA neighborhoods. Attractions here are recreational rather than cultural.

Manhattan Beach

The northernmost South Bay community is Manhattan Beach, 19 miles southwest of Downtown LA. It's an affluent, well-educated and young community that includes many USC graduates, now firmly ensconced on the career ladder, with respectable salaries that account for the city's average annual income of $70,000.

Between the beach – jam-packed on summer days with surfers and volleyball players – and the American-as-apple-pie residential areas inland is an upscale downtown lined with boutiques and restaurants, indicating a high degree of attention to modern city planning. Most of the activity centers along Manhattan Beach Blvd and the intersecting streets of Manhattan and Highland Aves.

Manhattan Beach Blvd culminates in the 928-foot pier, which leads to the **Roundhouse Marine Studies Lab & Aquarium** (☎ *310-379-8117; donations appreciated; open 3pm-sunset weekdays, 10am-sunset weekends*). Stocked with several tanks, this small facility is a clear winner with children, who get a kick out of getting close-up looks at moray eels, an octopus, reef sharks, tropical fish and a 50-year-old gargantuan lobster. They also get to finger various tide pool creatures in a touch tank.

In 1998, Hollywood came to Manhattan Beach with the opening of the **Raleigh Manhattan Beach Studios** (☎ *310-727-2700, 1600 Rosecrans Ave*), the first new studio to open in Los Angeles in about 60 years. It was conceived by Roy Disney (nephew of Walt); the TV hit series *The Practice* and *Ally McBeal* are being taped here.

Hermosa Beach

The Hermosa Pier of Hermosa Beach, located 16 miles southwest of Downtown, is 1½ miles south from Manhattan Beach's pier. A long-standing rivalry has existed between the two beach communities. Closer to the airport and the aerospace industries, Manhattan Beach has always been tidier and more affluent, while Hermosa has been more alternative, grungy and fun.

In the late 1990s Hermosa thoroughly revamped its downtown, resulting in a pleasant pedestrian zone in the area where Pier Ave meets the beach. Dozens of funky bars and restaurants provide outdoor seating, with a couple of shops and even a hostel thrown into the mix.

Workers replace a sign on one of LA's fabled freeways.

Tepid temps and tight tunes make the Hollywood Bowl a hit for outdoor concerts.

Extreme mural, Venice

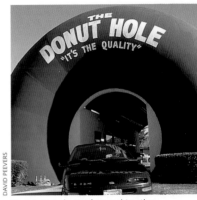

Donuts taste better from a drive-thru.

The famous Mann's Chinese Theater, Hollywood

Dino dining at Ripley's Believe It or Not!

Oscar delivery in one hour or your money back

In summer, especially, Hermosa takes on the feel of a laid-back college town, with throngs of boys and girls showing off their taut, bronzed bods. Both Manhattan and Hermosa have active professional volleyball scenes (16th St in Hermosa and Marine Ave in Manhattan are both good spots to see the pros bump, set and spike); tournaments take place frequently.

Similar to Manhattan, Hermosa was a sleepy village until a couple of railroad tycoons developed the land to attract business and passengers for their Los Angeles Pacific route. Since the end of WWII, Hermosa (like its South Bay neighbors) has been an enclave of well-to-do beachside residents.

Redondo Beach

Redondo is perhaps the most intriguing of the South Bay communities. At its north end is King Harbor, a small-boat marina and fisherfolk haven. In the heart of town, at the end of Torrance Blvd, are Monstad Pier and Fisherman's Wharf, the biggest surfside

pleasure complex south of Santa Monica. Joined at their seaward end, the pier and the wharf are chockablock with restaurants, bars, souvenir shops and a fishing dock. It's an oddly angular convoluted construction, typical of the multilevel interlocking concrete monstrosities built during the '70s.

Another attraction is the **Seaside Lagoon** (☎ 310-318-0681, 200 Portofino Way at Kings Harbor; admission adults $3.50, children 2-17 $2.50; open 10am-5:45pm daily late May to early Sept). This is a large saltwater lagoon heated by the nearby steam-generating plant and framed by sandy and grassy areas, picnic tables, volleyball courts and a snack bar.

Few clues survive to indicate that Redondo began as an early LA seaport, instrumental in bringing lumber and other cargo from ships to the blossoming city. The first wharf was completed in 1889, but Redondo's dream of winning the competition for biggest deepwater port in Los Angeles died in the 1910s when a series of major storms destroyed several of the city's

George Freeth: King of the Surfer Dudes

The Beach Boys, Frankie and Annette, Surfin' USA – surfing mythology and California have long been synonymous, and we may owe it all to land baron and railroad tycoon Henry Huntington's genius for promotion. Having developed Redondo Beach and brought the railroad there, Huntington planned to sell off his parcels of oceanfront property to the well-heeled. In 1907, to help lure prospective buyers to the area, he hired an Irish-Hawaiian athlete named George Freeth to perform his miracle of 'walking on the water' for visitors to Redondo. The crowds came, and Huntington sold a lot of land.

It was Freeth who fathered the surfing revolution that would eventually become an enormous industry and a lifestyle in California. As a child in Hawaii, after seeing an old painting showing his mother's ancestors riding the waves, he decided to try his luck at this ancient art. When the gargantuan, traditional 16-foot hardwood boards proved too hard to handle, he cut one in half, thus creating the first 'long board' – and modern surfing was born. Until 1915, Freeth held the Redondo beach crowds in thrall with daily performances and eventually became the first lifeguard in Southern California. (He received a Congressional Medal for bravely rescuing a boatload of stranded fishermen.) A bronze memorial to him on the Redondo Pier is frequently draped with leis from surfers who come from around the world to pay their respects.

Freeth died in the great influenza epidemic of 1919 at age 36, but the mark he left on world culture surpassed even the legacy of Huntington himself. Freeth's short sweet life was the original 'Endless Summer.' He was awesome, dude.

wharves, and business went to the neighboring port of San Pedro.

Tourism has always played an important role in Redondo, thanks to the efforts of Henry Huntington and others who connected the South Bay towns to LA by railway. The luxurious Hotel Redondo (no longer there), a saltwater plunge and several piers were among the early attractions, as was surfer dude George Freeth, hired by Huntington to delight visitors with his 'wave-walking' (see the related boxed text).

PALOS VERDES PENINSULA (MAP 4)

A rocky precipice rising from the sea and separating Santa Monica Bay from San Pedro Bay, the Palos Verdes Peninsula is among the most spectacular neighborhoods in LA County. Driving along its quiet, tree-lined roads, past opulent gardens and immaculately groomed Spanish-style villas, one feels transported to the Mediterranean Riviera. Views of the bay are positively sublime.

It should not be surprising that this is a neighborhood of affluence, further evidenced by the profusion of bridle trails. If you're lucky, you may not only see horses but also encounter a few of Palos Verdes' resident population of peacocks. These were introduced back in the 1920s by wily real estate developers who hoped to entice future home owners. The peacocks thrived to the point that the city exiled most of them in 1985, leaving only a few dozen to surprise visitors.

The Palos Verdes coastline is unspoiled and comprises a series of coves. The only easily accessible sandy beach is Malaga Cove; Abalone Cove is an ecological reserve with large tide pools. Surfers ride the waves at Royal Palms State Beach, while scuba divers plow the waters at White Point.

Point Vicente Interpretive Center

Landlubbers can spot migrating Pacific gray whales from the observation area of this facility (☎ 310-377-5370, 31501 Palos Verdes Dr W; exhibit prices adults/discounts $2/1;

open 10am-5pm, extended hours in summer). The whales travel by here en route from the Arctic Seas to Baja California and back between December and April. A small exhibit enlightens you about these amazing sea mammals and doubles as a Palos Verdes historical museum. Among the tidbits learned here is that Palos Verdes was originally an island and was only gradually linked to the mainland. The facility was closed at the time of research but may well have reopened by the time you're reading this. Call ahead to check.

Wayfarer's Chapel

On a knoll above the cliffs of Portuguese Bend, this enchanting chapel (☎ 310-377-1650, 5755 Palos Verdes Dr S) was designed in 1949 by Lloyd Wright, Frank's son. It was built as a memorial to Emanuel Swedenborg, an 18th-century religious reformer, and was almost entirely made of glass; note the recurrent use of the triangle, a symbol of spirituality. A canopy of trees adds to the fairytale-like quality of the place, which is constantly booked for weddings, some 700 of which are conducted here assembly-line style annually. The Swedenborgian Christian church, which owns the chapel, holds Sunday services at 11am.

South Coast Botanical Garden

An amazing example of land reclamation is this botanical garden (☎ 310-544-6815, 26300 Crenshaw Blvd; admission adults $5, students $3, children 5-12 $1; open 9am-5pm daily). Formerly it was an open pit mine for diatomite, used in making dynamite, insulators and filters. In 1957 more than 3.5 million tons of trash landed here before the area was converted into a garden in 1961. Today, some 200,000 plants representing 2000 species, plus 200 bird species, completely conceal the fact that you are standing on a pile of trash. Bisected by a stream and anchored by a lake, the gardens are divided into about 20 sections, including the Fuchsia Garden, Succulent and Cactus Garden, Children's Garden and Flower Garden. A tram operates on the weekends and plant and flower shows take place year-round.

SAN PEDRO (MAP 15)

About 21 miles south of Downtown LA, San Pedro is the burial place of Charles Bukowski but is more commonly known as the slow-paced harbor community on the northern fringe of Worldport LA, one of the busiest ports in the world. Much of the ethnically diverse population hovers near the lower end of the economic spectrum. While not blessed with great aesthetics (its seaside location aside), trendy restaurants or high culture, San Pedro still has numerous pockets of charm and interest for the visitor.

Before statehood, the Spanish allowed only two foreign ships a year to bring goods to the growing Los Angeles area, an act that fueled an active smuggling trade. In the 1870s, when Los Angeles was seeking a deepwater harbor after the arrival of the railroad, dredging work and construction of a breakwater began at San Pedro. The town incorporated in 1888 but was annexed to LA in 1909. Five years later, with the opening of the Panama Canal, San Pedro boomed.

Downtown San Pedro centers along 6th and 7th Sts between Pacific Ave and Harbor Blvd.

A good way to get around San Pedro is by Electric Trolley, which shuttles from the SS *Lane Victory* along Harbor Blvd to downtown San Pedro along 6th and 7th Sts to the Los Angeles Maritime Museum and Ports O'Call Village every 15 minutes Thursday to Sunday for a mere 25¢.

Worldport LA

The Port of Los Angeles forms the western half of Terminal Island, the port area between San Pedro and Long Beach, with the eastern half taken up by the Port of Long Beach. Together, the twin ports are the third largest in the world, after Singapore and Hong Kong. Fishing is still a main activity here, though container and cargo ships abound. Fuel, coal, chemicals, machinery and food are among the most commonly transported products. The majority is destined for Asian ports, especially Japan, South Korea, Hong Kong and China. The ballet of leviathan tankers gliding slowly out to sea is an impressive sight.

Los Angeles Maritime Museum

A former Streamline Moderne car ferry terminal (1941) has been transformed into the Los Angeles Maritime Museum (☎ 310-548-7618, Berth 84, bottom of 6th St; $1 suggested donation; open 10am-5pm Tues-Sun). The 75,000-sq-foot facility contains more than 700 ship models, figureheads, navigational equipment and an operating amateur radio station.

The battleship section has models of the USS *Hartford*, the Civil War flagship of Admiral David Farragut, and the USS *Washington*, which sank the most combat tonnage in the Pacific theater of WWII without losing a man. A highlight of the passenger-ship section is an 18-foot model of the *Titanic* constructed as a cutaway to expose the lavish interiors. Historic ships, such as Columbus' *Pinta, Niña* and *Santa Maria*, Charles Darwin's HMS *Beagle*, the Pilgrims' *Mayflower* and Sir Francis Drake's *Golden Hinde* are represented as well.

Ports O'Call Village

About half a mile south of the Maritime Museum, Ports O'Call Village is a hopeless tourist trap, supposedly evocative of 19th-century New England seaside towns. Cutesy shops hawk overpriced trinkets, and there are ice cream parlors and restaurants as well. Ports O'Call is the main departure point for harbor tours offered several times daily by Spirit Cruises (☎ 310-548-8080, Berth 77). One-hour narrated tours cost $7.50; 90-minute cruises are $9. A two-hour tour ($15) takes in the *Queen Mary* and the Navy base as it circles all of Terminal Island. Whale-watching excursions lasting 2½ hours ($15) also leave from here December through March. If it's fish you're after, deep-sea fishing launches depart for half-day and full-day excursions around 7am every day. Try LA Harbor Sportfishing (☎ 310-547-9916, Berth 79), which offers overnight, half-day and three-quarter-day trips.

Angels Gate Park & Around

A short uphill walk from Point Fermin takes you to Angels Gate Park. You'll find the impressive **Korean Friendship Bell** here; it was a gift from South Korea to the US on the latter's bicentennial in 1976 and fashioned after an 8th-century bronze bell. Some 12 feet high and weighing 17 metric tons, it's canopied by a pagoda-shaped belfry with a blue-tiled roof and a beamed, pillared, fan-like substructure. A small building houses a photo history of US-Korean relations from 1800 to today.

West of here is the **Fort MacArthur Military Museum** (*☎ 310-548-2631, 3601 S Gaffey St; donations appreciated; open noon-5pm Tues, Thur & weekends*). Fort MacArthur was established as a military reservation in 1888 and developed for military purposes just before WWI. It is now a residential community for personnel of the Air Force Space Division at El Segundo. Only the museum, housed in the Battery Osgood Farley, is open to the public. A defense post for enemy attacks from the sea between 1916 and 1945, it housed four batteries with 14-inch guns, which had a range of 14 miles. The museum documents the fort's history as a defensive post.

Cabrillo Marine Aquarium
A Frank Gehry–designed structure houses the lovely Cabrillo Marine Aquarium (*☎ 310-548-7562, 3720 Stephen White Dr; admission free, parking $6.50; open noon-5pm Tues-Fri, 10am-5pm weekends*). Recently upgraded and expanded, it is a fun and educational place, sure to keep kids entertained. And best of all, it's free.

There are 38 saltwater tanks, displaying colorful fish and other marine life from three major habitats: rocky shores, beaches and mudflats, and the open ocean. Out back is a touch tank where visitors are encouraged to handle starfish, sea urchins, sea cucumbers and other denizens of the sea.

The aquarium also offers numerous educational programs for children of all ages and runs a 'Meet the Grunion' program (March to July). Grunion are silvery fish that spawn on sandy beaches following high tide. Females deposit thousands of eggs in the sand; the eggs are instantly fertilized by the males, hatch in two weeks, and are then swept out to sea by the next tide.

Other Things to See & Do
About a mile north of the maritime museum is the SS *Lane Victory* (*☎ 310-519-9545; Berth 94, next to World Cruise Center; admission adults $3, children 5-15 $1; open 9am-4pm*). It is one of 500 'victory' ships used during WWII to transport cargo to the Allies. Today it houses a museum. On several summer weekends, the ship actually heads out to sea for an all-day cruise. Reservations are mandatory and tickets are $100.

The 1931 **Warner Grand Theater** (*☎ 310-548-7466, 478 W 6th St*), a lovely Art Deco movie palace with intricate wood carvings, underwent a major face-lift and reopened in 2000 for film screenings (mostly American classics) and live performances.

Landlubber whale-watchers have a great observation post at Point Fermin Park, Paseo del Mar at Gaffey St, San Pedro's southernmost cape. Occupying a cliff top 22 miles due north of Santa Catalina Island (which is visible on clear days), the park has tree-shaded lawns, sheltered pergolas, gardens and a palisade promenade. You can walk around, but cannot enter, the park's Victorian lighthouse (1874).

WILMINGTON (MAP 4)
Just north of San Pedro off the I-110 (Harbor Fwy) is the small town of Wilmington. The 1864 Greek Revival home of Phineas Banning, the founding father of San Pedro's harbor, has been turned into the **Banning Residence Museum** (*☎ 310-548-7777, 401 East M St; $3 donation requested; tours hourly 12:30pm-2:30pm Tues-Thur & weekends, also 3:30pm weekends*). The museum can only be seen on one-hour tours covering the mansion's kitchen, dining room and private quarters and, time permitting, also the schoolhouse and stagecoach barn. The museum is surrounded by a city park.

Two blocks south is the only Civil War–era structure in Southern California: **Drum Barracks Civil War Museum** (*☎ 310-548-7509, 1052 N Banning Blvd; $3 suggested donation; tours hourly 10am-1pm Tues-Thur, half-hourly 11:30am-2:30pm weekends*). Also built in Greek Revival, it was named for post commander Richard Drum and was in operation from 1862–1866. More than 13,000 Union soldiers were processed through here before going off to battle in the Southwest. The museum, in the former officers' quarters, can only be visited on guided tours and displays artifacts, weapons, furniture, photographs, uniforms and a 34-star Union flag.

LONG BEACH (MAP 16)

Long Beach is the county's southernmost city and its second-largest. Despite its nearly half a million inhabitants, it has maintained an easy-going small-town atmosphere, reminiscent of Santa Monica until the late 1980s. The Aquarium of the Pacific, opened in June 1998, and the majestic ocean liner *Queen Mary*, are the flagship attractions. But Long Beach also has a lively downtown, centered along Pine Ave and a pleasant shoreline around Queensway Bay. The upscale neighborhood of Belmont Shore, about 3 miles east of downtown, is a fun area and offers interesting shopping and dining along 2nd St. Farther on is the elite borough of Naples, distinguished by its canals.

On Saturday mornings, the nonprofit Long Beach Heritage organization (☎ 562-493-7019) conducts historical walking tours around downtown and through the East Village ($5).

Long Beach is easily reached from Downtown LA by the Metro Rail Blue Line. The center of town is equally easily explored on foot or by local bus – called the Passport with four routes hitting just about every place of interest (free within downtown, 90¢ otherwise). Passport bus Nos A and D both go out to Belmont Shore. The AquaBus, a water taxi, travels hourly from 11am-6pm around Queensway Bay, with stops at the aquarium, the *Queen Mary*, Pine Avenue and Shoreline Village ($2 per trip). The Transit Information Center at 223 E 1st St *(next to the Transit Mall; open 7:30am-4:30pm weekdays)* has details about getting around. Also here is Bikestation (☎ 562-436-2453) which rents city, mountain and road bikes from $5 to $7 hourly, $20 to $28 daily.

Aquarium of the Pacific

In this age of aquariums, when watery zoos proliferate faster than sea slugs on Viagra, Long Beach has fielded a contender that swims along with the best of them. A must-see on everyone's list should be the $117-million Aquarium of the Pacific (☎ 562-590-3100, www.aquariumofpacific.org, 100 Aquarium Way; admission adults $15, seniors $12, children $8, parking $6; open 10am-6pm daily).

Seventeen large habitats and 30 smaller focus tanks cover three Pacific Rim regions: Southern California & Baja, Northern Pacific and Tropical Pacific. More than 10,000 fish, and a few mammals and birds, call the museum home.

The journey kicks off in the **Great Hall of the Pacific**, dominated by a full-scale model of a blue whale, the world's largest animal. Also here is the titanic 30-foot Predator Exhibit tank – part of the **Southern California & Baja** section – whose simulated kelp forest is shared by prey and predator alike. Other aquatic residents in this gallery are the frisky seals and sea lions, and gracefully drifting, otherworldly moon jellies.

Upstairs, the icy waters of the **Northern Pacific** await. This gallery is entered through a misty 'surge channel,' to the sound of waves and screeching sea birds. Puffins, murres and other diving birds give way to a large habitat featuring playful sea otters, which were once on the verge of extinction. Wonderfully chilling are the giant spider crabs, whose football-sized bodies and spiny 3-foot-long arms make them look like fugitives from the movie *Alien*.

The final – and most impressive – gallery takes you to the tepid waters of the **Tropical Pacific**, in particular, the island archipelago of Palau in Micronesia (north of Australia), which is blessed with some of the world's most fecund and dazzling coral reefs. Fish in this environment sport a kaleidoscope of colors and include such species as angelfish, sweetlips, hawkfish, squirrelfish and several types of wrasses. As you move through the exhibit, you 'descend' farther down the reef, encountering stunning varieties of soft and hard coral (which are animals, not plants).

You will also see fragile anemones and bizarre creatures like the sea dragon, a relative of the sea horse, whose camouflage makes it look like a piece of kelp.

Laminated dive charts identifying species are available at the entrance to each section. Several touch labs provide hands-on encounters with sea cucumbers, sea urchins, sea hares, bat rays, limpets and other underwater dwellers. Enthusiastic volunteers are on hand to answer questions throughout the museum.

There's also an Information Kiosk next to the aquarium (open 10am-6pm daily Mar-Sep, 10am-4pm Fri-Sun Oct-Feb).

RMS *Queen Mary* & Around

The *Titanic* may have captured all the headlines, but the grand dame of oceanliners was the RMS *Queen Mary* (☎ 310-435-3511, 1126 Queens Hwy; admission adults $17, seniors & military $15, children $13, parking $8; open 10am-6pm daily most of the year, extended summer hours). The 81,237-ton liner was launched in 1934 and made 1001 crossings of the Atlantic before being retired in 1964 and moored in Long Beach three years later. The lavish vessel was favored by celebrities and royalty, including Fred Astaire, Greta Garbo, Bob Hope and Marlene Dietrich. The Duke and Duchess of Windsor hold the record for most steamer trunks (72), and Winston Churchill signed the D-Day invasion papers in the 1st-class ladies' drawing room.

More than 1000 feet long and 12 decks high, the *Queen Mary* accommodated its passengers in three classes: 3rd class in the bow (front) where the ride was the roughest, 2nd class in the stern (back) where propeller vibrations were the worst, and 1st class amidships. At $600, a 1st-class ticket cost three times as much as a 3rd-class ticket. The journey from Southampton to New York took 4½ days.

Much of the *Queen Mary* can be explored on a self-guided tour. It kicks off with introductory exhibits, followed by a short historical video, and then takes in the engine room, re-created state and dining rooms, the children's playroom, the gymnasium and the kitchen. A separate exhibit chronicles the ship's WWII role, when it transported 10,000 to 15,000 GIs to Europe with each journey.

Also included in the admission price is a one-hour tour that celebrates the *Queen Mary's* reputation as the stomping ground of the supernatural. Apparitions of people who died on the ship as well as voices and crying babies form the fodder for this slightly hokey trip, which provides access to areas that were previously off-limits.

Those who would like to see even more of the ship can join the Royal Historic Guided Tour for an additional $8.

Part of the ship is now a pleasant hotel with 365 state rooms, elegant restaurants and lounges, a wedding chapel and gift shops (see the Places to Stay chapter). If you like champagne brunches, the *Queen Mary's* on Sunday is among the best.

The *Queen Mary* entrance path weaves through the **Queen's Marketplace**, a fairly tacky takeoff on 19th-century British architecture. The huge adjacent dome-like shell once served as the hangar for billionaire aviator Howard Hughes' bizarre flying boat, the *Spruce Goose*. A few years ago, the plane was sold and moved to Oregon's Air Venture Museum. At the time of writing, the dome was to be converted into a new terminal for Carnival Cruise Lines.

In 1998, the *Queen* got a new neighbor, the **Scorpion** (☎ 562-435-3511; admission adults/discounts $10/9, combination tickets with Queen Mary $27/25/21; open 10am-6pm daily most of the year, extended summer hours). This Russian submarine is open for touring but has a cramped interior. Built in 1973, it was retired in 1994. After a short introductory film, you're guided via voiceover narration by a 'Russian commander' through the front torpedo room, living quarters, engine room and kitchen – all on a suffocatingly Lilliputian scale. It's hard to fathom how 78 crew members, sharing 27 bunks and two bathrooms, coexisted for months at a time.

Directly across Queensway Bay from the two vessels are **Shoreline Village** (☎ 310-435-2668), a shopping-and-dining complex, and **Rainbow Harbor**, the home of as many as 50 commercial boats offering harbor, dinner and whale-watching cruises as well as deep-sea fishing expeditions. Boats include several tallships and the *Na Hoku*, a beach-docking catamaran.

Museum of Latin American Art

Contemporary Latin American art is showcased at this fine museum (☎ 562-437-1689, 628 Alamitos Ave; admission adults $7, students & seniors $5, free for children under 12; open 11:30am-7:30pm Tues-Sat, noon-6pm Sun). It's housed in a complex that integrates the historic Hippodrome Skating Rink from 1920 and the former silent-movie Balboa Studio. There's also an adjacent multipurpose performing-arts and entertainment center to get the community involved. The museum claims the distinction of being the only museum dedicated to modern Latin American art in the western US and functions as the eastern anchor of the East Village Arts District, a slow-moving effort at revitalizing a not-terribly-vital part of town.

Long Beach Museum of Art (Map 4)

The dramatic oceanfront location is not the only strength of this museum (☎ 562-439-2119, 2300 E Ocean Blvd; admission adults $5, students & seniors $4, children under 12 free; open 11am-5pm Tues-Sun). Exhibits here are drawn from a permanent collection of about 5000 paintings, drawings and sculptures with particular strengths in 20th-century European art, California Modernism and contemporary art, including about 3000 artists' videos. The museum is also known for its American decorative arts. In 2000 it got sparkling new galleries in a two-story pavilion overlooking the ocean. It stands next to a 1912 Craftsman mansion, which now houses the administrative offices, a store and a cafe.

NAPLES (MAP 4)

Hugging the Orange County line, this upscale residential community consists of a trio of islands surrounded by Alamitos Bay.

The islands were reclaimed from marshland starting in 1903 by Arthur Parsons, a chronological and philosophical contemporary of Venice's Abbot Kinney. The **Rivo Alto Canal** still circles a network of curving lanes lined by garden-shrouded cottages. It's a pleasure to stroll around the canals on waterfront walkways, although perhaps the most enchanting way to experience Naples' beauty is by water.

When in Naples, do as the Venetians do. You can take a one-hour gondola cruise along the Naples canals through **Gondola Getaway** (☎ 562-433-9595, 5437 E Ocean Blvd; price $55 per couple, up to four additional persons $10 each, reservations necessary; open 11am-11pm daily). You get to relax with a loaf of bread, cheese and salami (bring your own wine); PS: Don't forget to kiss your sweetie under each and every bridge. The fleet includes 30-foot authentic Venetian vessels, which have a loose oar, and the larger American boats steered with two fixed oars. Each year, Naples' gondoliers participate in the *Vogalonga* race in Venice, Italy. In fact, they beat the Italians their first time out.

South Central

Gangs, drugs, poverty, crime and drive-by shootings are just a few of the negative images – not entirely undeservedly – associated with this district. Yet pockets of this area are surprisingly appealing, both culturally and historically. Early LA bigwigs built grand mansions here, while culture and the arts – especially jazz music – thrived to the point where South Central invited comparison to New York's Harlem.

Most of the area's neighborhoods and commercial strips were hard hit by the 1992 riots, as they were by the Watts riots of 1965 (see the boxed text 'The Los Angeles Riots: 1992 & 1965' in the Facts about Los Angeles chapter). While not a traditional tourist destination, South Central has a culture and history entirely its own; especially for those interested in LA's African American heritage, it should not be overlooked.

LA Street Gangs

Although gangs have been around in California since before the gold rush, the LA-based Crips and the Bloods are two of the country's most infamous gangs. Originally close-knit neighborhood affiliations, these gangs battled over turf and control of the drug trade for more than 20 years. Other players in LA's past and present crime circuit include Latino gangs, which are, in fact, even more prevalent than African American ones, and Asian and white gangs. It's estimated that almost 9600 people died in gang-related crimes in Los Angeles between 1971 and 1998 and there are reportedly over 1100 street gangs in the city.

The Crips-Blood truce in the early '90s and targeted civic measures have helped stunt the growth of a new generation of gangs. But perhaps the most startling anti-gang effort has come from the alleged co-founder of the Crips, Stanley 'Tookie' Williams. In 1971, Williams was branded a menace to society, perhaps achieving the highest aspiration of a gangbanger, and sentenced to death for four robbery-related murders. A stint in solitary confinement (euphemistically called the 'Adjustment Center') in the early '90s awoke remorse in Williams. He renounced his gang life and wrote a series of children's books advocating nonviolence. The series *Tookie Speaks Out Against Gang Violence* and his autobiography *Life in Prison* caught the attention of a member of the Swiss Parliament, who nominated Williams for the 2001 Nobel Peace Prize. While winning the prize is unlikely, Williams' nomination poses California with an unprecedented predicament: Will the state execute a nominee for the highest peace prize in the world? Stay tuned or visit Williams' Web site at www.tookie.com.

Unfortunately, the crime rate in sections of this area is rather high, and while it's unlikely that you will become a target, it's better to exercise extra caution and to restrict visits to the daytime.

WEST ADAMS

In the late 19th and early 20th century, the West Adams district, encompassing the area just south of the I-10 (Santa Monica Fwy) between Crenshaw Blvd to the west and Vermont Ave to the east, was one of LA's best addresses. Hollywood movie stars like Fatty Arbuckle lived here, as did industrial magnates like the Doheny family. Although West Adams has long since been supplanted by other fashionable communities farther west, many of the district's historic mansions, churches and other notable buildings still survive.

Doheny Mansion (Map 5)

One of the finest examples is the Doheny Mansion *(8 Chester Place)*, a lavish French Gothic chateau dating back to 1898 and

designed by Theodore Eisen and Sumner Hunt. It featured the first elevator in a private home; its Pompeiian Room is decked out in marble and topped by a Tiffany glass ceiling. It now stands on the grounds of the Downtown campus of Mount St Mary's College and often hosts chamber music concerts organized by the Da Camara Society *(☎ 310-440-1351)*. Other late-Victorian-era buildings are in the immediate area as well.

William Andrews Clark Memorial Library (Map 2)

One of LA's best kept secrets is this gem of a library *(☎ 323-731-8529, 2520 Cimarron St; reading rooms open 9am-4:45pm Mon-Fri)*. Today an adjunct to UCLA, it was built in 1926 by noted architect Robert Farquhar for William Andrews Clark Jr, the son of a copper-mining millionaire. Clark amassed an extraordinary book collection, particularly focused on English history and literature of the 17th and 18th century and the works of Oscar Wilde. While the written works are primarily of interest to scholars and researchers, everybody will be able to appreciate the library's idyllic garden atmosphere and sumptuous Italian Baroque interior.

The vestibule is a symphony in multihued, patterned marble, crowned by a painted ceiling depicting Apollo with his mother, Leto, and the Nine Muses. The grand music room was modeled after a chamber in the doge's palace in Venice, Italy; it is clad in oak walls and velvet drapery and features a Steinway grand piano, Persian carpet and a richly carved ceiling. The two book rooms are lined by two levels of bookcases as well as alabaster chandeliers and trompe l'oeil decorations. The reading rooms are open to the public during library hours, but appointments are needed to see the other rooms. Chamber music concerts and other events sometimes take place here, but tickets are very limited and often only available on a lottery basis.

CENTRAL AVENUE (MAP 3)

The northern end of Central Ave, just south of Downtown, was the center of African American life from the 1920s until the 1960s, though not entirely by choice. Kept from moving to other neighborhoods by restrictive racial covenants, LA blacks essentially became ghettoized around the time of WWI. Other restrictions kept black actors and musicians out of the evolving movie industry. As a result, Central Ave became a center of jazz and other entertainment.

The **Dunbar Hotel** (☎ 323-234-7882, 4225 S Central Ave), which opened in 1928 as a hotel for black visitors (who were barred from staying at other, white only, hotels), took on unofficial headquarters status. Every major black musician or singer, including Lena Horne, Ella Fitzgerald, Count Basie and Duke Ellington, stayed in this hotel. Clubs such as the Parisian Room, Ivy's Chicken Shack and Club Alabam thrived until the start of the area's decline in the '50s. As the clubs closed, the Dunbar fell into decay and even faced the threat of demolition in 1988. Restored since, it's now

a senior citizens home. To get a sense of Central Ave's heyday, visit the small exhibition in the Dunbar lobby.

LEIMERT PARK (MAP 2)

The Leimert Park neighborhood is south of Martin Luther King Jr Blvd and east of Crenshaw Blvd in the Crenshaw district. The park that anchors it is a nicely kept swath of green surrounded by quiet streets with towering trees and handsome single-family homes. Leimert Park was named after architect Walter Leimert, who conceived the space as a community for upper middle-class whites. Ironically, it is now predominantly inhabited by upper middle-class African Americans and has even been called 'Brenthood' by clever punsters (a take-off on the wealthy Westside enclave of Brentwood). In recent years, the neighborhood has witnessed a steep cultural ascent and it is now the hub of cutting-edge arts. The action is centered in Leimert Village, a two-block strip of Degnan Blvd between 43rd St and Leimert Park, where you'll find restaurants, coffeehouses, shops and performance spaces, most of them black-owned. (For recommendations for clubs in Leimert Park, see the Entertainment chapter.)

Museum in Black

Unusual masks, fertility and spiritual figures, instruments, jewelry and other artifacts imported from Africa can be found at this museum-cum-gallery (☎ 323-292-9528, 4331 Degnan Blvd; admission free; usually open noon-6pm Mon-Fri). It is owned by the quirky Brian Breye, an outspoken community advocate who began his career as a dealer in Asian antiques. An avid collector for over 30 years, he shops for art in Mali, Nigeria, Côte d'Ivoire and other African countries. Most of the pieces are for sale and are considered highly collectible. Ask to see the back room jammed with an astonishing collection of 'Negro' memorabilia – cookie jars, salt and pepper shakers, books, dolls, photos, etc – attesting both to the humiliation and the accomplishments of American blacks over the past decades.

Museum of African American Art

The 3rd floor of the Robinsons-May department store, in the mall at Baldwin Hills Crenshaw Plaza, is home to this small museum (☎ 323-294-7071, 4005 S Crenshaw Blvd; admission free; open 11am-6pm Thur-Sat, noon-5pm Sun). Look for the works of Palmer Hayden, a leading artist of the Harlem Renaissance, as well as art objects from Africa, the Caribbean, South America and the US. The mall is partly owned by basketball superstar Magic Johnson and contains a movie multiplex named for him.

CITY OF VERNON (MAP 3)

There's not much reason to go to industrial Vernon, about 2 miles southeast of Downtown. Its only redeeming value for the traveler is a highly unusual – some might even say macabre – landmark: the **Farmer John Pig Mural** (3049 E Vernon Ave). The gigantic mural, which covers the exterior facade of a sausage factory, depicts a bucolic landscape inhabited by happy oinkers romping and frolicking in the lush countryside, clearly oblivious to their future as pork rinds. It's the design of Les Grimes who, alas, didn't live to see his finished work; he fell to his death from a scaffold while painting the mural.

WATTS (MAP 3)

Watts is about 7 miles due south of Downtown and is served by the Metro Rail Blue Line to Long Beach. Trains have passed through Watts since 1902 when the Pacific Electric Company built a railway junction here. In those days, Watts was a multiethnic farming community of working-class Italian, German, Japanese, Chinese and Latino immigrants. Within a couple of decades, it became dominated by African Americans, largely because of racial covenants prohibiting them from settling in other neighborhoods in LA. In the 1990s, the area's ethnic makeup changed again; now about half of the population is Latino.

Watts has repeatedly been in the headlines for its violent, drug-related gang activity. It was a hotbed during both the 1965 and 1992 riots. It is not advisable to come here at night.

Watts Towers

One of the most beloved sights in Los Angeles is the Watts Towers (☎ 213-847-4646, 1765 E 107th St). On the National Register of Historic Places, this is the life's work of Italian immigrant Simon Rodia. It is a curious and unique folk-art monument that has the same whimsical and filigree aspects often associated with Spanish architect Antonio Gaudí. It's hard to fathom, though, that the towers are the product of a solitary and unskilled laborer, working with no architectural training and only simple

DAVID PEEVERS

Watts Towers

tiling tools. In that sense, the Watts Towers are nothing less than a testament to human imagination, vision and perseverance.

In 1921, Rodia set out to 'make something big' – and then spent the next 33 years doing just that. Supporting his towers are slender columns containing steel reinforcement, which he tied with wire, wrapped with wire mesh and covered by hand with cement. Incorporated into the facade are glass, mirrors, sea shells, rocks, ceramic tile and pottery. Most of the glass comes from soda bottles, especially green 7-Up bottles. When, in 1954, he decided his work was finished, the sculpture consisted of several towers (the tallest standing almost 100 feet), a gazebo with a circular bench, three bird baths and other sections. The same year, he suddenly gave the land to a neighbor and moved to the San Francisco Bay Area, where he died 11 years later having never returned to LA.

In the 1960s the towers were scheduled for an appointment with the wrecking ball. Luckily, neighbors banded together and the towers were saved. The riots left them unscathed, though the 1994 earthquake did not. A recent restoration is likely to be complete by the time you're reading this and tours (weekends only) should have resumed; for details, call the number above. To visit, take the Metro Rail Blue Line to the 103rd St/Kenneth Hahn station.

Watts Towers Art Center

Adjacent to Rodia's structure is the Watts community arts center (☎ 213-485-1795 or 213-847-4646, 1727 E 107th St; admission free; 10am-4pm Wed-Sun). It houses an interesting gallery with an excellent permanent display of folk instruments and changing exhibits of contemporary fine art by local and national artists. The center also sponsors free art classes, dance and theater workshops, and other programs designed to involve the community and help locals express themselves artistically. Begun in 1970, it was funded entirely through a community campaign known as 'One Square Inch,' whereby each dollar donated 'bought' the donor a square inch of the center.

Watts Labor Community Action Center

In the historic heart of Watts, this 7-acre complex is simply known as the Center (WLCAC; ☎ 213-563-5642, 10950 S Central Ave; open daily, call for hours). It was founded by union activist Ted Watkins after the 1965 riots and provides such social services as day care, job training and senior services. The Center has been operating from its current facilities since 1992, after the original structure was torched during the 1992 riots. It has been instrumental in bringing a hospital, two shopping centers, a park and other infrastructure to Watts. Through its exhibits and cultural events, the Center also strives to bring Angelenos from other parts of the city, as well as tourists, to Watts in an effort to reverse the negative perceptions of the area.

Anchoring a water garden is *The Mother of Humanity*, a bronze sculpture by Nigel Binns, which blends physical features and spiritual symbols of all races in a celebration of contributions by women to civilization. The northern edge of the complex features the Mudtown Flats, a row of facades intended to re-create Central Ave in its '20s and '30s heyday. Depicting such places as the Plantation Night Club and the Largo Theater, it often serves as a backdrop for movie shoots.

Off to the east is the Ted Watkins Center for Communication, a 35,000-sq-foot space named for the Center's founder who died in 1992. Inside are several performance spaces, a gallery and the interesting free Civil Rights Museum. A tour of the latter starts with a peek into the hull of a slave ship filled with human figures and continues with a walk down a virtual Mississippi Delta dirt road, complete with crickets, wagons, trees and other props. It leads to the Countdown to Eternity, an exhibit focused on telling the story of Martin Luther King Jr and the 1960s Civil Rights Movement through photographs and artifacts.

The Center also sponsors concerts and other events. You can explore on your own, but free guided tours are available as well (call ahead).

East LA

Driving into East LA – just beyond the LA River, east of Downtown – feels a bit like crossing the border from San Diego into Tijuana. More than 90% of its one million residents are Latino, a trend that began in the 1920s; today East LA's 15 sq miles have the largest concentration of Mexicans outside of Mexico. Before the '20s, the area had been more heterogeneous, with large pockets of Jewish, Armenian and Russian populations.

Life in the barrio is tough but lively. People shop and mill about in the streets lined with bakeries *(panaderías)*, convenience stores *(tiendas)*, stores selling herbal cures *(botanicas)* and toy shops. Brightly colored murals adorn many facades. But behind the color, life can look pretty grim. The district suffers from high unemployment and crime, low income and poor schools and infrastructure. One thing East LA has plenty of is cemeteries, a sad fact that underscores the violence so prevalent in this gang-infested neighborhood.

In general, East LA is not conducive to tourist visits. Though unlikely, the risk of becoming the victim of a crime is greater here than almost anywhere else in LA (with the possible exception of Compton). What little there is to see is pretty much located in the district of Boyle Heights, the first you'll get to from Downtown LA. It is best to visit in the daytime and communication may be easier if you speak at least a few words of Spanish.

Crisscrossed by four freeways, East LA's main artery is Cesar E Chavez Ave, named for the famous farm worker and union organizer, which is basically a continuation of Sunset Blvd. It was formerly known as Brooklyn Ave, because in the old days stores along here sold bagels and gefilte fish rather than tamales and *bolillos* (bread rolls).

Those familiar with Joseph Wambaugh's crime novels might want to check out **Hollenbeck Police Station** *(2111 E 1st St)*, which was his base as a cop.

Good streets to see are **Cesar E Chavez Ave, Mission Rd** and the neon-festooned **Whittier Blvd**, whose section between the I-710 (Long Beach Fwy) and Atlantic Blvd has been dubbed 'East LA's Sunset Strip' for its concentration of clubs, bars and restaurants. A darker moment in Whittier Blvd's history came on August 29, 1970, when an anti-Vietnam-War demonstration in Belvedere Park, just north of here, was interrupted by police and resulted in rioting. In the melee, Ruben Salazar, a noted Latino journalist covering the incident for the *Los Angeles Times*, was killed by a gas pellet fired by a sheriff's deputy. A park at 3864 E Whittier Blvd was recently named after Salazar.

BREED STREET SHUL (MAP 3)

Today it's hard to imagine that, between 1910 and 1950, some 80,000 Jews called Boyle Heights home and that there were 27 active synagogues. The only one to survive as a building, though no longer as an active congregation, is the 1923 Breed Street Shul *(247 N Breed St)*, one block west of Soto St. Until WWII it was the largest Orthodox shul west of Chicago. The brick facade, in Renaissance style, features leaf ornamentation and Jewish symbols around an arched portal. Inside, there's stained glass, wood carvings and murals. Badly damaged in the 1987 Whittier earthquake, it has been closed since 1992 and has been subjected to vandalism. In 1998, during a visit to LA, it caught the eye of then-first lady, now-senator Hillary Clinton, who made it part of the Save America's Treasures program, a bipartisan partnership between the government and private individuals and corporations. Restoration is now imminent.

MARIACHI PLAZA (MAP 5)

Mariachis are traditional Mexican musicians who play an endless repertory of folkloric songs on trumpet and guitar. They are usually dressed in black ranchero suits and often wear broad sombreros. Every day in the afternoon, freelance mariachis congregate beneath wall-sized murals, suitably depicting a group of musicians, at the corner of

Boyle Ave and 1st St, where they wait to be hired for restaurant performances or social gatherings.

SELF-HELP GRAPHICS GALLERY (MAP 3)

This community arts center (☎ 323-881-6444, 3802 Cesar E Chavez Ave; open 10am-4pm Tues-Sat and noon-4pm Sun) was founded in 1972 by Sister Karen Boccalero, a Franciscan nun with a strong belief in the healing powers of art. It's housed in a clunky building that would be nondescript were it not for its cheerful mural of broken glass and pottery shards. Inside is a gallery with changing exhibits, as well as a shop. The center is renowned for its workshop where students learn how to make multi-hued silkscreen prints.

EL MERCADO (MAP 3)

If you only visit one place in East LA make it El Mercado (☎ 323-268-3451, 3425 E 1st St), a wonderfully boisterous, sticky and colorful indoor market. Exuberantly decorated stalls sell a wide assortment of such 'must-haves' as tortilla-making machines and mariachi outfits for toddlers. At butcher shops you learn that no animal part is unfit for consumption. Tripe, beef tendon and pig snout are hawked next to ham, steak and chorizo. Fresh fish, shrimp and ceviche are here, as are handmade tamales and other delicacies. At a couple of lively restaurants upstairs you might be serenaded by mariachi musicians (see the Places to Eat chapter for restaurant recommendations).

PLAZA DE LA RAZA (MAP 3)

Plaza de la Raza (☎ 323-223-2475, 3540 N Mission Rd) is a multidisciplinary community arts center that in many ways is the cultural and artistic heart of this area. Spread over several buildings in 46-acre Lincoln Park, it was founded in 1970 by Mexican-born actress and singer Margo Albert and unionist Frank López. Its primary mission is to provide free or inexpensive after-school classes in theater, dance and the fine arts to neighborhood children. Two theaters, one of them outdoors near the park's pond, are

To Save & Protect

She is beautiful, dark-skinned and wears an innocent smile and flowing robes. She's also the most powerful woman in Latino-dominated East LA. Revered and feared, she stops robberies, inspires people to treat each other with respect, protects store owners and keeps graffiti from defacing buildings. And she's just about everywhere: you see her around every street corner, gracing stores, apartment buildings and churches.

Who is she? She is the Virgen de Guadalupe and she's a strong spiritual symbol among Mexican Catholics living in neighborhoods where violence and destruction of property are as normal as the sunrise. Her image acts as a deterrent to criminals, perhaps more effectively than an entire battalion of cops. Shop owners especially have discovered that having the image of her on their facade will keep business out of harm's way. Gang bangers and grandmothers cross themselves when walking by the paintings. One tough guy in an interview with the *LA Times* said 'I don't really trip on her...but I respect her because she's the mother of God. She was pregnant through the spirit.'

the venues of frequent dance, drama and other events. The Margo Albert Festival takes place twice annually and celebrates the traditions of LA's Mexican people with crafts, food, music and dance. More important, though, is Con Sabor Latino, a free summer concert series (on weekends), which brings nationally recognized musicians and dancers to East LA.

There's also a small gallery and La Tiendita, a store selling folk art and crafts. Lincoln Park itself, created in 1870, is notable for its 300 species of trees.

North Central (Map 3)

Thetwo neighborhoods of Mt Washington and Highland Park wrap around the Arroyo Seco, a gorge following a dry riverbed that runs from the San Gabriel Mountains to the LA River. It was flooded with artists and architects in the early 20th century, but lost its idyllic setting to the I-110 (Pasadena Fwy) in 1940. Several of its attractions still spotlight a pre-metropolitan LA.

SOUTHWEST MUSEUM

Looking out over the Arroyo Seco from its perch atop Mt Washington is the Southwest Museum (☎ 323-221-2164, 234 Museum Dr; admission adults $6, seniors & students $4, children 7-18 $3; open 10am-5pm Tues-Sun). The museum holds one of the most formidable collections of Native American art and artifacts in the US. It's also LA's oldest museum, founded in 1907 by Charles F Lummis (see the boxed text 'Don Carlos' Crusade'). Built in the Mission Revival style, the museum sports a distinctive seven-story tower and is reached via a steep driveway.

The Southwest Museum boasts an astonishing array of items, from prehistoric to contemporary, with each of the four halls dedicated to a native North American culture: the Great Plains, the Northwest Coast, the Southwest and California. This division allows visitors to compare the widely differing traditions, rituals, clothing, crafts, religious ceremonies, and social and political organizations. Notable items include moccasins, flaring feather headdresses, jewelry, work tools such as fleshers and knives, a Lakota teepee, dioramas of Indian scenes made in the 1930s, totem poles, winnowing trays and a replica of a sacred site with petroglyph carvings.

The museum also owns one of the largest basket collections in the USA (11,000 items), as well as some 7000 pieces of pottery and 6600 paintings, textiles, religious icons and decorative and folk art from Latin America. Because of crippling space restrictions, only 7% of the museum's extraordinary holdings are displayed at one time. A major draw for scholars from around the world is the Braun Research Library.

EL ALISAL

From 1898 and 1910, LA preservationist Charles F Lummis built El Alisal, also known as the Lummis House (☎ 323-222-0546, 200 E Ave 43 at Carlota Blvd; donations appreciated; open 1pm-4pm Thur- Sun). Trying to capture the Western spirit in its construction, Lummis used granite boulders from the adjacent Arroyo Seco for walls, telephone poles for ceilings and iron railroad rails as wall reinforcements. Today the Historical Society of Southern California is based here and maintains a small exhibit about Lummis, who was LA's first city librarian, a prolific writer and editor, and almost single-handedly preserved LA's original 18th-century missions at San Gabriel and San Fernando.

HERITAGE SQUARE MUSEUM

Eight vintage Victorian buildings dating from 1865 to 1914 were rescued from the wrecking ball by the LA Cultural Heritage Board. These treasures were moved to an open-air museum known as Heritage Square (☎ 626-449-0193, 3800 Homer St, just off the Ave 43 exit of the I-110/Pasadena Fwy; admission adults $5, seniors & teens $4, children 7-12 $2; open 10:30am-3:30pm Fri, 11:30am-4:30pm Sat, Sun & holiday Mon).

Don Carlos' Crusade

By the mid-1880s, Los Angeles had proven itself a city capable of generating huge amounts of capital. Many men had made fortunes, and these same men, now the oligarchs of a large city, became suddenly aware that for all of its growth and potential, Los Angeles still didn't seem to have any culture.

That's when Charles Fletcher Lummis arrived. Suffering from malaria, Lummis (1859–1928) left his Cincinnati home in 1884 for the Southern California sun – walking the entire way! During his five-month, 3000-mile hike, he cabled installments of an illustrative travel series to the *LA Times*, and on reaching his destination he accepted a job as editor for the paper.

Lummis very quickly asserted himself as a preacher of Southern California culture. As a writer of books and editor of a highly popular magazine called *Land of Sunshine*, he spread the notion that the California sun made life healthier and more productive. He also developed the dubious idea that California's mission heritage was an example of a new, more leisurely way of life – far more humane than life in East Coast cities. He urged Angelenos to build their city in the spirit of the missions and other Spanish models of civilization.

But in his enthusiasm for Spanish culture Lummis was a bit eccentric. He called himself 'Don Carlos' and dieted strictly on chili, tamales and refried beans. And though he'd originally come to Los Angeles for his health, in just four years he nearly worked, drank, ate and smoked himself to death, suffering a massive stroke before the age of 30. He recovered and then spent 15 years building his highly original mansion, which he named El Alisal (meaning 'sycamore'). The building still stands in the Mt Washington area near the Southwest Museum, which he co-founded, and is a fascinating tribute to this unusual man's life. It now houses the headquarters of the Historical Society of Southern California.

Ironically, Lummis' gospel was distributed throughout the East and Midwest by real estate promoters – and the mass society and industrialism that resulted were the exact opposite of what he seemed to have in mind.

Some structures have already been restored; others are still awaiting their face-lifts.

Highlights include the 1876 Perry House with its Italianate facade, and the Hale House, built in the Queen Anne/Eastlake style in 1885. The Longfellow Hastings Octagon House of 1893 is one of only three surviving octagonal houses, a style popular in the late 19th century. Another standout is the Lincoln Ave Methodist Church from 1897. The museum ticket booth is housed in a former railroad depot (1887) of the Southern Pacific Railroad.

The grounds are open for self-guided tours but you'll only get to marvel at the building's interiors during tours offered on the hour from noon to 3pm (included in the admission price).

San Gabriel Valley

The San Gabriel Valley refers to an ill-defined area northeast of Downtown LA, snuggled against the southern rim of the San Gabriel Mountains (the range that forms the northern border of the LA Basin – also see Mountains, later in this chapter). Although the district derives its name from the city of San Gabriel, the cultural center of the region is Pasadena. Originally inhabited by Gabrieleño Indians, the San Gabriel Valley was claimed in 1769 by missionaries, who established Mission San Gabriel Archangel near the banks of the San Gabriel River in 1771. In the following century, land-grant ranchos were broken into smaller tracts and a series of orchard towns emerged. As the population expanded, these towns grew together and today the valley has become a continuous suburban sprawl, extending more than 25 miles east from Alhambra and Pasadena in the west all the way to Claremont on the border of San Bernardino County. Large pockets of the San Gabriel Valley, Monterey Park and Alhambra in particular, are now home to large enclaves of Asian Americans.

PASADENA (MAP 17)

The Tournament of Roses may have given Pasadena long-lasting fame, but it's the progressive spirit of this stately city that characterizes it today. From its impressive early-20th-century mansions to its fine art museums and culinary pleasures, Pasadena is a happening place.

Approximately a 15-minute drive northeast of Downtown, Pasadena rests in the shadow of the San Gabriel Mountains. The city was founded in 1873 by Midwestern settlers who gave it a Chippewa name meaning 'crown of the valley.' Pasadena incorporated in 1886, and before long five commuter trains a day linked it with Downtown LA. Wealthy Easterners, drawn by the temperate climes, made Pasadena a fashionable winter haunt in the late 19th century. Those who stayed permanently included Henry Huntington, whose estate – now the Huntington Library, Art Collection and Botanical Gardens – is one of LA's greatest cultural treasures.

In the early 20th century, Pasadena became a haven for writers, painters and especially architects. In 1891, Amos G Throop founded Throop University, which evolved into the renowned California Institute of Technology. In 1940, Southern California's first freeway opened, the Arroyo Seco Pkwy – since designated as the I-110 (Pasadena Fwy). This freeway connected the city with Downtown LA, and even more commuters settled in Pasadena. About 139,000 people now call the city home. The mountains are often obscured by smog, but when it's clear there are few prettier places in LA County.

A fleet of free Pasadena ARTS buses regularly shuttles people between Old Pasadena, the Pasadena Playhouse District and South Lake Ave. Buses operate from 11am-7pm Monday to Thursday, to 10pm Friday, noon-8pm weekends.

Old Pasadena

Remember surf rockers Jan and Dean's 'Little Old Lady from Pasadena,' who was 'the terror of Colorado Blvd'? That was back in the '60s, but Pasadena's main street, Colorado Blvd, is still cruisin' territory for the college and yuppie crowd and, perhaps, an occasional little old lady.

Old Town is the heart of Pasadena, a 20-block historic district with early-20th-century buildings stretching out along Colorado Blvd between Arroyo Seco Pkwy and Pasadena Ave. In the early 1990s, this area underwent a renaissance that brought restaurants and coffeehouses, retail chain stores, bookstores, galleries, nightclubs and cinema complexes.

For a glimpse at Pasadena's heyday as a resort town, head one block south of Colorado Blvd on Raymond Ave to Green St, where you'll find an imposing Moorish and Spanish Colonial structure. Featuring a domed tower connected to the main building via a bridge, this complex contains the **Hotel Green** and the **Castle Green**. Built at the end of the 19th century, they were popular lodges for vacationers arriving at the nearby railroad station on Raymond Ave. While the glory of the Hotel Green (entrance at 50 E Green St) seriously faded as it became a low-income and senior citizens' residence, the Castle Green was given a thorough face-lift and converted into condominiums (closed to the public).

Norton Simon Museum

The new Getty Center may get all the attention these days, but visitors shouldn't overlook the Norton Simon Museum (☎ 626-449-6840, 411 W Colorado Blvd; admission adults $6, seniors $3, children under 18 free; open noon-6pm Wed-Mon, to 9pm Fri). It boasts an outstanding collection of European art, from the Renaissance to the

The World 'Tourns' Its Attention to Pasadena

Every year Pasadena enters the world's limelight on New Year's Day as it stages the Tournament of Roses Parade, seen locally by about a million spectators and beamed to millions more in some 100 countries via satellite. Conceived by the Valley Hunt Club in 1890, the event originally consisted of a parade of flower-festooned horse-and-buggies followed by young men competing in foot races and tugs-of-war.

So why 'tournament'? That name hails from a third event called the 'tourney of rings,' which is similar to a medieval jousting. It involved mounted horsemen equipped with 12-foot lances trying to spear three rings hung 30 feet apart while riding at top speed. Today's Rose Parade no longer includes that event, but it does feature marching bands, horses and humongous floats, all smothered in flowers and floral material. Average floats consume about 100,000 blossoms and cost $250,000 and up. After the parade, floats can be admired close-up for two days at Victory Park, 2575 Paloma St.

Since 1902, a football game has traditionally followed the parade. The contest, known as 'The Granddaddy of Them All,' was hugely successful and prompted the construction, in 1922, of a 100,000-seat stadium, the Rose Bowl. The New Year's Day game still matches the best Pac-10 (West Coast) university team with the best from the Big 10 (Great Lakes region).

20th century, and an exquisite sampling of 2000 years of Asian sculpture from India and Southeast Asia.

Botticelli, Cézanne, Degas, Goya, Matisse, Monet, Picasso, Raphael, Rembrandt, Renoir, Rubens, Toulouse-Lautrec and Van Gogh are just a few of the big-name artists found here.

Norton Simon (1907–1993) was a skilled entrepreneur who started out, in 1924, by investing in a bankrupt orange-juice bottling plant, eventually growing his empire into a multinational corporation that included Hunt-Wesson Foods, McCalls Corporation and Canada Dry. Simon's love for art, evidenced by his 25 years of collecting, culminated in his reorganizing of the Pasadena Museum of Modern Art (founded in 1924) in 1974. The museum was renamed in his honor. To improve the lighting and display conditions for the exquisite art works, the museum recently underwent a $5 million remodel under the auspices of Frank Gehry. At the same time, noted landscape designer Nancy Goslee Power turned the outdoor space into a lovely sculpture garden in the tradition of Claude Monet's Giverny.

In the opinion of many an expert, Norton Simon had far better taste in art than J Paul Getty, amassing a collection superior in quality, if not in size. Indeed, rare works by history's most skilled and renowned artists are found here. Among the oldest pieces in the collection are depictions of religious figures – including a stunning *Madonna and Child* by Paolo Veneziano done in tempera and gold leaf. Veneziano presents his subjects in an oddly detached way, with the baby Jesus bearing distinct adult features. This contrasts sharply with versions of the same characters by 15th-century Italian Renaissance artists Botticelli and Raphael, who show mother and son in a soft and natural way, wrapped up in a tender embrace and with Jesus as a chubby tot.

Other highlights in the old masters galleries are the stylized double painting *Adam and Eve* (c. 1530), by the German Lucas Cranach the Elder, and *The Resurrection* (1455), which is anchored by a strangely one-footed Jesus, by the Flemish artist Dietric Bouts.

Examples of the Baroque period include several portraits by Rembrandt, including a portrait in progress of his son Titus (1650).

Also look for several works by Canaletto, an opera-set designer turned landscape artist who specialized in realistic landscapes painted with postcard-like precision.

Well-represented as well are the French impressionists. Leading the pack are Edgar Degas' more than 100 pastels, drawings, oils and bronze sculptures. Degas' artistic worship of the female figure shines through brightly in his series of ballet dancers and seated nudes. Usually portrayed facing away from the viewer, their individual identities are less important than the aesthetics of their bodies and their movement. The hauntingly colored *Tahitian Woman and Boy* (1891) is a striking work by bourgeois-turned-bohemian Paul Gauguin; he traded his life as a stockbroker in France for that of a painter in the South Seas.

Works by Pablo Picasso share gallery space with those of Matisse, Gris, Braque and Seurat. A perennial favorite work is Claude Monet's rendition of his garden at Vétheuil, a sun-splashed burst of pigment and flowers radiating happiness and beauty. A more somber style is employed by Edouard Manet in *The Ragpicker* (1865–69), showing a singular figure whose loneliness is visually enhanced by a neutral gray background.

Simon's collection of Indian, Nepalese, Thai and Cambodian sculpture will be dramatically displayed in redesigned basement galleries. Examples of Western sculpture, on view in the museum garden, include Auguste Rodin's *Burghers of Calais*, Renoir's version of his friend Rodin and abstract works by Henry Moore.

Wrigley Mansion & Gardens

South of the Norton Simon stands the imposing Wrigley Mansion *(1914; ☎ 626-449-4100, 391 Orange Grove Blvd; admission to gardens free; open year-round)*. This ornate Italian Renaissance villa was once owned by chewing-gum magnate William Wrigley Jr and now houses the headquarters of the Tournament of Roses Association. The home has warm wood paneling, Italian marble fireplaces and brocade wallpaper.

The lush gardens, ablaze with roses and camellias, are open to the public, but the house itself is closed until at least February 2002. Call for an updated schedule.

Rose Bowl & Arroyo Seco

Among Pasadena's grandest architectural achievements is the 98,636-seat Rose Bowl stadium *(1922; ☎ 626-577-3100, 1001 Rose Bowl Dr)*. Home of the UCLA Bruins football team, the Rose Bowl is also the site of the famous Rose Bowl Game played on New Year's Day. The second Sunday of each month, a huge flea market is held on the surrounding grounds (see the boxed text 'Flea Markets' in the Shopping chapter).

The Rose Bowl sits in the midst of the 61-sq-acre **Brookside Park**, a broadening of Arroyo Seco. Once an orange grove, this gorge is now popular for hiking, biking and horseback riding. In the early 20th century, this was the center of Arroyo Culture, an aesthetic movement involving many of the craftspeople, artists and architects behind some of Pasadena's great homes. Dating from that period is the imposing former **Vista del Arroyo Hotel** *(1903; ☎ 626-441-2797, 125 S Grand Ave; free tours by appointment)*, restored in the 1980s to house the Ninth Circuit Court of Appeals.

Spanning the arroyo is the city's most infamous landmark, the **Colorado St Bridge** (1913). 'Suicide Bridge,' as it has come to be known, became the area's favorite jumping spot for those hard hit by the stock market crash in 1929, and it has since remained popular among forlorn souls. The restored bridge is open for pedestrians and auto traffic.

Art Center College of Design

Looking out over the Rose Bowl from a ridgetop is this world-renowned arts college *(☎ 626-396-2200, 1700 Lida St; tours free; tours 2pm Mon-Thur, 1:30pm Fri during school year; reservations required)*. Founded in 1930, it runs a widely respected undergraduate program and has an international student body. Majors include advertising, film, fine art, graphic design, illustration, photography and product design. Besides a sculpture garden, it contains several public galleries *(admission free; open noon-5pm Tues-Sun, to 9pm Thur)* with rotating shows of top-name artists and designers (as well as the usually excellent student work) in various media.

Pasadena Civic Center Area

This complex along Garfield Ave, a few blocks east of Old Pasadena, contains intricately detailed structures blending Italian Renaissance, Spanish Colonial and Beaux Arts styles. At the top end of this north-south axis is the **Public Library** *(1927; ☎ 626-405-4066, 285 E Walnut St)*. On the southern edge stands the **Civic Auditorium** *(1931; ☎ 626-449-7360, 300 E Green St)*, occasional home to television's Emmy Awards ceremony. In the center, on the east side of Garfield Ave, is the beautifully domed Spanish Renaissance **City Hall** *(1927; ☎ 626-744-4000, 100 N Garfield Ave)*, built around a courtyard garden and fountain. Directly east, across Euclid Ave, is Plaza Las Fuentes, a 6-acre hotel, office and restaurant complex.

Just east of this ensemble is one of Pasadena's most impressive religious structures, the **First United Methodist Church** *(500 E Colorado Blvd)*. This humongous Gothic Revival structure dates to 1924 and boasts some surprising architectural twists. Although its basic layout is cross-shaped, the sanctuary is actually in the form of a semicircle. A magnificent four-manual Skinner organ, embedded in a hand-carved wooden case, looms behind the altar. There are stained-glass windows, and the ceiling has delicate fan-vaulting. The church is closed except during services, but if you ask nicely at the adjacent office, someone will gladly let you inside.

Pacific Asia Museum

With its upturned roofs, dragon motifs and serene courtyard, this Chinese-imperial-style building houses the Pacific Asia Museum *(☎ 626-449-2742, 46 N Los Robles Ave; admission adults $5, seniors & students*

$3, free for children under 12; open 10am-5pm Wed-Sun, to 8pm Thur). The building was commissioned in the 1920s by art collector Grace Nicholson, who inhabited her 'Chinese Treasure House' until her death in 1948. The museum, with its five-millennia compilation of both rare and common art and artifacts, opened in 1961.

The permanent collection consists of 17,000 objects, displayed on a rotating basis and supplemented by major touring exhibits. The museum is strongest in the field of Chinese ceramics from several dynasties. (Unlike the Western cultures, the Chinese chronicle their history not in centuries but in dynasties, with each epoch producing distinct styles, colors and shapes of ceramics.) Other exhibits include Japanese paintings and drawings by Hiroshige and Hokusai and unusual items such as the assortment of Chinese cricket cages.

Despite their extraordinary collection, museum curators might give some thought to improving the way objects are presented. Dozens of items are normally crammed into glass cabinets, often devoid of any apparent chronological, geographical or thematic connection. Another problem is the museum assumes visitors already have some knowledge of Asian art, which may explain the paucity of informative panels.

South Lake District

Pasadena's premier financial and shopping district wraps around Lake Ave, south of Colorado Blvd about 10 blocks east of Old Pasadena. There are major department stores along this strip, but Lake Ave's distinction is its several European-style arcades. The **Burlington Arcade** *(380 S Lake Ave)* is a replica of the 19th-century London original with its skylights and arches. The **Colonnade** *(350 S Lake Ave)* is similarly elegant with its grand columns.

Kidspace

Looking for a way to keep kids entertained in an intelligent fashion? Try this hands-on children's museum *(☎ 626-449-9143, 390 S El Molino Ave; admission* *adults and children 2 and older $5, seniors $3.50, children under 2 $2.50; hours vary, closed Mon).* Just past the entrance are three environments that invite interaction: a supermarket, fire station and post office. Beyond are Eco Beach with murals, aquariums and a sandy pit, which kids explore equipped with shovels and buckets. Visiting shows from other children's museums from around the country often add another dimension to the permanent exhibits.

California Institute of Technology

Twenty-six Nobel laureates and 43 winners of the National Medal of Science are faculty members or alumni of California Institute of Technology *(Caltech; ☎ 626-395-6327, www.caltech.edu, 551 S Hill Ave; tours free; tours 2pm weekdays, except holidays, rainy days & winter break).* This is just one of the reasons why Caltech is regarded with awe in academic circles. (Yes, Albert Einstein did sleep here.) Now one of the world's most important research centers, this diminutive university has just 800 undergraduates and 1000 graduate students. Among their recent notable projects: designing the automated gene sequencer that had a cameo in *Jurassic Park.*

Caltech actually began life in 1891 as a school of arts and crafts called Throop University, after its founder, Amos G Throop. Thanks to the instigation of astronomer George E Hale, who joined the board of trustees in 1907, the school quickly evolved into a scientific and engineering institution and was renamed California Institute of Technology in 1920.

Campus tours include a visit to the renowned seismology laboratory. Tours leave from the visitors center *(☎ 626-395-6327, 315 S Hill Ave).* Architectural campus tours are conducted on the fourth Thursday

Famous Names of Caltech

Dozens of Caltech scientists have helped pave the way for progress in the 20th century. Earthquake studies were essentially pioneered here in the 1920s, when geologist Harry Wood invented the first seismograph. Charles Richter, along with Beno Gutenberg, invented the Richter scale, which is still used to express the magnitude of an earthquake. Ever since, Caltech has become a clearinghouse for earthquake measurements anywhere in the world, and its scientists are usually the first to appear on TV whenever a 'shaker' rattles through California or elsewhere in the world.

One of the college's most famous Nobel recipients was two-time winner Linus Pauling. His discovery of the nature of the chemical bond – how atoms link up to form molecules in both living and nonliving systems – facilitated breakthroughs both in chemical and molecular biology and in the creation of synthetic products. This netted him the Chemistry prize in 1954. He was also awarded the Nobel Peace Prize in 1962.

Another revolutionary breakthrough came in the early 1960s when physicist Murray Gell-Mann (1969 Nobel winner) detected that the smallest building blocks of matter were not protons and neutrons, but even smaller particles he named quarks. This led to new findings in subatomic physics and to greater understanding of the Big Bang. Another famous name is that of psychobiologist Roger Sperry (1981 Nobel winner), who figured out left-brain/right-brain designations.

Many of Caltech's accomplishments have been in the field of astronomy, prompting a leading British scientist to say, 'The universe of astronomy has no center, but the universe of astronomers does.' Achievements include the first map of the sky as seen from the Northern Hemisphere in 1948; discovering countless new stars, galaxies and comets (a second survey is currently underway); and the 1964 discovery that quasars were the most powerful and distant objects, allowing astronomers a glimpse at how the universe looked long before the birth of our galaxy.

of the month at 11am (no tours in July, August and December). Reservations are mandatory (call the visitors center).

Jet Propulsion Laboratory (Map 3)
Located in La Cañada just north of Pasadena proper is the Caltech-operated JPL (☎ 626-354-9314, 4800 Oak Grove Dr), NASA's main center for robotic exploration of the solar system with some 5700 employees. Though not open to the public, JPL provides glimpses of its activities on its website at www.jpl.nasa.gov and through an annual open house (usually in June).

JPL was an outgrowth of Caltech's Graduate Aeronautical Laboratory, headed by Theodore von Karman, whose experiments in the 1930s laid the scientific foundation of modern aviation and jet flight. JPL spacecraft have visited all of our solar system's planets except Pluto (the 'Pluto-Kuiper Express' is in the planning stages).

Current missions include the Cassini (orbits Saturn), the Galileo Europa (orbits Jupiter), the Mars Global Surveyor (orbits Mars) and Ulysses (sun fly-by). Its Pathfinder probe landed on Mars on July 4, 1997.

Huntington Library, Art Collection & Botanical Gardens
Railroad tycoon Henry E Huntington named his baronial estate, built in 1910, after an Italian enclave: tiny San Marino, the world's smallest republic. Today Huntington's 207-acre manor and grounds are one of Southern California's not-to-be-missed attractions (☎ 626-405-2100, www.huntington.org, 1151 Oxford Rd; admission adults $8.50, seniors & students $8, children $6, under 12 free; open 10:30am-4:30pm daily June-Aug; call for non-summer hours and docent-led garden tours).

The Huntington Library, Art Collection and Botanical Gardens is at once a cultural center, a research institution and a wonderful place to spend a relaxing afternoon. The sprawling **botanical gardens** alone – with some 14,000 species of trees, shrubs, flowering and nonflowering plants – are worthy of a visit. A highlight is the Desert Garden, featuring the widest array of mature cacti

and other succulents in the US. Other visitor favorites are the Japanese Garden and the Shakespearean Garden. The Rose Garden tea room (☎ 626-683-8131) serves English tea noon-3:30pm Tuesday to Friday and from 10:45am on weekends. Call for reservations.

Even more impressive is the **library** collection of rare English-language books, maps and manuscripts, including a 1455 Gutenberg Bible, the Ellesmere manuscript of Chaucer's *The Canterbury Tales* (1410), Benjamin Franklin's handwritten autobiography and a double folio edition of Audubon's *Birds of America*.

The **Huntington Art Gallery**, in the former family mansion, boasts a collection of 18th-century British and French paintings (among them Thomas Gainsborough's 1770 *Blue Boy*). European period sculptures, porcelains and tapestries are also displayed. Nearby, the Virginia Steele Scott Gallery of American Art exhibits works from the 1730s to the 1930s, including paintings by Mary Cassatt, Edward Hopper and John Singer Sargent alongside furniture by Gustav Stickley and others. There's also a permanent exhibit on the work of Gamble House architects, Charles and Henry Greene (see the Los Angeles Architecture special section for more about these architects).

Not far from the Huntington Gardens, the California Historical Society operates **El Molino Viejo** (☎ 626-449-5450, 1120 Old Mill Rd; admission free; open 1pm-4pm Tues-Sun). Built in 1816 by Gabrieleño Indians for the Mission San Gabriel, 'The Old Mill' was the very first water-powered grist mill in Southern California. Historical exhibits include a working model of the mill.

SAN GABRIEL (MAP 3)
The city of San Gabriel, about 3 miles south of Pasadena, is home to one of two historic missions in the LA area, the **Mission San Gabriel Archangel** (☎ 626-457-3048, 537 W Mission Dr; admission adults $4, seniors $3, children 6-12 $1; open 10am-5:30pm daily June-Sept; 9am-4:30pm daily rest of year). The mission was fourth in the line of 21 missions built in California. Originally founded

THINGS TO SEE & DO

Adobe Buildings

Built with mud and clay bricks dried under the sun, adobe buildings are a signature of the southwestern US. Greater Los Angeles has numerous examples of Spanish-era adobe architecture, starting with the area's two missions at San Gabriel and San Fernando. If you're interested in this regional tradition, you may want to seek out more of these historic structures, most of which are located in the San Fernando Valley.

Andrés Pico Adobe (☎ 818-365-7810, 10940 Sepulveda Blvd, Mission Hills, San Fernando Valley; admission free; open 10am-3pm Mon). Named after the military commander in Mexican LA, this house was restored after the 1994 Northridge quake and is now home to the Mark Harrington Library. Built in 1834, it's the second-oldest house in Los Angeles and contains period furnishings.

Avila Adobe This is LA's oldest house. See El Pueblo de los Angeles in this chapter for details.

Leonis Adobe (☎ 818-222-6511, 23537 Calabasas Rd, Calabasas; admission $2; open 1pm-4pm Wed-Sun). Dating from 1844, this two-story, Monterey-style ranch house has been restored to its appearance during its mid-19th-century heyday. Back in the day it was home to the colorful Don Miguel Leonis, the 'King of Calabasas' and third-richest man in California at the time. Note the 600-year-old oak tree; there's also a bar, blacksmith shop and horno (adobe oven).

Los Encinos State Historical Park (☎ 818-784-4849, 16756 Moorpark St, Encino; admission free; open 10am-5pm Wed-Sun). This 5-acre park preserves a mid-19th-century stagecoach stop, including a nine-room adobe built in 1849 (it was huge by standards of the time) and a two-story limestone cottage from 1870. Both sustained severe earthquake damage in 1994; restoration was expected to be completed in late 2001.

Pio Pico State Historic Park (☎ 310-695-1217, 6003 Pioneer Blvd, Whittier; admission free; open 10am-5pm Wed-Sun). The adobe building here dates from 1850 and also suffered serious damage in the 1994 earthquake. It's a two-story adobe hacienda built by Don Pio Pico, the last Mexican governor of California, next to the San Gabriel River and deeded to the state in 1917. It's been the centerpiece of a 9000-acre state historic park since 1927.

in 1771 by Pedro Cambon and Angel Somera 4 miles south of its current location, it was forced to relocate by heavy flooding in 1791. The capped-buttress design by Father Antonio Cruzado incorporates many Moorish elements inspired by the cathedral in his native Córdoba in southern Spain. The Franciscans got the local Gabrieleño natives workers to construct the church from stone, brick and mortar between 1791 and 1805, but already in 1804 an earthquake damaged the roof; another one in 1812 brought down the bell wall. Despite such setbacks, the mission itself was quite prosperous, reaping proceeds from the fertile land and producing soap and candles for all the other missions. It also maintained California's oldest and largest winery. The last wave of damage came during the 1987 Whittier earthquake, but the mission has since been restored.

Inside the church is a copper baptismal font and an altar made in Mexico City in 1790, plus various wooden statues of saints. The cemetery harbors, among many others, 6000 Indians who are honored with a memorial. Also on the grounds are soap and tallow vats, fireplaces, fountains and a replica of a kitchen. The museum contains Bibles, religious robes and Indian artifacts.

Indian artifacts and early photographs are displayed at the **San Gabriel Historical**

Association (☎ 626-308-3223, 546 W Broadway; free admission; open 1pm-4pm weekends). Nearby is the **San Gabriel Civic Auditorium** (☎ 626-308-2865, 320 S Mission Dr), a 1927 playhouse modeled after the Mission San Antonio de Padua in Monterey County. King Alfonso XIII of Spain donated coats of arms of each Spanish province for the theater's grand opening. Today it is used for concerts, stage plays and classic movies.

San Fernando Valley

One-third of the population of the city of Los Angeles (about 1.3 million) lives in what is known simply as 'the Valley,' a broad flat region of 220 sq miles. The Valley is as well-known for its earthquakes (the devastating 1971 Sylmar and the 1994 Northridge both were centered here) as for its seemingly endless commercial strips and tract homes. Major communities are Sherman Oaks, Van Nuys, North Hollywood, Burbank and Studio City.

Framed by mountain ranges that trap the air, the Valley is often blanketed by a thick layer of smog and is about 20°F hotter than Westside and beach communities. Now often mocked by outsiders, living in the Valley was actually quite fashionable in the early days of Hollywood, when movie moguls including Walt Disney and John Wayne had their private homes here. Along with them came most major studios, most of which settled in and around the Burbank area. And another branch of movie making established itself here as well: The Valley is the capital of the adult-film industry, fed by a steady stream of wannabe actors unable to get into mainstream movies.

Car culture was basically invented here, and the automobile rules supreme. Framed by four freeways, the Valley takes credit for giving birth not just to the mini-mall but also to the drive-in movie theater, the drive-in bank and of course the drive-in restaurant. This is where you'll still find plenty of these '50s vestiges sporting rocket rooflines last seen in *American Graffiti*, plus the last place in town that still does car-hop service.

GLENDALE (MAP 3)

Glendale, LA County's third-largest city with a population of 180,000, is about 7 miles north of Downtown and forms the transition between the San Fernando Valley and the San Gabriel Valley to the east. Languishing in obscurity for centuries, Glendale finally made it onto the map in the late 19th century, when real estate holder and civic pioneer Leslie C Brand sold off 1000 acres in the Verdugo Hills (a subrange of the San Gabriel Mountains) to settlers; Brand also convinced Henry Huntington to extend the Pacific Electric Railway from Downtown to the fledgling community. The town incorporated in 1906 and its growth mushroomed from there. Though Glendale is ethnically diverse, it is also home to the largest concentration of Armenian immigrants in the county.

Glendale has two main thoroughfares, Brand Blvd and Central Ave. A highlight on Brand is the 1939 **Alex Theater** (☎ 800-414-2539 in LA only, or 818-243-2611, 216 N Brand Blvd), a Streamline Moderne ex-movie palace, restored and converted into a popular multiuse entertainment venue. Nearby is the **Glendale Galleria**, Central Ave and Colorado St, a 250-store shopping mall (Map 8).

Brand Library & Art Center

Brand Park, in northeast Glendale, is home to the Brand Library and Art Center (1903; ☎ 818-548-2051, 1601 W Mountain Ave; open 1pm-9pm Tues-Thur, to 6pm Wed, to 5pm Fri & Sat). Originally the center was the private mansion, called El Miradero, of the 'father of Glendale,' Leslie C Brand. Inspired by the East Indian Pavilion at the 1893 Columbian Expo in Chicago, Brand commissioned his own phantasmagoric Taj Mahal, complete with turrets and porticoes fronted by scalloped arches. The Victorian interior features the original fireplace and oak wainscoting and houses a collection of some 50,000 books primarily on art and music. A new wing containing art studios, gallery space and a recital hall was added in 1969. The most impressive approach to the park is via Grandview Ave which leads directly to the house past a gate and along an avenue of palms.

The complex's other attraction includes the **Doctors' House** *(☎ 818-242-4290; tours $1, free if under 16; tours 2pm-4pm Sun except during holiday, July & rain)*. This 1890 Queen Anne/Eastlake is named for the quartet of doctors that once lived in it. Salvaged from demolition in 1979, it was moved here and subsequently restored. Tours introduce you to late-19th-century medical equipment and an early intercom. Just south of here is a traditional **Japanese garden** *(admission free; open 10am-3pm Mon-Thur)* with a teahouse that demonstrates the link of Glendale with its Japanese sister city, Higashiosaka.

Forest Lawn Memorial Park – Glendale

Often cheekily called 'country club for the dead,' this humongous cemetery *(☎ 818-241-4151, 1712 S Glendale Ave; open 9am-5pm)*, is even more grandiose than its sister in the Hollywood Hills (see the Griffith Park section).

Come here to view a copy of Michelangelo's *David* and a stained-glass rendition of

LA Car Culture

Detroit may have given birth to the car, but it was only after that 1000-mile cruise down Route 66 that Los Angeles added the culture. From hot rods to lowriders, the City of Angels has seen style and steel come together in a roaring contribution to America's artistic heritage.

It all began in the Roaring '20s, when Henry's fine Model T Fords, or 'T-buckets,' were adapted by speed demons for Los Angeles' unusually wide, straight streets. Despite the Great Depression, young people continued to modify their favorite '32 Fords, their 'little deuce coupes,' to go ever faster, tearing out seats, fenders and even removing the roofs entirely in their quest for speed. Detroit responded by building the first convertibles, but 'hot rods,' as these cutdown cruisers came to be called, remained LA's favorite example of American ingenuity.

America's booming post-WWII economy came on strong in Los Angeles, with more young people purchasing cars than ever before. Hot rodding became so popular it diversified, its practitioners splitting into two groups: the speed demons, who preferred to shoot across the salt flats of Utah in their sleek Lake Bonneville racers, reaching such dizzying speeds that their cars were made illegal on public highways, and the more urban, style-conscious cruisers, who remained partial to piling into their tamer 'street rods' for leisurely jaunts down Van Nuys Blvd and Wilshire Blvd's Miracle Mile. Showing little interest in these distinctions, newspapers simply decried the car-crazy youths as a public menace, signaling the beginning of the most mobile generation gap in history. Meanwhile, enterprising 'bad kids' Willie Parks and Jim Peterson institutionalized the craze, founding the National Hot Rod Association and Hot Rod Magazine, still two of the strongest automotive organizations in America.

In 1949, Los Angeles legend George Barris bought a brand-new Mercury and, with welder in hand, transformed it into a work of art. He 'chopped' the car's top for a speedy low look, raked the windshield backward and shortened the side columns. He also altered the body by welding and re-shaping the Mercury's boxy nose for a sleeker profile, and stripped and filled the chrome from fender to fender for a look as smooth as silk. Calling his outrageous new car a 'custom,' Barris snared automotive artisans Gil Ayala and 'Big Daddy' Roth into his colorful camp. Custom cars were

Leonardo da Vinci's *Last Supper*. Also here are two of the world's largest paintings, *The Crucifixion* (195 feet x 45 feet) and *The Resurrection* as well as three churches, modeled after their medieval English and Scottish originals.

Despite the obvious kitsch factor, it is worth a visit, if only to catch a glimpse of death culture so powerfully satirized by Evelyn Waugh's *The Loved One* (1948). It was Hubert L Eaton, a mining engineer from Missouri, who in 1917 invented the slick combination of business and death. (If you've ever gotten a call from a 'pre-need

counselor,' you know what we're talking about.) The company prides itself on arranging everything for you or grandpa with just one phone call (plus a bundle of cash). Eaton's boneyards look like parks. Upright headstones are discouraged; instead there's precision landscaping and replicas of historical buildings and 'artwork.'

However one feels about this concept, Forest Lawn is a popular posthumous destination, also favored by celebrities. Most of them are literally kept under lock and guard in mausoleums. The cemetery staff is instructed to keep celebrity-hoppers out, so

LA Car Culture

far more stylish than hot rods, with less emphasis on the engine. Their streamlined shapes and chopped tops created the illusion of speed, even as their chassis dropped so low that they scraped over speed bumps. Reshaped bodies were enhanced with luxurious interior furnishings and paint jobs featuring flames and contour-conscious murals. Barris' 'Mercs' raced through movies like *Rebel Without a Cause*, defining American cool. An entire industry of drive-through restaurants, drive-in movies and 'speed shops' made the '50s fun and California car culture a booming business.

Detroit attempted to cater to these trends with bigger engines and bolder shapes, from the fabulously finned '57 Chevy to muscle cars – but Angelenos still found ways to improve on these. Long, low Chevrolets soon filed down thoroughfares like Whittier Blvd in East LA, sparkling with chrome veneers and glittering, translucent paint and dropped to street-scraping levels on the tiniest tires available. When police protested that these 'lowriders' were too low, cruisers salvaged airplane hydraulics able to lift a car to the legal height at a moment's notice. South Central youths established their own lowered look, and adapted hydraulics to make cars hop and dance, even lifting all 3500lbs of steel into gravity-defying angles. The Sunday afternoon cruise on South Central's Crenshaw Blvd is still a great spot to see the city's best rides.

Today, hot rods, customs and lowriders cruise LA's streets alongside the Lamborghinis, Rolls Royces, SUVs (sport utility vehicles) and Hummers beloved by the upper classes, as well as the 'monster trucks' and 'art cars' built by more rural Californians. Car culture continues to grow and change. Check out the current cruisers created from Japan's best designs: the new 'pocket rockets,' Hondas and other small cars adapted for speed and style with plenty of chrome. Los Angeles' prolific gearheads won't rest as long as steel, gasoline and the wide open freeways continue to come together so seamlessly in Southern California.

Curse the freeways and smog if you must, but LA's automotive enthusiasts combine form and function like no other art form save architecture. And, when you're stuck in traffic – the quintessential LA experience – you may understand how one glimpse of a gleaming '59 Cadillac or souped-up '62 Corvette can transform your stressful situation into a moment of transcendental beauty.

– Paige R Penland

you'll need ingenuity, an innocent bat of the eye or chutzpah to get inside the Great Mausoleum, where legends such as Clark Gable, Carole Lombard and Jean Harlow have made their final home. Access is easier to the Freedom Mausoleum, where you can behold the crypts of Clara Bow, Nat 'King' Cole, Gracie Allen and George Burns. Walt Disney is buried in the Court of Freedom, not far from Errol Flynn.

BURBANK (MAP 18)

Ever since *Rowan and Martin's Laugh-In* joked about broadcasting from 'beautiful downtown Burbank' in the late 1960s, this city has been maligned by one TV comic after another. But Burbank got the last laugh. It now calls itself America's entertainment center – with good reason. Walt Disney Productions, Warner Brothers Studios, the National Broadcasting Company (NBC) and Columbia Pictures' television division all call Burbank home, as do several recording companies.

Located some 11 miles north of Downtown in the eastern San Fernando Valley, Burbank got its name from a New Hampshire dentist, David Burbank, who came to the area in 1866. Despite growing at a glacial pace, Burbank was the first Valley city to incorporate in 1891 with just 500 residents; today it has 94,000. Besides the movie industry, the manufacturing of aircraft began buttering people's bread; Lockheed set up shop near today's Burbank Airport in the 1930s, just in time to build bombers for WWII. Dating back to roughly the same time is Burbank's City Hall, an Art Deco jewel built by the Works Progress Administration at the corner of Olive Ave and 3rd St.

Warner Brothers Studios Tour

Don't expect razzle-dazzle special effects and thrilling theme rides when visiting the Warner Brothers Studios *(☎ 818-972-8687, 4000 Warner Blvd; tours $32; tours every half-hour 9am-4pm weekends, reservations required, children under 8 not allowed)*. Instead, you will get a unique and realistic glimpse behind the scenes at one of Hollywood's oldest movie and TV production facilities (1998 was its 75th anniversary). The excellent 2½-hour tour kicks off with a 15-minute 'greatest hits' film collage followed by a visit to the Warner Brothers Museum, both an archive and an altar to the stars. It's filled with costumes, letters and other paraphernalia, including James Dean's work shirt from *Giant* and the frilly hats from *My Fair Lady*.

Next up is a drive through the 110-acre backlot with its 33 sound stages where interior scenes are shot. The exact route depends on production schedules and may include a visit to the sets of *Friends*, *ER* or the 98-foot-high Stage 16, the tallest sound stage ever built. There may also be stops at technical departments such as Properties, the Garage (home of the Batmobile) and Costumes. Nearing the end of the tour, you will canvass several outdoor sets such as the Western-style Laramie St *(Bonanza* and *Roots)* and the Jungle Set *(Jurassic Park* and *Camelot)*. However, there is no guarantee that you'll see any stars, especially during the summer TV hiatus.

Tours start at the visitors center next to Gate 4 at the intersection of Hollywood Way and Olive Ave. Parking next to the visitors center is free.

NBC Studios Tour

The only major TV network that offers tours of its facilities is NBC *(☎ 818-840-3537, 3000 W Alameda Ave; tours adults $7, seniors $6.25, children 6-12 $3.75; tours 9am-3pm daily, extended hours in summer)*. NBC has been an LA mainstay since 1952, producing such legends as Bob Hope and Johnny Carson. Today, Jay Leno carries the torch as host of the famous *Tonight Show*. Tours usually take you behind the set of this program and into the Wardrobe, Makeup, Set Construction, Special Effects and Sound Effects departments. Parking is free. Make reservations in summer, as the 70-minute tours sell out early. For information on how to obtain tickets for a taping at NBC, see the boxed text 'Getting Into a Studio' in the Entertainment chapter.

Valley Secession & the Balkanization of LA

If a group called Valley Voters Organized Towards Empowerment (VOTE) has its way, the city of Los Angeles may soon be a lot smaller and a new city will have been spawned. The San Fernando Valley is technically a part of the city of LA, but in recent years anger, impatience and resentment with City Hall have grown so strong that a large group of Valley residents is pushing to secede and to form its own independent city. In March 1998, VOTE began collecting the 135,000 signatures needed to launch a feasibility study about breaking away from LA. More than enough names were presented by year's end, but the process is stalled over talks on who will foot the bill for the study.

Secessionists complain that the Valley is not receiving its fair share of services in proportion to the tax revenue it generates. They hope that independence will lead to greater control over land use, more efficient government, less bureaucracy, smaller council districts and faster and better responsiveness towards local needs. Opponents argue that more cities actually mean more government, that a break-up would reduce LA's clout and that diversity would decrease.

As of early 2001, the Local Agency Formation Commission concluded a preliminary study on the viability of the new city and found it could survive as an independent city but should pay a proposed $68 million in 'alimony' to LA for lost tax revenue. In addition, the new city would be dependent upon LA for water, power, sewer and 911 emergency dispatch services. Secessionists and their opponents are arguing the details of such a relationship so that the cityhood issue can be placed on the 2002 ballot.

Already waiting in the wings are groups in other parts of LA ready to plunge ahead with their own cityhood petition drives if the Valley effort proves successful. Besides San Pedro-Wilmington in the South Bay, they are Eagle Rock, Venice, Westchester and other Westside communities.

NORTH HOLLYWOOD (MAP 18)

A district just west of Burbank and some 11 miles northwest of Downtown LA, North Hollywood has recently come into its own with the creation of the **NoHo Arts District**. It is centered where Lankershim and Magnolia Blvds meet, right next to the Academy of Television Arts and Sciences, and is the last stop on Metro Rail's Red Line from Downtown. The area is best known for its lively theater scene with more than 30 companies producing everything from the mainstream to the avant-garde. One of the most anticipated openings was that of the **El Portal Center for the Arts** (☎ *818-508-4200, 5269 Lankershim Blvd*), a magnificent Spanish Renaissance edifice. See the Entertainment chapter for specifics about some of the theaters.

Also in North Hollywood is **Campo de Cahuenga** (*3919 Lankershim Blvd*), a recreated adobe building commemorating the site where the peace treaty ending the US-Mexican War was signed in 1847.

UNIVERSAL CITY (MAP 18)

Although it's a workplace for thousands and is visited by millions every year, Universal City is a city without residents – literally (the last two died sometime in the 1980s). About 9 miles north of Downtown, Universal City's only purpose is being home to Universal Studios, the production company as well as the theme park, and the entertainment complex around Universal City Walk.

Universal Studios Hollywood

The world's largest movie and television studios and the one of the county's grandest theme parks can be found at Universal Studios Hollywood (☎ *818-622-3801, 100 Universal City Plaza; admission adults $41, seniors $36, children 3-11 $31, annual passes*

$49/44/39; open 8am-10pm daily summer, 9am-7pm daily rest of year). Carl Laemmle founded Universal in 1912 and built the studio on the site of a chicken farm. To make a little extra money, he sold eggs and also invited the public to watch films being made. Formal studio tours began in 1964 and have since been experienced by 100 million visitors.

A few general words of advice: You'll need to devote a full day to Universal, and to beat the crowds you should get there as early in the morning as possible. The summer months are not just the hottest but also the busiest, so be prepared for long waits in stifling heat. Bring a hat, sunblock, patience and – if cutting costs is your aim – bottled water. Overall, though, prices for sodas ($2) and snacks (less than $10) here are not nearly as extortionate as they are at Disneyland. Beer and margaritas are served as well. Some rides, including the popular Back to the Future and Jurassic Park, have minimum height requirements (usually 42 or 46 inches).

Universal Studios is spread across 415 acres, the upper and lower sections connected by a quarter-mile-long escalator. To get your bearings, head straight for the recently revamped **Studio Tour**, a 45-minute part-educational, part-thrill ride behind the scenes of movie making. A tram whisks you and about 250 other visitors past the studio's maze of 35 sound stages. Each tram is equipped with a top-notch audio system and four video monitors. The tour is narrated by Ron Howard and also features other film directors and celebrities, including Steven Spielberg and Jason Alexander sharing their experiences on the set of Universal. As the tram rumbles past sound stages where such films as *Jurassic Park* and *Apollo 13* were filmed, you can see on the video screen how the barren stage is transformed into a realistic-looking movie set. The tram also travels past outdoor sets such as Courthouse Square, best known from *Back to the Future*, and the Bates Hotel featured in Hitchcock's *Psycho*. During the thrill portion of the tour you'll experience such special effects as an 8.3-magnitude earthquake, a flash flood, a

collapsing bridge, volcanic lava and close encounters with a plastic shark and King Kong. A new installation is based on the movie *The Mummy*.

Universal doesn't have a huge number of rides, but this actually keeps the overwhelm quotient down, as it's usually possible to experience them all in one day. One favorite is **Back to the Future – The Ride**, which blasts you through time and space in a DeLorean and has you free-falling into volcanic tunnels, plunging down glacial cliffs and colliding with dinosaurs (go for a seat in the front). **The ET Adventure** is a gentle flight aboard a monorailed 'bicycle' through a charming fantasy world. **Backdraft** is a pyrotechnic walking adventure that lets you catch a glimpse of amazing special effects. The climactic conclusion has you engulfed by an inferno roaring through a chemical factory, with ruptured fuel lines and tanks exploding all around you.

Terminator 2:3D is a futuristic adventure that combines live action stunts with eye-popping digital imaging technology and audience-involving special effects.

Top billing, though, goes to **Jurassic Park – The Ride**, a float through a prehistoric jungle past friendly herbivores before coming face to face with vicious velociraptors and a ravenous *Tyrannosaurus rex*. The ultimate thrill is…well, let's not spoil the surprise. (Hint: You'll get wet.)

Live shows, staged several times daily, also form part of the Universal experience. **Water World** features jet-ski stunts, giant fireballs and a crashing seaplane. Fancy quick-draws and fist fighting are at the heart of the old standby **The Wild, Wild, Wild West Stunt Show**, though learning about special effects at **The World of Cinemagic** may be more worthwhile. Children howled with glee at the cute birds, pigs, dogs and cats that form the cast of the **Animal Actors Stage**. Also targeted to the kids is the new **Rugrats Magic Adventure**, a fun experience of music, magic and mayhem. The illusions and stunts in this show stem from the imagination of famous magicians (think: levitating diapers), including David Copperfield and Lance Burton.

While walking the grounds you may run into Charlie Chaplin, Marilyn Monroe, Frankenstein or Woody Woodpecker, though it was Lucy and Ethel from *I Love Lucy* who seemed to be most omnipresent.

For a complete Universal immersion, get the VIP Experience ($125), which gives you VIP lounge access, a private tram and personalized backlot and theme park tour, no waiting in line and reserved show seating. The Southern California Value Pass entitles the holder to one-time admission to Universal Studios and Sea World in San Diego within a two week period and costs $75 ($55 for children ages three to 11).

Universal City Walk

Adjoining Universal Studios is this hugely popular artificial outdoor mall, dreamed up to provide a controlled environment of shops, restaurants, cinemas and nightclubs for those too intimidated by the – largely imagined – dangers of urban reality. (It is telling that the mall opened in 1993, just one year after the Rodney King riots.) Plenty of inspiration, imagination and innovation went into the critically acclaimed design by Jon Jerde. There are lots of whimsical visual surprises, including a '57 Chevy bursting through a freeway sign and a 27-foot gorilla guarding a music-store entrance. A recent expansion more than doubled the number of restaurants and also added Jillian's Hi-Life Bowling, a rock 'n' roll bowling experience; Club Rumba, a Latin dance nightclub, and an IMAX 3-D theater. The best time to visit is at night, when vibrant neon signs transform the promenade into a miniature Vegas-style strip. Parking is $7.

ELSEWHERE IN THE VALLEY
Paramount Ranch

In the western Valley community of Agoura Hills is the Paramount Ranch (☎ *818-597-9192, ext 201, Paramount Ranch Rd, off Cornell Rd; admission & parking free; open 8am-sunset daily*). This 450-acre western movie set was bought by Paramount Pictures in 1927 as a location for such movies as *The Cisco Kid*, the popular TV show *Dr Quinn, Medicine Woman* and other projects.

You can walk around the set by yourself (if you're lucky, filming may take place during your visit) or join a free ranger-led one-hour tour usually offered at 9:30am on the first and third Saturday of the month.

Take the US-101 (Ventura Fwy) west to the Kanan Rd exit, head south on Kanan Rd for three-quarters of mile and turn left on Cornell Rd (stay to the right). Continue for about 2½ miles and look for the entrance on your right.

Mission San Fernando
Rey de España

The second Spanish mission built in the LA area (after San Gabriel, see earlier in this chapter) – and the 17th in California – was Mission San Fernando Rey de España (☎ *818-361-0186, 15151 San Fernando Mission Rd, Mission Hills; admission adults $4, seniors & children 7-13 $3, children under 7 free; open 9am-4:30pm daily, Sunday mass 9am & 10:30am*). The mission is located in the northern Valley, roughly where the I-405 (San Diego Fwy) and Hwy 118 (Ronald Reagan Fwy) meet. Founded in 1797, it has twice been destroyed by earthquakes (in 1818 and 1971), but each time has risen like a phoenix with major efforts by parishioners. The highlight is the mission's 1822 convent, built with 4-foot-thick adobe walls and 21 Roman arches. The walls of the Old Mission Church are 7 feet thick. Inside the convent is an elaborate Baroque altarpiece from Spain.

The museum deals with mission history and displays Native American artifacts. Peacocks strut around the grounds, which are sprinkled with statues and a 35-bell carillon.

Mountains

SAN GABRIEL MOUNTAINS
(MAP 1)

The mountain range to the north of urban LA contains the **Angeles National Forest**, another major adventure playground and getaway for stressed-out Angelenos. About 30 million visitors, mostly locals, descend upon its trails, roads and campgrounds each year. One of the nicest drives is along the Angeles Crest Highway, which winds through the forest for 65 miles and offers spectacular views over the LA Basin at many turns.

Attractions within the forest include the **Mt Wilson Observatory** (☎ 626-793-3100), atop 5710-foot Mt Wilson and built in 1903 under the direction of George E Hale, who would go on to lay the groundwork for Caltech. Also here is LA County's tallest mountain, whose official name is Mt San Antonio but is referred to as **Old Baldy** for its treeless top at an elevation of 10,080 feet. A popular ski area in winter, Old Baldy is fairly easy to climb during snowfree months.

The general information center (☎ 626-335-1251, 701 N Santa Anita Ave; open 8am-4:30pm weekdays) is in Arcadia, about 20 miles east of Pasadena. The Mt Baldy Visitors Center (☎ 909-982-2829, on Mt Baldy Rd) is on the only road leading to the mountain. This is where you can pick up trail maps and information.

SANTA MONICA MOUNTAINS (MAP 2)

Few visitors to LA realize that the metropolis actually borders wilderness in the Santa Monica Mountains National Recreation Area. Consisting of more than 150,000 acres, it's a playground cherished by LA residents. The park is often overlooked by travelers, which is a shame because it's an easily accessible sample of the rugged beauty found throughout California. Even taking a few hours for a short hike makes for a refreshing break from urban sightseeing and will increase your appreciation of the city and its natural surroundings.

The Santa Monica Mountains stretch from west of Griffith Park in Hollywood to the east of the Oxnard Plain in Ventura County. Their northern border is the US-101 (Ventura Fwy), while in the south, they rise dramatically above the Pacific Ocean. Several canyon roads cut through the mountains, providing easy access to trails. Outdoor activities in the park include hiking, mountain biking, horseback riding and bird watching. Nearly 600 miles of trails

crisscross the area, including the popular 65-mile Backbone Trail. (See Activities, later in this chapter, for detailed trail coverage.)

The park was founded in 1978 by the US Congress with the intent to protect one of the world's last Mediterranean-type ecosystems (only four others still exist worldwide). Appearing relatively barren at first glance, the park actually boasts 26 ecological communities, such as oak woodlands, chaparral and coastal lagoons. More than 450 animal species, including deer, mountain lions and coyotes, make their home here. Hawks, falcons and eagles circle above, while rattlesnakes reside beneath the brush.

Spring, when temperatures are moderate and wildflowers are in bloom, is the most pleasant time to visit the park. Avoid midday hikes in summer (the mercury can climb to more than 100°F), and head out in the early morning or late afternoon instead. Fall can be nice, too, though there's the threat of fire. Winter often brings rain, which may result in trail closure due to the possibility of mud slides. In general, most trails are rugged and require sturdy footwear (sneakers or light hiking shoes are OK). For longer hikes, layer your clothing, bring sunscreen, a hat and lots of water. Look out for poison oak, which has waxy, glistening leaves that cause a rash on contact.

If you get bitten by a rattlesnake (the chances are slim), you will experience rapid swelling, severe pain and possible temporary paralysis. Victims rarely die, but in any case seek medical help immediately. Mountain lions are scarce in this neck of the woods, though there was a fatal attack in 1994. If you meet a lion, hold your ground and try to appear large by raising your arms or grabbing a stick. If the lion gets aggressive, fight back, shout and throw objects at it.

In the very western San Fernando Valley, the National Park Service (NPS) maintains a visitor center (☎ 805-370-2300, 401 W Hillcrest Dr, Thousand Oaks; open 8am-5pm Mon-Fri, 9am-5pm Sat-Sun, closed major holidays). Take the Lynn Rd exit from the US 101 (Ventura Fwy), head north on Lynn Rd, east on Hillcrest Dr, left on McCloud

Ave, and turn at the first driveway on your right. The center dispenses information and sells maps, hiking guides and books. (See the Activities section, later in this chapter, for recommendations on hiking trails; see Organized Tours in the Getting Around chapter for guided hikes.)

Activities

The following are a few of the many activities LA has to offer. See the previous section, Mountains, for additional hiking information. For surfing and fishing, see the boxed text 'Life's a Beach,' earlier in this chapter.

BICYCLING & IN-LINE SKATING
Although most of urban LA is not particularly inviting to cyclists or in-line skaters, the county has more than 200 miles of designated bike trails. Best of the bunch is the South Bay Bicycle Trail, a flat 22-mile paved path that follows the beach south from Santa Monica to Torrance Beach, with a detour around the yacht harbor at Marina del Rey.

There are other more adventurous paths from Azusa to Long Beach (the 37-mile San Gabriel River Trail), from Long Beach to Newport Beach (the 21-mile Oceanside Bike Path), and through Griffith Park (an 8-mile trail that passes the LA Zoo and the Autry Museum of Western Heritage).

Another trip from Griffith Park is along the newly expanded LA River Bikeway, which parallels a surprisingly wild and pleasant 5-mile stretch of the river from Atwater Village to Burbank. A good place to enter the bikeway is where Zoo Dr meets Riverside Dr.

The city Department of Transportation (☎ 213-485-2265, 200 N Spring St, 12th floor) has detailed maps.

Bike-rental places include Perry's Rentals (☎ 310-452-7609) with four outlets renting beach cruisers, tandems and in-line skates along the beach bike path in Santa Monica. Rates are $6/hour or $18/day. Skating lessons are offered on weekends.

Others to try are the Venice Pier Bike Shop (☎ 310-301-4011, 21 Washington Blvd, Venice) or Spokes 'N Stuff (branches: ☎ 310-306-3332, Jamaica Bay Inn, 4175 Admiralty Way, Marina del Rey; ☎ 310-395-4748, Loews Hotel, 1700 Ocean Ave, Santa Monica).

HIKING
With 580 miles of trails in the Santa Monica Mountains, it's impossible to describe every possible hike, but here are some favorites. If you want more guidance than just a trail map, check out the excellent series of guides by Los Angeles Times columnist John McKinney. His Day Hiker's Guide to Southern California ($15) and Walking Los Angeles: Adventures on the Urban Edge ($14) each explore several dozen hikes in great detail, providing not just route descriptions but also trailhead directions and historical background. Both guides, plus four other McKinney guides, are available in bookstores. (See Organized Tours in the Getting Around chapter for information on guided hikes.)

Santa Ynez Canyon
This easy-to-moderate trail (about 6 miles roundtrip) leads through a lovely shaded canyon along Santa Ynez Creek and it terminates at a waterfall tumbling into a rockface-enclosed pool, which makes for nice swimming in early summer. The easier, though less scenic, option to get onto this trail is from the Palisades Highland Trailhead. (Turn north off Sunset Blvd on Palisades Dr and turn left on Verenda de la Montura.) More ambitious hikers should start from Topanga State Park. (Turn east off Topanga Canyon Blvd onto Entrada Rd, then make two left turns to the park entrance; parking is $6.)

Sycamore Canyon
Sycamore Canyon is part of Point Mugu State Park on the northern fringe of LA County, about 30 miles northwest of Santa Monica. Hiking along the canyon floor makes for a lovely, easy walk, especially enjoyable in the fall when there is falling

LA Garden Culture

Traffic and freeways? Sure. But gardens? Absolutely. LA's antidote to the 'overwhelm factor' has been the creation of many peaceful and exotic garden settings. The following list includes gardens throughout LA County where only your own thoughts will interrupt you.

Descanso Gardens (☎ 818-952-4400, 1418 Descanso Dr, La Cañada Flintridge, San Fernando Valley; admission adults $5, seniors & students $3, children $1; open 9am-4:30pm daily). This 160-acre delight for flower lovers boasts some 100,000 camellias in bloom from October through March. Lilacs and orchids are at their best in April, while roses and other annuals blossom around the beginning of May. Wooded sections, streams, a lake and a bird sanctuary form part of the gardens.

Hannah Carter Japanese Garden (☎ 310-825-4574, 10619 Bellagio Rd, Bel Air; admission free, reservations required; open 10am-3pm Tues, Wed & Fri). A harmonious marriage of serenity and symbolism, this Kyoto-style terraced garden opened in 1961. Water plays a central role here, as expressed in a lily pond, waterfalls and a lively little brook. Other elements are a traditional tea-house, bonsai trees, bridges, antique stone carvings and symbolic rocks.

Japanese Gardens at Tillman Water Reclamation Plant (☎ 818-756-8166, 6100 Woodley Ave, Van Nuys; admission adults $3, seniors $2; open noon-4pm Mon-Thur; Map 2). The Bureau of Sanitation came up with an inventive and pleasant way to put tax dollars to work in this 6½-acre area, which includes Zen and tea gardens. It is entirely fed with reclaimed water.

The Arboretum of Los Angeles County (☎ 626-821-3222, 301 N Baldwin Ave, Arcadia; admission adults $5, seniors & students $3, children 5-12 $1, free on 3rd Tues of month; open 9am-5pm daily; Map 3). This large park in the San Gabriel Valley (near the Santa Anita racetrack) re-creates many of the world's major landscapes, arranged by continent, around a spring-fed lake. That's one reason this 127-acre garden has been so popular with filmmakers – including John Huston, who filmed much of The African Queen (starring Humphrey Bogart and Katharine Hepburn) here. A tram ($2 per person) travels throughout the park.

Orcutt Ranch (☎ 818-346-7449, 23600 Roscoe Blvd, West Hills, San Fernando Valley; open 8am-5pm daily). Huge live-oak trees, some perhaps as old as six centuries, shade a Spanish-style ranch house built in 1921 as a vacation home of William Orcutt, vice president of Union Oil, and his wife Mary. It's all surrounded by a lovely, secluded garden that's popular for weddings and filming.

Rancho Santa Ana Botanic Garden (☎ 909-625-8767, 1500 N College Ave, Claremont, San Gabriel Valley; admission free but donation requested; open 8am-5pm daily). This 86-acre garden at an elevation of 1350 feet displays the world's largest array of native California plants. Trails writhe through species from deserts, mountain woodlands and the coast.

Also see coverage in this chapter of the Huntington Library, Art Collection & Botanical Gardens (San Gabriel Valley); the Virginia Robinson Gardens (Beverly Hills) and the South Coast Botanical Gardens (Coastal Communities).

foliage and when Monarch butterflies stop by on their southward migration. More challenging trails, such as the Overlook Trail, head into the mountainous flanks of the canyon and provide glorious views over the ocean. The trailhead is at the Big Sycamore Canyon Campground, reached via Pacific Coast Hwy.

Modern art and architecture meet at the Museum of Contemporary Art.

RMS *Queen Mary*, Long Beach

The ever perky and hairy West Hollywood Cheerleaders

DAVID PEEVERS

Tournament of Roses Parade float, New Year's Day

DAVID PEEVERS

Bob's Big Boy, an American classic

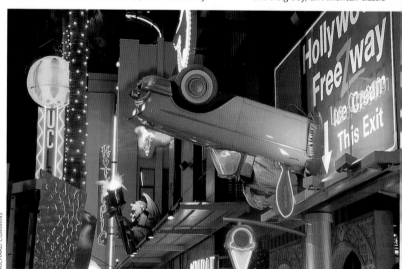

RICHARD CUMMINS

Freeze-dried LA at Universal City Walk

Runyon Canyon Park

This slice of wilderness lies just a few blocks north of the bustle of Hollywood Blvd. Trails steep enough to provide a moderate workout take you to a hilltop plateau with sweeping views of the city and the Hollywood Hills. Largely ignored by tourists, the park crawls with dog owners, many of them wannabe actors hoping the friendship between their Labrador and the boxer of the casting agent or producer will result in an audition. The easiest trailhead is at the end of Fuller St, off Franklin St; Mulholland Dr is the park's northern boundary (street parking is available).

The ruins near the Fuller St entrance are all that's left from the estate of Irish tenor John McCormack. He sold the estate to George Huntington II, heir to the A&P grocery-store chain, whose plan to turn it into a country club was defeated by neighbors. Errol Flynn lived in the pool house in the late '50s. The city purchased the park in 1984, but several fires have left only its foundations.

Ferndell–Griffith Observatory–Mt Hollywood

Ferndell is a lovely shady glen at the southern edge of Griffith Park. Lined by ferns, alder trees, sycamores and even coastal redwoods, it leads uphill to the Lower West Observatory Trail. From the observatory, where you'll enjoy great views of the city, walk to the north end of the parking lot where the Mt Hollywood path is clearly marked. This trail, while not home to the Hollywood sign, gives you repeated views of the landmark. The moderate hike is about 5½ miles roundtrip. The Ferndell trailhead is reached by taking Ferndell Dr north off Los Feliz Blvd. (Street parking is available.) For more hiking ideas through Griffith Park, visit the Griffith Park Ranger Station (☎ 323-665-5188, 4730 Crystal Springs Dr).

Solstice Canyon

This easy 2-mile trail (roundtrip via the canyon floor) is suitable even for families with strollers. Solstice Canyon, which opened on summer solstice 1988, was created on the site of the former Roberts Ranch, which burned down in 1982. The path leads past the 1865 Matthew Keller House (presumed to be the oldest in Malibu) to the ranch foundations at Tropical Terrace (named for the bamboo trees, agaves and palms planted here). The Roberts once kept a menagerie of exotic animals, including giraffes, buffalo, African deer and camels. Also look for the waterfall behind the former estate.

You can return the same way or, for a more strenuous workout, climb the canyon wall on the Rising Sun Trail, which has great views and returns to the parking lot in about 1½ miles. For the trailhead, turn inland off Pacific Coast Hwy on Corral Canyon Rd; turn left to the parking lot after a quarter mile. There's a $6 parking fee.

Inspiration Loop Trail

This 2-mile, easy-to-moderate hike leads through Will Rogers State Historical Park in Pacific Palisades. It begins at the west end of the tennis courts and affords superb vistas over Santa Monica Bay. It also connects with the Backbone Trail, which stretches along the mountain ridge for some 65 miles. Enter the park from Sunset Blvd (look for the signs).

GOLFING

Golfing is a popular pastime among Angelenos; it's no longer reserved for the country-club elite or the gray-haired set. Young professionals (males especially) are drawn to the greens, and LA's many public courses are often booked. (Note that most of the 18-hole courses are located in the distant suburbs and are not covered in this book.) With 13 courses, the city of LA maintains the largest municipal golf system in the US, and other cities also operate their own public courses. In order to tee off on an LA city course, you can either just show up, put your name on a waiting list and hope for the best; chances are best weekdays after noon. Or you can buy a reservation card (☎ 213-473-7055) for $35/year for residents and $90/year for non-residents; the card lets you book a tee time on an automated 24/7 system. City courses are open from dawn to dusk. In general, green fees are $12/15 weekday/weekend for 9-hole courses and $18/25 for 18-hole courses. The following are all within easy reach from central and west LA.

The Rancho Park Golf Course (☎ 310-838-7373, 10460 W Pico Blvd; fees $17-22; Map 2) has both a challenging 18-hole and a 9-hole course. Nicely laid out, the course is always crowded and getting a tee time as a visitor may be difficult. The Harding and Wilson courses in Griffith Park (☎ 323-663-2555, 4730 Crystal Springs Dr; Map 8) also both have 18 holes. The Harding course is more scenic and somewhat more difficult though shorter than Wilson. Penmar Golf Course (☎ 310-396-6228, 1233 Rose Ave, Venice; Map 13) is a 9-hole course that was recently overhauled and is quite busy now.

There are two courses near LAX airport, where land is relatively cheap. Just north of LAX is Westchester Golf Course (☎ 310-649-9166, 6900 W Manchester Blvd; fees $8-19; open 5am-10pm Mon-Fri, from 4:30am Sat-Sun; Map 2). It's an oddity because it has just 15 holes that are a bit noisy and relatively easy, but at least it's well-maintained. The other course is Lakes at El Segundo (☎ 310-322-0202, 400 S Sepulveda Blvd; fees $9-11; open 6am-10pm daily; Map 4).

HEALTH CLUBS

Angelenos' obsession with their bodies translates into a profusion of health clubs featuring the latest in exercise equipment and workout classes. New trends (aerobics, step aerobics, kick-boxing, spinning) are usually spawned here before moving on to the rest of the country and the world.

Many mid-range and practically all top-end hotels have their own fitness center or an agreement with a nearby club. Most outside gyms are membership-based; however, there are ways to get in. Most offer a free initial workout for nonmembers who are considering joining (you have to pretend). The downside is you will probably have to take a guided club tour and then endure the inane sales banter of commission-crazed counselors. Family Fitness Centers and

Bally's (see the Yellow Pages for branches) are clubs that operate in this way.

To avoid this hassle, go to gyms that offer day passes. If you want to pump iron with the pros, head to the legendary Gold's Gym (☎ 310-392-6004, 360 Hampton Dr, Venice; day rates $15; open 4am-midnight Mon-Fri, 5am-11pm Sat-Sun; Map 13). You might catch a glimpse of the next Mr Universe. (This is the gym where Arnold Schwarzenegger once bulked up for the title.) Fees include access to all equipment, classes and sauna.

The giant Crunch Gym (☎ 323-654-4550, 8000 Sunset Blvd, Hollywood; Map 10) is famous not just for its innovative fitness classes (including karaoke spin, gospel aerobics and yoga grooves), but also for being popular with the celebs. The 30,000-sq-foot facility has all the latest in workout equipment and more than 50 private trainers as well. Day passes are $23, though you may get in for free if you let it slip that you're considering joining.

More low-key athletic clubs specializing in aggressive workouts (like kick-boxing and boxing) include Bodies in Motion (branches: ☎ 310-264-0777, 2730 Santa Monica Blvd, Santa Monica; Map 13; ☎ 626-583-9206, 900 S Arroyo Parkway, Pasadena; Map 17). It also offers the usual array of workout machines and aerobics, and charges $10 a day, though you may get a discount if you're staying longer.

HORSEBACK RIDING

Griffith Park is ideal territory for horseback riding. Leaving the urban sprawl behind to negotiate the hilly terrain and forested bridle trails definitely feels like entering another world. Several riding stables have set up shop on the northern periphery of the park, where the LA Equestrian Center (818-840-9066, 480 Riverside Dr) is located as well.

Circle K Riding Stables (☎ 818-843-9890, 914 S Mariposa St, Burbank; Map 18) rents horses for $18 for the first hour and $12 for each subsequent hour. During warm weather, they do barbecue rides (in groups of five or more), which include an all-you-can-eat feast for $29. Griffith Park Horse Rental (☎ 818-840-8401, 480 Riverside Dr) has horses for $20/hour.

In operation for more than 80 years, Sunset Ranch (☎ 323-469-5450, 3400 Beachwood Dr) rents horses and offers guided rides daily. The charge is $20 for the first hour, $15 for each subsequent hour; if you take along a guide, the only additional cost is a tip. On Friday nights it offers the popular and romantic sunset ride, which takes you from below the Hollywood sign over the mountains to drinks and dinner at a Mexican cantina in Burbank, and back by moonlight ($35 plus dinner, three hours of horse-time).

RUNNING

Joggers abound on city streets especially in the early morning and evening hours. Favorite running places are along the beaches, in the sand or along paved walkways. Palisades Park atop the bluffs in Santa Monica and the green median strip along San Vicente Blvd are popular as well. Many joggers here combine a run with a session up and down the ultimate al fresco Stairmaster: the Santa Monica Steps, a steep 190-step stairway at 4th St and Adelaide Dr. Jogging in Griffith Park (Vermont Canyon Rd to Griffith Park Observatory) makes for a strenuous uphill workout and rewards you with great city views.

TENNIS

Tennis courts are plentiful in LA, though not all are open to the public. If your budget allows, you can stay at a hotel with a private court. Other options are courts at schools, which are not always perfectly maintained but, outside of school hours, are usually empty and cost-free. The recreation departments of the various cities within LA County operate public courts and should be able to refer you to the nearest one; check the phone book for the number of the closest City Recreation Department. Griffith Park has tennis courts as well.

Places to Stay

Tourism is a major industry in Los Angeles and there are plenty of accommodations in all price categories. Clearly, where you stay in LA will dictate how much you'll have to pay. Budget lodgings are scarce in Beverly Hills and West Hollywood but more abundant in Hollywood, Downtown and Pasadena, for example. Seasonal price fluctuations also affect room rates. Summer rates – especially in the beach communities and trendy areas – may increase by 50% or more to reflect the greater demand for rooms. The same is true around major holidays such as July 4, Labor Day, Thanksgiving, Christmas and New Year's.

Hotels that cater to business travelers often charge considerably higher rates during the week, when corporate expense accounts rule, than on weekends. As a result, a fancy suite will run $140 Sunday to Thursday but only $85 on Friday and Saturday. In Malibu and other beach cities, however, weekend rates are jacked up for the hordes of LA refugees scurrying to the seashore.

While differences between single and double occupancy are usually minor, the number of beds does make a difference. The cheapest rooms are those with one queen-size bed, which sleeps one or two people. Larger rooms have two queen-size beds or one king-size bed and sleep up to four; sometimes a surcharge of $10 to $25 applies for the third and fourth person. Room location (with or without a view) or recent renovations may also affect the price.

The cheapest option – about $15 to $20 – is a bunk in a hostel. Hostels are communal affairs with four- to eight-bed dorms (sometimes gender-segregated), shared washrooms and showers, kitchens and laundry and TV rooms. Some hostels also have private rooms for about $35 to $60 per night, double occupancy, or about the same rates as those at cheap motels. Expect the latter to be low-frill places with the basic amenities (including TV and phone), adequate to rest your head but not to hang out. You'll find them listed under 'Budget' in this book.

The closer you are to the coast or to upscale neighborhoods such as Beverly Hills or Santa Monica, the more likely you'll be staying at motels and hotels that typically run $100 to $150 per room. Spending just a little extra, from $150 to $200, generally buys more comfort and amenities, including in-room refrigerators and spa and voice mail services. This spectrum of accommodations is listed as 'Mid-Range.'

LA has many luxurious properties in the $200-plus category (these fall under 'Top End'). Amenities tend to be extravagant; rooms and public areas are beautifully furnished, adorned with art and fresh flowers. Often the location is central and there are special touches such as a rooftop swimming pool, tennis court or in-house massages. The sky's the limit in terms of price, and some suites and penthouses may cost several thousand dollars a night. Most of these hotels are clustered in Downtown, West Hollywood, Beverly Hills, Westwood and Santa Monica.

The rates quoted in this book should serve merely as a guideline. Whenever possible, a range of seasonal rates has been provided. If a season has not been indicated, the quoted rates are typically for the high season. Rates listed in this book do not – in fact, cannot – take into account special promotional rates that may become available at any given time, especially at the larger chain hotels. In general, make it a habit to ask about discounts when booking a room.

Discounts & Reservations

In many places, travelers who are members of the American Automobile Association (AAA) or a foreign affiliate or the American Association of Retired People (AARP) qualify for discounts of 10% or more off published rates. You might also cash in on discounts for university students, military personnel and travel-industry workers. Some hotels give better rates if you book over the Internet. Also look out for freebie ad rags packed with hotel discount coupons at gas stations and tourist offices.

If you have trouble finding accommodations, consider using one of the free hotel-reservation services. These companies include the Hotel Reservations Network (☎ 800-964-6835, www.hoteldiscount.com) and the Central Reservation Service (☎ 800-873-4683, www.reservations-services.com).

Taxes & Tips

Your final hotel bill will swell with taxes, tips, and parking and phone charges in proportion to the cost of your accommodations. The 'transient occupancy' tax on all hotel rooms in the city of Los Angeles is 14%. Percentages vary slightly in other cities, ranging from 11.85% in Pasadena to 13% in West Hollywood and 14% in Beverly Hills.

Other charges will be less of a concern unless you stay in a top-end hotel, where you are expected to tip bellhops and concierges in addition to cleaning staff, restaurant servers and bartenders. While parking is generally free at budget and many midrange properties, it will run $7 to $20 daily at upscale hotels, plus tips for valets. And while motels rarely charge more than 25¢ for local phone calls (often these are free), big hotels will charge up to $1 per call. If you're calling long distance, you'll pay through the nose unless you use a credit or calling card, but they'll still hit you with that pesky connection fee.

CAMPING

LA County has plenty of private, county and state campgrounds, but most are not very central and/or cater exclusively to RVs. Generally open year-round, they quickly fill to capacity in summer; early reservations are a good idea between May and October, especially for weekend travel. If you drive an RV, check whether your equipment is compatible with that of the campground.

In addition to the campgrounds mentioned here, the California Department of Parks & Recreation maintains dozens of camping facilities, often in more remote, rural locales. For information and reservations, contact Reserve America (☎ 800-444-7275, 8am-5pm daily, www.reserveamerica .com). There's a $7.50 fee per reservation.

Leo Carrillo State Beach Campground *(☎ 805-488-5223, 800-444-7275 for reservations, 9000 Pacific Coast Hwy)* Tent sites $12. This shady, kid-friendly site, about 28 miles northwest of Santa Monica, is extremely popular and fills up quickly. It has 138 tent and RV sites, a general store, flush toilets and hot showers (for a fee). There's a sandy beach, off-shore kelp beds and tide pools for exploring.

Dockweiler Beach RV Park *(☎ 310-322-4951, 800-950-7275, 8255 Vista Del Mar, Playa del Rey; Map 2)* RV sites $12-17 winter, $15-25 summer. Those who don't mind camping out near an oil refinery, noisy LAX and a sewage treatment plant should check out this large RV-only park. Its main assets are a central location and low rates. There are also hot showers and tables at each of the 117 sites (82 of them have full hookups).

Malibu Beach RV Park *(☎ 310-456-6052, 800-622-6052, fax 310-456-2532, 25801 Pacific Coast Hwy at Coral Canyon Rd, Malibu)* RV sites $25-40, tents $16-20. This popular ocean-side park is well-maintained and safe and has 150 sites with full and partial hookups, plus 52 tent spaces. Rates include tax, showers and hot-tub access.

Walnut RV Park *(☎ 818-775-0704, 800-868-2749, 19130 Nordhoff St, Northridge)* RV sites $30. In the San Fernando Valley, this park has 114 sites with full hookups. Take the I-405 (San Diego Fwy) to the Nordhoff St exit and head west for 4½ miles. From the US 101 (Ventura Fwy), get off at Tampa Ave and drive north for 4½ miles.

HOSTELS

LA has numerous hostels, including two affiliated with Hostelling International/ American Youth Hostels (HI/AYH). All take credit cards, and none has a curfew. Reservations are essential in summer and a good idea the rest of the year. The hostels' websites typically have additional details, including directions on how to get to each hostel by public transport. (Access the hostels' individual websites via HI/AYH's site at www.hiayh.org.) Prices include taxes.

HI/AYH Hostels

At HI/AYH hostels, dormitories are gender-segregated and alcohol and smoking are prohibited. Both LA hostels take reservations by phone, fax and email with a credit card. If you're using snail mail, you'll need to include a check, US bank draft or money order and a self-addressed and stamped envelope. To access the online reservation system, visit www.hiayh.org. You can also call the code-based reservation service at ☎ 800-909-4776. You will need the access code for the hostel to use this service (05 for Santa Monica, 26 for South Bay). Non-HI members will be charged an additional $3 per night.

HI-Los Angeles/Santa Monica Hostel (☎ 310-393-9913, fax 310-393-1769, reserve@ HILosAngeles.org, 1436 2nd St; Map 12) Dorm beds $23-25, private rooms $62. In an ivy-covered brick building, this hostel is near Third Street Promenade as well as the beach. It has a huge kitchen, courtyard, library, theater, laundry, travel store and offers discounted pick-ups from LAX. Though it's got a lot going for it, several of our readers have reported negative experiences. One reader called it 'very big and therefore a little impersonal but clean and well-situated.' A couple of people reported problems with 'mean staff' and one even called it a 'hostile hostel.' Keep us posted.

HI-Los Angeles/South Bay Hostel (☎ 310-831-8109, fax 310-831-4635, hisanpedro@ aol.com, 3601 S Gaffey St No 613; Map 15) Dorm beds $14, private rooms $39; check-in & check-out 11:45am. This San Pedro hostel, in pleasant bluff-top Angels Gate Park overlooking the Pacific Ocean, gets the top award for scenic location. Each dorm and public area sports a different theme, from 'African jungle' to 'American jazz' to 'Native American culture.' There's a big kitchen and a variety of entertainment and game equipment, plus a volleyball court and free mountain-bike rentals. The quiet

garden has hammocks, a barbecue patio and a vegetable garden, where guests may help themselves. Dorms sleep three to five with a total of 60 guests. There's a maximum stay of seven days. Make reservations at least two weeks in advance between June and September. MTA bus No 466 stops right outside at the Korean Friendship Bell.

Independent Hostels

LA's private hostels have comparable rates to HI/AYH hostels but no alcohol or smoking restrictions. In addition to dorms, most also have a few singles/doubles, sometimes with private bathrooms. Communal facilities include a kitchen, laundry, notice board and TV room. Most of these hostels are geared towards non-US travelers only; hostels accepting US citizens are noted below and typically require a passport and proof of travel (a rail, bus or plane ticket).

Hollywood (Map 9) *Orange Drive Manor* (☎ 323-850-0350, fax 323-850-7474, 1764 N Orange Dr)Dorm beds with showers $18 for international travelers or $22 for US travelers, singles/doubles with shared shower $33/39. This friendly and nonsmoking hostel, mere steps from Mann's Chinese Theater, offers plenty of privacy and a peaceful atmosphere. It's housed in a rambling 1920s manor, complete with creaky hardwood floors, steep staircases and high ceilings; it's not signed, so just look for the house number. This one's a winner – reservations are recommended.

USA Hostels – Hollywood (☎ 323-462-3777, 800-524-6783, fax 323-462-3228, Hollywood@usahostel.com, 1624 Schrader Blvd) Dorm beds $16, private rooms $36-44, including a free pancake and waffle breakfast; US travelers accepted. Rooms at this newish hostel are good-sized and have satellite TV and private bathrooms. Guests gather in the well-stocked kitchen or meet during free comedy nights, which are staged twice a week and present local talent. Call for free pick-ups from LAX and Greyhound.

Student Inn International Hostel (☎ 323-462-9269, 800-557-7038, no fax, 7038½ Hollywood Blvd) Dorm beds $13, dorm queen beds $22, private rooms $30, includes breakfast. Another new arrival on the Walk of Fame, this hostel emphasizes security and has the usual kitchen, Internet kiosk and lounge. Distinctive features include the large dorm beds for couples and free pick-ups from anywhere in the LA area.

Hollywood International Hostel (☎ 323-463-0797, 800-750-6561, fax 323-969-8829, 6820 Hollywood Blvd) Dorm beds $16, private rooms $40. A lively option, this hostel has 42 dorms sleeping three to four, and a few private rooms. Facilities include a tiny kitchen, gym, laundry room and TV lounge, as well as free coffee and tea. Pick-ups from LAX, Greyhound or Union Station are free with a stay of more than one night ($5 otherwise). This hostel attracts a rambunctious, sociable and international crowd.

Banana Bungalow Hollywood (☎ 323-851-1129, 800-446-7835, fax 323-851-1569, hwres@bananabungalow.com, 2775 N Cahuenga Blvd) Dorm beds $15-20, private rooms $59/68/76 double/triple/quad, including breakfast; US travelers accepted with proof of international travel. International party animals love this friendly and raucous place, converted from a rambling motel in the Hollywood Hills. It's less central than other Hollywood hostels, but public buses to central Hollywood and beyond stop right outside. Dorms sleep four, six or 10, and have cable TV, bathrooms and lockers. Extensive amenities include a large swimming pool, restaurant (dinners $2.25-6), small store, guest kitchen, Internet access, weight room, laundry and library. There are nightly movies on a large-screen TV, parties during the week and free shuttles to area attractions. LAX pick-ups are free with a three-night minimum stay.

Fairfax District (Map 10) *Orbit Hostel* (☎ 323-655-1510, 877-672-4887, reservations@orbithotel.com, 7950 Melrose Ave) Dorm beds $15-17, private room $45-59, includes breakfast; US travelers accepted only in private rooms. Retro decor with bold colors, a convivial ambience and a location near LA's epicenter of hipness make this spot a clear asset to the city's hostel scene. Rooms

and public areas are clean, modern and carpeted; there's an Internet kiosk, a large lounge, outdoor patio and coin laundry. Dorms sleep four to six, and private rooms are good-sized and have TV; some even have balconies. All rooms have a full bath. There are free pick-ups from the airport and Greyhound and Amtrak stations.

Venice (Map 13) Venice's youthful flair is a major magnet for backpackers and young travelers, which is probably why this funky beach town offers the greatest concentration of hostels. The area's not as safe as, say Santa Monica or Hermosa Beach, but great for sopping up that SoCal vibe. Just be careful after dark.

Share-Tel Apartments (☎ 310-392-0325, fax 310-392-9804, rooms@Share-Tel.com, 20 Brooks Ave) Dorm beds $20, private rooms $46-50. On a quiet street half a block from the beach, this charming hostel takes the cake. Freshly spruced up, it has pleasant four- to eight-bed dorms with private kitchens and bathrooms and small safes. Rates include linen, breakfast daily, dinner Monday to Friday and coffee and tea all day. There's a lounge with cable TV, an Internet kiosk, big lockers and a small laundry facility. The private rooms are sparse and a bit pricey for what you get.

Cadillac Hotel (☎ 310-399-8876, fax 310-399-4536, 401 Ocean Front Walk at Dudley Ave) Dorm beds $20; US travelers accepted. This is another great beach place; for a full review, see Venice & Marina del Rey under Hotels, later in this chapter.

Venice Beach Hostel (☎ 310-452-3052, fax 310-821-3469, pv@caprica.com, 1515 Pacific Ave) Dorm beds $19-21; private rooms $55; check-out 9am; US travelers accepted. A friendly atmosphere reigns at this large, multistory affair, one block inland from the beach. The large kitchen and recreational area, complete with piano, are welcome assets. Some hallways and rooms have been brightened with murals. Dorms sleep four to six people and some are women-only; all have their own bathrooms. Some private rooms (No 314 is a good one) even have kitchens and phones.

Venice Beach Cotel *(☎ 310-399-7649, fax 310-399-1930, 25 Windward Ave)* Dorm beds without/with ocean view $15/17.50; private rooms $35-49; check-out 11am; US travelers accepted. As its brochure explains, a 'cotel is a hostel with hotel standards.' This means ready-made beds; towels and soap; free boogie board, volleyball and paddle tennis rentals; wake-up service and airport transfers ($7); a cafe/lounge with free coffee, tea and a complimentary cocktail; Internet kiosk; and 24-hour security. Dorms (all mixed) sleep three to six, and some have baths. Private rooms are small but have decent furniture and TV. (No 319, with an ocean view, is a good choice.) On the downside, it's right above a popular nightclub and can get noisy.

Hostel California *(☎ 310-305-0250, fax 310-305-8590, Kschmahle@aol.com, 2221 Lincoln Blvd)* Dorm beds $12-17, private rooms $34-40, free parking; US travelers accepted. You have to be a pretty social animal to camp out in the 30-bed dorm, but for those needing more privacy there's also carpeted six-bed dorms (some women-only) and private rooms (with TV). All baths are shared. Amenities include a lounge with a big-screen TV, Internet kiosk, coin-op laundry and a kitchen. Bed linen, lockers and airport pick-ups (by prior arrangement) are free. It's about a 20-minute walk to the beach.

Hermosa Beach (Map 14) ***Surf City Hostel*** *(☎ 310-798-2323, 26 Pier Ave)* Dorm beds $15-18, private rooms $35-40, including small breakfast. Several of our readers have written glowing endorsements of this friendly hostel, steps from the beach and in the middle of Hermosa's 'bar row.' Interesting murals by talented former guests decorate the hallways leading to the rooms, kitchen and two small lounges with TV, VCR and Internet kiosk. Several dorms have en suite baths, though some are in pretty bad repair. From May to October, reservations are a good idea. Call for free airport pick-ups; Amtrak and Greyhound pick-ups are $15.

B&BS

Visitors should be aware that North American B&Bs are much less the casual, inexpensive sort of accommodations found in Europe or in Britain. While they are usually family-run, many if not most B&Bs require advance reservations, though some will be happy to oblige the occasional drop-in. Most have substantial breakfasts included in their prices, but lighter continental breakfasts are not unheard of.

Inn at 657 *(☎ 213-741-2200, 800-347-7512, 657 W 23rd St; Map 5)* Singles $95-120, doubles $125, suites $125-200, including tax, free parking. This gem of a place is right in the historic West Adams district south of Downtown LA, near USC and Exposition Park. Recently expanded to the adjacent house, it now has seven rooms and four suites, as well as lovely breakfast and sitting rooms. Antique furniture and nice decor abound.

Channel Road Inn *(☎ 310-459-1920, fax 310-454-9920, 219 W Channel Rd, Santa Monica; Map 13)* Rooms $150-335. This romantic place has 12 rooms and two suites facing the Pacific Ocean. Built in Colonial Revival style in 1910, it's set into a hillside garden and offers a library, spa and laundry, as well as free bicycles for riding along the beach on the South Bay Trail.

Venice Beach House *(☎ 310-823-1966, fax 310-823-1842, 15 30th Ave, Venice; Map 13)* Rooms $120-165, parking and kids under 5 free. This tasteful, homey retreat with nine sun-drenched rooms is draped in ivy. Charlie Chaplin used to stay here when it was the beach house of a local developer, and you can still dream of *City Lights* in the 'Tramp's Quarters.'

Inn at Playa del Rey *(☎ 310-574-1920, fax 310-574-9920, 435 Culver Blvd, Playa del Rey)* Rooms $150-345, suites $250-345. Romantic touches abound here. The office is in the middle of a busy kitchen, which produces amazing aromas, and there's an unobstructed view of the city over the Ballona Wetlands. Homemade breakfast; tea, wine and hors d'oeuvres in the afternoon; and freshly baked cookies and desserts in the truly lovely dining and seating areas make this place well worthwhile.

Lord Mayor (*☎/fax 562-436-0324, 435 Cedar Ave, Long Beach; Map 16*) Rooms $85-125. Historic B&Bs with rooms starting at under $100 are pretty rare, which makes this place all the more remarkable. The 1904 Edwardian house was once the home of the city's first mayor and has been meticulously restored by community preservationists Reuben and Laura Brasser. Each of the 12 rooms (10 with private bath) get their character from stylish antique furniture rather than frilly over-decoration; bathrooms have claw-foot tubs, and there's an ample sundeck.

The Turret House (*☎ 562-983-9812, 888-488-7738, fax 562-437-4082, 556 Chestnut Ave, Long Beach; Map 16*) Rooms $100-140. This friendly place, in a restored 1906 Queen Anne villa, is owned by a woman with a penchant for floral patterns, which cover everything from walls and carpets to pillows and furniture. Fluffy robes await in your antique armoire, the furniture is polished to a tee, and bathrooms have claw-foot tubs and lacy shower curtains. Each of the five rooms has a different theme and color scheme but none has a TV or telephone.

Artists' Inn & Cottage (*☎ 626-799-5668, 888-799-5668, fax 626-799-3678, artistsinn@artistsinn.com, 1038 Magnolia St, South Pasadena; Map 3*) Rooms $110-205. Each of the five rooms and four suites in this lovely Victorian farmhouse has decor recalling various artists and periods. All have private baths. Rooms in the cottage are quieter.

Bissell House (*☎ 626-441-3535, 800-441-3530, fax 626-441-3671, 201 Orange Grove Blvd, Pasadena; Map 17*) Rooms $115-160. This is a lovingly restored 1887 Victorian estate on 'Millionaire's Row.' Charming rooms, five in all, have leaded-glass windows and private baths with pedestal sink and claw-foot tub.

HOTELS
Downtown (Map 5)
Staying downtown has many advantages: You're near interesting sights and shopping

and good restaurants, as well as the Staples Center and Convention Center. It's also a public transportation hub, making it easy to get to places like Long Beach, Hollywood and Santa Monica. Walking around at night, though, cannot be recommended.

Budget Downtown has no hostels but there's no dearth of affordable accommodations. Most lower-priced properties cluster in the area around the Convention Center, along Wilshire Blvd west of the I-110 (Harbor Fwy) and in Chinatown. A few hotels are even housed in historic buildings and give you the added benefit of a glimpse of the area's faded 1920s grandeur. Prices quoted here may surge during convention activity.

Stillwell Hotel (*☎ 213-627-1151, 800-553-4774, fax 213-622-8940, 838 S Grand Ave*) Rooms $49-80. This historic property has been treated to a comprehensive makeover and now features 250 nicely appointed rooms, all with private bath, TV and air-con. Gill's Cuisine of India, a popular restaurant, and the eccentric Hank's Bar (see Entertainment) are on the premises.

Orchid Hotel (*☎ 213-624-5855, fax 213-624-8740, 819 S Flower St*) Rooms $33-38 daily, $184 weekly. The 63-room Orchid, two blocks west, is dirt-cheap but quite Spartan and not for those with exacting standards of cleanliness.

Milner Hotel (*☎ 213-627-6981, 800-827-0411, fax 213-623-9751, 813 S Flower St*) Rooms $60-70, including breakfast. A step up in comfort, the adjacent Milner has a multilingual staff and 177 generic and smallish rooms.

In Town Hotel (*☎ 213-628-2222, 800-457-8520, fax 213-623-1350, 913 S Figueroa St*) Rooms $55-65, free parking. Rooms at this dependable standby are decent and functional but don't expect too much in the charm department. There's also a fairly shabby coffee shop and a cocktail lounge. The location, though, is excellent.

Metro Plaza Hotel (*☎ 213-680-0200, 800-223-2223, fax 213-620-0200, 711 N Main St*) Rates $69-84, free parking. On the edge of

Chinatown, near Olvera St and Union Station, this four-story, 80-room hotel is noted more for convenience than for character. Rooms have refrigerators and contemporary furnishings in pastel colors.

Best Western Dragon Gate Inn (☎ 213-617-3077, 800-282-9999, fax 213-680-3753, 818 N Hill St, Chinatown) Rooms $89-$159, children under 18 free. This family-run place is one of the best Downtown deals. The Kwong family's 52 comfortably furnished rooms have Chinese decorative accents throughout and feature data ports, hair dryers, coffeemakers, cable TVs and refrigerators. Atrium shops include an English-speaking herbalist and acupuncturist, and there's also a tea house-dim sum restaurant with a Jackie Chan movie-set theme.

Royal Pagoda Motel (☎ 323-223-3381, 995 N Broadway) Rooms $59-79. This place is the Kwong family's other plainer property, but rooms were being spiffed up at the time of research.

Motel de Ville (☎ 213-624-8474, fax 213-624-7652, 1123 W 7th St) Rooms $40-45, free parking. Just north of the I-110 (Harbor Fwy) but still within easy access to the Staples Center and other attractions, this motel has classic neon signage, a small and poorly maintained pool and 62 plain, fairly clean rooms. The owners have zero charm but it's central and cheap. If traffic noise bothers you, ask for a room in the back.

City Center Motel (☎ 213-628-7141, 800-816-6889, fax 213-629-1064, 1135 W 7th St) Rooms $40-50, including small breakfast, free parking. Virtually identical in style and (lack of) atmosphere to the Motel de Ville, this is another place to simply rest your head after a day of exploring. It is also located a few blocks west of Downtown proper but still within easy access to major attractions.

Mid-Range *Hotel Figueroa* (☎ 213-627-8971, 800-421-9092, fax 213-689-0305, 939 S Figueroa St) Rooms $88-124. A favorite mid-priced Downtown hotel is this 1927 gem with the feel of an oversized hacienda. The striking lobby boasts such design flourishes as colored tiles, muralled doors, and

wrought-iron chandeliers and beamed ceilings. There's a poolside restaurant, a coffee shop and a stylish bar upstairs. The spacious rooms have a pastel color scheme and a good range of amenities. This place fills up quickly, so call ahead.

Kawada Hotel (☎ 213-621-4455, 800-752-9232, fax 213-687-4455, 200 S Hill St) Rooms $139, ask for discounts. This hotel has Japanese ownership and European appeal. Extra amenities include in-room VCRs (video rentals in the lobby) and refrigerators; some rooms have luxurious kitchenettes. The Epicentre restaurant, on the ground floor, is quite good.

Miyako Inn (☎ 213-617-2000, 800-228-6596, fax 213-617-2700, 328 E 1st St, Little Tokyo) Rooms $114-168. Many guests are charmed by this hotel where many of the 174 rooms are Japanese-style, with tatami mats, shoji screens and low beds. It has a restaurant, health club and karaoke lounge.

New Otani (☎ 213-629-1200, 800-421-8795, fax 213-622-0980, 120 S Los Angeles St, Little Tokyo) Rooms $189, suites $500, ask for discounts. Catering largely to a business clientele, the Otani's public areas are an awkward stab at integrating East and West, and rooms are more functional than stylish. Pleasant touches include a half-acre Japanese garden and several top-quality restaurants. Worth a splurge is the 'Japanese Experience' package at $649 per couple. It includes a night in an authentic Japanese suite with tatami mats, dinner at the signature restaurant and a miraculous shiatsu massage from tiny masseuses with hands of steel.

Los Angeles Athletic Club Hotel (☎ 213-625-2211, 800-421-8777, fax 213-689-1194, 431 W 7th St) Rooms $179, suites $300. This hotel has 72 large rooms adorned in rich, warm decor with all the trappings, including terry cloth robes. Rates also buy access to the posh in-house athletic club, complete with a 25-yard, sky-lit swimming pool, a gym, and racquetball and squash courts.

Hyatt Regency (☎ 213-683-1234, 800-233-1234, fax 213-629-3230, 711 S Hope St) Rooms $129, suites $600. The Hyatt Regency is above the Macy's Plaza shopping mall and offers the full range of amenities for business travelers.

Best Western Mayfair Hotel (☎ 213-484-9789, 800-528-1234, fax 213-484-2769, 1256 W 7th St) Rooms $99-129. Just north of the I-110 (Harbor Fwy), this former luxury hotel (built in 1928) maintains a touch of elegance in its sky-lit lobby. The Art Deco Orchid Restaurant serves a popular buffet lunch ($13), and there's also a lounge, fitness center and rooftop sundeck. Rooms are standard but comfortable.

Holiday Inn Downtown (☎ 213-628-5242, 800-465-4329, fax 213-628-1201, 750 Garland Ave) and ***Holiday Inn City Center*** (☎ 213-748-1291, 800-465-4329, fax 213-748-6028, 1020 S Figueroa St) Rooms $99-$199. Both of these places are popular with the convention crowd. Rooms feature coffee-makers, irons and hair dryers.

Top End ***Westin Bonaventure Hotel*** (☎ 213-624-1000, 800-228-3000, fax 213-612-4800, 404 S Figueroa St) Rooms $247, suites $307. Featured in nearly as many movies as City Hall, the five glass cylinders of this hotel tower a mere 35 stories above LA. With 1199 guest rooms and 157 suites, 20 restaurants, five bars, 40 retail stores, a swimming pool and a fitness deck the size of a football field, this hotel is definitely one of LA's landmarks.

The Regal Biltmore (☎ 213-624-1011, 800-245-8673, fax 213-612-1545, 506 S Grand Ave) Rooms $239-259, suites $500. Hugging the western edge of Pershing Square is Downtown LA's poshest hotel. Built in 1923, this landmark hotel has the feel of a European palace and has hosted a galaxy of US presidents, celebrities and dignitaries. Its rooms epitomize luxury. (See also the Biltmore in the Los Angeles Architecture special section).

Wyndham Checkers Hotel (☎ 213-624-0000, 800-996-3426, fax 213-626-9906, 535 S Grand Ave) Rooms $204-279, suites $300. Across the street, the intricate stone facade of this hotel dates from 1927. Besides an intimate lobby and sophisticated restaurant, antique furniture, marble bathrooms and a rooftop spa are among the elegant touches

in this first-class, 188-room European-style hotel. Amenities include free newspaper and shoe shine.

Hollywood (Map 9)

Budget Hollywood is dotted with cheap motels, but some are of questionable repute. If none of the ones listed here do the trick, try the string of chains and independents along Sunset Blvd between La Brea Blvd and Vine Ave; rates are in the $40 to $60 range.

Hollywood Best Inn (☎ 323-467-2252, fax 323-465-8316, 1822 N Cahuenga Blvd) Rooms $40-55. Low on character but with adequate facilities, this is your basic downtown Hollywood option. Rooms are of recent vintage and also have microwaves and refrigerators.

Liberty Hotel (☎ 323-962-1788, 800-750-6561, fax 323-463-1705, 1770 Orchid Ave) Rooms $40-55, free parking. Right behind Mann's Chinese Theater, this is a nice hotel with 21 large and bright rooms with private bath. There's a communal kitchen and free coffee, though rooms with private kitchens cost just an additional $5. A guest laundry is right on the premises.

Highland Gardens Hotel (☎ 323-850-0535, 800-404-5472, fax 323-850-1712, 7047 Franklin Ave) Rooms $70/95 winter/summer, suites with kitchens $85-130 winter, $95-150 summer. Also central to this family-friendly hotel. Comfortable rooms and suites wrap around a leafy, quiet courtyard. The hotel is associated with a bit of Hollywood trivia: Janis Joplin overdosed in room 105 on October 3, 1970.

Magic Hotel (☎ 323-851-0800, 800-741-4915, fax 323-851-4926, 7025 Franklin Ave) Rooms $69-125, free parking. This is easily the best value for your money in central Hollywood. Its large suites sleep up to four people. All have kitchens and modern decor, and there's a large heated pool as well. Rates are slightly lower in winter. As a bonus, the hotel can make reservations for the Magic Castle, a private dinner club, normally closed to the public featuring (what else?) the talents of top-flight magicians; the show is not cheap but definitely memorable.

Orchid Suites Hotel (☎ 323-874-9678, 800-537-3052, fax 323-874-5246, 1753 N Orchid Ave) Rooms $59-89 winter, $75-109 summer, free parking. Nearby, this hotel is another good-value establishment located on a quiet side street near Mann's Chinese Theater. Owner Joe's a friendly guy, and each of the 36 small apartments is nicely appointed and has a full kitchen; some also have balconies. There's even a large heated swimming pool.

Hollywood Celebrity Hotel (☎ 323-850-6464, 800-222-7017, fax 323-850-7667, 1775 N Orchid Ave) Rooms $80, including breakfast. Two doors down, this is another good option in a stylish, if slightly neglected, Art Deco building. Each of the 40 rooms is spacious and quiet, and there's a free shuttle to Universal Studios.

Saharan Motor Hotel (☎ 323-874-6700, 877-815-1938, fax 323-874-5163, 7212 Sunset Blvd) Rooms $45-90. Behind a garish Las Vegas-style neon sign awaits a better than average motel with a well-kept pool. The location (near a couple of strip clubs) is not the most savory, though, so don't plan on walking around at night.

Dunes Sunset Motel (☎ 323-467-5171, 800-443-8637 in CA, 800-452-3863 outside CA, fax 323-469-1962, 5625 Sunset Blvd) Rooms $65-75, higher in summer. The old-fashioned decor here is almost endearingly campy, but rooms are furnished with such modern amenities as air-con, satellite TV and direct-dial phones.

Mid-Range & Top End *Hollywood Metropolitan Hotel* (☎ 323-962-5800, 800-962-5800, fax 323-466-0646, 5825 Sunset Blvd) Rooms $99, suites $129, including breakfast, free parking. Rooms at this contemporary obelisk, near the US-101 (Hollywood Fwy) on the less savory eastern side of Hollywood, are stuck in the '80s. The flamboyant Art Deco lobby, though, sports a library and an aquarium; there is also a restaurant with a view.

Hollywood Roosevelt Hotel (☎ 323-466-7000, 800-950-7667, fax 323-462-8056, 7000 Hollywood Blvd) Rooms $99-299. If you want to experience those bygone days of glamour and glory, consider checking in at this place, mere steps from Mann's Chinese Theater. (Also see the entry in the Things to See & Do chapter).

Fairfax District (Map 10)

The area around the Farmers' Market has a bunch of good-value establishments.

Beverly Laurel Hotel (☎ 323-651-2441, 800-962-3824, fax 323-651-5225, 8018 Beverly Blvd) Rooms $75-79, with kitchenette $10 extra. This one's a winner – and not just for its great location near the Farmers' Market. Rooms wrap around a decent-sized pool with doors – painted a cheerful turquoise – leading to large rooms with modern furnishings and more than a modicum of style. Arty black-and-white photographs integrated into the headboards juxtapose nicely with diamond-patterned bedspreads. The attached Swingers diner, owned by Rosanna Arquette's husband, is open all day with nothing costing over $10.

Farmer's Daughter Motel (☎ 323-937-3930, 800-334-1658, fax 323-932-1608, 115 S Fairfax Ave) Rooms $58-95, free local calls. If the idea of merely crossing the street for breakfast at the historic Farmers' Market appeals to you, book yourself a room at this dependable motel. Rooms are adequately furnished and count coffeemakers and refrigerators among their amenities. There's also an outdoor pool.

Bevonshire Lodge Motel (☎ 323-936-6154, fax 323-924-6640, 7575 Beverly Blvd) Rooms $49-58. Nearby, this quiet and friendly place is another well-priced option. Rooms are clean and comfortable and come with air-con, TV and phone. There's a pool as well.

Park Plaza Lodge (☎ 323-931-1501, fax 323-931-5863, 6001 W 3rd St) Rooms $60-85. Those looking for excellent value will like this friendly place whose large rooms have antique-style furniture, refrigerators and air-con.

West Hollywood (Map 10)

Budget & Mid-Range *Holloway Motel* (☎/fax 323-654-2454, 888-654-6400, 8465 Santa Monica Blvd) Rooms $70-80 Sun-Thur,

$90-100 Fri & Sat, including breakfast, free parking. In the heart of WeHo, this friendly place can get a bit noisy but is otherwise a good value. Rooms have voice mail services, data ports and safes.

The Standard (☎ *323-650-9090, fax 323-650-2820, 8300 W Sunset Blvd*) Rooms $99-225, suites $650. Anything but standard, this young, fashionable and hip hotel has lots of boundary-pushing design surprises. The pool is pink and surrounded by blue Astroturf; the lobby is made of recycled glass. All rooms have CD players, VCRs, cordless phones and platform beds. There's a 24-hour coffee shop as well. It's an excellent value, especially if you can score one of the cheaper rooms.

Best Western Sunset Plaza Hotel (☎ *323-654-0750, 800-421-3652, fax 323-650-6146, 8400 W Sunset Blvd*) Rooms $99-150, including generous breakfast buffet. This place, in the heart of the Sunset Strip, attracts a mixed crowd of families and couples with its high-energy, cosmopolitan flair and reasonable prices. It has 100 nicely decorated and spacious rooms, some with full kitchens. A nice sundeck offers vistas of the city.

The Grafton on Sunset (☎ *323-654-4600, 800-821-3660, fax 323-654-5918, 8462 W Sunset Blvd*) Rates $165-300. This lovely boutique hotel, a couple of doors down from the House of Blues, was designed in accordance with Feng Shui principles. Facilities include a heated pool and a fitness center. Cozily outfitted rooms sport such nice touches as organic bath amenities, robes, speaker phones and voice mail services. Staying here also gives you VIP access to some area clubs.

Beverly Plaza Hotel (☎ *323-658-6600, 800-624-6835, fax 323-653-3464, info@ beverlyplazahotel.com, 8384 W 3rd St*) Rooms $159-268. Another place in the European mode is this trendy boutique hotel with 98 rooms located near the Beverly Center. Special touches include bed turndown service, daily $10 taxi vouchers, a gourmet coffee bar, fitness center, spa facilities and the popular restaurant Cava (see the Places to Eat & Entertainment chapters). Rooms are large, fashionably ap-

Gay Accommodations

By law, no hotel may turn away gay couples, though some may pretend to be full or frown upon homosexual guests. You can assume any hotel located in West Hollywood to be gay-friendly, so also check the accommodations listed in that section. Properties catering predominantly to a gay and/or lesbian clientele include:

San Vicente Inn/Resort (☎ *310-854-6915, fax 310-289-5929, 845 N San Vicente Blvd, West Hollywood; Map 10*) Rooms $69-209. Gay men should check out this pleasant hostelry. It has rooms with private or shared bath, as well as cottages and suites. All have stylish, contemporary furnishings and overlook a tropical garden. Facilities include a heated swimming pool, hot tub, sauna and clothing-optional sun patio. Free continental breakfast is served on the patio.

Grove Guest House (☎ *323-876-8887, 888-524-7683, fax 323-876-0890, 1325 N Orange Grove Ave, West Hollywood; Map 10*) Rooms $179. Stay in a spacious villa with separate living room and bedroom and a full kitchen. It's all set in a tropical garden and there's a pool and spa as well. Both men and women are welcome.

Coral Sands Motel (☎ *323-467-5141, 800-367-7263, 1730 N Western Ave, Hollywood; Map 9*) Rooms $63-73. Not in the nicest part of town, this little motel doesn't cater exclusively to a gay clientele, although its pool, hot tub and sauna have a reputation for being very cruisey. It's across the street from The Study, a bar and club popular with African American gay men.

pointed and have data ports and voice mail services.

Ramada West Hollywood (☎ *310-652-6400, 800-272-6232, fax 310-652-2135, 8585 Santa Monica Blvd*) Rooms $165, suites $185-275. This hotel is in the heart of 'Boys' Town' and has a nice Art Deco lobby. Standard rooms are smallish, so spend an extra $20 for the small suite, which has such nice touches as fluffy robes, speaker phones, hair dryers, coffeemakers and small refrigerators. A heated swimming pool and restaurants are on the premises as well.

Le Montrose Suite Hotel (☎ 310-855-1115, 800-776-0666, fax 310-657-9192, 900 Hammond St) Suites $165-560. Time at this cozy hideaway seems to move a bit slower than in the rest of LA. It boasts a $2 million art collection and 120 large suites with sunken living rooms and fireplaces; some have kitchenettes and private balconies. Views from the rooftop swimming pool, framed by private cabanas, are breathtaking. Bicycles to scoot around are included in the room rates.

Top End

Hyatt West Hollywood (☎ 323-656-1234, 800-233-1234, fax 323-650-7024, 8401 W Sunset Blvd) Rates $200-250. Ostensibly just another installment in this chain of contemporary luxury hotels, this facility actually has carved out a special status in LA rock 'n' roll history. A favorite haunt of headlining musicians in the '70s, it came to be dubbed 'Riot House.' The action here was wild indeed: Led Zeppelin once rented six floors and rode motorcycles in the hallways, according to Art Fein's *LA Musical History Tour*. Fein also reports that Jim Morrison was once kicked out for hanging out of a window by his fingertips. Following a recent renovation, rooms and public areas now sport Art Deco touches. Views from the rooftop swimming pool are dramatic.

The Argyle (☎ 323-654-7100, 800-225-2637, fax 323-654-9287, 8358 W Sunset Blvd) Rooms $250, suites $300. A perfect paean to original Art Deco, the 1931 Argyle has an impressive exterior as well as such charming interior touches as an undulating steel and brass staircase. Furnishings include replicas of historic pieces from major museum collections. Old-time Hollywoodians such as Errol Flynn and John Wayne (who allegedly once kept a cow in his 12th-floor penthouse) rented rooms here. The Fenix restaurant gets rave reviews from locals and guests alike.

Château Marmont (☎ 323-656-1010, 800-242-8328, fax 323-655-5311, 8221 W Sunset Blvd) Rooms $250, suites $325-$1950. Get ready for French-flavored indulgence at this swank 1927 hangout whose design takes its cue from a Loire Valley castle. In years past, regular guests were such luminaries as Greta Garbo and Howard Hughes (who is said to have used binoculars to watch bikini-clad swimmers from his suite). These days it still beds pop stars and actors who like its whimsical charm, gorgeous gardens, special services and legendary discretion. On a tragic note: Comedian John Belushi overdosed in Bungalow 2 (or 3, depending on your source) in 1982.

Mondrian (☎ 323-650-8999, 800-525-8029, fax 323-650-5215, 8440 W Sunset Blvd) Rooms $310-385, suites $370-570. Like the gates to heaven, two giant doors – but no marquee – announce your arrival at LA's beacon for the beautiful and celebrated. Ex-Studio 54 impresario Ian Schrager has sheathed his boutique hotel in melodramatic minimalism that juxtaposes harsh geometry with playful lighting effects. An air of exclusivity prevails. Rooms are top-notch, and 'basics' such as a 24-hour gym and gourmet restaurants are supplemented by a yoga studio and private physical trainers. The hotel is home to the (in)famous Sky Bar (see Entertainment).

Sunset Marquis Hotel & Villas (☎ 310-657-1333, 800-858-9758, fax 310-652-5300, 1200 N Alta Loma Rd) Suites $260-$320, villas $600-$1200. This is a discreet retreat and recording industry favorite (it has its own recording studio). Eric Clapton, Billy Joel and Bruce Springsteen have been among those checking into its luxurious digs set in a lush landscape of rolling lawns, koi pond and tropical gardens.

Mid-City

Chancellor Hotel (☎ 213-383-1183, fax 213-385-6657, 3191 W 7th St; Map 7) Rooms $40-45. While not terribly central, this hotel offers excellent value and is near a couple of cool underground restaurant/bars. The building, a 1924 castle-like confection, is a frequent movie location with a huge lobby and communal area. Rooms are small but clean, with adequate comforts and private baths. There's a sizable population of long-term residents, including international students and senior citizens.

Dunes Wilshire Motor Hotel (☎ 323-938-3616, 800-452-3863, fax 323-938-9661, 4300 Wilshire Blvd, Hancock Park; Map 10) Rooms $64-74. This older property has a swimming pool and laundry. Rooms are adequate, and kitchenettes are available (with a surcharge) by request.

Wilshire Royale Howard Johnson Plaza (☎ 213-387-5311, 800-421-8072, fax 213-380-8174, 2619 Wilshire Blvd, MacArthur Park; Map 5) Rooms $110-130 winter, $130-150 summer. This vintage place is a real surprise. The grand lobby revives the grandeur of the 1920s and rooms are graciously furnished with style and comfort.

Oxford Palace Hotel (☎ 213-389-8000, 800-532-7887, fax 213-382-3434, 745 S Oxford Ave; Map 7) Rooms $165-250, free valet parking. This handsome hotel has Asian aesthetics and upscale comforts. The lobby boasts a small waterfall and marble, and the rooms are outfitted with such amenities as coffeemakers and hair dryers.

Beverly Hills & Bel Air (Map 11)

Budget & Mid-Range *Beverly Hills* **Reeves Hotel** (☎ 310-271-3006, fax 310-271-2278, 120 S Reeves Dr) Rooms $85-95, including breakfast, free parking. Those who can't afford the glamour but would like to be close to it, should stay at this older but spanking clean property on a quiet street just south of Wilshire Blvd. Rooms have a microwave, small refrigerator and color TV.

Hotel del Flores (☎ 310-274-5115, 409 N Crescent Dr) Rooms $95-150. A homey environment and a central location are the assets of this place, which otherwise has a bit of a downtrodden air. The cheaper rooms come with shared baths.

Maison 140 (☎ 310-281-4000, 800-432-5444, fax 310-281-4001, 140 S Lasky Dr) Rates $140-215, including breakfast. This stupendous charmer, housed in the former villa of silent movie star Lilian Gish, redefines value for money. Designer Kelly Wearstler has created fantasy settings for each of the 46 rooms, largely achieved by

sheathing its walls and ceilings in boldly patterned and colored wallpaper. All have eclectic artwork and vintage furnishings blending French frivolity and Asian simplicity. Chenille throws and Frette bed linens are typical luxury touches.

Beverly Crescent Hotel (☎ 310-247-0505, 800-451-1566, fax 310-247-9053, 403 N Crescent Dr) Rooms $149-249, including continental breakfast. This newly renovated hotel wears its fresh look with pride. With just 38 rooms, personal attention is assured. All rooms are outfitted with voice mail services, computer modems and comfy robes and slippers. Rates include afternoon tea.

Top End *Luxe Hotel Rodeo Drive* (☎ 310-273-0300, 800-468-3541, fax 310-859-8730, 360 N Rodeo Dr) Rooms $255-355, suites $355-455, including breakfast. The only hotel right on Rodeo Dr opened in late 2000 and has a clean, contemporary and uncluttered look. The 88 airy rooms are outfitted in relaxing beiges and pastels and sport the ultimate in amenities, including luxurious linens and bath accouterments by Rene Furterer.

Avalon Hotel (☎ 310-277-5221, 800-535-4715, fax 310-277-4928, 9400 W Olympic Blvd) Rooms $200-250, suites $250-425. Mid-century modern meets amenities fit for the new millennium at this stylish boutique hotel. Furnishings include such retro touches as bubble lamps by George Neison and Eames cabinets; the pool is in the shape of a figure eight. Marilyn Monroe lived in this building for two years, and Lucy and Desi came and went as well.

Hotel Bel Air (☎ 310-472-1211, 800-648-4097, fax 310-476-5890, 701 N Stone Canyon Rd) Rooms $375-510, suites $650-3000. One of LA's classiest addresses, the emphasis here is on privacy; Tom Hanks and Joan Collins are among the celebs (though not as a couple) who have enjoyed the hotel's secluded bungalows, fountain courtyards and 11-acre gardens. In such a peaceful place, it's hard to imagine you're still in LA. Visit, if only to stroll the grounds and enjoy afternoon tea or a drink. (Also see the Bel Air restaurant in the Places to Eat chapter.)

JANET FRIES

The Beverly Hills Hotel, another legendary star

Beverly Hills Hotel (☎ 310-276-2251, 800-283-8885, fax 310-281-2905, 9641 Sunset Blvd) Rooms $335-425, suites and bungalows $725. If you fancy (and can afford) dwelling in the utmost of luxury in an ambience oozing opulence and infused with historical charm, this is your place. For historical background, see the Things to See & Do chapter.

The Regent Beverly Wilshire (☎ 310-275-5200, 800-427-9354 in CA, 800-421-4354 outside CA, fax 310-274-2851, 9500 Wilshire Blvd) Rooms $345-385, suites $560-900. This bastion of style, glamour and top-notch comforts has anchored Rodeo Dr since 1928. Yes, it's the hotel from which Julia Roberts first stumbled, then sashayed, in Pretty Woman. Not surprisingly luxury is taken very seriously here. If you want that historical feel, ask for a room in the Wilshire Wing. To experience the grandeur without becoming a major stockholder, treat yourself to afternoon tea in the Lobby Lounge.

Four Seasons Hotel (☎ 310-273-2222, 800-819-5053, fax 310-859-3824, 300 S Doheny Dr) Rooms $350-435, suites $590. This is one of those exceptional hotels that dazzle with class, not glitz. A natural color scheme, tasteful art and sculptures, and smart furniture bring to mind the sophistication of time-tested European hotels. Attention to detail is impeccable – even the restaurant bathrooms have fresh flowers and plush towels.

Westwood & Century City (Map 11)

Budget *Westwood Inn* (☎/fax 310-474-4262, 10820 Wilshire Blvd) Rooms $60-70, including small breakfast and free local calls; 7th night free. There is absolutely nothing fancy about this place, but it's run by friendly folks and close to UCLA and Westwood Village.

Royal Palace Westwood Hotel (☎ 310-208-6677, 800-631-0100, fax 310-824-3732, 1052 Tiverton Ave) Rooms $70-119, including breakfast, children under 12 stay free. Despite its name, this is no palace, but its location in Westwood Village makes it a bargain. The more expensive rooms have been newly renovated.

Mid-Range *Hilgard House Hotel* (☎ 310-208-3945, 800-826-3934, fax 310-208-1972, 927 Hilgard Ave) Rooms $124-134, including room-service breakfast, free parking. This snug boutique hotel has Old World charm and an academic ambience. Rooms have antique-style furnishings, refrigerators and ice-makers, and some have Jacuzzis.

Hotel del Capri (☎ 310-474-3511, 800-444-6835, fax 310-470-9999, 10587 Wilshire Blvd) Rooms $90-110, suites $115-235, including continental breakfast, free parking. This hotel is a charmer. Its 36 rooms and 45 suites in four stories surround a terrace and swimming pool. More than half of the rooms have kitchenettes and there's a free shuttle to Beverly Hills and Westwood.

Century Wilshire Hotel (☎ 310-474-4506, 800-421-7223, fax 310-474-2535, 10776 Wilshire Blvd) Rooms $95-125, including continental breakfast, free parking. Converted from a time-worn apartment building, this hotel has preserved a homey feel with differently decorated rooms. There's also a large swimming pool.

Top End The *W* (☎ *310-208-8765, 877-946-8357, fax 310-824-0355, 930 Hilgard Ave)* Suites $300. Even before checking in, you know that the W is no ordinary hotel: the valets wear headsets, the staircase doubles as a fountain and the dramatic lobby-bar has a game table where chic adults engage in a round of tic-tac-toe or dominoes. East Asian simplicity meets Western modernism describes the stylish decor that carries over to the rooms. Amenities are first-rate and comprehensive, and there are two pools, a spa and a fitness center.

Doubletree Hotel (☎ *310-475-8711, 800-472-8556, fax 310-475-5220, 10740 Wilshire Blvd)* Rooms $250, suites $400. The 295 rooms here have the usual range of upscale amenities. Rates include free unlimited access to a lovely sauna, Jacuzzi and fitness center. Shuttle service to UCLA is free.

Century Plaza Hotel (☎ *310-277-2000, 800-937-8461, fax 310-551-3355, 2025 Ave of the Stars)* Rooms $200. Swank and elegant, this is the kind of place that appeals to presidents of countries and corporations. Steps from the Shubert Theatre and Century City shopping mall, this hotel is sumptuously pleasant despite its size and cubic exterior. Rooms are spacious and appointed with delightfully frivolous knickknacks; many have nice views from private balconies. Rates vary widely but special weekend and promotional rates are frequent.

LAX Area

Budget Apart from the inexpensive chain hotels, you'll find numerous other affordable accommodations near the airport. Most offer free shuttle service to and from LAX.

Vista Motel (☎ *310-390-2014, 4900 Sepulveda Blvd; Map 12)* Rooms $49-80. This small motel is clean and fairly quiet and has 22 decent-size rooms with cable TV.

Super 8 (☎ *310-670-2900, 800-336-0025, fax 310-410-1787, 9250 Airport Blvd)* Rooms $65-85, suites $95-110. Another good choice is this place, which has 69 rooms, an outdoor pool and an on-site restaurant.

Sunburst Motel (☎ *310-398-7523, 3900 Sepulveda Blvd; Map 12)* Rooms $69-149. This motel has pleasant architecture and

The Chains

National hotel chains are heavily represented in greater Los Angeles. A few individual properties are included in the chapter itself, but space limitations prevent us from including more. Call the following toll-free reservation numbers to find additional hotels and motels in the LA area.

Budget

Days Inn	☎ 800-325-2525
Econo Lodge	☎ 800-446-6900
Motel 6	☎ 800-466-8356
Super 8 Motels	☎ 800-800-8000
Travelodge	☎ 800-255-3050
Vagabond Inns	☎ 800-522-1555

Mid-Range

Best Western	☎ 800-528-1234
Comfort Inns	☎ 800-228-5150
Howard Johnson	☎ 800-654-2000
Quality Inn	☎ 800-228-5151
Radisson Hotels	☎ 800-333-3333
Ramada Inns	☎ 800-272-6232

Top End

Doubletree Hotels	☎ 800-222-8733
Hilton Hotels	☎ 800-445-8667
Holiday Inns	☎ 800-465-4329
Hyatt	☎ 800-228-9000
Marriott Hotels	☎ 800-228-9290
Sheraton Hotels	☎ 800-325-3535

PLACES TO STAY

nicely furnished rooms with hair dryers and cable TV. The motel also has a hot tub for relaxing.

Hampton Inn (☎ *310-337-1000, 800-426-7866, fax 310-645-6925, 10300 La Cienega Blvd, Inglewood; Map 2)* Rooms $69-99, including breakfast, newspaper, free local calls. This place has 148 rooms.

Culver Hotel (☎ *310-838-7963, 888-328-5837, fax 310-815-9618, 9400 Culver Blvd; Map 12)* Rooms $79-109, free parking. This venerable property opened in 1924, during MGM's early heyday. During the filming of *The Wizard of Oz*, many of the Munchkins stayed here; they were, apparently, a party-hearty bunch. When the hotel reopened in

1997, the 14 surviving Munchkins met for a reunion. Rooms here are nothing glamorous but are comfortable and furnished with antiques.

Four Points by Sheraton (☎ 310-645-4600, fax 310-649-7047, 9750 Airport Blvd) Rooms $99, suites $129. A homey, light-flooded lobby welcomes guests to this good-value hotel. Each of its 573 rooms come with such extras as hair dryers, voice mail services and weekday newspapers; executive level rooms also have data ports and a breakfast buffet. Relax in the large pool, framed by thoughtful landscaping, or work out the kinks at the 24-hour fitness center.

Furama Hotel (☎ 310-670-8111, 800-225-8126, fax 310-337-1883, 8601 Lincoln Blvd; Map 2) Rooms $99-$119. This 770-room place is a pleasant, resort-style property. It's right across from a recreation park with access to tennis courts, a golf course and a driving range. On the premises are a swimming pool, bowling alley and supermarket. Shuttle service to the airport and Marina del Rey is free.

Mid-Range *Crowne Plaza LA Airport* (☎ 310-642-7500, 800-255-7606, fax 310-417-3608, 5985 W Century Blvd; Map 2) Rooms $129-159, suites $350-750. This 15-story place is your typical corporate hotel, big on efficiency and service, but low on atmosphere. The 615 rooms have amenities such as hair dryers and irons. The staff is unusually adept in anticipating the needs of clients; services include free airport pickups and drop-offs.

Los Angeles Airport Hilton & Towers (☎ 310-410-4000, 877-414-8014, fax 310-410-6250, 5711 W Century Blvd; Map 2) Rooms $153, suites $255. Biggest of the big, with similar facilities and services, is this 1200-room place.

Los Angeles Airport Marriott (☎ 310-641-5700, 800-228-9290, fax 310-337-5358, 5855 W Century Blvd; Map 2) Rooms $189/104 weekdays/weekends, suites $325. This hotel, which weighs in with 1100 rooms, is another anonymous behemoth with the upscale facilities typically associated with this chain.

Sheraton Gateway LA Airport Hotel (☎ 310-642-1111, 800-325-3535, fax 310-410-1852, 6101 W Century Blvd; Map 2) Rooms $145-175, suites $250. This massive property has 727 rooms and 83 suites.

Renaissance Los Angeles Hotel (☎ 310-337-2800, 888-293-0523, fax 310-216-6681, 9620 Airport Blvd; Map 2) Rooms $179, suites $229. Another huge place, this hotel features public areas and 499 rooms with a relative dash of personality.

Malibu

Most accommodations in Malibu lie on the Pacific Coast Hwy and are easy to spot.

Topanga Ranch Motel (☎ 310-456-5486, fax 310-456-1447, 18711 Pacific Coast Hwy; Map 2) Rooms $65-85. Although budget stays in Malibu are hard to come by, try this funky place, still reasonably close to Santa Monica, with 30 trim white cottages across the highway from the beach.

Malibu Riviera Motel (☎ 310-457-9503, no fax, 28920 Pacific Coast Hwy) Rooms $90-100, including tax, less in winter. This place between Zuma Beach and Paradise Cove has a sundeck and a hot tub.

Casa Malibu Inn (☎ 310-456-2219, 800-831-0858, fax 310-456-5418, casamalibu@earthlink.net, 22752 Pacific Coast Hwy; Map 2) Rooms $99-349. This lovely property overlooks a private beach. Some of the 21 rooms have private decks, fireplaces and kitchenettes. A continental gourmet breakfast is included in the price. Be sure to make reservations at least a few days ahead of your arrival.

Malibu Country Inn (☎ 310-457-9622, 800-386-6787, fax 310-457-1349, 6506 Westward Beach Rd) Rooms $125 Sun-Thur, $165 Fri & Sat, rooms with Jacuzzi $175-190, suites $200-250. This nicely restored 1943 Cape Cod-style inn is a quiet retreat in a great location 7 miles north of the Malibu town center. Each of the 16 rooms has different country-style decor and there's a heated pool.

Malibu Beach Inn (☎ 310-456-6444, 800-462-5428, fax 310-456-1499, 22878 Pacific Coast Hwy; Map 2) Rooms with partial ocean views $189-259, rooms with private outdoor Jacuzzi $249-329, suites $289-379, including continental breakfast. This breezy ocean-side hideaway is right on a tranquil swimming beach near the Malibu Pier. The decor is hacienda-style, and the ocean-facing patio makes a lovely breakfast setting.

Santa Monica (Map 13)

Budget True budget lodgings have become nearly as rare as an Elvis sighting in trendy Santa Monica. Most of the cheaper digs are away from the beach, but a couple of older motels are still holding forth on Ocean Ave. The price range is huge and what you end up paying depends on the season, demand and the mood of the receptionist. Bargaining may get you a discount.

Pacific Sands Motel (☎ 310-395-6133, fax 310-395-7206, 1515 Ocean Ave) Rooms from $80. Bathrooms here are less than sparkly but rooms are adequately sized and come with TV and phone.

Santa Monica Beach Travelodge (☎ 310-451-0761, 800-578-7878, fax 310-393-5311, 1525 Ocean Ave) Rooms $105-250. Next door, this place is one step up, with clean, comfortable rooms with coffeemaker, TV and phone.

Ocean Lodge (☎ 310-451-4146, 800-393-6310, fax 310-393-9621, 1667 Ocean Ave) Rooms $69-250. Another unpretentious motel, this one counts updated and nicely furnished rooms and free Internet access among its assets.

Sea Shore Motel (☎ 310-392-2787, fax 310-392-5167, 2637 Main St) Rooms & suites $70-119. Good value, clean and well-run, this motel is only two blocks from the beach and usually crawls with European travelers. Renovated rooms have lots of amenities and breakfast is available at the adjacent cafe (separate charge).

Mid-Range *Cal Mar Hotel Suites* (☎ 310-395-5555, 800-776-6007, fax 310-451-1111, 220 California Ave) Suites $99-159. On a quiet residential street, yet within a block of the beach and shopping, this older facility is a good choice for families or people in need of plenty of space. All suites have full kitchens and are arranged around a decent-sized swimming pool.

Hotel California (☎ 310-393-2363, 800-537-8483, fax 310-393-1063, 1670 Ocean Ave) Rooms $135-325 winter, $25 more from late May to mid-Sept. The Eagles may have been right: You may never (want to) leave the Hotel California although, unlike in the namesake song, there's nothing sinister about this charming 26-room beachside property. You'll be greeted by whimsical surf-inspired decor, and sunny rooms come with sparkling hardwood floors, private patios and kitchenettes. This place is good value for the money.

Hotel Shangri-La (☎ 310-394-2791, 800-345-7829, fax 310-451-3351, 1301 Ocean Ave) One- or two-person studios or suites $160-240, four-person suites $330, including breakfast. This swank 1939 Art Deco building has long been the sentimental favorite of those whose names appear in the newspaper in bold type, including Diane Keaton, Bill Murray and Gene Hackman. There is no swimming pool or restaurant, but the airy rooms are outfitted with retro-style furniture and most have full kitchens. Oceanfront suites come with huge living room and terrace.

Best Western Ocean View Hotel (☎ 310-458-4888, 800-452-4888, fax 310-458-0848, 1447 Ocean Ave) Rooms $149-189. This one's a standard affair in a terrific location. Rooms are pleasingly furnished and those with ocean view have petite verandas.

Top End *Georgian Hotel* (☎ 310-395-9945, 800-538-8147, fax 310-451-3374, reservations@georgianhotel.com, 1415 Ocean Ave) Rooms $235-400; $25 higher in July-Aug. This striking Art Deco landmark has decor so Great Gatsby-esque that a straw boater wouldn't feel out of place. In fact, during 1920s Prohibition, its speakeasy was favorite turf of Bugsy Siegel, Clark Gable, Carole Lombard, 'Fatty' Arbuckle and other legends. With 56 rooms and 28 suites, this property is small enough to be called intimate but also sports the full range of modern amenities. The personable staff adds another notch on the comfort level.

The Fairmont Miramar Hotel (☎ 310-576-7777, 800-866-5577, fax 310-458-7912, 101 Wilshire Blvd) Rooms $250-900. This classy property stands in the place of the former mansion of Senator John Jones, the founder of Santa Monica. It was he who planted the massive 120-year-old Moreton Bay fig tree in the driveway. Betty Grable was discovered here and notables from Marilyn Monroe to Bill Clinton have stayed in the luxurious guest rooms or bungalows set among quasi-tropical gardens.

Loews Santa Monica Beach Hotel (☎ 310-458-6700, 800-235-6397, fax 310-458-6761, 1700 Ocean Ave) Rooms $250-450, suites $575-2500. The original of the phalanx of luxury beach hotels in Santa Monica has undergone a makeover and now features subdued Asian decor and a lobby lined by fake palm trees. Amenities and facilities are top-notch. The hotel's Lavande restaurant is a far cry from the usual hotel eatery (see the Places to Eat chapter).

Shutters on the Beach (☎ 310-458-0030, 800-334-9000, fax 310-458-4589, 1 Pico Blvd) Rooms $355-600, suites $750-2000. Nearby, this elegant Cape Cod–style resort hotel has two fancy restaurants and a gallery's worth of original artwork by Roy Lichtenstein, David Hockney and others. Some rooms feature fireplaces and private Jacuzzis and most have complimentary books, magazines, videos and even waterproof shower radios.

Hotel Casa del Mar (☎ 310-581-5533, 800-898-6999, fax 310-581-5503, 1910 Ocean Front Walk) Rooms $345-875. If you wish to relive the grandeur of a 1920s beach club and resort, book yourself into this posh new player right next to the sand. The elegant Renaissance Revival-style building has been completely restored to its sumptuous pre-WWII heyday. Wallow in style and luxury in Mediterranean-flavored rooms distinguished by gauzy drapes, hand-painted armoires and wicker chairs. Most rooms are ocean-facing.

Hotel Oceana (☎ 310-393-0486, 800-777-0758, fax 310-458-1182, 849 Ocean Ave) Suites $360-600. For a special treat, ensconce yourself in the serenity of this all-suite luxury boutique hotel. The Italianate pool area and tastefully furnished and quiet rooms – featuring refrigerators loaded with gourmet pizzas – will appeal to the well-heeled. Think sooooothing…. On a sadder note, Stan Laurel died here in 1965, when this was still an apartment building.

Venice & Marina del Rey (Map 13)

Budget *Jolly Roger Hotel* (☎ 310-822-2904, 800-822-2904, fax 310-301-9461, 2904 Washington Blvd) Rooms $75-85, motel annex $55-65. Close to the beach, a cool pub and trendy Abbot Kinney Blvd, this friendly place is definitely hip to international travelers. Basic rooms with large bathrooms are a great value. More budget minded? Stay in the motel section. Public buses to the beach leave from right outside. Prices include continental breakfast and may drop a few dollars in winter – ask.

Cadillac Hotel (☎ 310-399-8876, fax 310-399-4536, 401 Ocean Front Walk at Dudley Ave) Dorm beds $20, rooms $69-79, suites $120. Right on the beach, this place is one of the best bargains in LA. Inside a gracefully restored 1930s Art Deco landmark, it has rooms and suites with ocean views, color TVs, safes, phones and private baths. There's also a gym and sauna, rooftop sundeck and coin laundry. There are 30 private rooms, as well as bunks in four-person dorms.

Sunbay Motel (☎ 310-306-7081, 12841 Washington Blvd) Rooms $58-65. A couple of miles farther inland, this simple motel has large and clean rooms with generic but modern furnishings, including microwave and refrigerator.

Inn at Venice Beach (☎ 310-821-2557, 800-828-0688, fax 310-827-0289, 327 Washington Blvd) Rooms $89-145 Sun-Thurs, $10 more Fri & Sat, including breakfast. The purple awnings and balconies are an indication of the fresh and cheerful decor that awaits inside this pleasant spot about two blocks from the beach. Rooms have high ceilings and are nicely furnished; amenities such as refrigerators and hair dryers are standard.

Ramada Limited (☎ 310-821-5086, 800-272-6232, fax 310-821-6167, 3130 Washington

Blvd) Rooms $89, suites $139. A recent renovation makes this a fine place to stay. Rooms have refrigerators, microwaves and data-port phones, and there's an outdoor Jacuzzi. *Definitely* ask for special deals, as rates vary by season and may be negotiable.

Mid-Range & Top End *Foghorn Harbor Inn (☎ 310-823-4626, 800-423-4940, fax 310-578-1964, info@foghornhotel.com, 4140 Via Marina, Marina del Rey)* Rooms $119-149, including breakfast. Rooms at this family-owned hotel, right on placid Mother's Beach, are smallish and fairly plain, but all have marina views, refrigerators and voice mail services. Rates also include 24-hour coffee, daily newspaper and shuttle to LAX.

Marina Pacific Hotel (☎ 310-452-1111, 800-421-8151, fax 310-452-5479, 1697 Pacific Ave) Rooms $119-159, suites $169-249, $10-20 more May-Sept; including breakfast. This hotel is a pleasant island of civilization in freaky Venice. Large and bright rooms are decked out in natural colors, and many have balconies with partial ocean views. Suites are spacious and have a full kitchen and fireplace.

Ritz-Carlton Marina del Rey (☎ 310-823-1700, 800-241-3333, fax 310-823-2403, 4375 Admiralty Way) Rooms $240-420. If you're going to spend big, it might as well be at this classy place. This lavish property comes with its own marina and charter yachts, as well as lighted tennis courts, a swimming pool and spa. The 12-story hotel has 294 luxurious rooms with all the trappings, as well as deluxe units and suites.

South Bay (Map 14)
Budget & Mid-Range Motels charging $40 or less per room abound along the Pacific Coast Hwy, which barrels through all the South Bay communities. Not all of the motels are in the best of shape, though.

Manhattan Beach Hotel (☎ 310-545-9020, 4017 Highland Ave, Manhattan Beach) Rooms $70-90. The upstairs rooms of this friendly little place, with full views of the waves a block away, are one of the best deals in town. The ones downstairs, though, are smaller, noisier and face the street.

There are no other amenities, aside from a sundeck.

Sea View Inn (☎ 310-545-1504, fax 310-545-4052, 3400 Highland Ave, Manhattan Beach) Rooms $95-225. A mere 300 feet from the shore, this friendly property has 31 newly renovated rooms and suites decked out in fresh colors. Most have ocean views, microwaves, refrigerators, VCRs and voice mail services. The 'executive suites,' essentially mini-apartments with full kitchens (granite counters!), are great for families. If the ocean's too cold, there's a heated pool for aquatic frolicking. Bicycles for scooting around town or along the South Bay Trail are available at no charge. There's a two-night minimum on weekends. A slew of bars and restaurants, including the popular Local Yolk breakfast haunt, are just a few steps away.

Barnabey's Hotel (☎ 310-545-8466, 800-317-7446, fax 310-545-8621, 3501 Sepulveda Blvd, Manhattan Beach) Rooms $109-179. Lots of lace, dark oak trimmings, thick carpets and a stately atmosphere make this homey inn look a bit like a cross between a Louisiana bordello and a Victorian manor. Rooms are nice and well-appointed. There's a lovely patio for afternoon tea, a pub and a popular restaurant.

Hermosa Beach has a couple of terrific choices for those wanting to be close to the ocean, sand and nightlife:

Grandview Motor Hotel (☎ 310-374-8981, fax 310-374-8983, 55 14th St) Rooms $83-90, rooms with ocean views $99-110. This safe, quiet and spanking clean establishment offers excellent value. Rooms are huge and count refrigerators and patios among their extra amenities. The lobby is on the 2nd floor (ring the bell to enter).

Sea Sprite Motel (☎ 310-376-6933, fax 310-376-4107, 1016 The Strand) Rooms $94/115 without/with view, winter rates 10% less. It's pretty noisy and some of the staff is attitudinous, but the location right on the beach is excellent. Units vary in size and some have microwave and refrigerator.

Best Western Sunrise Hotel (☎ 310-376-0746, 800-334-7384, fax 310-376-7384, 400 N Harbor Dr, Redondo Beach) Rooms

$119-129, including continental breakfast. This sprawling place near the King Harbor pier area has cheerfully decorated rooms with desk, refrigerator, two phones and a coffeemaker. There's also a good-size swimming pool.

Palos Verdes Inn (☎ *310-316-4211, 800-421-9241, fax 310-316-4863, 1700 S Pacific Coast Hwy, Redondo Beach*) Rooms $110-120. The exterior may not be much to look at, but this place actually has plenty of assets. Besides a location three blocks from the beach, there are comfortable rooms and free bicycle rentals. There's also a glass-encased pool with retractable roof, for swimming in all conditions. The restaurant, Chez Mélange, is one of the area's finest (see Places to Eat).

Top End Beach House (☎ *310-374-3001, 888-895-4559, fax 310-372-2115, 1300 The Strand, Hermosa Beach*) Rooms $209-359; free valet parking. Wallow in total luxury at this spanking new beachfront hotel with the feel of a luxurious cottage. Expect large rooms with separate sitting area, small patios and all the amenities you could wish for. The in-house day spa lets you work out the kinks.

Portofino Hotel & Yacht Club (☎ *310-379-8481, 800-468-4292, fax 310-372-7329, 260 Portofino Way, Redondo Beach*) Rooms with marina views $199-239, ocean-view $215-251, ask for off-season specials. This is the South Bay's ticket to ocean-side elegance. Occupying a private peninsula that separates the King Harbor marina from the Pacific Ocean, this neat property offers the gamut of amenities. The warmly appointed three-story atrium lobby bursts with stunning floral arrangements and also has a fireplace. A 24-hour fitness center is on the premises.

Long Beach (Map 16)

Also see the Bed & Breakfast section earlier in this section for additional listings in this city.

Budget Brooks College (☎ *562-597-6611, 800-421-3775, fax 562-597-2661, patti@*

brookscollege.edu, 4825 E Pacific Coast Hwy) Doubles $25 per person, including 3 meals; available July 1-end of Aug. A steal of a deal is offered by this arts and design college, which makes a limited number of rooms available to travelers. There are shared bathrooms, a linen service, cafeteria, laundry and a swimming pool. Several bus lines stop directly in front of the college for the 10-minute trip into downtown Long Beach. There's 24-hour security and gender-separated floors. For information and reservations, call 8am-5pm weekdays and ask to be connected to Student Services.

Beach Inn Motel (☎ *562-437-3464, fax 562-436-4541, 823 E 3rd St)* Rooms $60. A central, if somewhat noisy, location and fairly modest room rates make this place appealing. You can expect clean rooms with few amenities, but with these wallet-friendly prices, who's complaining?

Inn of Long Beach (☎ *562-435-3791, 800-230-7500, fax 562-436-7510, innoflb@hotmail.com, 185 Atlantic Ave)* Rooms $65-105, including breakfast, free parking and local calls. This friendly and central establishment is great value. Rooms have cable TV and VCRs (with free video rental), refrigerator and modem hook-up. All face a central courtyard with heated swimming pool and spa.

Mid-Range & Top End Hotel Queen Mary (☎ *562-435-3511, fax 562-499-1622, 1126 Queens Hwy)* Rooms $105-275, suites $350-400. If you've ever longed to experience the atmosphere of a classic ocean liner, this place offers you a chance. The original (refurbished) 1st-class staterooms of this permanently moored liner are cramped, to be sure, and portholes do not provide a lot of light, but the mood of Art Deco afloat is unmatched.

Dockside Boat & Bed (☎ *562-436-3111, 800-436-2574, fax 562-436-1181, Rainbow Harbor, Dock 5, 316 E Shoreline Dr)* Rooms $220-240. Salty types with a sense of romance should check out – and maybe check into – this floating hostelry. Let yourself be rocked to sleep by the waves aboard your own private yacht (choices include a 50-foot

Chinese junk), moored close to downtown and with a view of the *Queen Mary*.

Pasadena (Map 17)

Budget Pasadena's 'motel row' runs along E Colorado Blvd between Lake Ave and Rosemead Blvd. There are literally dozens of budget-priced motels along this strip, some in better shape than others, including such chain properties as Comfort Inn, Econo Lodge, Holiday Inn, Ramada and Travelodge. Several independent motels (especially those clustered between Sunnyslope and Eastern Aves) advertise rooms for just $25 a night, and these are popular with transients and low-income people.

Westway Inn (☎ 626-304-9678, fax 626-449-3493, 1599 E Colorado Blvd) Rooms $62-89. This friendly place is across from Pasadena City College. Each of the 61 modern rooms has a refrigerator, coffeemaker and hair dryer, and there's even a small swimming pool and spa. Some rooms have a private Jacuzzi.

Saga Motor Hotel (☎ 626-795-0431, 800-793-7242, fax 626-792-0559, 1633 E Colorado Blvd) Rooms $63-93, including continental breakfast. This spacious, nicely landscaped and well-kept three-story inn is next door. It has a pleasant swimming pool and spa area. There are 69 fairly spiffy rooms.

Best Western Colorado Inn (☎ 626-793-9339, fax 626-568-2731, 2156 E Colorado Blvd) Rooms $58-71, including continental breakfast. A bit farther east is this place, an older property with a peanut-size swimming pool. Rooms are not too generously proportioned, but bathrooms are quite large.

Pasadena Inn (☎ 626-795-8401, fax 626-577-2629, 400 S Arroyo Parkway) Rooms $55-65. Not even 1 mile south of Old Downtown is this well-maintained standard affair with a pool and free coffee and donuts for breakfast. Rooms have cable TV and phones, but refrigerators and microwaves must be rented for an extra fee.

Mid-Range & Top End *Sheraton Pasadena Hotel* (☎ 626-449-4000, 800-457-7940, fax 626-584-1390, 303 E Cordova St) Rooms $129-144. This newly remodeled five-story hotel has 312 rooms and is centrally located between Pasadena's civic auditorium, the convention center and a major shopping mall. It has a swimming pool, fitness center and 24-hour business center.

Pasadena Hilton (☎ 626-577-1000, 800-445-8667, fax 626-584-3148, 150 S Los Robles Ave) Rooms $109-249; check for Internet discounts. This 12-story hotel makes tasteful use of marble and skylights, and rooms are warmly furnished in dark wood. Amenities include a fitness center and swimming pool. The more expensive rooms are larger and have a view.

Doubletree Hotel (☎ 626-792-2727, 800-222-8733, fax 626-795-7669, 191 N Los Robles Ave) Rooms $179-229 Mon-Thur, $139-170 Fri-Sun. Pasadena's other central top property is a modern 12-story, 360-room hotel connected to the City Hall complex through a fountain-laden Mediterranean courtyard.

Ritz-Carlton Huntington Hotel (☎ 626-568-3900, 800-241-3333, fax 626-568-3700, 1401 S Oak Knoll Ave) Rooms $245-310. This sumptuous 392-room hostelry is surrounded by a magnificent 23-acre garden. Built in the Mission style in 1907, the hotel was fully upgraded following serious earthquake damage. Special touches include the covered picture bridge and California's first Olympic-size swimming pool. Rooms are the embodiment of refinement.

Glendale (Map 3)

Chariot Inn Motel (☎ 818-507-9774, fax 818-507-9774, 1118 E Colorado St) Singles $42-52, doubles $50-60, including breakfast. This motel has refrigerators and pay-per-view movies in its 31 spacious rooms.

Glendale Lodge (☎ 818-507-6688, fax 818-507-8103, 1510 E Colorado St) Rooms $62-82, suites $92-120, including continental breakfast. This is a solid if unexciting option amid a row of inexpensive motels close to the Hwy 134 (Ventura Fwy) and US-2 (Glendale Fwy).

Hilton Glendale (☎ 818-956-5466, 800-733-5466, fax 818-956-5490, 100 W Glenoaks Blvd) Rooms $214/139 weekdays/weekends. This handsome 19-story hotel has earned a good reputation with business travelers for its services and facilities, including free shuttles to Burbank Airport. Views from the 19th-floor bar are truly panoramic. For relaxation, there's an outdoor swimming pool, sauna, spa and fitness center. All 350 rooms have refrigerators.

Burbank & Universal City (Map 18)

Budget *Universal City Inn (☎ 818-760-8737, fax 818-762-5159, 10730 Ventura Blvd, Studio City)* Rooms $70-90. Within walking distance of Universal Studios, just off the busy US 101 (Hollywood Fwy), this flower-festooned place offers excellent value. The inn's 37 rooms are modern, large and have air-conditioning.

Holiday Lodge (☎ 818-843-1121, fax 818-559-6424, 3901 Riverside Dr, Burbank) Rooms $69-90. This 30-room motel has friendly service and tastefully appointed, fairly quiet rooms (some with extra-large tubs).

Burbank Inn & Suites (☎/fax 818-842-1114, 180 W Alameda Ave, Burbank) Rooms $79-99. This place has 34 standard rooms and 17 mini-suites. It's just west of the I-5 (Golden State Fwy).

Mid-Range *Safari Inn (☎ 818-845-8586, 800-782-4373, fax 818-845-0054, 1911 W Olive Ave, Burbank)* Rooms $109-129, suites $169. With its classic 1950s neon sign, the Safari Inn looks like a throwback to another era (it's even been used as a movie set). A recent renovation, though, has added a host of decidedly modern touches including data port phones and voice mail services. It's a stone's throw from the studios and also has a pool, sundeck and fitness room. This is one of the best bargains in this part of town. Suites have full kitchens and sleep up to five people.

The Annabelle Hotel (☎ 818-845-7800, 800-426-0670, fax 818-845-0054, 2011 W Olive Ave, Burbank) Rooms $174, suites $194-204, free parking, daily newspaper. Also sporting a fresh new look from top to bottom, the Annabelle Hotel is the upscale sister property to the Safari Inn and perfect for those traveling on business. A sky-lit

atrium lobby leads to 47 nicely appointed rooms with large desks, coffeemakers and the full range of comforts and communication devices.

Sportsmen's Lodge Hotel (☎ 818-769-4700, 800-821-8511, fax 818-769-4798, 12825 Ventura Blvd, Studio City; Map 2) Rooms $140-165. Emulating a British country estate, this lovely lodge is surrounded by a handsome garden complete with waterfalls and swan pond. Rooms ooze Old World charm, and there's a clubby restaurant and pub to continue the theme. Facilities include a fitness center and large pool. All rooms have a private patio. Shuttle service to/from Universal Studios is free.

Holiday Inn (☎ 818-841-4770, 800-465-4329, fax 818-566-7886, 150 E Angeleno Ave, Burbank) Rooms $149. If you want predictable comforts, check in at this 490-room property with its impressive lobby.

Top End *Burbank Airport Hilton & Convention Center (☎ 818-843-6000, 800-445-8667, fax 818-842-9720, 2500 Hollywood Way)* Rooms $139-159. Convenient to this regional airport, this nine-story hotel has 488 rooms, a restaurant, bar, two swimming pools, a sauna and fitness center. Rates usually go up when a convention is in town.

Sheraton Universal Hotel (☎ 818-980-1212, 800-325-3535, fax 818-985-4980, 333 Universal Terrace Pkwy) Rooms $180-250. This typical luxury chain hotel is basically on the Universal Studios lot. Amenities at this 21-story high-rise include in-room movies, a Jacuzzi, coffeemaker and morning newspaper, plus transportation to the theme park. A huge lobby gives access to 442 rooms.

Universal City Hilton & Towers (☎ 818-506-2500, 800-445-8667, fax 818-509-2053, 555 Universal Terrace Pkwy) Rooms $135-200. This monolithic place is the Sheraton's 24-story, steel-and-glass neighbor. It has another 446 rooms, all with views of the San Fernando Valley, and the standard Hilton amenities.

LONG-TERM RENTALS

Hotels often have attractive rates for stays of a week or longer. Your best bet, however, is to scan the newspapers: The *LA Times* has sections for apartment and room rentals in its classified supplement. Or select the neighborhood in which you want to live and pick up one of the free local papers usually found in retail stores (especially bookstores), restaurants and bars. Also check out the universities, which may offer subletting services. UCLA, for instance, has a Community Rental Housing Office (☎ 310-825-4491). It finds people who will be vacating their house or apartment for a limited time and puts them in touch with those in need of accommodations for that period.

Places to Eat

Folks in San Francisco may disagree, but the fact remains: Los Angeles is the culinary capital of the US West Coast. Some would even argue, with reason, that it represents the cutting edge of cuisine in the Western Hemisphere. Why? The number one reason, perhaps, is the willingness to experiment. As a cosmopolitan crossroads, LA attracts people from around the world, and with them their food. Creative chefs take bits and pieces from different cuisines and combine them in ways that would have been unimaginable in an earlier day. There are restaurants, for example, espousing the gastronomic glory of California Thai, Chinese Italian, Kosher Mexican and Australian American.

Unless noted otherwise, restaurants mentioned in this chapter are open daily for lunch and dinner. Changes do happen all the time, so call ahead.

Food

Eating healthy is very much part of the California lifestyle, which gave birth to California cuisine in the mid-1980s. Pioneers like Berkeley-based Alice Waters and LA's own star chef Wolfgang Puck created gourmet concoctions revolving around fresh seasonal ingredients, unusual flavor fusions and artistic presentations. A typical dish would be a serving of grilled mahi mahi with a side of sautéed spinach greens and wild rice pilaf. A good place to try classic California cuisine is Puck's own Spago Beverly Hills.

An offshoot of California cuisine is California Asian (Cal-Asian). Its focus is on the blending of local ingredients with Chinese or Japanese seasonings and cooking methods. Meats and fish are seasoned with adventurous combinations of turmeric, cilantro (fresh coriander), ginger, garlic, chili paste and fresh fruit juices (usually citrus), and served with Asian staples like rice, sweet potatoes or *udon* (buckwheat noodles). Try it at such places as Chaya Brasserie in Beverly Center District, Traxx

in Downtown LA, Chinois on Main in Santa Monica or Mum's in Long Beach.

Another variation of California cuisine is California French (Cal-French), which is a slimmed down version of Gallic fare, banishing much of the butter and cream and instead relying on the flavors produced by top quality vegetables and other ingredients. Good places to sample this kind of food are Citrus on Melrose Ave, JiRaffe in Santa Monica and Joe's in Venice.

With nearly 50% of LA's population being Latino, it's not surprising that south-of-the-border food – especially Mexican – is ubiquitous. For the budget traveler, it's a godsend: It's cheap, delicious and filling. (See the boxed text 'Whimsical Mexican Food' for more information on tasty dishes.)

A fairly recent trend in LA is the upscale version of Latin food commonly referred to as Nuevo Latino cuisine. Long popular on the East Coast, it combines the food culture from numerous Latin American countries – from Panama to Patagonia. Dishes are veritable flavor bombs blending exotic produce like jicama, plantains, yucca and mango with chiles, epazote and other spices in bold combinations. Ciudad in Downtown LA, the Border Grill in Santa Monica and Alegria in Long Beach all specialize in Nuevo Latino fare.

Fish and shellfish figure big on menus in Los Angeles from the lowly, but delicious, fish taco to oysters on the half-shell and seared ahi tuna. What is served at most restaurants often depends on the day's catch, which has the obvious advantage of complete freshness. You'll find some good seafood restaurants in the coastal communities; Ocean Avenue Seafood in Santa Monica comes to mind, although the Water Grill in Downtown reigns supreme.

Because LA is the quintessential ethnic cauldron, you'll find cuisines from just about every other country: from Ethiopia (Nyala in the Fairfax District), Cuba (Versailles in Culver City, El Floridita in Hollywood) to

China (Ocean Star in Monterey Park, Empress Pavilion in Chinatown). Thai and Italian are other prevalent cuisines.

Predictable, unexciting and certainly not healthy, fast food chains are cheap, reliable standbys any time of the day. For hamburgers, the California chain is the venerable In-N-Out Burger, which has a short menu and a die-hard clientele.

Dining Etiquette

Dining out in LA tends toward the casual, although you should still dress appropriately. That definitely means shoes and shirt; a jacket is appropriate for men at some upscale restaurants. If in doubt, call ahead and ask about the dress code. Classic dinner time is 8pm. In general, make reservations for all top end and mid-range restaurants several days ahead, especially if dining out on a Friday or Saturday night.

When you arrive at a restaurant, it's customary to wait by the entrance until the host seats you; only in very casual places may you choose a table yourself.

Most restaurants count on several seatings per night, so the expectation is that you'll leave soon after you've finished your meal. In most cases, your server will bring you the bill automatically; in some top restaurants it may be presented only after you've requested it (though to hustle you along, a server might come by your table asking if you'd like to order anything else). Smoking inside restaurants and bars is prohibited by state law, although outdoor areas are usually exempt.

Costs

If you don't insist on lavish, sit-down meals, you need not spend much money on food. Besides the ubiquitous fast-food chains, you can fill up cheaply at often excellent, if simple, establishments. If you want a more substantial hot meal, lunch is usually cheaper than dinner. Chinese and Thai restaurants are among those offering special set lunches for $7 or less. Dinners too can be affordable – even at fancy restaurants – if you stick to one main course and a single non-alcoholic beverage.

The LA scene: more chatting than chowing

Restaurants are notorious for huge markups on beer, wine and even bottled water. If you're concerned about money, stick with LA tap water; it's perfectly safe to drink. If you want alcohol, order beer or wine by the glass and avoid expensive cocktails.

Remember that your final bill will swell thanks to sales tax (8%) and a tip (15%); valet parking can also add another $2.50 to $5 to your total. Thus, a moderately priced $35 dinner for two (food only) will actually run you about $50.

In this book, restaurants are divided into three price categories: 'Budget' (most main courses cost $10 or less), 'Mid-Range' ($10 to $18) and 'Top End' ($18 and up).

DOWNTOWN (MAP 5)
Budget

The Grand Central Market at 317 S Broadway is a dream come true for the cash-strapped – and a terrific place to sop up Downtown LA's mélange of ethnicities, languages and cuisines. Eating here is super casual; simply pick an eatery and sidle up to the counter where you may rub elbows with mustachioed Mexicans, chirpy Korean housewives or legal eagles in $1000 suits. Choices are numerous, but these are some favorites:

Maria's Pescado Frito *(no ☎, central aisle)* Mains $1.25-2. For fresh fish and seafood, head here. Best bets are generously filled fish tacos, as well as tostadas topped with tangy ceviche, a marinated fish and vegetable salad.

Sarita's Pupuseria *(☎ 310-626-6320, north aisle)* Mains $1.50-4. This place serves mouthwatering Salvadoran food including *pupusas*, pastries filled with cheese, pork or beans.

Roast to Go *(☎ 213-625-1385, central aisle)* Mains $1.50-3.50. Beneath their trademark neon sign the Penilla family has been serving delicious tacos and burritos since 1952. Typical fillings include chicken, lamb, fish and *carnitas* (slow-cooked and shredded pork), although there are also more 'gutsy' choices such as hog maw, beef brains and tripe.

China Cafe *(no ☎, upper level)* Mains $2.50-4.50. This place offers 'counter culture' at its democratic best. Join the multiethnic throngs scarfing down giant platters of egg fong su and chow mein (one easily feeds two); the soups are huge, steamy and cheap.

Clifton's Brookdale Cafeteria *(☎ 213-627-1673, 648 S Broadway)* Mains $2-6; open daily 6:30am-7pm. This venerable eatery was founded in 1931 by a Salvation Army captain who doled out free grub to starving Angelenos during the Great Depression. 'Grub' is still what is served here, but the ultra-campy setting is what makes it special. Sprawling over several open levels, Clifton's is an enchanted forest with fake trees, squirrels and deer. For spiritual sustenance, duck into the diminutive chapel.

Angélique Cafe *(☎ 213-623-8698, 840 S Spring St)* Mains $5.45-9; open 7am-4pm Mon-Sat. French expats, downtown workers and dedicated gourmets flock to this charming establishment for delicious homemade French food at prices that are a veritable steal. Owner-chef Bruno has his way with interesting sandwiches and such classic bistro fare as coq au vin, spinach quiche or

salade niçoise. His superb pâtés, sold here for under $6 per pound, pop up at premium prices in swank restaurants around town.

Philippe The Original *(☎ 213-628-3781, 1001 N Alameda St)* Mains $2-4; cash only; open 6am-10pm daily. Whether this legendary establishment is truly the 'home of the French Dip sandwich' (as they claim) is beside the point. It has a pedigree going back to 1908, and some of the city's best chefs regularly join the throngs at the long service counter. Watch retro-clad 'carvers' prepare juicy roast beef sandwiches for dipping into fragrant juice from the roasting pan. To show you're not a novice, order a side of coleslaw or potato salad and a surprisingly decent glass of red wine. Coffee is just 9¢ (no misprint). Then hunker down at the long communal tables parked on the sawdust-covered floor and chow down.

Barragan's *(☎ 213-250-4256, 1538 Sunset Blvd)* Mains $4-13.50. A bit north of central Downtown, in a seedy section of Echo Park, this Mexican family operation has fed the cash-strapped for more than four decades. Traditional fare such as chicken enchiladas are a good bet, though the *cocido*, a flavorful broth with vegetables, is great on a winter night.

Patinette *(☎ 213-626-1178, 250 S Grand Ave)* Mains $4-10; open 10am-5pm Tues-Sun, to 8pm Thur. This is star chef Joachim Splichal's casual Downtown bistro at the Museum of Contemporary Art. It serves small meals and snacks with a Mediterranean bent. Also see Patina in the Central Hollywood – Top End section.

Suehiro *(☎ 213-626-9132, 337 E 1st St)* Mains $4-15; open 11am-1am Sun-Thur, to 3am Fri & Sat. For steaming bowls of *udon* soup (thick noodles and vegetables swimming in an aromatic broth), check out this Little Tokyo spot. Rice dishes, sukiyaki (sliced beef or chicken cooked with vegetables) and other dishes are served as well. Bargain hunters might like the Okonomi Plate (get it?), a huge platter plus soup and rice ($7.60). Open late, this place draws a lot of red-eyed night owls.

Yakitori East *(☎ 213-437-0563, 329 E 1st St)* Mains $4.50-16. Nearby, this youthful eatery, engagingly furnished with rough wooden tables and Japanese glamour movie posters, is a good choice for those wanting to sample a variety of foods. Sushi, yakitori (small kebabs), noodle soups, tempura and teriyaki chicken are all prepared reliably. The combination platters are the best value.

Mid-Range

Traxx (☎ 213-625-1999, 800 N Alameda St) Lunch $10-18 Mon-Fri, dinner $15-27 Mon-Sat. Train station dining is usually as exciting as a picnic next to a sewage pipe, but this classy candidate inside historic Union Station is a major exception. Repeat customers, including downtown suits, politicians and accidental travelers, go for the patio tables, then peruse the menu for chef Tara Thomas' latest Cal-Asian creations. If you want to stick with dependable classics, order the ahi tuna napoleon or the endive salad.

Original Pantry Cafe (☎ 213-972-9279, 877 S Figueroa St) Mains $8-14; open 24 hours. This cafe has occupied its corner spot for about 75 years and is owned by former LA mayor Richard Riordan. The city's movers and shakers rub shoulders here with out-of-work actors, welfare recipients, construction workers and people like you. Leave your calorie counter at home, grab a seat at the Formica counter and dig into omelets, steaks and fries, pork chops and other artery-clogging fare. Its famous sourdough bread, though, is preservative-free.

Frying Fish Sushi (☎ 213-680-0567, 120 Japanese Village Plaza) Sushi rolls $1.50-2.50. Little Tokyo is the obvious place for fresh sushi and this spot has some of the best prices. Sushi servings, sitting on plates colored to correspond with the price, buzz by you on a conveyor belt installed in the oval bar; you just pick up the ones you want. Your final tab is calculated by adding up the plates. The Tres Amigos roll (tuna, yellowtail and salmon) is among the best anywhere.

Shabu Shabu House (☎ 213-680-3890, 127 Japanese Village Plaza) Lunch $8-9.60, dinner $11-13.60; closed Mon. *Shabu-shabu* is a Japanese-style fondue, which involves briefly dipping wafer-thin slices of beef and vegetables into a simmering broth. In the

Dining Around the Clock

Hunger can strike travelers at any time, especially when jet lag sets in. The following places are among those that serve food 24/7. (For reviews, see individual entries under the respective sections.)

Canter's Deli (Fairfax District)
Fred 62 (Los Feliz & Silver Lake)
Jerry's Famous Deli (Beverly Center District)
The Kettle (South Bay)
Original Pantry Cafe (Downtown)
Van Go's Ear (Venice & Marina del Rey)

end, the remaining broth, now thick with flavor, is spooned up. This place is one of the best to engage in this culinary ritual. Lines are guaranteed, but the wait's worth it.

Hama Sushi (☎ 213-680-3453, 355 E 2nd St) Sushi combinations $12-15. Sublime sushi and sashimi is all that's ever served at this pocket-sized bar, which draws connoisseurs from around town.

Top End

Ciudad (☎ 213-486-5171, 445 S Figueroa St) Lunch $9-18.50 Mon-Fri, dinner $15-26 nightly. The latest Feniger/Milliken entry (also see Border Grill in Santa Monica later in this chapter) regales diners with a pioneering pan-Latino menu. The spirited decor matches such sizzling creations as the Peruvian ceviche appetizer or the Brazilian *moqueca* (seafood in coconut-lime broth). Even the desserts are worth the hip-expanding indulgence.

Cicada (☎ 213-488-9488, 617 S Olive St) Lunch $15-24 Mon-Fri, dinner $22-30 Mon-Sat. A gilded ceiling with the loftiness of a cathedral, shiny black leather booths and fresh flower bouquets are the hallmarks of this theatrical restaurant popular with the power crowd. It is housed in the Art Deco Oviatt Building, a former men's clothing store, and has received kudos for its contemporary Italian fare. A sweeping double staircase leads to the classy bar and a marble dance floor.

PLACES TO EAT

Café Pinot (☎ 213-239-6500, 700 W 5th St) Lunch $14-18 Mon-Fri, dinner $15-25 Mon-Sat. For some of LA's most pleasant outdoor dining head to this place, set in the quirky Maguire Gardens at the Central Library. Part of the restaurant empire of German master chef Joachim Splichal and his wife, Christine, Pinot specializes in sophisticated Cal-French cuisine. The menu is seasonal, although the rotisserie chicken is a perennial favorite, and the desserts are decadence on a plate. Free shuttle service to the Music Center makes this a popular pre-theater supper spot (make reservations several days ahead).

Water Grill (☎ 213-891-0900, 544 S Grand Ave) Lunch $22-30 Mon-Fri, dinner $25-38 nightly. This place screams either 'special occasion' or 'expense account,' but the dock-fresh and impeccably prepared seafood and fish are actually worth the steep tab. Start with a sampling from the oyster bar before moving on to such piscatorial delights as ahi tuna tartare or garlic shrimp teamed up with seasonal vegetables. Try to leave room for the signature chocolate bread pudding.

CHINATOWN (MAP 5)

Sinophiles will want to make the trip to Chinatown for some authentic chow. Restaurants here come essentially in two types: the formal banquet hall where the seafood is so fresh it often comes straight from the tank; and the casual cafeteria where they serve huge platters of chow mein, Mongolian beef, lemon chicken and other quickly prepared meals at rock-bottom prices (usually around $5-7). Several of the banquet halls are also dim sum parlors. Literally meaning 'touching your heart a little at a time' in Cantonese, dim sum involves selecting bite-sized portions of various dishes from carts maneuvered around the dining room by an army

of servers. Places always brim with chatty Chinese Americans, and English is definitely the second language here. Most dim sum items are priced between $2-4 each and served between 9am-3pm.

Ocean Seafood (☎ 213-687-3088, 757 N Hill St) Lunch $15-35, dinner $25-35. This is a large Hong Kong–style place and a dim sum favorite.

Empress Pavilion (☎ 213-617-9898, 3rd floor, Bamboo Plaza, 988 N Hill St) Lunch $10-12, dinner $20-25. This place is even bigger but the quality is at least as good as Ocean Seafood.

Golden Dragon (☎ 213-626-2039, 960 N Broadway) Mains $5-22. Owned by Pedro Chan – Chinese doctor, entrepreneur and magician – this place also does dim sum, but is more renowned for its seafood dishes and smoky chow fun (rice noodles).

Cheap chow houses abound, but these are among the best: *Full House (☎ 213-617-8382, 963 N Hill St)*; *Hong Kong Harbor (☎ 213-617-2983, 845 N Broadway)*; *Sam Woo (☎ 213-680-7836, 727 N Broadway)* and *Hop Woo (☎ 213-617-3038, 855 N Broadway)*.

KOREATOWN (MAP 7)

Koreatown Plaza International Food Court (☎ 213-382-5959, 928 S Western Ave) Mains $6 or less. 'Pan-Asian' – rather than 'international' – more aptly describes the fare served by the half dozen eateries in the basement of the snazzy Koreatown Plaza (which people have dubbed Koreatown's Beverly Center). Try Vietnamese *pho* (noodle soup), Japanese tempura or Korean kimchi.

Guelaguetza (☎ 213-427-0601, 3337½ W 8th St) Mains $2-10. For an immersion in the mysterious flavors of Oaxacan cuisine (Oaxaca is a state in southern Mexico), come to this super-casual eatery where saffron-colored walls provide a lively backdrop for delicious home-cooking. Many dishes revolve around mole, a rich sauce of Aztec origin that contains dozens of 'secret' ingredients, including spices, seeds, nuts and chocolate. The sauce is also sold in the little store out front. Come for breakfast or lunch as the area gets quite seedy after dark.

Papa Cristo's Taverna (☎ 323-737-2970, 2771 W Pico Blvd) Mains $5-8. Cap off a visit to the fabulous St Sophia Cathedral with lunch at this lively Greek eatery. Pita bread, tangy *tsatsiki*, potatoes and salad share the plates with such meaty favorites as lamb chops, souvlaki (marinated lamb) or *kefta* kebabs (spicy meat patties). It's part of the C&K Importing deli market, which sells canned and fresh Greek products.

El Cholo (☎ 323-734-2773, 1121 S Western Ave) Mains $8-12. A festive atmosphere and tasty food has been the recipe for success at this 1923 original, one of LA's favorite Mexican restaurants. Come in a group and kick things off with a Fiesta Platter ($16, serves 4), a smorgasbord of taquitos, nachos, chimichangas and other lip-smacking delicacies. From May through October, Grandma Rosa's famous green corn tamales are the big hit. It all washes down well with a frosty margarita.

Buffet Land (☎ 213-380-9292, 1925 W Olympic Blvd) Lunch $11, dinner $17; $1 extra on Fri & Sat. The quality is only so-so but for variety this all-you-can-eat buffet is unbeatable. This is a good introduction to Korean cuisine.

Soot Bull Jeep (☎ 213-387-3865, 3136 W 8th St) Mains $13-15. This funky and friendly establishment is one of the best places for Korean barbecue. Eating here is drama at its finest. Order a plate of marinated meat – ribs, pork or beef – then grill it to perfection over hardwood coals right in the center of your table. Dress casually: thick smoke and flying sparks are guaranteed.

LOS FELIZ & SILVER LAKE (MAP 9)
Budget

Fred 62 (☎ 323-667-0062, 1850 Vermont Ave) Mains $2.62-13.62; open 24 hours. This updated '50s-style diner in the heart of Los Feliz Village has a jazzy lime-green facade and a host of cool customers. Huge plates of polyethnic sandwiches, salads, noodles and more are dished out daily around the clock to hungry hipsters on small budgets. All prices end in '62.'

Palermo (☎ 323-663-1178, 1858 Vermont Ave) Lunch $7-12, dinner $8.50-13; closed Tues. Crowds are huge at this boisterous neighborhood Italian joint. The family-run operation is as welcoming and comfortable as a hug from an old friend. Pizzas are generously topped and buried beneath a pound of cheese, and the small antipasto salad is enough – as an appetizer – for four. A veritable cross-section of LA hunkers down at booths and tables – cops to rockers, families to gay couples, people of all ages, classes and colors. Service is fast and super-friendly. There's usually a wait, which isn't all that bad since you'll get an (almost free) glass of wine; it used to be complimentary, but free alcohol was apparently not in compliance with local laws.

El Siete Mares (no ☎, 3145 Sunset Blvd) Mains $5 or less. Casual taco stands abound in LA, but this one is famous for its consistently excellent – and huge – fish tacos, burritos and ceviche tostadas. There's free parking behind the stand and a full restaurant (☎ 323-665-0865, 3151 Sunset Blvd) next door.

ChaChaCha (☎ 323-664-7723, 656 N Virgil Ave) Lunch $8-13, dinner $11-18. This brightly pigmented eatery serves Caribbean cuisine, as well as various pizzas and pastas, in a lively ambience.

El Chavo (☎ 323-664-0871, 4441 Sunset Blvd) Mains $6-10.50, $8.50 per person minimum; cash only. This windowless Mexican classic is more of a visual than a culinary experience. Kaleidoscopic Christmas lights, saddles and other vaquero gear beneath a ceiling festooned with fluorescent sombreros give this place superior camp value. The owners claim that Dolly Parton stops by on occasion; look for her photograph near the bar.

Yuca's (☎ 323-662-1214, 2052 Hillhurst Ave) Mains $3-6. Fresh ingredients, clever spicing and rock-bottom prices are what keep business constant at this little hut with a few parking lot tables. Burritos, tacos and tortas – bulging with such Yucatan-style fillings as *machaca* (shredded meat) and *cochinita pibil* (pit-roasted pork) – fly nonstop through the service window.

Mid-Range

Sunset Blvd provides myriad dining options in this price category.

El Conquistador (☎ 323-666-5136, 3701 Sunset Blvd) Mains $9-13.50. The food's traditional but it's the friendly people, a festive indoor garden with twinkling lights and a bar straight out of a fishing village that set this Mexican mainstay apart.

Cobalt Cantina (☎ 323-953-9991, 4326 Sunset Blvd) A lively Cal-Mex eatery with a popular gay bar attached to it. For a full review, see West Hollywood.

Cafe Stella (☎ 323-666-0265, 3932 Sunset Blvd) Mains $14-24. For a slice of France, head to this snug bistro tucked away in a secluded courtyard at Sunset Junction (look for the red star). The small and select menu, written on a blackboard, features such traditional favorites as steak au poivre; all mains come with two side dishes.

Red Lion Tavern (☎ 323-662-5337, 2366 Glendale Blvd; Map 5) Mains $6-17. For a completely different experience, head to this tavern, serving the best of German country cooking in a venerable haunt cluttered with Germaniana. Beer steins, black-and-white glossies of old-time German movie stars and a jukebox stocked with cheesy German songs from the '50s are part of the decor. The dirndl-dressed waitresses serve up plates of beef roulade, schnitzel, a variety of sausages and other hearty fare. The beer garden buzzes year-round (see also Pubs & Microbreweries in the Entertainment chapter).

Top End

Vermont (☎ 323-661-6163, 1714 Vermont Ave) Lunch $9-16 Tues-Fri, dinner $12-26 Tues-Sun. Medieval-style vaulted ceilings meet concrete floors at this elegant restaurant. The menu's mostly Mediterranean, impeccably prepared with top-quality, fresh ingredients and usually featuring at least a couple of meatless mains.

Vida (☎ 323-660-4446, 1930 Hillhurst Ave) Mains $15-28; dinner only. Chef Fred Eric often pushes the boundaries of California cuisine at this chi-chi establishment. If you appreciate eccentric presentation and

like to surprise your taste buds with unusual flavor combinations, you'll find plenty to like. The smoked porterhouse steak for two ($38) – a 22oz wonker – is a specialty.

CENTRAL HOLLYWOOD (MAP 9)
Budget

Hamburger Hamlet (☎ 323-467-6106, 6914 Hollywood Blvd) Mains $5-13. Across from Mann's Chinese Theater, this predictable tourist place is perfect for grabbing a quick, casual burger, sandwich, salad or pasta. If you like it, check the Yellow Pages for other locations.

The Green Room (☎ 323-860-0775, 6752 Hollywood Blvd) Mains $4-7. This little cafe with an outdoor patio gives you an excellent vantage point for watching the endless parade of freaks and tourists milling down the Hollywood strip. Breakfast is served till 4pm daily and there are also decent salads and sandwiches.

Old Spaghetti Factory (☎ 323-469-7149, 5939 Sunset Blvd) Mains $6-9; lunch Sun-Fri, dinner nightly. The Hollywood branch of this small chain follows the familiar formula: a gloriously over-the-top setting, friendly service and heaps of filling, unbelievably cheap and actually quite good pasta. You can sit inside a Big Red streetcar, in roomy leather booths or in 'Seuss-ian' armchairs. All orders come with salad, fresh bread, coffee or tea and dessert.

Sanamluang (☎ 323-660-8006, 5176 Hollywood Blvd) Mains $4-6. Tucked into a nondescript mini-mall, this is considered one of LA's best Thai restaurants. The menu is as long and complex as an algebra equation, so let's make it simple: order a noodle dish, especially the delectable *pad thai* or *pad kee mow*.

Zankou Chicken (☎ 323-665-7842, 5065 Sunset Blvd) Mains $2.40-7.50. The decor at this little fast-food eatery may be conventional but the food is not. Even virgins of Armenian cuisine are likely to become instant fans when trying the lip-smacking rotisserie chicken, especially after slathering on the garlic sauce. Half a bird costs just $6 and comes with creamy hummus, salad and pita bread.

Birds (☎ 323-465-0175, 5925 Franklin Ave) Mains $6-12. This coffee shop on a hip two-block stretch of Franklin is famous for its marinated chicken, which is rotisseried for that light and crispy tan. It is served in the company of tasty dipping sauces, bread and a side dish. Sandwiches, salads, burgers and more are available as well.

La Poubelle (☎ 323-465-0807, 5907 Franklin Ave) Mains $8-22; dinner only. Have you ever noticed how yucky words always sound so much nicer in French. How would you like to eat at a place called 'Garbage Pail'? But how about 'La Poubelle'? The food here is simple but considerably better than the name suggests. The decor, though, does look thrown together from the reject bin, but perhaps that's just part of the charm.

Mid-Range

Miceli's (☎ 323-466-3438, 1646 N Las Palmas Ave) Lunch $7-12 Mon-Fri, dinner $9-17 nightly. Hollywood's oldest Italian restaurant (1949) is an atmospheric affair with live jazz nightly. You sit in oak booths carved as elaborately as choir stalls, while hundreds of empty Chianti bottles dangle from the beamed ceiling. The menu consists of toothsome pizzas and hearty Italian pastas, and the house wine is a steal at $12 a bottle.

El Floridita (☎ 323-871-0936, 1253 N Vine St) Mains $10-13. Cubans aren't the only ones who give this place, wedged into a mini-mall, an enthusiastic thumbs up for its authentic food, energetic atmosphere and live entertainment. Perennial favorites include the Cuban roast pork sandwiches and a dish called *ropa vieja* (literally, 'old clothing'), which consists of shredded beef simmered in Creole sauce. Reservations are advised (also see the Entertainment chapter).

Top End

Les Deux Cafés (☎ 323-465-0509, 1638 N Las Palmas Ave) Mains $18-32; lunch Mon-Fri, dinner nightly. One of LA's hottest French restaurants draws a cool crowd heavy on brass, beauty and power and greeted with air kisses by owner Michele

Great Celebrity Spotting

Given LA's fickle restaurant scene, what's hot with celebs today may have plunged out of favor tomorrow. The places listed below are among those that have demonstrated staying power. (For reviews, see individual entries under the respective sections.)

Caffè Luna (Melrose/La Brea)
Chaya Brasserie (Beverly Center District)
Chinois on Main (Santa Monica)
Dan Tana's (West Hollywood)
Geoffrey's (Malibu)
Hugo's (West Hollywood)
KoKoMo (Fairfax District)
Les Deux Cafés (Central Hollywood)
Locanda Veneta (Beverly Center District)
Matsuhisa (Beverly Hills)
Neptune's Net (Malibu)
Newsroom Café (Beverly Center District)
Ocean Avenue Seafood (Santa Monica)
Orso (Beverly Center District)
Pink's Hot Dogs (Melrose/La Brea)
Real Food Daily (Santa Monica)
Spago Beverly Hills (Beverly Hills)

PLACES TO EAT

Lamy. Preferred seating is on the secluded patio around a log-shaped reflecting pool, although the cozy cottage with its dark-wood furniture, fireplace and comfy banquettes is nice too. The bar, reached through a concrete tunnel, is open some nights and has live jazz occasionally. Enter the restaurant via Grants parking lot.

Musso & Frank Grill (☎ 323-467-7788, 6667 Hollywood Blvd) Mains $20-35; open 11am-11pm Tues-Sat. This hallowed Hollywood haunt, in business since 1919, was a hit with the heroines and swashbucklers of the silent film era. Later, its vinyl booths and dark dining room hosted literati from Raymond Chandler to Ernest Hemingway plus a catalog of celebs. The timeless spot still pulls in Industry heavyweights digging into a menu that includes a politically incorrect milk-fed veal cutlet and stick-to-the-ribs steak with gravy. Service is smooth, and so are the martinis.

Dar Maghreb (☎ 323-876-7651, 7651 Sunset Blvd) 7-course dinner $36; open 6pm-11pm nightly. Journey from Tinseltown to Tangier by simply stepping through giant shiny bronze portals into a replica Moroccan palace. You'll dine here pasha-style while reclining on fluffy cushions orbiting a low wooden table. As you dig into a seven-course mouthwatering feast – served family style and eaten without utensils – you may find your neck tickled by the tassel of a beautiful belly dancer.

Yamashiro (☎ 323-466-5125, 1999 N Sycamore Ave) Mains $18-35; dinner only; closed Mon. Seductively perched on a southerly slope of the Hollywood Hills, this landmark restaurant overlooks the sea of glitter that is the city at night. A replica of a Japanese palace, its name suitably translates as 'castle in the hill'; movies filmed here include *Sayonara* with Marlon Brando. Do what you must to score a window table, then sit back to savor the sushi and the view with petite, kimono-clad Japanese waitresses at your beck and call. The cash-strapped can come just for a drink in the adjacent lounge.

Patina (☎ 323-467-1108, 5955 Melrose Ave) Mains $20-30; set dinner $70-80; lunch Fri, dinner nightly. Serious food zealots with deep pockets shouldn't leave LA without worshipping here, the flagship restaurant of Joachim and Christine Splichal. Joachim has dug deep into his seemingly bottomless culinary purse to create a menu that miraculously fuses Californian tastes and European touches. The restaurant recently underwent an intense renovation that added 19-foot ceilings, blue French limestone floors and a new patio.

MELROSE/LA BREA (MAP 10)
Budget
Pink's Hot Dogs (☎ 323-931-4223, 709 N La Brea Ave) Hot dogs $2.35-3.65; open 9:30am-2am Mon-Fri, till 3am Sat-Sun. Regulars and out-of-towners make pilgrimages to this landmark 'doggeria,' which has been serving delicious all-beef dogs buried beneath aromatic chili and onions since 1939. Pink's enjoys cult status among night owls, and even famished celebs such as Kim

Basinger and Demi Moore have been seen downing a dog here.

Santé La Brea (☎ 323-857-0412, 345 N La Brea Ave) Mains $5-10; open 8am-11pm daily. Good food that's not bad for your waistline, heart or mental balance is the specialty of this small cafe. The kitchen prepares vegan versions of burritos, lasagna, risotto, chow mein and pizza that are best consumed in the leafy outdoor patio. The eggplant lasagna is outstanding. Breakfast is served as well.

East India Grill (☎ 323-936-8844, 345 N La Brea Ave) Mains $7-15; lunch specials $4.50-9. This critically acclaimed cafe, next door, treats you to a range of fragrant curries and tasty tandoori dishes, though it's easy to build a full meal around its delectable appetizers and breads.

Lala's (☎ 323-934-6838, 7229 Melrose Ave) Mains $7-13. On perennially hip Melrose Ave, this Argentine grill has a meat-heavy menu but light-hearted decor. Come for lunch, grab a table on the sidewalk patio and watch the stream of humanity flowing down Melrose.

Mid-Range
Caffè Luna (☎ 323-655-8647, 7463 Melrose Ave) Mains $9-13; open 10am-midnight Sun-Thur, to 3am Fri & Sat. Solid if standard country Italian fare (pizza, pasta, salads) can be found on the menu at this popular late-night haunt and occasional celebrity hangout. On a balmy night, the secluded, flower-festooned courtyard is a good place to bring a date, although the frenzied dining room is pretty nice too. Breakfast is served any time, and there's no corkage fee for the first two bottles of wine.

Bouchon (☎ 323-852-9400, 7661 Melrose Ave) Mains $9-14; lunch Tues-Sat, dinner Tues-Sun, brunch Sun. Walls the hue of Dijon mustard, booths the color of burgundy, a bar the shade of chocolate – the mere palette of this popular bistro is a feast for the eyes. It becomes a feast for the taste buds as soon as you dig into such French country favorites as beef bourguignon, coq au vin or steak au poivre. The crusty bread is perfect for sopping up the onion soup.

Tommy Tang's (☎ *323-937-5733, 7313 Melrose Ave)* Mains $8-17. A dependable Melrose favorite since 1982, Tommy Tang's serves updated versions of Thai classics and also has a decent sushi bar. Favorites include the Original Tommy Duck, though noodle and rice dishes are tasty as well. Sit on the outdoor deck, in the cafe-style front room or in the more formal back dining room with its booths and benches.

Frankie's (☎ *323-937-2801, 7228 Melrose Ave)* Mains $11-22; closed Sunday. For a taste of Little Italy, ex-New Yorkers gravitate to this airy, uncluttered supper club complete with a shiny baby grand and Old Blue Eyes' tunes. Manhattan seafood chowder and osso buco are both good. At night, the place is chock-full with behind-the-scenes Industry types, most of them greeted personally by Frankie himself. Scorcese and DeNiro would dig this place.

Ca' Brea (☎ *323-938-2863, 346 S La Brea Ave)* Mains $10-20; lunch Mon-Fri, dinner Mon-Sat. This sister property to Locanda Veneta (see Beverly Center District) offers superb Northern Italian selections in a homey, sectioned dining room enlivened by colorful canvasses.

Top End

Citrus (☎ *323-857-0034, 6703 Melrose Ave)* Mains $17-33; 4/5-course prix fixe dinner $55/65; lunch Mon-Fri, dinner nightly. One of LA's gastronomic jewels, master chef Michel Richard's artsy emporium keeps rolling in rave reviews for its imaginative Cal-French cuisine. Crab cakes and ahi tuna carpaccio are perennial bestsellers, as is the tuna burger. The Industry-heavy crowd means that mere mortals are often relegated to lesser tables.

Sonora Cafe (☎ *323-857-1800, 180 S La Brea Ave)* Mains $18-28; lunch Mon-Fri, dinner nightly. The fad for Southwestern food may be passé, but you wouldn't know it when trying to get a reservation at this place. Price tags are hefty, but the chef's use of meats, seafood and vegetables, plus ingenious preparation, justifies the cost. The tangy salsas are great, as are the wild mushroom enchiladas and barbecue pork chops.

Campanile (☎ *323-938-1447, 624 S La Brea Ave)* Lunch $12-18 Mon-Fri, dinner $24-38 Mon-Sat, brunch Sat-Sun. Down the street, this place has defined 'urban rustic' cooking. Chef Mark Peel comes up with new culinary creations daily, but staples include excellent grilled meats and fish with a few dollops of inspiration from the sun-drenched Riviera of France and Italy. This is also the home of the La Brea Bakery (its excellent rustic breads are sold all over town), where Nancy Silverton reigns as the queen of the dessert.

WEST HOLLYWOOD (MAP 10)
Budget

French Quarter Market (☎ *323-654-0898, 7985 Santa Monica Blvd)* Mains $5-13. This popular gay hangout is also a long-time favorite for casual California cuisine. Mountains of fresh, delicious salads are the house specialty. Unless you're starving, splitting an appetizer and a salad between two will probably do nicely (just inform your waiter; splits are no problem). This place is abuzz at all times, but Sunday brunch is especially chatty. Sit either on the outdoor patio facing the noisy boulevard or in the New Orleans–inspired interior. The surrounding shops are eccentric, to say the least.

The Abbey (☎ *310-289-8410, 692 N Robertson Blvd)* Mains $7-10; open 7am-3am daily; breakfast to 2pm. This popular place in the heart of Weho draws a mixed crowd of body- and budget-conscious patrons. The kitchen delivers inspired variations of such classics as chicken Dijon and grilled salmon, best enjoyed on the pretty patio dappled with terracotta statuettes and anchored by an outdoor bar. The desserts are heavenly, but service can be on the slow side. At night, it's one of the strip's hottest bars (see the Entertainment chapter – Gay & Lesbian Venues).

Hugo's (☎ *323-654-3993, 8401 Santa Monica Blvd)* Mains $8-10. This no-nonsense cafe may not look 'Hollywood' but it does attract a host of Industry insiders and wanna-bes, especially for breakfast. Much of the menu has a wholesome bent, including the Tantric veggie burgers, turkey

PLACES TO EAT

Romantic Dining Spots

Leisurely, romantic dinners are integral and memorable parts of any journey. Whether you like secluded patios, flower-festooned courtyards, candlelight, quiet piano music or stunning views over the sparkling city, you'll find all or some of it at the following places. (For reviews, see individual entries under the respective sections.)

Bel Air Restaurant (Westwood)
Bistro Garden at Coldwater (Ventura Blvd)
Ca' del Sole (North Hollywood)
Campanile (Melrose/La Brea Area)
Cicada (Downtown)
Geoffrey's (Malibu)
I Cugini (Santa Monica)
Inn of the Seventh Ray (Malibu)
Le Colonial (Beverly Center District)
Les Deux Cafés (Central Hollywood)
L'Orangerie (West Hollywood)
Orso (Beverly Center District)
Patina (Central Hollywood)
Sofi (Fairfax District)
Yamashiro (Central Hollywood)

meatloaf and grilled tuna filet sandwiches. Breakfast selections are great and paired with potatoes, turmeric rice or fresh fruit.

Basix (☎ 323-848-2460, 8333 Santa Monica Blvd) Mains $8-16. This place has an 'Ellis Island' salad menu (Italian, Greek, Chinese) and respectable thin-crust pizzas grilled over fruitwood.

Mid-Range

Cobalt Cantina (☎ 310-659-8691, 616 N Robertson Blvd) Tapas $3-9, mains $11-18. A party atmosphere reigns at this cheerful restaurant-bar with a large patio. A mixed (straight and gay) clientele indulges in such flavor bombs as Cajun chicken spring rolls or the hurricane shrimp; interesting Cal-Mex sandwiches and chicken dishes are among the main courses. On some days (usually Sun-Tues), specials like two-for-one mains or two-for-one tapas keep the place hopping.

House of Blues (☎ 323-848-5123, 8430 Sunset Blvd) Mains $8-23, Sunday brunch $32/16 adults/children. Most people come for the music, but this is also a restaurant serving so-so Deep South food, such as gumbo, crawfish risotto and baby back ribs. On Sunday, an all-you-can-eat brunch is accompanied by some mighty fine gospel singing; seatings are at 9:30am, noon and 2:30pm and reservations are obligatory.

Top End

Dan Tana's (☎ 310-275-9444, 9071 Santa Monica Blvd) Mains $16-41; dinner nightly. In this day and age of chic bistros, this nononsense chophouse is something of an anachronism. Steaks and dependably strong drinks are among the prime assets cherished by the loyal clientele, including a sizeable number of celebs in search of much needed privacy.

L'Orangerie (☎ 310-652-9770, 903 N La Cienega Blvd) Mains from $30, set dinners $90-95; dinner Tues-Sun. This formal French restaurant has decor that some might consider over the top, but it's incredibly romantic if you like Louis XIV–inspired pomp. The best French restaurant in LA by many critics' standards, it's an excellent place for those who truly know what good food, wine and service are about – and are able to pay for it.

Yujean Kang (☎ 310-288-0806, 8826 Melrose Ave) This elegant restaurant offers anything but your typical run-of-the-mill Chinese. For the full review, see Pasadena, later in this chapter.

BEVERLY CENTER DISTRICT (MAP 10)
Budget

Hard Rock Cafe (☎ 310-276-7605, ground floor, northwest corner, Beverly Center mall) Mains $7-17. John Lennon's handwritten lyrics to *Help*, Buddy Holly's high school yearbook and Madonna's slinky silver dress are among the memorabilia on view at the original LA branch of this ubiquitous chain dubbed the 'Smithsonian of Rock 'n' Roll' by Andy Warhol. The food is predictable but good and comes in huge portions.

Tail O' the Pup (☎ 310-652-4517, 329 N San Vicente Blvd) Mains $2.30-4.25. Eddie Blake's hot-dog-shaped stand is one of the few remaining pieces of mimetic architecture in LA. In business since 1938, it was once a favorite of Orson Welles, and its dogs and burgers continue to attract a loyal following. (We'll be discreet and simply tell you that the enormous protruding hot dog and soft buns of this shack are...suggestive. Ahem.)

Kings Road Cafe (☎ 323-655-9044, 8361 Beverly Blvd) Mains $5-11. Tables here are usually bustling with a young crowd, thanks to delicious bistro fare at budget prices. Penny-pinchers could make a meal of just a soup or salad and the crusty, fresh-baked country bread served with it. But they'd miss out on the generously stuffed gourmet panini or tasty pastas. The breakfast menu is extensive too. Seating is inside or at sidewalk tables, and there's an international newsstand next door.

Newsroom (☎ 310-652-4444, 120 N Robertson Blvd) Mains $5-12.50. Health gurus will be in heaven at this breezy, spacious cafe with large mirrors and a bamboo-fringed patio. Chef/owner Eddie J Caraeff uses only organic grains and produce and exiles as much dairy, fat and sodium as possible. Everything sounds tasty, but the veggie burger and 'fun-filled' ravioli are tops. News junkies can pick up the latest tidbits from ticker-tape displays or peruse a magazine at the in-house newsstand. Breakfast is served all day. A second, smaller branch is in Santa Monica.

Jerry's Famous Deli (☎ 310-289-1811, 8701 Beverly Blvd) Mains $4.50-13; open 24 hours. This popular deli has a menu as long and confusing as a Dostoyevsky novel. Offerings such as Mexican burritos and pizza may deviate from the usual deli format, but Jerry's returns to its roots with New York-style pastrami sandwiches and chicken soup with matzo balls. Breakfast is served anytime. For locations of the seven other branches, check the Yellow Pages.

Menjin (☎ 323-782-0039, 8393 Beverly Blvd) Mains $3.50-8.50. This unassuming mini-mall restaurant serves an international culinary medley revolving around the lowly noodle, which are bathed in fragrant broths, stir-fried with meat, seafood or vegetables or served cold as a salad. Dining takes place in a clean, little-adorned space with an open kitchen.

Real Food Daily (☎ 310-289-9910, 414 N La Cienega Blvd) Great vegan food in a friendly spot with clean-cut decor and unpretentious artwork. For the full review, see Santa Monica, later in this chapter.

Mid-Range

Cava (☎ 323-658-8898, 8384 W 3rd St) Tapas $5-10, mains $10-26, Sun champagne brunch $20; breakfast, lunch and dinner daily. This happening spot at the Beverly Plaza Hotel (see Places to Stay) sizzles with Spanish/Latin decor, live flamenco dancing (Wed nights) and the table-side sorcery of master chef Octavio who sears and flambees filet mignon and scallops right before your eyes (Wed-Sat dinner). For tapas, you can't go wrong with the superb ceviche served in a half coconut shell. (See also the boxed text 'LA's Best Happy Hours' in the Entertainment chapter.)

Barefoot Café (☎ 310-276-6223, 8722 W 3rd St) Mains $9-20. The reliable Italian trio of pizza, pasta and salads gets the California treatment at this fresh spot in a pretty, ivy-covered building across from Cedars-Sinai Hospital. Choose from a table in the carpeted dining room, the bistro-style bar area or the leafy sidewalk terrace. It also has a popular happy hour (see boxed text 'LA's Best Happy Hours' in the Entertainment chapter).

Locanda Veneta (☎ 310-274-1893, 8638 W 3rd St) Mains $10-26; lunch Mon-Fri, dinner Mon-Sat. The thick aroma of garlic welcomes diners to this classy and timeless eatery whose Northern Italian menu puts substance before culinary pyrotechnics. It is popular with Hollywood bigwigs digging into linguine with baby lobster and clams while talking deals and dollars.

Orso (☎ 310-274-7144, 8706 W 3rd St) Mains $10-25. This nearby restaurant hides its entrance behind a discreet 6-foot wall. You might glimpse the occasional celebrity, as well as Industry wheelers and dealers, munching on crunchy thin-crust pizza or imaginative pasta dishes. Make reservations for a table on the patio – an oh-so-romantic setting on a warm summer night.

Top End

Le Colonial (☎ 310-289-0660, 8783 Beverly Blvd) Starters $8-12, mains $18-28; lunch Mon-Fri, dinner nightly. With its cool tiled floor, lazy ceiling fans and rattan chairs, this place makes you feel like you've stepped onto the set of *Indochine*. The exotic Vietnamese cuisine has complex flavors and tends toward the spicy. Dishes are served family-style in the pleasant dining room or the patio. The lovely upstairs lounge is a popular hipster hangout that turns elitist on Thursday and Saturday nights when you need a dinner reservation or your name on the guest list in order to gain access.

Pastis (☎ 323-655-8822, 8114 Beverly Blvd) Mains $14-19; lunch Mon-Fri, dinner nightly. For sublime Provençal cooking, head to this intimate dining room. It's the kind of relaxed place where yellow walls bring the sunshine indoors and meals become culinary celebrations that comfortably stretch out for an entire evening. The menu changes frequently but may include bouillabaisse, wild mushroom ravioli or lemon-sautéed frogs' legs.

Chaya Brasserie (☎ 310-859-9833, 8741 Alden Dr) Mains $14-28; lunch Mon-Fri, dinner nightly. The menu here is as tantalizing as the Zen-meets-industrial dining room where special touches include mirrors and Japanese prints. Executive chef Shigefumi Tachibe performs miracles with Cal-French cuisine complimented by Asian inflections. The menu changes often but usually includes the house specialties of grilled Ji-Dori chicken Dijon and roast venison.

Indochine (☎ 323-655-4777, 8225 Beverly Blvd) Mains $6-20; dinner nightly. Owner Jean-Marc Houmard has re-created the lost world of French Indochina with sensual lighting, banana leaf frescos and snug green leather banquettes at this swank restaurant. Patrons are mostly of the hip persuasion and munch on intricately flavored and beautifully presented dishes, such as *amok cambodgien* (striped bass with coconut milk steamed in a banana leaf). Portions are small because the idea is to order two or three items. Be sure to leave room for the coconut crème brûlée.

FAIRFAX DISTRICT (MAP 10)
Budget

The Farmers' Market brims with food choices, including these favorites:

Gumbo Pot (☎ 323-933-0358, 6333 W 3rd St) Mains $4-8. Expect to wait in a long line before sinking a spoon into a bowl of gumbo or your teeth into a po' boy sandwich. All mains come with delicious corn bread and a choice of side dish.

KoKoMo (☎ 323-933-0773, 6333 W 3rd St) Mains $5-8. Belly up to the Formica counter of this hip Art Deco eatery whose big breakfasts provide enough carbs to sustain you through the entire day. It's a popular hangout of Industry types from neighboring CBS, as well as gay couples.

Doughboys (☎ 323-651-4202, 8136 W 3rd St) Mains $6-8. A few blocks west of the market, this little cafe serves terrific breakfast all day. Eclectic menu items include malted cornmeal pancakes with berries, homemade muesli and crispy sourdough and semolina waffles. The menu also features nutritious salads and imaginative sandwiches.

Canter's Deli (☎ 323-651-2030, 419 N Fairfax Ave) Mains $5-14; open 24 hours. The food is average at best, the service is slow and rude, but this vast deli has been packing 'em in since 1948, selling more than 10 million matzo balls and 2 million pounds of lox. The Reuben with pastrami is acceptable, but the soggy potato chips are not. There are also six different soups, including one called mishmosh, which combines the other five into one (yuk!). Canter's Kibitz Room lounge fills up after the clubs close (see Entertainment).

Damiano Mr Pizza (☎ 323-658-7611, 412 N Fairfax Ave) Slices $1.71, full pies $9.25, pasta $4.50; open to 6am Sun-Thur, to 7am Fri-Sat. Opposite Canter's, this low-key night-owl favorite keeps its staff firing up

Great Breakfast Haunts

Enjoying a leisurely breakfast is one of life's great pleasures and only too rarely indulged. What follows are the best breakfast spots that do a bit more than brew hot coffee and scramble a few eggs. (For reviews, see individual entries under the respective sections.)

The Abbey (West Hollywood)
Backburner Cafe (South Bay)
Beach Hut No 2 (South Bay)
Bob's Big Boy (Burbank)
Caffè Luna (Melrose/La Brea)
Doughboys (Fairfax District)
French Quarter Market (West Hollywood)
Good Stuff (South Bay)
Hugo's (West Hollywood)
Jerry's Famous Deli (Beverly Center District)
Kings Road Cafe (Beverly Center District)
KoKoMo (Fairfax District)
Newsroom (Beverly Center District)
Omelette Parlor (Santa Monica)
Rose Cafe (Venice & Marina del Rey)
Sidewalk Cafe (Venice & Marina del Rey)
Uncle Bill's Pancake House (South Bay)

New York–style pies until sunrise and also makes energy-restoring pastas.

Mid-Range

Sofi (☎ *323-651-0346, 8030¾ W 3rd St)* Mains $12-23; lunch Mon-Sat, dinner nightly. The enchantment of a Greek taverna can be reached through a bowling alley of a passageway that spills onto a shaded patio deck canopied by bougainvillea and leafy trees. This romantic hideaway serves all the staples, including rack of lamb and a mean moussaka. Alternatively, it's fun to simply graze on a selection of *meze* (appetizers; $10, two-person minimum) including creamy tsatziki and feta, olives and spanakopita.

Nyala (☎ *323-936-5918, 1076 S Fairfax Ave)* Lunch $5.50-7, dinner $9-11. The stretch of Fairfax between Olympic and Pico Blvds, known as Little Addis Ababa, is full of Ethiopian restaurants of which this one is the best known. In a dining room decked out with African art and artifacts, you'll be noshing on *doro wot* (intricately flavored chicken stew) or *kitfo* (Ethiopian-

style tartar). Instead of utensils, you'll be using *injera*, a spongy crepe that soaks up the sauces and can be folded around meat and vegetables. Wash it all down with African beer or honey wine. The all-vegetarian, all-you-can-eat lunch buffet is just $5.

BEVERLY HILLS (MAP 11)
Budget

Ed Debevic's (☎ *310-659-1952, 134 N La Cienega Blvd)* Mains $10 or less; lunch and dinner daily. Come here for a make-believe flashback to the age of beehives, hula hoops and Elvis. Munch on the signature Blue Moon Burger (with blue cheese sauce) while squeezed into sparkling turquoise Naugahyde booths fitted with table-side miniature jukeboxes. Tourists love this place for the prices and the wisecracking servers ('Good Food – Fresh Service' is the motto here).

Versailles (☎ *310-289-0392, 1415 S La Cienega Blvd)* Cuban-style pork or rotisserie chicken are among the staples at this casual landmark eatery. For the full review, see Culver City, later in this chapter.

Natalee Thai *(☎ 310-855-9380, 998 S Robertson Blvd; Map 10)* Come here, to the far eastern edge of Beverly Hills, for creative Thai food. For the full review, see Culver City, later in this chapter.

Mid-Range

The Farm *(☎ 310-273-5578, 439 N Beverly Dr)* Mains $11-21. If you want to pack 'em in, it doesn't hurt to be the son of Harrison Ford. But the casual crowds at The Farm are also there for Benjamin Ford's creative takes on American favorites, all freshly prepared in an open kitchen. Burgers with caramelized onions and blackened ahi tuna are typical concoctions served either in a warehouse-type dining hall or on the sidewalk patio beneath lemon-colored awnings. This restaurant also does a weekend brunch.

Barney Greengrass *(☎ 310-777-5877, 9570 Wilshire Blvd)* Mains $8-18; open to 7pm most nights. It's worth visiting this stylish deli on the top floor of the glamorous Barneys New York department store just for a terrace table with a view of the hills. As for the food, it helps if you're into fish: whitefish, sturgeon and smoked selections such as pastrami lox are available.

Stinking Rose *(☎ 310-652-7673, 55 N La Cienega Blvd)* Mains $12-30. The whimsical fantasy decor may well be the best thing about this place that makes you feel as if you just stepped into a wizard's lair. The 'rose' in question here is garlic, prepared in infinite varieties. The 40-clove garlic chicken is killer (vampires beware); thank goodness the breath mints are free.

The Taj *(☎ 310-652-3838, 50 N La Cienega Blvd)* Mains $9-18; set dinners $18-25; buffet lunch Mon-Sat, brunch Sun, dinner nightly. This elegant banquet hall serves nouvelle Indian with the best deals being the set dinners of soup, various appetizers and curries, dessert, tea and coffee.

Top End

Spago Beverly Hills *(☎ 310-385-0880, 176 N Cañon Dr)* Mains $17-32; lunch Mon-Sat, dinner nightly. With the original Spago closed, Wolfgang Puck's new flagship restaurant has quickly moved to the speed dial of many Industry folk. The seasonal menu here transcends the traditional fare of pizza and pasta and is best enjoyed on the romantic patio, which is anchored by ancient olive trees. If you can't snag a table there, don't despair: the gorgeous decor, courtesy of Puck's wife Barbara Lazaroff, offers as much eye candy as the often star-studded clientele. Make reservations early or hope for no-shows.

Crustacean *(☎ 310-205-8990, 9646 S Santa Monica Blvd)* Starters $8, mains $18-38; lunch Mon-Fri, dinner Mon-Sat. This tony restaurant is a tribute to owner and executive chef Elizabeth An's Vietnamese roots. The stunning decor, which recreates the slightly wicked French Colonial era of the 1930s, includes an undulating sunken aquarium where plump koi tumble lazily. Seafood reigns supreme here, with top honors going to the whole roasted Dungeness crab and the garlic noodles with tiger prawns, both treated to an aromatic balm of An's 'secret spices.'

Nic's *(☎ 310-550-5707, 453 N Cañon Dr)* Mains $23-28; lunch Tues-Sat, dinner Mon-Sat. Booths, banquettes and big mirrors characterize this hip supper club. Los Angeles restaurateur Larry Nicola has laced his menu of solid California dishes with the occasional Far Eastern touch. Sautéed oysters with spinach and walnuts are a famous appetizer (as the menu will tell you). For cocktails, head to the stylish martini lounge.

Matsuhisa *(☎ 310-659-9639, 129 N La Cienega)* Mains $20, tasting menu $100-120. Master chef Nobu Matsuhisa presides over one of LA's top-ranked restaurants and counts Madonna, Warren Beatty and Harrison Ford among his fans. Trained in Japan, he's as deft with the sushi knife as he is at blending Japanese and Peruvian flavors in creative seafood dishes. The 35-plus page menu may be the culinary equivalent of *War and Peace* – epic, intimidating and heroic. If unsure what to order, simply ask for a recommendation.

WESTWOOD (MAP 11)
Budget
Gypsy Café (☎ 310-824-2119, 940 Broxton Ave) Mains $4-9. Sure, this little Middle Eastern cafe serves the predictable pot-pourri of falafel, kebabs, humus and tabouli (plus, more incongruously, pizza and pasta), but here's the twist: for $10 you can order a hookah (water pipe) and choose from a range of fruit-flavored tobacco. On weekend nights, it's the thing *du jour* for curious UCLA coeds.

Taiko (☎ 310-207-7782, 11677 San Vicente Blvd, Brentwood; Map 13) Mains $7-20. This prim Japanese cafe inside a stylish Brentwood mall is the place to slurp succulently flavored soba and udon soups, either hot or cold, or dig into delectable rice bowls topped with a variety of meats and vegetables. Prepare for a wait: low prices and top quality are an irresistible combo.

Mid-Range & Top End
Cowboy Sushi (☎ 310-208-7781, 911 Broxton Ave) All-you-can-eat sushi $16/19 lunch/dinner; combination plates $5-7. Sushi lovers short on time and money should come to this small upstairs restaurant, which serves all the made-to-order sushi you can wolf down within one hour at one fixed price. A la carte choices include tempura, yakitori and other Japanese food.

Eurochow (☎ 310-209-0066, 1099 Westwood Blvd) Mains $9-20. Upon returning to Italy from his travels in Asia, Marco Polo introduced the noodle to the Boot. Eurochow marries the two cuisines (Italian and Asian) in an effective and only occasionally affected way. The colorful food looks good against the all-white backdrop, and so does the *très chic* clientele. In general, the less imaginative the name of the dish, the better it is: try The Chicken, The Duck or The Pork Chop. Pizza, pasta and fish also make steamy appearances.

Bel Air Restaurant (☎ 310-472-1211, 701 Stone Canyon Rd, Bel Air) Breakfast $25, lunch $45, dinner $85. This restaurant, at the namesake hotel, is one of the most romantic dining spots in town. Just getting there is enough to get you in the mood, sashaying along flower-festooned paths through a lush garden and past a pond where swans preen. Impeccable service, a superb menu and out-of-this-world prices make eating here even more memorable.

CULVER CITY (MAP 12)
Empanada's Place (☎ 310-391-0888, 3811 Sawtelle Blvd) Empanadas $2 each. This shoebox of a place makes super-fresh and creative Argentine empanadas – pockets of filo dough filled with 16 delicious choices, eight of them meatless – that are great for picnics and parties.

Versailles (☎ 310-558-3168, 10319 Venice Blvd) Mains $6-11. Come here for some of the best Cuban food this side of Havana. The lip-smacking roast garlic lemon chicken will make you cluck with delight, although others swear by the succulent roast pork. In either case, the meat is wonderfully juicy and shares the platter with black beans, rice, sweet onions and fried plantains.

Natalee Thai Cuisine (☎ 310-202-7003, 10036 Venice Blvd) Mains $6-10. Sony Studios grips and execs gravitate to this simple but stylish Thai eatery. The kitchen produces all the traditional staples, healthily prepared and wittily introduced on the extensive menu. The chicken *satay* appetizer and the pad thai are recommended.

Café Brasil (☎ 310-837-8957, 10831 Venice Blvd) Mains $5-17, set lunch $6.45. In the heart of Venice Blvd's 'Little Rio,' this tropical eatery serves hot sandwiches, pasta, salads, grilled fish or meats and (on weekends only) *feijoada*, a traditional Brazilian pork stew. The ambience is urban beach shack with mix-and-match furniture fenced off from the boulevard by a curtain of leafy plants.

MALIBU
Neptune's Net (☎ 310-457-3095, 42505 Pacific Coast Hwy, near Ventura County line) Mains $5-20; open 10:30am-7pm Sun-Thur, 9am-10:30pm Fri & Sat. People from all over LA drive to this casual place for superbly fresh seafood at decent prices. Come around sunset, when you can sit at the sturdy wooden tables, look out over the sea,

PLACES TO EAT

peel a pile of shrimp, chow on some corn and wash it all down with a cold beer. Harley Davidson fanatics with receding hairlines, families and Industry yuppies all love this convivial and unpretentious place.

Saddle Peak Lodge (☎ 818-222-3888, 419 Cold Canyon Rd; Map 2) Mains $23-44; dinner Wed-Sun, brunch Sun. As soon as you enter this place, all thoughts of urbanity are immediately banished. Rustic beyond belief, this rural oasis serves up a gamey menu in a setting featuring stuffed and mounted versions of the same. This is possibly the best place in LA to eat pheasant, venison and buffalo, or even quail and ostrich. Reservations are recommended, and casual dress is discouraged.

Geoffrey's (☎ 310-457-1519, 27400 Pacific Coast Hwy) Mains $14-30; open noon-9:30pm Mon-Fri, 11am-10:30pm Sat, to 9:30pm Sun. Listen up: If you want to impress that hot date, take him or her to this sublimely romantic – and celebrity-heavy (featured in *The Player*) – restaurant clinging to an ocean bluff. Deep pockets are de rigueur for a full indulgence in delicious California cuisine, although an appetizer, a glass of champagne, the sunset and ocean waves might just do the trick. Also come for the weekend brunch.

Inn of the Seventh Ray (☎ 310-455-1311, 128 Old Topanga Canyon Rd; Map 2) Lunch $7-15 Mon-Sat, dinner $17-27 nightly, Sun brunch buffet $17-21. An idyllic canyon setting and a karmically correct menu are among the main draws of this New Age establishment. The food's mostly meat-free, suitable for vegans and vegetarians and actually quite tasty. Seating is inside or on a shaded patio.

SANTA MONICA (Map 13)
Budget
Eatz (Santa Monica Place, ground floor) Mains $2-10. This is, hands-down, the best shopping mall food court. Choices cover the four corners of the world, from Chinese stir-fry to Middle Eastern kabobs, Indian curries, French croissants and American coffee. Highlights include the *pizza joint*, on the left as you enter from Broadway, where

hot slices draw a constant crowd; beware of being kneecapped by fellow patrons' shopping bags. A hilarious sideshow develops at *Hot Dog on a Stick* when the lissome girls in tight-fitting, clown-colored hot pants start whipping up their next batch of lemonade.

Wolfgang Puck Express (☎ 310-576-4770, 1315 Third Street Promenade) Mains $7-10. This casual eatery gives gourmets on a budget a chance to sample some of Puck's best-sellers such as the Chinese chicken salad. Sandwiches bulging with grilled or roasted meats and veggies and the wood-fired pizzas are excellent as well. Consume it all on the terrace with a bird's-eye view of the shenanigans unfolding on the promenade below.

Real Food Daily (☎ 310-451-7544, 514 Santa Monica Blvd) Mains $6-12. This casual eatery is one of Los Angeles' best organic vegan restaurants and has a sizeable celebrity following.

Omelette Parlor (☎ 310-399-7892, 2732 Main St) Mains $7 or less; breakfast & lunch only. This place has been whipping up some of the best egg dishes and breakfasts in town since opening during the 'Summer of Love' in 1967. Omelets are industrial-weight, and the beefy sandwiches pack a serious punch. Expect a line on weekend mornings.

Laredo (☎ 310-829-4550, 2909 Pico Blvd) Mains $6.50-14. For the past 20 years, this has been one of Santa Monica's best Mexican restaurants. Service is friendly and swift, and the menu features creative versions of traditional favorites. There's even occasional live music. The carnitas are a house specialty.

Newsroom (☎ 310-319-9100, 530 Wilshire Blvd) A great place for gourmet health food. For a full review, see Beverly Center District, earlier in this chapter.

Mid-Range
I Cugini (☎ 310-451-4595, 1501 Ocean Ave) Mains $11-35. This place has become a bit too popular for its own good, and higher prices for the pasta and seafood dishes have not always translated into higher quality. Dining on the lovely patio with a view of

Santa Monica's famous palm trees, though, is still a memorable experience.

Serenata di Garibaldi (☎ *310-656-7017, 1416 4th St)* Mains $9-22. The indoor Mexican courtyard decor may be a tad cheesy, but the food at this popular place is first rate. Traditional dishes like enchiladas and *gorditas* are given the gourmet treatment here, and there's also a respectable selection of meat and fish platters paired with exotic spices. Prices are high for Mexican food, but so is the quality.

Border Grill (☎ *310-451-1655, 1445 4th St)* Mains $13.50-24.50; lunch Tues-Sun, dinner nightly. The original outpost of Susan Feniger and Mary Sue Milliken (the 'Two Hot Tamales' from their Food Network TV show) looks as if it were designed by a six-year-old – walls are splashed in a rainbow of colors and decorated with naïve drawings – but that's just part of the charm. The kitchen serves a sizzling fiesta of south-of-the-border flavors. Rock shrimp ceviche or *mulitas de hongos* (portabella mushrooms layered with guacamole and other ingredients) are good choices.

Ye Olde King's Head (☎ *310-451-1402, 116 Santa Monica Blvd)* Mains $6.50-13. This is the unofficial HQ of the Westside's huge British expat community, and if you don't mind the fusty odor of 25 years worth of deep-fried fish and chips, you'll feel quite Piccadilly here. Great Brits from Churchill to the Royals to the Beatles look down on the scene from walls cluttered with ever-so-British bric-a-brac and big-game heads. Dinners are served in a series of connecting rooms well away from the dangers of the dartboard. Bangers and mash or steak and kidney pie go quick, but the King's fish and chips are the best in town.

The Galley (☎ *310-452-1934, 2442 Main St)* Mains $15-26. Loyal patrons put down the anchor at this seafood and chop house, which pegs its inception way back to 1934. There's sawdust on the floor and hokey maritime junk throughout (think giant clam fountains). For a special treat, see if you can get current owner Captain Ron to divulge the tale of how a foul-mouthed waitress first welcomed him to the restaurant.

Jake & Annie's (☎ *310-452-1734, 2700 Main St)* Mains $10-19. The Dust Bowl meets the Pacific via Brigadoon at this Irish-American neighborhood favorite. Slide into a deep, comfy booth and order from the creative menu, where the Oklahoma barbecue platter is as at home as the Irish roast chicken. The black linguine with rock shrimp is a personal favorite.

17th Street Cafe (☎ *310-453-2771, 1610 Montana Ave)* Breakfast $6-10, lunch $9-13, dinner $10-20. This is a comfortable eatery and standard meeting place for Brentwood moms, as well as shoppers relaxing after a stroll along this trendy boutique row. Its fresh, wholesome ingredients and low-fat cooking don't compromise on taste. The chicken pasta is great, though the balsamic grilled salmon convinces too. Don't be afraid to make dietary requests; in fact, they encourage it. The cafe also has weekend brunches.

El Cholo (☎ *310-899-1106, 1025 Wilshire Blvd)* This is one of the most popular Mexican restaurants in town. For full review, see the Koreatown section.

Top End

JiRaffe (☎ *310-917-6671, 502 Santa Monica Blvd)* Lunch Tues-Fri $10-12.50, dinner nightly $18-24. Walnut furniture, crystal chandeliers and original art – JiRaffe's setting has 'private mansion' written all over, but there's nothing stuffy about it. The Cal-French food is as elegant as the surroundings and the service is attentive yet discreet.

Ocean Avenue Seafood (☎ *310-394-5669, 1401 Ocean Ave)* Mains $17-25; lunch Mon-Sat, dinner nightly, brunch Sun. For fresh seafood this place is tops. The oyster bar serves some 180,000 portions a year of this slimy royalty, straight from a menu that must have been written by Jacques Cousteau. If you're fishing for celebrities, chances are quite good that you'll catch an 'A-list' member attacking a Maine lobster or slurping clam chowder.

Knoll's Black Forest Inn (☎ *310-395-2212, 2454 Wilshire Blvd)* Mains $15-28; closed Mon. If you think German food is all

Vegetarian Delights

The vegetarian and vegan scene in Los Angeles is quite established and eateries abound for those who have banished meat, eggs and other animal products from their plates. A good Web site with general and LA-specific information is www.vegparadise.com, a monthly Internet magazine. Practically all restaurants mentioned in this chapter offer one or more meat-free dishes, but the following are dedicated to the vegetarian lifestyle. (For reviews, see individual entries under the respective sections.)

The Green Temple (South Bay)
Inn of the Seventh Ray (Malibu)
Leonor's Vegetarian Restaurant
  (North Hollywood)
The Naked Garden (South Bay)
Real Food Daily (Santa Monica & Beverly Center District)
Santé La Brea (Melrose/La Brea)

about sausage and sauerkraut, you're in for a surprise – and a treat – at this elegant family-run establishment, which insiders regard as the best German restaurant in the western US. The châteaubriand and the veal with chanterelle mushrooms are favorites.

Lavande (☎ 310-576-3180, *The Loews, 1700 Ocean Ave*) Lunch $14-18, dinner $21-30. This stylish culinary forum proves that good hotel food is not an oxymoron. The French-flavored fare makes a perfect companion for the Mediterranean setting with its panoramic, ocean-facing windows, colorful ceramics and comfortable wicker chairs. Breakfast is served as well.

Röckenwagner (☎ 310-399-6504, *2435 Main St*) Mains $22-32, brunch $10-15; dinner nightly, brunch weekends. Ensconced in the Frank Gehry–designed Edgemar Complex, this is the fabled namesake restaurant of one of the city's most accomplished chefs. Hans himself will often come out to make recommendations, though regulars swear by the crab meat strudel or the sloe gin-roasted venison.

Chinois on Main (☎ 310-392-9025, *2709 Main St*) Lunch $25 Wed-Fri, dinner $45 nightly. You may spot Tom Cruise (sans Nicole Kidman) or other celebs as they sashay to their limos from this classic Wolfgang Puck outpost. Well sure, the food's expensive, the portions small and the noise barely tolerable, but foodies keep coming back for more of 'Wolfie's' innovative Cal-Asian cooking. Weekend dinner reservations are hard to get, and it's wise to call several days ahead even for lunches and weekday dinners.

Schatzi on Main (☎ 310-399-4800, *3110 Main St*) Breakfast $3.50-13, mains $11-30. By sheer dint of personality, the 'Terminator' himself has willed his eatery into success. The food is solid and international, although the chef shines most when making forays into Schwarzenegger's Austrian roots with such dishes as *Zwiebelröstbraten* and the pancake-based *Kaiserschmarrn* dessert. On Cigar Night, the first Monday of the month, $85 buys a four-course dinner, two prime cigars, a glass of wine and entertainment – plus a pretty good chance of meeting 'Ah-nold' himself.

VENICE & MARINA DEL REY (MAP 13)
Budget

Sidewalk Cafe (☎ 310-399-5547, *1401 Ocean Front Walk*) Mains $8-12. This is the most popular eatery on the Venice Boardwalk, and there's almost always a line. The long menu offers good, old-fashioned American food to a steady stream of locals and tourists alike. Portions are huge and can easily be shared (no split charge). Burgers are dependable, but it's the salads that lure most, especially the Chinese chicken salad (here inexplicably baptized 'the Andy Warhol'). For front-row seats to the stream of freaks lurching along the boardwalk, this is the place to be.

Jody Maroni's Sausage Kingdom (☎ 310-306-1995, *2011 Ocean Front Walk*) Mains $4. The exotically spiced sausages at this place, near the southern end of the boardwalk, are a satisfying fast-food option. The Yucatán (a tantalizing combination of chicken and duck with cilantro, chilies and beer) is a favorite, though any variety is of gourmet quality.

Rose Cafe (☎ 310-399-0711, 220 Rose Ave) Cafe mains $4 or less, restaurant mains $6-16. This Euro-feel place has been a Venice institution since 1979 and is frequented by beefcakes from nearby Gold's Gym, students and artists. Fresh croissants, muffins and other baked goods are available in the cafe section, while the restaurant offers such California classics as roasted vegetable sandwiches or Caesar salads. Both areas have outdoor seating.

Van Go's Ear (☎ 310-396-1987, 796 Main St) Mains $7-10; open 24 hours. This nearby cult cafe is ensconced in a yellow house festooned with a pierced portrait of the painter himself. The food makes stabs at being healthy but is far from gourmet. The place is busiest during weekend wee hours, when a post-clubbing crowd descends on its old-fashioned upholstered chairs orbiting tiled tables. Replenish your energy with a Fruit Fuck, a nutritional cocktail made with psyllium husks, soy protein, wheat grass and lots of fruit juices to make it all palatable.

Tortilla Grill (☎ 310-581-9953, 1357 Abbot Kinney Blvd) Mains $3-8. Healthy Mexican food is not an oxymoron at this buzzing eatery where service can be slow but the food is tasty. Complement your order with fresh salsa from the self-serve bar, then grab a seat on the sidewalk and watch the scene.

Abbot Pizza (☎ 310-396-7334, 1407 Abbot Kinney Blvd) Slices $2.50, whole pies $12.50-16. This little walk-in joint makes addictive bagel-crust pizzas with such gourmet toppings as wild mushrooms, barbecue chicken and olive pesto. Possibly one of the best pie places in town.

Tamara's Tamale (☎ 310-305-7714, Marina Plaza, 13352 Washington Blvd) Mains $2.50-6; closed Mon. This postage-stamp-size joint serves up some of LA's best tamales. The motto here is 'hand-made, home-made, always fresh,' with 30 concoctions to choose from including seafood, fat-free and vegan varieties. Staples such as chicken verde and red pork chili are always

popular alongside such gourmet twists as pumpkin, wild mushroom and cilantro pesto; items are cheaper by the dozen.

Mid-Range

Lilly's (☎ 310-314-0004, 1031 Abbot Kinney Blvd) Mains $10-19; lunch Sun-Fri, dinner nightly, brunch Sun. At this mellow neighborhood bistro the best tables are in the flowery, secluded courtyard, although some prefer the high-backed upholstered banquettes beneath bright abstract canvasses. The best deals are the $10 lunches, which pair a choice of main course with soup or salad.

Fabio's (☎ 310-452-6364, 1025 Abbot Kinney Blvd) Mains $8.50-20. Just as France and Italy are neighbors, so are Lilly's and Fabio's. The latter has a similarly idyllic courtyard, similar banquettes and $10 lunches, but the food bears the distinct imprint of the Boot. Pastas, risottos, fish and meat dishes are all represented on the menu.

Top End

Chaya Venice (☎ 310-396-1179, 110 Navy St) Lunch $10-15 Mon-Fri, dinner $12-39 nightly. Leather-covered booths, a chic, deep-pocketed clientele and Asian-style art make this sleek eatery more Beverly Hills than Venice. Bouillabaisse and roasted Dungeness crab are highlights from the mostly 'fishy' menu. At lunch, the chef's daily medley for $11 is a good choice for the undecided. There's also a sushi happy hour from 5pm-7pm daily.

Hal's Bar & Grill (☎ 310-396-3105, 1349 Abbot Kinney Blvd) Mains $14-25. Lunch Mon-Fri, dinner nightly, brunch Sat & Sun. The name may evoke brass and wood, but Hal's dining room is all cool industrial with a tall exposed ceiling and postmodern artwork. The menu, which changes frequently, features an international cast of ingredients, such as French lentils, Italian pancetta and Asian daikon paired with ahi tuna, duck breast and other fishy and meaty companions.

Joe's (☎ 310-399-5811, 1023 Abbot Kinney Blvd) Mains $18-24; 4-course meals $30-40; closed Mon. Long before Lilly's and

Fabio's moved in next door (see Mid-Range above), there was Joe's, a classic neighborhood eatery. Owner/chef Joe Miller serves up uniformly sophisticated Cal-French food from a kitchen the size of a walk-in closet. Simple dishes like arugula salad will linger on the palate and in the memory.

SOUTH BAY (MAP 14)
Budget

The Naked Garden (☎ 310-372-2509, 424 Pier Ave, Hermosa Beach) Mains $3.25-10; closed Sun night and Mon. All animal products (including dairy) are banished from the menu at this snug eatery filled with whimsical knickknacks and mostly local art. Chef Francois Galipeau whips organic vegetables, tofu and tempeh, soba, udon and other healthful ingredients into delicious dishes. The grilled vegetable burrito is outstanding.

Backburner Cafe (☎ 310-372-6973, 87 14th St, Hermosa Beach) Mains $2.25-7.25; closes around 2pm. Buckwheat pancakes and giant omelets are what distinguish this place from the rest.

Beach Hut No 2 (☎ 310-376-4252, 1342 Hermosa Ave, Hermosa Beach) Mains $3-6; closes around 2pm. Come here to soak up the surfer vibe and watch buff dudes and dudettes load up on carbs before hitting the waves.

El Gringo (☎ 310-376-1381, 2620 Hermosa Ave, Hermosa Beach) Mains $4-8.50. Colorful blankets for tablecloths and cheesy but charming decor make the ambience here *muy auténtico*. The succulent *pollo asada* (chicken that's been soaked in an interesting mix of spices and juices) is a winner.

La Playita (☎ 310-376-2148, 37 14th St, Hermosa Beach) Mains $3.50-8; closed Mon. This easygoing shack, half a block from the sand, has delicious tacos and big burritos and is a perfect stopover to wrap up a day at the beach.

The Kettle (☎ 310-545-8511, 1138 Highland Ave, Manhattan Beach) Mains $5-13; open 24 hours. A mass of humanity almost always congregates at this updated coffee shop. They come for hefty sandwiches and burgers, fresh salads and meaty mains like

the barbecue beef ribs. The nicest tables are on the patio separated from the sidewalk by a curtain of exotic flowers and plants.

El Sombrero (☎ 310-374-1366, 1005 Manhattan Ave, Manhattan Beach) Mains $3-7.50. A long-time locals' favorite, this Mexican eatery has red booths and tables and sidewalk seating. There's often a line.

Uncle Bill's Pancake House (☎ 310-545-5177, 1305 Highland Ave, Manhattan Beach) Mains $3-7.50; closes at 2pm. Grab a table on the ocean-view patio, then make up your mind about whether to get eggs and bacon or a creative variations such as potatoes stroganoff or the Istanbul omelet (made with *turkey* – duh!).

Good Stuff (☎ 310-545-4775, 1300 Highland Ave, Manhattan Beach; ☎ 310-374-2334, 1286 The Strand, Hermosa Beach; ☎ 310-316-0262, 1617 Pacific Coast Hwy, Redondo Beach) Mains $6-13. This place has airy lifeguard-theme decor and indoor-outdoor, upstairs-downstairs seating, making it a perfect beach hangout. Like most South Bay restaurants, the menu offers mostly popular standbys (burgers, salads, sandwiches and a few Mexican dishes). Breakfast is served until 5pm.

Fun Fish Market (☎ 310-374-9982, 121 International Boardwalk, lower level 3, Redondo Beach) Mains $10 or less. This super-casual eatery won't win any prizes for its functional decor, but it does serve some of the best and freshest seafood in town. During lobster season, it charges just $10 per spiny fellow, and it always offers full meals such as whole charbroiled fish or snow crab.

Quality Seafood (☎ 310-372-6408, 130 International Boardwalk, lower level 3, Redondo Beach) Mains $8-16. Opposite, this place is much pricier but has some nice outdoor tables and live mariachi music on Sunday.

The Green Temple (☎ 310-944-4525, 1700 S Catalina Ave, Redondo Beach) Mains $5-10; closed Mon. Vegans and vegetarians may want to give this funky place a try. The dining room is a Far Eastern dreamscape with Oriental carpets, rainbow-colored mosaic tabletops and a smiling Buddha for good measure. The food is more down-to-earth. Good choices include the three bean soup and the savory steamers, which combine tofu or tempeh with rice, lots of vegetables and a delicious mysterious sauce.

Mid-Range

Chez Mélange (☎ 310-540-1222, 1716 S Pacific Coast Hwy, Redondo Beach) Mains $9-24. Breakfast & lunch Mon-Fri, dinner nightly, brunch Sat & Sun. This popular brasserie attached to the Palos Verdes Inn (see Places to Stay) serves reliably good, global fare in an elegant, bourgeois dining room. The Cajun meatloaf, one of its signature dishes, comes with a delectable sauce and mashed potatoes; there's also a caviar and oyster bar for deep-pocketed gourmets.

Gina Lee's Bistro (☎ 310-375-4462, 211 Palos Verdes Blvd, Redondo Beach) Mains $8-21. The mini-mall location may not be the most dazzling but the food here makes up for any visual shortcomings. Pan-Asian dishes are prepared California-style with little fat and much flavor. The wontons are crispy and plump, the duck breast juicy and the spinach salad doused with an intriguing dressing.

Buca di Beppo (☎ 310-540-3246, 1670 S Pacific Coast Hwy, Redondo Beach) Mains $10-20. This fast expanding empire of energetic eateries serves Southern Italian comfort food: big portions of pasta drenched in tangy sauces, saucer-sized pizzas, and desserts worthy of a hiatus from dieting. Murals, framed glossies of Sinatra, Loren and Lollobrigida, and gaudy paintings create a milieu that's both kitschy and fun. The sauces are made daily, as are the humongous bread loaves. Bring some friends and dig in – leftovers are guaranteed.

Tony's Fish Market (☎ 310-376-6223, 112 Fisherman's Wharf, upper pier plaza, Redondo Beach) Mains $13-22; lunch Sat-Sun, dinner nightly. For character and a surreal '50s flashback, head for this classic fish house, where seafood and meat is served with typically Italian *abondanza* ('abundance'). The clam chowder is so

---

Great Places to Go with Kids

These restaurants are all casual and sure to be winners: All have imaginative decor, a kid-friendly menu and affordable prices. (For reviews, see individual entries under the respective sections.)

Bob's Big Boy (Burbank)
Buca di Beppo (South Bay)
Good Stuff (South Bay)
Hard Rock Cafe (Beverly Center District)
Marvel Mania (Universal City)
Old Spaghetti Factory (Central Hollywood)
Sidewalk Cafe (Venice & Marina del Rey)
Stinking Rose (Beverly Hills)
Tail O' the Pup (Beverly Center District)

---

thick, it makes your spoon stand up. Enjoy the view through the panoramic windows or sit around the fireplace. (There's also a bar on top of the restaurant; see Entertainment.) There's a newer branch at 210 Fisherman's Wharf (☎ 310-374-9241).

Top End

Soleil (☎ 310-545-8654, 1142 Manhattan Ave, Manhattan Beach) Mains $12-28; lunch Tues-Fri, dinner Tues-Sun. Inspired Mediterranean food served in a casual, rustic setting with a high-beamed ceiling is what awaits you at this pleasant gourmet eatery. An extensive wine list, including 70 selections by the glass, complements the menu where many dishes are built around fresh fish and seafood.

Le Beaujolais (☎ 310-543-5100, 522 S Pacific Coast Hwy, Redondo Beach) Mains $13-26. A hint of Paris in Redondo is what you'll find at this place, which has been serving top-notch French selections since 1983. Savor intricately spiced rack of lamb or fresh halibut in an old-fashioned candlelit dining room. Sunday brunch offers the best value with main courses costing about $11 and served with fresh orange juice, two glasses of champagne, muffins, soup or salad and vegetables.

PLACES TO EAT

SAN PEDRO & LONG BEACH
Budget

Taco Company (☎ *310-514-2808, 447 S Gaffey St, San Pedro; Map 15*) Mains $1.50-3.50. When it comes to eating Mexican food, simpler is often better, and taco stands such as this sun-colored one often yield inexpensive gourmet experiences. The best bet here is anything containing fish, either fried or grilled. Only the soupy salsa needs a bit of improvement.

Egg Heaven (☎ *562-433-9277, 4358 E 4th St, Long Beach; Map 4*) Mains $3-8. Come to this old-fashioned diner in Belmont Heights for scrumptious breakfasts and lunches.

Taco Surf (☎ *562-434-8646, 5316 E 2nd St, Long Beach; Map 4*) Mains $2-9. This spit-and-sawdust cantina straight out of Baja caters to substantial appetites with its hearty and delicious Mexican standards. Seating is inside in oversized wooden booths or on the sidewalk patio.

Mid-Range

Pine Ave is downtown Long Beach's 'Restaurant Row,' with more than a dozen restaurants to choose from, including the following favorites:

Mum's (☎ *562-437-7700, 144 Pine Ave; Map 16*) Mains $12-30. One of Long Beach's top restaurants, Mum's is elegant, but, as befits a beachside town, anything but stuffy. Preferred tables are on the spacious sidewalk terrace, which gives you front row people-watching seats. The menu is Cal-Asian, with selections ranging from sushi (respectable but not first-rate) to miso poached salmon with couscous and Asian vegetables. Upstairs is Club Cohiba, a martini lounge with cigar and billiard rooms (see Clubs & Live Music in the Entertainment chapter).

Alegria (☎ *562-436-3388, 115 Pine Ave; Map 16*) Tapas $6-10, mains $14-20. The trippy, Technicolor mosaic floor, an eccentric Art Nouveau bar and trompe l'oeil murals form an appropriately spirited backdrop to the spicy and exotic Nuevo Latino cuisine. Selections include classic Spanish paella and grilled filet mignon in a red wine

mushroom sauce, though you could make this a budget place by sticking to tapas. Stay away from the wimpy and overpriced margaritas and order the sangria instead. There is live entertainment nightly, including a flamenco show on Sunday.

For a culinary experience with a decidedly local flavor, head south to happening Belmont Shore. *Malvasia* (☎ *562-433-5005, 5316 E 2nd St; Map 4*) Mains $8-20; dinner nightly. Next to Taco Surf (see Budget), this more upscale restaurant allows for a culinary journey around the Mediterranean: from Spanish olives to French escargot to Italian penne to Greek dolmades to Israeli humus. There is a sidewalk patio, interior patio and main dining room with exposed rafters and brick walls.

Belmont Brewing Company (☎ *562-433-3891, 25 39th Place; Map 4*) Mains $9-19. Everybody's favorite brewpub and restaurant, BBC has a great beachfront location next to Belmont Pier, a large outdoor deck (perfect for watching sunsets), fresh and handcrafted brews, and a well-priced menu that goes far beyond pub grub. Try Seafood Leo, a fishy bonanza packaged in filo dough with a lobster cream sauce.

Top End

Papadakis Taverna (☎ *310-548-1186, 301 W 6th St, San Pedro; Map 15*) Mains $15-25; dinner only. Many people make the trip to San Pedro just to indulge in the authentic Greek food served here. This family-style restaurant has friendly waiters and such delectable classics as lamb and moussaka. Stay for the sirtaki dancing, glass-smashing and other riotous rituals.

Sky Room (☎ *562-983-2703, 40 S Locust Ave; Map 16*) Mains $20-35; dinner Tues-Sat, brunch Sun. Long Beach's launch into stellar dining came with the opening of the Sky Room, a refurbished Art Deco supper club on the 15th floor of the historic Breakers Building. Part of the experience is a sashay up the red carpeted stairs, where you'll be escorted to the elevators by a guy in a tuxedo and top hat. Perhaps even better than the continental food is the 360° view. Leave room for Fred & Ginger, a decadent crème brûlée served in a chocolate top hat ($10). Dancing and live music make it a popular place for dates and anniversaries.

EAST LA (MAP 3)

You won't find many sushi bars or fancy Italian restaurants here, but East LA offers some of the best Mexican food around.

El Tepeyac Cafe (☎ 323-268-1960, 812 N Evergreen Ave) Mains $7.50-9; closed Tues. This is one restaurant that draws a huge following. Burritos come smothered in cheese and bulging with anything from machaca to chorizo (spicy sausage) to scrambled eggs and pork. The Big Burrito ($12.40) feeds four. It's a small, simple place, anchored by a heavy bar and framed by mirrored walls festooned with Christmas lights.

El Tarasco, *El Gallo* & *La Perla (☎ 323-263-1662 or 323-262-4507, 3425 E 1st St)* Mains $6-14, slightly higher during mariachi shows. These three lively and *auténtico* restaurants are all managed by the same woman and located side by side on the cavernous mezzanine level of El Mercado, a colorful indoor market (also see Things to

See & Do). Decor, food and ambience are identical. The locals boast that everything on the menu is excellent, but investigation uncovered the best dish: the *ricas botanas* ('rich appetizer'), which is piled high with fresh shrimp, calamari, and more shrimp and appetizingly served with cocktail sauce. The small *(chica)* plate is enough for two ($26).

MONTEREY PARK (MAP 3)

Some call it 'Little Taipei,' others 'Chinese Beverly Hills,' but regardless, Monterey Park is replete with food palaces where you can sample some very authentic dishes in a setting that will feel quite exotic unless you are of Chinese descent yourself. You'll pass dozens of restaurants just driving down Garvey Ave or Atlantic Blvd, but here are a couple worth keeping an eye out for:

Ocean Star (☎ 626-308-2128, 145 N Atlantic Blvd) Mains $15-35. This vast gourmet emporium, made of several rooms with glass, brass and marble touches, serves dim sum from 9am-3pm. For dinner, seafood – so fresh the tanks actually form part of the decor – is the name of the game.

Whimsical Mexican Food

Antojitos, or 'little whims,' are traditional Mexican snacks or small meals. They can be eaten at any time of day, on their own or as part of a larger meal. Here are some of the more popular ones:

burrito – any combination of beans, cheese, meat, chicken and seafood, seasoned with salsa or chili and wrapped in a flour tortilla

chile relleno – poblano chili stuffed with cheese, meat or other ingredients, dipped in beaten egg, fried and baked in a sauce

enchilada – ingredients similar to the burrito, wrapped in a corn tortilla and then baked in a sauce

gordita – fried maize dough filled with refried beans, topped with sour cream, cheese and lettuce

guacamole – avocados mashed with onion, chili, lemon, spices and sometimes tomato and typically served as a dip or condiment

machaca – cured, dried and shredded beef or pork, reconstituted, mixed with eggs, onions, cilantro and chilies and fried

quesadilla – flour tortillas filled with melted cheese and sometimes other ingredients

taco – ingredients similar to the burrito, wrapped in a soft or crisp corn tortilla and then topped with a range of condiments (onion, tomato, sour cream, shredded cabbage etc)

tamale – corn dough stuffed with meat, beans or chili, wrapped in corn husks and then steamed

torta – ingredients similar to a burrito served in a sandwich roll

tostada – flat, crisp tortilla topped with meat or cheese, tomatoes, beans and lettuce

PLACES TO EAT

Charming Garden (☎ *626-458-4508, 111 N Atlantic Blvd*) Mains $7-20. Try this clean and simple Hunan eatery for its excellent spicy chicken and intricately flavored seafood dishes.

LEIMERT PARK (MAP 2)

Phillip's House of Barbecue (☎ *323-292-7613, 4307 Leimert Blvd*) Sandwiches $4.50-6.50, mains $6.75-12. Banish any worries about love handles or clogged arteries before coming to this local institution. Smoky and innocuous, this hole in the wall serves some fingerlickin' pork and beef ribs. Go easy on the hot sauce unless you're auditioning as a fire-eater. Hours are erratic, so call ahead.

Elephant Walk (☎ *323-299-1765, 4336 Degnan Blvd*) Mains $15-35; dinner only, closed Mon. This classy place is tastefully furnished with antiques and originals by local artists, and has tables topped with crisp linen cloths and candles. The fare is soul and Cajun and there's also a coffee bar. On Sunday, there's a gospel brunch.

PASADENA (MAP 17)
Budget

Marston's (☎ *626-796-2459, 151 E Walnut Ave*) Mains $6-10; closed Sun & Mon. Join the locals at this unpretentious breakfast and lunch hangout inside a homey cottage. Only fresh ingredients make it into the delicious sandwiches and salads, and there's a dozen burgers to choose from as well, including a vegetarian version. (The best tables are out on the porch.)

Akbar (☎ *626-577-9916, 44 N Fair Oaks Ave*) Mains $6-18, lunch specials $6.25. This easygoing eatery has great Indian food, including succulent Tandoori staples like chicken tikka, fragrant lamb and chicken and seafood curries. Some of this restaurant's spicier dishes will definitely jumpstart your senses.

Buca di Beppo (☎ *626-792-7272, 80 W Green St*) Down-home and powerfully flavored fare is doled out in mega-portions in a fun atmosphere. For a full review, see South Bay, earlier in this chapter.

Zankou Chicken (☎ *626-405-1502, 1206 E Colorado Blvd*) Mains $2.40-7.50. Great rotisserie chicken. For full review, see Hollywood earlier.

Mid-Range

Twin Palms (☎ *626-577-2567, 101 W Green St*) 2-course lunch $6.95 Mon-Sat, dinner $9-28 nightly, brunch $6-15 Sun. This casual California eatery, owned by Cindy, Kevin Costner's ex, is named for a pair of palms towering above its large canopied patio. The menu features meat and fish dishes prepared with a Mediterranean touch as well as pizza and pasta. There's live entertainment (cover is charged on weekends) and a daily happy hour.

Mi Piace (☎ *626-795-3131, 25 E Colorado Blvd*) Mains $8-18. The name is Italian for 'I like it,' and that's what the throngs of trendoids seem to think as they crowd into this high-ceilinged restaurant. This is one of the most popular restaurants on the Colorado strip, though the true draw isn't clear. The food's pretty bland and unimaginative, but the sidewalk tables provide front row seats for see-and-be-seen types. There are several other, similarly priced, Italian eateries nearby, including **Trattoria Farfalla** (☎ *626-564-8696, 43 E Colorado Blvd*) and **Trattoria Sorriso** (☎ *626-793-2233, 46 E Colorado*).

Rack Shack (☎ *626-405-1994, 58 E Colorado Blvd*) Mains $7-22. The intoxicating aroma of Southern home-style cooking pulls people into this tunnel-shaped eatery. Feast on the crazy Cajun chicken soaked in mystery spices and delivered with a sauce that could very well take the enamel off your teeth, or play it safer with such meaty fare as beef back ribs. All meals come with two side dishes (green salad, baked beans, yams, among others) and cornbread.

Café Bizou (☎ *626-792-9923, 91 N Raymond Ave*) Lunch $7.50-13 Tues-Fri, dinner $11-16 Tues-Sun. Gourmet French at fair prices served in an upscale bistro ambience with satin-sheathed booths and blonde wood. For full review, see Ventura Blvd, later in this chapter.

Top End

Yujean Kang *(☎ 626-585-0855, 67 N Raymond Ave)* Lunch $7-8.50, dinner $12-18. As soon as you step inside, you know that this is not your typical Chinese restaurant. The walls are copper-stained and decorated with delicate sumi paintings. Dishes are artworks, especially the duck and mushroom soup topped with a meringue and featuring a little drawing. Tea smoked duck is paired with pancakes, and prawns team up with fava beans as well as black and enoki mushrooms.

Xiomara *(☎ 626-796-2520, 69 N Raymond Ave)* Lunch $9-15 Mon-Fri, dinner $18-28 nightly. Next door to Yujean King is this equally stylish place, which serves world cuisine at its finest. Ceviche, foie gras, risotto, goat cheese salad and lamb shank are all comfortable neighbors on the limited menu. It's all served in a bistro ambience highlighted by a sleek marble bar, a black ceiling and large Art Deco mirrors.

GLENDALE (MAP 3)

Glendale's main artery, Brand Ave, is packed with fast-food and chain eateries, but there are several exceptions. ***Fresco Ristorante*** *(☎ 818-247-5541, 514 S Brand Blvd)* Mains $10-22; lunch Mon-Fri, dinner Mon-Sat. Patrons sit at white linen–bedecked tables in an intimate dining room that's civilized without being stodgy. The solid Italian menu is particularly strong in the pasta department, although the risotto also shows the quality touch.

Zankou Chicken *(☎ 818-244-2237, 1415 E Colorado St)* Mains $2.40-7.50. Great rotisserie chicken. For the full review, see Hollywood, earlier in this chapter.

Baklava Factory *(☎ 818-548-7070, 1415 E Colorado St)* Mains $6 per pound. In the same mini-mall as Zankou Chicken, this unassuming bakery is baklava nirvana. Fluffy filo dough – wrought into interesting shapes – wraps around such delectable fillings as pistachio, almond, pecan and walnut; these confections are all lightly dipped into rosewater syrup, achieving just the right amount of gooeyness.

BURBANK (MAP 18)
Budget

Several low-key, inexpensive eateries cluster in Burbank Village along San Fernando Blvd between Olive Ave and Magnolia Blvd.

The Great Grill *(☎ 818-567-0060, 126 N San Fernando Blvd)* Mains $4-8. This mock '50s diner has the predictable gamut of burgers, sandwiches, fries and salads. The imaginative decor includes a giant vinyl record suspended from the ceiling. A bottle of wine is just $9, and there's outdoor seating as well.

Knight *(☎ 818-845-4516, 138 N San Fernando Blvd)* Mains $2.50-8.75. Another option on the block, this cafe has a lofty ceiling, copper-colored walls and contemporary metal furniture. Here you can chow down on gyros, falafels, shish kebabs and other Middle Eastern specialties.

India's Tandoori *(☎ 818-846-7500, 142 N San Fernando Rd)* Mains $5-11. Fragrant meat and vegetarian curries as well as succulent dishes from the tandoor (clay oven) are the specialty here. The lunch buffet ($7) and Sunday champagne brunch ($9) are both popular. It's all served in an exotically decorated dining room.

Poquito Más *(☎ 818-563-2252, 2635 W Olive Ave)* Mains $3.50-7. Lines are always long at this shacklike Mexican eatery, which serves some of the most healthful fast food around. The ahi tacos and chicken burritos reach gourmet quality; also try the tortilla soup.

Bob's Big Boy *(☎ 818-843-9334, 4211 Riverside Dr)* Mains $5-9. For a genuine slice of Americana, check out this classic coffee shop from the late '40s, fronted by a sculpture of cheeky Bob himself. This is the oldest remaining outlet of what used to be a large chain of restaurants. This branch is an architectural landmark, built in Streamline Moderne by Wayne McAllister. On Saturday and Sunday nights between 5pm-10pm, the car hop service (sans the roller-skates) lets you catch that *American Graffiti* vibe. Friday is classic car night. Breakfast is served anytime.

Mid-Range

Market City Cafe (☎ *818-840-7036, 164 E Palm Ave*) Mains $7-13. Italian staples in their infinite variety are on the menu here, including pasta, pizza, panini and salads. By far the best deal, though, is the all-you-can-eat antipasto bar for $8 (or $5.25 with main course). It's all best enjoyed on the nice patio.

Piero's Seafood Restaurant (☎ *818-842-5159, 2825 W Olive Ave*) Mains $10-28. Lunch Mon-Fri, dinner nightly. Piero himself may greet you as you step into this neighborhood favorite, which serves classic Italian fare. All main courses are partnered with a house salad. Special treats are the daily seafood and fish selections and the flambéed shrimp prepared tableside.

NORTH HOLLYWOOD & UNIVERSAL CITY (MAP 18)

Leonor's Vegetarian Restaurant (☎ *818-980-9011, 11403 Victory Blvd*) Mains $5-9.50. A loyal clientele has been flocking to Leonor's dark cavern for more than 21 years. Pizzas, Mexican food, salads, sandwiches are all given the homemade, vegan treatment. The chicken salad, made with soy chicken, is a good choice.

Ca' del Sole (☎ *818-985-4669, 4100 Cahuenga Blvd*) Mains $8-17; lunch Mon-Fri, dinner nightly, brunch Sun. One of the Valley's best restaurants, this is a slice of Italy in the midst of suburbia. Curvaceous booths, panoramic windows and an airy atmosphere welcome diners who are wowed by tantalizing, flavor-intensive Northern Italian fare.

Tokyo Delve's (☎ *818-766-3868, 5239 Lankershim Blvd*) Mains $20; dinner Mon-Sat. There are certainly places with better sushi, but the food here is – almost – an afterthought. It's the boisterous party atmosphere – fueled by insane, tap-dancing sushi chefs – that draws in a mostly college-age crowd. There's almost always a line waiting by the roped entrance, so make reservations, which don't always guarantee admission.

Barsac Brasserie (☎ *818-760-7081, 4212 Lankershim Blvd*) Mains $13-27; lunch Mon-Fri, dinner Mon-Sat. No animal is safe from appearing on the menu here, where an open kitchen dishes out everything from scallops, snails and brains to the more mainstream lamb, veal and pork. Lively crowds of studio executives have kept this restaurant busy for years. If you're on a tight budget, just order an appetizer: portions are almost the same size as other restaurants' main courses.

Recently expanded, **Universal City Walk** now has nearly 30 restaurants. Some good choices are:

Camacho's Cantina (☎ *818-622-3333*) Mains $8-16, Sun brunch $12.95. This is an average Mexican restaurant with daily happy hour specials, and a budget-priced Sunday brunch with strolling mariachis.

Karl Strauss Brewery (☎ *818-753-2739*) Mains $6-15. This comfortable brew-pub serves American food infused with Germanic touches. It goes down especially well with a mug of the house brew. The sandwiches, pizzas and salads are big enough for a meal and inexpensive enough for the budget-conscious.

Gladstone's (☎ *818-622-3485*) Sandwiches $8-15, mains $20 and up. This is the place to come for superbly fresh seafood, some of which still swims around in large tanks in the back. There's an oyster bar and a salad bar.

Other Universal City Walk options are clones of successful eateries around town; see the relevant sections for full reviews.

Jody Maroni's Sausage Kingdom (☎ *818-622-5639*) Gourmet sausages; see Venice & Marina del Rey, earlier in this chapter.

Versailles (☎ *818-505-0093*) Superb Cuban chicken and roast pork; see Culver City, earlier in this chapter.

Buca di Beppo (☎ *818-509-9463*) Huge portions of Southern Italian fare in a wildly imaginative setting: see South Bay, earlier in this chapter.

VENTURA BLVD (MAP 2)

The Valley's main drag stretches for miles and is littered with restaurants mostly centered around Sherman Oaks and Studio City. *Bamboo Inn* (☎ *818-788-0202, 14010*

International Food Markets for the Adventurous

Los Angeles has become a second home for hundreds of thousands of people from around the world who've brought with them their culture, music and, of course, their food. The city is filled with markets and stores catering to these recent arrivals. Browsing through here is a quick culinary journey to a foreign land and also allows you to stock up on all the exotic ingredients needed to experiment in your own kitchen.

Farm Fresh Ranch Market (☎ 323-957-7373, 5520 Sunset Blvd, Hollywood; Map 9) Located in Little Armenia, this amazing market is famous for its United Nations of edibles *and* shoppers. Pick up fresh Bulgarian feta, Greek Kalamata olives, banana leaves for tamales, chorizo from El Salvador, Russian-style pickled herring or freshly baked Mexican *bolillos* (buns). Prices are low, especially for produce, meat, fish and baked items.

Bangluck Market (☎ 323-660-8000, 5170 Hollywood Blvd, Hollywood; Map 9) This diminutive but well-stocked store in the heart of Thai Town has every conceivable type of noodle, curry, spice and condiment to please aficionados of Thai cuisine. Dishes, candles and even fresh meat and produce are also available; prices are very reasonable.

Koreatown Plaza Market (☎ 213-385-1100, 928 S Western Ave, Koreatown; Map 7) Stock up on kim chi, buckwheat noodles, fresh fish and tasty sweet treats at this upscale supermarket. The deli counter, filled with pickled, dried and sliced mysteries, looks like something from another universe but everything is clean and attractively presented.

Liborio Market (☎ 213-386-1458, 864 S Vermont Ave, Koreatown; Map 7) This place is claustrophobically crammed with spices, dried beans, *crema, masa* flour, canned fruit purees and other Central American staples, but the friendly staff is happy to help you find anything. There's a special meat counter as well as a Salvadoran bakery and a good selection of tamales.

Mitsuwa (☎ 213-687-6694, 333 S Alameda St, Little Tokyo; Map 5; ☎ 310-398-2113, 3760 Centinela Ave, West LA; Map 13) For Japanese ingredients, there's no bigger market than this – choose from various types of tofu, enoki mushrooms, entire shelves of sake and everything you'd need to make sushi, sukiyaki or tempura.

India Sweets & Spices (☎ 310-837-5286, 9409 Venice Blvd, Culver City; Map 12) This aromatic, if chaotic, store has shelves piled high with everything you'd need to make your own Indian feast: rice, spices, exotic vegetables, chutneys, relishes and teas. Don't fancy doing your own cooking? Pick up some of the cheapest curries, dhal and sweets from the busy take-out counter.

Gourmet Coffee Warehouse (☎ 310-392-6479, 671 Rose Ave, Venice; Map 13) This barn-like store is dedicated to the cult of the bean. Wholesale prices (about $7 per pound), freshness and about 40 varieties (including blends and organic kinds) account for its popularity. The beans are roasted in a back room every three days and stored in old-fashioned, self-service wooden bins. Several varieties are available for tastings. It also sells fine tea and accessories.

Ventura Blvd, Sherman Oaks) Mains $5-10. This is one of the best Mandarin Chinese restaurants in the Valley, with minimalist decor and very good seafood; the fish in black bean sauce is recommended.

Café Bizou (☎ 818-788-3536, 14016 Ventura Blvd, Sherman Oaks) Lunch $7.50-13 Mon-Fri, dinner $11-16 nightly. Beg, borrow, steal or lie to procure a table at this charming establishment where French food receives the royal treatment at prices even paupers can afford. Add soup or salad to your main course for just a $1 more; corkage fee is $2.

Teru Sushi (☎ 818-763-6201, 11940 Ventura Blvd, Studio City) Lunch $15-20 Mon-Fri, dinner $20-25 nightly. This place is busy, theatrical and allegedly one of the sushi bars that helped launch the unabated raw fish craze among non-Japanese Americans. The dishes are creatively named and prepared; for instance, the 'sea flower' is a petal-shaped fish filet.

La Pergola (☎ 818-905-8402, 15005 Ventura Blvd, Sherman Oaks) Mains $12-21; lunch Mon-Fri, dinner nightly. This old Valley favorite keeps the faithful coming. Owner/chef Tino Pettignano has astutely adapted a wide range of Italian classics to the neurotic tastes of modern-day yuppies. The pasta is eggless, the vegetables and herbs are organically grown in a big garden behind the restaurant, and it's all prepared with little fat but much imagination.

Bistro Garden at Coldwater (☎ 818-501-0202, 12950 Ventura Blvd, Studio City) Mains $15-30; lunch Mon-Fri, dinner nightly. Romantic dining in the Valley means going to this Euro-style winter garden and digging into premium selections of seafood, meats and pastas paired with delectable vegetables and lovely sauces.

MARKETS

Ralphs, *Vons*, *Pavilions* and *Albertsons* are the most ubiquitous supermarket chains, while the discount *Food 4 Less* is slightly less common. All have different specials every week. To qualify for the steepest discounts, Ralphs, Vons and Pavilions require you to become a 'club' member, a formality that's instantly accomplished by filling out a short form (you don't have to live in LA to do this). In return, you'll be given a credit-card sized club card that must be presented at the cash register. The Sunday *LA Times* has coupons to help cut costs further.

Looking for shaved truffles, French brie or smoked salmon? You'll find them at these upscale markets. *Trader Joe's* (☎ 800-746-7857) Gourmets on a budget swear by this Euro-style discount warehouse with near-legendary cheese, wine and beer selections. It also has delicious breads, frozen foods, dairy and ready-made salads and wraps. For the nearest branch, phone the number above, then punch in your zip code.

Bristol Farms (☎ 323-845-1699, 7860 Sunset Blvd, Hollywood; ☎ 310-474-4317, 1570 Rosecrans Ave, Manhattan Beach; Map 14) This small chain of gourmet supermarkets has attractive presentation, stellar selection and out-of-this-world prices.

Gelson's (☎ 323-656-5580, 8330 Santa Monica Blvd, West Hollywood; Map 10; ☎ 310-306-2952, 13455 Maxella Ave, Marina del Rey; Map 13) Gelson's excels at anything fresh – produce, meat, fish, flowers, baked goods etc – and is dependable in all other departments. Prices are rather high.

Health-conscious shoppers with designs on organic products and vitamin and food supplements should check out these stores, which seem to cluster in trendy Westside communities. Prices are generally higher than at traditional markets, but some (especially Erewhon) might be good for celebrity spottings:

Wild Oats Food Market (☎ 310-854-6927, 8611 Santa Monica Blvd, West Hollywood; Map 10; ☎ 310-576-4707, 1425 Montana Ave, Santa Monica; Map 13; ☎ 310-395-4510, 500 Wilshire Blvd, Santa Monica; Map 13)

Whole Foods (☎ 323-848-4200, 7871 Santa Monica Blvd, West Hollywood; Map 10; ☎ 310-996-8840, 11666 National Blvd, West LA; Map 13; ☎ 310-826-4433, 11737 San Vicente Blvd, Brentwood; Map 13)

Erewhon Natural Foods Market (☎ 323-937-0777, 7660 Beverly Blvd, Fairfax District; Map 10)

Entertainment

To keep your finger on what's hot in LA, your best sources of information are the *Los Angeles Times* (especially the daily Calendar section and the magazine-like Sunday supplement) and the free *LA Weekly*, published Fridays (but usually available Thursday nights) and available at many restaurants, shops and bars throughout Los Angeles.

Buying Tickets

In most cases, tickets for concerts, sporting events, theater, musicals, etc are available by phone or in person through the venue's box office, usually with no or only a small booking fee. Many also allow reservations via the Internet. The central reservation agency, Ticketmaster (☎ 213-480-3232, www.ticketmaster.com), however, collects exorbitant handling fees and service charges in addition to the base ticket price. Tickets are then charged to your credit card and either mailed to you or made available for pick-up before the show at the will-call counter of the respective venue. A smaller agency is Telecharge (☎ 800-233-3123).

For information on half-price theater tickets, see the Theater section later in this chapter. Details about movie tickets are included in the Cinemas section next.

CINEMAS

Cinemas – usually multiplexes with up to 20 screens – are ubiquitous in the movie capital of the world. Major chains showing mainstream first-release movies include Cineplex Odeon, Mann, United Artists, Edwards, General Cinema, Pacific Theaters and AMC. First-run films sell out early on Friday and Saturday nights, and you may have to stand in line twice: once to buy tickets and then again to get into the theater.

The first screening is usually around noon and the last one at about 10pm. Shows after 6pm cost $9; shows before 6pm can be up to 50% off. To guarantee that you will get tickets, you can make advance credit card bookings by calling ☎ 213-777-3456 or ☎ 310-777-3456, or by logging on to www.moviefone.com; there's no surcharge for this service.

Historic theaters include the Cinerama Dome (under renovation), the El Capitan, the Egyptian and Mann's Chinese Theater in Hollywood, the Warner Grand in San Pedro and the Orpheum in Downtown (see the Things to See & Do chapter for details about these). You'll find other clusters of theaters on the Third Street Promenade in Santa Monica, on Colorado Blvd in Old Pasadena and in Westwood Village.

Neighborhood Cinemas

Only several of these independently run, single-screen theaters survive. Many show first-release movies on the verge of going to video. The sound may not be THX, but low prices still bring in the crowds.

Aero (☎ 310-395-4990, 1328 Montana Ave, Santa Monica; Map 13) This old-timey theater has uncomfortable seats, cheap prices and a loyal following among Brentwood millionaires. Tickets are $6.

Cineplex Odeon Fairfax Cinema (☎ 323-653-3117, 7907 Beverly Blvd, Fairfax District; Map 10) This place is a steal: all tickets for all show times for first-run movies are just $2.50.

Vista Theater (☎ 323-660-6639, 4473 Sunset Blvd, Silver Lake; Map 9) Recent-release movies are shown here, with tickets costing just $4.50 before 6pm.

Los Feliz Theatre (☎ 323-664-2169, 1822 N Vermont Ave, Los Feliz; Map 9) In addition to mainstream movies, this theater shows the occasional foreign or art film.

Revival & Art Houses

Mainstream filmic fare definitely dominates in LA, but the following places offer foreign, offbeat, non-commercial, cult, documentary or classic films.

Nuart (☎ 310-478-6379, 11272 Santa Monica Blvd, West LA; Map 13) This is con-

Murder & Mischief at the Silent Movie Theatre

The history of the Art Deco **Silent Movie Theatre** is a roller coaster of tragedy and triumph, dedication and greed, full of the kind of melodrama found in the flicks rolling off its projection spool. The theater was founded in 1942 by old-time movie buffs John and Dorothy Hampton, but the inaugural screening of Cecil B DeMille's *King of Kings* had barely finished when the theater went dark as John went to prison for protesting US involvement in WWII. Upon his release four years later, he reopened and stayed in business until lung cancer forced another abrupt closure in the late 1970s. Encouraged by family friend Lawrence Austin, Dorothy breathed new life into the place in 1990. But calamity struck again in 1997 when Lawrence was shot to death in the theater lobby by a hit man hired by his lover. Then, one day in 1999, Santa Monica songwriter Charlie Lustman saw a 'For Sale' sign on the boarded-up property. He bought the historic landmark, restored it and reopened in late 1999 with Charlie Chaplin's *Modern Times*. Let's all wish him well....

sidered the best art house in town; the midnight Saturday screenings of the cult-flick *Rocky Horror Picture Show* are legendary.

The Royal (☎ 310-477-5581, *11523 Santa Monica Blvd, West LA; Map 13*) A few blocks west, this comfortable theater specializes in arty European films.

NuWilshire Cinema (☎ 310-394-8099, *1314 Wilshire Blvd, Santa Monica; Map 13*) Recent-release foreign films with an offbeat bent are on the menu at this Santa Monica classic.

Laemmle Theater (☎ 310-394-9741, *1332 2nd St, Santa Monica; Map 13*) High-brow independent US and foreign films are shown at this fourplex.

Warner Grand Theater (☎ 310-548-7672, *478 6th St, San Pedro; Map 15*) Classic Hollywood flicks show at this Art Deco temple.

Other Film Venues

Silent Movie Theatre (☎ 323-655-2520, *611 N Fairfax Ave, Fairfax District; Map 10*) Admission adults/children, students and seniors $9/6; screenings 8pm Thur-Sun, 1pm & 4pm Sun. This is the only theater in the US dedicated to silent movies. Screenings are accompanied by live music and preceded by cartoons and shorts. (Also see the boxed text 'Murder & Mischief at the Silent Movie Theatre.')

Egyptian Theater (☎ 323-466-3456, *6712 Hollywood Blvd, Hollywood; Map 9*) Admission adults/students and seniors $8/6.

The nonprofit American Cinematheque presents a nightly program of independent, classic, foreign and avant-garde films. Showing twice daily except Monday is *Forever Hollywood*, a one-hour documentary about Hollywood history. Call for times.

Bing Theater (☎ 323-857-6010, *5905 Wilshire Blvd, Miracle Mile District; Map 10*) Intelligent, classic, obscure and arty fare is offered in this theater at the Los Angeles County Museum of Art (LACMA).

Goethe Institute (☎ 323-525-3388, *5750 Wilshire Blvd, Suite 100, Miracle Mile District; Map 10*) Nearby, this German cultural organization offers occasional screenings of new and classic works by German filmmakers; you might find a Fassbinder retrospective or a Brecht series.

James Bridges Theater (☎ 310-206-3456, *302 E Melnitz, Westwood; Map 11*) Drawing on the collection of the UCLA Film & TV Archive, this theater on UCLA's campus revives classics, often in themed presentations.

Museum of Television and Radio (☎ 310-786-1000, *465 N Beverly Dr, Beverly Hills; Map 11*) This museum and archive presents retrospectives and restored TV classics.

THEATER

Theater has long been a lively and integral part of LA's cultural scene. Choices range from glittery international hit musicals and plays to ensemble shows and independent fringe theater in unconventional venues.

Theaters are great places to catch both the budding stars of tomorrow and to see major film and television actors return to their roots on the live stage.

Half-price theater tickets for same-day evening or next-day matinee shows are sold on the Internet by Theatre LA, an alliance of 160 large and small theaters in the LA area. The Web site, at www.theatrela.org, provides details about what performances are on sale that day (and sometimes two or three days in advance); a service fee of $2-6 applies. Tickets must be picked up at the box office half an hour before the show; seating is assigned at that time.

Large Venues
Mark Taper Forum (☎ 213-628-2772, Music Center, 135 N Grand Ave, Downtown; Map 5) This venue is considered the leading theater in Southern California yet, with only 760 seats, it is actually rather intimate. Its resident ensemble specializes in developing new plays and many of its high-caliber productions have gone on to Broadway and from there to win Tony and Pulitzer awards *(Angels in America* and *Children of a Lesser God* among them). Famous actors from TV and film often lead the cast. The Taper has a public rush for last-minute $10 tickets, starting 10 minutes before curtain.

Ahmanson Theater (☎ 213-628-2772, Music Center, 135 N Grand Ave, Downtown; Map 5) In the same complex, this theater seats between 1300 and 2000 for top-notch Broadway musicals and plays such as *Miss Saigon, Phantom of the Opera* or Neil Simon comedies.

Shubert Theater (☎ 310-201-1500, 800-447-7400, 2020 Ave of the Stars, Century City; Map 11) Another good place to catch leading musical productions (such as *Sunset Blvd* and *Beauty and the Beast)* is this huge, state-of-the-art venue.

Pantages Theater (☎ 323-468-1770, 6233 Hollywood Blvd, Hollywood; Map 9) A wonderfully restored, historic venue with eye-popping Art Deco decor, especially in the lobby. In 2000, it catapulted back into the limelight with a stellar production of the musical *The Lion King*.

Small Venues
LA County's small, fringe theater scene has been thriving since organizers have been allowed to pay non-equity (nonunion) rates to actors under the Equity Waiver Program, regardless of whether the actors are professional or amateur. One requirement is that a theater cannot have more than 99 seats. While this usually doesn't allow performers to make a living off their acting, it gives them a chance to hone their skills, showcase their talent and act just for the love of it. For theatergoers, it means a varied menu of new plays, revival shows, experimental performances and classic productions that are often cutting edge and surprisingly good.

Downtown (Map 5) *East West Players (☎ 213-625-4397, Union Center for the Arts, 120 N Judge John Aiso St, Little Tokyo)* Founded in 1965, this pioneering company is the top-ranked Asian Pacific American ensemble with a repertory that ranges from classics to Broadway to plays specific to the community's experience. Alumni have gone on to win Tony and Emmy Awards.

Japan American Theater (☎ 213-680-3700, 244 S San Pedro St, Little Tokyo) This theater puts on an annual season of plays and concerts, including Kabuki, Noh and Bunraku theater performances.

Los Angeles Theatre Center (☎ 213-485-1681, 514 S Spring St) In a former bank building, this is one of the leading theater venues in Downtown. It's run by the city's Cultural Affairs Department, which rents out the four stages to performing-arts groups.

Central Hollywood (Map 9) Hollywood's 'Theater Row' stretches along Santa Monica Blvd with a series of small venues, some of them in bad shape and struggling, but often providing quality productions.

Actors' Gang Theatre (☎ 323-465-0566, 6209 Santa Monica Blvd) Among the standouts is the 'Gang,' founded in 1981 by Tim Robbins and fellow UCLA acting school graduates. It presents daring and offbeat interpretations of classics as well as new works produced during ensemble workshops. This troupe provokes, stimulates and amuses, making it one of the most rewarding theatrical experiences in LA.

Hudson Theatres (☎ 323-856-4249, 6539 Santa Monica Blvd) This sophisticated theater actually houses a quartet of stages – each with a different flavor – plus a restaurant and a coffeehouse. You'll find a checkered schedule that ranges from modern stalwarts to experimental productions to perennial crowd-pleasers like Neil Simon's The Odd Couple.

Open Fist Theatre (☎ 323-882-6912, 1625 N La Brea Ave) This cutting-edge company, founded in 1989 by five graduates of Cal State Fullerton, presents thought-provoking theatrical fare with themes relevant to contemporary society. Plays are often difficult and obscure works by 20th century playwrights such as Rainer Werner Fassbinder, Sam Shepard and Carlo Goldoni.

The Cinegrill (☎ 323-466-7000, 7000 Hollywood Blvd) Cover $10-25, plus 2-drink minimum. A fixture in the Hollywood Roosevelt Hotel since the 1920s, the Cinegrill's varied program ranges from impersonators to cabaret-style acts to readings to jazz concerts. The sprawling room lacks the historic feel permeating the rest of the hotel.

Gardenia Restaurant & Lounge (☎ 323-467-7444, 7066 Santa Monica Blvd) Cover $10, plus 2-drink minimum; open Mon-Sat. This is an intimate, no-nonsense space where you might catch Kurt Weill–type chanteuses, jazz musicians or straight cabaret. Expensive Italian-style food is also served.

West Hollywood (Map 10) As LA's creative hub of art and design, West Hollywood is also rich in live theater.

Coast Playhouse (☎ 323-650-8587, 8325 Santa Monica Blvd) This place attracts major actors from other cities and has maintained a fine reputation for putting on quality productions.

Celebration Theater (☎ 323-957-1884, 7051 Santa Monica Blvd) This 64-seater is among the nation's leading producers of gay and lesbian plays, winning 35 awards in 1996 alone. Its playbill includes both mainstream and provocative, cutting-edge experimental works.

Coronet Theatre (☎ 310-657-7377, 366 N La Cienega Blvd) Bertolt Brecht saw the premiere of his famous work Galileo here in 1947. Ever since, this small but illustrious venue has hosted a slew of 'pre-fame' actors as well as such big names as Richard Dreyfuss, Peter Falk and Gwyneth Paltrow. On some Monday nights, the theater also hosts free staged readings of new plays cooked up by the resident writers' workshop, Playwrights' Kitchen Ensemble (☎ 310-285-8148).

Tiffany Theater (☎ 310-289-2999, 8532 Sunset Blvd) In a former movie palace with a stunning lobby, the Tiffany consists of two state-of-the-art, 99-seat theaters. The schedule is heavy on fine stagings of works by accomplished young playwrights and premieres that often launch the careers of both writers and actors.

West Coast Ensemble (☎ 323-525-0022, 522 N La Brea Ave) An LA fixture for more than two decades, this professional ensemble puts on four main stage productions (one drama, comedy, musical and ethnic work each), as well as three smaller experimental plays per season. It has been repeatedly recognized by regional and national organizations.

Westside & Coastal Communities The **Cañon Theatre** (☎ 310-859-8001, 205 Cañon Dr, Beverly Hills; Map 11) Originally a movie house, this venue turned to theater in the late '70s and is usually booked for extended runs of productions like Love Letters by AR Gurney and The Vagina Monologues by Eve Ensler, which both featured rotating celebrity casts.

Geffen Playhouse (☎ 310-208-5454, 10886 Le Conte Ave, Westwood; Map 11) Affiliated with the UCLA School of Theater, Film & Television, this quaint brick building houses cutting-edge productions by leading American playwrights, including Pulitzer Prize–winner Margaret Edson.

Odyssey Theatre (☎ 310-477-2055, 2055 S Sepulveda Blvd, West LA; Map 13) The oldest and one of LA's most revered 99-seat theaters, the Odyssey puts on reliably excellent productions under the stewardship of artistic director Ron Sossi, who founded the company in 1969. It has three separate 99-seat theaters and specializes in innovative stagings of modern classics like Mamet's *Speed the Plow* and international works by Bertolt Brecht and others.

Highways Performance Space (☎ 310-453-1755, 1651 18th St, Santa Monica; Map 13) This is LA's only venue dedicated primarily to performance art, most of it by artists from under-represented segments of society, such as gay and lesbians, the physically challenged and those of non-European background. Events usually have a provocative, sometimes shocking, nature. Sir Ian McKellan and Annie Sprinkle are among the big names that have performed here, although the emphasis is on giving emerging artists a forum for expression.

Santa Monica Playhouse (☎ 310-394-9779, 1211 4th St, Santa Monica; Map 13) Comedies, musicals, dramas and even fairy tales are performed here, sometimes with a cast that includes major actors.

Pacific Resident Theatre (☎ 310-822-8392, 703 Venice Blvd, Venice; Map 13) This artistic laboratory is one of the most well-respected stages in the area. The varied menu ranges from lesser known works by famous playwrights (Maxim Gorky, Raymond Chandler, William Shakespeare) to new works by emerging talent.

Powerhouse Theater (☎ 310-396-3680, 3116 2nd St, Santa Monica; Map 13) Head here for new and avant-garde plays.

Beyond Baroque (☎ 310-822-3006, 681 Venice Blvd, Venice; Map 13) This literary arts center hosts a variety of readings that offer an excellent introduction to the diversity of voices that make up LA's cultural mosaic. Writers of all ages, ethnicities and socioeconomic backgrounds are featured here and at such satellite venues as Self-Help Graphics Gallery in East LA (see the Things to See & Do chapter) and World Stage in Leimert Park (see Jazz & Blues, later in this chapter).

Will Geer Theatricum Botanicum (☎ 310-455-3723, 1419 N Topanga Canyon Blvd; Map 2) Nestled in Topanga Canyon, this is a magical natural outdoor amphitheater, founded by – and named for – the man most remember as 'Grandpa Walton.' Throughout the summer, its resident professional acting company performs Shakespeare and more modern playwrights like Tennessee Williams or Thornton Wilder. Quality can be pretty hippy-dippy, though it's always fun to enjoy a performance shaded by sycamores.

The Valley The North Hollywood ('NoHo,' for short) Arts District brims with about 30 theaters, including this outstanding trio.

El Portal Center for the Arts (☎ 818-508-4200, 800-233-3123, 5269 Lankershim Blvd; Map 18) Built in 1926 in Spanish Renaissance Revival style, the El Portal was badly damaged during the 1994 Northridge earthquake but got a new lease on life in 2000 as an artistic complex with three theaters and an art gallery. The resident company is Actors Alley, which was founded in 1971 with Tyne Daly (currently starring in the TV drama *Judging Amy*) and David Soul as original cast members.

Deaf West Theatre (☎ 818-762-2773, 5112 Lankershim Blvd; Map 18) Bridging the gap between deaf and hearing-impaired artists and their audiences, Deaf West, founded in 1991, was the first professional sign language theater west of the Mississippi. Its repertory includes classic revivals, contemporary and original works, all performed in sign language with voice interpretation and/or super-titles.

Interact Theatre (☎ 818-773-7862, 5215 Bakman Ave; Map 18) This ensemble features about 50 actors, many with film, TV and national stage experience, in readings, workshops and full-scale productions that range from the new to the tried and true. Free readings take place on alternate Mondays.

A Noise Within (☎ 323-953-7795, 234 S Brand Blvd, Glendale; Map 3) 'Classical' has always equated with 'classy' at this respected theater inside a historic Masonic Temple. Founded by alumni of the American Conservatory Theater in San Francisco, the repertory ranges from Shakespeare to Calderón de la Barca to Noel Coward.

Getting Into a Studio

To see a particular TV star while in LA, your best bet is to watch a taping of his or her show. Doing so is easy, and tickets are free – but plan well ahead. The most coveted shows, such as *Friends*, are usually booked for months. The production season runs August to March and all shows have minimum age requirements (usually 16 or 18).

The easiest way to get tickets is through **Audiences Unlimited** (☎ 818-753-3483, 100 Universal City Plaza, Building 153, Universal City, CA 91608), which handles the distribution for some 30 shows, mostly sitcoms, including the popular *Friends* and *Spin City*. Tickets are available by phone 24 hours a day up to 30 days prior to the show's taping date. Using the Web site (www.tvtickets.com) is even more convenient as it allows you to specify a date, check ticket availability, reserve and even print out your own tickets.

The following studios also distribute tickets directly, either by phone, by mail or in person. When writing for tickets, specify your preferred date plus three alternate dates and the number of tickets; also enclose a self-addressed and stamped envelope.

Paramount Studios (☎ 323-956-5575 for recorded show schedule, ☎ 323-956-1777 for tickets, 860 N Gower St, Hollywood) This studio's crowd pleasers include *Becker*, *Frasier* and *Moesha*. Tickets are available five days before the show taping. Both general admission (first-come, first-served without seat guarantee) and a small number of reserved tickets are available. They are best obtained by phone but also available in person at the box office; hours are 8am-4pm weekdays.

NBC Television Studios (☎ 818-840-3537 for recorded information, 3000 W Alameda Ave, Burbank, CA 91523) Jay Leno's *Tonight Show* is the biggest draw and the only one handled directly by the studio box office. Tickets are available by mail (order at least six weeks in advance) and in person at the box office on a first-come, first-served basis starting at 8am on the day of the taping at 5pm. Tickets to NBC sitcoms are available through Audiences Unlimited (see above).

CBS Television City (☎ 323-575-2458, 7800 Beverly Blvd, LA, CA 90036) Game shows like *The Price Is Right* and *Hollywood Squares* and the sitcom *Just Shoot Me* tape here. Tickets are available by mail or in person at the box office on the Fairfax Ave side of the building from 9am-5pm weekdays.

Another way to see live filming is by obtaining a **shoot sheet**. This is a list detailing the locations where movies, TV programs, videos and commercials are being shot that day. It's available for free on the Internet at www.seeing-stars.com/ShootSheet or in person for a small fee from the Los Angeles Film & Video Permit Office (☎ 323-957-1000, 7083 Hollywood Blvd near Mann's Chinese Theater). The list does not reveal which actors are involved in the shoot or whether it's an indoor or outdoor shoot.

Pasadena Playhouse (☎ 626-356-7529, 39 S El Molino Ave, Pasadena; Map 17) One of LA's most popular venues, this theater has been in business since 1924. A major refurbishment in the '80s returned it to its former glory, and it has been a doing box-office business ever since. There are only 18 rows, so views are quite good from all seats. Performances are of high quality but mostly of the safe and crowd-pleasing variety.

Knightsbridge Theatre (☎ 626-440-0821, 35 S Raymond Ave, Pasadena; Map 17) This company is one of the most acclaimed little theaters in Los Angeles and has recently expanded operations to Silver Lake (☎ 626-440-0821, 1944 Riverside Dr, Silver Lake; Map 3). The company's ambitious schedule ranges from works by Oscar Wilde to Woody Allen, with three or four productions running concurrently.

COMEDY CLUBS

On any given night, comedy stars – some of them very famous – may be polishing their chops in one of LA's many comedy clubs. At the very least, you'll be treated to a hilarious evening with an up-and-coming comic – LA is where funny people come to make it big. Because most clubs are rather intimate, with a limited capacity, it's best to call ahead for a reservation. Most have a two-drink minimum in addition to the cover charge; unless otherwise mentioned, you must be 21 or older to be admitted to these clubs.

The greatest concentration of comedy clubs is in West Hollywood.

Groundlings Theater (☎ 323-934-9700, 7307 Melrose Ave; Map 10) Cover $12-18.50; all ages; open Thur-Sun. Best of the bunch is this improv school and company that's tickled people's funny bones for more than 20 years. Many of its graduates go on to careers on *Saturday Night Live, Mad TV* and the big screen, and its alumni include Lisa Kudrow, Pee-Wee Herman, Jon Lovitz, Phil Hartman and Julia Sweeney. Shows feature students, alumni, guests or a combination thereof. The theater foyer, usually open all day, every day, has a photographic who's who of current and past members (free).

The Improv (☎ 323-651-2583, 8162 Melrose Ave; Map 10) Cover $10-15. David Letterman and Billy Crystal got their starts at this legendary haunt. Nightly shows feature rising and established stars, including Latino and African American comics, with big name stars like Drew Carey or Chris Tucker popping in on occasion.

Laugh Factory (☎ 323-656-1336, 8001 Sunset Blvd; Map 10) Cover $10-12; ages 18 and over. This is a high-tech club that keeps cranking out mainstream comics and stand-up comedians. Jim Carrey, Ellen DeGeneres and Rodney Dangerfield are among those who have performed here. The owner, Jamie Masada, garners lots of press each year at Thanksgiving when he turns the club into a soup kitchen.

Comedy Store (☎ 323-656-6225, 8433 Sunset Blvd; Map 10) Cover up to $15.

David Letterman, Robin Williams and Roseanne Barr (as she then called herself) were relative unknowns when they first appeared here. Originally the club was called Ciro's and was a famous (and somewhat shady) hangout in the '40s and '50s. There are three separate rooms to showcase both young and established stand-up talent, with special nights devoted to ethnic groups and female comics.

Acme Comedy Theater (☎ 323-525-0202, 135 N La Brea Ave; Map 10) Cover $8-15. Small but choice, this venue is renowned for its offbeat sketch and improv comedy.

Bang Improv Studio (☎ 323-653-6886, 457 N Fairfax Ave; Map 10) Cover $5-10. You'll get lots of bang – and laughs – for your money at this pint-sized improv stage.

Comedy & Magic Club (☎ 310-372-1193, 1018 Hermosa Ave, Hermosa Beach; Map 14) Cover $10-20; ages 18 and over. Jay Leno makes regular Sunday night appearances to test out new material for the *Tonight Show*, and other big stand-up comedians like Jerry Seinfeld and George Carlin are occasional headliners. Leno's bandleader Kevin Eubanks also plays Sundays at the adjacent Lounge at the Beach.

Ice House (☎ 626-577-1894, 24 N Mentor Ave, Pasadena; Map 17) Cover $2.50-12.50. This place went through an earlier life as a pop and folk club before becoming one of LA's top comedy clubs. It attracts the major professional talents of today and the stars of tomorrow.

CLASSICAL MUSIC & OPERA

Dorothy Chandler Pavilion (☎ 213-972-0700, Music Center, 135 N Grand Ave, Downtown; Map 5) This is the main venue for highbrow music, home to the LA Philharmonic (until completion of the Walt Disney Hall; see the Things to See & Do chapter), the LA Opera and LA Master Chorale.

LA Philharmonic Orchestra (☎ 213-850-2000, www.laphil.org, Dorothy Chandler Pavilion, Music Center, 135 N Grand Ave, Downtown; Map 5) Admission $10-70. Since

ENTERTAINMENT

Outdoor Venues

Going to a concert at the **Hollywood Bowl** (☎ 323-850-2000; Map 9) is an experience that should not be missed. The music is just one reason to spend a tepid summer night in this historic outdoor amphitheater at 2301 N Highland Ave. Most concertgoers start off the evening with a picnic on the park-like grounds or in the bleachers before show time, and then relax beneath the starry skies to the sounds of Beethoven or Mozart with a glass of wine (bring your own). Carry along a pillow and blanket, as it can get a bit chilly. Bowl prices are most democratic, with tickets starting at just $1 on some nights. As the summer home of the LA Philharmonic and the Hollywood Bowl Orchestra, the program is heavy on symphonic crowd-pleasers, though jazz, mariachi music and pop concerts round out the schedule.

The **John Anson Ford Theatre** (☎ 323-461-3673; Map 9) is another historic outdoor venue near the Bowl at 2580 E Cahuenga Blvd. With 1200 seats it is comparatively intimate and no seat is more than 96 feet from the stage. It presents a far-ranging program of music, dance and family events from May to October, including the popular 'Summer Nights at the Ford' series.

The **Greek Theater** (☎ 323-665-1927; Map 8), in a natural bowl in Griffith Park at 2700 N Vermont Ave, opened in 1929 and seats more than 6000. Top rock and pop bands usually pass through here on their summer tours. Try to get seats close to the stage for better acoustics.

From July 4 to Labor Day (in early September), cheap concerts are held Sunday afternoons at the **Starlight Bowl** (☎ 818-238-5300; Map 2). This 7000-seat amphitheater is at 1249 Lockheed View Dr in Burbank. All musical tastes are covered, including rock, reggae, classical and big band.

1992, the orchestra has been under the stewardship of Esa-Pekka Salonen, a charismatic young Finn. He has enjoyed a loyal following despite insisting on programs that often focus on works by obscure composers, or obscure works by famous composers. The performing season runs October to May; the orchestra then moves to its summer home in the Hollywood Bowl (see the boxed text 'Outdoor Venues'). In 2003, the orchestra will move to the new Walt Disney Hall (see the Things to See & Do chapter).

LA Opera (☎ 213-972-8001, *Dorothy Chandler Pavilion, Music Center, 135 N Grand Ave, Downtown; Map 5*) Admission $28-148. LA has had its own opera since 1985 and in 2000, none other than one third of the Three Tenors, Plácido Domingo, came aboard as artistic director. The varied and high-caliber repertory includes popular operas like *Carmen* and the *Barber of Seville* but also less mainstream ones like *The Flying Dutchman* and *Werther*.

Los Angeles Master Chorale (☎ 800-787-5262, 213-626-0624, www.lamc.org, *Dorothy Chandler Pavilion, Music Center, 135 N Grand Ave, Downtown; Map 5*) The 120-voice chorus has been critically acclaimed. Founded in 1964, it presents stand-alone recitals and also serves as the chorus for the LA Philharmonic and the LA Opera.

Other notable classical groups include:

Los Angeles Chamber Orchestra (☎ 213-622-7001, ext 215) This orchestra performs at UCLA's Royce Hall and at the Alex Theater at 216 N Brand Blvd in Glendale. It specializes in a wide repertory of chamber music ranging from baroque and early classical works to 19th- and 20th-century compositions and contemporary works.

Da Camera Society (☎ 310-440-1351) This organization is dedicated to staging chamber concerts in historic venues, including the elegant Doheny Mansion in the West Adams district (see the Things to See & Do chapter).

DANCE

Dance doesn't nearly enjoy as great a following in LA as theater, and there are far fewer local companies. Historically, though,

LA has played an important role in modern dance, with Martha Graham, Alvin Ailey and Bella Lewitzky among those who got their start here. Groups tend to perform at different venues around town; check the listings in the local press. Companies to look out for include:

American Repertory Dance Company (☎ 323-664-0553, www.ardc-la.org) Founded in 1969, this is one of the oldest local dance companies. Artistic directors Janet Eilber and Bonnie Oda Homsey have made it their mission to keep alive the legacy of early 20th-century modern dance pioneers, including Martha Graham and Isadora Duncan. (Both trained and danced with the Martha Graham Company for several years.)

Avaz International Dance Theatre (☎ 323-663-2829) Since 1977, this company has been dedicated to preserving the heritage of Middle Eastern dances – from Greece to Uzbekistan. Founder and artistic director Anthony Shay puts on energetic and entertaining shows with dancers clad in flashy, colorful costumes.

Diavolo Dance Theatre (☎ 818-773-7454, www.diavolo.org) Fascinating, if slightly bizarre, this troupe practices a cutting-edge dance form called hyperdance, which sprang from the vision of company founder Jacques Heim in 1992. It involves dancers performing in custom-built spaces by literally slamming their bodies into walls, doors or objects. Its dramatic movement is filled with physical danger and often results in bruises, sprains and even the occasional broken bone. Diavolo has been critically acclaimed internationally and has a very loyal following.

Jazz Tap Ensemble (☎ 310-475-4412) As its name suggests, this ensemble hones the art of tap dancing, which it skillfully blends with jazz music. Performing locally, nationally, abroad and on celluloid for almost two decades, the permanent troupe – under the leadership of Lynn Dally – is often joined by such top tap talent as Jimmy Slyde.

Loretta Livingston & Dancers (☎ 213-627-4684, www.livingstondance.com) Another LA jewel, this modern dance company is led by Loretta herself, who danced with the now-retired Bella Lewitzky for 10 years. She stages innovative, avant-garde programs.

Lula Washington Dance Theater (☎ 323-936-6591, www.lulawashington.com) This is one of the premier African American dance companies on the West Coast. It has toured internationally and is known for its unique blend of African, modern and jazz techniques, as well as performance art and humor.

CLUBS

LA's club scene is one of the liveliest in the country and caters to everyone's tastes and expectations, from pale-faced college-age ravers to designer-chic yuppies and ex-hippie baby boomers. No 20th-century era is off-limits these days, be it '20s jazz, '30s and '40s big band swing, '50s rockabilly, '60s rock 'n' roll, '70s disco, '80s punk and new wave, or the techno, house, gothic, industrial, hip hop, trip hop, trance, etc, sounds of today. Unless mentioned otherwise, you have to be 21 or over to be admitted to any of these clubs. As everywhere, the scene changes constantly, so check the *LA Weekly* for up-to-date listings. Also look for free or discounted admission coupons in this newspaper.

Downtown (Map 5)

Al's Bar (☎ 213-625-9703, *305 S Hewitt St*) Cover $5, free Tues & Wed. From hippies to punks to goths, Al's has been a master of survival no matter what's been touted as the current hot trend. Dark, dank and divey, it's in the heart of Downtown LA's revitalized arts district – though the jury's still out on the artistic value of the post-atomic graffiti obliterating every square inch of wall space. Drinks are cheap ($2.50 for beer or wine), bands – usually several a night, unusually unsigned – are wild and edgy, and so is the audience. Wednesday is 'no talent night.'

Silver Lake (Map 9)

The Garage (☎ 323-662-6802, *4519 Santa Monica Blvd*) Cover up to $5. In a former garage that was also once a gay cowboy bar, this place looks like the headquarters of Silver Lake's self-styled grunge-meisters. Come here for bands that are provocatively bizarre and sometimes even talented.

ENTERTAINMENT

Spaceland *(☎ 323-661-4380, 1717 Silver Lake Blvd)* Cover $5-10, usually free on Mon. This is the epicenter of Silver Lake's underground rock scene and the best place to catch local bands hoping for a career breakout (Beck and The Eels played at this venue). Put on your thrift-shop finest and be sure to drop into the smoking lounge with its mind-bending satellite dishes.

Central Hollywood (Map 9)

Knitting Factory *(☎ 323-463-0204, 7021 Hollywood Blvd)* Cover $5-15; all ages. Tucked in the back of the garish Galaxy mall, this branch of the well-known New York club opened in Hollywood in late 2000, but the verdict is still out on how much of an impact it will make. The avant-garde lineup ranges from upwardly hopeful local bands to veteran musicians testing new material: Midget Handjob to Goo Goo Dolls. Headliners take the main stage, the rest make do with the intimate AlterKnit Lounge. The large bar has interactive computer terminals to play with if conversation with your date runs dry.

Blue *(☎ 323-462-7442, 1642 Las Palmas Ave)* Cover $5-10; ages 18 and over; closed Tues. Ensconced in the old Las Palmas Theatre, this nicely renovated venue draws a heavy goth crowd most nights and runs an after-hours club on Friday and Saturday. It has two rooms filled with black couches and booths for lounging. Music is strictly DJ and varies nightly with a mix of hip hop, techno, industrial and dark wave. It's unmarked; just look for the cobalt blue facade.

Arena *(☎ 323-462-0714, 6655 Santa Monica Blvd)* Cover $10-15; open Thur-Sun. A young and energetic crowd heats up this former ice factory. Themes vary nightly, from retro to house to hip hop to salsa. On Saturday, it's currently *the* gay Latino disco, in partnership with the adjacent Circus (see Gay & Lesbian Venues later this chapter).

Dragonfly *(☎ 323-466-6111, 6510 Santa Monica Blvd)* Cover $5-15. Easily recognized by the giant namesake painted on the outside wall, this hipster haven books mostly rock bands, although the occasional reggae or Latin band may make it into the mix. From Thursday to Saturday, DJs spin dance music after the bands leave. The patio is great for bumping into people.

Opium Den *(☎ 323-466-7800, 1608 Cosmo St)* Cover $4-10. Get your henna tattoo before lining up at this exotic slice of India right in the heart of Hollywood. Bands are mostly of the up-and-coming, homegrown variety, producing an ambience that's low in attitude but high in energy. Later on weekends, it turns into a dance club.

Goldfinger's *(☎ 323-962-2913, 6423 Yucca St)* Cover $3-5, cash only. Catering to hard-core clubbers, this raucous little joint offers live bands plus DJs on weekends, keeping the crowds grooving with a frenzied mix of funk, glam rock and techno. Its Liberace-style, over-the-top decor is a flashback to the Kennedy era. Don't miss the great martinis.

Vynyl *(☎ 323-465-7449, 1650 N Schrader Blvd)* Cover $10-20. Warehouse-sized, yet somehow intimate, this club opens up the stage for everyone from local garage rockers to on-the-verge-of-stardom acts. A comfy lounge gives way to the main stage flanked by raised seating and the main bar.

The Palace *(☎ 323-467-4571, 1735 N Vine St)* Cover $10-12; ages 18 and over. Opposite Capitol Records, this is a huge, glamorous Art Deco landmark dating to 1924. It has a 20,000-watt sound system and fits about 1500 people. Bands range from local and obscure to international and famous; on Friday and Saturday, the big dance floor sizzles with Top 40 dance tunes.

Fairfax District (Map 10)

Kibitz Room *(☎ 323-651-2030, 419 N Fairfax Ave)* No cover. Skip the matzo balls at next door Canter's, but check out the late night action at this compact lounge that spills over with adrenaline- (and who knows what else) powered hipsters with energy left to burn after the clubs close. The live menu includes cabaret, rock and the occasional blues jam.

Largo *(☎ 323-852-1073, 432 N Fairfax Ave)* Cover $2-12; all ages. Largo has garnered a soft spot among accomplished acoustic musicians and the audiences that

RICK GERHARTER

Boyle Heights, East LA

DAVID PEEVERS

Got junk? Melrose Ave

ROBERTO SONCIN GEROMETTA

Old-school rollerskating on Venice boardwalk

The famous and fashionable crossroads of Beverly Hills

Pasadena's domed City Hall

Couture capital, Via Rodeo

love them. The intimacy of the space (just 135 seats) is both a drawback (it's hard to get in) and an asset (once in, the concerts feel like private performances). Bookings occasionally include such big-name musical poets as Beck, Elvis Costello and Rickie Lee Jones.

Genghis Cohen (☎ 323-653-0640, 740 N Fairfax Ave) Cover varies; all ages. Skip the fairly pricey Chinese food and head straight to the mellow lounge that features performers nightly, many of them from the acoustic camp, delivering homegrown songs. Vonda Shepard, a friend of Michelle Pfeiffer and now of *Ally McBeal* fame, often played here before being hired by show creator (and Pfeiffer hubby) David Kelley.

West Hollywood (Map 10)

Coconut Teaszer (☎ 323-654-4773, 8117 W Sunset Blvd) Cover up to $12; ages 18 and over most nights. The 18-and-over policy definitely brings the median age down at this established club known mainly for its hard rock acts. Up to six bands heat up the stage nightly, most of them Hollywood stalwarts, with the occasional musical heavy hitter thrown in.

House of Blues (☎ 323-848-5100, 8430 W Sunset Blvd) Cover varies. The LA branch of the successful chain co-owned by Dan Aykroyd features the customary faux Mississippi Delta decor and so-so Southern food. An in-house store hawks logo merchandise, but the big name stars appearing onstage make up for such annoying commercial transgressions. Top talents of all stripes, not just the blues, come here, and shows often sell out. (See the Places to Eat chapter for the popular Sunday Gospel brunch.)

Viper Room (☎ 310-358-1880, 8852 W Sunset Blvd) Cover $10 and up. This small, ultra-hip hangout for musicians, celluloid celebs, hyper show-biz types and their hangers-on started out as the Melody Room mobster lounge in the 1940s (frequented by Bugsy Siegel and his cohorts). Now owned by Johnny Depp, the club gained notoriety once more in 1993 when 23-year-old actor River Phoenix died of a drug overdose outside the front door. Today, the Art Deco interior plays host to everyone from

up-and-comers to headliners. Sunday and Thursday are the best nights.

Whisky a Go Go (☎ 310-652-4202, 8901 W Sunset Blvd) Cover $10-15; all ages. Rock dominates at this fire-engine-red haunt whose continued popularity rides on the coattails of having been the place where Jim Morrison was discovered. The fine art of go-go dancing was allegedly invented here as well. These days, it schedules everybody from national circuit bands to upwardly hopeful locals.

Cat Club (☎ 310-657-0888, 8911 W Sunset Blvd) Cover $5-8. Next door, this unpretentious small club is owned by Slim Jim Phantom, formerly of the Stray Cats, and presents mostly multi-act lineups of solid rock 'n' roll. There's an upstairs lounge and patio for relaxing your ears in between sets.

Roxy (☎ 310-276-2222, 9009 W Sunset Blvd) Cover varies; ages 18 and over. A Sunset fixture since 1973, this venue often doubles as a launch pad for bands on the verge of stardom. Most nights, the lineup mixes local and national rock bands, but a big act like Neil Young or Bruce Springsteen also makes the occasional appearance.

Key Club (☎ 310-274-5800, 9039 W Sunset Blvd) Cover $10-30. This ultrachic club with galactic decor and a top-notch sound system is more memorable for its earlier incarnation as Gazzarri's, the club that launched the Doors and the Byrds. During the so-called 1966 Sunset Riots, it was one of the leading forces behind thwarting the city's attempt to close down all rock 'n' roll clubs. There's an eclectic schedule of live acts, followed by DJs and dancing on Friday and Saturday.

Doug Weston's Troubadour (☎ 310-276-6168, 9081 Santa Monica Blvd) Cover varies; all ages. The Troubadour has been an LA mainstay for more than 40 years, hosting a who's who of class acts, from Elton John to the Barenaked Ladies.

Club 7969 (☎ 323-654-0280, 7969 Santa Monica Blvd) Cover $6-10. This place attracts the more bizarre set of LA clubbers with different theme parties nightly. Whips and worse come out in the Fetish Room in back during the Saturday 'Sin-A-Matic' club.

ENTERTAINMENT

Drag parties, topless women dance revues, gothic balls and ladies-only male strip shows are also part of the no-holds-barred repertory.

Westside & Coastal Communities

The Mint (☎ 323-954-9630, 6010 W Pico Blvd, Mid-City; Map 2) Cover $5-10. The Mint has been dishing out live blues, rock and jazz to the faithful in a no-nonsense environment that's changed little since 1937. The acoustics are so good, they've even got a built-in studio for live recordings. Headliner stars (including, allegedly, the Rolling Stones) occasionally drop by to test out new material (they'll appear under a fictitious name to avoid getting mobbed).

The Gig (☎ 310-444-9870, 11637 W Pico Blvd, West LA; Map 13) Cover $5-10. This comfortable, neighborly place has staved off the influence of trends. Fluffy sofas, a mirrored disco ball and an aquarium make for relaxed decor, attracting an audience that's similarly laid back. Gigs run the gamut from reggae to blues to disco. It also has a satellite on Melrose Ave (☎ 323-936-4440, 7302 Melrose Ave; Map 10) Cover $5-10.

14 Below (☎ 310-451-5040, 1348 14th St, Santa Monica; Map 13) Cover up to $15. This locals' hangout has two bars and three rooms plus a fireplace in winter. Bands, mostly from around LA, cover the spectrum from alternative to reggae, rock to ska.

Temple Bar (☎ 310-393-6611, 1026 Wilshire Blvd, Santa Monica; Map 13) Cover $3-12. Popular if probably not worth a trip across town from, say, Hollywood, this Westside joint books bands nightly, most of them of the funk, hip hop and rock persuasion. There are deep booths and sofas to lounge in, a decent-sized dance floor and a solid menu of small dishes.

Rusty's Surf Ranch (☎ 310-393-7437, 256 Santa Monica Pier; Map 13) Cover varies. The Ranch, right on the pier, has nightly bands playing to a casual crowd of college kids and tourists. The phalanx of surfboards lining the walls and ceiling should help get you into the beach mood.

The West End (☎ 310-313-3293, 1301 5th St, Santa Monica; Map 13) Cover up to $10.

Emanating a distinct London vibe, this club attracts lots of expat Brits and other Euro types to its lively, party-like dance nights that cover the musical spectrum from disco to '80s flashbacks, hip hop, reggae and rock.

McCabe's Guitar Shop (☎ 310-828-4403, 3101 Pico Blvd, Santa Monica; Map 13) Cover $10-25; all ages. LA's longtime main folk venue is an intimate (some might say cluttered) room that puts you face to face with performers. Nearly everyone worth their salt in the genre – Joni Mitchell, John Lee Hooker, Dan Hicks and the Hot Licks, and Jackson Browne, among them – have made their way to this West Coast mecca of musicianship. You never know who will show up to join in on a set. The adjacent store sells the best in guitars and music books.

Lighthouse Cafe (☎ 310-372-6911, 30 Pier Ave, Hermosa Beach; Map 14) Cover up to $5. This timeless beachside mainstay is particularly strong on rock and blues. Originally a Chinese restaurant, it became a major jazz venue in the '50s and '60s.

Club Caprice (☎ 310-316-1700, 1700 Pacific Coast Hwy, Redondo Beach; Map 14) Cover usually $10-15; ages 18 and over. This is the top dance club in the South Bay, with big-name live acts most weekends. There is a two-drink minimum unless you're having dinner.

Club Cohiba (☎ 562-491-5220, 144 Pine Ave, Long Beach; Map 16) Above Mum's restaurant, this dance club has a martini lounge, a cigar sanctuary and billiard room.

JAZZ & BLUES
Leimert Park (Map 2)

Some of the best venues for catching established and up-and-coming jazz talent are in the Leimert Park Village, immediately north of the park itself, in the Crenshaw district.

World Stage (323-293-2451, 4344 Degnan Blvd) No cover Sun-Thur, $10 Fri & Sat. This no-nonsense space was under the stewardship of Billy Higgins, considered one of the leading drummers of progressive jazz, until his untimely death in May 2001. There's no food or drink, just good music from some of the finest jazz musicians around. The Thursday jam session has people grooving until 2am.

Fifth Street Dick's (☎ 323-296-3970, 3347 W 43rd Place) Cover varies. This hole-in-the-wall coffeehouse attracts a racially mixed crowd to its upstairs loft where the jazz house band holds forth. When it stops at 1am, more often than not a raw and raucous jam session starts up that can go on till the wee hours.

Babe & Ricky's (☎ 323-295-9112, 4339 Leimert Blvd) Cover up to $8. LA's oldest blues club is a slice of the American South and has been presided over by 'Mama' Laura Mae Gross for the past 36 years. Every night the darkish room, rimmed with burgundy booths and vintage guitars, is home to finger-lickin' barbecue ribs and chicken and top blues talent from around the city and beyond. The Monday night jam session often brings the house down.

Elsewhere in Los Angeles

Atlas Supper Club (☎ 213-380-8400, 3760 Wilshire Blvd; Map 7) Cover $5-10; open Tues-Sat. For time travel back to the 1930s, when men were suave in their tuxedos and women were called ladies and wore little black dresses, head to this Art Deco marvel at the historic Wiltern Theater. Live entertainment ranges from Latin rock and Creole jazz to funk, salsa and R&B, while dining takes place beneath a high, midnight-blue ceiling and lamps shaped like Zorro's mark. The menu (mains $12-24) covers the United Nations of culinary tastes – from pizza to Cajun crab cakes to paella – though results can be uneven.

Catalina Bar & Grill (☎ 323-466-2210, 1640 Cahuenga Blvd, Hollywood; Map 9) Cover $10-18; open Tues-Sun. This classic jazz venue is one of LA's finest and draws big name musicians of international stature, including Chick Corea and Branford Marsalis. A big poster of John Coltrane hangs on the off-pink walls next to the small stage. There is a two-drink minimum unless you're having dinner.

Lunaria (☎ 310-282-8870, 10351 Santa Monica Blvd, Century City; Map 11) Cover

$5-10, free Tues & Wed and with dinner; all ages. The elegant restaurant has a bar/lounge area that hums with classy, subdued jazz six nights a week.

Jazz Bakery (☎ 310-271-9039, 3233 Helms Ave, Culver City; Map 12) Cover $15-25, half-price student rush Sun-Thur; all ages. The warehouse-like setting inside a former bakery forms the perfect backdrop for serious performances by heavy hitters on tour mixed in with top-notch local talent. Charlie Haden, David Murray and Milt Jackson have all played here.

Harvelle's (☎ 310-395-1676, 1432 4th St, Santa Monica; Map 13) Cover varies. This hole-in-the-wall blues joint has delighted generations of music lovers since 1931. Accomplished local groups perform blues, R&B, funk and rock nightly.

Cafe Boogaloo (☎ 310-318-2324, 1238 Hermosa Ave, Hermosa Beach; Map 14) Cover up to $10. Live blues is featured at this relaxed joint, where you can also enjoy two dozen microbrews on tap and a Southern-influenced menu.

Blue Cafe (☎ 562-983-7111, 210 The Promenade, Long Beach; Map 16) Cover $5-10. Farther south, check out this raucous tavern with its huge sidewalk terrace. Live bands perform nightly and the owners are good at hauling in some pretty surprising talent. Bands also play Wednesday and Sunday afternoons, usually for free. Upstairs is a big billiard room.

The Valley

BB King's Blues Club (☎ 818-622-5464, Universal City Walk; Map 18) Cover varies. This club usually bustles with tourists expecting the quality of the club to match its legendary namesake. Depending on the act, this is not always the case, though the multilevel venue's Southern feel (also reflected in the menu) is not unattractive.

Baked Potato (☎ 818-980-1615, 3787 Cahuenga Blvd, North Hollywood; Map 18) Cover $10-12; all ages. This small place has been dishing out great jazz for about three decades, served alongside a 21-varieties menu of huge but somewhat overpriced spuds. There's a bigger but otherwise similar

ENTERTAINMENT

branch in Central Hollywood called **Baked Potato-Hollywood** (☎ 323-461-6400, 6266½ Sunset Blvd; Map 9).

La Vé Lee (☎ 818-980-8158, 12514 Ventura Blvd, Studio City; Map 2) Cover varies; all ages; open Tues-Sat. Latin, jazz and blues form the musical menu at this venue. La Vé Lee also serves pretty decent Mediterranean cooking.

SWING

The swing craze of the late '90s has died down a bit, allowing the real aficionados to take the dance floor back from those who only got briefly into the 'swing of things' after watching the movie *Swingers*. The two clubs listed here were there before, during and after the trend caught fire.

The Derby (☎ 323-663-8979, 4500 Los Feliz Blvd, Los Feliz; Map 9) Cover $5-10, includes free lesson (8pm-9pm). This classy club has been LA's 'swing central' since 1993 and was even featured in *Swingers*. Some of the best dancers in town jump 'n' jive around the pint-size dance floor, while stylish retro bands play on. Consider yourself lucky if you can snare one of the booths with purple velvet curtains. Food is provided by Louise's Trattoria next door.

Coconut Club (☎ 310-285-1358, 9876 Wilshire Blvd, Beverly Hills; Map 11) Cover $20; open from 7:30pm Fri & Sat. LA's most sophisticated swing nightclub is a ballroom-sized venue in the Beverly Hilton Hotel, with theatrical, yet classy, decor that makes you feel like you're in a pre-war movie. Watching sleek ladies with '40s-style hairdos and vintage dresses doing the lindy hop or jitterbug with suave zoot-suited guys is superb entertainment in itself, though the catchy tunes of the live orchestra will have you bustin' a move in no time. A small but exquisite supper menu complements a full bar. Seating is in sinuous booths or at cafe tables where you can order drinks or continental food from the small menu.

LATIN MUSIC

Salsa, merengue, flamenco, samba, marimba and other exotic rhythms – thanks to LA's sizable Latino population, Spanish roots and proximity to Mexico, fiery Latin sounds have sizzled here long before the Ricky Martin explosion. Also check out the Web site www.salsaweb.com for one-time events.

Mayan Theater (☎ 213-746-4287, 1038 S Hill St, Downtown; Map 5) Cover $15; open Fri & Sat. Many patrons of this established club live *la vida loca* on a daily basis and come here to kick back with authentic, fiery live salsa. The club is housed in a fantastic pre-Columbian-style ex-movie palace from 1927 where, rumor has it, Marilyn Monroe appeared as a stripper in 1948. If you're serious about salsa and merengue, this is *the* place to do it up and also to watch some beautiful dancers in action. It is extremely dressy – definitely don't wear jeans or sneakers. Admission for women is free before 10pm Friday; come for free salsa lessons 8pm-9pm.

El Floridita (☎ 323-871-8612, 1253 N Vine St, Hollywood; Map 9) Cover $10, no cover with dinner; open Mon, Wed, Fri & Sat; all ages. The original Floridita in Havana was Hemingway's favorite hangout and the Hollywood version is *the* place to go *cubano* in LA. Floor-to-ceiling mirrors may make the rhythmically challenged feel a tad self-conscious, but it's fun to just sit back and watch the sleek dancers jiggle every conceivable body part to the live music (or try a free lesson 8pm-9pm Monday.) The Monday night jams are legendary; make reservations at least a week in advance.

El Cid (☎ 323-668-0318, 4212 W Sunset Blvd, Hollywood; Map 9) Cover $9 without dinner, $26 for dinner and show; closed Mon & Tues. This is one of the best places in town to catch live flamenco. The rambling hillside hacienda actually began life in the 1920s as Hollywood's first sound stage for DW Griffith's movie studio. As a theater in the 1950s, it helped launch many acting careers, including Marlon Brando's. In 1961, in its third incarnation, it became a flamenco bar and restaurant drawing top singing and dancing talent from Spain, the US and other countries. Three flights of stairs lead down to an intimate room with tables set up before the stage, veiled by a lipstick-red velvet curtain. There's also an outdoor patio.

Rudolpho's *(☎ 323-669-1226, 2500 Riverside Dr, Silver Lake; Map 3)* Cover $7-8. Inside this ivy-draped brick building, salsa fever explodes on Monday and Wednesday with either live bands or DJs; the clientele is predominantly gay on the first and last Saturday of the month.

Conga Room *(☎ 323-549-9765, 5364 Wilshire Blvd, Miracle Mile District; Map 10)* Cover $10-20 general admission, $20-45 VIP admission (reserved tables with cocktail service); open Wed-Sat. Chic Westside folks who wouldn't dare go Downtown to the Mayan mix with upscale Latinos at this classy venue. A roster of celebs headed by Jimmy Smits and Jennifer Lopez co-owns this trendy club with the heady feel of pre-revolution Havana. Top acts like Ruben Gonzales and Albita hold forth in the 'sound-sational' ballroom where ladies in spiky heels and nattily dressed gents writhe to the beat. There's a tiny smoking patio and the glam La Boca restaurant to tank up on sustenance and rest weary feet.

Zabumba *(☎ 310-841-6525, 10717 Venice Blvd, Culver City; Map 12)* Cover $3-8; open Thur-Sat. Bossa nova, jazz, *axé*, samba, salsa – those are the rhythms that make this one of the hottest spots in town – especially during Carnival. It's popular with Brazilian ex-pats; authentic Brazilian food is served as well (mains $10-15).

COUNTRY & WESTERN

In fast-moving, urban LA, the country & western scene is suffering from an 'achy breaky heart' these days. Less than a handful of clubs remains in business, drawing a stalwart clientele that didn't move on to swing or salsa when the fad for line-dancing died down sometime in the early '90s. There's usually no cover and, with so little competition, a rollickin' good time can be had. Most places also offer free dance lessons.

Culver Saloon *(☎ 310-391-1519, 11513 Washington Blvd, Culver City; Map 12)* The

most central surviving club sports Western decor and a neighborly ambience that's more rural Montana than urban LA.

A couple more candidates are tucked away in the suburban sprawl of the San Fernando Valley.

The Cowboy Palace Saloon *(☎ 818-341-0166, 21635 Devonshire St, Chatsworth)* This is your quintessential honky-tonk: ten-gallon hats, finger-licking barbecues, line dancing and even horses hitched to the post outside. City slickers are welcome to make the journey to the northwestern San Fernando Valley. Yee-ha!

Crazy Jack's *(☎ 818-845-1121, 4311 W Magnolia Blvd, Burbank; Map 18)* This bar and restaurant is a local Burbank institution. The owner keeps unusual hours – 6:30am-2:30am – making it a popular hangout with the post-graveyard-shift of cops and studio employees.

BARS

No matter where you are in LA, you are never far from a bar. You have to be 21 or over to get in and may be asked to show ID to enter. Note that smoking is officially illegal inside California bars; some places, though, get around this ban by offering smoking patios or outdoor seating or, in a few rare cases, by blatantly ignoring the ban altogether.

Downtown (Map 5)

Hank's Bar *(☎ 213-623-7718, 838 S Grand Ave)* On the ground floor of the Stillwell Hotel, this classic tunnel-shaped watering hole is in dungeon-like darkness, making you feel like you're caught in a Raymond Chandler novel. Former LA Mayor Richard Riordan used to down screwdrivers here with his friend the bar owner, Hank Holzer, who died a few years ago.

Grand Avenue Bar *(☎ 213-612-1925, 506 S Grand Ave)* One of Downtown's most popular sports bars is on the ground floor of the swank Regal Biltmore Hotel. There's a free snack buffet weeknights. A more grown-up atmosphere reigns at the hotel's knockout ***Gallery Bar*** upstairs.

Top of Five (☎ 213-612-4743, 404 S Figueroa St) If you can ignore the dated decor and aren't fazed by the steep drinks prices, you may actually enjoy the eye-popping Downtown views from this rotating bar atop the Westin Bonaventure Hotel. The ride up here, aboard a glass bubble elevator, quite possibly provides the best kick.

Silver Lake (Map 9)

Good Luck Bar (☎ 323-666-3524, 1514 Hillhurst Ave) Behind the nondescript doors of

LA's Best Happy Hours

OK, these days it may not be politically correct to send anybody to a bar to booze up on cheap drinks during 'happy hour.' But fact is, LA has some of the best in the business and they're a gold mine not just for the imbibing crowd but also for the cash (and food) starved. All places listed here offer either free or heavily discounted goodies with which to sop up the alcohol to ensure you don't get wasted before sundown, naughty you.

Ciudad (445 S Figueroa St; Map 5) Come here for gourmet morsels at paupers' prices. The discounted *cuchifritos* (appetizers) are great and a couple of glasses of sangria ($2) will definitely have you happy in no time – at least from 3pm-7pm weekdays. (See also the Places to Eat chapter.)

McCormick's & Schmick (633 W 5th St; Map 5 and 206 N Rodeo Dr; Map 11) This serial fish house has won repeated votes for 'best happy hour.' Choose from around a dozen food items costing just $1.95 each and served 4pm-6:30pm weekdays. Selections vary by branch but may include quarter-pounder cheeseburgers, Caesar salad, ahi tuna carpaccio, chicken tacos or steamed black mussels. Maine lobsters weighing 1¼ pounds cost just $14.95. Drinks are full price.

Barefoot Café (8722 W 3rd St, Beverly Center District; Map 10) Rumor has it that the happy hour at this bustling bistro is a great place to meet docs and other medical staff from Cedars-Sinai Medical Center across the street. But even if you've said goodbye to the singles' scene, pop in for $3 glasses of wine, beer or liquor, $6 pizzas and discounted appetizers. It's on 4:30pm-7pm weekdays, with Thursday being one of the busiest nights. (See also the Places to Eat chapter.)

Cava (8384 W 3rd St, Beverly Center District; Map 10) During *hora feliz* (4:30pm-7pm weekdays) you get to sip exotic cocktails for $3 or put away the famous sangria for just $2. Enjoy free hors d'oeuvres or order the most popular tapas at bargain prices. There's even live entertainment on Thursday, Friday and Saturday nights.

Toppers (1111 2nd St; Map 13) The best happy hour on the Westside takes place on the top floor of Santa Monica's Radisson Huntley Hotel from 4:30pm-7:30pm daily. Come to this lively sports bar for ocean sunsets, $5.25 baby pitchers of margaritas (ask for them 'on the rocks') and a free buffet of nachos, pizzas, hot dogs, chili and rice and salads. (While here, women should check out the 'toilet-with-a-view.')

World Café (2820 Main St; Map 13) Starving pizza lovers should flock to this chic restaurant/bar to feast on wood-fired versions for free while sipping a beer, wine or cocktail in the lounge. Come between 5pm-7pm Tuesday to Friday.

this cultish watering hole opens up a Chinese fantasy world looking like it might have been an opium den in an earlier incarnation. The decor is all carmine red and paper lanterns add a touch of the exotic. The crowd's cool, the jukebox music loud and the drinks seductively strong (Yee Mee Loo Blue and a Chinese herb-based whisky are popular choices).

Tiki Ti *(☎ 323-669-9381, 4427 Sunset Blvd)* Sadly, owner Rae has passed away since the last edition of this book, but his spirit lives on in this garage-sized tropical tavern over which he presided for nearly 40 years. Order a Rae's Mistake, jostle up to the bar next to show-biz folks, blue-collar types and Silver Lake trendoids and ponder the wickedly wonderful collection of nautical kitsch and junk that makes up the surreal decor. Credit cards are not accepted and – damn the torpedoes! – smoking is permitted.

Dresden Room *(☎ 323-665-4294, 1760 N Vermont Ave)* This swank and old-timey place recaptured the spotlight for a couple of years after being featured in the 1996 movie *Swingers*. The campy singing duo of Marty & Elaine, a fixture since 1981, still croons on, but, alas, most of the fickle trend-mavens have moved on.

Central Hollywood (Map 9)

Beauty Bar *(☎ 323-464-7676, 1638 N Cahuenga Blvd)* This pint-sized cocktail bar gives new meaning to the word 'retro': it's entirely decorated with hair salon paraphernalia from the Kennedy era. Sip your martini while seated in swivel chairs beneath plastic hair dryers. On some nights, you can even get your nails done.

Daddy's *(☎ 323-463-7777, 1610 N Vine St)* Once your eyes have adjusted to the dimness, you'll discover a quintessential American cocktail lounge: chic yet simple and with understated decor. Sidle into one of their sensuous booths, order a martini and pretend you're Rita Hayworth or Cary Grant.

Formosa Cafe *(☎ 323-850-9050, 7156 Santa Monica Blvd)* Sop up some Hollywood nostalgia along with your cocktail at this onetime watering hole of Bogart,

Monroe and Gable. The walls of this dimly lit lounge are plastered with autographed celebrity photographs, most faded along with the fame of those pictured. Time has also worn out the carpets and the plastic booths (some are held together with duct tape), but a gritty charm survives, especially in the section built into a 1902 Big Red Streetcar. Smokers will appreciate the roof deck and patio. Mai tais and martinis are beverages of choice. Skip the food.

The Frolic Room *(☎ 323-462-5890, 6245 Hollywood Blvd)* This quintessential noir dive in the dark heart of Hollywood announces itself with a blazing neon sign. Vice still rules here, with everyone jostling up to the heavy bar and downing a few stiff ones while blatantly ignoring the smoking ban. Drinks are cheap, and there's a cool jukebox and a wall of Hirschfeld-style caricatures of Hollywood legends.

Lava Lounge *(☎ 323-876-6612, 1533 N La Brea Ave)* Cover about $5. Despite the name, you will not find any lava lamps in this trendy spot (but check out the 'lobster lamp'). A seductive tropical feel lingers in the cigarette-perfumed air, helped along by curvaceous booths, tiny tiki lamps, bamboo and palm fronds. Mostly local talent takes to the small stage, enlivening the place with everything from disco to soul, jazz to funk. To get that special Maui buzz, order a Blue Hawaiian ($8).

West Hollywood (Map 10)

The Sky Bar *(☎ 323-848-6025, 8440 Sunset Blvd)* A line of people from here to Timbuktu will tell you that you have arrived at LA's most exclusive bar, ensconced at the Mondrian Hotel. But, alas, you haven't truly 'arrived' unless your name is on the guest list. Should you make it inside, you'll see that the best thing is the poolside setting, even if the place itself is basically a shack and you'll be imbibing expensive drinks from plastic cups (because of the pool). Still, this is one of the choicest spots to indulge in big helpings of eye candy.

Whiskey Bar *(☎ 310-657-1337, 1200 N Alta Loma Rd)* At the Sunset Marquis Hotel is another über-chic lounge, co-owned, like the Sky Bar, by Rande Gerber, also known as 'Mr Cindy Crawford.' If you make it past the velvet rope, you may be sipping expensive drinks in the company of music industry heavyweights (U2, Beck) as well as A-list celluloid faces (Leo, Matt, Gwyneth).

El Coyote (☎ 323-939-2255, 7312 Beverly Blvd) This down-home cantina has a reputation for serving some of LA's worst Mexican food and stiffest margaritas, which provide a cheap buzz at just $3.50. The interior, featuring colored-glass lamps and large booths, is as dark as a Gothic cathedral, but there's also a courtyard.

Koreatown (Map 7)

The Prince (☎ 213-389-2007, 3198 W 7th St, Koreatown) Join 20-something Koreans and other hipsters at this campy 1940s hangout anchored by a big bar and rimmed by comfy booths. Bordello red is the color of choice, with everything (carpets, wallpaper, tablecloths and lampshades) all decked out in a seductive carmine. Come for a stiff one or even to sample the mysterious garlicky Korean concoctions emanating from the kitchen. Smoking is fine.

HMS Bounty (☎ 323-385-7275, 3357 Wilshire Blvd) A throwback to the era when the fancy Coconut Grove at the Ambassador Hotel across the street was in full swing, this barely-lit tavern now woos a new generation of scenesters with its retro Naugahyde booths and stiff drinks at wallet-friendly prices. After a few of those, the barmaids and the campy pseudo-nautical decor will seem a lot less bizarre.

Westside & Coastal Communities

Liquid Kitty (☎ 310-473-3707, 11780 Pico Blvd, West LA; Map 13) If you thought all the cool lounges were in Hollywood and Silver Lake, the 'Kitty' is here to prove you wrong. The neon martini sign announces you have arrived at one of the city's grooviest cocktail bars, with DJ-spun sounds and live jazz on Sunday (no cover). Order the namesake drink which is, shall we say, most memorable.

Harbor Room (☎ 310-821-6550, 195 Culver Blvd, Playa del Rey; Map 13) Near the beach, south of Venice, the Harbor Room legitimately calls itself the 'smallest bar in LA County.' When the local publicans gather here to drown their sorrows, you'll be lucky to elbow your way in. The crowd is friendly, crusty and as real as it gets, and it's been that way since 'sometime in the '50s,' according to imperfect local recollection.

Baja Sharkeez (☎ 310-545-6563, 3801 Highland Ave, Manhattan Beach; Map 14) This spit-and-sawdust cantina with its wild and wacky decor brings the Mexican beach party indoors. Different drink and food specials daily (like the Tuesday Taco-Margarita Madness with two-for-one tacos and $1.75 margaritas) draw in a young party crowd.

Aloha Sharkeez (☎ 310-374-7823, 52 Pier Ave, Hermosa Beach; Map 14) The party's even wilder at this related branch with a Hawaiian theme. Just remember: hang loose. Both branches also feature raucous happy hours weekdays 3pm-6:30pm.

Poopdeck (☎ 310-376-3223, 1272 Strand, Hermosa Beach; Map 14) This charmingly named bar is another sweaty and smelly watering hole with nightly drink specials and cheap beer. You may feel like you're crashing a frat party, but it's one of Hermosa's most revered boozing institutions.

Naja's Place (☎ 310-376-0466, 154 International Boardwalk, lower level 3, Redondo Beach; Map 14) Bars abound here at Fisherman's Wharf, including this funky rock 'n' roll bar and club with live bands and a small dance floor. The huge beer selection (777 selections, they say) is definitely the biggest draw.

Tony's Bar (☎ 310-376-6223, 210 Pier Plaza level, Redondo Beach; Map 14) For cocktails, head to the flying-saucer-shaped glasshouse which has landed right atop the 'old Tony's' restaurant (see the Places to Eat chapter). The bar and tables in this establishment haven't changed since a young Elvis topped the charts.

PUBS & MICROBREWERIES

LA pubs are popular with musicians of all stripes as well as the full range of scenesters, tourists and trendoids.

Cat & Fiddle Pub (☎ 323-468-3800, 6530 *Sunset Blvd, Hollywood; Map 9)* This sprawling affair has several rooms, but the nicest place to sip UK brews and surprisingly decent cocktails is the laid-back courtyard with a fountain and twinkle lights (smoking permitted). If you cherish having your personal space, don't come on weekends after 11pm.

Coach & Horses (☎ 323-876-6900, 7617 *Sunset Blvd, Hollywood; Map 9)* This is a half-pint-sized pub that's dark and divey and sometimes attracts a pretty rough crowd.

Coronet Pub (☎ 310-659-4583, 370 N La *Cienega Blvd, West Hollywood; Map 10)* This more civilized pub is popular with patrons of the nearby Coronet Theater.

Molly Malone's (☎ 310-578-5591, 575 *Fairfax Ave, Miracle Mile District; Map 10)* This comfortable Irish local watering hole also has the requisite Irish folk music most nights (cover up to $5).

Red Lion Tavern (☎ 323-662-5337, 2366 *Glendale Blvd, Silver Lake; Map 5)* For imported German brews on tap, head here. Choices include the popular pilsners Warsteiner and Dortmunder, and the Spaten Weissbier from Munich, all served by dirndl-clad waitresses. You may find yourself sharing the bar or table with expat Germans, downtown attorneys, Silver Lake grungemeisters and working class stiffs.

O'Brien's (☎ 310-829-5303, at Wilshire *Blvd & 23rd;* ☎ 310-396-4725, 2941 Main St, *Santa Monica; Map 13)* This comfortable Irish entry is popular with the college crowd and can get boisterous. There's a crowded smoking patio and a long bar where friends are made over a pint of Guinness.

Ye Olde King's Head (☎ 310-451-1402, 116 *Santa Monica Blvd, Santa Monica; Map 13)* Possibly the best English pub this side of the Thames, the lager flows profusely, and Cockney and Queen's English mix easily in a way they never would back home (see also the Places to Eat chapter).

Scruffy O'Shea's (☎ 310-821-0833, 822 *Washington Blvd, Venice; Map 13)* Farther south, this place is party central most nights, with a happening happy hour, English pub grub and live bands playing reggae, rock, salsa, swing and Irish music seven days a week.

Manhattan Beach Brewing Co (☎ 310-798-2744, 124 Manhattan Beach Blvd, Man-*hattan Beach; Map 14)* Shiny steel brewing vats line up like organ pipes behind the bar at this comfortable watering hole and favorite frat hangout. Simple but satisfying pub fare (pizza, burgers, pasta, salads) is washed down here with homemade brews.

Whale & Ale (☎ 310-832-0363, 327 W 7th *St, San Pedro; Map 15)* Heavy on polished brass, leather and oak, this British-style pub lays on the Victoriana pretty thick. It has friendly service and a decent selection of lagers, ales and stronger German-style beers. Alas, the food's British (need we say more?) and overpriced. Stick to the liquids. There's a happy hour with $3 drafts 3pm-6pm Monday to Friday.

Yard House (☎ 562-628-0455, 401 Shore-*line Village Dr, Long Beach; Map 16)* The bartenders here command an oval bar that looks like a spaceship helm. They serve some 250 beers on tap, connected to 5 miles of beer lines and 27 pumps. Serious boozers consume their brew from yards.

Gordon Biersch Brewery (☎ 626-449-0052, 41 Hugus Alley, off Colorado Blvd, *Pasadena; Map 17)* This ever-so-popular microbrewery (part of a chain) works with original German recipes, churning out respectable, smooth-tasting brews, including a crisp pilsner, the slightly sweet Märzen and the full-bodied Dunkles. They also serve mid-priced lunches and dinners daily.

COFFEEHOUSES

Major chains like Starbucks have insured that you'll never have to walk more than a couple of blocks for a jolt of java. Competing franchises in Hollywood include the Coffee Bean & Tea Leaf, Seattle's Best Coffee and Dietrich's, all of which serve up a whole slew of coffee concoctions from caffè latte to cappuccino to iced mocha to macchiato to – who knows what else. The following independent coffee and tea emporia offer a less corporate and more distinctive ambience.

ENTERTAINMENT

Central Hollywood (Map 9)

Highland Grounds (☎ 323-466-1507, 742 N Highland Ave) One of LA's oldest coffeehouses also has a menu with simple but superb food and even a liquor license, which helps draw people in. Seating for their varied entertainment, offered almost nightly ($2 cover), is inside, on the balcony or on the outdoor patio.

Bourgeois Pig (☎ 323-962-6366, 5931 Franklin Ave) Walk in here and you will soon lose any sense of whether it's day or night. Red plastic covers the large window, creating a perpetual netherworld with quasi-Gothic faux gold fixtures and black carpeting. Well-worn couches contrast with the bustling pool tables. Brad Pitt and Sandra Bullock have allegedly been spotted here (though not together).

West Hollywood (Map 10)

Insomnia Cafe (☎ 323-931-4943, 7286 Beverly Blvd) The ceiling of this cafe is as tall as its opening hours are long. After dark, wannabe writers with laptops give way to a flock of night owls in desperate need of stimuli. Hunker down at dark wooden tables or, better yet, grab the coveted cushiony sofas neatly tucked away in a private alcove.

Doughboys (☎ 323-651-4202, 8136 W 3rd St) This closet-sized cafe and bakery also serves yummy breakfasts all day (see the Places to Eat chapter).

Urth Caffe (☎ 310-659-0628, 8565 Melrose Ave) At Urth, everything down to the curtains is organic, which makes it popular with New Agers and the karmically correct. Tables inside and on the nice terrace, which spills out onto the sidewalk, are packed at all hours. For sustenance, there are salads and sandwiches ($7-11).

Santa Monica & Venice (Map 13)

Anastasia's Asylum (☎ 310-394-7113, 1028 Wilshire Blvd) An eclectic crowd of writers, grannies, working stiffs and bohemians all seem to feel at home in this cafe with its velvet couches, bistro tables and sunset-colored walls. The counter crew makes strong coffee and sells baked goods and a full vegetarian menu. You'll also be serenaded nightly with acoustic music from the loft stage.

Novel Cafe (☎ 310-396-8566, 212 Pier Ave) Bohemianism is alive and well at this unpretentious cafe with its cozy couches, book-lined walls, snug corners and friendly staff. The people next to you may be discussing the merits of the latest Tom Wolfe novel, pecking away on a laptop, reading or practicing their foreign language skills.

Abbot's Habit (☎ 310-399-1171, 1401 Abbot Kinney Blvd) This corner cafe serves hot latte by the gallon alongside scones, muffins and sticky caramel buns. It also has healthy, freshly prepared sandwiches for $6 and bagels with cream cheese for $1.50.

The Valley

Lulu's Beehive (☎ 818-986-2233, 13203 Ventura Blvd; Map 2) Lulu's is cult in the Valley, especially on Friday nights when Midnight Comedy Hour comes on (at 11pm, actually). A home away from home for local hipsters, there's great music too.

Eagles Coffee Pub (☎ 818-760-4212, 5231 Lankershim Blvd, North Hollywood; Map 18) Ideas and creativity have been brewing at the Eagles along with the coffee for more than a decade. Originally an artists' hangout, this pub has changed its stripes over the years and is now more of a neighborhood bar, coffeehouse and live music venue.

Equator Coffeehouse (☎ 626-564-8656, 22 Mills Place, Pasadena; Map 17) Tucked away in an alley, this comfy and cozy cafe serves its high-octane brews in a historic carriage repair shop filled with plump armchairs. It offers 10 minutes of free Internet access with purchase (otherwise it's

$3.50/hour), karaoke on Friday nights and bands all other nights except Sunday. Inexpensive pastries, sandwiches and salads are served as well.

GAY & LESBIAN VENUES

West Hollywood (WeHo) is the heart of LA's gay and lesbian scene, and there's practically 24/7 action in the bars, restaurants, clubs, coffeehouses and gyms along Santa Monica Blvd. Most cater primarily to gay men, though there are a few for lesbian and mixed audiences. Beauty reigns supreme in 'Boys' Town' and the intimidation factor can be high unless you're buff, bronzed and styled. Silver Lake is cruising heaven for the Levi's and leather crowd and also has a few Latino bars. The beach towns have more relaxed, neighborly scenes, while venues in the San Fernando Valley are generally more mundane and mainstream. For updates and specifics about the various scenes, check out the free gay and lesbian magazines available in bars, restaurants and gay-friendly establishments.

Dance Clubs & Bars

West Hollywood (Map 10) *The Factory/ Ultra Suede* (☎ 877-447-5252 hot line, ☎ 323-659-4551 direct line, 652 La Peer Dr & 661 N Robertson Blvd) Cover varies; open Wed, Fri & Sat. This chic twin disco in the former Axis/Love Lounge space is the largest dance club in WeHo. It's got an edgy New York feel and is gay, lesbian, straight or mixed, depending on the night's theme. The music is mostly techno, top 40 remixes and '80s. It also hosts clubs like 'Girl Bar,' a popular lesbian club, and 'Buddha Lounge,' which draws gay Asian Americans.

Rage (☎ 310-652-7055, 8911 Santa Monica Blvd) This two-story bar and dance club for men sparkles after a recent makeover. The crowd and music change nightly, but a high energy buzz keeps things interesting despite attitudinous service and high prices.

The Palms (☎ 310-652-6188 hotline, 310-652-1595 direct line, 8572 Santa Monica Blvd) The oldest lesbian bar and party venue in WeHo, the schedule here changes

constantly and may include karaoke, live bands, theme parties and salsa nights.

Micky's (☎ 310-657-1176, 8857 Santa Monica Blvd) It's 'raining men' at this posing, preening and cruising club where nonstop high-energy dance music creates an electric party atmosphere. Go-go boys further heat up the ambience. There's also free food during happy hour.

The Abbey (☎ 310-289-8410, 692 N Robertson Blvd) This was once WeHo's coffeehouse of record, but now it is Boys' Town's most fashionable bar, where you and your friends can sip flavored martinis on a divan in your own private booth. It also serves pretty decent food (see the Places to Eat chapter).

Mother Lode (☎ 310-659-9700, 8944 Santa Monica Blvd) Less pretentious types might prefer this large but neighborly bar with gold-rush inspired decor. Check out its cocktail hour specials and Sunday beer parties.

Revolver (☎ 310-659-8851, 8851 Santa Monica Blvd) This is a stylish video bar with music, film and comedy clips playing continuously to a handsome crowd. It's mostly gay men, but women won't feel uncomfortable. During Monday karaoke nights, you can hear off-work professional singers give free performances.

Trunks (☎ 310-652-1015, 8809 Santa Monica Blvd) More mature men gravitate toward this sociable sports bar with pool tables.

Benvenuto (☎ 310-659-8635, 8512 Santa Monica Blvd) Open 10:30pm-3am Wed-Sat. Tiny space, cool bartenders and good drinks equals lots of fun for the lesbians and occasional gay man hanging out here. The Italian food served in the mixed restaurant below is pretty good too.

Hollywood (Map 9) *Circus* (☎ 323-462-1291, 6655 Santa Monica Blvd) Cover $5-15. This club (mostly men) is big on dance music and has a huge patio. It goes mixed on Saturday when it draws a roster of international DJs.

Tempo (☎ 323-466-1094, 5520 Santa Monica Blvd) Wedged into a nondescript mini-mall in a *muy latino* neighborhood in eastern Hollywood near Western Ave is this dance club. The crowd's friendly and blue collar and enthusiastic about the twice nightly drag shows of serious pro caliber. On weekends, you may be serenaded by live mariachi, *banda* or *norteña* bands.

Faultline (☎ 323-660-0889, *4216 Melrose Ave, Hollywood*) Open 4pm-2am Tues-Sun. This is a cavernous joint with dark corners and a cruisey ambience: the leather and Levi's scene predominates. There are four bars and a patio with a fire pit.

Silver Lake (Map 9) *Dragstrip 66 @ Rudolpho's* (☎ 323-969-2596, *2500 Riverside Dr, Silver Lake; Map 3*) Cover $10-15. On the second Saturday of the month, eyelashes the size of tarantula legs, stiletto heels the size of miniature coffins and platinum wigs the size of beehives rule at this 'mother' of all drag clubs. The theme changes monthly (eg Trailer Trash, Catholic Schoolgirl) and the music ranges from '70s to metal, so call ahead for the scoop. Non-drag queens make up the majority of patrons but pay more to enter. By day, and most nights, this is a Mexican restaurant. (See also Latin Music earlier in this chapter.)

Cuffs (☎ 323-660-2649, *1941 Hyperion Ave*) A no-frills, no-nonsense bar for the hardcore leather crowd that can get pretty intense at times. Leave your shyness at the door.

Akbar (☎ 323-665-6810, *4356 W Sunset Blvd*) This neighborhood nook is trendy sans the attitude. It's hot with laid-back gay men and straight women who come for cocktails, conversation and jukebox music. Complexion-friendly candlelight, Moorish arches and dangling cylindrical wicker lamps add a touch of the exotic. Smoking is tolerated.

Gauntlet II (☎ 323-669-9472, *4219 Santa Monica Blvd*) This is a sexy pick-up joint for the tattoo, uniform and leather set and hosts infamous underwear party contests on Thursday.

Elsewhere in Los Angeles *Roosterfish* (☎ 310-392-2123, *1301 Abbot Kinney Blvd, Venice; Map 13*) Check out this low-key

hangout where you can strike up new friendships while playing pool, shooting electronic darts or nursing your drink. There's a fun jukebox and patio as well and things get really crowded on Friday nights.

The Study (☎ 323-464-9551, *1723 N Western Ave; Map 9*) Friday and Saturday are happening but Sunday nights are the hottest at this cozy bar popular with African American men. There are pool tables, video games and even a fireplace encircled by seats for making friends.

Que Sera (☎ 562-599-6170, *1923 E 7th St, Long Beach; Map 4*) Melissa Etheridge devotees may want to make a pilgrimage to this Long Beach landmark where the rock star once played acoustic solo sets. No longer exclusively a lesbian lounge, its red and black boudoir decor now brings in a broader crowd for drink specials, DJ-spun techno or even the occasional alternative rock band.

The Silver Fox (☎ 562-439-6343, *411 Redondo Ave, Long Beach; Map 4*) Long Beach's oldest video bar has more than two decades to its credit. The arsenal of more than 7000 music and comedy videos is a major draw, but so is the eccentric and fun decor, the friendly vibe and the cute staff. It's mostly for gay men, although lesbians and some heteros also find their way here. Those on a budget should come on Monday for the all-night happy hour.

Rumors (☎ 818-506-9651, *10622 Magnolia Blvd, North Hollywood; Map 18*) Lesbian-owned and operated, this gossipy neighborhood joint offers drinks specials plus dancing, darts, pool, karaoke and other entertainment.

Coffeehouses

WeHo Lounge (☎ 310-659-6180, *8861 Santa Monica Blvd; Map 10*) You'll find this an easy-going java joint with sofas, sidewalk seating and Internet access. It's also a community center and offers HIV testing, free condoms, education forum and support groups.

City Bean (☎ 323-848-8500, *8457 Santa Monica Blvd; Map 10*) Not exclusively a gay hangout, this is noted for micro-roasting its

25 bean varieties and for dishing out pretty good desserts.

SPECTATOR SPORTS

Los Angeles has an on-again, off-again love affair with its sports teams – the action heats up when they're winning, but drops off the radar when teams are merely mortal. Still without a professional football team, the city nonetheless has other teams with power, pride and traditions that – when they are playing at the top of their games – are well worth the price of admission.

Baseball

By all accounts, the history of baseball in LA *is* the Dodgers, at least ever since they moved here from Brooklyn in 1958. The team plays April to October at **Dodger Stadium** (☎ 323-224-1500, www.dodgers.com, 1000 Elysian Park Ave; Map 5). Tickets are usually available at the box office on game day and typically cost $6-17 adults, $4 children 4-12. (For information about the team's history, see the Things to See & Do chapter.)

Basketball

Los Angeles Lakers The Lakers came to LA from Minneapolis in 1960, and with players like Jerry West, Wilt Chamberlain, Kareem Abdul-Jabbar and Magic Johnson, the team pretty much set the standard for excitement in the 'round-ball' game. It was a non-sports episode, though, that brought the Lakers to the attention of the world. When Earvin 'Magic' Johnson announced that he had tested positive for HIV, it was a turning point, both for athletes and the fans.

For the 1996 season, the Lakers acquired another superstar: Shaquille O'Neal. From 1997–98, Shaq was a close second in scoring to the now-retired Michael Jordan of the Chicago Bulls. Under the stewardship of former Bulls coach Phil Jackson, and after signing the talented Kobe

Bryant, the Lakers recaptured the NBA Championship in 2000. In the ensuing season, though, a petty rivalry between O'Neal and Bryant, the two most highly paid players, weakened the team. Both have been trash-talking each other and acting like kids in a sandlot game. Fans and even Jackson have grown tired of this squabbling and at the time of writing it looked as if – at season's end – one of these colossal 'children' may well be playing for another team.

This rivalry, however, did not prevent them from winning the championship in 2001 and inspiring hopes of a 'three-peat' the following year.

The Lakers play at the **Staples Center** (☎ 800-525-3775 information, ☎ 213-742-7340 box office, 1111 S Figueroa St; Map 5). Tickets ($21-160) are hard to come by and mostly sold through Ticketmaster (see Buying Tickets earlier in this chapter), although a few may also be available at the box office.

Los Angeles Clippers The city's second – and secondary – men's basketball team also plays at the **Staples Center** (☎ 213-742-7500/55 information, ☎ 213-742-7340 box office, 1111 S Figueroa St; Map 5). Tickets are $10-85 and available through Ticketmaster or the Staples Center box office.

Los Angeles Sparks The LA Sparks is the city's women's basketball team, which, in the 2000 season, had three all-star players and made it to the semi-finals. It also plays at the **Staples Center** (☎ 877-447-7275 information, ☎ 213-742-7340 box office, 1111 S Figueroa St; Map 5). Tickets are customarily $5-35 and are available from Ticketmaster and at the box office. The season starts in June and ends in August.

Magic Johnson

ENTERTAINMENT

UCLA Bruins UCLA's basketball team, the Bruins, is one of the best college teams in the US. The team have racked up 11 men's basketball championships, and during the 1971–74 seasons went an astonishing 88 games without defeat. UCLA has appeared on the cover of *Sports Illustrated* 91 times, represented by the likes of Kareem Abdul-Jabbar, who after starring for the Bruins went on to become the only man to win six MVP Awards in the NBA (National Basketball Association). The team plays on the UCLA campus in ***Pauley Pavilion*** (☎ 310-825-2101 *box office; Map 11*). Tickets are $17-35.

Football
Los Angeles no longer has a professional football team, but the USC Trojans and UCLA Bruins compete in the Pacific 10 (Pac-10) Conference for the right to play in Pasadena's Rose Bowl game on January 1. The Bruins also play their regular games at the ***Rose Bowl*** (☎ 310-825-2101, *1001 Rose Bowl Dr; Map 17*) . Tickets are $12-15 for adults, $4 children. The Trojans play at the ***LA Coliseum*** (☎ 213-640-4672, *3911 S Figueroa St; Map 6*). Tickets are $27-50.

Soccer
It may be a cold day in hell before Major League Soccer catches fire in this country, but that's not stopping the LA Galaxy from putting on an impressive show since their 1995 launch. By winning 12 consecutive games their first year out, they announced that they would be a team to be reckoned with and in 2000, they advanced as far as the semi-finals. Games are played at the ***Rose Bowl*** (☎ 626-535-8300 *or* ☎ 877-342-5299 *for tickets and information, 1001 Rose Bowl Dr, Pasadena; Map 17*). Tickets are $12-22 and with nearly 100,000 available seats, getting one is never a problem.

Hockey
The LA Kings play in the National Hockey League and with no moderate success. Although the glory days of the 'Great Gretzky,' who took the team to the Stanley Cup Finals in 1993, are over, new star player Ziggy Palffy has helped put the team in the playoff hunt in the 2000–01 season. The LA Kings play at the ***Staples Center*** (☎ 213-742-7100 *or* 888-546-4752 *information,* ☎ 213-742-7340 *box office, 1111 S Figueroa St; Map 5*) with tickets costing $19.50-100 and available through Ticketmaster or at the box office. The season runs October-April.

Horse Racing
Santa Anita Racetrack (☎ 626-574-7223, *www.santaanita.com, 285 W Huntington Dr, Arcadia, Map 3*) Horse racing enthusiasts consider this one of the best tracks in America. Thoroughbred season runs from the day after Christmas to April 16 and from late September to early November. Admission is $5 for adults, free for children under 18 if accompanied by an adult.

Hollywood Park Race Track (☎ 310-419-1500, *www.hollywoodpark.com, 1050 S Prairie St, Inglewood; Map 2*) Live racing season is from April to July, while the Fall Meeting is from November to December. There's also a casino next door where you can play cards and bingo and wager on races at other tracks. Admission is $7 (includes parking and program) for adults, free for children under 18.

Shopping

Shopping in LA does not mean spending huge amounts of money. You'll find everything from $1 vintage sweaters at flea markets to walnut-sized diamonds on Rodeo Dr. Shopping here can be as adventurous as you want it to be. To be sure, 'Gapification' (the proliferation of retail chains like the Gap, Banana Republic, Pottery Barn and others) is widespread and malls abound, but countless offbeat shops in LA's many distinct neighborhoods will reward those with a knack for browsing and a flair for the unusual.

WHERE TO SHOP

Most Angelenos do their serious shopping in multi-story malls, some with upwards of 200 stores in a single building. But when they want to take a less frantic approach to shopping, locals head for a handful of streets where the people-watching is as much fun as the window browsing.

Shopping Districts

There are several areas to come for 21st-century funk and cutting-edge designs. **Melrose Ave** between La Brea and Fairfax Aves has a great concentration of quirky and hip boutiques. Silver Lake and Los Feliz have a flurry of funky club-wear stores as well as thrift and vintage clothing shops. Check out **Los Feliz Village** along Vermont Ave as well as the 3000 and 4000 blocks of **Sunset Blvd**.

On N Robertson Blvd between Beverly Dr and W 3rd St in the **Beverly Center District** are the boutiques of young upscale designers. Farther north near Robertson Blvd's intersection with Melrose Ave, you'll find LA's center for design, with furniture and accessory stores abundant. Also check out **La Brea Blvd** in Hollywood.

In Beverly Hills, **Rodeo Dr** is known the world over for its up-up-upscale designer boutiques and jewelry stores, art galleries and antique shops. Start at the Two Rodeo Dr complex on Wilshire Blvd opposite the Regent Beverly Wilshire Hotel; from there, follow Rodeo north for three blocks. One block east of Rodeo, Beverly Dr is home to the mainstream retail stores.

Santa Monica's **Third Street Promenade** is a pedestrian mall anchored by the Frank Gehry–designed Santa Monica Place mall on Broadway. Street musicians, not to mention Hollywood entertainment scouts, keep this strip busy day and night. This is where you will find a Disney store, mainstream fashions at Gap and Banana Republic, novelties and casual clothing at Urban Outfitters, funky fashions at NaNa and much more. Other good shopping streets in Santa Monica are **Main St**, for galleries, furnishings and fashions, and tony **Montana Ave** for one-of-a-kind clothing boutiques, specialty gifts and knickknacks for the home.

Cheap and crazy goodies are what you'll find along the **Ocean Front Walk** in Venice Beach. Especially on weekend afternoons, ambulatory vendors display their wares on the ocean side of this beachfront promenade; permanent shops and cafes line the city side. Need a silk Italian tie or a velvet hat to rival the Mad Hatter's? A bronze dancing Shiva icon or a bronze cowbell from Switzerland? A spiked leather hat for your dog or a spiked leather bikini for your sister (or vice versa)? Whatever it is, this is where you'll find it.

Gentrified **Colorado Blvd** in Old Pasadena has plenty of bookstores, boutiques, houseware and specialty stores.

Highlights include Sur La Table cookware, Restoration Hardware home furnishings, Crate & Barrel home accessories and a huge Barnes & Noble bookstore. Also in Pasadena is **South Lake Ave**, notable for its London-style shopping arcades.

Broadway, **Olvera St** in Downtown and **El Mercado** in East LA are good places to find Mexican handcrafted leather and handwoven clothing as well as children's toys and piñatas. **Chinatown** has many shops selling imported porcelain, furniture and silk clothing, as well as chopsticks and soapstone Buddhas. Little Tokyo's main shopping center is the **Japanese Village Plaza**, a 40-shop pedestrian lane that winds between 1st and 2nd Sts. Look for imported kimonos and books, origami art and fine spun pottery. For African art – masks, sculptures, paintings and crafts – head to **Degnan Ave** in Leimert Village.

Fanciful **Universal City Walk** in Universal City has about 40 shops, restaurants and entertainment venues. Check out Adobe Road, which sells Native American crafts; the Nature Company, where a walk through a simulated rain forest inspires purchases of eco-sensitive gifts; or Things From Another World, for science-fiction lovers.

Fashion District

Bargain shoppers from throughout the city flock to this frantic warren of fashion in southwestern Downtown every day of the week. The district is subdivided into several distinct retail areas. Stores specializing in women's wear can be found on Los Angeles St between Olympic and Pico Blvds and along 11th St between Los Angeles and San Julian Sts. Men's wear stores are concentrated along Los Angeles St between 7th and 9th Sts and 14th and 16th Sts. For fabrics, beads and crafts supplies head to 9th St between Los Angeles and San Pedro Sts and Wall St between 8th St and Olympic Blvd. Children's clothing is sold on Wall St between 12th St and Pico Blvd. Jewelry and accessory stores cluster along Santee St between Olympic Blvd and 11th St. *Art Box* (☎ 213-746-7929, 1017 S Santee St; Map 5) has some of the best prices and styles.

Those with a knack for haggling should head to Santee Alley, just east of Santee St between Olympic Blvd and 12th St, where knockoff Calvin Klein and Tommy Hilfiger sweat suits go for around $20 and faux Kate Spade handbags command between $15-25. This is also the place for bargains on leather jackets, cosmetics, toys, underwear and more.

The *Cooper Building* (☎ 213-627-3754, 860 S Los Angeles St; Map 5) was California's first outlet store and has two crammed floors of boutiques, many with changing rooms.

Shopping in this 56-block bazaar of bargains can be a lot of fun but it helps to know the rules. Shops with signs reading 'Wholesale Only' or *'Mayoreo'* are off-limits to the public. Leave your credit cards at home because most vendors will only accept cash. Haggling is OK, but don't expect to get more than 10% or 20% off. There are usually no refunds or exchanges, so choose carefully and make sure the item is in good condition (many items sold here are 'seconds,' meaning they're slightly flawed). Most stores don't have dressing rooms. You can sometimes get around this by wearing an outfit conducive to trying on garments while ducking behind a rack of clothing. Stores are usually open 10am-5pm Monday to Saturday, to 4pm on Sunday.

For an overview, take a free guided bus tour, departing at 10am, 11am and noon on the last Saturday of every month from the California Mart on Olympic Blvd between Main and Los Angeles Sts. Call ☎ 213-488-1153 for reservations.

The Things to See & Do chapter has more information on the Fashion District.

Shopping Malls

Nothing defines shopping in LA more than the mall, a Southern California invention resulting from reliance on the car. Much more than a place to shop, malls define and reflect the culture of vanity and commercialism so prevalent here. The mall is a home away from home, a safe haven where meeting friends and having a cappuccino is as much part of the itinerary as browsing the sales racks at Bloomingdale's. Movies have been made about this phenomenon, including *Scenes from a Mall* and *Mall Rats*. Frank and Moon Zappa's song *Valley Girl* was inspired by the Sherman Oaks Galleria. (In a bizarre twist, this prototypical mall was forced to close in 1999 for lack of customers; it is being converted into a business center.) Nevertheless LA malls are surprisingly different and are actually fun and convenient places to shop.

7+Fig (☎ 213-955-7150, 735 S Figueroa St, Downtown; Map 5) Open 10am-7pm Mon-Fri, 10am-6pm Sat, noon-5pm Sun (selected stores). The unique architecture of this mall is at least as eye-catching as the window displays of its 50 stores. Descending three floors beneath street level, it's built around a circular atrium and is open to the sky. A profusion of flowers, iron grillwork stairs and a bird-cage elevator are among the creative flourishes.

The Beverly Center (☎ 310-854-0070, 8500 Beverly Blvd at La Cienega; Map 5) Open 10am-9pm Mon-Fri, 10am-8pm Sat, 11am-6pm Sun. This is the mall where you're most likely to spot a celebrity trying on shoes at Charles David or buying a skimpy dress at Betsey Johnson. Those not born to shop might find this huge place a bit overwhelming; there are about 160 upscale shops (anchored by Bloomingdale's and Macy's), a Warner Brothers Studio store and about 25 men's clothing stores. The food court is quite a disappointment, though the 13 cinemas on the 8th floor are not. The first five levels of this bunker-like building are reserved for parking; stores are on floors six to eight.

Century City Shopping Center (☎ 310-553-5300, 10250 Santa Monica Blvd; Map 11) Open 10am-9pm Mon-Fri, 10am-6pm Sat, 11am-6pm Sun. Flanked by glass and concrete stalagmites of offices, this is a pleasant outdoor mall. The roughly 140 stores are elegant but still affordable and largely mainstream. The big department stores are Bloomingdale's and Macy's. There's a 14-screen cinema complex and an excellent food court.

Santa Monica Place (☎ 310-394-5451, 395 Santa Monica Place; Map 13) Open 10am-9pm Mon-Fri, 10am-10pm Sat, 10am-

6pm Sun. Though not overwhelmingly large, this is one of the most popular malls in the LA area. Anchored by Robinsons-May and Macy's, it houses a full range of retail clothing, furniture, music and household stores, as well as a branch of the wonderful KCET Public Broadcasting's Store of Knowledge. The space itself, designed by Frank Gehry, is imaginative and pleasant, while the food court, Eatz, is definitely the best around.

Westside Pavilion (☎ 310-474-6255, 10800 W Pico Blvd, Westwood; Map 2) Open 10am-9pm Mon-Fri, 10am-8pm Sat, 11am-6pm Sun. Although the designers did well in conceiving this pretty, glass-covered mall, parking is a nightmare of impacted entranceways and tightly spiraling ramps. Once inside, it's a pleasure to browse through the 160 indoor and outdoor shops, including the upscale Nordstrom and the more down-to-earth Robinsons-May department stores. There's also a cinema complex and a supermarket.

The following are other major malls:

Macy's Plaza (☎ 213-624-2891, 7th & Flower Sts, Downtown; Map 5) Open to 6:30pm Mon-Fri. There are 30 boutiques, anchored by Macy's.

Glendale Galleria (☎ 818-240-9481, 2148 Glendale Galleria; Map 8) Open 10am-9pm Mon-Fri, 10am-7pm Sat, 11am-6pm Sun. This giant mall has 260 stores, anchored by Macy's, Robinsons-May, JC Penney, Nordstrom and Mervyn's.

Fox Hills Mall (☎ 310-390-7833, 294 Fox Hills Mall, Culver City; Map 12) Open 10am-9pm Mon-Fri, 10am-7pm Sat, 11am-6pm Sun. Features 140 shops, anchored by Macy's, Robinsons-May and JC Penney.

Fashion Square Mall (☎ 818-783-0550, 14006 Riverside Dr, Sherman Oaks, San Fernando Valley; Map 2) Open 10am-9pm Mon-Fri, 10am-7pm Sat, 11am-6pm Sun. There are 135 stores, anchored by Bloomingdale's and Macy's.

Outlet Malls

Outlet malls, where famous and mainstream chain stores sell off their stock at reduced prices, have become all the rage with many visitors. While bargains here are possible, it's worth noting that items are often damaged, irregular or leftover from the previous season, or rejected from regular department stores. That lime-green shirt that was so fashionable last year may get you ticketed by the fashion police this summer. Service in these stores is also kept to a minimum; there are generally fewer employees, dressing rooms and mirrors.

Citadel Factory Stores (☎ *213-888-1220, 5675 E Telegraph Rd; Map 3*) Open 10am-8pm Mon-Sat, 10am-6pm Sun. The only outlet mall in LA County is 9 miles south of Downtown, right off the I-5 Washington exit. A planned expansion is supposed to add 35 stores to what is a relatively small complex of shops including Corning Revere, London Fog and Eddie Bauer.

Ontario Mills (☎ *909-484-8300, 4557 One Mills Circle, Ontario*) Open to 10pm Sun-Thur, to midnight Fri & Sat. With more than 200 stores spread over 131 acres, this is the Godzilla of California's outlet malls. It's about a 40-minute drive east of Downtown LA. Headliners include Saks Fifth Avenue, Guess?, Ann Taylor and Warner Brothers Studio. Besides a food court with 13 eateries, this center also integrates an entertainment complex featuring the American Wilderness Experience, which re-creates a variety of California ecosystems, including a redwood forest, the desert and Yosemite Valley. There's also a 30-screen movie theater as well as an UltraScreen Theatre, featuring a six-story screen and 30-speaker sound system.

Farmers' Markets

California is famous for its year-round produce, and vendors at weekly neighborhood farmers' markets offer the best in quality and selection. Come here to stock up on groceries or just to put together a beach picnic. As elsewhere in the world, markets are also great for people-watching, catching glimpses of local life and browsing, even without buying. Some also allocate space to artisans and/or offer live entertainment. Here's a selection:

Hollywood – Ivar and Selma Aves between Sunset and Hollywood Blvds (8:30am-1pm Sun)

West Hollywood – Plummer Park at 7377 Santa Monica Blvd (9am-2pm Mon)

Beverly Hills – 200 block of Cañon Dr north of Wilshire Blvd (9am-1pm Sun)

Culver City – 9070 Venice Blvd at Culver Ave (3pm-7pm Tues)

Santa Monica – Arizona and 2nd Sts (9am-2pm Wed, 9:30am-2pm Sat); Pico and Cloverfield Blvds (8:30am-1pm Sat); and Ocean Park Blvd and Main St (9am-noon Sun)

Venice – Venice Blvd at Venice Way (7-11am Fri)

Hermosa Beach – 13th St and Hermosa Ave (noon-4pm Fri)

Long Beach – 3rd St and Broadway on the Promenade North (10am-4pm Fri)

Pasadena – Villa Park Community Center at 363 East Villa St (9:30am-1:30pm Tues); and Victory Park between Altadena Dr and Sierra Madre at Paloma St (8:30am-1pm Sat)

Glendale – 100 N Brand Blvd (9:30am-1:30pm Thur)

Burbank – 3rd St and Orange Grove Ave (8am-1pm Sat)

Galleries

Consult the Calendar section of the *LA Times* for information on galleries and openings. Also check out the free magazine *Arts Scene* (☎ *213-482-4724, artscene@ artscenecal.com, www.artscene.com*), available at shops and restaurants around LA. Most galleries are open from 10am or 11am to 5pm or 6pm Tuesday to Saturday.

West Hollywood (Map 10)

Daniel Saxon Gallery (☎ *310-657-6033, 552 Norwich Dr*) – many leading Chicano artists working in the media of glass, painting, print and sculpture

Fahey-Klein Gallery (☎ *323-934-2250, 148 S La Brea Ave*) – one of America's foremost photography galleries, with provocative shows of vintage and contemporary images, representing Robert Doisneau, Allen Ginsberg, Robert Mapplethorpe and Herb Ritts among others

Herbert Palmer Gallery (☎ *310-278-6407, 9003 Melrose Ave*) – modern and contemporary masters such as Christo, Claes Oldenburg, Man Ray and Picasso

Iturralde Gallery (☎ *323-937-4267, 154 S La Brea Ave*) – contemporary Latin American artists and new talent, including works by Tijuana artist Marcos 'Erre' Ramirez, Ernesto Pujol and Javier Marin

Jack Rutberg Fine Arts Gallery (☎ 323-938-5222, 357 N La Brea Ave) – modern and contemporary paintings, drawings, prints and sculptures by such masters as Chagall, Kollwitz, Picasso, Warhol and Manet

Jan Baum Gallery (☎ 323-932-0170, 170 S La Brea Ave) – international contemporary art, primitive art and art by emerging LA artists

Paul Kopeikin Gallery (☎ 323-937-0765, 138 S La Brea Ave) – fine-art photography, especially California Pictorialism and Modernism by lesser-known artists

Tasende Gallery (☎ 310-276-8686, 8808 Melrose Ave) – contemporary drawings, paintings and sculptures by modern masters such as José Luis Cuevas, Henry Moore and Andrés Nagel

Tobey C Moss Gallery (☎ 323-933-5523, 7321 Beverly Blvd) – fine prints, drawings, paintings and sculptures. Specializing in California Modernism, abstract art and Post-Surrealism

Santa Monica & Venice (Map 13)

Bergamot Station Arts Center (2525 Michigan Ave, Santa Monica) – nearly 40 galleries of top-notch works by local, national and international artists working in all media; outstanding galleries include **Patricia Correia Gallery** (☎ 310-264-1760), **Sherry Frumkin Galleries** (☎ 310-453-1850) and **Bobbie Greenfield Gallery** (☎ 310-264-0640)

Eames Office Gallery (☎ 310-396-5991, 2665 Main St, Santa Monica) – the furniture and designs of Ray and Charles Eames through rotating exhibits, photos and artifacts (This gallery is run by the Eames family, keeps Sunday hours and has a gift shop of Eames-related merchandise.)

Ernie Wolfe Gallery (☎ 310-473-1645, 1653 Sawtelle Blvd, West LA) – large-scale traditional sculptures from Africa, including granary ladders and house posts, as well as tribal furniture and contemporary paintings and sculptures from Kenya, Ivory Coast, Ghana and Mali

Impolitic (☎ 310-396-2720, 2665 Main St, Santa Monica) – rare and collectible original and limited cartoon art, the collection of local attorney Josh Needle (open Wed-Sun)

James Corcoran Gallery (☎ 310-966-1010, 1633 Electric Ave, Venice) – highly regarded exhibit spaces for the work of local talent, including big names like Laddie John Dill and Annette Bird

Jurassic Inc (☎ 310-899-2992, 131 Broadway, Santa Monica) – art produced by nature, including giant geodes, fossilized birds and petrified dinosaur eggs

LA Louver Gallery (☎ 310-822-4955, 45 N Venice Blvd, Venice) – contemporary American and European art, including works by Wallace Berman, Tony Berlant, David Hockney, and Edward and Nancy Kienholz

Leslie Sacks Fine Art (☎ 310-820-9448, 11640 San Vicente Blvd, Brentwood) – superb collection of modern and contemporary masters, as well as Impressionist, German Expressionist and African art

Ten Women (☎ 310-452-2256, 1237 Abbot Kinney Blvd, Venice; ☎ 310-314-9152, 2651 Main St, Santa Monica) – an all-women co-op of now 23 artists working in the fields of painting, jewelry, basketry, stained glass, hand-painted fabric and more

Elsewhere in LA

Brewery Art Complex (Map 3) – several galleries, all specializing in contemporary, cutting-edge art (open to the public from noon-5 pm Fri-Sun); outstanding galleries include **At the Brewery Project** (☎ 323-222-3007, 676 S Ave 21, Suite 33), **Eye Five Gallery** (☎ 323-227-8816, 2100 N Main St, Suite A-9), **Coagula Projects** (☎ 323-221-7912, 2100 N Main St, Suite A-8) and **LA Artcore Annex** (☎ 213-276-9320, 650A S Ave 21)

Cirrus Gallery (☎ 213-680-3473, 542 S Alameda St; Map 5) – a fine-arts press and gallery of emerging and established California artists, including John Baldessari, Lita Albuquerque and Ed Ruscha

La Luz de Jesus Gallery (☎ 323-666-7667, 4633 Hollywood Blvd, Silver Lake; Map 9) – underground artists working in post-pop painting and sculpture; themes range from folk to religious to sexually deviant

Gagosian Gallery (☎ 310-271-9400, 456 N Camden Dr, Beverly Hills; Map 11) – top US names in contemporary painting and sculpture, including Richard Serra, Ed Ruscha and Maya Lin in a spectacular space

Latin American Masters (☎ 310-271-4847, 264 N Beverly Dr; Map 11) – big names in Latin American art, including Diego Rivera, Rufino Tamayo and Armando Morales

Pace Wildenstein (☎ 310-205-5522, 9540 Wilshire Blvd, Beverly Hills; Map 11) – top names in international contemporary art such as Claes Oldenburg and Georg Baselitz (enter from the back)

Thrift Shops

These charity-operated stores are a treasure trove of donated formerly owned clothing, household items, books, furniture and other stuff sold at often ridiculously low prices.

Many people enjoy the hunt for bargains, but for those traveling on a tight budget thrift stores can be a godsend. For a fraction of what you would pay in most department stores, you can replace that only pair of shorts you ruined by spilling red wine. The cash-strapped can look stylish in a thrift store dress or blazer when showing up at that unexpected dinner party.

Used clothing stores selling designer and brand-name clothing abound in fashion-conscious Beverly Hills and Santa Monica, where – in some circles – wearing the same dress twice is considered gauche. Here's a small selection of the city's best stores:

Out of the Closet (☎ 323-644-0525, 4398 *Sunset Blvd, Silver Lake; Map 9;* ☎ 323-848-9760, 8224 Santa Monica Blvd, West Holly-*wood; Map 10;* ☎ 310-664-9036, 214 Lincoln *Blvd, Venice; Map 13;* ☎ 626-440-1719, 1726 *E Colorado Blvd, Pasadena; Map 17).* Style-savvy Angelenos poke through the racks of this chain of thrift stores benefiting HIV- and AIDS-related charities. For additional branches, see the Yellow Pages or call any of the locations listed.

Goodwill Industries (☎ 213-628-1748, 235 S Broadway, Downtown; Map 5; ☎ 323-*644-1517, 4575 Hollywood Blvd, Los Feliz; Map 9;* ☎ 310-442-9655, 11726 Santa

---

Calling All Pack Rats: Flea Markets Abound

Flea markets or swap meets: Call them what you will, LA has plenty of them. Nourished by a remarkably diverse population with some equally eclectic tastes, these gatherings can make for the best bargain shopping around and unearth some pretty unusual treasures. Whether you're hunting for a '57 Chevy hubcap or a Hopalong Cassidy pocket knife, arrive early, bring a bag and small bills, wear those walking shoes and get ready to haggle.

Melrose Trading Post (Map 10) – About 120 vendors of hip and bizarre collectibles make the Trading Post, at Fairfax High School on Melrose and Fairfax Aves, one of LA's coolest markets; it happens every Sunday, 9am-5pm.

Santa Monica Outdoor Antique & Collectible Market – On Airport Ave off Bundy Ave, you'll find Victorian to Postmodern wares along with tasty food; it happens the fourth Sunday of the month, 8am-3pm; admission is $5.

Venice High School Flea Market – Antiques, crafts, bric-a-brac, furniture, music, toys, jewelry and clothes wait for the collector at 13000 Venice Blvd, every second Saturday of the month, 9am-4pm.

Long Beach Outdoor Antique & Collectible Market – Over 800 antique and collectible dealers sell quality stuff at the Veteran's Memorial Stadium, on Conant St between Lakewood Blvd and Clark Ave, every third Sunday of the month, 8am-3pm.

Pasadena City College Flea Market – Over 500 vendors selling mostly used merchandise, including clothes, crafts, jewelry and collectibles take over 1570 E Colorado Blvd on the first Sunday of the month, 8am-3pm. This is the best flea market for music.

Rose Bowl Flea Market – The largest in the land, this flea market has over 2200 vendors who descend upon Pasadena's scenic Arroyo Seco, 1001 Rose Bowl Dr, Pasadena, on the second Sunday of the month, 7:30am-3pm; admission is $5, or $10 before 9am.

Glendale Community College Swap Meet – On Mountain Ave near Verdugo is where 200 antique and collectible dealers set up every third Sunday of the month, 8am-3pm.

Burbank Monthly Antique Market – About 125 dealers collect at the Pickwick, on Main St and Riverside Dr, to sell antiques, clothing, furniture, art and other collectibles every fourth Sunday of the month, 9am-3pm; admission is $3.

Monica Blvd; Map 13). This nonprofit provides education, training and jobs to people with disabilities and vocational disadvantages. Its collection is very mainstream, but it's all clean, color-coordinated and most branches even have dressing rooms. There's a total of 28 branches throughout the county.

Garage Sales

As you're driving through LA's neighborhoods on Friday and Saturday, you'll probably notice signs attached to traffic signals and telephone poles announcing a 'Moving Sale,' 'Estate Sale,' 'Multi-Family Sale' or 'Garage Sale,' along with an address and the date. Whatever they're called, these sales are an LA institution, and serious bargain hunters will hit the streets early for the best finds. For those holding the sale, it's a way to clean out closets and make a buck on the side. For treasure hunters, garage sales can yield everything from vintage earrings to furniture at rock-bottom prices. Haggling, of course, is just part of the fun.

WHAT TO BUY
Books

LA may not have a reputation as a literary town but you wouldn't know it from the number of bookstores here. Aside from chains like Barnes & Noble, Borders and Crown, there are plenty of independent stores, many of which regularly host book signings and readings. Call the individual store for upcoming events.

General *Skylight Bookshop* (☎ 323-660-1175, 1818 N Vermont Ave, Los Feliz Village; Map 9) A living ficus tree anchors this small bookstore, which has plenty of LA-related titles and a magazine rack with such cult glossies as *Bizarre* and *Bitch*.

Book Soup (☎ 310-659-3110, 8818 Sunset Blvd, West Hollywood; Map 10) Open to midnight daily. Students, Sunset hipsters and even celebrities are drawn to this eclectic store, which includes a sizeable gay and lesbian section, a big international newsstand and lots of books about LA, its history and scene.

Dutton's (☎ 310-476-6263, 11975 San Vicente Blvd, Brentwood) Dutton's caters to a well-read and educated clientele and specializes in the humanities, with large selections of history, philosophy and poetry. The store itself is rambling and cluttered, but service is tops.

Midnight Special Bookstore (☎ 310-393-2923, 1318 Third Street Promenade, Santa Monica; Map 13) This place owes its name to the popular blues song about a train passing a prison at the stroke of midnight. If its headlight shone through the prison bars onto one of the inmates, he would be the next to be set free. The store makes no bones about its political leanings, reflected in its solid representation of minority, feminist and radical writers.

Small World Books (☎ 310-399-2360, 1407 Ocean Front Walk, Venice; Map 13) Chock-full of literary criticism, fiction and poetry, much of it from small presses, this shop also has plenty of foreign-language novels and a legendary Mystery Annex (as in mystery books).

Vroman's (☎ 626-449-3220, 695 E Colorado Blvd, Pasadena; Map 17) This is Southern California's oldest (since 1894) bookstore and also one of its largest. It's a favorite among LA literati.

Used *Heritage Bookshop* (☎ 310-659-3674, 8540 Melrose Ave, West Hollywood; Map 10) Closed Sun. In a turreted building, this shop offers a vast assortment of rare books, including many first editions and manuscripts; it also does book binding. The autograph gallery showcases the writings of Hemingway and others.

Acres of Books (☎ 562-437-6980, 240 Long Beach Blvd, Long Beach; Map 16) This has to be the mother of all bookstores. It takes time, patience and a hunter's instinct to unearth gems from this labyrinth. The staff, however, is knowledgeable and friendly and will help you find what you need from the densely packed shelves.

Cookbooks (☎ 818-848-4630, 321 N San Fernando Blvd, Burbank; Map 18) If you want a recipe for Waldorf salad from the 1950s, you'll probably find one here. The shop also has fiction, books on the history of food, and culinary magazines.

House of Fiction (☎ 626-449-9861, 663 E Colorado Blvd, Pasadena; Map 17) Open to 9pm Mon-Sat, to 5pm Sun. This store is favored by students and has a big selection of novels.

Travel & Specialty **Thomas Bros Maps**
(☎ 213-627-4018, 521 W 6th St; Map 5) Located in Downtown for 30 years, Thomas Bros produces the most thorough and accurate city maps. Shelves here bend with any city, county, regional, national and world map you can imagine. Bestsellers are the laminated maps that you can write on and erase later.

Traveler's Bookcase (☎ 323-655-0575, 8375 W 3rd St, Beverly Center District; Map 10) Small but excellent, every inch of wallspace in this diminutive store is swathed with guides, dictionaries, novels, atlases and a decent selection of maps.

California Map & Travel (☎ 310-396-6277, 3312 Pico Blvd, Santa Monica; Map 13) This shop has it all, including topographical, hiking, biking and driving maps of places around the world. Check out its selection of travel books, globes and accessories. Slide shows take place weekly.

Nations (☎ 310-318-9915, 800-546-8060, 500–504 Pier Ave, Hermosa Beach; Map 14) Make your travel arrangements at the in-house American Express travel agency, then pick up all the guidebooks you'll ever need at this one-stop travel haven. Owner Jan displays only the latest editions at his well-stocked, well-sorted and immaculately kept South Bay institution. Maps, travel accessories and globes round out the assortment. There's another branch (☎ 310-921-2242) at the Del Amo Fashion Center in Torrance.

Distant Lands Bookstore (☎ 626-449-3220, 56 S Raymond Ave, Pasadena; Map 17) Besides a vast assortment of travel books, this store also sells travel accessories and shares space with a Council Travel branch. Frequent book signings and slide shows are hosted here.

Geographia Map & Travel Store (☎ 818-848-1414, 4000 Riverside Dr, Burbank; Map 18) This Valley store is another good source for specialty maps as well as general travel books.

Bodhi Tree (☎ 310-659-1733, 800-825-9798, 8585 Melrose Ave, West Hollywood; Map 10) Come to this tranquil store, which specializes in inner healing, astrology, spiritual enlightenment and other New Age subjects for a clientele that includes Shirley MacLaine. For psychic readings and used books, check out the annex in back (open until 7pm).

Cooks Library (☎ 323-655-3141, 8373 W 3rd St, Beverly Center District; Map 10) Give your friends a good meal and make them gourmets for a day; give them a good cookbook and make them gourmets for life. This ought to be the motto of this small store, which stocks every conceivable culinary bible ever created and featuring recipes from American apple pie to Zambian zebra steaks.

Hennessy & Ingalls (☎ 310-458-9074, 1254 Third Street Promenade, Santa Monica) Spacious, well-lit and well-organized, Hennessy & Ingalls reflects its specialization in interior design, art and architecture. It has materials on all the visual arts, including graphic design and landscape architecture.

Gay & Lesbian **A Different Light Bookstore** (☎ 310-854-6601, 8853 Santa Monica Blvd, West Hollywood; Map 10) This is the area's number-one gay bookstore and is also a fine place to go to start learning your way around. You can browse the stacks daily until midnight.

Unicorn Bookstore (☎ 310-652-6253, 8940 Santa Monica Blvd, West Hollywood; Map 10) Nearby A Different Light, this store has a smaller selection.

The Sisterhood Bookstore (☎ 310-477-7300, 1351 Westwood Blvd, Westwood; Map 11) Books, music, jewelry and crafts by women for women are sold here, though the store does not cater exclusively to lesbians.

Sports & Outdoor Gear
REI (☎ 310-727-0728, 1800 Rosecrans Ave, Manhattan Beach) This warehouse-sized store is the top shop for all-around outdoor

Taking Home a Piece of Tinsel

So you've stood in the footsteps of Douglas Fairbanks at Mann's Chinese Theater, sat on the chair that may once have been occupied by Cameron Diaz at Spago Beverly Hills, and seen Mel Gibson in the flesh during a taping of the *Tonight Show with Jay Leno*. But now the end of your LA trip is sadly in sight and Kansas City, Canberra or Nottingham just don't seem as glam as the City of Angels. To keep the tinsel glittering for a bit longer, pick up a souvenir from these stores, all of which stock a bit more than plastic Oscar statuettes and Hollywood Sign fridge magnets.

Clothes

It's a Wrap (☎ 818-567-7366, 3315 W Magnolia Ave, Burbank; Map 18) Fancy those pants worn by Kevin Spacey in *American Beauty* or the skimpy outfit Heather Locklear pranced about in *Spin City*? This is the place that hawks – for surprisingly little money – the wardrobes previously worn by the stars during movies, commercials, sitcoms, soaps and other shoots. Many are even designer labels. Tags tell you the name of the show and sometimes that of the actor, so you'll know what to brag about.

Reel Clothes & Props (☎ 818-508-7762, 12132 Ventura Blvd at Laurel Canyon, Studio City; Map 2) This place is similar but much smaller and more into higher-priced collectibles, many of which are also sold on the Internet at www.reelclothes.com. Tags only specify the studio but not the show or actor.

Memorabilia

Moletown (☎ 323-851-0111, 900 N La Brea Ave; Map 10) If you have your heart set on a Rugrats mug, a T-shirt emblazoned with the cast of the *Drew Carey Show* or a Pamela Anderson Barbie doll, check out this stage-sized emporium of TV and movie memorabilia.

Scripts, Stills, Books

Larry Edmunds Bookshop (☎ 323-463-3273, 6644 Hollywood Blvd, Hollywood; Map 9) The small storefront belies the Tinseltown treasures that can be unearthed at this long-time purveyor of scripts, posters, stills and books about films, theater and TV.

Samuel French Theatre & Film Bookshop (☎ 323-876-0570, 7623 Sunset Blvd, Hollywood; Map 9) Aspiring and accomplished actors can be found trawling this amazing repository of filmic, dramatic and musical fare. In need of the script to the *Godfather* or the score of the *Sound of Music*? You'll find it here.

Book City (☎ 323-466-2525, 6627 Hollywood Blvd, Hollywood; Map 9; ☎ 818-848-4417, 308 N San Fernando Blvd, Burbank; Map 18) If it's rare books about art and cinema, or movie scripts and celebrity autographs you're after, you'll find them here in this well-organized store. The Hollywood branch is less movie-oriented.

Movie World (☎ 818-845-1563, 212 N San Fernando Blvd, Burbank; Map 18) Crammed and chaotic, this is another place to dig up movie-related tomes, stills and posters; some of the coolest stuff is stored in cardboard boxes and metal filing cabinets.

---

needs. The knowledgeable staff sells everything from wool socks to stoves, and rents tents, skis, stoves, bikes, kayaks and more.

Adventure 16 (☎ 310-473-4574, 11161 W Pico Blvd) This outfitter is smaller but has a more central Westside location.

ZJ Boarding House (☎ 310-392-5646, 2619 Main St, Santa Monica; Map 13) Surf-boards, snowboards and skateboards – all the tools needed for that laid-back SoCal lifestyle are sold at this funky store.

Niketown (☎ 310-275-9998, 9560 Wilshire Blvd, Beverly Hills; Map 11) The trademark swoosh of Nike products is everywhere at this huge emporium of sneakers, sweats and sporting equipment. You can't miss the

SHOPPING

'shoe elevators,' which suck sneakers out of the inventory room and spit them out to the salespeople.

Roger Dunn Golf Shop (☎ *310-556-0914, 9970 Santa Monica Blvd, Century City; ☎ 818-763-3622, 4744 Lankershim Blvd, North Hollywood; Map 18)* Beginners and pros head to this megastore for every sort of golfing equipment imaginable by such makers as Lynx, Etonic, Armour, Nike and Odyssey.

Music

Rockaway Records (☎ *323-664-3232, 2395 Glendale Blvd, Silver Lake; Map 5)* This is a great source for used CDs and vinyl, with everything from Kiss to Smashmouth at fair prices; there are plenty of booths for listening before buying. Classical music, 45s, laser discs, videos and music memorabilia complete the assortment. The store also buys CDs.

Vinyl Fetish (☎ *323-660-4500, 1750 N Vermont Ave, Los Feliz Village; Map 9)* Come here for esoteric tunes – gothic, industrial, electronica etc – sold at pretty steep prices. Though it specializes in 33⅓-rpm albums, it also has a few CDs and a smallish 45-rpm section.

Tower Records (☎ *310-657-7300, 8801 W Sunset Blvd, Hollywood; Map 10)* Chart hounds, import freaks, classical connoisseurs – they all will find their fill at this chain music store. The service is only so-so, but the selection is great, especially for mainstream stuff. Check the Yellow Pages for other branches around the city.

Tower Records Clearance Center (☎ *323-461-6901, 7021 Hollywood Blvd, Hollywood; Map 9)* Come here for discounted CDs and movies.

Penny Lane (☎ *323-651-3000, 7563 Melrose Ave, Hollywood; Map 10; ☎ 626-564-0161, 16 Colorado Blvd, Pasadena; Map 17)* Smaller, but still a good standby for used CDs, this store has listening stations and also buys music. Check the Yellow Pages for additional branches.

Rhino Records (☎ *310-474-8685, 1720 Westwood Blvd, Westwood; Map 11)* Inde-pendent labels and promotional overstock are the bread and butter of this legendary store and label founded in the early 1970s; it launched such home-grown talent as Phranc and Billy Vera and the Beaters.

Hear Music (☎ *310-319-9527, 1429 Third Street Promenade, Santa Monica; Map 12)* For choice music from around the world – Celtic to African to Cuban – this is the place to be. You can browse the racks and also preview numerous preselected CDs.

Record Surplus (☎ *310-478-4217, 11609 W Pico Blvd, West LA; Map 13)* Hands-down the best place for vinyl LPs with prices that won't give your wallet a heart attack.

Opus (☎ *626-685-2800, 38 E Colorado Blvd, Pasadena; Map 17)* The selection at this all-CD store is small but choice, with an emphasis on world music and electronica, including some used and discounted. Listening stations abound.

Jewelry

LA's historic Jewelry District (Map 5) is Downtown on South Hill St between 6th and 7th Sts. Prices for watches, gold, silver or gemstones are 40% to 70% less than elsewhere in the city. Much of the merchandise sold here, however, comes from the Middle or Far East and is not always the best in terms of quality – buyer beware. *St Vincent Jewelry Center* (☎ *213-629-2124, 650 S Hill St)* and *Fox Jewelry Plaza* (☎ *213-627-8907, 608 S Hill St)* are two places where dozens of outlets cluster.

You're guaranteed superior quality at any of the shops on Rodeo Dr (Map 11) in Beverly Hills, where you can buy upscale and one-of-a-kind baubles. For those of us who failed to triple our incomes during the '90s, even a pair of tiny diamond stud earrings remains elusive at $4000. Others might actually find something to buy at this trio of treasure chests: *Tiffany* (☎ *310-273-8880, 210 N Rodeo Dr)*, *Van Cleef & Arpels* (☎ *310-276-1161, 300 N Rodeo Dr)* and *Cartier* (☎ *310-275-4272, 220 & 370 Rodeo Dr)*.

Maya (☎ *323-655-2708, 7452 Melrose Ave; Map 10)* Pocketbooks of all sizes will find something affordable here. This eclectic store stocks a huge selection of funky silver jewelry – including toe rings, waist chains and ear curls – sold alongside an equally impressive collection of imported Asian and African masks, fertility figures and other carved items.

Tantau Smith (☎ *310-392-9878, 1353 Abbot Kinney Blvd, Venice; Map 13)* Handmade, classy silver jewelry – much of it incorporating semi-precious stones – is nicely displayed in glass vitrines along with cotton clothing, candles, picture frames and other home accessories.

Antiques

Antiquarius (☎ *310-274-2363, 8840 N Beverly Blvd; Map 10)* There are 40 shops in this place near West Hollywood's Pacific Design Center.

The Antique Guild (☎ *310-838-3131, 3231 Helms Ave, Culver City; Map 12)* Great selection is what you'll find on 2 acres within the former Helms Bakery.

Santa Monica Antique Market (☎ *310-314-4899, 1607 Lincoln Blvd; Map 13)* This market is a major antique venue with more than 150 dealers and 20,000 sq feet of display space.

Off the Wall (☎ *323-930-1185, 7325 Melrose Ave; Map 10)* This mini-warehouse is filled with wacky collectibles and feels somewhat like a movie studio prop room. Depression-era radios, a roulette wheel, a bear skeleton or life-size plastic penguins – you never know what you'll find.

LA's flea and antique markets, held on Sunday in various locales, are other good sources for antiques and collectibles (see the boxed text 'Calling All Pack Rats: Flea Markets Abound' for details).

Mainstream & Designer Clothing

The obvious places to look for mainstream clothing are the malls (see Where to Shop, earlier in the chapter), which have department stores and retail chains. Chanel, Dior, Armani, Gucci, Hermès, Prada and Tommy Hilfiger, among other designer duds, can be found on Beverly Hill's Rodeo Dr and adjacent streets. West Hollywood and Santa Monica host boutiques of young, cutting-edge designers.

The Place & Co (☎ *310-645-1539, 8820 S Sepulveda Blvd, Westchester; Map 2)*. So you're into logo mania but don't have a trust fund? This long-time store near LAX sells barely worn couture at steep discounts. Many of the clothes were once owned by celebrities but, alas, their identities remain concealed.

Aero & Co (☎ *323-665-4651, 4651 Kingswell Ave, Los Feliz Village; Map 9)* This sparsely decorated boutique specializes in unique designs by LA designers and features unusual fabrics – many of them handmade – and fabric combinations (for example, cowhide and denim).

Fred Segal (☎ *323-651-4129, 8100 Melrose Ave, West Hollywood; Map 10; ☎ 310-458-9940, 500 Broadway, Santa Monica; Map 13)* Fashionistas like Cameron Diaz and Helen Hunt have been spotted hunting for eclectic urban clothes in this classy boutique.

Curve (☎ *310-360-8008, 154 N Robertson Blvd, West Hollywood; Map 10)* The two Jennifers (Aniston and Love Hewitt) are among those making pilgrimages to this loft-like emporium in the stylish Beverly Center District. Creative and sometimes off-the-wall couture by both underground and established designers mingle with co-owner Delia Seaman's own creations and jewelry by her partner Nevena Borissova.

Lisa Kline (☎ *246-0907, 136 S Robertson Blvd, West Hollywood; Map 10)* Post-pubescent shoppers are more likely to find their fill at this boutique a few doors south. Bright colors dominate the collection, which is big on both progressive and traditional styles.

Jon Valdí (☎ *323-653-3455, 8111 Melrose Ave, West Hollywood; Map 10)* Celebrities from Lisa Kudrow to Sir Ian McKellan have draped themselves in classy Valdí outfits, which are distinguished by a mix of top-quality fabrics and a slim, body-hugging fit.

Red Balls on Fire (☎ *323-655-3409, 7365 Melrose Ave, Melrose/La Brea; Map 10)* The eye-catching facade looks like an assemblage of upturned hub caps. Inside, you'll

The Sick, the Bizarre & the Twisted

There's no final frontier to your shopping experience in LA. Anything goes, and apparently anything sells, as this list of the more bizarre boutiques shows.

Panpipes Magickal Marketplace (☎ 323-462-7078, 1641 Cahuenga Blvd, Hollywood; Map 9) Open 10am-7pm Mon-Sat. LA's oldest occult supply shop (since 1961) is ideal for stocking up on your basic powdered lizard, crystal balls ($200), Ouija boards ($24.95) and magical potions (from $3.25). Owner and modern-day alchemist George Hiram Derby, who sports pentagram tattoos and jewelry, is trained in voodoo, pagan crafts and other ritualistic and spiritual fields – even Catholicism. He will mix up more than 6500 wet and 4600 dry metaphysical blends to help you solve problems relating to love, money, sex or whatever you desire. Ingredients, kept in neatly stacked glass vials, can be as common as essential oils and as rare as mummy dust – and you don't want to know what the latter costs.

Necromance (☎ 323-934-8684, 7220 Melrose Ave, Hollywood; Map 10) During a recent visit, a grungy surfer-dude barreled into this small store, lugging a brown paper bag. 'Do you want to buy some pig skulls?' Owner Nancy Smith barely raised a well-plucked eyebrow before declining politely. 'Not in good enough condition,' she later revealed. Skulls, though, are the stock in trade of bayou-born Smith's bazaar of the bizarre. Neatly displayed behind glass are everything from mouse heads (a steal at $8) to the full-blown human head (about $500) for your next Hamlet impression. A frog in formaldehyde for your mantel? A vampire repellant kit complete with garlic, holy water and a wooden stake for your emergency kit? Plastic bug bracelets? Necromance is full of surprises. Who buys this stuff? 'It's pretty much everybody,' confides Nancy. So there's no need to feel weird when paying a visit.

Mondo Video a Go-Go (☎ 323-953-8896, 1718 N Vermont Ave, Los Feliz Village; Map 9) The easy pick for weirdest LA emporium is this cluttered video store, operated by a giggly couple right out of the *Twilight Zone*. Among the most 'normal' selections are music videos by Heino, a blind

---

find edgy club wear, including Red Balls' own label, plus plenty of jewelry, belts, hats and other accessories.

Sacks SFO (☎ 323-939-3993, 652 N La Brea Ave, Hollywood; Map 10) This place stocks everything from trendy club wear to cashmere turtlenecks or leather jackets at 40% to 80% off retail prices. Check the Yellow Pages for locations of the other six branches.

Loehmann's (☎ 310-659-0674, 333 S La Cienega Blvd, Beverly Center District; Map 10) Catering to mature men and women, this sprawling shop has rack after rack of discounted snazzy designer labels, especially dresses, suits, silk blouses and other career gear as well as accessories. The back room has evening wear.

DNA (☎ 310-399-0341, 411 Rose Ave, Venice; Map 13) Tiny DNA is jam-packed with a small but choice assortment of hip garb by local and national designers for men and women, much of it with a stylish European flair.

Betsey Johnson (☎ 310-452-7911, 2929 Main St, Santa Monica; Map 13) This New York–based designer has rocked women's fashions for more than three decades. Exuberant colors, a sexy fit, flowing fabrics and whimsical detailing are among her many hallmarks.

Vintage Clothing

Pull My Daisy (☎ 323-663-0608, 3908 Sunset Blvd, Silver Lake; Map 9) This place is crammed with vintage goodies useful for the office or for a period costume party. In the mix are 1940s pumps, '50s sunglasses and '60s corsets, as are such irresistible gift items as syringe-shaped pens.

The Sick, the Bizarre & the Twisted

German singer with a platinum wig. Also available are crude videos showing violent neo-Nazis in action, though the Bad Taste Award definitely goes to the Lustful Midgets porn section.

Skeletons in the Closet (☎ 323-343-0760, 1104 N Mission Rd, Downtown; Map 5) Open 8am-4:30pm, closed noon-1pm. This ghoulish gift shop, operated by the LA County Coroner's Office, is located two floors above the morgue. Personalized toe-tags are among the most popular purchases, but there's also plenty of practical stuff such as beach towels, baseball hats and refrigerator magnets, all adorned with a dead body outline. Other items include body-shaped sticky notes, aprons and mugs with the department's mascot, Sherlock Bones. Proceeds benefit the Youthful Drunk Driving Visitation Program, an alternative sentencing option.

Naughty tales, Mondo Video a Go-Go

Koma Bookstore (☎ 213-239-0030, 548 S Spring St, Suite 1033, Downtown; Map 5) Ever since yet another rent increase forced Koma owner Dan to vacate his former store in increasingly trendy Los Feliz Village, he's been holed up on the 10th floor of a venerable old bank building in the heart of Downtown. Surrounding him is his trademark assortment of the most warped, bizarre, sleazy, controversial and anarchic material that was ever committed to print. Let's just say, Jesse Helms and other pro-censorship types would be risking a heart attack browsing around here. Dan deals in most media: new and used books, records, CDs and videos. He's usually around from noon to 7pm, but call ahead just to make sure.

Squaresville (☎ 323-669-8464, 1800 N Vermont Ave, Los Feliz Village; Map 9) Come here to stock up on the goods for that funky Left Coast look, at prices that won't require a bank robbery. The store buys, sells and trades, and the quality is high.

Jet Rag (☎ 323-939-0528, 825 N La Brea Ave, Melrose/La Brea; Map 10) Missiles crash into the facade and animal skeletons double as mannequins at this warehouse-sized store with quality retro clothing and accessories. During the Sunday parking lot sales, you can do battle with thrifty hipsters foraging for treasures among the bales of used clothing – just a $1 apiece.

Golyester (☎ 323-931-1339, 136 S La Brea Ave, Melrose/La Brea; Map 10) This beautifully decorated store has immaculate couture fashions (some up to 100 years old), eccentric accessories (like harem slippers) and top-quality antique textiles, linens, laces and accessories.

Buffalo Exchange (☎ 323-938-8604, 131 N La Brea Ave, Melrose/La Brea; Map 10) This youthful store stocks more mainstream hand-me-downs, with a few Calvins and Versaces thrown into the mix, as well as shoes and accessories.

Wasteland (☎ 323-653-3028, 7428 Melrose, Melrose/La Brea; Map 10) The window displays and facade are at least as eye-catching as the top-quality vintage and contemporary designer fashions on sale at this huge place. The store also buys or trades old clothing and jewelry.

Lingerie & Erotica
Tacky to tasteful – whatever is your fancy, in freewheeling LA there's no shortage of stores to get your nocturnal niceties.

Frederick's of Hollywood (☎ *323-466-8506, 6608 Hollywood Blvd, Hollywood; Map 9)* This is one of the oldest lingerie stores and still among the most popular. The assortment runs from the mainstream to the professional but it's all displayed tastefully with no need to blush.

Playmates (☎ *323-464-7636, 6438 Hollywood Blvd, Hollywood; Map 9)* This place is somewhat more hardcore, so to speak, and a favorite of exotic dancers, actresses and ladies of the night. In other words, it stocks everything a girl with imagination might need for a night of debauchery: leopard-patterned robes, fluffy feather boas, latex bustiers, tasseled pasties, and lace, satin and – ouch! – vinyl thongs. Check out the basement for deals. Swimwear and every-day lingerie is sold as well.

Hustler Hollywood (☎ *310-860-9009, 8920 Sunset Blvd, West Hollywood; Map 10)* 'Relax – it's just sex' is the motto of this emporium of erotica run by the daughter of top porno purveyor Larry Flynt. Lots of logo wear, books and magazines, toys, love lotions and lingerie orbit the 'inner sanctum' where you can purchase XXX-rated videos starring some of the people who might be standing next to you in the check-out line.

Trashy Lingerie (☎ *310-652-4543, 402 N La Cienega Blvd, Beverly Center District; Map 10)* Those who worship at the altar of hedonism should also check into this cluttered store, which has custom-made corsets and other imaginables made from leather, vinyl and lace, much of it designed locally. To keep out lookyloos, the store charges a $2 'membership fee' good for one year.

Pleasure Chest (☎ *323-650-1022, 7733 Santa Monica Blvd, West Hollywood; Map 10)* This sexual-hardware store is LA's kingdom of kinkiness. The huge assortment caters to every conceivable fantasy and fetish, though more of the naughty than the nice kind. Handcuffs, dildos and nipple clamps are among the more mainstream items, but there's also lace-up leather hoods, whips and a full range of unprintable stuff.

Dreamdresser (☎ *323-848-3480, 8444 Santa Monica Blvd, West Hollywood; Map 10)* This is another pleasure pit, with wearable vinyl and rubber gadgets as well as spiky anythings and very friendly service.

One-of-a-Kind

Hollywood Toys & Costumes (☎ *323-464-4444, 6600 Hollywood Blvd; Map 9)* Fancy having a hairdo à la Marilyn? A pair of angel wings? Or how about some werewolf hands? This place has been in business since 1950 and has a huge assortment of costumes, wigs, feathers, hats and other accessories to fulfill any fantasy. Right by the entrance is a sunken monster pit covered with glass and flanked by rows of campy masks. Giant plastic spiders can be had for less than $5, and those wigs – from realistic brunette to crazed pink – start at $40.

Wacko (☎ *323-663-0122, 4633 Hollywood Blvd, Silver Lake; Map 9)* Books on were-wolves, cocktail stirring sticks topped by mermaids and inflatable plastic chairs make great birthday gifts – for someone. These and many more novelties bordering on the absurd are what's in store at the appropriately named Wacko.

Allied Model Trains (☎ *310-313-9353, 4411 S Sepulveda Blvd, Culver City; Map 12)* The hearts of serious train aficionados will skip a beat when entering this gargantuan repository of any make, model and choo-choo accessory. Everyone else will delight at the many scale-model landscapes, which include a Bavarian village and an Old West town, navigated by fleets of buzzing miniature trains.

Audrey's Good Vibrations (☎ *310-664-1180, 1204 Abbot Kinney Blvd; Map 13)* At this quintessentially Venice store, you can have your chakra tested (free) before stocking up on organic oils, gem elixirs and flower essences to purge yourself of negative energy and restore karmic balance.

Eddie Brandt's Saturday Matinee (☎ *818-506-7722, 5006 Vineland Ave, North Hollywood; Map 18)* In the day and age of chain video superstores, this one is a survivor, largely because of its incredibly eclectic selection: From samurai sex movies to collections of the TV programs *Ozzie & Harriet* and *Fawlty Towers*, you'll find it here.

Excursions

There are many points of interest just a short hop from Los Angeles. This chapter covers Southern California's major theme parks, followed by some popular overnight destinations, including Laguna Beach and Santa Barbara. The offshore Santa Catalina Island, actually part of LA County, is also covered. And for those who haven't seen enough glitz and glamour in Hollywood, there's also an overview of Las Vegas, a popular destination for both Angelenos and visitors. For more getaways close to LA, check out Lonely Planet's *California & Nevada* or *San Diego & Tijuana*.

ANAHEIM

Anaheim, the home of Disneyland and the hub of Orange County, is getting a $4.2 billion face-lift thanks to the new Disneyland California Adventure and a revamped and updated Convention Center. The helpful Anaheim/Orange County Visitor & Convention Bureau (☎ 714-765-8888, 800 W Katella Ave; open 8am-5pm Mon-Fri) in the Convention Center across from Disneyland has countywide lodging, dining and transportation information.

Disneyland

For many first-time visitors to LA, the *de rigeur* trip to Disneyland (☎ 714-781-4000, www.disneyland.com, 1313 Harbor Blvd) is as important as visiting the Eiffel Tower in Paris. And, probably, much more fun. The addition of a second park, Disney's California Adventure, and Downtown Disney, a restaurant and retail mall, in 2001 further increased Disneyland's appeal as a tourist destination.

When Walt Disney trotted out his famous mouse in 1928, it was the beginning of a commercial bonanza that's been relentlessly refined ever since. Fueled by the dreams of children worldwide, Disney has become a legend of corporate success – and excess – in virtually every field it has entered: movies, TV, publishing, music and merchandise. You'll see many of Disney's classic visions reflected here. But, after a day in the 'happiest place on earth' – braving crowds, standing in long lines in the stinging Southland sun, and trying to ignore the feeling that you're being manipulated (and you are) – you may well flee back to your hotel room, pour yourself a beer and watch the sun set, feeling the desperate need for reality.

So what remains of the charming dream that originally launched Disneyland in 1955? The twofold answer is very much, and very little. The original Disneyland was successful because it understood its purpose well: Cater to the imagination of kids, and the parents will foot the bill. But over the years, children have become more adult while adults have become more childlike. Disney has adapted completely. The gentle rides of yore have given way to spectacular thrills catering to over-stimulated children with cyberspace expectations. And, the parents don't come along just to hold their tots by the hand. They scream right along with them.

Some charm remains in Disneyland – the Pirates of the Caribbean, the Haunted Mansion and the perennial favorite of the under-3-feet-tall set, It's a Small World. But you'd better be prepared for some major manhandling and manipulation. The shiny, happy 'cast members' grin to the point of rictus. There are, however, only a few places to sit down other than in a restaurant. And during the summer months, the park is jammed with visitors, and the waiting lines – up to three hours for some rides – will eventually take their toll on all but the hopelessly good-natured.

Of course, Disney doesn't want you to do so, but you can save time and money by sneaking in your own sandwiches and drinks. The best advice is to pace yourself and don't push to the point of exhaustion and family feuds. Hey – you're in Disneyland! So make the most of it.

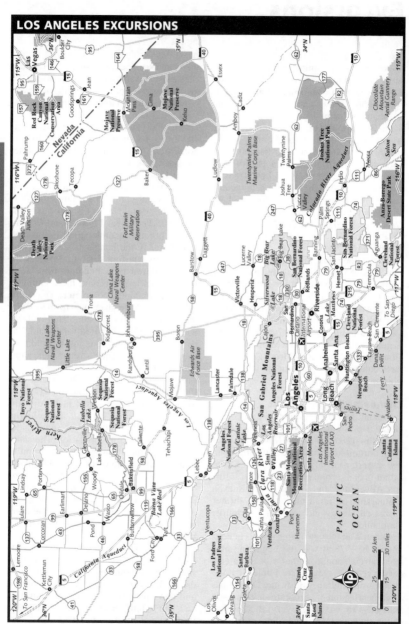

LOS ANGELES EXCURSIONS

Tickets Admission prices for Disneyland and the new Disney's California Adventure are the same, and several different types of tickets are available. One-day admission for each park is $43 adults, $33 children; three-day passes are $111/87, four-day passes $137/107. If you're not planning to visit on consecutive days, you can also buy a Flex Ticket, which allows you to get in on any three (or four) days within a 14-day period. Prices are the same as for regular three- and four-day tickets. The multi-day tickets give you access to both parks, although only one park per day may be visited (meaning you can't go to Disneyland in the morning and California Adventure in the afternoon). Parking is an additional $8.

Hours Park hours are highly arbitrary and depend upon the marketing department's projected attendance numbers. Typical summer hours are 8am-10pm Monday to Thursday, 10am-10pm or midnight Friday to Sunday. Typical off-season hours are 10am-8pm Monday to Thursday, 10am-10pm Friday, 10am-midnight Saturday, 10am-9pm Sunday.

Information Disneyland has a baby-care center, currency-exchange stations, banks and a kennel for your pet. Four-hour guided tours are offered for $15/14, plus admission. Lines throughout the park are the longest during summer and around major holidays. In general, visiting midweek is better than Friday, Saturday or Sunday, and arriving early in the day is best. Also keep in mind that many rides have minimum age and height requirements, so avoid tantrums by preparing the kids.

In early 2001, Disneyland introduced the Fastpass system, which allows you to pre-book time slots for particular rides in order to cut back on the time spent waiting in line. Simply go to the attraction of your choice and, if the wait is too long, look for the Fastpass ticket machine. It shows the next available time period. If it suits your schedule, insert your admission ticket and you'll be issued a Fastpass ticket showing the time slot when you can arrive and go straight to

the Fastpass line instead of the regular line. There may still be a wait, but it'll be much shorter. The system is only available at the most popular attractions, like Indiana Jones and Splash Mountain, where wait times can otherwise be as long as 2½ hours in the summer. (Note that you can only hold a Fastpass ticket for one ride at a time.)

Rides & Attractions You enter Disneyland on **Main Street USA**, a cheery re-creation of small-town America circa 1900, with myriad shops including the Candy Emporium. Resist the temptation to buy overpriced peanuts, but stop to have your picture taken with Mickey and Minnie, or any of the other Disney characters that usually hang around here. Plunge on into the seven Disney 'lands' centered around Sleeping Beauty's Castle, which was inspired by Germany's Neuschwanstein palace.

Main Street ends in the Central Plaza. Immediately on your right is **Tomorrowland**, the high-tech showpiece of the park, where lines tend to be longest. On the Star Tours ride, you're clamped into a StarSpeeder vehicle, piloted by a dysfunctional android, for a wild and bumpy ride through deep space. Space Mountain hurtles you into complete darkness at frightening speed, and you *will* scream long and loud. It's hard to recommend this one for anyone under 12.

The latest ride in this Wagnerian paean to space travel is the journey to Imagination and Beyond on the new Rocket Rods XPR. You blast off on a four-minute indoor and outdoor breakneck tour of Tomorrowland that is the longest and fastest of all the Disney rides. (This ride is undergoing renovation to make it even more thrilling.) Honey, I Shrunk the Audience also draws huge crowds, all anticipating the experience of becoming subminiature and being threatened by insects.

Adventureland, located to the left of Central Plaza, is a favorite. The highlight is the Indiana Jones Adventure, definitely a not-to-be-missed jungle hoot. While you're waiting in line, you'll pass by a jungle office filled with ancient tomes, a vintage radio and exotic treasures that will have you

EXCURSIONS

smelling Harrison Ford in the air; such is the genius of Disney designers. Enormous Humvee-type vehicles lurch off for encounters with pyrotechnic, near-death experiences in re-creations of themes and stunts from the Indiana Jones movie trilogy.

Little ones will love climbing up to Tarzan's House nearby where they will cross a suspension bridge and can play with shipwreck toys. Also here is the Jungle Cruise, a mellow expedition through tropical rainforests, featuring encounters with roaring hippopotami and jungle denizens.

Just beyond is **New Orleans Square**, where charming offerings include the Haunted Mansion. Here, you will be beguiled by the hokey Vincent Price School of Horror frights and sights. It's low-tech but creepy, and some of the phantasms and sounds will stay in your mind. Not to be missed is the subterranean cruise through the tawdry land of Pirates of the Caribbean. Sail past buccaneers' skeletons perched atop their mounds of booty and hilariously made-up pirates who loot, plunder and pillage while the villages burn. It's great stuff, created from the imagination that built the Disney myth.

Next up, **Frontierland** harkens back to the rip-roarin' Old West, when cowboys made their own kind of law and order. This is a fairly low-key area of the park, and even small children will emerge unshaken after a ride on the Big Thunder Mountain Railroad roller coaster. Another family favorite here is a churning trip aboard the Mark Twain Riverboat stern-wheeler.

From here it's only a short walk to **Critter Country**, the land of Davy Crocket and a cast of rabbits and bears that harkens back to the early days of North American exploration. The highlight here is Splash Mountain, a high-speed wild water ride aboard hollowed-out logs.

In the park's center, **Fantasyland** can be approached through Sleeping Beauty's Castle. It's filled with the characters and experiences of classic children's stories. Here you'll find Dumbo the Elephant, Peter Pan, Winnie the Pooh, Merlin the Magician and some quaint rides straight out of *Alice in*

Wonderland. The amazing It's a Small World ride floats past hundreds of animatronic children representing the world's cultures, brought together by the Disney theme song. Children are enthralled by this musical voyage, but be warned: Days after you've finished picking Disney popcorn out of your teeth, this song will still be batting around in your head. (The only sure antidote is listening to the entire collection of Led Zeppelin.) Another classic ride is the Matterhorn Bobsled, a roller coaster that's certainly gentle by today's standards but fun nonetheless.

At the northern section of the park is **Mickey's Toon Town**, another favorite with the elementary-school set. This is where Mickey and Minnie make their home (separate ones, of course – this *is* Disney), Donald keeps his boat, Goofy has a Bounce House, Chip 'n Dale have a Treehouse and Roger Rabbit invites you to a Car Toon Spin.

Downtown Disney

Linking Disneyland with the new Disney's California Adventure (see next in this chapter) is this quarter-mile-long mall à la Universal City Walk. Like its LA cousin, Downtown Disney presents a fun, though sanitized, mix of dining, shopping and entertainment venues. Highlights include the *House of Blues* (☎ 714-778-2583), which has live concerts and Southern food; the *ESPN Zone* (☎ 714-300-3776), a 35,000-sq-foot sports and drinking emporium with 175 TV monitors; and *Y Arriba Y Arriba* (☎ 714-533-8272), which pulsates with a sizzling Latin dance show nightly. Dining options include gourmet Mediterranean by star chef Joachim Splichal at *Catal Restaurant* (☎ 714-774-4442) and tropical fare from Mexico, Asia and the Caribbean at the *Rainforest Cafe* (☎ 714-772-0413).

Disney's California Adventure

Opened in February 2001, Disney's California Adventure is right next to the original Disneyland but is not so much of an expansion as it is a park in its own right. It presents the state as an idealized fantasy environment, focusing on its natural and

Manhattan Beach pier

Hermosa Beach's popular pastime

Worry-free livin' along the Pacific Coast Hwy

Venice canals once covered 16 miles.

Point Vicente lighthouse, Palos Verdes

STEPHEN SAKS

Soaking up picturesque Santa Barbara

DAVID PEEVERS

Mission Santa Barbara – the queen of missions

ALISON WRIGHT

Catalina's casino (really a theater and museum) was built by chewing-gum tycoon, William Wrigley Jr.

human-made treasures while blissfully ignoring its problems and troubles. It is, as Richard Corliss of *Time* Magazine put it, 'a G-rated make-over of the tarnished Golden State; a living movie fantasy – the reel thing.' (For telephone numbers, hours and tickets, see Disneyland, earlier in this chapter.)

The park is divided into four main sections: You enter onto **Sunshine Plaza**, anchored by a 50-foot-tall sun that glistens and sparkles in the real California sunshine. Off to the left is the **Hollywood Pictures Backlot**, while straight ahead is the thematic heart of the park, appropriately called **Golden State**. This is subdivided into six districts, each celebrating a region, from Pacific Wharf to Condor Flats (a desert airfield), from Bountiful Valley Farm to the Golden Vine Valley (wine country) to the Bay Area (San Francisco) and Grizzly Peak Recreation Area. Beyond here is **Paradise Pier** where you'll find most of the major rides.

The new park sits on 55 acres and contains about two dozen attractions, many of which are fun but, overall, don't have the heart-stopping, techno-driven velocity of, say, the Indiana Jones ride at Disneyland. Not to be missed is Soarin' Over California in the Condor Flats district, a ride that simulates a hang-gliding experience over the state's mountains, ocean and cities and, of course, Disneyland itself. For more birds-eye views of the park, head to Sun Wheel at Paradise Pier, a giant Ferris wheel modeled after the 1927 Coney Island Wonder Wheel. Also here is California Screamin', a roller coaster built around a Mickey Mouse silhouette; it looks tame but packs a 360° loop and a 108-foot drop, enough to give most people an adrenaline rush.

Some of the park's areas are disturbingly commercial. The main attractions of Pacific Wharf, for instance, are a Boudin Bakery sourdough bread-making factory and a tortilla factory sponsored by Mission Tortilla. Another district, the Golden Vine Valley, offers wine tastings hosted by mega-winemaker Robert Mondavi.

The park also has several attractions that appeal primarily to the elementary-school set. Kids can get 'bug-eyed' during a hilari-ous 3D look at the challenges of insect life in It's Tough to Be a Bug. Jim Henson's Muppet Vision is another low-key 3D treat located in the Hollywood Pictures Backlot.

Perhaps the most visually interesting is the Bay Area district which re-creates typical San Francisco architecture and landmarks. Also here is the Golden Dreams Theater, which shows a 20-minute movie about the history of the state from Native American settlements to today.

Knott's Berry Farm

Just 4 miles northwest of Disneyland, off the I-5 (Santa Ana Fwy) is Knott's Berry Farm (☎ 714-220-5200, *8039 Beach Blvd, Buena Park; admission adults $40, seniors & children 3-11 $30, after 4pm on days the park is open past 6pm all admission $16.95, annual pass $110/50, parking $7; hours vary seasonally, call for specifics*). This park is much less crowded and a kinder, gentler place that lacks the crush and desperation of Disneyland. In fact, many Southern Californians prefer Knott's over subjecting themselves to Mouse-mania.

The park opened in 1932, when Mr Knott's boysenberries (a blackberry-raspberry hybrid) and Mrs Knott's fried-chicken dinners attracted crowds of local farmhands. Mr Knott built an imitation ghost town to keep them entertained, eventually hiring local carnival rides and charging admission. Mrs Knott kept frying the chicken, but the rides and Old West buildings became the main attraction.

The park keeps the Old West theme going at Ghost Town which features buildings brought here from actual historic mining towns in California and other western states. There are staged gunfights, gold-panning demonstrations and steam-train rides. Knott's also acknowledges pre-gold-rush history with Aztec dancers and a California Missions exhibit – there's even mariachi music in Fiesta Village.

Ghost Town is home to GhostRider, one of the world's longest wooden coasters, which rides along a 4530-foot track – 118 feet tall at its highest point – then drops them 108 feet with a G-force of 3.14.

EXCURSIONS

Other roller coaster highlights include Montezuma's Revenge, which makes a loop as high as a three-story building and then does it again backwards; the Corkscrew, which has a triple upside-down loop; and the six-loop Boomerang. The newest scream on the block is Perilous Plunge. Billed as 'just 34 feet shorter than Niagara Falls,' it sends passengers to a height of 127 feet, then drops them down a 115-foot water chute at a 75-degree angle. You *will* get soaked on this one. Also popular is Supreme Scream which plunges you 254 feet (30 stories) at 50 mph with a G-force of 4, then bounces you upward with a G-force of -1.5 – all in about 45 seconds.

For a slightly tamer adventure, Big Foot Rapids sloshes down a faux whitewater river, leaving you absolutely drenched. Camp Snoopy is a kiddy wonderland where you'll meet Snoopy, Charlie Brown, Lucy, Linus and all the other Peanuts characters.

If you pace your day, you might have enough energy left to enjoy the Edison International Electric Nights multimedia/laser/pyrotechnics show. It is accompanied by wild water effects, and the 'ooohs' and 'aaahs' are justified by this high-tech but old-timey show.

Throughout the month of October, Knott's hosts what is possibly Southern California's best and scariest Halloween party. Professional performers in costume haunt the park, special rides and attractions are put up for the occasion, and lights around the park are dimmed or turned off.

Places to Stay

Although Anaheim gets the biggest chunk of its business from Disneyland tourism, it is also a popular year-round convention destination, and room rates shift accordingly.

Budget *HI Fullerton Hacienda Hostel* (☎ *714-738-3721, fax 714-738-0925, hifull@ aol.com, 1700 N Harbor Blvd)* Dorm beds $13-15. This clean and friendly hostel is the cheapest lodging option, with 20 beds in three dorms. Bus No 47 runs to the hostel from the Greyhound station; from the Anaheim Amtrak station, take bus No 41.

The area surrounding Disneyland teems with reasonably priced accommodations; all the major chains (Motel 6, Travelodge, Econo Lodge, etc) are represented. Most rooms here are reliably clean, have all the basic amenities and cost $60 or less; rates sometimes even include continental breakfast. Most hotels offer shuttle service to Disneyland. Prices may be slightly higher between May and October. Independent motels and hotels near Disneyland include the following.

Alamo Inn (☎ *714-635-8070, 800-378-9696, fax 714-778-3307, 1140 W Katella Ave)* Rooms $60-80. This fairly pleasant place has rooms with coffeemakers and cable TV, and there's a swimming pool and Jacuzzi as well. It's a block and a half from the park.

Little Boy Blue (☎ *714-635-2781, 800-284-3804, fax 714-635-4254, 416 W Katella Ave)* Rates $60-90, includes continental breakfast. Rooms sparkle after a recent face-lift and are stocked with such amenities as microwaves and coffeemakers.

Castle Inn & Suites (☎ *714-774-8111, 800-227-8530, fax 714-956-4736, 1734 S Harbor Blvd)* Rooms $80-110. Those willing and able to spend slightly more should check out this place, which has a pool, spa and free parking.

Candy Cane Inn (☎ *714-774-5284, 800-345-7057, fax 714-772-5462, 1747 S Harbor Blvd)* Rooms $80-110. Across the street, this place was recently overhauled and is another good bet.

Mid-Range & Top End *Disneyland Hotel* (☎ *714-778-6600, fax 714-956-6597, 1150 W Cerritos Ave)* and *Disneyland Pacific Hotel* (☎ *714-999-0990, fax 714-956-6508, 1717 S West St)* Rooms $110-275, discounts for multiple nights (call ☎ 800-523-9000). These two hotels are connected to the park by monorail. On some days, hotel guests get to enter the park 1½ hours before the general public.

Hilton Anaheim (☎ *714-750-4321, 800-222-9923, fax 714-740-4252, 777 Convention Way)* Rooms $140-285. This dependable giant both in reputation and size (1580 rooms) caters to the convention crowd. It recently underwent a $18.5 million restoration and is two blocks from Disneyland.

Places to Eat

Within the Disneyland theme park, the nicest restaurants are the **Blue Bayou** for Louisiana-style cuisine and **Bengal Barbecue** for more healthful salads and chicken. Otherwise it's mostly burgers, fries, ice cream and buckets of popcorn.

Outside the park, choices are slim besides hotel and chain restaurants, with a few notable exceptions.

Millie's Restaurant (☎ 714-535-6892, 1480 S Harbor Blvd) Mains $6-10; open 6am-midnight. Across from Disneyland's main entrance, this family restaurant has an all-you-can-eat buffet and is famous for its banana splits.

Sonic Drive-In (☎ 714-992-4500, 1632 N Lemon Rd) Mains under $5. For a flashback to the days of Elvis and Eisenhower come to this place where your burgers, hot dogs and fries are delivered straight to your car by friendly carhops.

Disney's PCH Grill (☎ 714-956-6755, 1717 S West St) Mains $11-20. PCH artfully presents California eclectic cuisine at the Disneyland Pacific Hotel. Creative wood-fired pizzas, pastas and seafood are all pretty good.

Cuban Pete's (☎ 714-490-2020, 1050 W Ball Rd) Mains $12-22. With some imagination you may feel yourself transported to Hemingway's 1940s Havana. Otherwise, just enjoy the Cuban food flavored with exotic spices.

Getting There & Away

Disneyland is about 30 miles south of Downtown LA. Take the Disneyland exit off the I-5 (Santa Ana Fwy) and follow the copious signs. Another option is booking yourself on a tour (see Organized Tours in the Getting Around chapter).

From the Greyhound station (☎ 714-999-1246, 100 W Winston Rd), buses to LA depart at least hourly; the trip takes from one half to 1½ hours and costs $8 each way. The AirportBus (☎ 800-772-5299) runs between LAX and Anaheim hotels at fre-

quent intervals; tickets are $14/25 one way/roundtrip.

Amtrak's *Pacific Surfliner* goes to Downtown LA's Union Station with Anaheim up to nine times daily (41 minutes, $8 each way). The station is at Edison International Field.

Knott's Berry Farm is south of I-5 (Santa Ana Fwy) and the 91 Fwy about 40 miles south of Downtown LA. Take the Beach Blvd exit from the I-5, 91, 22 or 405 Fwys. Amtrak's Fullerton Station (☎ 714-992-0530), on the LA-San Diego route, is connected to the park by bus No 99 ($1). MTA bus No 460 connects the park to Downtown LA.

SANTA CATALINA ISLAND

Santa Catalina – called Catalina locally – is one of the largest of the Channel Islands, a chain of semi-submerged mountains that rise from the floor of the Pacific between Santa Barbara and San Diego. It's a 'deer park' for the privileged and protected, to be sure. But it's also, literally, a breath of fresh air for impacted Angelenos, such as a medical student who rented a room there to study for exams and a screenwriter whose writer's block dissolved after a week in Avalon (the island's only town).

'Discovered' by Juan Rodriguez Cabrillo in 1542, the island was relatively untouched until 1811, when the native seafaring Indians were tragically resettled on the mainland. Most of the island has since been privately owned. Catalina was purchased in 1919 by chewing-gum magnate William Wrigley Jr (1861–1932), who built a mansion and a casino. He also briefly made Catalina the spring training headquarters for his major-league baseball team, the Chicago Cubs.

Even after the Mediterranean-flavored port town of Avalon began attracting tourists in the 1930s, Catalina's interior and most of its coastline remained largely undeveloped. In conjunction with LA County, the nonprofit Santa Catalina Island Conservancy (☎ 310-510-1421) was able to buy 86% of the 8-by-21-mile island from the Wrigley family in 1975, assuring that it remains free of future development.

The island has a unique ecosystem, with 400 plant species, including eight endemic ones, more than 100 types of birds, and numerous animals such as deer, goats, boar and foxes. There are also several hundred wild American bison descended from those brought to Catalina in 1925 for the filming of Zane Grey's *The Vanishing American*.

Catalina's main tourist season is June to September, when prices are steepest, especially on weekends. Rates plunge for midweek travel and during the off-season, though some activities may not be available during those times.

Avalon

Most of Catalina's 3500 permanent residents (and up to four times as many in summer) live in tiny Avalon, on the southeast shore facing Avalon Bay. Hotels, restaurants and shops line the recently overhauled shorefront, Crescent Ave, and its side streets. The Catalina Visitors Bureau (☎ 310-510-1520, www.catalina.com; open daily) has a booth on the Green Pleasure Pier, with maps, brochures, tour and general information.

Catalina's most noticeable landmark is the circular white Spanish Moderne **Casino** *(☎ 310-510-0179, 1 Casino Way)*, built for Wrigley in 1929. This is no gambling joint: The top-floor grand ballroom once featured dancing to the big-band tunes of Benny Goodman, Glenn Miller and other such legends; beneath is a gorgeous 1184-seat Art Deco theater with an organ and murals of underwater scenes. Visit during nightly first-run movie screenings ($7.50), or join a 40-minute tour ($9). Also here is the **Catalina Island Museum** *(☎ 310-510-2414; admission $1.50; open 10:30am-4pm daily)*, which explores 7000 years of island history.

The **Wrigley Memorial and Botanical Garden** *(☎ 310-510-2595, 1400 Avalon Canyon Rd; admission adults $3, children under 12 free; open 8am-5pm daily)* is about 1½ miles inland from Avalon Bay. A spiral staircase climbs the 130-foot tower of the memorial, built in 1934 of blue flagstone and decorative glazed tile to honor Wrigley. Surrounding it is the 38-acre garden with

its impressive cacti groves, succulents and samples of the eight plant species endemic to Catalina. The best time to visit is during wildflower season around February and March.

Two Harbors

Besides Avalon, the only development on Santa Catalina is Two Harbors, which occupies an isthmus near the island's northeastern end. There's a beachfront campground, picnic area, dive shop, general store, restaurant and saloon and hilltop lodge.

In the summer, you can reach this remote and pretty area by Coastal Shuttle boat from Avalon ($13, 45 minutes) and directly from San Pedro's Catalina Sea & Air Terminal ($36, 90 minutes). It's also served by the Safari Shuttle Bus (see Getting Around, later in this chapter).

Water Sports

Those with a love of water sports – above and below sea level – will find plenty to do on Catalina. Most outfitters have set up shop on Avalon's Green Pier, where you can gather information, rent equipment and book tours.

Swimmers can take to the water from the small beach next to the pier, though a better option is the club-like Descanso Beach just beyond the Casino. It's privately owned and

Shark got your oar?

there's a $2 admission, but it's one of the few US beaches where alcohol is allowed.

Snorkelers should head to Lovers' Cove, on the southeastern end of Avalon Bay, which is hard to beat for density and variety of wildlife. Highlights include the sunset-colored, luminescent garibaldi (the official California state marine fish) and the occasional horn or leopard shark. Snorkeling gear can be rented for $5-7/hour or $10-12/day from a number of outfitters set up at the cove and also on the pier. Scuba divers will want to head to the spectacular Underwater Park, right at the Casino. Catalina Divers Supply (☎ 310-510-0330, 800-353-0330) rents equipment and operates guided dive tours from $75, including all gear.

Kayak rentals (no experience necessary) are available from Descanso Beach Ocean Sports (☎ 310-510-1226). Single kayaks cost $11/45 per hour/day. Guided kayak tours start at $36. Joe's Rent-A-Boat on the Green Pier (☎ 310-510-0330, 800-353-0330) rents kayaks as well as small boats, a good way to get away from Avalon and discover the secluded beaches along the rugged coastline. Rates start at $30/hour for a 16-foot utility boat, also good for fishing excursions.

Organized Tours

The easiest way to see Catalina is on an organized tour, offered by several operators including Santa Catalina Discovery Tours (☎ 310-510-8687, 800-626-1496) and Catalina Adventure Tours (☎ 310-510-2888). Options include exploration of the protected island interior ($36) and of Catalina's rich underwater gardens aboard a glass-bottom boat ($8 adults and $5 children, students and seniors). There are also scenic tours of Avalon and harbor and night cruises. Jeep Eco-Tours (☎ 310-510-2595, ext 0) run by the Catalina Island Conservancy, offers three-hour journeys on the island's back roads for $98.

Places to Stay

Hermit Gulch Campground (☎ 310-510-8368) Tent sites $12 late Mar-Labor Day, $6 rest of year. This lovely campground is in beautiful Avalon Canyon, a 1½-mile hike or a ride aboard the Island Hopper bus (see Getting Around) from Avalon. If you don't have your own tent or camping equipment, you can rent it here ($10/16 for a 2-person/4-person tent, $20 teepees). For information on campgrounds in the island's rugged interior, call ☎ 888-510-7979 or check www.catalina.com/twoharbors.

Hostel La Vista (☎ 310-510-0603, 145 Marilla Ave) Dorm beds $15; open June-Oct. This privately run affair offers bare-bones accommodations.

Catalina's hotels depend heavily on summer business, and rates vary widely between seasons. In general, rates go up during weekends year-round; some properties impose a two-night minimum stay.

Hermosa Hotel (☎ 310-510-1010, 888-684-1313, hermosa@usa.net, 131 Metropole St) Rooms $35-55 midweek, $50-100 weekend May-Oct, less Nov-Apr. Half a block from the beach, this hotel offers great value and friendly service. Some units have kitchens.

Catalina Beach House (☎ 310-510-1078, 800-974-6835, 310-510-1573) Rooms $75-145 summer, $35-105 rest of year. This newly remodeled place has rooms with TV, VCR (free movies), phone, microwave and coffeemaker. Divers are welcome.

Zane Grey Pueblo Hotel (☎ 310-510-0966, 800-378-3256, fax 310-510-1340, 199 Chimes Tower Rd) Rooms $135-165 summer, $80-110 rest of year. For a real retreat, hole up at this quiet 16-room inn (1926). The Zane Grey was formerly the pueblo adobe home of its namesake, the prolific American Western writer. Rooms have no phones but the best views around. Ask for weekend specials during the off season.

Inn on Mt Ada (☎ 310-510-2030, fax 310-510-2237, 398 Wrigley Rd) Rooms $330-620 summer, $280-570 winter, including breakfast & lunch. Top of the line is this stuffily stylish and luxurious six-room inn in the historic Wrigley mansion, with superb views of the bay. Rates include a golf cart, the main means of getting around on this largely car-free island.

EXCURSIONS

Places to Eat

In keeping with its upscale accommodations, Avalon's restaurants are similarly pricey. Most are concentrated along waterfront Crescent Ave.

Armstrong's Seafood (☎ 310-510-0113, *306 Crescent Ave*) Lunch $7-13, dinner $11-21. Come here for upscale steak and seafood, including sashimi, best consumed on the deck with a view of the bay.

Antonio's Pizzeria & Cabaret (☎ 310-510-0008, *230 Crescent Ave*) Breakfast from $5, lunch & dinner $6-17. Another place for waterfront dining, Antonio's serves pizza, pasta, burgers, salads and the like. Friday and Saturday are karaoke nights.

Blue Parrot (☎ 310-510-2465, *205 Crescent Ave*) Lunch $7-9, dinner $12-16. The Blue Parrot has casual American fare like salads and burgers and live entertainment on Friday and Saturday.

Casino Dock Cafe (☎ 310-510-2755, *1 Casino Way*) Mains $5-9; closed Dec-Mar. A bit off the beaten path, but en route to the Casino, this is a good place for simple fare and drinks.

Pancake Cottage (☎ 310-510-0726, *118 Catalina St*) Mains $4-8; closes at 2pm. Huge and satisfying breakfasts are served just off Crescent Ave at the slightly eccentric eatery.

Getting There & Away

Catalina Express (☎ 310-519-1212, 800-481-3470) offers the fastest and smoothest service with up to 30 departures daily. Boats leave from the Catalina Express Port next to the *Queen Mary* (Map 16; see Long Beach in the Things to See & Do chapter) and from the Catalina Sea & Air Terminal, Berth 95 in San Pedro (Map 15). Roundtrip fares are $39 adults, $29.50 ages two to 11, $35.50 if over 55; bikes or surfboards are an additional $6. The trip lasts about one hour from Long Beach and 1¼ hours from San Pedro. Boats also depart from San Pedro to Two Harbors (same fare, 1½ hours).

Fifteen-minute helicopter rides aboard Island Express (☎ 310-510-2525, 800-228-2566) from the boat terminals in San Pedro and Long Beach to Avalon cost $68/125 one way/roundtrip.

Getting Around

Only 10-year Catalina residents are allowed to have cars on the island. Bicycles and golf carts can be rented for travel around Avalon, but if you plan on going beyond the square-mile city limits, you'll need to buy a $50 permit (ask at the visitors bureau, which can also recommend bike rental shops).

The Island Hopper bus provides public transportation around Avalon for $1 per ride. For trips into the interior, including the airport, Little Harbor, Two Harbors and the Hermit Gulch Campground, take the Safari Shuttle Bus. In summer, the Coastal Shuttle boat operates between Avalon and Two Harbors ($13, 45 minutes).

LAGUNA BEACH

Laguna Beach is proof that there's more to Orange County than Disneyland and shopping. About 60 miles south of Los Angeles, this gorgeous Riviera-like stretch of seaside is defined by secluded beaches, low cliffs, glassy waves, waterfront parks, eucalyptus-covered hillsides and a host of art galleries and boutiques. Home to several renowned arts festivals (see the related boxed text), as well as the highly regarded Laguna Playhouse, the city draws artists, culture lovers and art collectors from all over the world. Laguna's population of 23,000 swells with tourists on summer weekends, but away from the Village (the central business district) and Main Beach (where the Village meets the shore), there is plenty of un-crowded sand and water.

History

Laguna's earliest inhabitants, the Ute-Aztecas and Shoshone tribes, called the area 'Lagonas' because of two freshwater lagoons in what is now Laguna Canyon. The name held until 1904, when it was changed to Laguna. At roughly the same time, San Francisco artist Norman St Claire came to Laguna to paint watercolors of the surf, cliffs and hills. His enthusiasm drew other artists, who, influenced by French impressionism, were known as the *plein air* (outdoors) school. The Laguna Beach Art Association, the precursor to the Laguna

Laguna Arts Festivals

Laguna Beach's landmark event is the **Festival of the Arts**, a seven-week, juried exhibit of 160 artists whose work varies from paintings to handcrafted furniture to scrimshaw. Begun in 1933 by local artists who needed to drum up buyers for their work, the festival now attracts patrons and tourists from all over the world and offers such added attractions as the Junior Art Gallery featuring children's art, free daily workshops conducted by artists, and live entertainment. The grounds are open from 10am (closing hours vary) daily July to August; season admission for adults is $7, seniors and students $5.

The most unique aspect of the fair, and a tremendous experience that will leave you rubbing your eyes in disbelief, is the **Pageant of the Masters**, where human models are blended seamlessly into re-creations of famous paintings. This also began in 1933 as a sideshow to the main festival. Tickets ($10 to $60) need to be ordered weeks in advance, though you can often pick up last-minute cancellation tickets at the gate. Nightly performances begin at 8:30pm. For information call ☎ 949-497-6582; for tickets call ☎ 800-487-3378. The Web site is at www.foapom.org.

In the 1960s, Laguna Beach artists who did not make the juried exhibition started their own festival to take advantage of the art-seekers passing through town. They set up directly across from the festival (935 Laguna Canyon Rd, half a mile from the Village), mocking its formal atmosphere by scattering sawdust on the ground. Local journalist Dick Nall coined the name **Sawdust Art Festival** (☎ 949-494-3030, www.sawdustartfestival.org), which, now juried itself, has remained ever since. Many people actually enjoy this festival more, as the arts and crafts are utilitarian and quite affordable. Hours are 10am-10pm. Day admission passes for adults are $6.50; seniors, $5.50; children, $2. Season passes are also available.

A third art festival, the **Art-A-Fair Festival** (☎ 949-494-4514), runs simultaneously and is a nationally juried show focused on watercolors, pastels and oil paintings, although photography, jewelry, ceramics and other arts and crafts are displayed as well. Its grounds are at 777 Laguna Canyon Rd, and it's open daily until 9pm or 10pm. Admission for adults is $5, seniors and students $3.50, children under 12 free. Buses (75¢) shuttle continuously from 10am-midnight between the festivals and the Village.

Art Museum, was founded in 1918. By the late '20s, more than half of the town's 300 residents were artists.

The 1920s and '30s brought the most lasting development to Laguna. In 1926, the Pacific Coast Hwy was opened between Newport Beach and Dana Point, allowing Laguna three access routes. Mary Pickford, Douglas Fairbanks, Mickey Rooney and Bette Davis vacationed here regularly and in 1932 helped establish the Laguna Playhouse (still in operation) and the Festival of the Arts, still the town's biggest attraction.

Orientation & Information

Though Laguna stretches for about 7 miles along Pacific Coast Hwy, the shops, restaurants and bars are concentrated in the Village, along Broadway, Ocean, and Forest Sts and their intersections with Pacific Coast Hwy (all within a quarter-mile). Across Pacific Coast Hwy from the Village, Main Beach offers the most public beach access. Just four miles south, the separate community of Laguna Niguel is home to the fancy Ritz-Carlton Hotel and Salt Creek Beach, a favorite with local surfers.

The Laguna Beach Visitors Bureau (☎ 949-497-9229, 800-877-1115, fax 949-376-0558, www.lagunabeachinfo.org, 252 Broadway; open 9am-5pm Mon-Fri, weekend hours vary by season) is a block off Pacific Coast Hwy. It offers information of all kinds and will make walk-in lodging reservations for free. The free weekly *Coastline News*, available here and around town, lists local news and events.

Parking is a perpetual problem. If you're spending the night in town, leave your car at your hotel and take the bus (see Getting Around). Parking lots in the Village charge $6 or more and fill up quickly in summer.

Laguna Art Museum

The Laguna Art Association showcases its collection at this museum (☎ 949-494-8971, 307 Cliff Dr; admission adults $5, seniors & students $4, children under 12 free, free for all on Tues; open 11am-5pm Thur-Tues, free tours 2pm Sat-Tues). There are three levels of exhibit space and an interesting gift shop. Changing exhibits usually feature one or two California artists, while the permanent collection consists primarily of works by early Laguna artists, California landscapes and vintage photographs.

Beaches

Laguna Beach has 30 public beaches and coves, and most are accessible by stairs off Pacific Coast Hwy; just look for the 'Beach Access' signs. Main Beach fronts the Village and has volleyball and basketball courts, a wooden boardwalk and colorful tile benches. This is the best place for swimming, as the water is calm, rocks are absent and lifeguards are on duty year-round. At the north end of this beach, a path heads up the bluff (past Las Brisas restaurant) to Heisler Park, a long, skinny stretch of grass accented by hibiscus, roses and bougainvillea. Several sets of stairs lead down to the sand; at the north end of the park is Diver's Cove, a deep protected inlet popular with guess who. On the north end of town, Crescent Bay is the best beach for body surfing, with big hollow waves. Parking is difficult; try the bluffs atop the beach.

About 1 mile south of the Village is one of Laguna's less crowded beaches, Victoria Beach. Besides volleyball courts, its main attraction is the 'La Tour' landmark from 1926, a Rapunzel-tower-like structure that provides private beach access from the house above. Everyone else has to take the stairs down Victoria Dr; there's limited parking on Pacific Coast Hwy. A bit farther south is Aliso Creek Beach, which is popular with surfers; there's also a fishing pier. Parking is fairly plentiful.

Places to Stay

Accommodations get booked far in advance for summer months, when prices are hiked up by 20% to 50%.

Hotel Laguna (☎ 949-494-1151, 800-524-2927, fax 949-497-2163, 425 S Coast Hwy) Rooms $100-185 May-Aug, $80-165 Sept-Apr. Right on the beach, the hotel features a pool, spa, sun terrace and a private beach club. A continental breakfast is delivered to the rooms.

Vacation Village (☎ 949-494-8566, 800-843-6895, fax 949-494-1386, 647 S Coast Hwy) Rooms without/with ocean view $90/163 summer, $80/118 rest of year. South of the Village, this is a good spot for families. It has 130 units, about half of them with kitchens, plus two pools and a spa.

Eiler's Inn (☎ 949-494-3004, fax 949-497-2215, 741 S Coast Hwy) Rooms $130-255 June-Sept, $95-175 Oct-May. Romantics should try to score one of the 12 rooms at this B&B just a few steps from the heart of the Village and the beach. Antique furniture, Art Nouveau lamps, lots of fluffy pillows and flowery wallpaper are just some of the idyllic touches. Rooms wrap around a central fountain courtyard, where wine and cheese are served nightly; breakfasts are memorable. There's also a sundeck with an ocean view.

Surf and Sand (☎ 949-497-4477, 800-524-8621, fax 949-494-7653, 1555 S Coast Hwy) Rooms $345-425 summer, $285-360 rest of year. One of Laguna's most elegant establishments sports a natural color scheme commensurate with its name. Luxurious rooms have all the trappings; some also have ocean views. The Splashes restaurant serves classy California cuisine right next to the private beach.

Inn at Laguna Beach (☎ 949-497-9722, 800-544-4479, fax 949-497-9972, 211 N Coast Hwy) Rooms $149-589 summer, $109-549 rest of year. If you're going to splurge, this should be your first choice: the inn perches dreamily atop the cliff between Main Beach and Heisler Park. Spacious rooms are appointed with French blinds, lots of special amenities like a selection of books and CDs and bathrobes. A lavish breakfast is delivered to your room, and the Las Brisas restaurant is immediately next door.

Ritz-Carlton Laguna Niguel (☎ 949-240-2000, 800-241-3333, fax 949-240-1061, Ritz-Carlton Dr) Rooms from $375, 10 times that for a deluxe suite. The flashiest hotel in the area is 'The Ritz,' west off Pacific Coast Hwy, offering lap-of-luxury accommodations in an opulent setting. There are two pools, a full spa, tennis courts, terraced paths to the beach (which happens to be a great surfing spot), a library and smoking lounge, and several restaurants. The most affordable experience here is a drink in the Lobby Lounge, a grand place to watch the sunset.

Places to Eat

Taco Loco (☎ 949-497-1635, 640 S Coast Hwy) Mains under $5. Open to midnight, to 2am weekends. Surfers, the budget-conscious and those wanting a late-night snack flock to this sidewalk cafe with a taco bar (from $1.50) as well as quesadillas, nachos and lots of vegetarian choices.

Las Brisas (☎ 949-497-5434, 361 Cliff Dr) Lunch $7-13, dinner $15-25. Next to the Laguna Art Museum, this institution has one of the best views on the coast. It serves Mexican seafood dishes in the dining room and snacks and soft tacos on the patio bar. It also has a great breakfast buffet with an omelet chef whisking up your favorites.

Cottage Restaurant (☎ 949-494-3023, 308 N Coast Hwy) Lunch $7-10, dinner $10-20. Across the street from Las Brisas, this place is equally popular in the morning. Assets here are the big rustic outdoor tables, free newspapers and lip-smacking cranberry orange pancakes ($3.95).

Dizz's As Is (☎ 949-494-5250, 2794 S Coast Hwy) Dinner $16-27; closed Mon. This local favorite is in a wood-shingled 1920s house with an Art Deco interior. The continental menu, changes daily but focuses on seafood and fowl. Complete dinners include paté, soup or salad and sourdough bread.

White House (☎ 949-494-8088, 340 S Coast Hwy) Lunch $6-9.50, dinner $9-20. This restaurant serves contemporary food and, after dark, turns into a bar and nightclub, often with live music.

Even more entertainment is provided by Laguna's two microbrewery pubs. Both have indoor and outdoor seating.

Laguna Beach Brewing Company (☎ 949-499-2337, 422 S Coast Hwy) Mains $8-18. At Laguna's first microbrewery, you can drink and eat with a view of the ocean. On Saturday nights, it has live magic performances. The food ranges from pizzas to ribs to salads and sandwiches.

Ocean Brewing Company (☎ 949-497-3381, 237 Ocean Ave) Lunch $8-12, dinner $12-20. Come here for handmade brews and Italian cuisine, which are served in a convivial atmosphere.

Getting There & Away

To reach Laguna from the I-405 (San Diego Fwy), take Route 133 (Laguna Canyon Rd) west; this passes the Festival of the Arts site and takes you right to the Village and beaches. An alternative to this curvy and fairly dangerous road is to take the Route 73 toll road at Costa Mesa ($2.50). Traveling to or from Laguna by public transportation is difficult.

Getting Around

Laguna Beach Transit (LBT; ☎ 949-497-0746) has its central bus depot on the 300 block of Broadway, a block inland from the visitors bureau, and operates three routes at hourly intervals (no service between noon and 1pm). The Gray Line covers Laguna Canyon, North Laguna and the Top of the World viewpoint. The Blue Line heads from central Laguna into the residential areas of Bluebird Canyon and Arch Beach Heights. For visitors, the most important is the Light Blue Line, which travels to the hotels and beaches along Pacific Coast Hwy, terminating at the Ritz-Carlton Hotel. Ask for the self-guided bus tour pamphlets at the visitors bureau. Each ride is 75¢.

EXCURSIONS

Several places in town rent bicycles, including Laguna Beach Cyclery (☎ 949-494-1522, 240 Thalia St) and Rainbow Bicycle Co (☎ 949-494-5806, 485 N Coast Hwy). A 24-hour rental is about $20.

GLEN IVY HOT SPRINGS

At the foot of the Santa Ana Mountains, about an hour and a half southeast of Los Angeles, is this lovely bathing complex (☎ 909-277-3529, ext 0, 25000 Glen Ivy Rd, Corona; admission $24 Mon-Thur, $29 Fri-Sun, minimum age is 16; open 9:30am-6pm Apr 1-Oct 31, to 5pm Nov 1-Mar 31). There are 15 pools and spas filled with naturally heated mineral water, surrounded by 10 acres of landscaped grounds profuse with bougainvillea, eucalyptus and palm trees. Spend a relaxing day wallowing in the hot pools, take an aqua aerobics class, treat yourself to a massage (extra fee) or swim some laps in a larger swimming pool.

The best part here, though, is the red-clay mud pool. Like some prehistoric animal wandering into the tar pits, you first soak yourself in muck. Then, apply what amounts to a full-body mask by grabbing a chunk of clay and smearing it all over your body before lounging in the sun until it's baked on to your skin. Whether this treatment truly has therapeutic effects is debatable, but it's certainly fun. Bring an old swimsuit, though, as the clay does stain a little.

From LA, take the I-10 (San Bernadino Fwy) east to the I-15 Fwy south; exit at Temescal Canyon Rd, turn right and drive 1 mile to Glen Ivy Rd, turn right and go to the end.

BIG BEAR LAKE

The main reason to come to Big Bear Lake, framed by the San Bernardino National Forest, is for outdoor recreation. The year-round, family-friendly mountain resort is an easy and enormously popular getaway for people from LA, the deserts and San Diego. In the warmer seasons, the lake itself is the main attraction. Eight miles long and 1 mile across at its widest point, it was formed in 1888 behind a dam built to provide water to citrus growers in Redlands. It's perfect for swimming, waterskiing, sailing, fishing, jet skiing and other water sports.

During the winter months, downhill skiers and snowboarders are drawn here by Southern California's two largest ski areas – Bear Mountain and Snow Summit – which are taken over by mountain bikers as soon as the snow melts. Big Bear Village is the town's cutesy and touristy center, which attempts to re-create the atmosphere of an Alpine resort.

Orientation & Information

Most of Big Bear town is sandwiched between the lake's southern shore and the mountains. It is bisected by Hwy 18, here called Big Bear Blvd. Big Bear Village sits right at the center, with most of the cabins and nicer motels located along the highway to the west. East of the Village is the more commercial part of town, with a number of motels, fast-food stores and a modern shopping center. The lake's northern shore, along Hwy 38 (here North Shore Blvd), is much quieter and is the departure point for most hiking trails.

Maps, brochures and information on area dining and activities can be found at the Big Bear Lake Chamber of Commerce (☎ 909-866-4607, info@bigbearchamber.com, www.bigbearchamber.com, 630 Bartlett Rd; open 8am-5pm Mon-Fri, 9am-5pm Sat-Sun). Also here in the Visitors Center is the Big Bear Lake Resort Association (☎ 800-424-4232, fax 909-866-5671, www.bigbearinfo.com), which can help with lodging at places that are organization members.

For suggestions on hiking trails, maps and wilderness permits, visit the ranger-staffed Discovery Center (☎ 909-866-3437, along Hwy 38; open 8am-6pm daily May-Oct, to 4:30pm Nov-Apr), on the northern shore (just look for the signs). This wonderful facility features educational exhibits, weekly events and a top-notch staff.

The Discovery Center also sells the National Forest Adventure Pass. Anyone visiting Southern California's forests by car must purchase this permit ($5/30 a day/year). It's transferable and should be displayed on the windshield if you're stopping

EXCURSIONS

Air Combat USA: The Ultimate Thrill Ride

Plunk down $895 and get ready for a life-changing experience. You'll drive to the Air Combat USA (☎ 714-522-7590, 800-522-7590, 230 N Dale Place) offices at Fullerton airport, about 30 miles southeast of Downtown LA, and meet with some of the top military pilots in the world. One of them will be your classroom instructor and another will be your copilot in a high-performance Marchetti aircraft, outfitted with an infrared video 'machine gun.' After a morning theory session, you will fly off, alongside an opponent in another plane, for your first experience of air combat. And you had best believe it's the real thing: Nothing on the ground will ever prepare you for what's about to happen in the sky.

You'll fly your aircraft to a 'combat' area over the Pacific Ocean and engage in a series of six dogfights, where you'll try to get the upper hand on your opponent, the 'bandit,' by lining him up in your gunsights and shooting him out of the sky. You will fly at 250mph and experience vertical climbs, dives, snap rolls and loops. You will fly your aircraft upside down – the world spinning around your head – and roar like an animal when the G-forces threaten to tear off your helmet. You will curse when a plume of smoke pours from beneath your fuselage (meaning you've been killed) and shout for joy when you've got that other sucker in the cross-hairs of your gunsights. And it'll all be there for you to view on the video that was made of your entire flight, complete with all the grunts, groans and victory screams.

Bungee jumping, whitewater river rafting, high-speed racecar driving – forget 'em! There is no on-the-edge experience that remotely compares with this; that is, until you try the same thing in an F-16.

– David Peevers

at a ranger station or parking at a fee-based campground or ski resort. If you're caught parking without the pass, the penalty is $100. However, displaying of the pass isn't required if you're just driving through the forest without parking your car.

Skiing

With an 8000-foot ridge rising above the lake's south side, Big Bear Lake is known for its downhill skiing and snowboarding. Snow usually falls by mid-December and lasts until March or April, with snowmaking machines producing supplementary powder whenever necessary. The best part about Big Bear skiing is the weather – sunshine 90% of the time, and shorts and T-shirt temperatures in spring. Very basic ski, boot and pole rentals start at $10/day (more for high-performance gear and discounts for week-long rentals), offered all along Hwy 18 and at ski lodges.

Both of Big Bear's ski mountains are off Hwy 18. There are 12 lifts and 1200 vertical

feet at **Snow Summit** (☎ 909-866-5766, 888-786-6481 for 24-hour snow information, www.snowsummit.com; adult day lift tickets $39, half-day tickets $30, night tickets $24, during holidays $49). Tickets come with a satisfaction guarantee and may be exchanged for vouchers (within 75 minutes of issue) good for another day.

There are 11 lifts and 1665 vertical feet at **Bear Mountain** (☎ 909-585-2519, 800-232-7686 for 24-hour snow information, www.bearmtn.com; adult day lift tickets $35). Its Outlaw Snowboard Park is a favorite with young hotdoggers. While Snow Summit has more terrain, Bear Mountain is favored for its steep upper runs.

A smaller area, which is good for beginners and iffy intermediates, is **Snow Valley** (☎ 909-867-2751), 11 miles west of Big Bear on Hwy 18.

Hiking

In summer, people trade their ski boots for hiking boots and hit the forest trails. The best hiking and most accessible trailheads are on the lake's north shore, off Hwy 38.

One of the nicest trails is the Pacific Crest Trail (PCT), an easy walk along a 2400-foot ridge, 2 miles long and parallel to the highway, offering great scenery and views. A moderately difficult hike up the Cougar Crest Trail starting near the Discovery Center accesses the PCT and offers grand views of Big Bear Lake and Holcomb Valley. Popular too is the Woodland Trail, an easy 1½-mile nature trail starting at the lake's eastern end.

Mountain Biking

Big Bear is hugely popular for mountain biking, and the town is the site of professional and amateur racing competitions. Most popular is the terrain atop Snow Summit, crisscrossed by 40 miles of roads and trails suitable for all levels of riders. A chairlift ($7 per ride, $19 unlimited all day rides) provides easy access to the top with your bike. Tickets, guides, maps and bike rentals are available from the Mountain Bike Center (☎ 909-866-4565) at the mountain base. Rental prices start at $9/50 hour/day and include helmets. Popular riding areas that don't require the chairlift are

Holcomb Valley, Delamar Mountain and Van Duesen Canyon off Hwy 38. Non-mountain cyclists will enjoy the gentle 2½-mile bike path along the lake's north shore.

Water Sports

Big Bear Lake is best experienced from the water, which provides cool respite from hot summer days. Swim Beach, just east of the Village, is the lake's only official swimming area and is popular with famili in a beautiful bay accented by islands made up of piles of boulders and the privately owned China Island. There's no access by road, es. The best swimming, however, is on the lake's far-western end, so the only way to get there is by boat or jet ski.

The rental place closest to China Island is North Shore Landing (☎ 909-878-4386, 38573 North Shore Dr). Jet skis (for one to three people) rent from $55-95/hour; a boat and equipment for water skiing is $95/hour; speed boats (for two to six) are $65-95/hour, plus gas; pontoon boats (for eight to 10) cost $50/hour or $185/day, plus gas; and sail boats (for two to six; two-hour minimum) are $25-45/hour.

The lake teems with trout, catfish, bass, carp and other fish, though catching them is not always easy. Those bent on success should sign up with the affable John Cantrell Guide Service (☎ 909-585-4017, 909-593-4309), which guarantees you'll catch a fish or your money back. You'll need to buy a fishing license ($9/27 day/year), available at sporting goods stores around town, and rent a boat ($40/hour). John will provide all the poles, bait, expertise – and fish.

Other Activities

Explorations of the mountains are offered by Jeep Tours (☎ 909-878-5337, 40687 Village Dr; open mid-May–mid-October). Tours start at $37.95 for a 90-minute outing, though the most popular is the three-hour White Mountain Tour ($52.95). Another way to see the mountains is on horseback. Guided tours are offered by several companies in town, including Rockin' K Riding Stables (☎ 909-878-4677, 731 Tulip Lane).

Alpine Slide (☎ 909-866-4626, on Big Bear Blvd just west of the Village) begins with a placid chairlift ride up Magic Mountain. This is followed by a thrilling wheeled bobsled ride that hurtles down a concrete track with you at the controls – more or less. Single rides are $3.50, five rides are $15. The complex also includes a water slide and a go-cart track.

For 9- or 18-hole golfing, sign up for tee time at the Bear Mountain Golf Course (☎ 909-585-8002).

Places to Stay

Accommodations in Big Bear Lake run the gamut from snug B&Bs and resort cabins to lodges, hotels, campgrounds and private homes. In general, rates drop during midweek (Sunday to Thursday) and go up on weekends, especially around holidays. Some places require two-night minimum stays. The Big Bear Visitors Center (see Orientation & Information earlier) has a thorough list and makes free reservations.

Camping There are numerous campgrounds, administered by the US Forest Service, in the Big Bear Lake area. For reservations, call ☎ 877-444-6777 or go online at www.reserveusa.com.

Pineknot Campground (☎ 909-866-8550, top of Summit Blvd) Tent sites $15, open May-late Oct. This 48-space campground is in a fir, pine and oak forest next to a ski area yet close to town.

Serrano (☎ 909-866-8550, off Hwy 38) Tent sites $18-36, RV sites $28, two-night minimum stay on weekends, open Apr 1-Sept 30. Near the Discovery Center on the north shore of the lake, this is the only area campground with showers and RV hookups. It has 132 spaces.

Cabins Renting a cabin is a good value for groups of four or more, but the privacy of your own place is also cherished by individuals and couples. Big Bear Lake has dozens of cabins, ranging from small and shabby to huge and elegant. Most have kitchens, fireplaces, sundecks and Jacuzzis. Prices vary

accordingly, starting at $70 and going up as high as $400 a night. Big Bear Lake Visitors Center can make referrals or try this place:

Grey Squirrel Resort (☎ 909-866-4335, 800-381-5569, info@greysquirrel.com, 39372 Big Bear Blvd) All the cabins here have TV, VCR, phone, microwave and fireplace. The resort also rents great private homes, which are located right in the woods.

Hotels & Lodges Dozens of lodgings, almost all independently owned, are strung along Big Bear Blvd.

Honey Bear Lodge (☎ 909-866-7825, 800-628-8714, fax 909-866-1958, 40994 Pennsylvania Ave) Rooms $44-84 midweek, $99-174 weekend, less for stays of two nights or more. The friendly Honey Bear, three blocks from the Village, has a wide range of rooms, including some with private spa. Each has a TV, microwave, refrigerator and fireplace.

Northwoods Resort (☎ 909-866-3121, 800-866-3121, fax 909-878-2122, 40650 Village Dr) Rooms $79-169 midweek, $119-209 weekends. This 1930s-style mountain lodge comes with all modern amenities and is a good place for a splurge.

Knickerbocker Mansion Country Inn (☎ 909-878-9190, 877-423-1180, fax 909-878-4248, 869 Knickerbocker Rd) Rooms $110-155, suites $200-225. The nine rooms and two suites in this historic lodge and adjacent converted carriage lodge have TVs, VCRs, telephones and lots of charm. It's three blocks from the Village and surrounded by 2 acres of gardens; rates include breakfast.

Places to Eat

Breakfast and dinner are the most important meals here, as lunch is usually eaten on a mountain or trail. For groceries, the *Vons* supermarket, with a deli and bakery, is located toward the east end of the lake on Hwy 38.

Grizzly Manor Cafe (☎ 909-866-6226, 41268 Big Bear Blvd) Mains under $7.50, open to 2pm. For bear-sized breakfasts, head to this popular hangout with twisted *Twin Peaks*-ish charm. Owner Jaymie Nordine

Tricky Dick & Gipper Libraries

Within easy reach from LA are two of the country's presidential libraries, honoring the lives of Richard Nixon and Ronald Reagan. No matter what your political leanings, you're likely to find these libraries surprisingly fascinating.

Visit the **Richard Nixon Library & Birthplace** (☎ 714-993-3393, 18001 Yorba Linda Blvd, Yorba Linda; open 10am-5pm Mon-Sat, 11am-5pm Sun; admission adults $5.95, seniors & students $3.95, children 8-11 $2, under 8 free). You can watch a film called Never Give Up: Richard Nixon in the Arena, listen to carefully edited White House tapes from the Watergate era, see the pistol given to Nixon by Elvis Presley and even view the telephone used to communicate with Apollo 11 astronauts on the moon. There's also a re-creation of the Lincoln Sitting Room, Nixon's favorite White House room. The museum's brochure emphasizes that this is the only presidential library built without using taxpayers' money – at a cost of $21 million. Don't miss the gift shop. To get there, take I-5 south to the 91 Fwy; head east on 91, then north on the 57 Fwy, exit east on Yorba Linda Blvd and continue straight to the museum.

Prefer to study up on the 'Reagan Revolution'? Come on down to the **Ronald Reagan Presidential Library & Museum** (☎ 800-410-8354, 40 Presidential Dr, Simi Valley; open 10am-5pm daily, except major holidays; admission adults $5, seniors $3, free if under 15). You can follow Reagan's career from his early days in radio and acting to his stints as president of the Screen Actors Guild and Governor of California. The museum features a re-creation of the White House's Oval Office and the Cabinet Room, Reagan family memorabilia, gifts from heads of state and an actual (disarmed) nuclear cruise missile. Reflecting Reagan's passion during the Cold War is a graffiti-covered slice of the Berlin Wall.

To get there, take the I-405 (San Diego Fwy) north to the US-118 (Ronald Reagan Fwy) west; exit at Madera Rd South, turn right on Madera and continue straight for 3 miles to Presidential Dr.

---

greets most guests by name, and then retires to the steamy kitchen to produce delicious pancakes the size of catchers' mitts, plus any number of huge plates of food.

Mozart's Bistro (☎ 909-866-9497, 40701 Village Dr) Mains $13-27. This is the closest to gourmet you'll get in Big Bear. It has imaginative crab cakes, juicy filet mignon, huge portions of pork ribs and other hearty upscale fare. There's plenty of fine outdoor seating here, allowing you to enjoy the good mountain air.

Stillwells (☎ 800-866-3121, ext 7885, 40650 Village Dr) Mains $7-26. Burgers, seafood, salads, steaks – the menu here at the Northwoods Resort has something for everyone. Service is swift and there's nice outdoor seating as well.

Captain's Anchorage (☎ 909-866-3997, 42148 Moonridge Way) Mains $20; dinner only. Locals like the steaks, prime rib and seafood at this rustic restaurant, in business since 1947.

Getting There & Away

Mountain Area Regional Transit Authority (MARTA; ☎ 909-584-1111) buses connect Big Bear with the Greyhound and Metrolink stations in San Bernardino four times each weekday and twice on Saturday ($5). Large groups might consider reserving the door-to-door Big Bear Shuttle (☎ 909-585-5514), which costs $150 for one person, then $10 per extra person up to 10 people. The shuttle will pick you up in any part of LA.

Big Bear Lake is about 100 miles northeast of Los Angeles, about a 2½ hour drive. Take the I-10 (San Bernardino Fwy) east to Hwy 30 in Redlands. Follow Hwy 30 to Hwy 330 to Hwy 18. For a more scenic route, exit

Orange St N in Redlands and follow the signs to Hwy 38.

SIX FLAGS MAGIC MOUNTAIN

For roller coaster lovers and thrill freaks, no other California theme park compares to Six Flags Magic Mountain (*☎ 661-255-4111, 818-367-5965, 26101 Magic Mountain Pkwy, Valencia; admission adults $41, seniors & children shorter than 4-feet tall $22.50, parking $7; open 10am daily Mar 31-Labor Day and on weekends and holidays after Labor Day-Mar 30, closed Christmas, closing hours vary from 6pm-midnight).*

Velocity is king here, which is why you'll have to deal with so many roving, raucous, hormone-crazed teens (though they're normally just a minor irritation).

You can go up, down, fast and inside out in more ways at Magic Mountain than anywhere else this side of the Space Shuttle. There are 15 coasters among more than 100 rides, shows and attractions in the 260-acre park. The latest addition is Goliath, the champion of the roller coaster world, which takes you on an 85mph ride with a 61°, 255-foot drop. Riddler's Revenge, purportedly the world's tallest and fastest stand-up roller coaster, hurtles you along at 65mph through vertical loops, barrel rolls and a drop of 146 feet. Somewhere in all this, you'll experience a G-force of 4.2, close to the point where combat pilots begin to black out.

Batman: The Ride serves up high-speed loops and corkscrews with a 0-gravity spin. Superman: The Escape blasts you from 0 to 100mph in seven seconds and then gives you 6½ seconds of weightlessness while you fall back to earth. Flashback has six spiral hairpin drops, and Viper falls 188 feet into a double-boomerang turn that puts you upside down, which can be most unpleasant if you're not ready for it. Colossus takes you along nearly 2 miles of track in classic wooden-coaster tradition.

Other rides include Tidal Wave, where you boat over a 50-foot waterfall. Purists will want to pay homage to Revolution, the first 360° looping steel roller coaster ever made. Tamer activities include a 1912 carousel, a Western stage and stunt show, and Bugs Bunny World for the toddlers.

Getting There & Away

From Downtown LA, take I-5 (Golden State Fwy) north about 30 miles and exit at Magic Mountain Pkwy. Getting here by public transport is cumbersome but not impossible. From Downtown LA, take the Metrolink train to the Santa Clarita station, then catch bus No 10 or 20 (every half hour) to the park. Organized tours are also widely available through LA-area hotels.

HURRICANE HARBOR

Adjacent to Six Flags Magic Mountain is Hurricane Harbor (*☎ 661-255-4527, 818-367-5965, off Magic Mountain Parkway; admission adults $20, seniors & children under 4 feet $13, free for children under 2; open 10am daily late May-early Sept, open weekends only May and Sept, closing hours vary).*

This water park with a tropical jungle theme gives children large and small the chance to frolic all day and get soaking wet. The park includes 22 slides splashing into awaiting pools, such as Black Snake Summit, a 75-foot speed slide; Bamboo Racer, six racing slides; and Lizard Lagoon, which has speed slides, water basketball and volleyball. There are also fanciful lagoons and wave pools. A note of caution: The sun in Southern California is fierce and *anyone* planning to romp outdoors should wear heavy sunscreen.

There is a special two-park admission deal of $50 for both Magic Mountain and Hurricane Harbor, but it's almost impossible to do both in a single day.

SANTA BARBARA

Sandwiched between the Pacific Ocean and Santa Ynez Mountains, Santa Barbara is an affluent and pretty city of 90,000, about 90 miles north of Los Angeles. Its charming red-tile roofs, white stucco walls and seaside lassitude evoke the atmosphere of a Mediterranean town. The city has outstanding architecture, including a masterpiece of a courthouse and noteworthy natural-history

EXCURSIONS

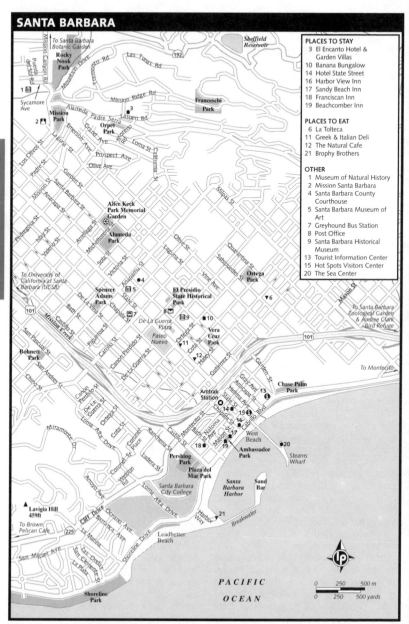

SANTA BARBARA

PLACES TO STAY
3 El Encanto Hotel &
  Garden Villas
10 Banana Bungalow
14 Hotel State Street
16 Harbor View Inn
17 Sandy Beach Inn
18 Franciscan Inn
19 Beachcomber Inn

PLACES TO EAT
6 La Tolteca
11 Greek & Italian Deli
12 The Natural Cafe
21 Brophy Brothers

OTHER
1 Museum of Natural History
2 Mission Santa Barbara
4 Santa Barbara County
  Courthouse
5 Santa Barbara Museum of
  Art
7 Greyhound Bus Station
8 Post Office
9 Santa Barbara Historical
  Museum
13 Tourist Information Center
15 Hot Spots Visitors Center
20 The Sea Center

PACIFIC
OCEAN

and art museums. Five colleges and universities in the area, including the University of California at Santa Barbara (UCSB), give the town a youthful vivacity and balance Santa Barbara's yachting and retirement communities.

History
Until about 200 years ago, Chumash Indians thrived in and around Santa Barbara. They watched when, in 1542, Juan Cabrillo entered the channel, raised a Spanish flag and went on his way. Sebastian Vizcaino, a cartographer for the Duke of Monterey, anchored in the harbor on December 4, 1602, (the feast day of St Barbara) and literally put Santa Barbara on the map. But being claimed and named by Spain didn't affect Santa Barbara's Chumash until the arrival of missionaries in the mid-1700s.

The padres converted the Chumash to Catholicism, made them construct the mission and presidio, and taught them to wear clothes and change their traditional diet. The Chumash were soon decimated by European diseases, but today the tribe is very much alive and well.

Easterners started arriving in force with the 1849 gold rush, and by the late 1890s Santa Barbara was an established vacation spot for the rich and famous. The American Film Company, founded here in 1910, was the world's largest for about three years of its decade-long existence. Thanks to the local film commission, the entertainment industry continues to thrive in the city. Each March, independent US and international films are screened at the Santa Barbara International Film Festival.

Orientation & Information
Downtown Santa Barbara is laid out in a square grid, the main artery of which is State St, running north-south. 'Lower' State St (south of Ortega St) has a greater concentration of bars and shady characters, while 'upper' State St (north of Ortega St) is where the nice shops and museums are. Cabrillo Blvd hugs the coastline and turns into Coast Village Rd as it enters the eastern suburb of Montecito.

Maps, brochures and a busy but helpful staff can be found at the Tourist Information Center (☎ 805-965-3021, on the corner of Garden St and Cabrillo Blvd; open 9am-5pm Mon-Sat May-Oct, 10am-5pm Sun, shorter hours Nov-Apr). The Hot Spots Visitors Center (☎ 805-564-1637, 800-793-7666, 36 State St; open 9am-9pm Mon-Sat, to 4pm Sun) is inside a 24-hour cafe.

Both of these offices maintain a touch-screen computer for information and free hotel reservations. You can also pick up a free map for the Red Tile Tour from the either office. This self-guided 12-block walking tour takes in all of the major downtown sights and historic landmarks, including the Santa Barbara County Courthouse, the Museum of Art and the Historical Museum.

Santa Barbara County Courthouse
One sight not to be missed in Santa Barbara is its 1929 courthouse (☎ 805-962-6464, 1100 Anacapa St; open 8:30am-5pm Mon-Fri, 10am-5pm Sat-Sun, free guided tour 2pm Mon-Sat & 10:30am Fri). Built in Spanish-Moorish Revival style, it features hand-painted ceilings, wrought-iron chandeliers and tiles from Tunisia and Spain. If you miss the tour, be sure to visit the mural room and go up the 80-foot clock tower for panoramic views of the city.

Santa Barbara Museum of Art
This is a well-regarded regional museum (☎ 805-963-4364, 1130 State St; admission adults $5, seniors $3, students $2, free if under 6, free for everyone Thur & 1st Sun of month; open 11am-5pm Tues-Thurs & Sat, 11am-9pm Fri, noon-5pm Sun). It has a varied permanent collection, with works by Monet, Matisse, Chagall, Hopper and O'Keefe, as well as Asian art and classical sculpture. A new wing added more exhibit space, a cafe and a children's gallery.

Santa Barbara Historical Museum
An exhaustive collection of Santa Barbara memorabilia is waiting to be discovered at

this educational museum (☎ 805-966-1601, 136 E De La Guerra St; admission free; open 10am-5pm Tues-Sat, noon-5pm Sun, guided tours 11:30am Tues & Sat and 1:30pm Sun). Located in an adobe complex, the museum features antique furniture and an intricately carved coffer that once belonged to Father Junípero Serra.

Mission Santa Barbara

Sitting on a majestic plot, half a mile north of downtown, is the Queen of the Missions, Mission Santa Barbara (☎ 805-682-4713, 2201 Laguna St; admission adults $4, free for children; open 9am-5pm daily). The mission was established on December 4, 1786, as the 10th California mission. Three adobe structures preceded the current stone one, built in 1820, with a main facade integrating Neoclassical columns. Today, the mission still functions as a Franciscan friary as well as a parish church and museum. Among Chumash wall decorations, the gardens in the courtyard are peaceful. Behind the mission is an extensive cemetery with 4000 Chumash graves and the elaborate mausoleums of early European settlers.

Museum of Natural History

While you're at the mission, go two blocks north to visit this museum (☎ 805-682-4711, 2559 Puesta del Sol Rd; admission adults $6, seniors & teens $5, children $4; open 9am-5pm Mon-Sat, 10am-5pm Sun). Its beautiful architecture and landscaping are worth the short walk. Highlights include an extensive Chumash exhibit and the entire skeleton of a blue whale, though other exhibits are quite mediocre. There's also a planetarium.

Santa Barbara Botanic Garden

A mile north of the Museum of Natural History is this 65-acre botanical garden (☎ 805-682-4726, 1212 Mission Canyon Rd; admission adults $5, seniors & students $3, children 5-12 $1; open 9am-sunset, guided tours 2pm daily and 10:30am Thur, Sat & Sun). Devoted to California's native flora, the botanic garden has 5½ miles of trails meandering through cacti, redwoods, wildflowers, and past the old mission dam, which

was built by the Chumash Indians to irrigate the mission's fields.

Santa Barbara Zoological Garden

You can see 650 animals from around the world, including big cats, monkeys, elephants and giraffes, and gorgeous gardens at the zoo (☎ 805-962-6310, 500 Niños Dr; admission adults $8, seniors & children ages 2-12 $6; open 10am-5pm daily). The zoo's 100-year-old vegetation was once part of a palatial estate.

Just west of the zoo, the **Andree Clark Bird Refuge** (1400 E Cabrillo Blvd; admission free) consists of a lagoon, gardens and a path from which to observe nesting freshwater birds.

Stearns Wharf

This rough wooden pier extending into the harbor from the south end of State St is a popular place for visitors to eat seafood and watch sea lions. Built in 1872 by John Peck Stearn, it is the oldest continuously operating structure of its kind on the West Coast. During the 1940s, the wharf was owned by the Hollywood star James Cagney and his two brothers.

Located on the wharf is the **Sea Center** (☎ 805-962-0885; admission adults $3, seniors & teens $2, children $1.50; open noon-5pm Mon-Fri, 10am-5pm Sat-Sun). Affiliated with the Natural History Museum, the center features full-size models of a gray whale cow and calf and touch tanks filled with starfish and sea anemones.

Places to Stay

In summer, budget accommodations are practically nonexistent in Santa Barbara. Even a cheap motel room that costs just $35 in November can go for as much as $150 between mid-May and September. In general, rates go down slightly during midweek (Sunday to Thursday). Some hotels impose a two-night minimum stay.

Banana Bungalow (☎ 805-963-0154, 800-346-7835, fax 805-963-0184, 210 E Ortega St) Dorm beds $18-19. Santa Barbara's only hostel is a 56-bed, fairly grungy affair in a barrel-like corrugated-tin structure. There's no curfew, no lockout, and no real chance of getting a good night's sleep when the place is full. In summer, there's a busy activity schedule with barbecues, hiking trips, volleyball competitions and the like. American travelers are accepted at the hostel for stays of up to three days.

Hotel State Street (☎ 805-966-6586, fax 805-962-8459, 121 State St) Rooms $35 midweek, $55-75 Fri & Sat. Clean and newly renovated, this is a good value and near the beach. It attracts Europeans and sophisticated budget travelers. Each room has a sink and towel, but bathrooms are shared.

Most of Santa Barbara's mid-range motels are along Cabrillo Blvd, west of State St.

Sandy Beach Inn (☎ 805-963-0405, 800-554-9324, fax 805-965-4577, 122 W Cabrillo Blvd) Rooms $95-175 winter, $165-295 summer. This place has a wide range of rooms, some with ocean views, furnished in a modern style. If the ocean's too cold, you can relax in the pool and Jacuzzi.

Beachcomber Inn (☎ 805-965-4577, 800-554-9324, fax 805-962-5946, 202 W Cabrillo Blvd) This nearby sister property to the Sandy Beach Inn (same price range) has 32 rooms, a small pool and a sundeck.

Another cluster of hotels is on Bath St just off Cabrillo Blvd.

Franciscan Inn (☎ 805-963-8845, fax 805-564-3295, 109 Bath St) Rooms $105-260 summer, $75-200 winter, including continental breakfast. Run with efficiency and charm, this place's cheaper rooms represent great value. All have nice furnishings and such extra amenities as VCRs and a free video library in the lobby. There's also a large heated pool and spa.

High-end accommodations are mostly north of downtown in the hills.

El Encanto Hotel & Garden Villas (☎ 805-687-5000, 800-346-7039, fax 805-687-0943, 1900 Lasuen Rd) Cottages with private patios $229-1450. Long considered *the* hotel in Santa Barbara, this place consists of 83 cottages and villas built in both Craftsman and Spanish Colonial style. Surrounded by 10 acres of lush gardens, it sits on a hill above the mission with a great view of downtown and the ocean.

Harbor View Inn (☎ 805-963-0780, 800-755-0222, fax 805-963-7967, 36 W Cabrillo Blvd) Rooms $200-350, suites $350-800. This one's a good choice near the beach and has a large pool, spa and nice landscaping.

Places to Eat
Santa Barbara's 'restaurant row' is on the 500 and 600 blocks of State St.

Greek & Italian Deli (no ☎, corner of State & Ortega Sts) Lunch around $5. A local institution, this deli has delicious sandwiches, gyros, Greek salads, dolmas and hot lunch specials.

The Natural Cafe (☎ 805-962-9494, 508 State St) Mains under $7. A couple of blocks south, the Natural Cafe serves Zen burgers, Buddha burritos and Yogananda lasagna.

La Tolteca (☎ 805-963-0847, 616 E Haley St) Mains $2-6. In an industrial part of town, this 'mexicatessen' has famously authentic enchiladas and tamales.

Brown Pelican (☎ 805-687-4550, 2981½ Cliff Dr) Breakfast $5-9, mains $5-25. West of town on Arroyo Burro Beach, this informal cafe has a view of the waves. Fare includes mouthwatering salads, sandwiches and seafood (the clam chowder is terrific). It's also a nice place for breakfast.

Brophy Brothers (☎ 805-966-4418, 119 Harbor Way) Mains $6-20. Overlooking the Santa Barbara Harbor, this reliably excellent, lively restaurant and oyster bar is where locals go for superb seafood. Top choices include clam chowder and cioppino, served with chewy sourdough bread.

Getting There & Away
Greyhound has 10 daily buses between LA and Santa Barbara ($14/24 one way/round-trip; two to 3½ hours). The Greyhound bus station (☎ 805-965-7551), a magnet for transient types, is downtown at 34 W Carrillo St.

Amtrak's *Pacific Surfliner* makes four trips daily between Los Angeles and Santa Barbara ($16/32, 1½ hours). The train depot (☎ 805-963-1015) is at 209 State St.

Santa Barbara is bisected by US-101. For downtown, take the Garden St or Cabrillo

EXCURSIONS

A River Roars Through It: The Killer Kern

Can't take the stress and sheer velocity of the LA freeway system? What better cure for big-city blues than a return to the 'serenity' of nature on one of the most awesome whitewater rivers in America, the aptly nicknamed 'Killer Kern.'

When the runoff from winter snows begins in spring, part of the Kern becomes a surging monster of a river charging through steep gorges in the Sequoia National Forest. At other times of the year, and on other sections, the passage can be enjoyed by nearly everyone. To Angelenos, the Kern has the distinct advantage of being only 150 miles north of the city, just a three-hour drive away.

Having been a guide on rivers of the Northwest in what seems like an earlier incarnation, I was ready to hit the water again on a tour of the Lower Kern with Whitewater Voyages (☎ 800-488-7238, fax 510-758-7238, www.whitewatervoyages.com), an outfitter with a permanent base on the river. Between April and September, this company runs one- to three-day trips on various stretches of the Kern – mild to menacing.

'Wet and wild' was definitely the norm on the Lower Kern (class III and IV) two-day run. It began rather placidly on day one with a lovely float through beautiful forests and past bizarrely carved granite boulders that – when the water's high – create enormous waves and treacherous hydraulic holes. We camped on a sublime bend in the river, where – after a gourmet dinner of steak, chicken, salads and Dutch-oven brownies – we slept like babes while the Kern murmured sweetly to us.

The following day, our group of four was joined by 23 other adventurers, and our armada of rafts headed into the class III and IV sections downriver. This was wild! I got to relive my former river-rat life by pulling three 'swimmers' – launched from other rafts while bumping through various cataracts – to sputtering safety. One of our boats wrapped around a boulder for half an hour and another raft popped, gimping home after a hasty patch job. There were bruises, cuts and abrasions to be sure, but the river did its work: The macho were meek, the reclusive were raucous, and the timid were tigers.

Whitewater Voyages also operates half-day and one-day trips on the Upper Kern (class III to IV) and the distinctly class V 'Thunder Run.' Those who hunger for the extreme should try the 'Forks of the Kern' run. The river drops 60 feet per mile through solid granite walls in an unending series of furious class IV and class V rapids that will all but erase your id, ego and all taints of civilization. But be warned: You have to be tough, experienced and comfortable running on the edge to go here. People do die – many are unprepared and/or drunken yahoos.

The two-day Lower Kern tour ranges from $264 midweek to $314 on Saturday; one-day tours cost $115-165. Half a day on the Upper Kern costs $94-108; one-day tours are $90-175. The 'Forks of the Kern' costs $645 for two days and $735 for three days. Rates include all meals and most equipment.

– David Peevers

Blvd exit. Parking on the street and in any of 10 municipal lots is free for the first 90 minutes daily and all day Sunday.

Getting Around

To get your bearings, consider taking the Santa Barbara Trolley (☎ 805-965-0353), which makes a narrated 90-minute loop past Stearns Wharf, the courthouse, the art museum and the mission. Tickets cost $5 and are valid all day, allowing you to get on and off. (If you get off, you'll have to wait the full 90 minutes for the next bus to arrive.)

The Downtown-Waterfront Shuttle bus runs south along State St from its intersection with Sola St down to Stearns Wharf every 10 to 15 minutes from 10:15am to 6pm. A second route travels from the zoo to the yacht harbor at 30-minute intervals. The fare is 25¢ per ride; transfers between routes are free.

Santa Barbara Metropolitan Transit District (MTD) buses cost $1 per ride and serve all of Santa Barbara and outlying communities.

LAS VEGAS

Las Vegas has grown in 90 years from nothing to nearly half a million people in 1998. It's an exciting place for a brief visit, and if you like gambling and glitter, you'll love it – at least until your money disappears, or the incessant ding-ding-ding of slot machines and the haggard faces of down-and-out gamblers wear you out.

Food and lodging, while not outrageous, are no longer inexpensive as Las Vegas is once again going after a more adult, big-spender audience. The best deal may be a special flight and accommodation package; check the travel supplement of the Sunday edition of the *LA Times* or see a travel agent.

Paiute Indians and Mormon missionaries were the only settlers in this arid region until 1902, when Las Vegas became a railroad town with ice works, hotels and saloons. The Great Depression brought a collapse in mineral and crop prices, so in 1931 the state government legalized gambling and created agencies to tax it, turning an illegal activity into a revenue source and tourist attraction.

By the '50s, gambling was well-established in Las Vegas, thanks to gangsters, who bankrolled its growth, and the Hoover Dam, a New Deal project that provided the water and electricity needed by the burgeoning city. LA mobster Bugsy Siegel's Fabulous Flamingo pioneered the new style of casinos – big and flashy, with lavish entertainment to draw in the gamblers – that is still in vogue today.

Orientation & Information

Las Vegas is about 300 miles, a five- to six-hour drive, northeast of Los Angeles. You enter the city on I-15, which parallels Las Vegas Blvd. Also known as the Strip, this is where all the big hotel/casinos are, so work out which cross street will bring you closest to your destination. If you want an introduction to the city, get off I-15 at Blue Diamond Rd (exit 33) and cruise the length of the Strip from south to north, all the way to downtown. This can take anywhere from 20 minutes to an hour, depending on traffic.

Downtown Las Vegas is the original town center. Its main artery, Fremont St, is now a covered pedestrian mall lined with low-key casinos and hotels, spiced up with nightly laser shows.

For maps and information about every nook and cranny of Sin City, consult the Las Vegas Visitor Center at the Convention Center (☎ 702-892-7575, 800-332-5333, www .lasvegas24hours.com, 3150 Paradise Rd; open 8am-6pm Mon-Fri, 8am-5pm Sat-Sun).

Casinos

Most casinos are gaudy, noisy and deliberately disorienting, with no clocks or windows. The Strip's new mega-casinos also feature gimmicky themes, attention-grabbing architecture and nongambling amusements.

Casinos listed here (from north to south along the Strip) are worth visiting as attractions in their own right. Except for poker, all

EXCURSIONS

gambling pits the player against the house, and the house always has a statistical edge. Some casinos offer introductory lessons in blackjack, roulette and craps. To enter a gambling area, you must be 18, and in some cases 21, years old.

Stratosphere *(☎ 800-998-6937)* This casino/hotel has a landmark 1149-foot tower with a restaurant and two rides up top – a roller coaster ($5) and the free-fall 'Big Shot' ($8).

Circus Circus *(☎ 800-634-3450)* – One of the original casino-cum-theme-parks, Circus Circus offers free circus acts in its tent-like interior.

The Venetian *(☎ 888-283-6423)* – Take a gondola ride or a stroll around Venice at this kitschy but impressive re-creation of the romantic Italian city.

Treasure Island *(☎ 800-944-7444)* – The pirate ship and man-of-war in the lagoon out front stage a sea battle every 90 minutes from 4:30pm to midnight.

Mirage *(☎ 800-627-6667)* – A fake volcano erupts out front every half hour. Inside are a tropical rain forest, a dolphin tank and the white tigers used in the 'Siegfried & Roy' stage show.

Caesar's Palace *(☎ 800-634-6001)* – You enter stylish Caesar's along a moving footpath, past classic columns and 'ancient' statues. Part of the hotel is the Forum Shops, a faux Roman street with a painted sky that changes from dawn to dusk every three hours.

Bellagio *(☎ 888-987-6667)* – Catering to upscale tastes and fat wallets, the Bellagio offers lovely architecture and decor; a $300-million art collection with works by Matisse, Van Gogh and others ($10 admission); 17 restaurants; and an impressive – and free – water fountain show. Also here is the most sophisticated show on the Strip: Cirque du Soleil's water-based *O*.

Paris Las Vegas *(☎ 888-266-5687)* – This 1999 arrival re-creates major Paris landmarks like the Arc de Triomphe and features a half-scale replica of the Eiffel Tower.

New York, New York *(☎ 800-693-6763)* – The hotel's facade re-creates the Manhattan skyline, with replicas of the Statue of Liberty, Empire State Building and more. The Manhattan Express roller coaster ($10) is a major rush.

Excalibur *(☎ 800-937-7777)* This humongous property is decorated like a medieval castle with an overworked Arthurian theme. Dinner shows feature jousting knights.

Luxor *(☎ 800-288-1000)* – This casino is a remarkable glass-covered pyramid with a sphinx and an imitation of Cleopatra's needle out front. Inside are Egyptian-themed rides ($7) and an IMAX movie theater ($9).

Mandalay Bay *(☎ 877-632-7000)* – This sophisticated billion-dollar hotel opened in 1999 and contains numerous fancy restaurants, a great vodka bar and a branch of the House of Blues. The 11-acre garden includes a sand-and-surf beach (with artificial waves) and a lazy river ride.

Other Things to See & Do

There are many things to do besides gambling, and discount coupons are available for most of them. The **Wet 'n Wild** water park *(☎ 702-737-3819, 2601 S Las Vegas Blvd; admission $26)*, looks mighty tempting on a hot day. There's an excellent collection of vehicles once owned by the rich and famous, from Hitler to Howard Hughes, to be seen at the **Imperial Palace Auto Museum** *(☎ 702-731-3311, 3535 S Las Vegas Blvd; admission $7)*. A Vegas favorite is the campy **Liberace Museum** *(☎ 702-798-5595, 1774 E Tropicana Ave; admission $8)*, with sequined capes, rhinestone jewelry, flashy cars and fabulous candelabra.

One of the best places to explore the charms of the Southwest and escape the madness of Vegas is **Red Rock Canyon**, a dramatic valley noted for the steep red-rock escarpment rising 3000 feet on its western edge. It's about a 20-mile drive west of Vegas on Charleston Blvd, which turns into Hwy 159. A 13-mile, one-way scenic loop starts at the BLM visitor center *(☎ 702-363-1921; open 8:30am-4:30pm daily; park day-use fee $5)* near Hwy 159. The visitor center has maps and information about several short hikes in the area. Sunset and sunrise are the best times for viewing.

Places to Stay

Las Vegas International Hostel (☎ 702-385-9955, lasvegashostel@aol.com, 1208 Las Vegas Blvd) Dorm beds/rooms $12-14/28. This no-frills hostel is four blocks north of the Strip in a converted apartment block. It's popular with international backpackers.

Las Vegas Backpackers Hostel (☎ 702-385-1150, 800-550-8958, fax 702-385-4940, vegasbackpackers@hotmail.com, 1322 Fremont St) Dorm beds/singles/doubles

$13/19/38/54. This hostel is on the not-so-nice outskirts of downtown, but has excellent facilities (including pool and Jacuzzi), caring management and low rates. Call for a free pick-up from the Greyhound station.

Las Vegas room rates vary wildly with demand. A standard room at the Bellagio, for example, usually goes for $159, but the same room can cost three times as much during busy convention periods. By the same token, some unbelievable bargains are available during lulls in visitor activity. Deals come and go by the hour, so call before you arrive.

Budget-friendly casinos include **Circus Circus** (☎ 800-634-3450, fax 702-734-2268, 2880 S Las Vegas Blvd), the **Sahara** (☎ 888-696-2121, fax 702-737-2027, 2535 S Las Vegas Blvd) and the **Barbary Coast** (☎ 888-227-2279, 3595 S Las Vegas Blvd).

Even the fancier casinos sometimes have great deals. Check **Caesar's Palace** (☎ 800-634-6001, fax 702-731-6636, 3570 S Las Vegas Blvd), the **Luxor** (☎ 800-288-1000, fax 702-262-4452, 3900 S Las Vegas Blvd) and the **MGM Grand** (☎ 800-929-1111, fax 702-891-1112, 3799 S Las Vegas Blvd).

Places to Eat

Larger casinos have multiple restaurants in all price ranges. The all-you-can-eat buffet is a Las Vegas institution and the best buffet in town is a subject of debate. Two hotels often mentioned by locals are the **Rio Suite Hotel & Casino** (☎ 702-252-7777, 3700 W Flamingo Rd) and **Main Street Station** (☎ 702-387-1896, 200 N Main St), neither of which are on the Strip. Good strip choices include **Bally's Big Kitchen** and the **Palatium Buffet** at Caesar's Palace. Prices are around $6 for breakfast, $7-10 for lunch and $10-15 for dinner.

Las Vegas' cuisine scene has recently come of age and there are plenty of good eateries found both in the casinos and outside.

Chin Chin (☎ 702-740-6969, at New York, New York) Mains $5-12. Come here for wonderful Chinese food in a cheerful cafe setting. The cafe's shredded chicken salad is a classic.

Yolie's Brazilian Steak House (☎ 702-794-0700, 3900 Paradise Rd) Lunch $6-13, set dinner $27. This place has outstanding grilled meats and also dependable salads.

Andre's (☎ 702-385-5016, 401 S 6th St) Mains $20-30. At perhaps the best restaurant in town, you'll be served delightful French cuisine in a 1930s house.

Picasso (☎ 702-693-7111, in the Bellagio) 4/5-course meal $70/80. Regional cuisine of France and Spain is on the menu at this exquisite restaurant where walls are graced by genuine Picasso paintings.

Entertainment

The best source for entertainment information is the free magazine *What's On in Las Vegas*. For nightlife listings with a more local flair, check the *New Times*, a free weekly paper. 'Big room' casino shows can include concerts by famous artists, Broadway musicals or flashy song-and-dance shows. Tickets cost $25-75, more for big-name acts. 'Lounge shows' are smaller productions, in smaller venues, for smaller prices ($8-20). Some recommended shows are the two permanent Cirque du Soleil shows, *Mystère* ($70) at Treasure Island and *O* ($90-100) at the Bellagio. The Riviera's *Evening at La Cage* ($30-35, including two drinks), starring a cast of over-the-top female impersonators, is also good.

There's no shortage of nightclubs in Las Vegas. **Club Utopia** (☎ 702-736-3105, 3765 S Las Vegas Blvd), across from the Monte Carlo, is a popular dance spot that plays techno-pop, hip-hop, alternative and Top 40 music. **Ra** (☎ 702-262-4000, in the Luxor) is a spectacular nightclub with an Egyptian theme and semi-naked go-go dancers.

Getting There & Around

The busy McCarran International Airport (☎ 702-261-5743) has direct flights to and from most LA-area airports, as well as most major US cities. Bell Trans (☎ 702-739-7990) and Gray Line (☎ 702-384-1234) provide airport shuttle service ($4-6 a person).

The Greyhound bus station (☎ 702-384-8009), downtown on Main St, has regular buses to and from Los Angeles ($33). The

Missing Link Tours operates a $39 shuttle between Las Vegas and Los Angeles. (See the Getting There & Away chapter for more information.)

Citizens Area Transport (CAT; ☎ 702-228-7433) runs local buses; bus No 301 cruises the Strip, 24 hours a day, all the way to downtown ($1.50). The Strip Trolley (☎ 702-382-1404) does a loop from the Luxor to the Stratosphere and out to the Las Vegas Hilton every 25 minutes until 2am ($1.30). Dozens of agencies along the Strip rent cars for $25-45 a day. Try Budget (☎ 702-736-1212) or Thrifty (☎ 702-896-7600).

Thanks

Many thanks to the following readers (apologies if your name is misspelled) who took the time to write in about their experiences in Los Angeles:

Ronalie Green, Adam Jones, Gareth Jones, Chris Leonard, Marti Matulis, Sara Parks, Bernie Robinson, Laurence Svirchev, Philip Weate, Eric Wilson, Paul Wyatt.

LONELY PLANET

You already know that Lonely Planet produces more than this one guidebook, but you might not be aware of the other products we have on this region. Here is a selection of titles which you may want to check out as well:

California & Nevada
ISBN 0864426445
US$19.95 • UK£12.99

San Diego & Tijuana
ISBN 1864502185
US$16.99• UK£10.99

San Francisco
ISBN 1864503092
US$15.99 • UK£9.99

Los Angeles City Map
ISBN 1864502584
US$5.99 • UK£3.99

Diving & Snorkeling Southern California & the Channel Islands
ISBN 1864502932
US$16.99 • UK£10.99

Las Vegas
ISBN 1864500867
US$15.95 • UK£9.99

Available wherever books are sold.

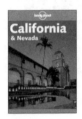
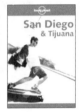

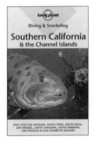

Index

Text

A

accidents 91
accommodations 196–217.
    See also Places to Stay
    index or individual
    neighborhoods
    B&Bs 200–1
    camping 197
    discounts 196–7
    gay 205
    hostels 53, 197–200
    hotels 201–6
    long-term 216–7
    reservations 196–7
    tipping 197
Adamson House 151
adobe buildings 182
African Americans 16, 17, 22
    museums 116–7, 169–70
    neighborhoods 49, 169,
        170
Ahmanson Theater 105,
    249
AIDS. *See* HIV/AIDS
Air Combat USA 299
air travel 78–82
airlines 82
    glossary 80
    museum 158
    tickets 78–9, 80
airports
    accommodations near
        209–10
    Burbank–Glendale–
        Pasadena 78, 87
    LAX 54, 78, 86–7, 209–10
    other 78
    transportation to/from
        86–7
Algren, Nelson 28

Ambassador Hotel 135
American Automobile
    Association (AAA) 70
Amtrak 84
amusement parks. *See* theme
    parks
Anaheim 285, 287–91
Anderson, Loni 143
Andrés Pico Adobe 182
Angeles National Forest
    189–90
Angelino Heights 40, 113
Angels Flight 101
Angels Gate Park 163–4
Angelus Temple 113
antiques 281
aquariums
    Aquarium of the Pacific
        165–6
    Cabrillo Marine Aquarium
        164
    Roundhouse Marine
        Studies Lab & Aquarium
        160
Arboretum of Los Angeles
    County 192
architecture 30, 33–48
    architects 34–6
    books on 62
    photos of 65
    styles 36–8
    tours 38–52
Arroyo Seco 178
art 30–1. *See also* museums
    festivals 295
    galleries 31, 112, 117,
        157, 173, 181, 274–5
    public 30, 99–100, 159
Art Center College of Design
    178–9
Art Deco 33, 37, 40
Arts District 112–3
ArtsCard LA 138
Asians 22, 108–10
ATMs 56
Autry, Gene 120

Autry Museum of Western
    Heritage 120
Avalon 292
aviation industry 15–6
Avila Adobe 107

B

Ballona Wetlands 160
banda 27
B&Bs. *See* accommodations
Banning Residence Museum
    164
Barnsdall Art Park 121–2
Barris, George 184–5
bars 261–4, 267–8
baseball 114, 269
basketball 111, 269–70
beaches 152–3, 296
Bear Flag Republic 13
Bel Air 144–6, 207–8, **Map 11**
Bergamot Station 157
Beverly Center District
    228–30, 271, 273, **Map 10**
Beverly Hills 139–44, **Map 11**
    accommodations 207–8
    art galleries 275
    entertainment 250, 260
    restaurants 231–2
    shopping 271
    tourist office 50
Beverly Hills Hotel 141, 208
bicycles 96, 191. *See also*
    mountain biking
Biddy Mason Park 104
Big Bear Lake 298–303
Big Blue Bus 89
Biltmore Hotel 39, 40
biographies 62
bird watching 306
blues 258–60
Bob's Big Boy 243
body modifications 132
books 61–3. *See also*
    libraries; literature
bookstores 277–8, 279
Bow, Clara 144, 151, 186

Boyle Heights 172
Bradbury Building 104
Bradley, Tom 20, 39, 71, 105
Brand Library & Art Center 183–4
breakfast 231
Breed Street Shul 172
Brentwood 144–6, **Map 2**
Brewery Art Complex 112
Broadway 102–3
Bullocks Wilshire Department Store 135–6
Bunker Hill Steps 99
Burbank 186, **Map 18**
    accommodations 216
    entertainment 261
    restaurants 243–4
Burbank–Glendale–Pasadena Airport 78, 87
buses 82–3, 87–9, 97
business
    doing 77
    hours 74

C

Cabrillo, Juan Rodríguez 11, 291, 305
Cabrillo Marine Aquarium 164
cafes. See coffeehouses
Cain, James M 23, 29
California African American Museum 116–7
California Heritage Museum 157–8
California Institute of Technology (Caltech) 180–1
California Science Center 115–6
calling cards 59
camping. See accommodations
Capitol Records Tower 127
Capote, Truman 148
cars 84–5, 91–5
    AAA 70
    accidents 91
    culture 183, 184–5
    driver's licenses 53
    freeways 84–5, 94

museum 138
parking 92–3
regulations 85, 92–3
renting 93–5
thefts 72–3
Carson, Kit 12, 13
casinos 292, 309–10
Catalina. See Santa Catalina Island
Cathedral of Our Lady of the Angels 106
celebrities. See also individual names
    biographies of 62
    burial sites of 121, 130, 148, 184–6
    clothing of 279
    hangouts of 225
    homes of 97, 142–4
Center for Motion Picture Study 140
Central Ave 169, **Map 3**
Central Library 38–9, 71, 98–9
Century City 148–9, **Map 11**
    accommodations 208–9
    entertainment 249, 259
    shopping 273
Chandler, Raymond 28–9, 225
Chaplin, Charlie 62, 102, 141, 142, 248
Chiat/Day Building 48
children
    activities for 116
    restaurants for 239
    traveling with 70
Chinatown 108, **Map 5**
    restaurants 222
    shopping 272
Chinese American Museum 108
Christ Church 45
Chumash 11, 305
churches 45–5, 106, 107, 118, 136, 179
cinemas 102–3, 247–8
Cinerama Dome 128
City Hall 105

CitySync 61
Civic Center 105–6, **Map 5**
Clark Memorial Library 168–9
classical music 253–4
climate 18–9
clothing
    of celebrities 279
    designer 281–2
    factory working conditions 112
    Fashion District 272
    laundry 66
    lingerie 283–4
    mainstream 281–2
    outlet malls 273–4
    vintage 282–3
clubs 255–61
    comedy 253
    country & western 261
    dance 267
    jazz & blues 258–60
    Latin music 260–1
    rock & pop 255–8
    swing 260
Coca–Cola Bottling Plant 37, 38, 112
coffeehouses 265–7, 268–9. See also cybercafes
Colburn School of Performing Arts 101
comedy
    clubs 253
    films 24–5
consulates 53–4
costs 56–7
country & western 261
Craft & Folk Art Museum 138
Craftsman style 33, 35, 36–7, 41–2
credit cards 56
crime 56, 72–3
    in film 23–4
    in literature 28–9
Crossroads of the World 128
cruises 97, 167
cultural centers 72
Culver City 149–51, **Map 12**
    entertainment 259, 261
    restaurants 233
    transportation 89

Culver Studios 150
currency 55
customs 54–5
cybercafes 60
cycling. *See* bicycles

D

dance 254–5
dance clubs 267
DASH 89
debit cards 56
Descanso Gardens 192
DiMaggio, Joe 134, 148
disabled travelers 69–70
Disneyland 285, 287–8
Disney's California Adventure
  288–9
diving 293, 296
documents 51–3
Dodger Stadium 114, 269
Doheny, Ed 15, 144
Doheny Mansion 168
Downtown 98–118, **Map 5**
  accommodations 201–3
  architectural tour 38–41,
    38
  Arts District 112–3
  Chinatown 108, 222, 272
  Civic Center 105–6
  Echo Park 113
  Elysian Park 113–4
  entertainment 249, 255,
    260, 261–2
  Exposition Park area
    114–8
  Fashion District 111, 272
  Financial District tour
    98–101, 100
  historic core tour 101–4,
    103
  Little Tokyo 108–10
  restaurants 219–22
  shopping 272
  South Park 110–2
Downtown Disney 288
driving. *See* cars

Drum Barracks Civil War
  Museum 164–5
Dunbar Hotel 169
Duncan-Irwin House 42

E

earthquakes 18, 73
East LA 172–4, **Map 3**
  restaurants 241
  shopping 272
Eastern Columbia Building
  37, 102
Eastlake style. *See* Victorian
  architecture
Eaton, Fred 14, 19
Echo Park 113, **Map 5**
economy 21
education 22
Egyptian Theater 126, 248
El Alisal 174, 175
El Capitan Theater 125–6
El Matador Beach 152
El Mercado 173
El Molino Viejo 181
El Pescador Beach 152
El Pueblo de los Angeles
  106–8
electricity 65–6
Elysian Park 113–4, **Map 5**
email 59–60
embassies 53–4
emergencies 73–4
employment 77
Ennis-Brown House 30, 44–5
entertainment 247–70
  bars 261–4, 267–8
  cinemas 247–8
  classical music & opera
    253–4
  clubs 255–61, 267–8
  coffeehouses 265–7,
    268–9
  comedy clubs 253
  dance 254–5
  gay & lesbian venues
    267–9
  pubs & microbreweries
    264–5
  spectator sports 269–70
  theater 29–30, 248–52

tickets 138, 247
environmental issues 19–20
erotica 283–4
exchange rates 55
excursions 285–312, 286
Exposition Park 114
Exposition Park area 114–8,
  Map 6

F

Fairbanks, Douglas 102, 124,
  126, 130, 140, 142, 295
Fairfax District 131, 133,
  Map 10
  accommodations 199, 204
  entertainment 256–7
  restaurants 230–1
Fante, John 27
farmers' markets 133, 274
Fashion District 111, 272
faxes 59
Feynes Estate 42
film industry 16, 21, 62. *See
  also* celebrities; Hollywood
films 22–4
Financial District 98–101, **100**
Fine Arts Building 41
First Congregational Church
  47
First United Methodist
  Church 179
Fisher Gallery 117
Fishermen's Village 160
fishing 300
Fitzgerald, F Scott 28, 126
flea markets 276
flower market 111–2
Flynn, Errol 143, 186
food 218–9, 241. *See also*
  markets; Places to Eat
  index; restaurants
football 75, 177, 178, 270
Forest Lawn Memorial Park
  121, 184–6
Fort MacArthur Military
  Museum 164
Frederick's of Hollywood
  Lingerie Museum 127
free activities 97, 147–8
Freeman House 131

Freeth, George 161, 162
freeways 84–5, 94
Frémont, John C 13

G

Gabrieleño (Shoshone) 11,
    12, 175, 294
Gamble House 30, 36, 42
gangs 72, 168
garage sales 277
gardens
    Arboretum of Los Angeles
        County 192
    Descanso Gardens 192
    Hannah Carter Japanese
        Garden 192
    Huntington Library, Art
        Collection & Botanical
        Gardens 181
    Japanese Gardens at
        Tillman Water
        Reclamation Plant 192
    Orcutt Ranch 192
    Rancho Santa Ana Botanic
        Garden 192
    Santa Barbara Botanic
        Garden 306
    South Coast Botanical
        Garden 162
    Virginia Robinson Gardens
        140–1
    Wrigley Mansion &
        Gardens 178
    Wrigley Memorial &
        Botanical Garden 292
Garment District. See Fashion
    District
Garnier Building 108
Gas Company Tower 39
gays & lesbians
    accommodations for 205
    bookstores 278
    travelers 68–9
    venues 267–9
Gehry, Frank 35–6, 47, 48,
    106, 110, 116, 117, 157,
    164, 177, 236
Gehry House 35, 48
geography 18
geology 18
Getty, J Paul 154, 177

Getty Center 33, 34, 47, 48,
    145
Getty Museum 154
Gin Ling Way 108
Glen Ivy Hot Springs 298
Glendale 183–6, **Map 3**
    accommodations 215–6
    entertainment 251
    restaurants 243
Globe Theater 103
Golden Triangle 139
golf 193–4, 280
gondolas 167
government 20
Grand Central Market 104
Grand Hope Park 110
Grauman, Sid 62, 124
Great Wall of Los Angeles 30
Greek Theater 119, 131
Green Tortoise 83
Greene, Graham 28
Greene & Greene 35, 41–2
Greyhound 82–3
Greystone Park & Mansion
    144
Griffith Observatory &
    Planetarium 119
Griffith Park 118–21, **Map 8**
guidebooks 61–2
Guinness World of Records
    Museum 126

H

Hahn, James K 20
Hammer Museum 148
Hannah Carter Japanese
    Garden 192
happy hour 262
Harrison, George 143
health 66–8
    immunizations 66
    insurance 67
    medical services 67–8
    precautions 66–7
health clubs 194
Hefner, Hugh 143, 148
Hemingway, Ernest 28, 225
Heritage Square Museum
    174–5
Hermosa Beach 153, 160–1,
    Map 14

    accommodations 200
    entertainment 258, 259,
        264
    tourist office 50
high schools 128, 129
highlights 99
hiking 190, 191–3, 299–300
    guides 62
    tours 96–7
hip-hop 26
history 11–8, 62
hitchhiking 85
HIV/AIDS 52, 68, 74
hockey 111, 270
holidays 74–5
Hollyhock House 30, 33, 34,
    122
Hollywood 122–34, **Map 9**.
    See also film industry
    accommodations 198–9,
        203–4
    Central Hollywood 122–30
    entertainment 249–50,
        256, 259, 260–1, 263,
        266, 267–8
    Fairfax District 131, 133,
        199, 204, 230–1,
        256–7
    historic tour 123–8, **123**
    Hollywood Hills 130–1
    Melrose Ave 131, 226–7,
        271
    restaurants 224–6
    shopping 271
    sign 65, 129–30
    tourist office 50
    West Hollywood 133–4,
        204–6, 250, 257–8,
        263–4, 266, 267,
        274–5
Hollywood & Highland
    124–5
Hollywood & Vine 127–8
Hollywood Athletic Club 128
Hollywood Blvd 24, 123
Hollywood Bowl 131, 254
Hollywood City Pass 138
Hollywood Entertainment
    Museum 123–4
Hollywood Forever Cemetery
    130

Hollywood High School 128, 129
Hollywood Hills 130–1, **Map 9**
Hollywood Roosevelt Hotel 124, 204
Hollywood Studio Museum 131
Hollywood Walk of Fame 123
Hollywood Wax Museum 126
Home Savings of America Tower 41
Hop On Hop Off Bus 83
horse racing 270
horseback riding 194–5
hostels. *See* accommodations
hot springs 298
hotels. *See* accommodations
Huntington, Henry 90, 161, 176, 183
Huntington Library, Art Collection & Botanical Gardens 181
Hurricane Harbor 303

I

IMAX Theater 116
Immanuel Presbyterian Church 47
immunizations 66
insurance
    car 93–4, 95
    travel 53, 67
International Driving Permit 53
International Society for Paranormal Research (ISPR) 125
International Style Modern. *See* Modernist style
Internet access 59–60. *See also* Web sites

J

Janes House 127
Japanese American Cultural & Community Center 110
Japanese American National Museum 109–10

Japanese Village Plaza 110, 272
jazz 25, 258–60
Jet Propulsion Laboratory (JPL) 181
jewelry 280–1
Jewelry District 102
Jews 31, 131, 133, 172
    cultural center 145–6
    museums 149
    synagogues 45–6
John Anson Ford Theater 131
John Drescher Planetarium 157
Johnson, Magic 269
Judson Studios 46

K

kayaking 293
Kern River 308
Kidspace 179–80
King, Rodney 17, 63
Kinney, Abbot 158–9
Knott's Berry Farm 289–90
Kong Chow Temple 108
Korean Friendship Bell 163
Koreatown 135–6, **Map 7**
    entertainment 264
    restaurants 222–3

L

La Brea Ave 226–7, 271, **Map 10**
La Brea Tar Pits 136–7
La Piedra Beach 152
La Plata Cigar Factory & Shop 111
LACMA. *See* Los Angeles County Museum of Art
LADOT 89
Laguna Art Museum 296
Laguna Beach 294–8
language 32
LAPD 17, 18
Las Vegas 309–12
Latin music 26–7, 260–1
Latinos 22, 49, 76, 170, 172
laundry 66
Laurel, Stan 121, 212
LAX 78

accommodations near 209–10
    customs 54
    transportation to/from 86–7
legal matters 74
Leimert Park 169–70, **Map 2**
    entertainment 258–9
    restaurants 242
Leo Carrillo State Beach 152
Leonis Adobe 182
lesbians. *See* gays & lesbians
libraries 71, 302. *See also* individual libraries
Library Tower 39
lingerie 127, 283–4
literature 27–9. *See also* books
Little Tokyo 40, 108–10, **Map 5**
Lloyd, Harold 142
Long Beach 153, 165–7, **Map 16**
    accommodations 214–5
    entertainment 258, 259, 268
    restaurants 240–1
    tourist office 50
Long Beach Museum of Art 167
Los Angeles Clippers 111, 269
Los Angeles Conservancy 40
Los Angeles Contemporary Exhibitions (LACE) 127
Los Angeles County Museum of Art (LACMA) 137–8
Los Angeles Department of Transportation. *See* LADOT
Los Angeles Dodgers 114, 269
Los Angeles International Airport. *See* LAX
Los Angeles Kings 111, 270
Los Angeles Lakers 111, 269
Los Angeles Maritime Museum 163
Los Angeles Memorial Coliseum & Sports Arena 117, 270
Los Angeles River 12, 15
Los Angeles Sparks 269
Los Angeles Theater 103

Bold indicates maps.

Los Angeles Times 63, 105
Los Angeles Zoo 119
Los Encinos State Historical
  Park 182
Los Feliz 121–2, **Map 9**
  entertainment 260
  restaurants 223–4
  shopping 271
Lovell House 44
luggage storage 66
Lummis, Charles Fletcher 174,
  175

M

MacArthur Park 135, **Map 5**
magazines 63
mail 57–8
Malibu 151, **Map 2**
  accommodations 210–1
  restaurants 233–4
  tourist office 50
Malibu Lagoon Museum 151
Malibu Lagoon State Beach
  153
malls 272–4
Manhattan Beach 153, 160,
  Map 14
  entertainment 264
  tourist office 50
Mann's Chinese Theater 124
Mansfield, Jayne 143
maps 50
Mariachi Plaza 172–3
Marina del Rey 159–60,
  Map 13
  accommodations 212–3
  restaurants 236–8
  tourist office 51
Mark Taper Forum 105–6,
  249
markets
  farmers' 133, 274
  flea 276
  food 173, 245, 246
McPherson, Aimee Semple
  113
measurements 66
medical services. *See* health
Meier, Richard 34, 36, 47,
  48, 141
Melrose Ave 131, **Map 10**

restaurants 226–7
  shopping 271
memorabilia 279
Metro Rail 89–90, **Map 19**
Metro Rapid 87, 89
Metrolink 90–1
Metropolitan Transportation
  Authority. *See* MTA
Mexican food 241
microbreweries 264–5
Mid-City 134–8, **Map 10**
  accommodations 206–7
  Koreatown 135–6, 222–3,
    264
  MacArthur Park 135
  Miracle Mile District 136–8
Miracle Mile District 136–8,
  Map 10
Missing Link Tours 83, 85
Mission Revival–style
  architecture 33, 36
missions 11–2
  San Fernando Rey de
    España 189
  San Gabriel Archangel
    181–3
  Santa Barbara 306
MOCA 100–1
MOCA Gallery at PDC 133
MOCA Geffen Contemporary
  110
Modernist style 33, 35, 38,
  43–5
MONA 110–1
money 55–7
Monroe, Marilyn 62, 123,
  134, 141, 143, 144, 148,
  149, 207, 212, 263
Monterey Park 241–2, **Map 3**
motorcycles 84–5, 91–2, 95
Mt Wilson Observatory 190
mountain biking 300
movies. *See* celebrities;
  cinemas; film industry;
  films; Hollywood
MTA 87, 88, 89, 96
Mulholland, William 14, 19
Muscle Beach 156, 158, 159
museums
  Autry Museum of Western
    Heritage 120

Banning Residence
    Museum 164
California Heritage
    Museum 157–8
California Science Center
    115–6
Chinese American
    Museum 108
Craft & Folk Art Museum
    138
Drum Barracks Civil War
    Museum 164–5
Fort MacArthur Military
    Museum 164
Frederick's of Hollywood
    Lingerie Museum 127
Getty Museum 154
guidebook of 62
Guinness World of Records
    Museum 126
Heritage Square Museum
    174–5
Hollywood Bowl Museum
    131
Hollywood Entertainment
    Museum 123–4
Hollywood Studio
    Museum 131
Hollywood Wax Museum
    126
Japanese American
    National Museum
    109–10
Kidspace 179–80
Laguna Art Museum 296
Long Beach Museum of
    Art 167
Los Angeles County
    Museum of Art
    (LACMA) 137–8
Los Angeles Maritime
    Museum 163
Malibu Lagoon Museum
    151
Museum in Black 169
Museum of African
    American Art 170
Museum of Contemporary
    Art (MOCA) 100–1
Museum of Death 127
Museum of Flying 158

Museum of Jurassic Technology (MJT) 150–1
Museum of Latin American Art 167
Museum of Natural History 306
Museum of Neon Art (MONA) 110–1
Museum of Television & Radio 141
Museum of Tolerance 149
Natural History Museum of LA County 114–5
Norton Simon Museum 176–8
Pacific Asia Museum 179
Page Museum at La Brea Discoveries 137
Petersen Automotive Museum 138
Santa Barbara Historical Museum 305–6
Santa Barbara Museum of Art 305
Santa Monica Museum of Art 157
Southwest Museum 174
Travel Town Museum 120–1
UCLA Hammer Museum 148
Wells Fargo History Museum 100
music 25–7
blues 258–60
country & western 261
hip-hop 26
jazz 25, 258–60
Latin 26–7, 260–1
outdoor venues 254
radio stations 64
rap 26
rhythm & blues 25–6
rock 26, 130, 255–8
stores 280
swing 260

Bold indicates maps.

Music Center of LA County 105–6, 249
Musso & Frank Grill 126, 225

N

Naples 167, **Map 4**
native peoples 22
Chumash 11, 305
Gabrieleño (Shoshone) 11, 12, 175, 294
Ute-Azteca 294
Natural History Museum of LA County 114–5
NBC Studios tour 186
Neutra, Richard 30, 33, 35, 38, 43–4, 121
Neutra Colony 43–4
newspapers 63, 105
Nixon, Richard 302
norteña 26–7
North Hollywood 187, **Map 18**
entertainment 251, 259, 266, 268
restaurants 244
Norton Simon Museum 176–8

O

Ocean Front Walk 271
oil industry 15
Old Plaza 107
Olvera St 107
One Bunker Hill 39
O'Neal, Shaquille 269
O'Neill House 140
opera 253–4
orange industry 15
Orcutt Ranch 192
Orpheum Theater 102
Oscar 124, 140
outlet malls 273–4
Oviatt Building 33, 40–1
Owens Valley 14, 109

P

Pacific Asia Museum 179
Pacific Coast Hwy (PCH) 85, 151
Pacific Design Center 133
Pacific Mutual Building 40

Pacific Palisades 154–5, **Map 2**
Pacific Park 156
Page Museum at La Brea Discoveries 137
The Palace 127
Palisades Park 156
Palos Verdes Peninsula 162, **Map 4**
Pantages Theater 127–8, 249
Pantages/Warner Brothers Theater 102
Paramount Ranch 189
Paramount Studios 130, 252
parking 92–3
parks
Angels Gate Park 163–4
Barnsdall Art Park 121–2
Biddy Mason Park 104
El Pueblo de los Angeles 106–8
Elysian Park 113–4
Exposition Park 114
Grand Hope Park 110
Greystone Park & Mansion 144
Griffith Park 118–21
Leimert Park 169
Los Encinos State Historical Park 182
MacArthur Park 135
Palisades Park 156
Pio Pico State Historic Park 182
Runyon Canyon Park 193
Topanga State Park 154
Zuma Beach County Park 153
Pasadena 176–81, **Map 17**
accommodations 215
architectural tour 41–2, 41
entertainment 252, 266–7
restaurants 242–3
shopping 271–2
tourist office 51
passports 51
Pelanconi House 107
Pepperdine University 154
Pershing Square 40, 101–2
Petersen Automotive Museum 138

phones 58–9
photography 64–5
Pickford, Mary 102, 124, 126, 140, 142, 295
Pio Pico State Historic Park 182
planetariums 119, 157
plastic surgery 132
Playa del Rey 264
Playboy Mansion 143
Plaza de la Raza 173–4
Point Dume Beach 153
Point Vicente Interpretive Center 162
police. See LAPD
politics 20, 62, 187
pollution 19
population 21–2
Porno Walk of Fame 134
Ports O'Call Village 163
postal services 57–8
Presley, Elvis 143
public art 30, 99–100, 159
public transportation 86, 87–90
pubs 264–5
Puck, Wolfgang 218, 232, 234, 236

Q

Queen Anne style. See Victorian-style architecture
Queen Mary 166–7

R

radio 63–4, 141
ranchera 37
rancheros 12–3, 14
Rancho Santa Ana Botanic Garden 192
rap 26
Reagan, Ronald 104, 144, 302
Red Rock Canyon 310
Redondo Beach 153, 161–2, **Map 14**
entertainment 258, 264
tourist office 51
Reeves, George 143
religion 31
restaurants 218–46. See also Places to Eat index

for breakfast 231
celebrities at 225
costs 57, 219
etiquette 219
kid-friendly 239
romantic 228
24-hour 221
vegetarian 236
Revival styles 37
Reynolds, Burt 143
rhythm & blues 25–6
Rialto Theater 102
Riordan, Richard 20, 221
riots 16–7
Ripley's Believe It or Not! 126
rock music 26, 255–8
Rock Walk of Fame 130
Rodeo Dr 139–40, 271
Rodia, Simon 170–1
Rose Bowl 75, 177, 178, 270
Roundhouse Marine Studies Lab & Aquarium 160
running 195
Runyon Canyon Park 193

S

safety
crime 56, 72–3
earthquakes 73
swimming 66–7, 152
St Basil's Roman Catholic Church 46
St John's Episcopal Church 118
St Sophia Cathedral 136
St Vincent De Paul Catholic Church 118
San Antonio Winery 112–3
San Fernando Valley 183–9
Burbank 216, 243–4, 261
entertainment 259–60, 266–7
Glendale 183–6, 215–6, 243, 251
North Hollywood 244, 251, 259, 266, 268
restaurants 244–6
Universal City 187–9, 216, 244, 259, 272
San Gabriel 181–3, **Map 3**
San Gabriel Mountains 175, 189–90

San Gabriel Valley 49, 175–83
Pasadena 41–2, 176–81, 215, 242–3, 252, 266–7, 271–2
San Gabriel 181–3
San Pedro 163–4, **Map 15**
restaurants 240–1
tourist office 51
Santa Barbara 303–9, **304**
Santa Barbara Botanic Garden 306
Santa Barbara County Courthouse 305
Santa Barbara Historical Museum 305–6
Santa Barbara Museum of Art 305
Santa Barbara Zoological Garden 306
Santa Catalina Island 291–4
Santa Fe Trail 13
Santa Monica 155–8, **Map 13**
accommodations 198, 211–2
art galleries 275
entertainment 251, 258, 259, 266
restaurants 234–6
shopping 271, 273
tourist office 51
transportation 89
Santa Monica Mountains 190–1
Santa Monica Museum of Art 157
Santa Monica Pier 155–6
Santa Monica State Beach 153
Santa Ynez Canyon 191
Schindler, Rudolph 30, 33, 35, 38, 43, 44, 121, 134
Schindler House 134
sculpture 30–1
Seaside Lagoon 161
Self-Help Graphics Gallery 173
Self-Realization Fellowship Lake Shrine 154–5
senior travelers 53, 70
Sepulveda House 107
Shoestring Corridor 49

shopping 271–84
  antique shops 281
  art galleries 274–5
  bizarre boutiques 282–3
  bookstores 277–8, 279
  clothing stores 272, 279,
    281–3
  districts 271–2
  farmers' markets 274
  flea markets 276
  garage sales 277
  jewelry stores 280–1
  lingerie & erotica stores
    283–4
  malls 272–3
  memorabilia stores 279
  music stores 280
  outlet malls 273–4
  specialty shops 284
  sporting goods stores
    278–80
  thrift shops 275–7
Shoshone. See Gabrieleño
Shrine Auditorium 117–8
Shubert Theater 149, 249
Siegel, Bugsy 130, 141, 144,
  211, 309
Silent Movie Theatre 248
Silver Lake 121–2, **Map 9**
  architectural tour 43–5, 43
  art galleries 275
  entertainment 255–6, 261,
    262–3, 268
  restaurants 223–4
Simpson, OJ 63, 117, 144–5
Six Flags Magic Mountain 303
skating, in-line 191
skiing 299
Skirball Cultural Center
  145–6
smog 19
snorkeling 293
soccer 270
Solstice Canyon 193
Sony Pictures Studios 150
South Bay 160–2, **Map 14**

  accommodations 198,
    213–4
  restaurants 238–9
South Coast Botanical Garden
  162
South Park 110–2, **Map 5**
Southern California Flower
  Market 111–2
Southwest Museum 174
Spadena House 140
Spanish Colonial style. See
  Mission Revival–style
  architecture
special events 75–7
Spelling, Aaron 143
sporting goods stores 278–80
sports 269–70. See also
  individual sports
Spring St 40, 103–4
stained glass 46
Staples Center 111, 269, 270
Starlight Bowl 131
State Theater 103
Stearns Wharf 306
Stockton, Robert F 13
Streamline Moderne 33, 37–8
students 53
Studio City 260
studios 122, 130, 133,
  149–50, 160, 186, 187–9,
  252
sunscreen 67
Sunset Strip 134
supermarkets 246
surfing 161
swimming 66–7, 152, 292–3,
  300. See also beaches
swing music 260
Sycamore Canyon 191–2
synagogues 45–6

T

Tate, Sharon 142
tattoos 132
taxes 57
taxis 87, 95–6
telephones 58–9
television. See also studios
  museum 141
  stations 63
tennis 195

theater 29–30, 248–52
theme parks 97, 156, 187–9,
  285, 287–90, 303
Third Street Promenade 157,
  271
thrift shops 275–7
tickets
  airline 78–9, 80
  entertainment 138, 247
  sports 269–70
  television studios 252
  theater 249
Tillman Water Reclamation
  Plant 192
time zones 65
tipping 57, 197
toilets 66
Topanga Canyon 154
Topanga State Park 154
tourism 21, 50
tourist offices 50–1
tourist seasons 49
Tournament of Roses Parade
  177
tours, organized 40, 85, 96–7.
  See also individual locations
tours, self-guided
  cutting-edge architecture
    47–8
  Downtown architecture
    38–41, 38
  Financial District 98–101,
    100
  historic Downtown core
    101–4, 103
  historic Hollywood 123–8,
    123
  Pasadena architecture 41–2,
    41
  Silver Lake architecture
    43–5, 43
  stars' homes 142–4
  Wilshire Blvd religious
    buildings 45–7, 45
Tower Theater 102–3
trains 84, 89–91
transportation
  air travel 78–82, 86–7
  bicycles 96
  buses 82–3, 87–9
  cars 84–5, 91–5

hitchhiking 85
motorcycles 84–5, 91–2, 95
public 86, 87–90
taxis 87, 95–6
trains 84, 89–91
walking 96
Web sites 61
travel agencies 51
travel insurance 53
Travel Town Museum 120–1
traveler's checks 55–6
Turner, Lana 144
TV. *See* television
Two Harbors 292

U

UCLA 71, 146, 148, 270
UCLA Ocean Discovery Center 156
Union Station 40, 107–8
United Artists Theater 102
Universal City 187–9, **Map 18**
accommodations 216
entertainment 259
restaurants 244
shopping 272
Universal Studios Hollywood 187–9
universities & colleges 71–2. *See also* individual schools
USC 71, 117, 270
Ute-Aztecas 294

V

Valentino, Rudolph 141, 143
The Valley. *See* San Fernando Valley
vegetarianism 236
Venice 158–9, **Map 13**
accommodations 199–200, 212–3
art galleries 275
entertainment 251, 266, 268
restaurants 236–8
shopping 271
Venice Boardwalk 158–9

Venice Canalwalk 159
Venice City Beach 153
Ventura Blvd 244–6
Vernon 170, **Map 3**
Victorian-style architecture 36
video 64–5
Virgen de Guadalupe 173
Virginia Robinson Gardens 140–1
visas 51–2, 77

W

walking 96. *See also* tours, self-guided
Walt Disney Hall 106
Warner Brothers Studios 186
Warner Grand Theater 164
water
conserving 50
history 14, 15
quality 66–7
supply 19–20
water parks 303, 310
Watts 16, 170–1, **Map 3**
Watts Labor Community Action Center (WLCAC) 171
Watts Towers 170–1
Watts Towers Art Center 171
Waugh, Evelyn 28
Wayfarer's Chapel 162
Web sites 60–1
Weissmuller, Johnny 143
Wells Fargo History Museum 100
West, Nathanael 27, 28
West Adams 168–9
West Hollywood 133–4, **Map 10**
accommodations 204–6
art galleries 274–5
entertainment 250, 257–8, 263–4, 266, 267
restaurants 227–8
tourist office 51
West Hollywood Cheerleaders 77
Westside 139–51

Bel Air 144–6, 207–8
Beverly Hills 139–44, 207–8, 231–2, 250, 260, 271, 275
Brentwood 144–6
Century City 148–9, 208–9, 249, 259, 273
Culver City 89, 149–51, 233, 259, 261
entertainment 250, 258, 264
Westwood 146, 148, 208–9, 233, 250, 273
Westward Beach 153
Westwood 146, 148, **Map 11**
accommodations 208–9
entertainment 250
restaurants 233
shopping 273
Westwood Memorial Park 148
whale watching 162, 164
whitewater rafting 308
Will Geer Theatricum Botanicum 154
Will Rogers State Beach 153, 154
Williams, Stanley 'Tookie' 168
Wilmington 164–5, **Map 4**
Wilshire Blvd 45–7, 45
Wilshire Boulevard Temple 44, 45–6
Wilshire Christian Church 46–7
Wiltern Theater 135
wine tasting 112–3
women travelers 68
work 77
Worldport LA 163
Wright, Frank Lloyd 30, 33, 34, 35, 44, 122, 139
Wright, Lloyd 34–5
Wrigley Mansion & Gardens 178
Wrigley Memorial & Botanical Garden 292

Z

zoos 119, 306
Zuma Beach County Park 153

Places to Stay

The Annabelle Hotel 216
The Argyle 206
Artists' Inn & Cottage 201
Avalon Hotel 207
Banana Bungalow Hollywood 199
Barnabey's Hotel 213
Beach House 214
Beach Inn Motel 214
Best Western Colorado Inn 215
Best Western Dragon Gate Inn 202
Best Western Mayfair Hotel 203
Best Western Ocean View Hotel 211
Best Western Sunrise Hotel 213–4
Best Western Sunset Plaza Hotel 205
Beverly Crescent Hotel 207
Beverly Hills Hotel 208
Beverly Hills Reeves Hotel 207
Beverly Laurel Hotel 204
Beverly Plaza Hotel 205
Bevonshire Lodge Motel 204
Bissell House 201
Brooks College 214
Burbank Airport Hilton & Convention Center 216
Burbank Inn & Suites 216
Cadillac Hotel 199, 212
Cal Mar Hotel Suites 211
Casa Malibu Inn 210
Century Plaza Hotel 209
Century Wilshire Hotel 208
Chancellor Hotel 206–7
Channel Road Inn 200
Chariot Inn Motel 215
Château Marmont 206
City Center Motel 202
Coral Sands Motel 205
Crowne Plaza LA Airport 210
Culver Hotel 209–10
Dockside Boat & Bed 214–5
Dockweiler Beach RV Park 197

Doubletree Hotel 209, 215
Dunes Sunset Motel 204
Dunes Wilshire Motor Hotel 207
The Fairmont Miramar Hotel 212
Farmer's Daughter Motel 204
Foghorn Harbor Inn 213
Four Points by Sheraton 210
Four Seasons Hotel 208
Furama Hotel 210
Georgian Hotel 211
Glendale Lodge 215
The Grafton on Sunset 205
Grandview Motor Hotel 213
Grove Guest House 205
Hampton Inn 209
HI-Los Angeles/Santa Monica Hostel 198
HI-Los Angeles/South Bay Hostel 198
Highland Gardens Hotel 203
Hilgard House Hotel 208
Hilton Glendale 215–6
Holiday Inn Burbank 216
Holiday Inn City Center 203
Holiday Inn Downtown 203
Holiday Lodge 216
Holloway Motel 204–5
Hollywood Best Inn 203
Hollywood Celebrity Hotel 204
Hollywood International Hostel 199
Hollywood Metropolitan Hotel 204
Hollywood Roosevelt Hotel 204
Hostel California 200
Hotel Bel Air 207
Hotel California 211
Hotel Casa del Mar 212
Hotel del Capri 208
Hotel del Flores 207
Hotel Figueroa 202
Hotel Oceana 212
Hotel Queen Mary 214
Hotel Shangri-La 211

Hyatt Regency 202–3
Hyatt West Hollywood 206
In Town Hotel 201
Inn at Playa del Rey 200–1
Inn at 657 200
Inn at Venice Beach 212
Inn of Long Beach 214
Jolly Roger Hotel 212
Kawada Hotel 202
Le Montrose Suite Hotel 206
Leo Carrillo State Beach Campground 197
Liberty Hotel 203
Loews Santa Monica Beach Hotel 212
Lord Mayor 201
Los Angeles Airport Hilton & Towers 210
Los Angeles Airport Marriott 210
Los Angeles Athletic Club Hotel 202
Luxe Hotel Rodeo Drive 207
Magic Hotel 203
Maison 140 207
Malibu Beach Inn 210–1
Malibu Beach RV Park 197
Malibu Country Inn 210
Malibu Riviera Motel 210
Manhattan Beach Hotel 213
Marina Pacific Hotel 213
Metro Plaza Hotel 201–2
Milner Hotel 201
Miyako Inn 202
Mondrian 206
Motel de Ville 202
New Otani 202
Ocean Lodge 211
Orange Drive Manor 198
Orbit Hostel 199
Orchid Hotel 201
Orchid Suites Hotel 204
Oxford Palace Hotel 207
Pacific Sands Motel 211
Palos Verdes Inn 214
Park Plaza Lodge 204
Pasadena Hilton 215
Pasadena Inn 215

Portofino Hotel & Yacht Club 214
Ramada Limited 212–3
Ramada West Hollywood 205–6
The Regal Biltmore 203
The Regent Beverly Wilshire 208
Renaissance Los Angeles Hotel 210
Ritz-Carlton Huntington Hotel 215
Ritz-Carlton Marina del Rey 213
Royal Pagoda Motel 202
Royal Palace Westwood Hotel 208
Safari Inn 216
Saga Motor Hotel 215
Saharan Motor Hotel 204
San Vicente Inn/Resort 205

Santa Monica Beach Travelodge 211
Sea Shore Motel 211
Sea Sprite Motel 213
Sea View Inn 213
Share-Tel Apartments 199
Sheraton Gateway LA Airport Hotel 210
Sheraton Pasadena Hotel 215
Sheraton Universal Hotel 216
Shutters on the Beach 212
Sportsmen's Lodge Hotel 216
The Standard 205
Stillwell Hotel 201
Student Inn International Hostel 198–9
Sunbay Motel 212
Sunburst Motel 209
Sunset Marquis Hotel & Villas 206
Super 8 209

Surf City Hostel 200
Topanga Ranch Motel 210
The Turret House 201
Universal City Hilton & Towers 216
Universal City Inn 216
USA Hostels-Hollywood 198
Venice Beach Cotel 200
Venice Beach Hostel 199
Venice Beach House 200
Vista Motel 209
W 209
Walnut RV Park 197
Westin Bonaventure Hotel 203
Westway Inn 215
Westwood Inn 208
Wilshire Royale Howard Johnson Plaza 207
Wyndham Checkers Hotel 203

Places to Eat

The Abbey 227
Abbot Pizza 237
Akbar 242
Albertsons 246
Alegria 240
Angélique Cafe 220
Backburner Cafe 238
Baklava Factory 243
Bamboo Inn 244–5
Bangluck Market 245
Barefoot Café 229
Barney Greengrass 232
Barragan's 220
Barsac Brasserie 244
Basix 228
Beach Hut No 2 238
Bel Air Restaurant 233
Belmont Brewing Company 240
Birds 225
Bistro Garden at Coldwater 246
Bob's Big Boy 243
Border Grill 235

Bouchon 226
Bristol Farms 246
Buca di Beppo 239, 242, 244
Buffet Land 223
Ca' Brea 227
Ca' del Sole 244
Café Bizou 242, 245
Café Brasil 233
Café Pinot 222
Cafe Stella 224
Caffè Luna 226
Camacho's Cantina 244
Campanile 227
Canter's Deli 230
Cava 229
ChaChaCha 223
Charming Garden 242
Chaya Brasserie 230
Chaya Venice 237
Chez Mélange 239
China Cafe 220
Chinois on Main 236
Cicada 221
Citrus 227

Ciudad 221
Clifton's Brookdale Cafeteria 220
Cobalt Cantina 224, 228
Cowboy Sushi 233
Crustacean 232
Damiano Mr Pizza 230–1
Dan Tana's 228
Dar Maghreb 226
Doughboys 230
East India Grill 226
Eatz 234
Ed Debevic's 231
Egg Heaven 240
El Chavo 223
El Cholo 223, 235
El Conquistador 224
El Floridita 225
El Gallo 241
El Gringo 238
El Perla 241
El Siete Mares 223
El Sombrero 238
El Tarasco 241

El Tepeyac Cafe 241
Elephant Walk 242
Empanada's Place 233
Empress Pavilion 222
Erewhon Natural Foods
    Market 246
Eurochow 233
Fabio's 237
The Farm 232
Farm Fresh Ranch Market
    245
Food 4 Less 246
Frankie's 227
Fred 62 223
French Quarter Market 227
Fresco Ristorante 243
Frying Fish Sushi 221
Full House 222
Fun Fish Market 238
The Galley 235
Gelson's 246
Geoffrey's 234
Gina Lee's Bistro 239
Gladstone's 244
Golden Dragon 222
Good Stuff 238
Gourmet Coffee Warehouse
    245
The Great Grill 243
The Green Room 224
The Green Temple 238-9
Guelaguetza 222-3
Gumbo Pot 230
Gypsy Café 233
Hal's Bar & Grill 237
Hama Sushi 221
Hamburger Hamlet 224
Hard Rock Cafe 228
Hong Kong Harbor 222
Hop Woo 222
Hot Dog on a Stick 234
House of Blues 228
Hugo's 227-8
I Cugini 234-5
India Sweets & Spices 245
India's Tandoori 243
Indochine 230
Inn of the Seventh Ray 234
Jake & Annie's 235
Jerry's Famous Deli 229
JiRaffe 235

Jody Maroni's Sausage
    Kingdom 236-7, 244
Joe's 237-8
Karl Strauss Brewery 244
The Kettle 238
Kings Road Cafe 229
Knight 243
Knoll's Black Forest Inn 235-6
KoKoMo 230
Koreatown Plaza International
    Food Court 222
Koreatown Plaza Market 245
La Pergola 246
La Playita 238
La Poubelle 225
Lala's 226
Laredo 234
Lavande 236
Le Beaujolais 239
Le Colonial 230
Leonor's Vegetarian Restaurant
    244
Les Deux Cafés 225
Liborio Market 245
Lilly's 237
Locanda Veneta 229
L'Orangerie 228
Malvasia 240
Maria's Pescado Frito 220
Market City Cafe 244
Marston's 242
Matsuhisa 232
Menjin 229
Mi Piace 242
Miceli's 225
Mitsuwa 245
Mum's 240
Musso & Frank Grill 225
The Naked Garden 238
Natalee Thai Cuisine 232, 233
Neptune's Net 233-4
Newsroom 229, 234
Nic's 232
Nyala 231
Ocean Avenue Seafood 235
Ocean Seafood 222
Ocean Star 241
Old Spaghetti Factory 224
Omelette Parlor 234
Original Pantry Cafe 221
Orso 229-30

Palermo 223
Papa Cristo's Taverna 223
Papadakis Taverna 240
Pastis 230
Patina 226
Patinette 220
Pavilions 246
Philippe The Original 220
Phillip's House of Barbecue
    242
Piero's Seafood Restaurant
    244
Pink's Hot Dogs 226
Poquito Más 243
Quality Seafood 238
Rack Shack 242
Ralphs 246
Real Food Daily 229, 234
Red Lion Tavern 224
Roast to Go 220
Röckenwagner 236
Rose Cafe 237
Saddle Peak Lodge 234
Sam Woo 222
Sanamluang 224
Santé La Brea 226
Sarita's Pupuseria 220
Schatzi on Main 236
Serenata di Garibaldi 235
17th Street Cafe 235
Shabu Shabu House 221
Sidewalk Cafe 236
Sky Room 240-1
Sofi 231
Soleil 239
Sonora Cafe 227
Soot Bull Jeep 223
Spago Beverly Hills 232
Stinking Rose 232
Suehiro 220
Taco Company 240
Taco Surf 240
Taiko 233
Tail O' the Pup 229
The Taj 232
Tamara's Tamale 237
Teru Sushi 246
Tokyo Delve's 244
Tommy Tang's 227
Tony's Fish Market 239
Tortilla Grill 237

Trader Joe's 246
Trattoria Farfalla 242
Trattoria Sorriso 242
Traxx 221
Twin Palms 242
Uncle Bill's Pancake House
    238
Van Go's Ear 237

Vermont 224
Versailles 231–2, 233, 244
Vida 224
Vons 246
Water Grill 222
Whole Foods 246
Wild Oats Food Market 246
Wolfgang Puck Express 234

Xiomara 243
Yakitori East 220–1
Yamashiro 226
Ye Olde King's Head 235
Yuca's 223
Yujean Kang 228, 243
Zankou Chicken 224, 242,
    243

Boxed Text

Accidents Do Happen 91
Adobe Buildings 182
Air Combat USA: The Ultimate Thrill Ride 299
Air Travel Glossary 80
As a River, It's a Washout 12
Best Shots in LA 65
Big Red Cars 90
Body Modifications 132
Calling All Pack Rats: Flea Markets Abound
    276
The Chains 209
Dining Around the Clock 221
Don Carlos' Crusade 175
Especially for Kids 116
Famous Alumni 129
Famous Names of Caltech 180
Free Tours 97
Gay Accommodations 205
George Freeth: King of the Surfer Dudes 161
Getting Into a Studio 252
Ghost Expeditions: If the Spirit Moves
    You…125
Great Breakfast Haunts 231
Great Celebrity Spotting 225
Great Places to Go with Kids 239
A Helping Hand for Public Art 30
Highlights 99
HIV & Entering the USA 52
Important Bus Routes 88
International Food Markets for the
    Adventurous Necessities 245
Judson Studios: A Legacy of Stained Glass 46
LA at a Discount 138
LA Car Culture 184–5

LA Garden Culture 192
LA Street Gangs 168
Laguna Arts Festivals 295
LA's Best Happy Hours 262
Life's a Beach 152–3
Literary Potshots 28
Los Angeles Conservancy Tours 40
The Los Angeles Riots: 1992 & 1965 17
Major Airlines Serving LA 82
Major Freeways 94
Murder & Mischief at the Silent Movie
    Theatre 248
Outdoor Venues 254
Purple People Greeters 105
A River Roars Through It: The Killer Kern 308
Romantic Dining Spots 228
Shake, Rattle & Roll: Earthquakes in LA 73
The Shoestring Corridor 49
The Sick, the Bizarre & the Twisted 282–3
The Story Behind the Garment Glitz 112
Taking Home a Piece of Tinsel 279
To Save & Protect 173
Tom Bradley – An LA Icon 20
Tricky Dick & Gipper Libraries 302
Valley Secession & the Balkanization of LA 187
Vegetarian Delights 236
Warning 78
Water for a Thirsty Giant 14
What's Free 147
Where to Log On 60
Whimsical Mexican Food 241
The World 'Tourns' Its Attention to Pasadena
    177
The WWII Battle of LA 16

Los Angeles Map Section

Map 1   Los Angeles

Map 2   Western Los Angeles

Map 3   Eastern Los Angeles

Map 4   Southern Los Angeles

Map 5   Downtown Los Angeles

Map 6   Exposition Park Area

Map 7   Koreatown

Map 8   Griffith Park

Map 9   Hollywood, Los Feliz & Silver Lake

Map 10   West Hollywood & Mid-City

Map 11   Beverly Hills & Westwood

Map 12   Culver City

Map 13   Santa Monica & Venice

Map 14   South Bay

Map 15   San Pedro

Map 16   Long Beach

Map 17   Pasadena

Map 18   Burbank, North Hollywood & Universal City

Map 19   Metro Rail System

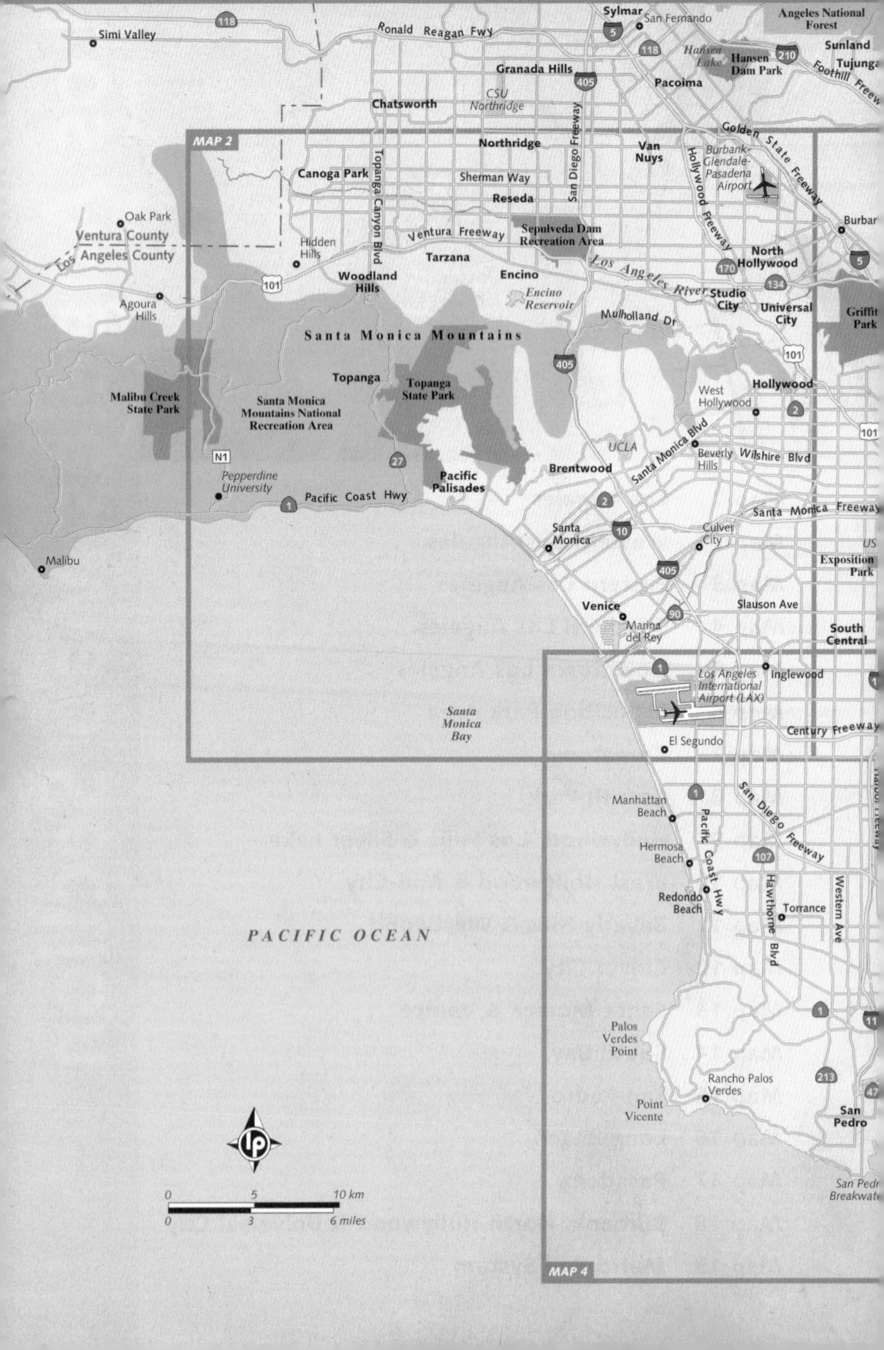

MAP 1 LOS ANGELES

Simi Valley

Ronald Reagan Fwy

118

Sylmar
San Fernando

5

Angeles National
Forest

Granada Hills

118

Pacoima

Hansen
Lake

Hansen
Dam Park

210

Sunland

Tujunga
Foothill Fwy

Chatsworth

CSU
Northridge

405

Burbank-
Glendale-
Pasadena
Airport

Golden State Freeway

MAP 2

Northridge

Van
Nuys

Burbar

Canoga Park

Topanga Canyon Blvd

Sherman Way

Reseda

Sepulveda Dam
Recreation Area

Hollywood Freeway

North
Hollywood

5

Oak Park

Ventura County
Angeles County

Hidden
Hills

Ventura Freeway

Tarzana

Encino

Los Angeles River

170

134

Studio
City

Universal
City

Griffith
Park

Los Angeles River

Agoura
Hills

101

Woodland
Hills

Encino
Reservoir

Mulholland Dr

101

Santa Monica Mountains

Topanga

Topanga
State Park

405

West
Hollywood

Hollywood

2

Malibu Creek
State Park

Santa Monica
Mountains National
Recreation Area

UCLA

Santa Monica Blvd

Beverly
Hills

Wilshire Blvd

101

Malibu

N1

Pepperdine
University

27

Pacific Coast Hwy

Pacific
Palisades

Brentwood

2

Santa Monica Freeway

US
Exposition
Park

1

Santa
Monica

10

Culver
City

405

Slauson Ave

South
Central

Venice

90

Marina
del Rey

Los Angeles
International
Airport (LAX)

Inglewood

1

Santa
Monica
Bay

El Segundo

Century Freeway

Manhattan
Beach

1

San Diego Freeway

Hermosa
Beach

Pacific Coast Hwy

107

Hawthorne Blvd

Western Ave

PACIFIC OCEAN

Redondo
Beach

Torrance

1

11

Palos
Verdes
Point

213

Rancho Palos
Verdes

47

Point
Vicente

San
Pedro

0   5   10 km
0   3   6 miles

San Pedr
Breakwate

MAP 4

MAP 3

San Gabriel Mountains

Angeles Crest Hwy

Bear Creek

Cogswell Reservoir

San Gabriel River

La Crescenta

Mt Wilson Observatory

Angeles National Forest

San Gabriel Reservoir

Morris Reservoir

La Cañada Flintridge

Jet Propulsion Laboratory

Altadena

Brookside Park

Rose Bowl

Pasadena

Foothill Freeway

Monrovia

Azusa

Glendora

Glendale

Caltech

Santa Anita Racetrack

Arcadia

Santa Fe Dam Recreation Area

Pasadena Freeway

San Marino

N Rosemead Blvd

Temple City

Baldwin Park

Covina

Bonelli Regional County Park

Alhambra

San Gabriel

El Monte

San Bernardino Freeway

West Covina

Pomona

Los Angeles

Monterey Park

Whittier Narrows Recreation Area

Industry

La Puente

San Gabriel River Freeway

Diamond Bar

Vernon

East Los Angeles

Santa Ana Fwy

Pico Rivera

Pomona Freeway

Rowland Heights

Schabarum Regional Park

Orange Freeway

Whittier

La Habra Heights

Los Angeles County

Orange County

Carbon Canyon Rd

Watts

Downey

La Habra

Imperial Hwy

Compton

La Mirada

Santa Ana Freeway

Brea

Richard Nixon Library

Long Beach Freeway

Paramount

Norwalk

Yorba Linda Blvd

CSU Fullerton

Yorba Linda

Artesia Freeway

San Gabriel River

Los Angeles River

Fullerton

Placentia

CSU Dominguez Hills

Lakewood

Cerritos

Buena Park

Riverside Freeway

Carson St

Lincoln Ave

Knott's Berry Farm

Anaheim

Villa Park

Irvine Regional Park

Willow St

Cypress

Katela Ave

Stanton

Disneyland & Disney's California Adventure

Edison International Field of Anaheim

Orange

CSU Long Beach

Long Beach

Garden Grove Fwy

Garden Grove

Eastern Transportation Corridor (toll)

United States Naval Weapons Station

San Diego Freeway

Westminster

Santa Ana

Tustin

Outer Los Angeles Harbor

Seal Beach National Wildlife Refuge

Beach Blvd

Tustin Air Station

Middle Breakwater

Long Beach Breakwater

Pacific Coast Hwy

San Pedro Bay

Santa Ana River

Costa Mesa Freeway

Irvine Center Dr

John Wayne Airport (Orange County)

Irvine

Concordia University

To Santa Catalina

Huntington Beach

Costa Mesa

UC Irvine

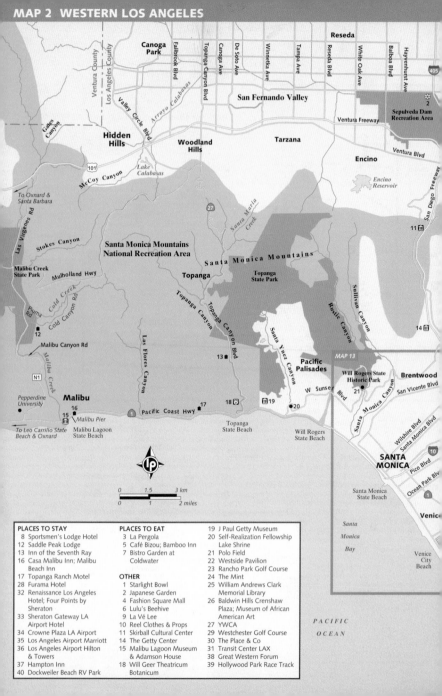

MAP 2 WESTERN LOS ANGELES

Reseda

Canoga Park

Fallbrook Blvd
Topanga Canyon Blvd
Canoga Ave
De Soto Ave
Winnetka Ave
Tampa Ave
Reseda Blvd
White Oak Ave
Balboa Blvd
Hayvenhurst Ave

405

San Fernando Valley

Ventura Freeway

☼ 2

Sepulveda Dam
Recreation Area

Valley Circle Blvd
Arroyo Calabasas
Los Angeles County
Ventura County

Gates Canyon

Hidden Hills

Woodland Hills

Tarzana

Ventura Blvd

Encino

McCoy Canyon

101

Lake Calabasas

Encino Reservoir

San Diego Freeway

To Oxnard & Santa Barbara

27

Santa Maria Creek

11 🏛

Las Virgenes Rd

Stokes Canyon

Santa Monica Mountains
National Recreation Area

Santa Monica Mountains

Malibu Creek State Park

Mulholland Hwy

Topanga

Topanga State Park

Sullivan Canyon

14 🏛

Cold Creek

Piuma Rd

Cold Canyon Rd

12

Topanga Canyon

Topanga Canyon Blvd

Rustic Canyon

MAP 13

Will Rogers State Historic Park

Brentwood

Malibu Canyon Rd

Las Flores Canyon

13 ■

Pacific Palisades

21

San Vicente Blvd

N1

Pepperdine University

Malibu Creek

Malibu

16

15 🏛

Malibu Pier

18 ☒

🏛 19

20

Santa Ynez Canyon

W Sunset Blvd

Santa Monica Canyon

1

Pacific Coast Hwy

17

Wilshire Blvd
Santa Monica Blvd

To Leo Carrillo State
Beach & Oxnard

Malibu Lagoon
State Beach

Topanga
State Beach

Will Rogers
State Beach

SANTA MONICA

10

Pico Blvd

Ocean Park Blvd

LP

0   1.5   3 km
0   1   2 miles

Santa Monica
State Beach

Venice

1

Santa
Monica
Bay

Venice
City
Beach

PACIFIC

OCEAN

PLACES TO STAY
8 Sportsmen's Lodge Hotel
12 Saddle Peak Lodge
13 Inn of the Seventh Ray
16 Casa Malibu Inn; Malibu Beach Inn
17 Topanga Ranch Motel
28 Furama Hotel
32 Renaissance Los Angeles Hotel; Four Points by Sheraton
33 Sheraton Gateway LA Airport Hotel
34 Crowne Plaza LA Airport
35 Los Angeles Airport Marriott
36 Los Angeles Airport Hilton & Towers
37 Hampton Inn
40 Dockweiler Beach RV Park

PLACES TO EAT
3 La Pergola
5 Café Bizou; Bamboo Inn
7 Bistro Garden at Coldwater

OTHER
1 Starlight Bowl
2 Japanese Garden
4 Fashion Square Mall
6 Lulu's Beehive
9 La Vé Lee
10 Reel Clothes & Props
11 Skirball Cultural Center
14 The Getty Center
15 Malibu Lagoon Museum & Adamson House
18 Will Geer Theatricum Botanicum

19 J Paul Getty Museum
20 Self-Realization Fellowship Lake Shrine
21 Polo Field
22 Westside Pavilion
23 Rancho Park Golf Course
24 The Mint
25 William Andrews Clark Memorial Library
26 Baldwin Hills Crenshaw Plaza; Museum of African American Art
27 YWCA
29 Westchester Golf Course
30 The Place & Co
31 Transit Center LAX
38 Great Western Forum
39 Hollywood Park Race Track

MAP 2 WESTERN LOS ANGELES

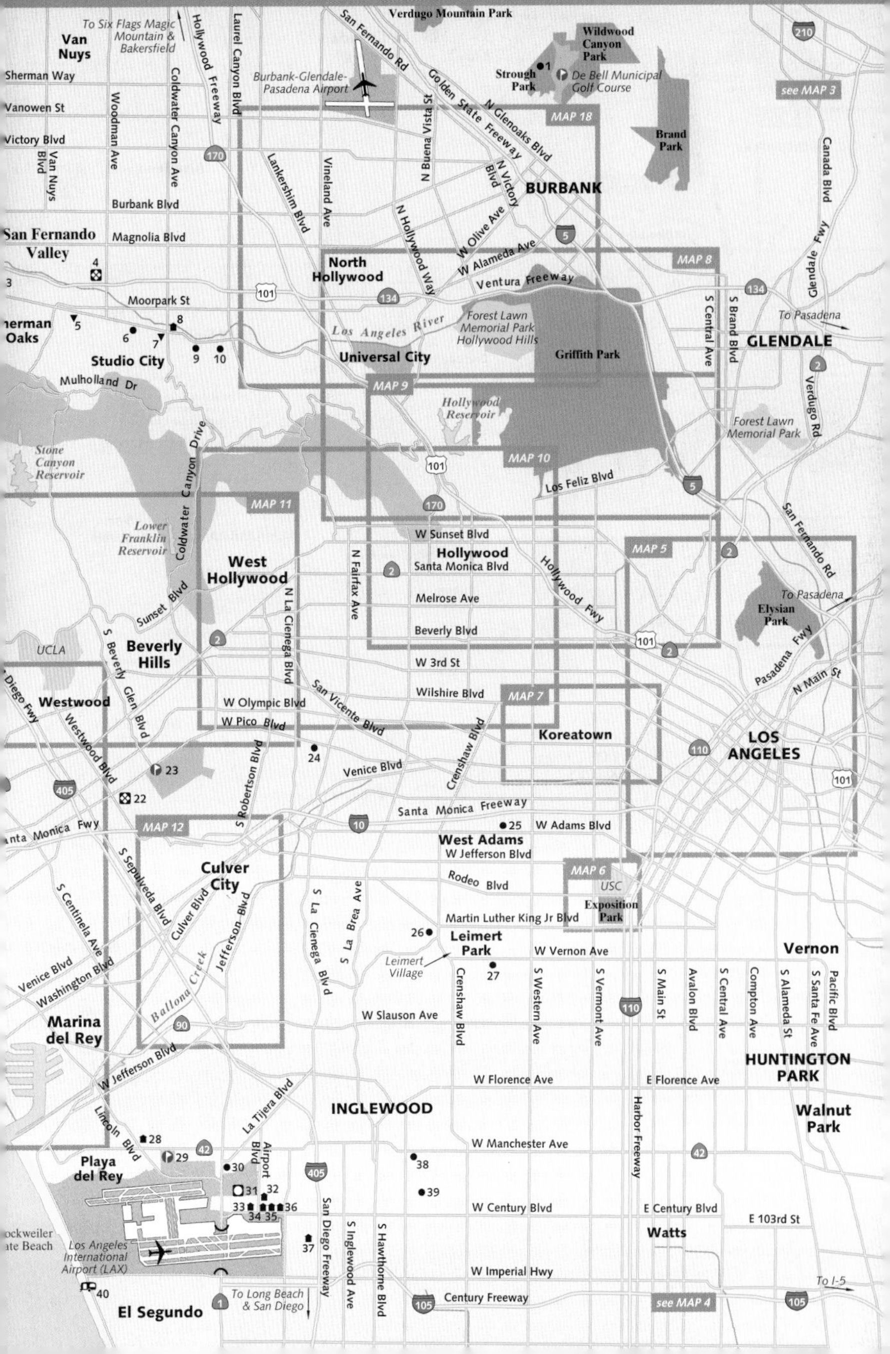

Van Nuys

To Six Flags Magic
Mountain &
Bakersfield

Sherman Way

Vanowen St

Victory Blvd

Van Nuys Blvd

Woodman Ave

Coldwater Canyon Ave

Laurel Canyon Blvd

Hollywood Freeway

Burbank Blvd

Magnolia Blvd

San Fernando Valley

Moorpark St

Sherman Oaks

Studio City

Mulholland Dr

Lankershim Blvd

Vineland Ave

N Hollywood Way

N Buena Vista St

Golden State Freeway

San Fernando Rd

Verdugo Mountain Park

Burbank-Glendale-
Pasadena Airport

Strough
Park

Wildwood
Canyon
Park

De Bell Municipal
Golf Course

MAP 18

Brand
Park

see MAP 3

210

Canada Blvd

N Glenoaks Blvd

N Victory Blvd

W Olive Ave

BURBANK

W Alameda Ave

5

MAP 8

Ventura Freeway

134

North Hollywood

101

170

Los Angeles River

Forest Lawn
Memorial Park
Hollywood Hills

Griffith Park

S Central Ave

S Brand Ave

134

GLENDALE

To Pasadena

Forest Lawn
Memorial Park

Verdugo Rd

Universal City

MAP 9

Hollywood
Reservoir

Stone
Canyon
Reservoir

101

MAP 10

Los Feliz Blvd

5

San Fernando Rd

170

MAP 11

Coldwater Canyon Drive

Lower
Franklin
Reservoir

West Hollywood

W Sunset Blvd

N Fairfax Ave

2

Hollywood

Santa Monica Blvd

Melrose Ave

Beverly Blvd

MAP 5

2

Elysian
Park

To Pasadena

Pasadena Fwy

N Main St

Sunset Blvd

S Beverly Glen Blvd

N La Cienega Blvd

Hollywood Fwy

101

2

UCLA

Beverly Hills

2

W 3rd St

Wilshire Blvd

MAP 7

101

Westwood

San Diego Fwy

Westwood Blvd

S Robertson Blvd

San Vicente Blvd

W Olympic Blvd

W Pico Blvd

24

Venice Blvd

Crenshaw Blvd

Koreatown

110

LOS ANGELES

101

405

23

22

Santa Monica Fwy

MAP 12

Santa Monica Freeway

10

25

W Adams Blvd

West Adams

W Jefferson Blvd

MAP 6

USC

S Main St

Avalon Blvd

S Central Ave

S Alameda St

Santa Fe Ave

Pacific Blvd

Vernon

S Centinela Ave

S Sepulveda Blvd

Culver Blvd

Jefferson Blvd

Culver City

Ballona Creek

S La Brea Blvd

S La Cienega Blvd

Rodeo Blvd

Martin Luther King Jr Blvd

26

Leimert
Park

Leimert
Village

27

W Vernon Ave

Crenshaw Blvd

S Western Ave

S Vermont Ave

110

Exposition
Park

HUNTINGTON
PARK

Compton Ave

Venice Blvd

Washington Blvd

Marina del Rey

90

W Slauson Ave

W Jefferson Blvd

W Florence Ave

E Florence Ave

Walnut
Park

Lincoln Blvd

28

La Tijera Blvd

Airport Blvd

INGLEWOOD

W Manchester Ave

Harbor Freeway

42

Playa del Rey

29

30

405

42

38

W Century Blvd

E Century Blvd

E 103rd St

Watts

San Diego Freeway

S Inglewood Ave

S Hawthorne Blvd

31 32

33 34 35 36

37

39

E Century Blvd

ockweiler
ate Beach

Los Angeles
International
Airport (LAX)

40

El Segundo

1

To Long Beach
& San Diego

W Imperial Hwy

105

Century Freeway

see MAP 4

To I-5

105

MAP 3 EASTERN LOS ANGELES

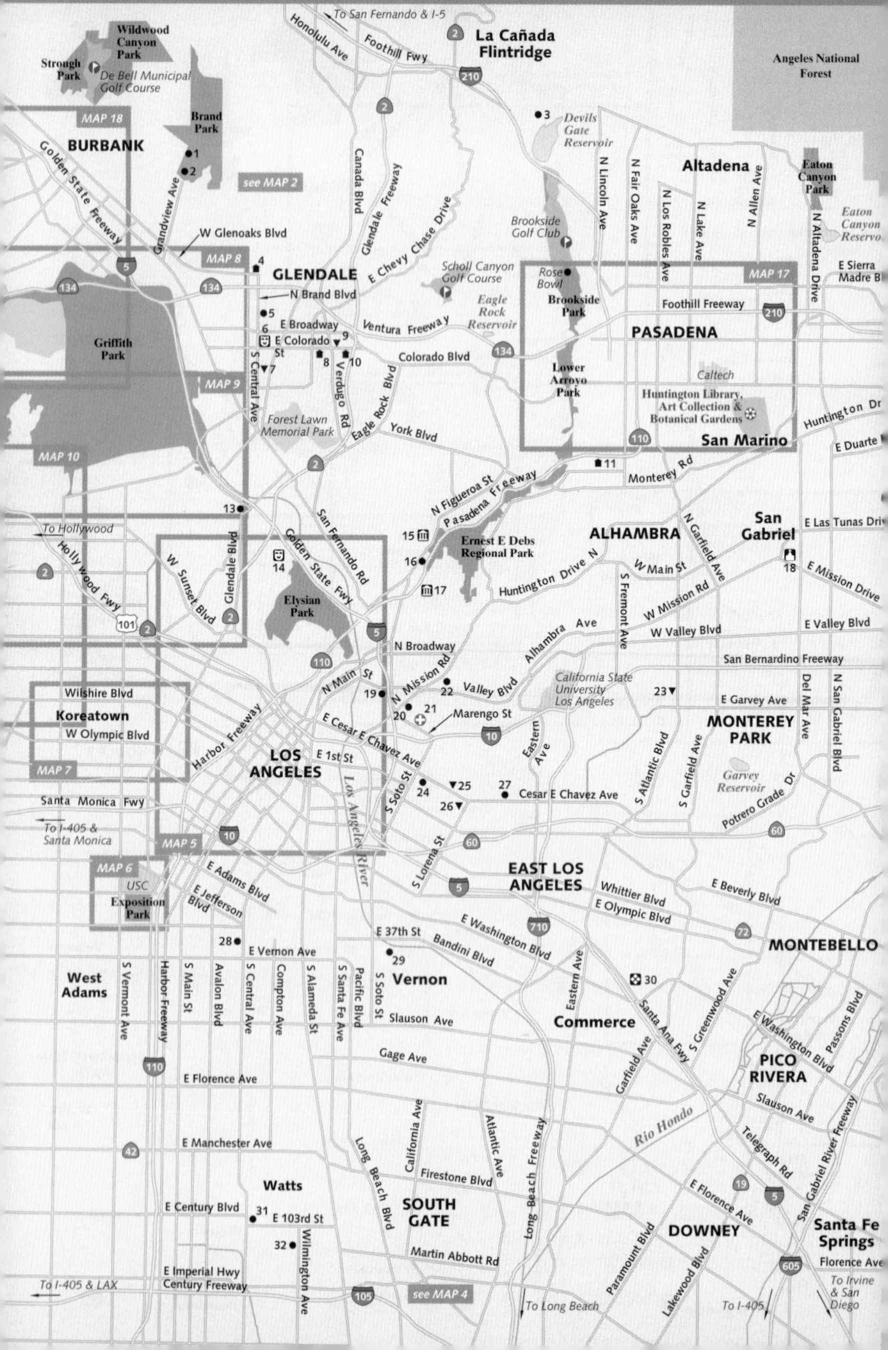

Wildwood Canyon Park

Strough Park

De Bell Municipal Golf Course

MAP 18

Brand Park

BURBANK

Grandview Ave

1
2

see MAP 2

W Glenoaks Blvd

MAP 8

Golden State Freeway

134

134

5

Griffith Park

MAP 10

S Central Ave

MAP 9

Forest Lawn Memorial Park

To Hollywood

Hollywood Fwy

2

W Sunset Blvd

Glendale Blvd

101

2

Koreatown

Wilshire Blvd

W Olympic Blvd

MAP 7

Santa Monica Fwy

To I-405 & Santa Monica

MAP 6

USC

Exposition Park

West Adams

S Vermont Ave

S Main St

Harbor Freeway

Avalon Blvd

S Central Ave

Compton Ave

110

42

Watts

E Century Blvd

31 E 103rd St

32

Wilmington Ave

E Imperial Hwy
Century Freeway

To I-405 & LAX

105

To San Fernando & I-5

Honolulu Ave

Foothill Fwy

La Cañada Flintridge

210

Canada Blvd

Glendale Freeway

2

E Chevy Chase Drive

GLENDALE

4

N Brand Blvd

5 E Broadway St

E Colorado St

7 8 9

Verdugo Rd

Eagle Rock Blvd

Ventura Freeway

Colorado Blvd

York Blvd

13

S San Fernando Rd

Golden State Fwy

14

Elysian Park

5

110

N Main St

N Mission Rd

19

20 21

Marengo St

N Broadway

Valley Blvd

22

Eastern Ave

10

LOS ANGELES

E 1st St

E Cesar E Chavez Ave

S Soto St

24 25

26

27

Cesar E Chavez Ave

S Lorena St

60

EAST LOS ANGELES

5

E Adams Blvd

E Jefferson Blvd

Harbor Freeway

Los Angeles River

MAP 5

10

28

E Vernon Ave

E 37th St

29

Vernon

Pacific Blvd

S Santa Fe Ave

S Soto St

Slauson Ave

S Alameda St

Gage Ave

California Ave

Atlantic Ave

Long Beach Blvd

Firestone Blvd

Long Beach Freeway

SOUTH GATE

Martin Abbott Rd

see MAP 4

To Long Beach

Angeles National Forest

3 Devils Gate Reservoir

Altadena

N Fair Oaks Ave

N Los Robles Ave

N Lake Ave

N Allen Ave

Eaton Canyon Park

Eaton Canyon Reservo

N Lincoln Ave

Brookside Golf Club

Scholl Canyon Golf Course

Rose Bowl

Brookside Park

Eagle Rock Reservoir

134

Lower Arroyo Park

MAP 17

E Sierra Madre B

Foothill Freeway

210

PASADENA

Caltech

Huntington Library, Art Collection & Botanical Gardens

110

San Marino

Huntington Dr

E Duarte

Monterey Rd

11

N Figueroa St

Pasadena Freeway

15

16

17

Ernest E Debs Regional Park

Huntington Drive N

ALHAMBRA

San Gabriel

E Las Tunas Dri

18

E Mission Drive

W Main St

W Mission Rd

E Valley Blvd

W Valley Blvd

N Garfield Ave

S Fremont Ave

Alhambra Ave

San Bernardino Freeway

California State University Los Angeles

23

E Garvey Ave

MONTEREY PARK

Del Mar Ave

N San Gabriel Blvd

Marengo St

S Atlantic Blvd

S Garfield Blvd

Garvey Reservoir

Potrero Grade Dr

60

E Washington Blvd

E Olympic Blvd

Whittier Blvd

710

E Beverly Blvd

72

MONTEBELLO

Bandini Blvd

Eastern Ave

Commerce

30

Santa Ana Fwy

Garfield Ave

S Greenwood Ave

E Washington Blvd

Passons Blvd

PICO RIVERA

Slauson Ave

Rio Hondo

Telegraph Rd

E Florence Ave

19

5

DOWNEY

Santa Fe Springs

Florence Ave

605

To Irvine & San Diego

To I-405

Paramount Blvd

Lakewood Blvd

San Gabriel River Freeway

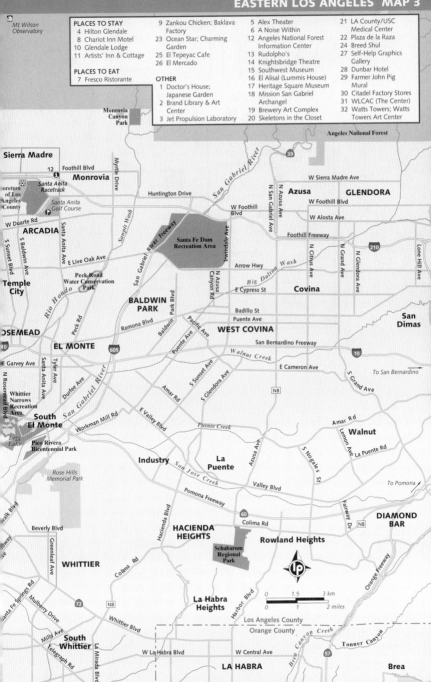

PLACES TO STAY
4 Hilton Glendale
8 Chariot Inn Motel
10 Glendale Lodge
11 Artists' Inn & Cottage

PLACES TO EAT
7 Fresco Ristorante

9 Zankou Chicken; Baklava Factory
23 Ocean Star; Charming Garden
25 El Tepeyac Cafe
26 El Mercado

OTHER
1 Doctor's House; Japanese Garden
2 Brand Library & Art Center
3 Jet Propulsion Laboratory

5 Alex Theater
6 A Noise Within
12 Angeles National Forest Information Center
13 Rudolpho's
14 Knightsbridge Theatre
15 Southwest Museum
16 El Alisal (Lummis House)
17 Heritage Square Museum
18 Mission San Gabriel Archangel
19 Brewery Art Complex
20 Skeletons in the Closet

21 LA County/USC Medical Center
22 Plaza de la Raza
24 Breed Shul
27 Self-Help Graphics Gallery
28 Dunbar Hotel
29 Farmer John Pig Mural
30 Citadel Factory Stores
31 WLCAC (The Center)
32 Watts Towers; Watts Towers Art Center

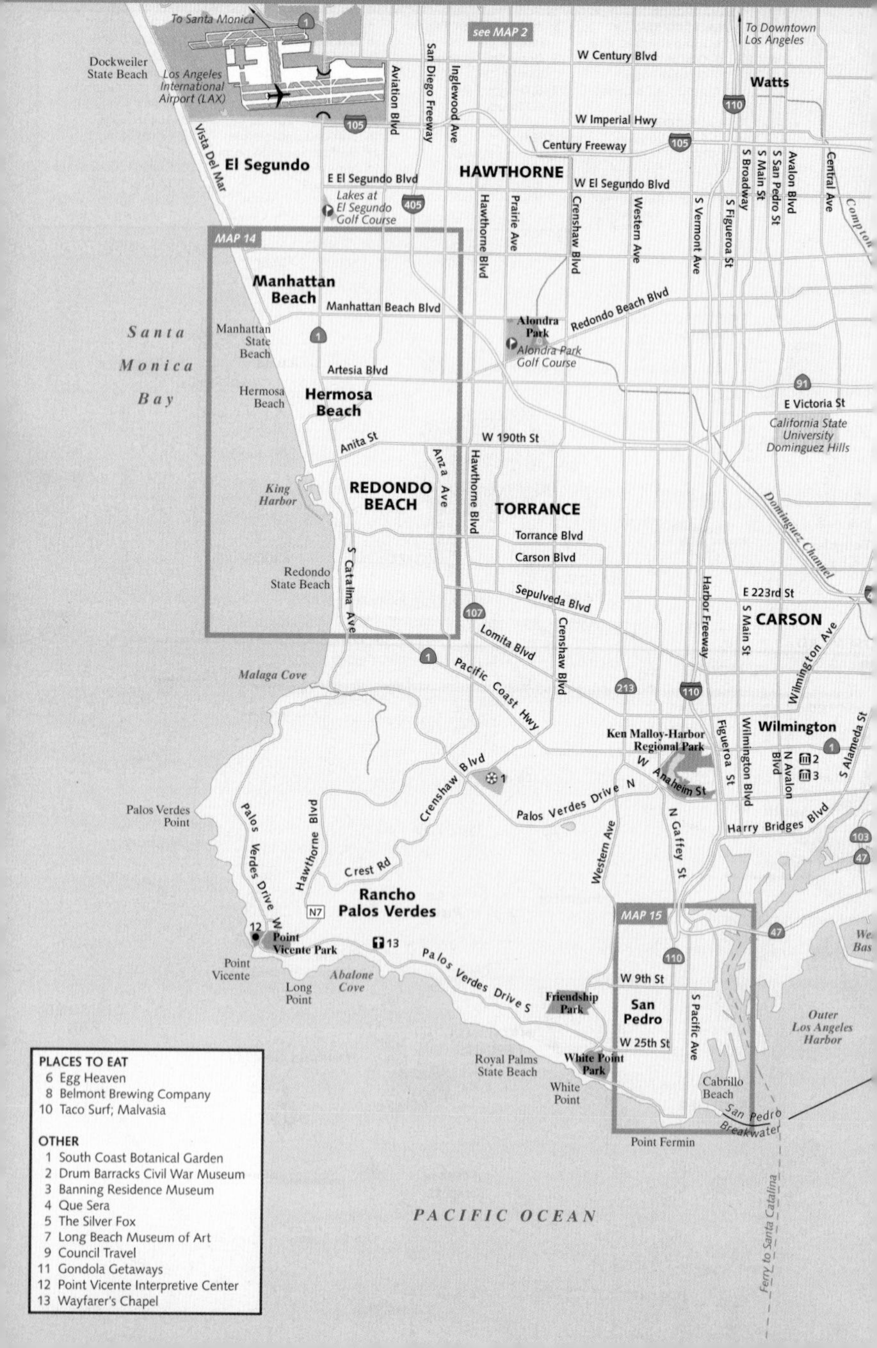

MAP 4 SOUTHERN LOS ANGELES

To Santa Monica

see MAP 2

To Downtown
Los Angeles

Dockweiler
State Beach

Los Angeles
International
Airport (LAX)

W Century Blvd

Watts

El Segundo

E El Segundo Blvd

HAWTHORNE

W Imperial Hwy

Century Freeway

W El Segundo Blvd

Lakes at
El Segundo
Golf Course

Vista Del Mar

Aviation Blvd

San Diego Freeway

Inglewood Ave

Aviation Blvd

Prairie Ave

Hawthorne Blvd

Crenshaw Blvd

Western Ave

S Vermont Ave

S Figueroa St

S San Pedro St

S Main St

S Broadway

Avalon Blvd

Central Ave

Compton

MAP 14

S a n t a
M o n i c a
B a y

**Manhattan
Beach**

Manhattan Beach Blvd

Manhattan
State
Beach

Hermosa
Beach

**Hermosa
Beach**

Artesia Blvd

Anita St

King
Harbor

**REDONDO
BEACH**

Redondo
State Beach

Malaga Cove

**Alondra
Park**

Alondra Park
Golf Course

Redondo Beach Blvd

E Victoria St

California State
University
Dominguez Hills

W 190th St

TORRANCE

Torrance Blvd

Carson Blvd

Sepulveda Blvd

Lomita Blvd

Pacific Coast Hwy

Hawthorne Blvd

Ana Ave

S Catalina Ave

Crenshaw Blvd

Dominguez Channel

E 223rd St

S Main St

CARSON

Harbor Freeway

Wilmington Ave

Ken Malloy-Harbor
Regional Park

Wilmington

Figueroa St

Wilmington Blvd

N Avalon Blvd

S Alameda St

W Anaheim St

Harry Bridges Blvd

Palos Verdes
Point

**Rancho
Palos Verdes**

Palos Verdes Drive W

Hawthorne Blvd

Crest Rd

Crenshaw Blvd

Western Ave

Palos Verdes Drive N

N Gaffey St

Point
Vicente

Point
Vicente Park

12

13

Long
Point

Abalone
Cove

Palos Verdes Drive S

MAP 15

W 9th St

**San
Pedro**

W 25th St

S Pacific Ave

Friendship
Park

Outer
Los Angeles
Harbor

We
Bas

Royal Palms
State Beach

White Point
Park

White
Point

Cabrillo
Beach

San Pedro Breakwater

Point Fermin

Ferry to Santa Catalina

PACIFIC OCEAN

PLACES TO EAT
6 Egg Heaven
8 Belmont Brewing Company
10 Taco Surf; Malvasia

OTHER
1 South Coast Botanical Garden
2 Drum Barracks Civil War Museum
3 Banning Residence Museum
4 Que Sera
5 The Silver Fox
7 Long Beach Museum of Art
9 Council Travel
11 Gondola Getaways
12 Point Vicente Interpretive Center
13 Wayfarer's Chapel

see MAP 3

SOUTH GATE

Rio Hondo

Martin Abbott Rd

Mulberry Drive

72

DOWNEY

19

605

Telegraph Rd

Mills Ave

La Mirada Blvd

Paramount Blvd

Lakewood Blvd

Firestone Blvd

Florence Ave

Leffingwell Rd

E Imperial Hwy

Atlantic Ave

710

Century Freeway

105

Carmenita Rd

Valley View Ave

Santa Ana Freeway

COMPTON

Rosecrans Ave

Los Angeles County

Orange County

E Compton Blvd

19

Alondra Blvd

Studebaker Rd

Pioneer Blvd

Norwalk Blvd

Artesia Blvd

5

S Alameda St

Long Beach Blvd

Artesia Freeway

San Gabriel River

91

Bloomfield Ave

Coyote Creek

Orangethorpe Ave

Atlantic Ave

Cherry Ave

Paramount Blvd

Lakewood Blvd

Bellflower Blvd

South St

La Palma Ave

39

Long Beach Freeway

LAKEWOOD

San Gabriel River Freeway

Del Amo Blvd

Knotts' Berry Farm

Los Angeles River

Carson St

W Lincoln Ave

Heartwell Park

Long Beach Municipal Airport

Skylinks Golf Course

Los Coyotes Diagonal

El Dorado Park

Wardlow Rd

W Ball Rd

San Diego Freeway

Cerritos Ave

39

Santa Fe Ave

E Willow St

El Dorado Park Golf Course

Katella Ave

LONG BEACH

710

19

E Pacific Coast Hwy

Atherton St

Los Alamitos Blvd

605

Garden Grove Fwy

22

MAP 16

E Anaheim St

Recreation Park Golf Course

California State University Long Beach

E 7th St

4

Redondo Ave

Ximeno Ave

Recreation Park

22

Cherry Ave

5

Garden Grove Fwy

San Diego Freeway

405

6

1

E Ocean Blvd

7

Naples

9

8

10

Long Beach Marina

Seal Beach Blvd

Westminster Ave

United States Naval Weapons Station

Bolsa Ave

Springdale St

Golden West St

405

Terminal Island Fwy

East Basin

11

Outer Long Beach Harbor

Seal Beach

Anaheim Bay

Seal Beach National Wildlife Refuge

Bolsa Chica Rd

Warner Ave

39

Middle Breakwater

Long Beach Breakwater

Sunset County Beach

San Pedro Bay

Ferry to Santa Catalina

Bolsa Chica State Beach

1

Pacific Coast Hwy

0   1.5   3 km
0   1   2 miles

Huntington City Beach

To Laguna Beach

To Irvine & San Diego

MAP 5 DOWNTOWN LOS ANGELES

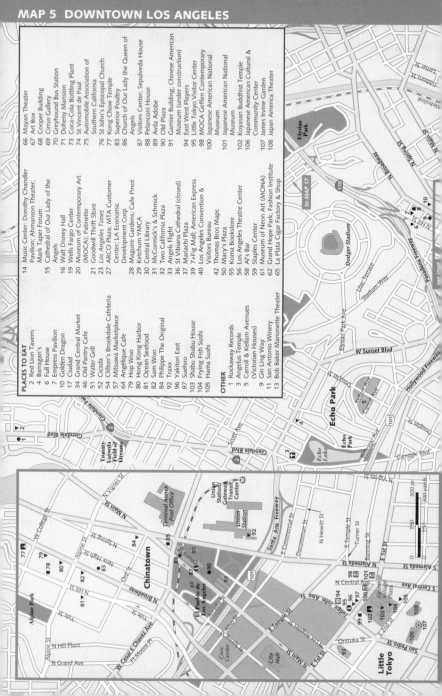

PLACES TO EAT

2 Red Lion Tavern
4 Barragan's
6 Full House
7 Empress Pavilion
10 Golden Dragon
17 Ciudad
34 Grand Central Market
46 Old Pantry Cafe
51 Water Grill
52 Cicada
54 Clifton's Brookdale Cafeteria
57 Mitsuwa Marketplace
64 Angelique Cafe
79 Hop Woo
80 Hong Kong Harbor
81 Ocean Seafood
82 Sam Woo
84 Philippe The Original
92 Traxx
96 Yakitori East
97 Suehiro
103 Shabu Shabu House
104 Frying Fish Sushi
105 Hama Sushi

OTHER

1 Rockaway Records
3 Angelus Temple
5 Carroll & Kellam Avenues
   (Victorian Houses)
9 Gin Ling Way
11 San Antonio Winery
13 Bob Baker Marionette Theater

14 Music Center: Dorothy Chandler
   Pavilion; Ahmanson Theater;
   Mark Taper Forum
15 Cathedral of Our Lady of the
   Angels
16 Walt Disney Hall
19 Wells Fargo Center
20 Museum of Contemporary Art
   (MOCA); Patinette
21 Goodwill Thrift Store
23 Los Angeles Times
27 ARCO Plaza; MTA Customer
   Center; LA Economic
   Development Corp
28 Maguire Gardens; Cafe Pinot
29 Ketchum YMCA
30 Central Library
31 McCormick's & Schmick
32 Two California Plaza
33 Angels Flight
37 Mariachi Plaza
39 7-Fig Mall; American Express
40 Los Angeles Convention &
   Visitors Bureau
42 Thomas Bros Maps
50 Macy's Plaza
55 Koma Bookstore
56 Los Angeles Theatre Center
58 Al's Bar
59 Staples Center
61 Museum of Neon Art (MONA)
62 Grand Hope Park; Fashion Institute
65 La Plata Cigar Factory & Shop

66 Mayan Theater
67 Art Box
68 Cooper Building
69 Cirrus Gallery
70 Greyhound Bus Station
71 Doheny Mansion
73 Coca-Cola Bottling Plant
74 St Vincent de Paul
75 Automobile Association of
   Southern California
76 St John's Episcopal Church
77 Kong Chow Temple
83 Superior Poultry
86 Church of Our Lady the Queen of
   Angels
87 Visitors Center; Sepulveda House
88 Pelanconi House
89 Avila Adobe
90 Old Plaza
91 Garnier Building; Chinese American
   Museum (under construction)
94 East West Players
95 Little Tokyo Visitor Center
98 MOCA Geffen Contemporary
100 Japanese American National
    Museum
101 Japanese American National
    Museum
102 Koyasan Buddhist Temple
106 Japanese American Cultural &
    Community Center
107 James Irvine Garden
108 Japan America Theater

PLACES TO STAY

8 Royal Pagoda Motel
12 Wilshire Royale Howard Johnson Plaza
18 Westin Bonaventure Hotel; Top of Five
22 Kawada Hotel
24 Best Western Mayfair Hotel
25 City Center Motel
26 Motel de Ville
38 Holiday Inn Downtown
41 Wyndham Checkers Hotel
43 The Biltmore; Grand Avenue Bar; Gallery Bar
44 Hotel Figueroa
45 In Town Hotel
47 Orchid Hotel
48 Milner Hotel
49 Hyatt Regency
53 Los Angeles Athletic Club Hotel
60 Holiday Inn City Center
63 Stillwell Hotel; Gill's Cuisine of India; Hank's Bar
72 Inn at 657
78 Best Western Dragon Gate Inn
85 Metro Plaza Hotel
93 New Otani Hotel
99 Miyako Inn

MAP 6 EXPOSITION PARK AREA

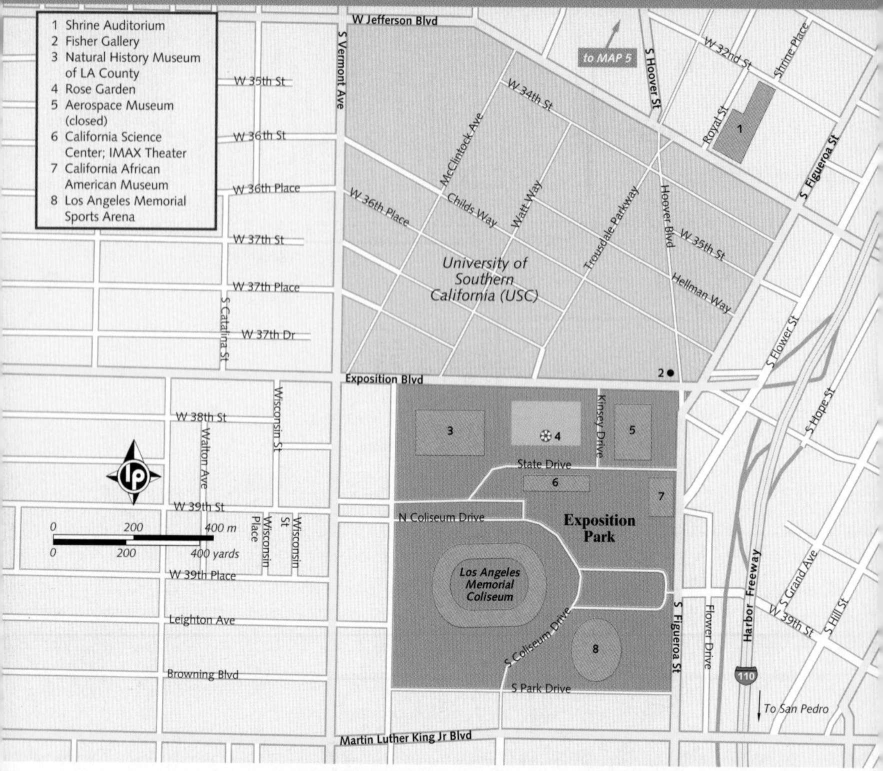

1 Shrine Auditorium
2 Fisher Gallery
3 Natural History Museum of LA County
4 Rose Garden
5 Aerospace Museum (closed)
6 California Science Center; IMAX Theater
7 California African American Museum
8 Los Angeles Memorial Sports Arena

W Jefferson Blvd
W 35th St
W 36th St
W 36th Place
W 37th St
W 37th Place
W 37th Dr
W 38th St
W 39th St
W 39th Place
Leighton Ave
Browning Blvd
Martin Luther King Jr Blvd

S Vermont Ave
S Catalina St
Walton Ave
Wisconsin St
Wisconsin Place
Wisconsin St

to MAP 5
W 32nd St
Shrine Place
S Hoover St
Royal St
S Figueroa St

W 34th St
McClintock Ave
Childs Way
Watt Way
W 36th Place
Trousdale Parkway
Hoover Blvd
W 35th St
Hellman Way

University of Southern California (USC)

Exposition Blvd
2 ●

3
4 ⚽
5
Kinsey Drive
State Drive
6
7
N Coliseum Drive
Exposition Park
S Flower St
S Hope St
S Grand Ave
S Hill St
W 39th St
Los Angeles Memorial Coliseum
S Coliseum Drive
S Figueroa St
Flower Drive
Harbor Freeway
8
S Park Drive
110
To San Pedro

0   200   400 m
0   200   400 yards

MAP 7 KOREATOWN

W 6th St
Wilshire/ Western
Wilshire Blvd
Wilshire/ Normandie
Wilshire/ Vermont
M
Lafayette Park
W 6th St
Metro Red Line
Wilshire Blvd
MacArthur Park

S Wilton Pl
S Western Ave
S Oxford Ave
S Serrano Ave
S Hobart Blvd
Kingsley Drive
S Ardmore Ave
Irolo St
S New Hampshire Ave
S Mariposa Ave
S Berendo St
S Vermont Ave
S Westmoreland Ave
Hoover St

W 7th St
1
5
M
6
3
4
8th St
W 8th St
9
James M Woods St
Koreatown Plaza
San Marino St
10
Ardmore Park
Catalina St
S Kenmore Ave
S Catalina Ave
S Normandie Ave
MacArthur Lake
Westlake/ MacArthur Park
S Park View St
S Alvarado St
James M Woods St
see MAP 5

W Olympic Blvd
S Normandie Ave
S Mariposa Ave
Fedora St
W Olympic Blvd
12

W 11th St
W 12th St
13
Country Club Dr
S Gramercy Pl
Manhattan Pl
W Pico Blvd
14
W 15th St
15
Normandie Park
Venice Blvd

0   300   600 m
0   300   600 yards
LP

PLACES TO STAY
5 Chancellor Hotel
7 Oxford Palace Hotel

PLACES TO EAT
8 Guelaguetza
9 Soot Bull Jeep
10 Liborio Market
11 Koreatown Plaza International Food Court

12 Buffet Land
13 El Cholo
14 Papa Cristo's Taverna; C&K Importing

OTHER
1 HMS Bounty
2 Wiltern Theater; Atlas Supper Club

3 Ambassador Hotel
4 The Prince
6 Former Bullocks Wilshire Department Store; Southwestern University School of Law
15 St Sophia Cathedral

MAP 8 GRIFFITH PARK

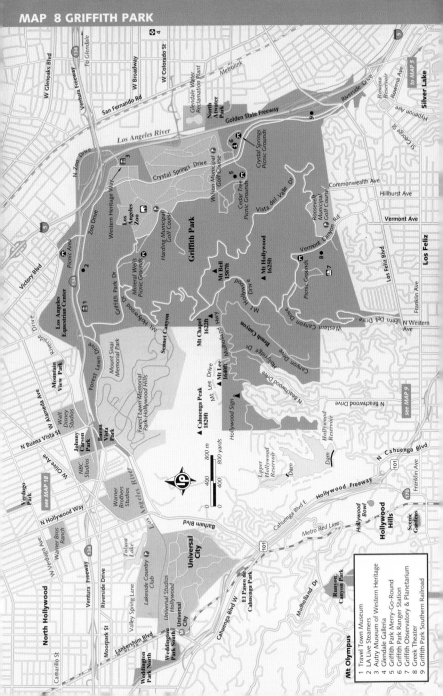

W Glenoaks Blvd
Ventura Freeway
To Glendale
W Broadway
W Colorado St
134

Glendale Water
Reclamation Plant
Metrolink

San Fernando Rd

North
Atwater
Park
Golden State Freeway

to MAP 5

Los Angeles River

Rowena
Reservoir
Rowena Ave

Silver Lake

Hyperion Ave

Riverside Drive

9

St George St

N Zoo Drive

Crystal Springs Drive

Crystal Springs
Picnic Grounds

K

Commonwealth Ave

Hillhurst Ave

Zoo Drive

Western Heritage Way

Wilson Municipal
Golf Course

5

Cedar Tree
Picnic Grounds

Vista del Valle Dr

Roosevelt
Municipal
Golf Course

Vermont Ave

M

Los
Angeles
Zoo

Griffith Park

Vermont Canyon Rd

Los Feliz

Picnic Area

Harding Municipal
Golf Course

Mt Bell
1587ft

Vermont Ave

8

7

Los Angeles
Equestrian Center

2

Griffith Park Dr

Mineral Wells
Picnic Grounds

K

Mt Hollywood
1625ft

Picnic
Grounds

Los Feliz Blvd

Victory Blvd

5

134

Mt Hollywood Hwy

Franklin Ave

1

Forest Lawn Drive

Mt Hollywood Dr

Sennet Canyon

Mt Chapel
1622ft

Brush Canyon

Western Canyon Drive

N Western Ave

Fern Dell Drive

Mount Sinai
Memorial Park

Mulholland Hwy

Mt Lee
1640ft

Hollyridge Dr

Canyon Drive

N Beachwood Drive

see MAP 9

N Beachwood Drive

Mountain
View Park

W Alameda Ave

Walt Disney
Studios

Forest Lawn Memorial
Park-Hollywood Hills

Cahuenga Peak
1820ft

Mt Lee Drive

Hollywood
Sign

Hollywood
Reservoir

N Buena Vista St

Buena
Vista
Park

Johnny
Carson
Park

N Olive Ave

NBC
Studios

Warner
Brothers
Studios

800 m

800 yards

400

400

Dam

Upper
Hollywood
Reservoir

Dam

N Cahuenga Blvd

Franklin Ave

see MAP 18

Verdugo
Park

N Hollywood Way

N Verdugo Ave

Ventura Freeway

Warner Bros
Ranch

Riverside Drive

134

Los Angeles River

Toluca Lake

Universal City

Barham Blvd

101

Cahuenga Blvd E

Hollywood Freeway

Metro Red Line

Hollywood
Bowl

Hollywood
Hills

170

Scenic
Gardens

101

North Hollywood

Camarillo St

Moorpark St

Valley Spring Lane

Lakeside Country
Club

Universal Studios
Hollywood

Universal City

El Paseo de
Cahuenga Park

Cahuenga Blvd W

Mulholland Dr

Runyon
Canyon
Park

Lankershim Blvd

Weddington
Park North

Weddington
Park South

Mt Olympus

1 Travel Town Museum
2 LA Live Steamers
3 Autry Museum of Western Heritage
4 Glendale Galleria
5 Griffith Park Merry-Go-Round
6 Griffith Park Ranger Station
7 Griffith Observatory & Planetarium
8 Greek Theater
9 Griffith Park Southern Railroad

MAP 9 HOLLYWOOD, LOS FELIZ & SILVER LAKE

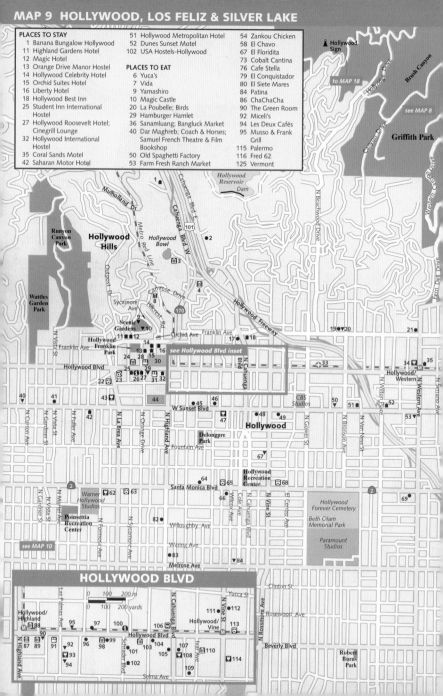

PLACES TO STAY
1 Banana Bungalow Hollywood
11 Highland Gardens Hotel
12 Magic Hotel
13 Orange Drive Manor Hostel
14 Hollywood Celebrity Hotel
15 Orchid Suites Hotel
16 Liberty Hotel
18 Hollywood Best Inn
25 Student Inn International Hostel
27 Hollywood Roosevelt Hotel; Cinegrill Lounge
32 Hollywood International Hostel
35 Coral Sands Motel
42 Saharan Motor Hotel

51 Hollywood Metropolitan Hotel
52 Dunes Sunset Motel
102 USA Hostels-Hollywood

PLACES TO EAT
6 Yuca's
7 Vida
9 Yamashiro
10 Magic Castle
20 La Poubelle; Birds
29 Hamburger Hamlet
36 Sanamluang; Bangluck Market
40 Dar Maghreb; Coach & Horses; Samuel French Theatre & Film Bookshop
50 Old Spaghetti Factory
53 Farm Fresh Ranch Market

54 Zankou Chicken
58 El Chavo
67 El Floridita
73 Cobalt Cantina
76 Cafe Stella
79 El Conquistador
80 El Siete Mares
84 Patina
86 ChaChaCha
90 The Green Room
92 Miceli's
94 Les Deux Cafés
95 Musso & Frank Grill
115 Palermo
116 Fred 62
125 Vermont

HOLLYWOOD BLVD

ENTERTAINMENT
2 John Anson Ford Theatre
5 The Derby
17 Goldfinger's
19 Bourgeois Pig
22 Open Fist Theatre
28 Mann's Chinese Theater
31 El Capitan Theater
34 The Study
43 Lava Lounge
47 Cat & Fiddle Pub
49 Baked Potato-Hollywood
56 Good Luck Bar
57 Vista Theater
59 Tiki Ti
61 Cuffs
62 Formosa Cafe
63 Gardenia Restaurant & Lounge
64 Arena/Circus
65 Hudson Theatres
66 Dragonfly
68 Actors' Gang Theatre
69 Tempo
70 The Garage

72 Akbar
74 El Cid
75 Gauntlet II
85 Highland Grounds
91 Faultline
91 Egyptian Theatre; American Cinematheque
93 Blue
101 Vynil
107 Catalina Bar & Grill
108 Beauty Bar
109 Opium Den
111 The Palace
113 Pantages Theater; Frolic Room
114 Daddy's
117 Los Feliz Theatre
121 Dresden Room

OTHER
3 Hollywood Bowl Museum
4 Hollywood Studio Museum
8 Freeman House
21 Immaculate Heart High School
23 Cyber Java
24 Hollywood Entertainment

Museum; Tower Records Clearance Center; Knitting Factory
26 Hollywood Chamber of Commerce
30 Hollywood & Highland Entertainment Complex
33 Los Angeles Free Clinic
37 Hollyhock House
38 Wacko; La Luz de Jesus Gallery
40 Guitar Center; Rock Walk of Fame
44 Hollywood High School
45 Crossroads of the World
46 Hollywood Athletic Club
48 Cinerama Dome
55 Hollywood Presbyterian Hospital
60 KCET Studios
71 Out of the Closet
77 Pull My Daisy
78 i2i World Café
81 Spaceland
82 A&I

87 Ripley's Believe It or Not!
88 Hollywood Wax Museum
89 Guinness World of Records Museum
96 Larry Edmunds Bookshop
97 Book City
98 Frederick's of Hollywood Lingerie Museum
99 Hollywood Toys & Costumes
100 Janes House; Visitors Center
103 LA Contemporary Exhibitions (LACE)
104 Playmates
105 Panpipes Magickal Marketplace
106 Greyhound Bus Station
110 Museum of Death
112 Capitol Records Tower
118 Skylight Bookshop
119 Squaresville
120 Funny Farm
122 Vinyl Fetish
123 Aero & Co
124 Mondo Vidéo a Go-Go

MAP 10 WEST HOLLYWOOD & MID-CITY

PLACES TO STAY
1 Château Marmont
6 Hyatt West Hollywood
7 The Grafton on Sunset
8 Mondrian; Sky Bar
10 Best Western Sunset Plaza Hotel
11 The Argyle
12 The Standard
13 Grove Guest House
24 Sunset Marquis Hotel & Villas
25 Holloway Motel
39 Le Montrose Suite Hotel
41 Ramada West Hollywood
48 San Vicente Inn/Resort
72 Orbit Hostel
98 Beverly Laurel Hotel; Swingers
105 Bevonshire Lodge Motel
118 Beverly Plaza Hotel; Cava
121 Farmer's Daughter Motel
123 Park Plaza Lodge
145 Dunes Wilshire Motor Hotel

PLACES TO EAT
9 House of Blues
27 Hugo's
28 Basix
29 Gelson's
33 French Quarter Market
35 Whole Foods
40 Wild Oats Food Market
44 L' Orangerie
54 Dan Tana's; Doug Weston's Troubadour
56 Yujean Kang
59 Cobalt Cantina
60 The Abbey
76 Bouchon
78 Citrus
81 Newsroom
84 Le Colonial
85 Chaya Brasserie
86 Jerry's Famous Deli
87 Tail O' The Pup
88 Hard Rock Cafe
90 Real Food Daily
94 Menjin
95 Kings Road Cafe
96 Indochine
97 Pastis
100 Canter's Deli; Kibitz Room
103 Damiano Mr Pizza
104 Erewhon Natural Foods Market
108 El Coyote
111 Santé La Brea; East India Grill
112 Barefoot Cafe
113 Orso
114 Locanda Veneta
119 Doughboys
120 Sofi
122 Gumbo Pot; KoKoMo
131 Sonora Cafe
134 Ca' Brea
135 Natalee Thai
144 Campanile
146 Nyala
148 Caffé Luna
153 Tommy Tang's
156 Lala's
157 Frankie's
161 Pink's Hot Dogs

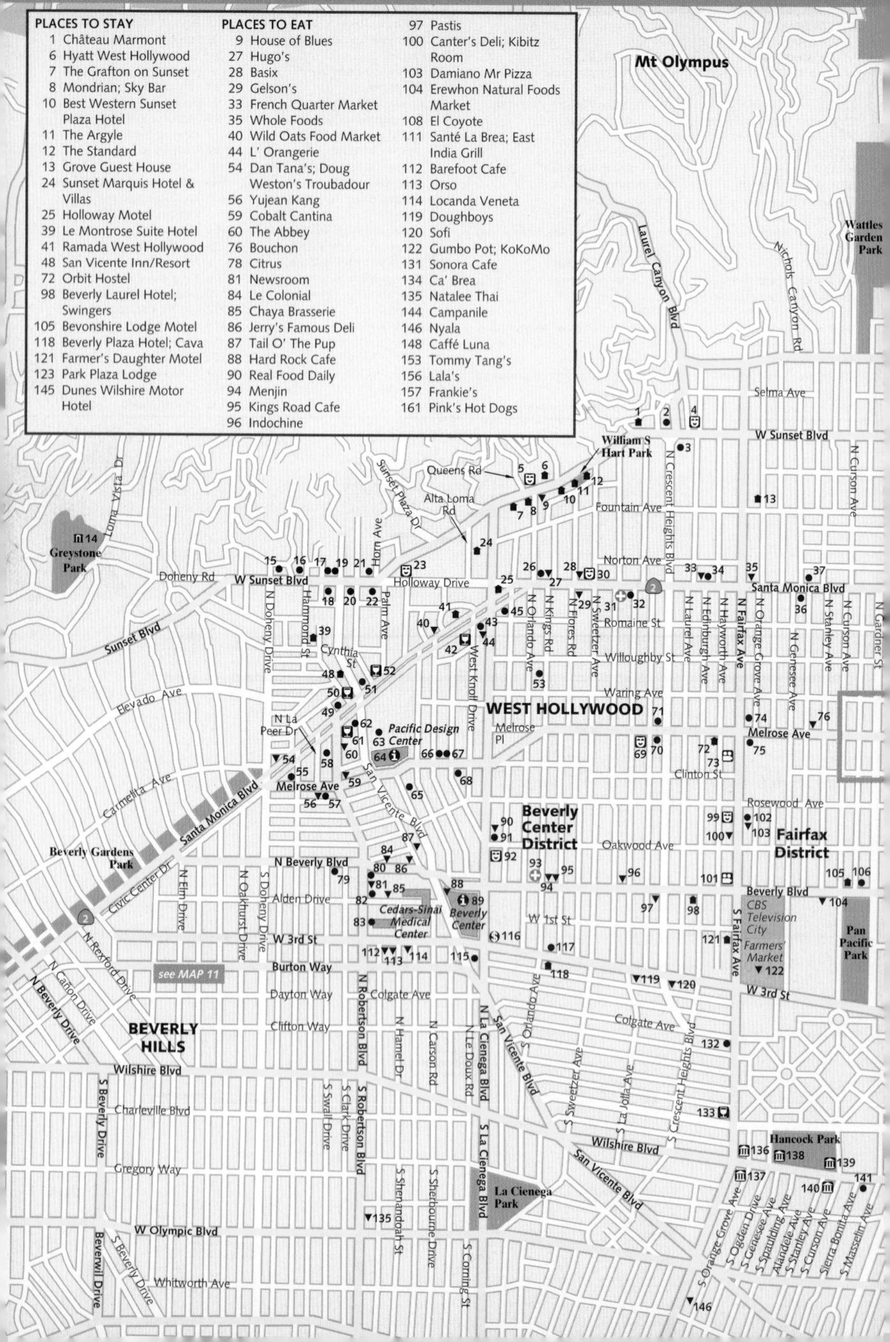

Mt Olympus
Wattles Garden Park
Laurel Canyon Blvd
Nichols Canyon Rd
Selma Ave
W Sunset Blvd
William S Hart Park
N Crescent Heights Blvd
N Curson Ave
Queens Rd
Alta Loma Rd
Fountain Ave
Sunset Plaza Dr
Greystone Park
Loma Vista Dr
Horn Ave
Doheny Rd
Holloway Drive
Norton Ave
Santa Monica Blvd
Romaine St
Willoughby St
Waring Ave
Sunset Blvd
N Doheny Drive
Hammond St
Palm Ave
Cynthia St
West Knoll Drive
N Orlando Ave
N Kings Rd
N Flores Rd
N Sweetzer Ave
N Laurel Ave
N Edinburgh Ave
N Hayworth Ave
N Fairfax Ave
N Orange Grove Ave
N Genesee Ave
N Stanley Ave
N Gardner St
Elevado Ave
WEST HOLLYWOOD
N La Peer Dr
Pacific Design Center
Melrose Pl
Melrose Ave
Clinton St
Carmelita Ave
Santa Monica Blvd
San Vicente Blvd
Rosewood Ave
Beverly Center District
Fairfax District
Oakwood Ave
Beverly Gardens Park
N Beverly Blvd
Civic Center Dr
N Elm Drive
N Oakhurst Drive
S Doheny Drive
Alden Drive
Cedars-Sinai Medical Center
Beverly Center
Beverly Blvd
CBS Television City
Farmers' Market
Pan Pacific Park
W 1st St
W 3rd St
S Fairfax Ave
Burton Way
see MAP 11
N Rexford Drive
N Cañon Drive
N Beverly Drive
Dayton Way
Colgate Ave
Clifton Way
N Robertson Blvd
N Hamel Dr
N Carson Rd
N Le Doux Rd
N La Cienega Blvd
S Orlando Ave
BEVERLY HILLS
Wilshire Blvd
S Sweetzer Ave
S La Jolla Ave
S Crescent Heights Blvd
S Beverly Drive
Charleville Blvd
S Swall Drive
S Clark Drive
S Robertson Blvd
S La Cienega Blvd
Hancock Park
Gregory Way
S Shenandoah St
S Sherbourne Drive
La Cienega Park
W Olympic Blvd
Beverwil Drive
Whitworth Ave
S Corning St
S Orange Grove Ave
S Ogden Drive
S Genesee Ave
S Spaulding Ave
Alandele Ave
S Stanley Ave
S Curson Ave
Sierra Bonita Ave
S Masselin Ave

ENTERTAINMENT
2 Coconut Teaszer
4 Laugh Factory
6 Comedy Store
15 Key Club
16 Roxy
17 Cat Club
19 Whisky A Go Go
20 Viper Room
23 Tiffany Theater
29 City Bean
30 Coast Playhouse
34 Club 7969
38 Celebration Theater
42 The Palms
43 Benvenuto
50 Rage; Thomas Cook
51 WeHo Lounge; A
   Different Light
   Bookstore; Micky's;
   Revolver
52 Trunks
58 The Factory/Ultra Suede
61 Mother Lode

67 Urth Caffe
69 The Improv
73 Silent Movie Theatre
74 Genghis Cohen
77 West Coast Ensemble
92 Coronet Theatre; Coronet
   Pub
99 Bang Improv Studio
101 Cineplex Odeon Fairfax
   Cinema
102 Largo
109 Insomnia Cafe
124 Acme Comedy Theater
133 Molly Malone's
142 Conga Room
154 Groundlings Theater
155 The Gig

SHOPPING
18 Hustler Hollywood
21 Tower Records
22 Book Soup
32 Out of the Closet
37 Pleasure Chest

45 Dreamdresser
46 Jet Rag
47 Moletown
55 Herbert Palmer Gallery
57 Tasende Gallery
62 Unicorn Bookstore
65 Daniel Saxon Gallery
66 Bodhi Tree
68 Heritage Bookshop
70 Fred Segal
71 Jon Valdí
75 Melrose Trading Post @
   Fairfax High School
79 Antiquarius
80 Curve
82 Storyopolis
83 Lisa Kline
91 Trashy Lingerie
106 Every Picture Tells a Story
107 Tobey C Moss Gallery
110 Jack Rutberg Gallery
115 Loehmann's
117 Traveler's Bookcase;
   Cooks Library
125 Buffalo Exchange
126 Fahey/Klein Gallery
127 Paul Kopeikin Gallery
128 Iturralde Gallery
129 Golyester
130 Jan Baum Gallery
147 Penny Lane
149 Maya Jewelry
150 Wasteland
151 Red Balls on Fire
152 Off the Wall
158 Necromance
162 Sacks SFO

OTHER
3 Crunch Gym
14 Greystone Mansion
31 Progressive Health Services
36 Porno Walk of Fame
49 Margo Leavin Gallery
53 Schindler House
63 MOCA Gallery at PDC
64 West Hollywood
   Convention & Visitors
   Bureau
89 California Information
   Center
93 Los Angeles Free Clinic
116 American Express
132 Samy's Camera
136 LACMA West
137 Petersen Automotive
   Museum
138 LA County Museum of
   Art; Bing Theater
139 La Brea Tar Pits; Page
   Museum at La Brea
   Discoveries
140 Craft & Folk Art Museum
141 Goethe Institute
143 MTA Customer Center
159 @Coffee
160 STA Travel

Hollywood Hills
Runyon Canyon Park
Metro Red Line
Hollywood Bowl
Outpost Drive
Scenic Gardens
Hollywood Franklin Park
Hollywood/Highland
Hollywood Blvd
Hawthorn Ave
see MAP 9

N Fuller Ave
N La Brea Ave
N Highland Ave
N Vista St

W Sunset Blvd
CBS Studios
101

Hollywood

Delongpre Park
Fountain Ave

Hollywood Recreation Center

Warner Hollywood Studios
N La Brea Ave
N Sycamore Ave
N Orange Drive
N Mansfield Ave
N Highland Ave
N Vine St

Santa Monica Blvd
Poinsettia Recreation Center
Willoughby Ave
Beth Olam Memorial Park
Hollywood Forever Cemetery
N Wilton Place

Waring Ave
Paramount Studios

see Melrose Ave inset

MELROSE AVE

Melrose/La Brea

Waring Ave
150   300 m
0   150   300 yards

N Sierra Bonita Ave
N Gardner St
N Vista Ave
N Martel Ave
N Fuller Ave
N Poinsettia Pl
N Alta Vista Blvd
N Formosa Ave
N Detroit St
N La Brea Ave

Melrose Ave

The Wilshire Country Club

W 1st St

S Fuller Ave
S Formosa Ave
S Alta Vista Blvd
S Detroit St
S La Brea Ave

W 2nd St

W 3rd St

W 4th St
MID-CITY
W 6th St

Miracle Mile District
S Cloverdale Ave
S Detroit St
S Sycamore Ave

W 8th St
W 9th St

Hancock Park
S Lucerne Blvd
S Plymouth Blvd

Wilshire Blvd
W Olympic Blvd
Los Angeles High Memorial Park

S Crenshaw Blvd
S Mullen Ave

S Wilton Place
S Western Ave

Wilshire/Western
Wilshire/Normandie
Metro Red Line

see MAP 7

Koreatown

MAP 11 BEVERLY HILLS & WESTWOOD

DOWNTOWN BEVERLY HILLS

Beverly
Hills City
Hall

W 3rd St

Burton Way

66

Beverly
Gardens
Park

67

68

69

70

71

74

75

73

72

76

77

79

80

81

82

78

Two
Rodeo

91

83

92

93

87

90

85

88

84

86

89

94

Santa Monica Blvd

S Santa Monica Blvd

Wilshire Blvd

S Spalding Drive

S Linden Drive

S McCarty Drive

S Roxbury Drive

Bedford Drive

Peck Drive

N Camden Drive

Rodeo Drive

N El Camino Drive

S Beverly Drive

N Reeves Drive

N Canon Drive

N Crescent Drive

Canon Drive

Park Way

N Beverly Drive

N Rodeo Drive

N Bedford Drive

Brighton Way

Dayton Way

Clifton Way

N Bedford Drive

Foothill Rd

Crescent Drive

Philbert Dr

1

2

Bella Dr

Cielo Dr

3

Green
Acres Dr

8

Benedict Canyon Drive

Carolwood Drive

12

15

13

14

Monovale
Drive

Charing
Cross Rd

19

4

7

6

N Beverly Glen Blvd

Saint Pierre Rd

Bel Air

Bella Dro Rd

Bel Air Rd

N Siena Canyon Dr

Clifton Rd

Cabot Rd

**Holmby
Hills**

Bel Air
Country Club

To Getty Center,
Brentwood &
San Fernando Valley

W Sunset Blvd

Reservoir

De Neve Drive

17

18

Circle Drive

Holmby
Park

20

Club View Drive

Mapleton Dr

Comstock Ave

Los Angeles
Country Clu

29

30

31

University of
California at
Los Angeles
(UCLA)

Circle Drive S

32

Warner Ave

Westholme Ave

Hilgard Ave

Malcolm Ave

S Beverly Glen Blvd

Cayley Ave

Circle Drive W

Westwood Plaza

405

Los
Angeles
National
Cemetery

San Diego Freeway

West Los Angeles
Veterans
Administration
Center

45

44

Le Conte Ave

37

41

39

40

51

49

50

43

42

46

47

48

Westwood

Thayer Ave

Weyburn Ave

38

Broxton Ave

52

53

Lindbrook Drive

Kinross Ave

54

56

57

58

55

Wilshire Blvd

Gayley Ave

Glendon Ave

Midvale Ave

Westwood
Memorial
Park

Selby Ave

Wellworth Ave

59

2

Santa Monica Blvd

Little Santa Monica Blvd

Westwood
Park

S Sepulveda Blvd

Veteran Ave

Westwood Blvd

To South Bay

Ohio Ave

65

see MAP 13

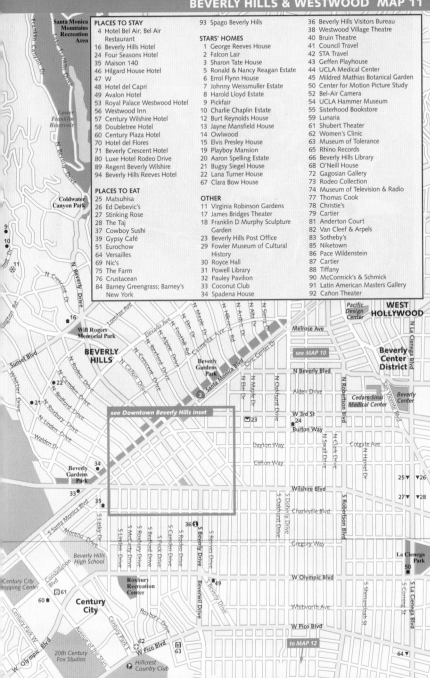

PLACES TO STAY
4 Hotel Bel Air; Bel Air Restaurant
16 Beverly Hills Hotel
24 Four Seasons Hotel
35 Maison 140
46 Hilgard House Hotel
47 W
48 Hotel del Capri
49 Avalon Hotel
53 Royal Palace Westwood Hotel
56 Westwood Inn
57 Century Wilshire Hotel
58 Doubletree Hotel
62 Century Plaza Hotel
70 Hotel del Flores
71 Beverly Crescent Hotel
80 Luxe Hotel Rodeo Drive
89 Regent Beverly Wilshire
94 Beverly Hills Reeves Hotel

PLACES TO EAT
25 Matsuhisa
26 Ed Debevic's
27 Stinking Rose
28 The Taj
37 Cowboy Sushi
39 Gypsy Café
51 Eurochow
64 Versailles
69 Nic's
75 The Farm
76 Crustacean
84 Barney Greengrass; Barney's New York

93 Spago Beverly Hills

STARS' HOMES
1 George Reeves House
2 Falcon Lair
3 Sharon Tate House
5 Ronald & Nancy Reagan Estate
6 Errol Flynn House
7 Johnny Weissmuller Estate
8 Harold Lloyd Estate
9 Pickfair
10 Charlie Chaplin Estate
12 Burt Reynolds House
13 Jayne Mansfield House
14 Owlwood
15 Elvis Presley House
19 Playboy Mansion
20 Aaron Spelling Estate
21 Bugsy Siegel House
22 Lana Turner House
67 Clara Bow House

OTHER
11 Virginia Robinson Gardens
17 James Bridges Theater
18 Franklin D Murphy Sculpture Garden
23 Beverly Hills Post Office
29 Fowler Museum of Cultural History
30 Royce Hall
31 Powell Library
32 Pauley Pavilion
33 Coconut Club
34 Spadena House

36 Beverly Hills Visitors Bureau
38 Westwood Village Theatre
40 Bruin Theatre
41 Council Travel
42 STA Travel
43 Geffen Playhouse
44 UCLA Medical Center
45 Mildred Mathias Botanical Garden
50 Center for Motion Picture Study
52 Bel-Air Camera
54 UCLA Hammer Museum
55 Sisterhood Bookstore
59 Lunaria
61 Shubert Theater
62 Women's Clinic
63 Museum of Tolerance
65 Rhino Records
66 Beverly Hills Library
68 O'Neill House
72 Gagosian Gallery
73 Rodeo Collection
74 Museum of Television & Radio
78 Thomas Cook
78 Christie's
79 Cartier
81 Anderton Court
82 Van Cleef & Arpels
83 Sotheby's
85 Niketown
86 Pace Wildenstein
87 Cartier
88 Tiffany
90 McCormick's & Schmick
91 Latin American Masters Gallery
92 Cañon Theater

I got this cop and motorcycle all on eBay.

Third Street Promenade's nightly neon display, Santa Monica

MAP 12 CULVER CITY

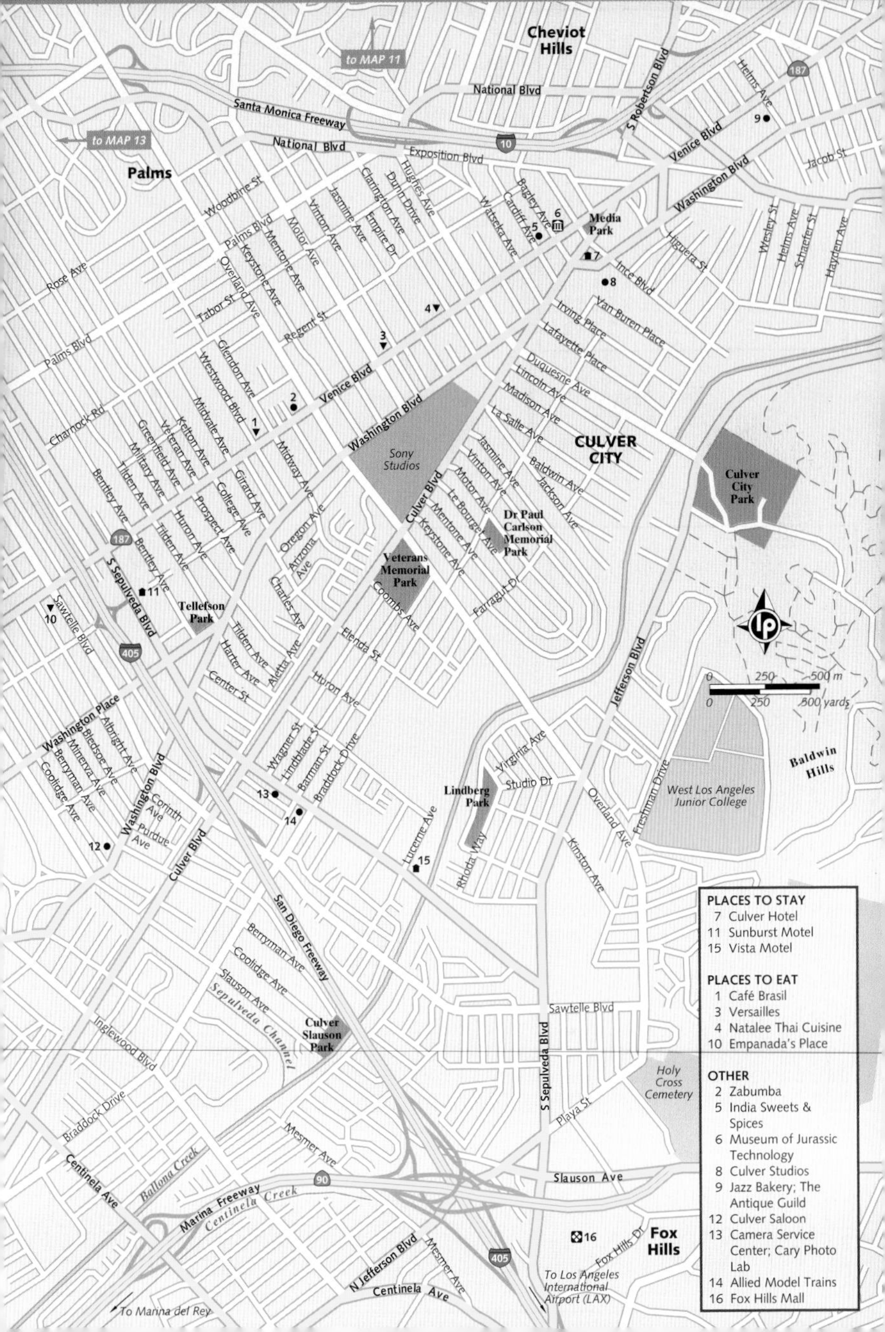

Cheviot
Hills

National Blvd

to MAP 11

Santa Monica Freeway

to MAP 13

National Blvd

Exposition Blvd

Palms

Woodbine St

Palms Blvd

Motor Ave

Keystone Ave

Jasmine Ave

Irvine Dr

Empire Dr

Duquesne Ave

Clarington Ave

Hughes Ave

Watseka Ave

Cardiff Ave

6
5
Media
Park
7

Ince Blvd

8

Higuera St

Washington Blvd

Venice Blvd

S Robertson Blvd

Helms Ave

187

9

Jacob St

Wesley St

Schaefer St

Hayden Ave

Rose Ave

Tabor St

Overland Ave

Mentone Ave

Vinton Ave

Jasmine Ave

Regent St

Palms Blvd

4

3

2

Venice Blvd

Washington Blvd

Irving Place

Van Buren Place

Lafayette Place

Duquesne Ave

Lincoln Ave

Madison Ave

La Salle Ave

CULVER
CITY

Culver
City
Park

Charnock Rd

Westwood Blvd

Glenbarr Ave

Kelton Ave

Midvale Ave

Greenfield Ave

Veteran Ave

Military Ave

Hilton Ave

Bentley Ave

Bentley Ave

187

Tilden Ave

Prospect Ave

College Ave

Girard Ave

Midway Ave

Oregon Ave

Arizona Ave

Coombs Ave

1

Sony
Studios

Culver Blvd

Le Bourget Ave

Keystone Ave

Mentone Ave

Motor Ave

Vinton Ave

Jasmine Ave

Jackson Ave

Baldwin Ave

Dr Paul
Carlson
Memorial
Park

Veterans
Memorial
Park

Farragut Dr

Jefferson Blvd

Freshman Drive

S Sepulveda Blvd

Sawtelle Blvd

10

11

Tellefson
Park

405

Tilden Ave

Charles Ave

Alexia Ave

Center St

Harter Ave

Huron Ave

Elenda St

Wagner St

Lindblade St

Barman Ave

Braddock Drive

Studio Dr

Virginia Ave

Lindberg
Park

13

14

15

Lucerne Ave

Rhoda Way

West Los Angeles
Junior College

0   250   500 m
0   250   300 yards

Baldwin
Hills

Washington Place

Washington Blvd

Albright Ave

Minerva Ave

Berryman Ave

Coolidge Ave

Rhodes Ave

Corinth Ave

Purdue Ave

Culver Blvd

12

San Diego Freeway

Berryman Ave

Coolidge Ave

Slauson Ave

Sepulveda Channel

Culver
Slauson
Park

Inglewood Blvd

Braddock Drive

Centinela Ave

Ballona Creek

Centinela Creek

Marina Freeway

90

S Sepulveda Blvd

Sawtelle Blvd

Playa St

Overland Ave

Kenston Ave

Holy
Cross
Cemetery

16

Slauson Ave

Fox
Hills

Fox Hills Dr

Mesmer Ave

N Jefferson Blvd

Centinela Ave

405

To Los Angeles
International
Airport (LAX)

To Manna del Rey

PLACES TO STAY
7 Culver Hotel
11 Sunburst Motel
15 Vista Motel

PLACES TO EAT
1 Café Brasil
3 Versailles
4 Natalee Thai Cuisine
10 Empanada's Place

OTHER
2 Zabumba
5 India Sweets &
   Spices
6 Museum of Jurassic
   Technology
8 Culver Studios
9 Jazz Bakery; The
   Antique Guild
12 Culver Saloon
13 Camera Service
   Center; Cary Photo
   Lab
14 Allied Model Trains
16 Fox Hills Mall

MAP 13 SANTA MONICA & VENICE

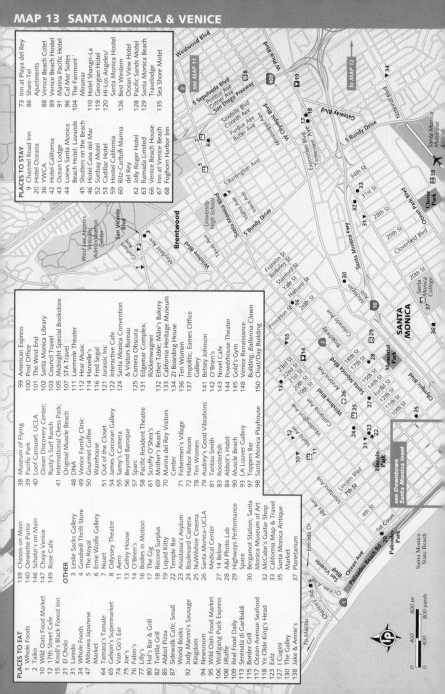

PLACES TO EAT
1 Whole Foods
2 Taiko
10 Wild Oats Food Market
12 17th Street Cafe
15 Knoll's Black Forest Inn
21 El Cholo
31 Laredo
34 Whole Foods
47 Mitsuwa Japanese Market
64 Tamara's Tamale
65 Gelson's Supermarket
74 Van Go's Ear
75 Joe's
76 Fabio's
77 Lilly's
80 Hal's Bar & Grill
82 Tortilla Grill
85 Abbot Pizza
87 Sidewalk Cafe; Small World Books
92 Jody Maroni's Sausage Kingdom
94 Newsroom
95 Wild Oats Food Market
106 Wolfgang Puck Express
108 JiRaffe
109 Real Food Daily
113 Serenata di Garibaldi
115 Border Grill
117 Ocean Avenue Seafood
118 Ye Olde King's Head
123 Eatz
127 I Cugini
130 The Gallery
138 Jake & Annie's
139 Chinois on Main
140 Omelette Parlor
146 Schatzi's on Main
147 Chaya Venice
149 Rose Cafe

OTHER
3 Leslie Sacks Gallery
4 Goodwill Thrift Store
5 The Royal
6 Ernie Wolfe Gallery
7 Nuart
8 Odyssey Theatre
11 Aero
13 Gethy House
14 O'Brien's
16 Bodies in Motion
17 The Gig
18 Record Surplus
19 Liquid Kitty
22 Temple Bar
23 Anastasia's Asylum
24 Boulevard Camera
25 NuWilshire Cinema
26 Santa Monica-UCLA Medical Center
27 14 Below
28 A&I Photo Lab
29 Wolfgang Puck Express
30 Bergamot Station; Santa Monica Museum of Art
32 McCabe's Guitar Shop
33 California Map & Travel
35 Santa Monica Antique Market
37 Planetarium
38 Museum of Flying
39 Pacific Park
40 Looff Carousel; UCLA Ocean Discovery Center; Rusty's Surf Ranch
41 International Chess Park; Original Muscle Beach
48 DNA
49 Venice Family Clinic
50 Gourmet Coffee Warehouse
51 Out of the Closet
54 James Corcoran Gallery
55 Samy's Camera
56 Beyond Baroque
57 Sparc
58 Pacific Resident Theatre
61 Scruffy O'Shea's
69 Mother's Beach
70 Marina del Rey Visitors Center
71 Fishermen's Village
72 Harbor Room
78 Ten Women
79 Audrey's Good Vibrations
81 Tantau Smith
83 Roosterfish
90 Abbot's Habit
93 LA Louver Gallery
97 Toppers Bar
98 Santa Monica Playhouse
99 American Express
100 Post Office
101 The West End
102 Santa Monica Library
103 Council Travel
105 Midnight Special Bookstore
107 STA Travel
111 Laemmle Theater
112 Hear Music
114 Harvelle's
116 Fred Segal
121 Jurassic Inc
122 Interactive Cafe
124 Santa Monica Convention & Visitors Bureau
125 Camera Obscura
131 Edgemar Complex; Rockenwagner
132 Ether Table; Mani's Bakery
133 California Heritage Museum
134 ZJ Boarding House
136 Ten Women
137 Impolitic; Eames Office Gallery
141 Betsey Johnson
142 O'Brien's
143 Novel Cafe
144 Powerhouse Theater
145 Gold's Gym
148 Venice Renaissance Building; Ballerina Clown
150 Chiat/Day Building

PLACES TO STAY
9 Channel Road Inn
20 Hotel Oceana
36 YWCA
42 Hotel California
43 Ocean Lodge
44 Loews Santa Monica Beach Hotel; Lavande
45 Shutters on the Beach
46 Hotel Casa del Mar
52 Sunbay Motel
53 Cadillac Hotel
59 Hostel California
60 Ritz-Carlton Marina del Rey
62 Jolly Roger Hotel
63 Ramada Limited
66 Venice Beach House
67 Inn at Venice Beach
68 Foghorn Harbor Inn
73 Inn at Playa del Rey
86 Share-Tel Apartments
88 Venice Beach Cotel
89 Venice Beach Hostel
91 Marina Pacific Hotel
96 Cal Mar Suites
104 The Fairmont / Miramar
110 Hotel Shangri-La
119 Georgian Hotel
120 HI-Los Angeles/ Santa Monica Hostel
126 Best Western Ocean View Hotel
128 Pacific Sands Motel
129 Santa Monica Beach Travelodge
135 Sea Shore Motel

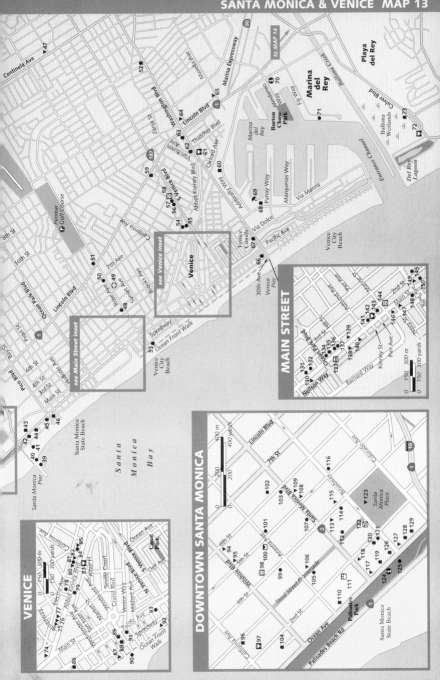

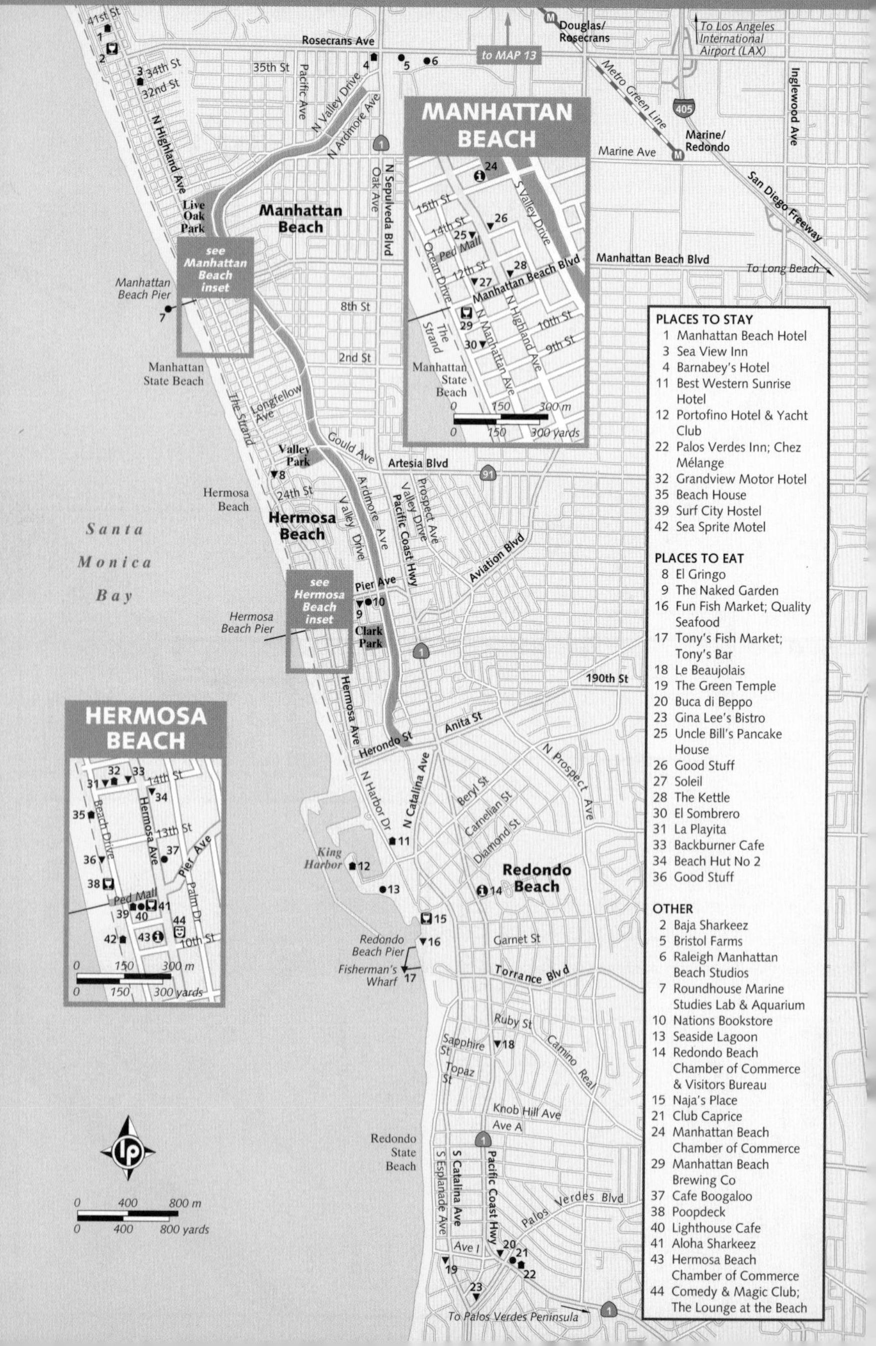

MAP 14 SOUTH BAY

41st St
2
3 34th St
32nd St
35th St
Rosecrans Ave
Douglas/
Rosecrans
To Los Angeles
International
Airport (LAX)
4 5 6
to MAP 13
Metro Green Line
405
Marine Ave
Marine/
Redondo
M
San Diego Freeway
To Long Beach
Inglewood Ave

Pacific Ave
N Valley Drive
N Ardmore Ave
Oak Ave
N Sepulveda Blvd
N Highland Ave

Live
Oak
Park

**MANHATTAN
BEACH**

24
15th St
25 Pel Mall
12th St
N Ocean Drive
27
30
29
26
28
Manhattan Beach Blvd
N Manhattan Ave
9th St
10th St
N Highland Ave
N Valley Drive

Manhattan Beach Blvd
To Long Beach

**Manhattan
Beach**

see
**Manhattan
Beach
inset**

Manhattan
Beach Pier
7

Manhattan
State Beach

8th St
2nd St

The Strand
Manhattan
State
Beach

0   150   300 m
0   150   300 yards

Longfellow Ave
Gould Ave
Valley Drive
Ardmore Ave
Pacific Coast Hwy

**Valley
Park**
8

Artesia Blvd
1

Hermosa
Beach

**Hermosa
Beach**

24th St

see
**Hermosa
Beach
inset**

Pier Ave
10
9

Prospect Ave
Valley Dr

Aviation Blvd

190th St

*Santa
Monica
Bay*

Hermosa
Beach Pier

Clark Park

Hermosa Ave

Herondo St

Anita St

N Harbor Dr
N Catalina Ave
Beryl St
Camelian St
Diamond St
N Prospect Ave

**HERMOSA
BEACH**

32 33
31 34
35
Beach Drive
Hermosa Ave
14th St
13th St
37
36
38
Pel Mall
39 40
42 43
Pier Ave
Palm Dr
41
44

0   150   300 m
0   150   300 yards

11
King
Harbor
12

13

14
15

Redondo
Beach Pier
16
Fisherman's
Wharf 17

Garnet St
Torrance Blvd

**Redondo
Beach**

Ruby St
Camino Real

Sapphire
St
18
Topaz
St

Knob Hill Ave
Ave A

Redondo
State
Beach

S Catalina Ave
S Esplanade Ave
Pacific Coast Hwy
Palos Verdes Blvd

Ave I
19
20 21
22
23

To Palos Verdes Peninsula
1

0   400   800 m
0   400   800 yards

PLACES TO STAY
1 Manhattan Beach Hotel
3 Sea View Inn
4 Barnaby's Hotel
11 Best Western Sunrise
   Hotel
12 Portofino Hotel & Yacht
   Club
22 Palos Verdes Inn; Chez
   Mélange
32 Grandview Motor Hotel
35 Beach House
39 Surf City Hostel
42 Sea Sprite Motel

PLACES TO EAT
8 El Gringo
9 The Naked Garden
16 Fun Fish Market; Quality
   Seafood
17 Tony's Fish Market;
   Tony's Bar
18 Le Beaujolais
19 The Green Temple
20 Buca di Beppo
23 Gina Lee's Bistro
25 Uncle Bill's Pancake
   House
26 Good Stuff
27 Soleil
28 The Kettle
30 El Sombrero
31 La Playita
33 Backburner Cafe
34 Beach Hut No 2
36 Good Stuff

OTHER
2 Baja Sharkeez
5 Bristol Farms
6 Raleigh Manhattan
   Beach Studios
7 Roundhouse Marine
   Studies Lab & Aquarium
10 Nations Bookstore
13 Seaside Lagoon
14 Redondo Beach
   Chamber of Commerce
   & Visitors Bureau
15 Naja's Place
21 Club Caprice
24 Manhattan Beach
   Chamber of Commerce
29 Manhattan Beach
   Brewing Co
37 Cafe Boogaloo
38 Poopdeck
40 Lighthouse Cafe
41 Aloha Sharkeez
43 Hermosa Beach
   Chamber of Commerce
44 Comedy & Magic Club;
   The Lounge at the Beach

MAP 15 SAN PEDRO

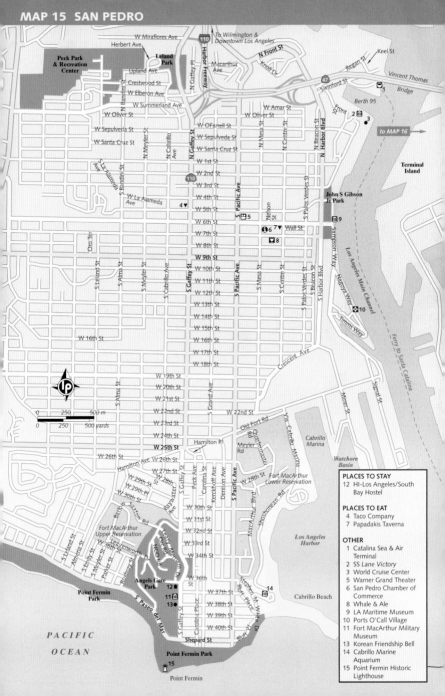

W Miraflores Ave
To Wilmington &
Downtown Los Angeles
Herbert Ave
Leland
Park
W Macarthur
Ave
N Front St
Keel St
Peck Park
& Recreation
Center
Knoll Dr
Regan St
Vincent Thomas
Bridge
Upland Ave
Crestwood St
W Elberon Ave
W Summerland Ave
W Oliver St
W Amar St
W Oliver St
W OFarrell St
Swinford St
Berth 95
Front St
N Beacon St
Harbor Blvd
2
3
to MAP 16
W Sepulveda St
W Santa Cruz St
W Sepulveda St
W Santa Cruz St
W 1st St
W 2nd St
W 3rd St
N Mesa St
N Centre St
N Beacon St
Terminal
Island
John S Gibson
Jr Park
W 4th St
W 5th St
4
5
Nelson St
S Palos Verdes St
9
W 6th St
1 6
7
Wall St
W 7th St
8
W 8th St
W 9th St
W 10th St
S Pacific Ave
S Mesa St
S Centre St
S Beacon St
S Palos Verdes St
S Harbor Blvd
Simpson Way
Nagoya Way
Los Angeles Main Channel
Ferry to Santa Catalina
W 11th St
W 12th St
W 13th St
W 14th St
10
W 15th St
Timms Way
W 16th St
W 17th St
W 18th St
Crescent Ave
W 19th St
W 20th St
W 21st St
S Alma St
S Grand Ave
Sigmal St
W 22nd St
W 22nd St
W 23rd St
Old Fort Rd
Miner St
W 24th St
Cabrillo
Marina
W 25th St
Hamilton Pl
Watchorn
Basin
W 26th St
Meyler
Rd
PACIFIC
W 27th St
Fort MacArthur
Lower Reservation
W 28th St
Los Angeles
Harbor
W 29th St
W 29th Pl
W 30th St
W 31st St
W 32nd St
W 33rd St
W 34th St
Fort MacArthur
Upper Reservation
W 36th St
Angels Gate
Park
12
Point Fermin
Park
11
13
Cabrillo Beach
W 37th St
14
W 38th St
W 39th St
W 40th St
OCEAN
Shepard St
Point Fermin Park
15
Point Fermin

PLACES TO STAY
12 HI-Los Angeles/South
Bay Hostel

PLACES TO EAT
4 Taco Company
7 Papadakis Taverna

OTHER
1 Catalina Sea & Air
Terminal
2 SS Lane Victory
3 World Cruise Center
4 Warner Grand Theater
6 San Pedro Chamber of
Commerce
8 Whale & Ale
9 LA Maritime Museum
10 Ports O'Call Village
11 Fort MacArthur Military
Museum
13 Korean Friendship Bell
14 Cabrillo Marine
Aquarium
15 Point Fermin Historic
Lighthouse

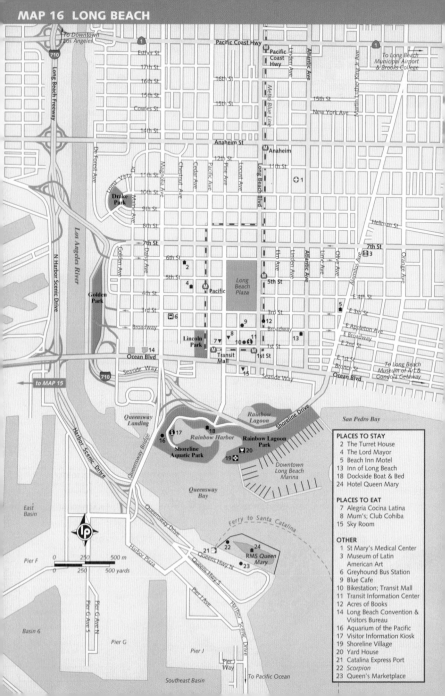

MAP 16 LONG BEACH

PLACES TO STAY
2 The Turret House
4 The Lord Mayor
5 Beach Inn Motel
13 Inn of Long Beach
18 Dockside Boat & Bed
24 Hotel Queen Mary

PLACES TO EAT
7 Alegria Cocina Latina
8 Mum's; Club Cohiba
15 Sky Room

OTHER
1 St Mary's Medical Center
3 Museum of Latin American Art
6 Greyhound Bus Station
9 Blue Cafe
10 Bikestation; Transit Mall
11 Transit Information Center
12 Acres of Books
14 Long Beach Convention & Visitors Bureau
16 Aquarium of the Pacific
17 Visitor Information Kiosk
19 Shoreline Village
20 Yard House
21 Catalina Express Port
22 Scorpion
23 Queen's Marketplace

MAP 17 PASADENA

PLACES TO STAY

3 Doubletree Hotel
14 Westway Inn
15 Saga Motor Hotel
17 Best Western
   Colorado Inn
19 Sheraton
   Pasadena Hotel
21 Pasadena Hilton
25 Pasadena Inn
28 Bissell House
29 Ritz-Carlton
   Huntington Hotel

PLACES TO EAT

1 Marston's
13 Zankou Chicken
30 Café Bizou
31 Xiomara; Yujean
   Kang
33 Akbar
34 Mi Place
35 Trattoria Farfalla
39 Trattoria Sorriso
40 Rack Shack
43 Twin Palms
44 Buca di Beppo

OTHER

2 Public Library
4 Greyhound Bus Station
5 Norton Simon Museum
6 City Hall
7 Pacific Asia Museum
8 First United Methodist
   Church
9 Pasadena Playhouse
10 House of Fiction
11 Vroman's Bookstore
12 Ice House
16 Out of the Closet
18 Vista del Arroyo Hotel;
   Court of Appeals
20 Pasadena Convention
   & Visitors Bureau
22 Colonnade
23 Burlington Arcade
24 Wrigley Mansion &
   Gardens
26 Kidspace
27 Bodies in Motion
32 Gordon Biersch
   Brewery
36 Penny Lane
37 Equator Coffeehouse
38 Opus
41 Knightsbridge
   Theatre - Pasadena
42 Distant Lands
   Bookstore; Council
   Travel
45 Hotel Green; Castle
   Green

DOWNTOWN

PASADENA

South Lake District

SAN MARINO

Huntington Library, Art Collection & Botanical Gardens

MAP 18 BURBANK, NORTH HOLLYWOOD & UNIVERSAL CITY

To San Fernando

Empire Ave
Lincoln St
Scott Rd
Victory Place
Golden State Freeway
Metrolink

McCambridge Park
N Glenoaks Blvd
N 3rd St
N San Fernando Blvd

BURBANK

Magnolia Blvd
Palm Ave
Orange Grove Ave
Olive Ave
S Angeleno Ave
Tulipang Ave
S Glenoaks Blvd
S 3rd St

Victory Blvd
W Burbank Blvd

N Mariposa St
N Victory Blvd

3 4
5 6 7 8
5 7
9

Metrolink Station
S San Fernando Blvd

Magnolia Park

Chandler Blvd
N Buena Vista St
N Keystone St
N Lamer St
N Orchard Drive
N Parish Place
N Magnolia Blvd

George Izay Park

N California St
N Niagara St
N Florence St
N Catalina St
N Naomi St
N Frederic St

8

Burbank Western Channel

Verdugo Park

W Verdugo Ave
19 20
W Olive Ave
Oak St
S Parish Place
S Lamer St

Alameda Ave
21
Golden State Freeway
Victory Blvd

5
To Downtown Los Angeles

25
24
N Avon St
W Alameda Ave

Mountain View Park

Walt Disney Studios

Chavez St
Riverside Drive

Los Angeles Equestrian Center

Main St

26

134

NBC Studios
Johnny Carson Park
Ventura Freeway
Zoo Drive
To Glendale

29
Riverside Drive
Buena Vista Park
Forest Lawn Drive
Forest Lawn Memorial Park-Hollywood Hills
Mount Sinai Memorial Park
see MAP 8

Griffith Park

Griffith Park Drive

Warner Brothers Studios
Los Angeles River
Forest Lawn Drive

Kenwood St
Maple St

LP

0   300   600 m
0   300   600 yards

Cahuenga Peak ▲
1820ft

Barham Blvd
to MAP 9

PLACES TO STAY	7 The Great Grill; Knight; India's Tandoori	14 Academy of Television Arts & Sciences
1 Burbank Airport Hilton & Convention Center	11 Tokyo Delve's	15 Deaf West Theatre
9 Holiday Inn	24 Piero's Seafood House	16 Rumors
19 The Annabelle Hotel	25 Poquito Más	17 Crazy Jack's
20 Safari Inn	27 Bob's Big Boy	18 It's a Wrap
21 Burbank Inn & Suites	30 Barsac Brasserie	22 Eddie Brandt's Saturday
29 Holiday Lodge	31 Ca' del Sole	Matinee
32 Universal City Inn		23 Roger Dunn Golf Shop
35 Sheraton Universal Hotel	**OTHER**	26 Circle K Riding Stables
36 Universal City Hilton & Towers	3 Cookbooks	28 Geographia Map & Travel Store
	4 Book City	33 Baked Potato Jazz Club
	6 Movie World	34 Campo de Cahuenga
PLACES TO EAT	8 Burbank City Hall	37 Universal City Walk;
2 Leonor's Vegetarian Restaurant	10 El Portal Center for the Arts	Gladstone's; Camacho's; Jody Maroni's; BB King's
5 Market City Cafe	12 Eagles Coffee Pub	Blues Club
	13 Interact Theatre	

STEPHANIE DIANI

Sunset on the Griffith Observatory & Planetarium

ANDREA SCHULTE-PEEVERS

Pacific Design Center in West Hollywood

ROBERTO SONCIN GEROMETTA

Say it loud, say it proud – vanity plates for the wealthy patriot.

MAP 19 METRO RAIL SYSTEM

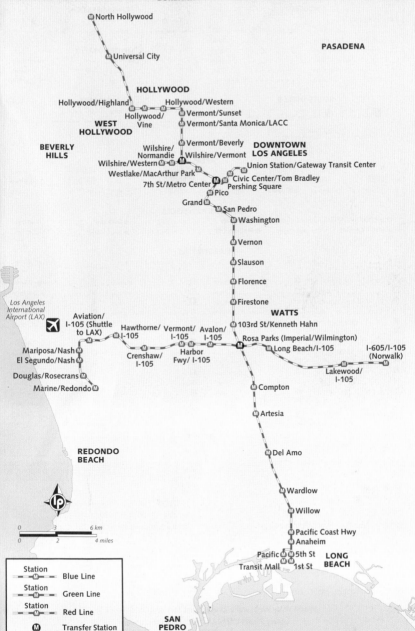

BURBANK

North Hollywood

Universal City

PASADENA

HOLLYWOOD

Hollywood/Highland
Hollywood/Western
Hollywood/Vine
Vermont/Sunset
Vermont/Santa Monica/LACC

WEST HOLLYWOOD

BEVERLY HILLS

Vermont/Beverly
Wilshire/Normandie
Wilshire/Vermont
Wilshire/Western
Westlake/MacArthur Park
7th St/Metro Center
Pico
Grand
San Pedro

DOWNTOWN LOS ANGELES

Union Station/Gateway Transit Center
Civic Center/Tom Bradley
Pershing Square

Washington

Vernon

Slauson

Florence

Firestone

WATTS

Los Angeles International Airport (LAX)

Aviation/I-105 (Shuttle to LAX)
Hawthorne/I-105
Vermont/I-105
Avalon/I-105
103rd St/Kenneth Hahn
Rosa Parks (Imperial/Wilmington)
Long Beach/I-105

Mariposa/Nash
El Segundo/Nash
Crenshaw/I-105
Harbor Fwy/I-105

I-605/I-105 (Norwalk)
Lakewood/I-105

Douglas/Rosecrans
Marine/Redondo

Compton

Artesia

REDONDO BEACH

Del Amo

Wardlow

Willow

Pacific Coast Hwy
Anaheim
Pacific 5th St
Transit Mall 1st St

LONG BEACH

SAN PEDRO

Station	
M	Blue Line
Station	
M	Green Line
Station	
M	Red Line
M	Transfer Station

MAP LEGEND

ROUTES

City Regional

.............Freeway
......Toll Freeway
....Primary Road
Secondary Road
...Tertiary Road
.........Dirt Road

Pedestrian Mall
..............Steps
............Tunnel
...................Lane
...............Trail
Walking Tour

TRANSPORTATION

............Train
............Metro

............Bus Route
............Ferry

HYDROGRAPHY

.....River; Creek
..............Canal
................Lake

...Spring; Rapids
........Waterfalls
....Dry; Salt Lake

ROUTE SHIELDS

Interstate Freeway
California State Highway
County Road
US Highway
Nevada State Highway

BOUNDARIES

....International
............State

...........County
...........Disputed

AREAS

.........Beach
........Building
........Campus

...........Cemetery
...............Forest
.......Garden; Zoo

.........Golf Course
...............Park
...............Plaza

..............Market
..........Sports Field
..............Swamp

POPULATION SYMBOLS

NATIONAL CAPITAL... National Capital
STATE CAPITAL............State Capital

Large City.....................Large City
Medium City.................Medium City

Small City..........................Small City
Town; Village..............Town; Village

MAP SYMBOLS

............Place to Stay
............Place to Eat
............Point of Interest

.... Airport Runway	.... Church	.... Museum	.... Skiing - Downhill
.... Airport	.... Cinema	.... Observatory	.... Stately Home
...... Archeological Site; Ruin	.... Dive Site	.... Park	.... Surfing
.... Bank	...... Embassy; Consulate	.... Parking Area	.... Synagogue
.... Baseball Diamond	.... Footbridge	.... Pass	.... Tao Temple
.... Battlefield	.... Gas Station	.... Picnic Area	.... Taxi
.... Bike Trail	.... Hospital	.... Police Station	.... Telephone
.... Border Crossing	.... Information	.... Pool	.... Theater
.... Buddhist Temple	...... Internet Café	.... Post Office	.... Toilet - Public
...... Bus Station; Terminal	.... Lighthouse	.... Pub; Bar	.... Tomb
...... Cable Car; Chairlift	.... Lookout	.... RV Park	.... Trailhead
.... Campground	.... Mine	.... Shelter	.... Tram Stop
.... Castle	.... Mission	.... Shipwreck	.... Transportation
.... Cathedral	.... Monument	...... Shopping Mall	.... Volcano
.... Cave	.... Mountain	... Skiing - Cross Country	.... Winery

Note: Not all symbols displayed above appear in this book.

LONELY PLANET OFFICES

Australia
Locked Bag 1, Footscray, Victoria 3011
☎ 03 8379 8000 fax 03 8379 8111
email talk2us@lonelyplanet.com.au

USA
150 Linden Street, Oakland, CA 94607
☎ 510 893 8555, TOLL FREE 800 275 8555
fax 510 893 8572
email info@lonelyplanet.com

UK
10a Spring Place, London NW5 3BH
☎ 020 7428 4800 fax 020 7428 4828
email go@lonelyplanet.co.uk

France
1 rue du Dahomey, 75011 Paris
☎ 01 55 25 33 00 fax 01 55 25 33 01
email bip@lonelyplanet.fr
www.lonelyplanet.fr

World Wide Web: www.lonelyplanet.com *or* AOL keyword: lp
Lonely Planet Images: lpi@lonelyplanet.com.au